A SOCIAL AND RELIGIOUS
HISTORY OF THE JEWS

Late Middle Ages and Era of European Expansion
1200–1650

VOLUME XVI
POLAND–LITHUANIA 1500–1650

A SOCIAL
AND RELIGIOUS
HISTORY OF
THE JEWS

By SALO WITTMAYER BARON

Second Edition, Revised and Enlarged

Late Middle Ages and Era of European Expansion
1200–1650

VOLUME XVI

POLAND–LITHUANIA 1500–1650

Columbia University Press
New York and London   1976

The Jewish Publication Society of America
Philadelphia   5736

COPYRIGHT © 1976 COLUMBIA UNIVERSITY PRESS

ISBN: 0-231-08853-1

LIBRARY OF CONGRESS CATALOG CARD NUMBER: 52-404

PRINTED IN THE UNITED STATES OF AMERICA

CONTENTS

A SOCIAL AND RELIGIOUS HISTORY

OF THE JEWS

PUBLISHED VOLUMES

Late Middle Ages and Era of European Expansion

POLAND-LITHUANIA 1500-1650

POLAND'S GOLDEN AGE

URING THE CRUCIAL ERA of Humanism and Reformation, there developed on the eastern periphery of Roman Catholicism a new center of Judaism, which was destined to play a vital role in the entire subsequent history of the Jewish people. While the lamps were going out in the Jewish quarters all over western and large parts of central Europe, new lights were being kindled in the less developed valleys of the Vistula, Dniester, Dnieper, and Niemen (Neman). Increasing waves of immigration from the West gradually transformed the area between the Baltic and the Black Sea into a major focus of Jewish culture. By the end of the sixteenth century, the dual Commonwealth of Poland-Lithuania achieved the hegemony of all Ashkenazic, in fact, of all world, Jewry.

Poland's sudden rise to the position of a great European power is well described by Aleksander Brückner, a leading historian of Polish culture:

The nation, hitherto almost mute, now raised its voice in political and religious affairs, as well as in problems of scientific and moral import; Polish pens excelled in Latin and raised the level of the national literature to heights far beyond those achieved by contemporary Czech and German letters. The nation had hitherto led a quiet, gray, humble life; it now exchanged it for a glittering, turbulent, and colorful way of living. The gold, which had theretofore in an unprecedented fashion streamed into it in return for its raw materials, was now lavishly spent on clothing, buildings, and drink; on armaments, horses, and spices; on scholars and poets, and artists from the South and the West. The nation, to which theretofore only the papal Curia and Venice had given any thought in connection with their anti-Turkish designs, now assumed considerable international importance as a result of the Jagiellon dynastic policies. The same royal family now reigned over Hungary, Bohemia, Poland, and Lithuania. Only the Habsburgs equaled it in this respect, both dynasties often entering into far-reaching liaisons.

Domestically, to be sure, there was a great, historic break when the Jagiellon succession ended with the death of Sigismund II

Augustus in 1572. As a result, the monarchy, theretofore essentially hereditary, became truly elective, the country soon being converted into a "nobles' commonwealth," which ultimately degenerated into mob rule by an unbridled gentry. But in the immediate sequel, internationally and culturally, the élan of the preceding decades carried over into the regime of the Transylvanian prince Stephen Báthory (Batory), under whom Poland's glory reached its pinnacle. It began to recede only during the reign of his successor, Sigismund III, and the onset of the rigid Counter Reformation, which also helped stifle the country's great literary and scientific creativity. In consequence, Poland entered a period of relative political and cultural stagnation.[1]

MASS IMMIGRATION

Poland's political and economic expansion opened up new avenues for Jewish migrants. We have seen that Jewish immigration into these vast open spaces from both East and West had proceeded apace for several centuries before 1500. That from the eastern regions, both Byzantine and Muslim, to be sure, and especially from the former Khazar territories, had largely ceased after the Tatar invasions, the rule of the Golden Horde, and the rise of Muscovite power. On the other hand, the Western expulsions, especially from German territories, furnished ever-new willing immigrants to Poland and Lithuania. However, the total Jewish settlement in both parts of the Jagiellon kingdom apparently did not exceed 30,000 persons at the end of the fifteenth century. This despite the fact that the German expulsions had set in motion an increasing number of émigrés from 1348 on. But in the 1500s there was an immediate acceleration of that eastward movement. A major propelling force was the progressive shrinkage of the outlets still open to German Jews in the territories of the Bohemian Crown and Hungary during the sixteenth century. In fact, the numerous local expulsions from Bohemia and Moravia, the decline of Hungary, and its final division into Habsburg, Ottoman, and Transylvanian sections after 1526 sent out new waves of Jewish wanderers looking for havens of refuge. The Czech areas now became the main source of Jewish manpower entering first western Poland, and then the other, still greatly underpopulated, provinces of the Polish Crown and the Grand Duchy of Lithuania. On their part, the Polish kings willingly opened their gates to this Jewish immigration, which now partly replaced the former large-scale German colonization of the eastern lands.[2]

Remarkably, Emperor Maximilian I, who himself consented in 1496 and 1515 to the expulsion of the Jews from Styria, Carinthia, and Carniola, recommended to Sigismund I (1506–1548) the admission of his Jewish agent Abraham of Bohemia, who was being forced to leave his country. Sigismund accepted this proposal, since he undoubtedly knew of the great financial services rendered by Abraham, not only to the emperor himself but also to Sigismund's elder brother, Vladislav Jagiellon, king of Bohemia and Hungary. In 1512 Abraham was appointed chief tax collector for all Jews in Great Poland and Mazovia. When he was subsequently accused by some "converted Jews and others" of various transgressions, Sigismund exonerated him completely, rejecting the accusations as based exclusively on the accusers' "envy and malevolence." The king also declared that he had "received sufficient testimony about his [Abraham's] honesty and integrity as may be expected from a good Jew." Before long Sigismund went further. In expectation of a growing influx of Bohemian Jews into Poland, he took many of those still living in Bohemia under his protection and, in 1517, warned the Bohemian chancellor Vladislav Sternbergk not to allow any persecution of Jews or interference with their legitimate use of possessions, since they were on the point of departing for Poland. In the following year Sigismund singled out a Jewish family in Litoměřice (Leitmeritz), consisting of one Isaac, his son-in-law, their wives and children, for special permission to come to Poland and enjoy there all the rights given to other Jews in the country. These rather audacious interventions in the internal affairs of a neighboring country are less amazing in the case of Sigismund, who had lived for years in the lands of the Bohemian Crown and had even served as governor of Silesia under the reign of his elder brother Vladislav, who had died in 1516. An even more sweeping privilege was extended by Sigismund to the Jew Joseph of Chomútov (Komotau), his sons, and family: the newcomer was given the right to settle in any Polish city of his choice.

At the same time the king specifically asked Sternbergk not to place any obstacles in the way of that family's departing, with its property, to Poland. Undoubtedly the documents cited here represent only a fraction of the similar privileges extended by the Polish Crown to prospective Jewish arrivals from Bohemian provinces. Evidently the Jagiellon rulers of Bohemia did not resent this interference of another Jagiellon king in the internal affairs of their country.[3]

Of course, the majority of arrivals came without invitation. Propelled by the growing insecurity of life in the Holy Roman Empire, they quickly realized that conditions in Poland did not greatly differ from those to which they had been accustomed in their native lands. Especially the numerous former residents of Bohemia, Moravia, and Silesia, many of whom had adopted Slavic names such as Czarny or Czarna, Chwała, or Morawczyk, had long been living in a Slavic environment. Those who came from other German states, too, found in many Polish cities a predominantly German-speaking population, although it was now in the process of being rapidly Polonized.[4]

Acclimatization to the new environment was somewhat more difficult for settlers hailing from Spain, Portugal, and Italy. While the expulsions from the Iberian Peninsula in the period 1492–98, as well as those from southern Italy in 1492, 1511, and 1540, had initiated a large-scale emigration of Jewish refugees seeking new homes, the conditions of life in still "backward" Poland and Lithuania exercised little attraction for exiles from the culturally more advanced, climatically milder, and economically more diversified Mediterranean lands. Less important in the Jewish case was the prevailing unfavorable opinion of Spaniards held by most Poles of the period, as well as by the French and many other northerners. Certainly, the *leyenda negra* (black legend), which attributed Jewish and Moorish origins to the majority of Spaniards—even if it had been widely accepted in eastern Europe, which is doubtful —could not have significantly increased the local antagonism to Jewish immigration as such. More decisively, the Muslim traditions still being very vivid in both Iberia and Sicily, made emigration to the upsurging Ottoman Empire and North Africa far more promising. Nonetheless, a growing number of Sephardic and Italian Jews found their way to Polish cities. We are most familiar with the names of such outstanding personalities as Isaac Hispanus. A distinguished physician, who had apparently enjoyed a considerable reputation in his home country, he was successively employed, as we recall, by John Albert, Alexander, and Sigismund I, as court physician. In 1504 Alexander did not hesitate to send him to the khan of the "trans-Volga," or Kipchak, Tatars. Quite likely the physician undertook this "long and arduous journey" not only for medical reasons but also to pursue some diplomatic negotiations between the two rulers, who were equally threatened by Tsar Ivan III of Moscow. Isaac could, indeed, invoke many precedents of Jewish physicians who had served as diplomatic envoys from his native country, whether under Muslim or Christian domination. (Conversely, a Tatar khan, probably from the Crimea, in 1567 dispatched a Jewish envoy to the king of Poland.) The services rendered by Isaac to the Crown were rewarded by Alexander and Sigismund I with many special privileges, which included exemption from all taxes and the placement of Isaac under direct royal jurisdiction. Upon Isaac's death the king assigned a pension to his widow. The doctor was but the first of an illustrious array of Jewish court physicians, for the most part recruited from Italian medical circles. Some other Italian arrivals accompanied, or followed, Queen Bona Sforza, who in 1518 became Sigismund I's second wife and whose native duchy of Milan still harbored remnants of important Jewish communities.[5]

Because of their superiority in numbers, wealth, and cultural attainments, the new arrivals succeeded, within a relatively short time in imposing their own rituals, customs, and speech upon the local Jews. Even the segment which had originally come from Khazar, Byzantine, or Muslim lands became totally submerged in the new Polish-Lithuanian community organized by the Western immigrants. This process had begun even before the mass immigration of the sixteenth century. Ever since the stoppage of the influx from the East some time before 1300, the amalgamation of Eastern and Western Jewry had progressed to such an extent that hardly any vestige is left in the sixteenth-century records of the existence of a substantial group of Jews of Eastern origin. Linguistically, too, the Yiddish dialect of German, used by the Western arrivals, began dominating the speech of all inhabitants of the Jewish quarters throughout the realm. Even those who came from the Bohemian areas seem to have incorporated but few Slavonic words into their ordinary speech. If we may judge from the sparse extant communal documents and the quotations in the contemporary rabbinic responsa and folk literature, only a few technical terms pertaining to names of certain objects, court procedure, and other official transactions were derived from the Polish or Ukrainian tongues. The major admixture to the Germanic vocabulary and sentence structure consisted in Hebrew abstract and religious terms, Hebrew influences on syntax, and other Hebraic borrowings. Of course, in time, the divergence of Yiddish from German increased, as Germany herself superimposed upon its various local dialects a more unified literary language, under the impact of Luther's translation of the Bible and the chancery idiom developed by the new bureaucracies of the German princes. In their general conservatism, Jews often continued to cultivate inherited modes of speech with greater fidelity than even the German colonists in Poland. They thus repeated a phenomenon attested earlier in the case of ancient Babylonian Jewry, which had carried into the Sassanian Empire linguistic reminiscences inherited from the Achaemenid age, long after the Persians themselves had given up these archaic forms. We shall see that a similar thing happened in the Balkans and the Middle East, where Spanish-Portuguese immigrants formed their new Ladino language on the basis of fifteenth-century Iberian, mainly Castilian, dialects which on the Peninsula itself were being abandoned by the Spanish and Portuguese peoples.[6]

The most important remnant of Eastern Jews which retained its identity was that of the Karaites, because it was distinguished from the Jewish majority by its religious teachings and practices and, partially, also by its language. The Karaites' immigration to Lithuania may also have had unusual aspects. If it is true, as has been suggested, that their string of earliest settlements was located along Lithuania's border with lands held by the Teutonic Order so that they might defend the country against these rapacious neighbors, their paramilitary posture must have differentiated them from the usual Rabbanite arrivals. By adhering, moreover, to their long-accepted deviations from Rabbanite Judaism, the Karaites of Troki, Halicz, and other communities preserved their separate communal life, at variance with the majority. In Troki they actually tried to keep the Rabbanite Jews at arm's length, generating a long-lasting animosity between the two communities. Often intertwined with the story of the Polish-Lithuanian Karaites was that of the so-called Krymchaki, who were in fact native Rabbanite Jews from the Crimean Peninsula. They cultivated a language of their own, which kept them apart from both the Karaites and other Rabbanite Jews.[7]

LOCAL RESISTANCE

Needless to say, the tremendous influx of Western Jews created great difficulties with non-Jewish groups. Certainly, the Church looked with a jaundiced eye upon the strengthening of dissident forces in religion. While on the whole trying to uphold the medieval treatment of Jews, it also had to bear in mind the royal determination to bring these "infidels" into the country and the obvious economic gains derived from their immigration by the Church itself, as well as by society at large. Even the Synod of Piotrków of 1542, which included various anti-Jewish proposals, demanded only a sharp limitation of the number of Jews admitted to Poland, especially to Cracow and Kazimierz. For this purpose the assembled churchmen objected to the Jews acquiring houses in localities in which they had not lived before. They demanded that the king ordain that such houses be disposed of by the Jews within a stated period or be taken away without compensation. The synod added:

He [the king] shall also order the destruction of all new synagogues, even in Cracow. While the Jews are tolerated by the Church in memory of the passion of our Saviour, their number should be allowed to increase in but a very limited way. According to the regulations of the sacred canons, they are to be permitted to repair old synagogues, but not to build new ones.

Yet, although this form of prohibition had indeed dated back to Roman times and had played a great role in Judeo-Christian and Judeo-Muslim relations throughout the Middle Ages, the six-

teenth-century Polish hierarchy did not harp on it in its meetings
and pronunciamentos. In some cases, to be sure, negotiations for
a building permit were protracted, even costly, but as a rule the
Jews erected their basic communal institutions without too much
delay; often even without requesting a permit. In view of the extensive self-government granted them from the outset by the law
of the land, this procedure seems not to have evoked any opposition in many areas. In general beset by tremendous difficulties
arising from the growing Protestant Reformation, the Church
probably considered the Jewish issue of relatively minor importance. Only with the full onset of the Counter Reformation, under
Sigismund III, did the Church's anti-Jewish influence make itself
more severely felt. The Synod of Gniezno of 1589 and its successors began to pursue the prohibition of new synagogues, too, with
more sustained vigor and determination. In 1638, finally, a royal
decree issued by Wladislaw IV generally outlawed the erection of
new synagogues. But by that time Jewish immigration and the resulting formation of new communities had greatly slowed down.[8]

Understandably, the strongest opposition to Jewish settlement
came from the burghers; it stemmed mainly from their economic
rivalries with the incoming Jewish merchants and artisans. The
artisan guilds, in particular, often tried to safeguard their monopolistic control. Remarkably, however, their vision was usually restricted to their own localities. Rarely do we hear of concerted
efforts by the burghers' class to influence general governmental
policies concerning the admission of Jews to Poland. We shall see
that even a rather exceptional interurban alliance between Lwów,
Cracow, and Poznań, in 1521, ultimately resulted in a quest for
special legislation for each particular municipality. Yet, when this
move failed to persuade either the king or the Diet, the cities
turned to separate negotiations, aimed at securing advantages for
their own local struggles, not only against Jews and other non-
burghers but also against other competing cities. Locally, however,
some municipalities obtained from the kings sweeping privileges
de non tolerandis Judaeis under this or another guise. No fewer
than eighteen cities are recorded to have received such privileges
in the period from 1520 to 1600. Of course, like other royal decrees in Poland, these privileges did not necessarily exclude all
Jews, the city councils themselves sometimes making exceptions

for favored individuals. Yet the residence rights of such preferred Jews were always more precarious and could easily be terminated.[9]

In most other metropolitan areas the hostile burghers succeeded only in segregating Jews in separate quarters within their cities or, occasionally, in forcing them to settle in outlying communities such as Kazimierz, outside Cracow. Nor was this segregationist policy limited to Judeo-Christian relations. For example, the Protestant township of Leszno existed side by side with Catholic Warsaw, while Stare Szkoty accommodated Anabaptists and other radical Reformers not tolerated in neighboring, predominantly Lutheran Gdańsk. In many areas Jewish residence within, or close to, the city limits was made possible only because numerous enclaves (so-called *jurydyki*) were under the control of nobles or churchmen and were thus outside the city's jurisdiction. Lwów actually had to accommodate two Jewish communities, one in the city proper and another in a suburb, the relationships between the two sets of elders often vastly complicating Jewish life in that Red Russian emporium. On the other hand, the effort of the Poznań city council, on the occasion of a great fire in 1536, to remove the Jews to the village of Rybaki, was frustrated by the intervention of the provincial governor, Luka Gurko. (Ultimately, with the further growth of Jewish population, there arose a separate Jewish community in nearby Swarzędz-Schwersenz.) But this struggle for admission to the cities was only a phase of the relationships between the burghers and the Jews, which were so ramified and infringed on so many aspects of Jewish life that they will have to be treated more fully in the next chapter.[10]

Remarkably, xenophobic manifestations also appeared within the Jewish camp. At least in the latter part of the sixteenth century, when most of the immigrants had developed their own vested interests and other characteristics of a settled population, some leaders began looking askance at the arrival of competing newcomers, whether from abroad or from other parts of Poland and Lithuania. Typical of the sentiments prevailing at the end of the century are the following drastic provisions of the Cracow Jewish community's ordinance of 1595:

He who, without having the right of sojourn [*ḥazaqah*], shall try to settle here without the permission of the elders and the *Kahal* and establish himself in either the Jewish quarter or elsewhere in Kazimierz,

Cracow, Kleparz, or Stradom, or the district belonging to these localities, be it man or woman, widower or widow [despite the rights of his or her deceased mate], shall be excommunicated from all the holiness of Israel, segregated from the two worlds [this world and the hereafter], have no child circumcised, and not be buried in a Jewish graveyard. Should such a one nevertheless deliberately attempt to settle here in the Jewish quarter, no houseowner shall venture to admit him, under the same penalty, the payment of a fine of 30 florins to the governor and 15 florins to charity, and the confiscation of the house by the community.

Equally extreme were the resolutions adopted by the Lithuanian Jewish Council in its first session of 1623. The assembled delegates declared: "No [Jew] from another country shall be allowed to establish a residence in any Lithuanian province without the knowledge and consent of the [Jewish] head of the province." They added a special safeguard for the community of Minsk by providing that "if a stranger from any part of Poland should settle near the city of Minsk, they should ruthlessly pursue him and expel him from this land." These sharply anti-alien regulations, to be sure, seem to reflect attitudes generated by the steadily diminishing economic opportunities for Jews and non-Jews alike under the regime of Sigismund III. They nevertheless reveal the extent to which even the Jewish leaders could be affected by the isolationist spirit animating most city councils.[11]

For the exercise of such controls over the admission of newcomers to their communities, the Cracow and Lithuanian elders could, indeed, invoke many legal precedents going back to the talmudic age. Known by the term *ḥezqat* (or *ḥerem*) *ha-yishub* (acquired right, or ban, of settlement), and subject to varying interpretations in the light of changing local conditions, the authority of the community to safeguard the interests of its members was vouchsafed by normative Jewish law, which in varying degrees mirrored conditions in the closed societies of Sassanian Babylonia and medieval Europe. Now the Polish Jewish communities secured confirmation of this right from Sigismund I in 1532. In the same connection, some communities even regulated the conditions under which a member might accommodate transients with the elders' permission. Even in the synagogue the leading in divine services by a stranger was subject to the elders' approval. Going further, some communities withdrew the right of settlement from a resident member convicted of a crime or immoral behavior, giving him the alternative of either leaving his residence or else joining the Christian community.[12]

The almost constant struggle of Jews for admission to Polish cities may well be illustrated by the developments in Lublin, Warsaw, and Vilna. All three cities were to play a great role in the cultural history of East-European Jewry, Warsaw and Vilna becoming, in the nineteenth century, leading intellectual centers. Only Lublin, however, had an important Jewish community in the sixteenth century, when the city's annual fairs attracted a vast cosmopolitan merchant group from both western and eastern countries. The resultant commercial opportunities, as well as Lublin's location in the center of the Polish Crown, accounted for the rapid growth of the city's population, which in the 1560s totaled some 10,000 souls. Unable to gain admission to the city proper (only one Jossko was granted such a permit by the intolerant local bourgeoisie), Jews began clustering around the castle, which was under the control of the district governor (*starosta*) and was thus outside the authority of the city council. As early as January 25, 1505, King Alexander issued a privilege in favor of "the Jew Szabdey Haniec residing outside the walls of our city of Lublin . . . to trade freely in Lublin and anywhere else in Our kingdom." Yet, when suggesting in 1523 to Sigismund I that a general privilege be granted to the Lublin Jewish community, the *starosta,* Johannes de Pilcza, did not stress the Jews' commercial and fiscal usefulness, but rather their assistance in cleaning the river (Vistula) and in maintaining the castle walls. The king complied and, in his decree of February 27, 1523, placed Lublin Jewry on a footing of equality with the other Jewish communities in Poland. The community soon flourished, establishing a famous academy of learning, successively headed by such great luminaries as Rabbis Solomon b. Yeḥiel Luria and Meir b. Gedaliah, often identified by the acronyms Maharshal and Maharam of Lublin, respectively. Because of its location and the visits of distinguished Jewish leaders to the fairs, the city was ultimately selected as the seat of the first all-Polish Jewish tribunal, which soon led to the formation of the Council of Four Lands, the great central authority of the Jews of Poland and, for a time, of Lithuania.[13]

The growth of medieval Warsaw Jewry was cut short in 1527

when the duchy of Mazovia was incorporated into the Polish Crown and Sigismund I granted the burghers the privilege *de non tolerandis Judaeis* (April 2). But the king did not hesitate to make an immediate exception in favor of one Moise, "Our old toll master to whom, because of his services in behalf of the dukes of Mazovia, We have given the permission to live in Warsaw." This lifetime permit was limited to Moise and his immediate family. While it lasted it proved very profitable to both the toll collector and the Crown; but upon Moise's death some five years later, the surviving members of the family had to leave, and no Jews were allowed to reside in Warsaw for several generations. Sigismund I's decree of 1527 was duly confirmed by Sigismund II Augustus in 1570, Stephen Báthory in 1580, and Wladislaw IV in 1633. Only a few Jews were able to circumvent that prohibition by settling in neighboring suburbs belonging to Polish noblemen. Later on, when the Polish Diet held its meetings in Warsaw, Jews and others had to be allowed to visit the city from two weeks before to two weeks after each parliamentary session. In 1596–1611 Warsaw became the capital of the realm. Thenceforth the *Sejm* held regular biennial sessions there lasting six weeks each, in addition to many special convocations (particularly for the election of a new king), which often continued for several months. Some Jews, moreover, were able to prolong their stays by various means. In this endeavor they were aided by Diet members who, for the most part coming from provincial towns or estates, were eager to acquire luxuries and industrial products in Warsaw at the best price available, often from Jewish traders. However, Jews were not allowed to form a regular community with a synagogue, cemetery, or other religious or educational institutions. At late as the eighteenth century, the so-called Warsaw Committee, a permanent joint delegation of the Polish and Lithuanian Jewish Councils, had to conduct its negotiations without any backing from local elders.[14]

Vilna, too, which as early as 1387 had been endowed with the privileges of the Magdeburg law, successfully excluded Jews, although the Jewish population of neighboring Troki, divided between Karaites and Rabbanites, had received an independent privilege from Grand Duke Vitovt in 1388. At late as 1527, Sigismund I's decree in favor of the Vilna burghers expressly barred Jews from residence or trade in the city. Nonetheless, twenty-four years later two Jewish arrivals from Cracow received permission to trade in Vilna under the jurisdiction of the governor's tribunal. Another event of 1551 even more peremptorily opened the gates to Jewish settlement. The Lithuanian Diet, controlled by the nobility, resolved to exempt from municipal jurisdiction all members of the grand duke's council who acquired houses in the city. Before long, many Lithuanian nobles began owning houses and renting or selling them to Jews, riding roughshod over the city's protests. When the Union of Lublin of 1569, between Lithuania and the Crown, fully established the predominance of the nobility, Jews began to settle in Vilna in larger numbers. By 1573 they already owned a synagogue. On the occasion of an anti-Jewish riot nineteen years later, the records mention the existence of a Jewish street. Because of the contradictory nature of the royal privileges, the frequent litigations between the city and the Jews often ended in a stalemate. Nevertheless, the Jews increasingly secured *de facto* residential rights, and gradually expanded their occupational activities as well. Ultimately, royal decrees of 1633 and 1643, and a decision by the royal tribunal presided over by the king himself in 1646, formally legalized the existence of the Jewish community. Even efforts to keep the Jews from owning houses outside their rapidly expanding quarter, as well as reciprocally to prohibit Christians from acquiring houses within that quarter, broke down in the face of the continued cooperation between the Jews and the nobles.[15]

GEOGRAPHIC EXPANSION AND
NUMERICAL GROWTH

Cities pursuing policies of total intolerance were a small minority of the Polish-Lithuanian urban complex, however. Most towns and hamlets followed the example of the provincial capitals Poznań, Cracow, Lwów, and Brest-Litovsk in accommodating themselves, be it only under royal pressure, to the influx of Jews. At the most they tried to segregate the Jews in special quarters or to keep them at arm's length by restricting their residence, though not all their trading privileges, to a neighboring locality, such as

Kazimierz, in the case of Cracow, or (in part) the suburbs of Lwów. It has been estimated that at the end of the fifteenth century there were only about 50 communities in Poland and 4 in Lithuania, but that by the 1560s their number had increased to 52 in Great Poland and Mazovia, 41 in Little Poland, and about 80 in Red Russia, Volhynia, and Podolia (or a total of 173 in the Polish Crown) while the number of Lithuanian communities jumped to over 20. In addition there were many lesser settlements of a few families each, some of which soon developed into peculiar subcommunities, called *przykahałki,* whose administration often was wholly under the control of the major communities. As a rule, the main community alone had secured specific governmental privileges, in addition to the country-wide royal charters, and thus had a stronger backing in public law, in return for the responsibility of collecting the ever-increasing Jewish taxes from both the main localities and the neighboring settlements.[16]

The vast authority exercised by the regional communities over their dependencies, based largely on judicial, funerary, and fiscal considerations, is well illustrated by the resolutions adopted by the Lithuanian Council at its constituent session of 1623, where only the three regional communities of Brest, Pinsk, and Grodno were represented. They read in part: "The communities of the entire region have no *hezqat ha-yishub* (exclusive residence rights) vis-à-vis the three major communities. . . . In commercial transactions the former may not protest against inhabitants of the major communities trading in their localities." Only in the case of a serious threat to the livelihood of the local shopkeepers could the dependent settlements seek redress from the regional elders elected by the major communities. In contrast, their members had no reciprocal right to settle or trade in the major cities without special permission from those elders. Such legislation and taxation "without representation" understandably irked the provincials. If they sometimes found ways of circumventing the rigid regulations, their evasions often gave rise to protracted disputes. This happened, for instance, in the community of Żółkiew at a later date, when it acted in defiance of the Lwów leadership. The smaller settlement could invoke the legal precedent established by the fifteenth-century rabbi Moses Menz in an analogous case in Germany. Menz had taught that, if the inhabitants of the hamlets had no share in passing particular ordinances, they "could not be subjected to them, and if they violated them they were not to be fined." [17]

A considerable number of Jewish families may also have settled in villages, including the new ones founded between 1450 and 1550. Polish historians have noted that in the century and a quarter from 1400 to 1523 no fewer than 950 villages are mentioned for the first time in the extant records of Great Poland alone. While some of these villages may merely have escaped previous notice, others undoubtedly were, for similar reasons, not recorded until after the first quarter of the sixteenth century. Such an increase of some 36 percent in Great Poland must have been vastly exceeded in the southeastern provinces of the Crown and in Lithuania, areas which were at that time the scene of intensive colonization and transformation of forest and marsh lands into agricultural settlements. In this process Jews seem to have actively participated. The best-known case is that of the Jewish merchant-banker, Wołczko the Tollman, in Lwów. As early as June 24, 1427, Wladislaw Jagiello appointed him bailiff of the village of Werbiż in the vicinity of Sambor. Wołczko, whose "industry, circumspection, and foresight" were praised by the king, was also given the right to erect a new village and "to settle persons of whatever status or sex, condition or kind." The tollmaster did indeed receive an allotment of land not far from Werbiż which he seems to have developed into another village, called Werbiża. Perhaps to appease objectors to such favors being extended to "infidels," the king mouthed the pious hope that his liberality might induce the Jewish bailiff to give up the "error of his unbelieving blindness" and stop practicing "his execrable ritual." Wołczko's failure to do so evidently did not prevent Jagiello from granting further privileges to his Jewish favorite, who on August 4, 1427, was able to transfer the bailiwick of the village of Karez to a Christian master for 40 marks. It stands to reason that the villages of Wołczków, Wolkowa, Wolków, and Wołkowce, mentioned in the late medieval sources, likewise owed their origin to Wołczko's initiative. We may also assume that, utilizing the royal privilege of freely choosing his settlers, the Jewish colonizer placed quite a few coreligionists in these villages, if for no other reasons than to have them help him supervise the progress of colonization and exercise some of his jurisdictional rights. Some of these Jews may well have joined the local peasantry. The name of one Chłopko Judaeus (the little Jew peasant), who appeared at a Lwów fair in the early fifteenth century, is probably indicative of his calling. To be sure, we know little about Jewish villagers in southeastern Poland before the seventeenth century, but our ignorance may be owing entirely to the paucity of records resulting from the general inarticulateness of the peasant class, non-Jewish as well as Jewish.[18]

Another vast area opened up to Jewish expansion in the adjacent territories which came under Polish overlordship in the late fifteenth through mid-seventeenth centuries. This was the period of Poland's greatest political and military power. Because the Polish Commonwealth extended considerable liberties to their ruling classes, some neighboring lands voluntarily sought its protection against their mighty enemies, especially the Muscovite Empire. It has been shown that Poland-Lithuania, which by 1582 embraced an area of 815,000 square kilometers (some 315,000 square miles), reached a peak of 900,000 square kilometers (about 347,000 square miles) after the peace treaties with the Muscovite and Ottoman empires in 1634. Of this area, the second-largest of any contemporary European state, only 180,000 square kilometers (some 70,000 square miles) formed the close Polish ethnographic settlement, although the Poles, together with the scattered Polish and Polonized groups, may have amounted to some 40 percent of the heterogeneous total population.

In the West the centuries-long struggle with the knights of the Teutonic Order ended with the Order's submission to Polish overlordship in the Treaty of Toruń (Thorn) of 1466. This surrender opened up the gates of Königsberg (now Kaliningrad) to Jewish settlement. Soon after the Order's secularization, two Jewish physicians were admitted to residence in the city, in 1538 and 1541, respectively. They and other Jewish settlers laid the foundation for a Jewish community which, despite a hostile resolution by the Three Estates in 1566 and a ducal decree on July 14, 1567, rescinding the earlier toleration of Jews (any Jew thereafter found in the duchy was to be deprived of all rights, regardless of any protective

document in his favor) gradually resumed its growth and ultimately played a leading role in Germany's eighteenth-century
Haskalah movement. In contrast, Gdańsk (Danzig) long resisted
the admission of Jews. In 1454, under the burghers' pressure, even
the relatively tolerant Casimir IV issued the so-called *Privilegium
Casimirianum,* which provided that "no Lombard, Nuremberger,
Scot, Englishman, or Jew shall enjoy the liberties of the city." Although in 1476 the same king authorized two Jews to trade
throughout the Prussian "province," the intolerant local citizenry
continued to bar Jews from Gdańsk itself in the following decades.
In reprisal, some Lithuanian Jewish merchants decided to boycott
the traders of that leading Polish port by entering into direct dealings with French and English agents. However, this arrangement
proved unsatisfactory to both sides, and individual Jews began
trading in Gdańsk in a sporadic fashion. Yet in 1577, when Poland formally recognized the free-city status of Gdańsk, the city
demanded the expulsion of its few Jewish residents. As late as
1595, the city council allowed Jews to visit Gdańsk only during
fairs, provided they would refrain from public worship. Yet in an
undated application, two Poznań Jews, Jochim and Isaac Manres,
appearing as "spokesmen of the Jewish nation," complained that
even during the two annual fairs they had to remain in the "Scot-
land" district and were not allowed to enter the main quarter
where the fair was held. Nonetheless, the city's division into three
autonomous entities facilitated circumvention of the hostile legislation, and by the end of the sixteenth century, it appears, perhaps
as many as 400–500 Jews were able to reside there. Similarly, when
in the sixteenth century Polish domination began to extend north-
eastward over what later became Latvia and Estonia, the Polish
regime slowly opened the gates for the influx of Jews to that Baltic
area. However, this immigration, too, became significant only late
in the century, and will be treated in Chapter LXIX.[19]

For this and other reasons, it is extremely difficult to estimate
the Jewish population in Poland-Lithuania during the Jagiellon
period. Only after the adoption of a general capitation tax
(*pogłówne*) in 1549 was the royal courtier Stanisław Lipnicki able
to compile from the early tax records an extensive description of
the Jewish inhabitants in the provinces of Sandomierz, Red Russia,

Podolia, Lublin, and Bełz. Soon thereafter the government also had at its disposal figures derived from more general censuses conducted in various regions in the 1560s and 1570s. The outcome of these so-called *lustracje* have been more fully examined only in recent years, and some areas still await the close scrutiny they deserve.[20]

In any case, as we shall see, the methods employed in these first census efforts were rather primitive. Their glaring deficiencies must have persuaded the government to negotiate with the Jewish leaders for special lump sum payments from the individual communities and, ultimately, from the Jews of the country at large. This system lasted almost until the end of the Commonwealth; that is, until 1764, when the Diet and Stanislaus II Augustus Poniatowski, the last king of Poland, disbanded the great Polish and Lithuanian councils and their regional subordinates. The deficiencies of these censuses have undermined the confidence of modern scholars in the results of all older censuses.[21]

Somewhat more acceptable are the estimates of the Jewish population in individual Jewish communities. Some of them are based on the number of houses in the Jewish street, a number which was steadily on the increase. For example, in Poznań—which, according to the censuses of 1550 and 1552, was one of the four communities having a Jewish population of over 1,000 souls, the others being Cracow, Lublin, and Lwów—the allowable quota of Jewish houses at that time was only 49. In 1558, however, even the antagonistic city council had to raise the quota to 83, and in the early 1600s to 138, buildings. The Jews were aided in this endeavor by a number of noble landlords, some of them high officials, who built houses for them both in the Jewish quarter and outside the city walls. In 1619 the number of such houses amounted to 22. For some reason, 5 plots belonging to nobles had not yet been built on, despite the great population density within the Jewish quarter, which in 1590 covered 16,025 square meters of the total area of 210,000 square meters within the city walls. In 1539 a Cracow Jew had claimed, in his now lost apologetic treatise *Ad quaerelam mercatorum Cracoviensium, responsum Judaeorum* (A Reply by Jews to the Accusation of the Cracow Merchants concerning Commerce), that in all of Poland there were only 500 Polish traders and almost no craftsmen, whereas the Jewish population embraced 3,200 merchants and three times as many artisans. This contrast doubtless was grossly exaggerated at that time, even if the author referred only to non-German Poles, but it quickly became realistic in the following decades.[22]

Jewish population growth would undoubtedly have been even greater if large-scale immigration and the substantial surplus of births over deaths had continued unhampered by natural catastrophes. However, like the rest of Europe of the period, Poland and Lithuania suffered from both recurrent pestilences and disastrous fires. True, Poland seems to have escaped the great ravages caused by the Black Death in other parts of Europe—even Silesia, as we recall, suffered only from its aftermath in the 1360s—and hence its nascent Jewish communities, except perhaps Cracow and Kalisz, were not "burned" in the German fashion. Yet, like almost all other countries, the Slavonic lands had their share of plagues. Other recurring contagious diseases must also have resulted in considerable loss of life. We learn from incidental references in private Yiddish letters written in 1588 that, at that time, some Cracow Jewish elders had fled the city to live in the small community of Olkusz, where the air was supposed to have been purer. But the majority remained behind in the capital and probably furnished their quota of victims. Moreover, even when there was no major catastrophe, the riot-prone Polish mobs sometimes killed Jews because they resented certain actions by individuals. It sufficed, for example, for some Poznań Jews in 1580 to persuade the wife of a convert not to follow her husband into the new faith, to cause a serious public disturbance which cost the lives of a number of Jews.[23]

Similarly, fires, which did not always result directly in the loss of human lives, frequently led to fatalities in anti-Jewish riots. As we recall, in sixteenth-century Bohemia, Jews were frequently accused of having started conflagrations because they allegedly wished to destroy their hated Christian neighbors. Here, too, for instance in Cracow in 1477, a fire which had started in the Jewish quarter and spread into the Christian areas, provoked the frenzied population not only to attack the Jewish street but also to demand the expulsion of the Jews from the city. This fire indeed contributed to the fateful compromise of 1485, whereby the Jews surrendered many commercial rights, and ultimately to the forcible transfer of the entire Jewish community to neighboring Kazimierz. Similarly, in 1536 a Poznań fire spreading from the Jewish quarter furnished the Poznań burghers a welcome opportunity to petition the king for total exclusion of Jews from the city. Anticipating royal objections, the city elders tried, through the Poznań-born Marchioness Hedwig, to induce her husband, Elector Joachim II of Brandenburg, to intervene with the Polish king. They claimed that the city, which was beginning to enjoy the fruits of prosperity, "has been burned by the infidel Jews and to a large extent turned into ashes. For God has decided to punish them, and us together with them, on account of the overbearing haughtiness with which they have undermined the livelihood of us Christians." The burghers succeeded in removing the Jews to the neighboring suburb of Rybaki. But, owing to a firm royal intervention, that exile proved to be short-lived. More serious was the 1590 conflagration which claimed 15 Jewish lives and destroyed 75 houses and 70–80 Torah scrolls. This time the Jews seem to have been the major victims of the fire; hence the accusation of their arson lacked all plausibility. For this reason the city council did not insist upon removal of the Jews, and even arranged for temporary accommodation of the homeless families in Christian houses. It stipulated that such hospitality should extend only for a very brief period, however, and that the Jews obligate themselves to rebuild their homes within two years and then move back to their quarter. So frequent had attacks on Jews become that, beginning in 1640, the Jewish elders placed a permanent guard at the entrance to the Jewish quarter whose duty it was to inform them of any incipient anti-Jewish riots. As late as 1725 when a violent storm destroyed a part of Poznań, miraculously leaving the Jewish quarter fairly intact, the Jewish communal organs, to forestall possible accusations, forbade their members to acquire any objects which might have come from the ruined Christian dwellings. In short, one cannot venture any estimate of the average life expectancy among the Polish or Lithuanian Jews. We are not even able to ascertain the accuracy of the contemporary observation, by the generally anti-

Jewish writer Mikołaj Rej, that most Jews were very fat and for this reason often died before their time.[24]

THE LAST JAGIELLONS

As in many Western countries, the relatively stablest relationship existed between the royal power and its Jewish subjects. The kings, who generally welcomed Jewish immigration, also endowed the Jews with privileges, whether country-wide in scope or addressed to specific localities. As elsewhere, these decrees greatly varied in detail; they depended on the ever-changing local and regional conditions and power struggles, and on the personal temperament of the rulers. Yet there existed a basic legislative and administrative continuity which, despite occasional disruptions, endured from the days of Casimir the Great to the end of the Commonwealth.

In contrast to the general constitutional developments in western Europe, however, those in Poland-Lithuania gradually weakened the royal prerogative and concentrated power in the hands of the gentry (*szlachta*). This process, begun in the middle of the fifteenth century, reached a climax in the *pacta conventa* of 1573. Thenceforth Poland-Lithuania was a "Nobles' Commonwealth" (*Rzeczpospolita szlachecka*) governed by an increasingly unruly mass of nobles, under an elective and often powerless king. In this degenerated form the country finally fell prey to its three predatory neighbors.[25]

In the meantime the trends toward "protoabsolutism" along the prevailing Western lines, which had manifested themselves during the long regime of Casimir IV (1447–92), were reversed under his sons and successors. His elder sons, John Albert and Alexander, reigned only a few years each (1492–1501, 1501–1506) and had little chance to develop major policies of their own. True, Grand Duke Alexander, after taking over the Polish crown in 1501, not only readmitted Jews to Lithuania but also decreed that the exiles be allowed to reclaim all their previous possessions (1503). Later he entrusted Prince Alexander Jurewicz with the task of aiding the Jews in collecting their loans from both nobles and burghers. The king also made concessions to other Jews under special circumstances. For example, in 1503, to alleviate the "poverty" of the Poznań Jews, he ordered their coreligionists in neighboring Gniezno and Międzyrzecze to share in their burdens. In 1506 Alexander freed the Jews, as well as the Christians, of Lwów from tolls and other indirect taxes and reduced the former's direct tax payments from 200 to 100 zlotys. In the same year he also renewed the privilege of Lwów Jewry prohibiting any municipal interference with their trade at fairs. However, all these measures were designed only to keep the Jewish economy intact for the benefit of the Polish Treasury. For the same reason Alexander also promoted the interests of certain Jewish favorites. Although he had to cancel a three-year contract with one Jossko for the collection of all tolls in the area of Lwów and Bełz, he nevertheless upheld Jossko's tax immunity from all imposts, both general and communal. He also exempted Jossko and his entire family from all but the royal jurisdiction. Equally extensive were his benefactions in favor of the newly arrived Spanish physician, Isaac Hispanus.[26]

On the other hand, in 1502 Alexander readily yielded to the entreaties of Duke Konrad of Mazovia to stop certain alleged "innovations" by a Jewish tollmaster in Główno. He also listened to the complaints of the Lwów district governor (*starosta*), Stanisław of Chodecz, that Jews were smuggling wax from Lithuania without paying the required customs duties. Stanisław claimed: ". . . these Jews act to the great detriment of Your Majesty's kingdom, than which there is no greater detriment," but added that their illicit traffic could not be checked in the deserted areas between the two countries. Most remarkably, Alexander never formally renewed the general royal Charter for Polish Jewry. When, on the king's order, Chancellor Jan Łaski compiled the existing Polish legislation in chronological sequence, the Jewish privilege was included, with the compiler's excuse that this was done "for the protection of Christians." [27]

Quite different was Alexander's younger brother Sigismund I (1507–1548). Though generally enlightened and honest, Sigismund was too weak and cunctatory to lend his regime enough force against the conflicting factions or to pursue any policy without wavering. His retreat on the international scene lowered the prestige of the monarchy internally as well. At the beginning of the sixteenth century Poland still was an expanding major power, playing a significant role in European affairs. However, owing in part to Sigismund's weakness, but in the main because of the Habsburg successes in extending their reign to the Netherlands, the Iberian Peninsula, and the New World, and the death of Louis II, the last Jagiellon ruler of Hungary, at the Battle of Mohács in 1526, Poland had to give up its great European ambitions. Only the Northeast still offered opportunities for Polish expansion, along the Baltic and into the interior of the Muscovite Empire. But after reaching a climax at the turn of the century the contest was reversed in Moscow's favor.[28]

Despite their political vagaries the monarchs still were the mainstay of Polish-Lithuanian Jewry. Here and there one could even hear faint echoes of the Western notion that Jews were "serfs" of the royal power. However, unlike their Western counterparts, the Polish rulers never employed that phrase; they merely indicated that the Jews' fiscal relationship with the Crown justified the general royal policy of extending protection to Jews against their numerous enemies. In Sigismund I's formulation the basic Charter expressly stated that the king "reserves them [the Jews] for Our Treasury" and that "these Jews belong to Our Treasury" (Arts. 9 and 36). Even its inclusion in Jan Łaski's compilation, ostensibly intended to shield the accepted text from future Jewish interpolations, such as were often bruited about by Jew-baiters, in effect reinforced its validity and the Jews' ability to invoke its articles for the defense of their rights. As reenacted by Sigismund I in 1539, this statute assumed its more or less definitive form. But its pro-Jewish implications and some of the more sweeping statements concerning the Jews' equality with their Christian neighbors in various local privileges were often hedged by limitations of specific Jewish rights when they conflicted with royal privileges granted to burghers and others. Sigismund was particularly guilty of such inconsistencies. Not even when dealing with different groups of Jews was he entirely of one mind. For example, when in 1519 he issued a decree placing the Jews residing in a Lwów suburb on an equal footing with their coreligionists in the inner city, he did not pursue that policy with any degree of firmness. In general, the king was easily swayed by whichever adviser he listened to last.[29]

Even Sigismund's deep attachment to his strong-willed second wife Bona Sforza, who tried to uphold the power of the monarchy, failed to strengthen his backbone at crucial moments. In fact, the queen's own rapacious policies and attempts to buy up numerous noble estates (including those of such eminent converts from Judaism as Jan and Constantyn Abrahamowicz, sons of Abraham Ezofowicz) antagonized not only the imperiled magnates but also much of Polish public opinion in general. So did many of the queen's Italian advisers—about 280 Italians, including three Jewish physicians, had arrived in Poland together with Bona after her marriage in 1518, and others followed in subsequent years—whose business ethics appeared to the Poles no less objectionable than their social behavior. One of the Italian Jewish doctors, Samuel b. Meshullam, came into conflict with the famous Cracow rabbi Jacob Polak, who had allegedly accused him of having an affair with a married Jewish woman, Klara. Through his connections with the royal house, Samuel succeeded in forcing Polak out of the country, notwithstanding the rabbi's excellent relations with the leading local Jewish family, Fiszel (Fischel), into which Polak had married. Yet, at times, Bona herself intervened in favor of Jews and sometimes even settled controversies within the Jewish community. For instance, in her capacity as queen mother, she issued three decrees in 1549–53 resolving a bitter conflict over the election of a rabbi in Grodno. Sometimes, however, Sigismund even defied the will of the Church, which was then on the defensive because of the incipient spread of Reform tendencies in the country. The king did not hesitate, for example, expressly to allow the construction of a second synagogue in Cracow and ordered the Cracow governor to set aside a plot for the new building (1537).[30]

Nor was Sigismund I persistent enough in his attempt to secure control over all Jewish communities by a centralized fiscal administration. Beginning in 1512 he appointed so-called chief rabbis for Great Poland, Little Poland, Red Russia, and Lithuania. Following precedents set by his predecessors in 1389–93 when one Pechno was appointed *episcopus Judaeorum Poznaniae*, Sigismund finally selected, in 1514, Abraham of Bohemia as the official

leader of Polish Jewry, and Michael Ezofowicz (brother of the
convert Abraham, who was making a career in the Lithuanian administration and ultimately became a nobleman, serving from
1510 on as *podskarbi;* that is, Secretary of the Treasury) as chief
of the Jews of Lithuania. Michael, though remaining a Jew, was
in 1525 raised to the ranks of the nobility during the festive ceremony of homage by Duke Albert of Prussia to his overlord Sigismund. Like their respective German coreligionists, however, the
Polish-Lithuanian Jews did not cooperate with such royal appoin-
tees, but preferred their own elected rabbis and elders, with a local
or at best regional jurisdiction. After a few years of experimenta-
tion, Sigismund yielded, and approved the election by the Jews
themselves of provincial chief rabbis and lay leaders who could
represent the Jews before the king as well as convey the monarch's wishes to the Jewish communities under their control. To
strengthen the hands of these provincial chiefs, the king confirmed
in 1518–19 the selection by Poznań Jewry of two new chief rabbis
for their province. He was more specific in his decree of 1527
which ratified the unanimous election of Rabbi Samuel Margolies
(Margaliot) for that post. He authorized the rabbi

as long as he may live, to judge all Jews in the lands of Great Poland
and the duchy of Mazovia in matters pertaining to law; to recognize,
bind or absolve, to impose censures and bans, in accordance with the
ritual and custom of Mosaic law; and to exercise all other forms of
authority in spiritual matters. It is hereby expressly stated, and, as the
said Jews have declared before Us, has been observed as an ancient
usage that, if any Jew should venture to take lightly the censures and
bans imposed upon him by the aforementioned Doctor [Rabbi] Samuel
and make no attempt to extricate himself therefrom within one
month, such a person, after being denounced to Us, shall be beheaded
and all his property shall be confiscated for Our Treasury.

In 1533 Sigismund also sanctioned the operation of an intercity
Jewish tribunal which began meeting in Lublin in connection
with the great fairs. These early joint efforts by the Polish-Lithuanian communities were ultimately crowned by the formation of
the two great Jewish Councils.[31]
     Many inconsistencies in Sigismund's policies were due to the
internal power struggles between factions and classes. While Casi-

mir IV had relied mainly upon the landowning oligarchy, its excesses forced the Polish kings of the early sixteenth century to promote the power of the poorer gentry. To be sure, the *szlachta* would not achieve complete ascendancy until later. But during Sigismund's regime many areas in Poland and Lithuania were removed from under the direct control of the king–grand duke and were handed over to the autonomous jurisdiction of their noble owners, as well as of churches.

This transition affected the Jews both favorably and adversely. On the one hand, Jews proved economically very useful, especially to the great landowners. As early as 1521 the anti-Jewish burgher-historian Justus Ludwig Dietz (Decius or Decyusz) observed that "there is hardly a magnate, even among the Commonwealth leaders, who does not hand over the management of his estate to a Jew. He thus entrusts to Jews dominion over Christians, and more zealously protects them against any wrong, real or imaginary, than he protects Christians." We have seen that many Jews found shelter in enclaves (*jurydyki*) of otherwise hostile cities because they were protected there by the secular or ecclesiastical lords. On the other hand, these masters often exercised arbitrary rule over the Jews under their control. The king often refrained from interfering in the "internal" operations of these separate entities, since the nobles could invoke not only the general constitution, *Nihil Novi* of 1505 (whereby the monarchy had promised not to enact any changes in the existing status without the agreement of the Diet), but also the specific privileges granted the nobles from time to time. Sigismund drew the logical consequence from that situation when in 1539 he promulgated a decision adopted by the Diet:

Those nobles who in their towns and villages keep Jews, are allowed by Us to receive all the fruits and emoluments from them. They shall also administer the law for the Jews according to their own judgment. In fact, We do not allow these Jews, from whom We derive no benefit, to make use of the Jew law enacted by Us and Our predecessors, nor do We wish them to appeal to Us in cases of infringement. Those from whom We receive no benefit shall have none of Our protection.

Like many other royal pronunciamentos, this threat, intending to stem the tide of private agreements between the Jews and the nobles, was never completely implemented. The nobles increasingly enjoyed much leeway, and at times completely arbitrary power, in dealing with their Jews. In discussing the situation of the Jewish community of Rymanów, R. Meir of Lublin, noted that the strict enforcement of rabbinic regulations affecting trade in wine would undermine the Jews' ability to make a living, and added: "It is known that their lord is a wild man of wide-ranging powers, so that it is even impossible for them to flee and escape from under his authority." Yet, the king continued to function as the permanent and overall protector of Jewish rights throughout the country.[32]

The traditional alliance between the Jews and the royal power found an even more telling expression during the reign of Sigismund II Augustus (1548–72). Much more gifted than his father, the new king inherited from his mother some of the Italian diplomatic techniques, and from the outset sought to strengthen the power of the monarchy. However, his passionate nature led him to devote much of his time and energy to hedonistic pursuits, and at crucial moments he neglected important public affairs. Having been associated with his father in the management of government (as early as 1530 he had been elected grand duke of Lithuania, to serve concurrently with Sigismund I, so as to assure his future succession to the throne of that country as well as of Poland), he realized the usefulness of the Jews to the Polish-Lithuanian economy and fiscal structure. He found the country's finances in grave disarray. Much of the public expenditure had theretofore been covered by revenue from the royal domains. Yet, like the earlier kings, his father was often much too liberal in handing over royal estates to favorite nobles, either as outright gifts or as pledges for insignificant loans. From the outset, therefore, the redemption (called "execution") of that domain through legislation loomed very large among the reform projects widely discussed at the Diet and by the publicists of the period. Hand in hand with that redemption went the problem of general fiscal reform, which was also to lay the foundation for the complete restructuring of the army. The employment of a small but efficient standing army of mercenaries, to supplement the nobles and other citizens called to arms at times of emergency, now became an urgent necessity. Needless to say, the maintenance of such a corps of hirelings was expensive, and required a royal Treasury able to finance it in peace and war.[33]

Apart from endeavoring to recapture the royal domain through a slow and cumbersome procedure, Sigismund Augustus sought to raise regular revenue by instituting in 1549 a general capitation tax (*poglówne*). Jews, Tatars, and Gypsies throughout the possessions of the Crown were required to pay an annual per capita tax of one zloty. This tax was extended in 1552 to the Jews inhabiting areas controlled by the nobles, as well as to those of Lithuania. It thus became clear that even those Jews who lived under the protection of magnates or the Church had to pay that poll tax, and hence legally came under the king's direct control. From the beginning of his reign Sigismund Augustus viewed the protection of Jews as a very important royal prerogative. In 1548, soon after his coronation as king of Poland-Lithuania, he solemnly confirmed the basic Charter of Polish and Lithuanian Jewry in the extended form promulgated by his father. He supplemented these decrees by special ordinances reaffirming the rights of Jews in various localities, such as Cracow (1549). In his confirmation of the rights of Przemyśl Jewry in 1559, he went so far as to declare sweepingly: "Otherwise these Jews shall enjoy all the liberties there . . . which are enjoyed by Our city of Przemyśl." With this assertion he did not intend to imply a complete equality of rights between Jews and burghers. Such an implication, in the face of the diverse specific privileges previously granted to the two groups, as well as the general legal structure which allowed for many exceptions through detailed regulations or customs, would have been quite anachronistic. But the statement did indicate the royal wish to protect those rights of Jews which were not specifically delimited by law.[34]

General political and religious struggles affected the Jews to an even greater extent than did the royal wishes. In its drive to power, the gentry, on whom the king leaned heavily in his attempt to reduce the power of the great landowners, pursued economic policies which were ultimately ruinous to the state. The magnates saw to it that their own products—particularly grain, lumber, and cattle—should be freely exported to other countries, thereby keeping the prices of agricultural produce very high. On

the other hand, they tried to keep the frontiers open to the importation of foreign industrial products with low customs duties
or entirely duty-free so as to hold down the prices of such commodities for their own consumption. This policy adversely affected
the Jewish tollmasters and customhouse administrators, but it favored those Jews who, in the landlords' service, were busy exporting agricultural produce and importing industrial goods. This
situation was further underscored by the provision that nobles
should not engage in retail trade or petty crafts. As a result the
Jews faced competition only in the cities, from the local burghers
and from foreign merchants whom Polish legislation encouraged
to come in person. At the same time, the Polish Crown inhibited
journeys of Polish merchants abroad. Jews, with their interterri-
torial relations, were able to utilize the opportunities thus created
to good advantage. Ultimately, of course, the economic ruin of the
country occasioned by the preponderance of the increasingly self-
seeking and anarchical gentry proved detrimental to Jewish interests as well.[35]

The socioeconomic and political consequences of this unbal-
anced class policy were intensified after the famous Union of Lublin in 1569, which established a permanent tie between Poland
and Lithuania. Among its other effects, the Union brought about
the emancipation of the Lithuanian gentry from the overlordship
of the magnates, and their increasing parity with their Polish compeers. As a result, the Jews, who had theretofore been permitted
to appear on Lithuanian streets in a garb resembling that of the
nobles and to wear swords and other marks of distinction, were
now forbidden to do so. Even the problem of a special Jewish
badge, as we shall see, also assumed increasing importance in the
debates of lawyers and politicians, though it never became a full-
fledged reality in either of the two realms. With the Union the
unusual privilege of Lithuanian converts from Judaism—who,
upon baptism, were to be raised immediately to the rank of nobility—lost some of its practical effect, although the First Lithuanian Statute of 1528 and even the Third Statute of 1588, promulgated after the Union (XII, 7, Art. 5), were quite explicit on
this matter. The provision that "should a Jew or Jewess join the
Christian faith such a person and his or her offspring shall be rec-

ognized as noblemen" was not formally abrogated until 1764, and even then the Diet made clear that the abrogation had no retro-active force. Yet there is relatively little evidence of its actual im-plementation. Perhaps because of the relative paucity of conver-sions of Lithuanian Jews after 1528, we know of very few ennobled apostates such as one Oszejko in 1499 and Abraham Ezofowicz a few years later. (After all, Abraham's brother Michael also re-ceived the noble title of De Leliwa while remaining a professing Jew and leader of his community.) Another result of the Union was that several Lithuanian provinces, including Volhynia, Pod-lasie, and parts of the Ukraine, were now incorporated into the Polish Crown. On this occasion five representatives each of the Rabbanite and the Karaite Jews of Łuck, and fifteen other Jews, led by one Habram Juryczyn, along with the nobles and the bur-ghers, took an oath of fealty to the Crown (June 1569). Apparently the nobles of Podlasie, and perhaps also those of the other areas, had to be persuaded to take such an oath by the royal pledge to take care of "whatever grievance and complaint [they might have] with respect to customs duties and tolls, in regard to Jews, or any other aspect." [36]

The rapid progress of the Protestant Reformation, as we shall see, likewise was a double-edged sword with respect to the Jewish status. On the one hand, the break-up of the ecclesiastical unity of the Polish people, and the formation of ever-new Christian sects, diverted the attention of the Church from the Jewish question. From time to time, to be sure, Catholic church gatherings still de-manded the implementation of all canon laws relating to new or enlarged synagogues, the badge, and other discriminatory and seg-regationist features which had long been an integral part of the Catholic attitude toward Jews. At times they even demanded the complete exclusion of Jews from certain localities. But these reso-lutions as a rule carried little conviction, and were not vigorously pursued. On the other hand, denominational conflicts stirred up much religious feeling, even fanaticism, in the populace. It is small wonder, then, that the old folkloristic accusations relating to ritual murder were now heard more and more frequently in both Poland and Lithuania. The Catholic-Protestant conflict over the Eucharist also aggravated allegations of Jewish desecration of the host, and such charges led to the martyrdom of a number of Jews.

Sigismund Augustus, himself a pious Catholic, did not believe any of these accusations. But at the crucial moment in Suchaczew in 1556 his intervention came too late to save the defendants. He blamed this tragedy in part on the Jews themselves, because they had neglected to register with the local authorities the earlier royal decrees outlawing both the blood libel and rumors about blood flowing from hosts allegedly pierced by Jews. In response to the Suchaczew libel, he issued a sharp law declaring that all accusations of host desecration or ritual murder by Jews should be adjudicated exclusively by the so-called Diet tribunal, that is, by the Sejm in session in the presence of the king or his delegates. This decree of January 1557 also provided that before any trial on this score, all accused Jews should be released from prison in the custody of the Jewish community, failing which they were to be detained but not in chains. The king went even further in 1564, on the occasion of a Blood Accusation in Lithuania. Here Sigismund Augustus decided that no defendant could be convicted of either of these highly improbable crimes without the positive testimony of four reliable Christian and three Jewish witnesses. True, these ordinances did not prevent the populace from renewing the accusations from time to time. But the good will of the enlightened king, who could not believe that any Jew would commit murder to obtain blood for ritual purposes (since, as he emphasized, this allegation had been consistently denied by popes and kings), was clearly demonstrated. Not surprisingly, therefore, the death of the friendly monarch was mourned by the Jewish communities, that of Cracow entering into its official minute book a special memorial passage recording his demise, on Monday, Tammuz 26, 5332 (July 8, 1572). The contemporary Jewish chronicler David Gans of Prague, likewise, recorded the passing of the "righteous" (ḥasid) king, adding the usual formula beseeching the divine grace to secure the immortality of the monarch's soul. On the whole, despite his hesitant and sometimes ambivalent policy, Sigismund Augustus' reign was one of the happier periods of Jewish sojourn in East-Central Europe. During that period the rapidly growing Jewish communities in the country struck deep roots which enabled them to weather the subsequent storms.[37]

TWO INTERREGNA AND BÁTHORY

Sigismund II's demise ended the Jagiellon dynasty's rule over Poland. The king's failure to provide for the election of a successor led to a prolonged electoral campaign, the candidacy of many foreign princes, and the exaction by the gentry of enormous concessions on the part of the would-be new kings. Among the most serious candidates were Ivan the Terrible, the tsar of Muscovy; and the Habsburg prince Ernest, son of Emperor Maximilian II. How much both these candidates pursued the interests of their respective countries, rather than of what might become their new royal responsibilities, was shown in their secret plans, which later came to light, contemplating the ultimate partition of Poland. In the end a measure of Polish patriotism prevailed and the electoral assembly turned to the more distant, and hence more disinterested, Prince Henry of Valois, duke of Anjou and brother of the reigning king of France, Charles IX. Henry accepted the election, although it took him several months to reach Poland.

Perhaps Henry's most significant royal act was his signing the so-called *pacta conventa* (though he refused to accept their further elaboration in the *artykuły henrykowskie* [Henry's Articles], which his successors signed), providing for the complete domination of Polish-Lithuanian affairs by the *szlachta*. Some Jews, like their Protestant neighbors, expected that religious intolerance would now spread in Poland, especially after they heard rumors that Henry had aided his mother, Catherine de Médicis, in staging the St. Bartholomew's Day Massacre of thousands of French Huguenots in August 1572. For this reason, on May 3, 1573, the so-called Warsaw Confederation of all parties at the electoral Diet agreed on the following safeguards for religious freedom:

Since Turks, Armenians, Tatars, Greeks, and Jews not only sojourn in Poland but also reside there and [freely] move from place to place, they ought [undisturbedly] to profess their faiths, enjoy their liberties, and benefit, so to say, from the same rights of citizenship [*una quasi civitate utantur*]. For this reason neither those who are convicted of heresies under whatever law, nor others who are entitled to enjoy immunities and equal rights with other nobles, shall be subjected to harsh censures.

Despite the failure of the large majority of bishops to sign this declaration, and their subsequent protests, a clause to this effect was inserted in the *pacta conventa*, to be signed by the new king after his election thirteen days later. On his part, Henry, perhaps to underscore his staunch Catholic loyalty, sponsored and attended the baptismal ceremony of an unnamed, impoverished Jewish woman—probably because no more prominent Jewish convert was then available (January 31, 1574). Whatever hopes or fears individuals may have entertained with regard to Henry were suddenly dissipated, however, after the death in Paris of King Charles, who was without progeny. As the legitimate heir to the throne of France, Henry understandably preferred it to that of Poland, although the dual Commonwealth covered an area twice the size of France, as was stressed by the French envoy Jean de Monluc, bishop of Valence. In the middle of the night of June 18, 1574, the king fled his adoptive country, in which he had resided for only five months, and returned to Paris, where he was crowned King Henry III. When repeated summonses by the Polish Diet to him for his return to Poland went unheeded, a new electoral campaign was begun which, fortunately for Poland, resulted in the election of the Transylvanian prince Stephen Báthory (1576–86).[38]

Curiously, as we shall see, Henry's religious bias did not deter some Jewish leaders, like Solomon Ashkenazi, the Italo-Turkish physician and diplomat, from promoting the Frenchman's candidacy. The Cracow Jewish community, too, recorded in its minute book that a *fraid feier* (joyful celebration) had taken place on the Jewish street during the night of Sivan 25, 5333 (May 27–28, 1573), on the occasion of Henry's coronation. The notation that this had occurred in the period of the weekly lesson *shelaḥ* (Num. 13–15) may have been an allusion to the main tenor of that scriptural portion, which emphasizes Israel's absolute religious conformity and unquestioned reliance on God's will in the face of threatening reports. The short duration of the king's reign may have given rise to the legend that Saul Wahl, a prominent Jewish citizen of Brest-Litovsk, had been elected king of Poland for one day. This legend, doubtless stimulated by the interpretation of the name Wahl as referring to the German term for election (though the name may in fact have been derived from the Polish *woł,* meaning ox, the equivalent of the Hebrew word *shor,* a frequent family name among Polish-Lithuanians and other Jews throughout the centuries), was for generations thereafter cherished by the descendants of Saul, himself a scion of the distinguished Italo-German family of Katzenellenbogen.[39]

The decade of Stephen's reign, following the turmoil of the two *interregna,* marked a high point in Poland's political power and internal consolidation. The Transylvanian prince succeeded not only in incorporating several Baltic provinces into his realm but also in pushing back the Muscovite armies almost to the gates of Moscow. A previously little-known Jewish engineer, Mendel Isack (Sax?) of Cracow, participated in this expedition, probably because he was an able bridge builder. At least, in his application to Emperor Rudolph II on July 4, 1589, he claimed that he "had built many bridges over large rivers in Russia and Muscovy for the late king Báthory." (Mendel was also involved after Báthory's death in Archduke Maximilian's unsuccessful campaign for election to the throne of Poland, and had to flee to Prague and Vienna. Yet after his return to Cracow he was sent by Sigismund III to Graz to negotiate the marriage between Anna Jagiellońska and an Austrian archduke.) With the acquisition of new territories, Báthory unwittingly opened new areas to Jewish settlement and, ultimately, to the establishment of a number of Jewish communities in them. Internally he could not quite stem the tide of the gentry's hegemony, but he honored, within his constitutional limitations, the royal obligation to protect Jews. He failed, as we shall see, to implement a number of anti-Jewish resolutions adopted by provincial or district gatherings of nobles (Cracow, 1577; Bełz district, 1584; and others). From the extant sources we learn only a little about his contacts with individual Jewish leaders. Outstanding among them was Báthory's Sephardic physician, Salomon Calahora, who had earlier served Sigismund Augustus in his professional capacity. In his decree of July 31, 1578, Stephen appointed Calahora as his "own and the Commonwealth's servant" and exempted him from the payment of taxes and from any other than the king's jurisdiction. Salomon apparently took no part, however, in the medical ministrations during Stephen's short but fatal illness in 1586, for he was not involved in the acrimonious public debate which ensued between the two attending Italian physicians about the causes of the king's death—a debate which has continued to the present day, without conclusive results. In addition to the practice of medicine, Calahora engaged in large business undertakings, especially in the exploitation of salines, for which he enjoyed royal support. Another Cracow Jewish businessman in close contact with the royal court was Jacob Ezdrasz (Ezra), banker and jeweler. An interesting entry in the royal account books records that in December 1576, shortly after Stephen's accession to the throne of Poland, the Jewish banker had advanced the king 5,000 zlotys to finance a journey. This loan, secured by a pledge of silverware, carried an interest rate of $6\frac{1}{2}$ percent, which was raised in January 1579 to 7 percent.[40]

In general, Báthory, who had learned to practice toleration of religious dissent in ethnically and denominationally divided Transylvania, proved to be a friendly monarch to his Jewish subjects. Soon after his coronation he reconfirmed the basic Jewish Charter (July 20, 1576). He also reaffirmed many local Jewish privileges, though referring to the general Charter, which would seem to make such special legislation superfluous. His reaffirmation was particularly important in Volhynia, which in 1569 had joined the Polish Crown. Here the king acted in response to a joint petition of the Rabbanite and Karaite communities of Łuck. Because of ducal Prussia's semi-independent status and traditional hostility to Jews, a special privilege there was likewise indicated. Protection of Jewish lives also loomed large in Stephen's mind. When a riot once again endangered the Jewish quarter in the city of Poznań, Stephen issued a sharp decree imposing severe penalties not only on the mob but also upon the city council. He threatened that if the council "did not, as was its obligation, restrain the passions of the populace, and failed to provide all that is necessary for the security of the said Jews," it would have to pay a fine of 10,000 marks to the Treasury. If the riot resulted in the slaying of a Jew, the guilty person would be executed, in accordance with the Charter originally promulgated by King Casimir. This decree, dated

February 10, 1577, had little effect; before long the Poznań Jewish quarter became the scene of another bloody riot (on May 29; or, according to another version, on March 8, 1578). The immediate cause for this disturbance was, as frequently elsewhere, of a minor nature. Apparently some Jew (according to one version, a Jewish woman) failed to undergo conversion to Christianity as expected. After the Jewish community obtained the intervention of the authorities, the very officer sent to release the prospective convert from the home of a Christian notary who was applying undue pressure on the purported catechumen, later incited some young Jesuit students to break into the Jewish street and indiscriminately attack its inhabitants. When the king tried to exact the prescribed penalty of 10,000 marks from the city council, however, both the councilors and the original inciter of the riot perjured themselves by swearing that they had had no part in the tumult. A contemporary chronicler (probably Leonard Gorecki), after giving his version of the events, bitterly commented on the shame of high officials perjuring themselves, an act which he considered even more reprehensible than the crimes committed by the rioters.[41]

Somewhat more effective appear to have been Stephen's two decrees of July 5 and August 6, 1576, outlawing blood and host accusations, and threatening willful and malicious rumormongers with capital punishment. This legislation was an act of great courage on his part. He must have realized that any decree aimed at ending false accusations of desecrating the host would antagonize not only large segments of the population, always ready to believe the most atrocious tales about Jewish enmity to the Christian faith, but also an influential segment of the Church. Just twenty years before, in June 1556, the then papal nuncio Aloisio Lippomano and Archbishop Stanisław Golański, the primate of Poland, had exchanged letters showing that the Papacy itself, then represented by the strongly anti-Jewish Pope Paul IV, had vigorously supported that accusation. On the basis of the archbishop's reports, the nuncio accused the palatine of Great Poland of being lax in prosecuting prepetrators of that crime because he had been bribed, and demanded the application of torture so that the guilty persons might confess and be "condemned to the extreme penalty." It was to suppress public criticism, relating to his other policies as well, that the strong-willed monarch decreed that no work should be printed or published in Poland without a royal permit. But he could not prevent preachers, even in his own presence, from castigating his permissive attitude toward religious nonconformity. Curiously, according to a report sent to the pope by Nuncio Alberto Bolognetti on January 6, 1583, it was a convert from Judaism called Severinus of Lublin or Cracow, a Dominican monk, who administered the sharpest rebuke to Báthory. Emulating a sermon previously delivered by the controversial papal diplomat Antonio Possevino, the preacher, who had studied in Paris and Salamanca and was both eloquent and well-informed, cited the passage "Why hast Thou thus dealt with us?" (Luke 2:48) to ask the king: "From among the princes of the entire world they have searched thee out and raised thee from thy house; why hast thou dealt with us by leaving unpunished such sins, such heresies, such persecutions of Catholics?" Severinus waved before the king's eyes a heretical book stamped with the royal arms and dedicated to Báthory. Addressing the king rather than the general audience, and noticing that Stephen's attention was flagging (perhaps because in the six years since his election, the king had not yet acquired a facility for listening to a sermon in Polish), the Dominican friar switched in the middle of his oration from Polish to Latin. According to Bolognetti, the king was sufficiently shaken upon leaving the chapel to inform the nuncio that, in accepting the dedication of the book, he had merely wished to do a favor to the author, but that he would now give orders to arrest the printer. Nonetheless, the king persisted in his outlawry of the two anti-Jewish accusations and, in his emphasis, in this connection, that Jews, like his other subjects, merited full royal protection. As usual, royal privileges were also issued in favor of certain individuals; they ranged from permission to acquire houses in certain localities and tax immunities to total exemption from any judicial authority other than the king's own, as was granted to Lazar Abrahamowicz Weiswasser of Tykocin and others. Characteristically, however, most of these pro-Jewish enactments date from the early years of Stephen's reign, although there is no evidence that he later submitted more readily to local Jew-baiting pressures.[42]

In his conversations with papal envoys, however, Stephen apparently spoke as a confirmed Catholic, perhaps even as a Jew-hater. He not only agreed with the papal nuncios that the printing of the Talmud, undertaken by the Jews of Lublin, should be forbidden, but he may indeed, in an unguarded moment, have made a statement which clearly ran counter to his publicly proclaimed policies. According to the reports sent to the Holy See by the nuncio Giovanni Andrea Caligari on November 25, 1579, January 16, and February 2, 1581, the king repeatedly assured him that royal orders had been sent out prohibiting the printing of the Jewish classic. On these occasions Báthory supposedly revealed to the envoy his innermost conviction "that Jews were a pernicious element in the Commonwealth and that, if he could, he would expel them all from his realm." It is possible, however, that the nuncio wishfully heard more than he was actually told.[43]

Be this as it may, Stephen could not abolish the established right of certain cities not to tolerate Jews, however, despite his own sweeping decree of 1578 allowing Jews to live and trade in all cities of the Polish Crown and annulling all contrary urban charters. He had to uphold, for instance, the highly restrictive agreement concluded by the burghers and Jews of Cracow in 1485 and repeatedly renewed in subsequent decades. The city of Warsaw secured from the king an interpretation whereby the prohibition against Jewish settlement there was extended to the area within a radius of two leagues from the city limits. This provision was intended to prevent Jews from settling on any noble or ecclesiastical estate in the immediate vicinity of Warsaw—which, as the frequent seat of the Diet, increasingly arrogated to itself the status of a second capital of Poland (it became the official capital a few years after Báthory's death). Curiously, so little informed were the Jews about the first two post-Jagiellon kings that, while they had participated in the public celebrations on Henry's accession to the throne, they apparently abstained from any overt rejoicing upon the arrival of the more sympathetic Stephen. Yet the impact of Stephen's personality and liberal policies was such that when, a fortnight after his death (on December 27, 1586), the senators and gentry of the three important provinces of Cracow, Lublin, and Sandomierz met and formed a confederation to achieve "peace and brotherly love," they specifically invited Jews, along with all others, to join them in the pursuit of these goals.[44]

INTERNATIONAL RAMIFICATIONS

Poland's sixteenth-century upsurge coincided with great changes in the power constellations of the European countries and in considerable redrawing of the maps of the Old and New Worlds. Simultaneously with the expansion of Poland's frontiers, the world witnessed the rapid growth of the Ottoman Empire, the rise of Muscovy as a new power in Eastern Europe, the tremendous agglomeration of territories under Charles V and his Habsburg successors, and the great overseas colonization by Spain and Portugal. Because of the ever-widening power struggles, everything happening in the Polish-Lithuanian Commonwealth attracted the close scrutiny of many European chanceries. Their attention was redoubled after the extinction of the Jagiellon dynasty, and the conversion of the Polish kingdom into a "Nobles' Commonwealth." The elective monarchy after 1572, in particular, which gave foreign bidders access to the crown of Poland-Lithuania, turned every election into a game of power politics among the neighboring countries, each of which tried to gain indirect control over its vast territories by placing a member of its own ruling dynasty on the throne of the dual Commonwealth.

While most local Jews steered clear of political entanglements, some influential Jewish leaders in foreign lands were unavoidably drawn into the vortex of this power struggle. Economic interests, too, were often closely tied to the outcome of these political conflicts, since Poland-Lithuania was located astride important trade routes from the Middle East to northern and northwestern Europe, in the commerce of which Jewish merchants began playing an increasingly active role. At the same time, the rise of the Ottoman Empire, which embraced another large concentration of Jewish immigrants, some of whose leaders had attained a high position in the councils of the Porte, opened up new opportunities for individual, if not collective, Jewish diplomatic activities.

At first the international negotiations concerning Jews related largely to favored individuals, whose interests were deemed worthy of protection by one or another monarch. We recall that in 1453 Casimir IV intervened in behalf of a Jewish merchant of Grodno with the grand master of the Teutonic Order, which was gradually becoming Poland's vassal state and could not easily deny the Polish king. More remarkable was Sigismund I's aforementioned attempt to take the Jews of the Bohemian Crown under his protection because he considered them potential immigrants into his country. He probably would not have dared to go so far in his attempt to influence a foreign government if Bohemia were not under the rule of his elder brother, Vladislav. In 1535 Sigismund intervened twice with the Austrian authorities in behalf of his Jewish subjects. In his letter to Ferdinand I of March 20, he complained that Polish Jewish merchants passing through Austria on their frequent travels to Venice and other Italian cities, were subjected to grave molestation by the local populace. He asked the emperor to protect these transients. Ferdinand replied on July 3, that any insults to Jewish travelers were perpetrated without his approval or knowledge. But he expostulated that, by disregarding the Austrian provisions regarding Jewish distinguishing marks, Polish Jewish travelers often aroused the ire of Christian onlookers through their strange behavior. In the meantime, the distinguished Cracow bishop and vice-chancellor of the Polish Crown, Piotr Tomicki, asked the high Austrian official Siegmund von Herberstein to secure from the emperor a letter of recommendation to the Venetian doge for the Jewish physician Moses, who had rendered faithful service to the Polish king. Sigismund I had already written directly to the doge in behalf of Moses, who had a litigation pending in the City of the Lagoons, but a similar imperial recommendation would, in Moses' opinion, prove of great assistance to him. On his part, Emperor Maximilian I did not hesitate to recommend to Sigismund his own faithful servant and creditor Abraham of Bohemia. Nor should we overlook the physician Isaac Hispanus' aforementioned journey to minister to the Tatar khan, a mission which doubtless also served some diplomatic purpose. But such individual interventions were soon overshadowed by activities directly or indirectly connected with what came to be called in western Europe the growing "Turkish menace." [45]

Ottoman expansion could, and ultimately did, become a threat to Poland's southeastern provinces, too. But in the sixteenth century it could also serve as a basis for an alliance against enemies threatening both countries. The expanding Muscovite Empire, in particular, not only tried to "liberate" Lithuania's "Russian" provinces but, in its southern drive became, along with the Habsburgs, an archenemy of Turkey. Poland, located between Russia and the Holy Roman Empire, often needed Ottoman diplomatic support. Hence hostile religious rhetoric—in part generated by the Papacy's reiterated calls for an anti-Turkish crusade (actual war preparations were made in 1544)—alternated with real Polish-Turkish cooperation, though beclouded at times by the two countries' conflicting policies relating to semidependent Moldavia. Ottoman hospitality to political and religious refugees from Poland, allegedly including some Polish converts to Judaism, irked determined Christian conformists like the chronicler Marcin Bielski. Many Poles readily believed his report that Suleiman had promised the Jews that he would come to Poland, "expel the Christians, safeguard peace for the Jews, and open for them a free road everywhere." Yet the image of Turkey and the Turks was not as distorted in the minds of the Poles as it was in most of western Europe. Not only did numerous pilgrimages to the Holy Land by Polish-Lithuanian aristocrats and others furnish the Poles with eyewitness accounts about conditions in the Balkan and West-Asian lands, but Poland herself accomodated quite a few Ottoman citizens. In the eastern emporia, especially Lwów and Vilna, there were more-or-less permanent settlements of Armenians, Greeks, and Tatars. These foreign traders often intermingled with the Jews, Germans, and even Dutch, English, French, and Italian merchants, but like all these groups, they retained their ethnoreligious identity. Almost to the same extent as the Jewish communities, those of the Armenians enjoyed considerable autonomy. Much has indeed been learned about the status of Polish-Lithuanian Jews from the study of legislation affecting their Armenian, Greek, and other minority-group neighbors.[46]

Needless to say, in its recurrent propaganda for a crusade against the "infidel" occupants of the Holy Land, the Papacy often agitated for Poland's participation in an anti-Ottoman expedition.

However, its appeal to the Poles, who were increasingly divided by denominational differences, was extremely limited; it carried little weight even in Catholic circles. Although Sigismund I watched with great anxiety the Ottoman attack upon Hungary and the death of his nephew, Louis II, at Mohács in 1526, he did nothing to help the beleaguered Hungarians. He intervened later by quietly helping John I Zapolya to wrest control of Transylvania from the Habsburg Ferdinand I. When the approach of the Turkish armies in 1542–44 seemed to threaten Poland herself, the Diet voted new taxes for the pursuit of war—the Jews were to furnish an additional 3,000 zlotys—but the response of the general population to this taxation was quite lukewarm. The Cracow clergy itself, when called upon by its bishop in 1542 to contribute 10 percent of its ecclesiastical tithe for the defense of the country, vigorously repudiated this "pretension." Queen Bona, moreover, an old adversary of the Habsburgs, agitated against any war with Turkey. Finally calmer counsels prevailed and, for the rest of the century, the Polish Commonwealth and the Ottoman Empire followed their own national interests by entertaining growingly amicable relations with each other.[47]

Under these circumstances, Polish and Turkish Jews not only could travel and even migrate in either direction but also could exert some influence on the international relations of the period. This is particularly true of the two leading Jewish diplomats in Constantinople, Solomon Ashkenazi and Don Joseph Nasi. Ashkenazi, in particular, could the more readily play a part in the diplomacy between the two countries as, though born in Udine in the Venetian Republic, he had spent sixteen years as court physician to Sigismund I and Sigismund II in Cracow before settling in Constantinople in 1564. It did not take him long to achieve eminence at the Sublime Porte as well. His meteoric rise to power, especially in collaboration with the sultan's leading vizier Mehemet Sokolli, gave Ashkenazi the opportunity to play a role in the election of Henry of Valois as the new Polish king in 1573. Like many Polish Protestants, he may have reasoned that, if Henry's hands were tied by strict *pacta conventa*, the French prince would have to abandon his religious intransigence. Since Polish-Turkish relations at the time were rather amicable, the sultan could use his good offices to promote the candidacy of a prince friendly to his own interests. To enlist Turkish support, the French king, Henry II, sent a special envoy to Constantinople, François de Noailles, bishop of Dax, who employed the usual means, including lavish bribes, and proved moderately successful. According to a brief summary in a Spanish report, Mehemet Pasha [Sokolli] addressed a letter to the Polish Estates in which he expressed his "condolences on the death of the Polish king, pledged himself to preserve the peace, and recommended the election of the French king's brother as king of Poland." The bishop of Dax later claimed full credit for whatever influence Turkish diplomacy had exerted in turning the votes of the *szlachta* to the French candidate. Henry himself recognized the value of Ottoman support; in a letter of July 24, 1573, he thanked Selim II for "the great demonstration of good will and the good offices which he [the sultan] displayed toward Us and Our election by the Diet." Ashkenazi, however, later asserted that the credit was due him. In his letter of February 18, 1580, to Henry III of France, the former Polish king, he insisted: "Particularly in the election of Your Majesty to the throne of Poland, it was I who was the cause of everything that was done here, although I believe that Monsieur d'Ax may have attributed it all to himself." Since in 1573 Ashkenazi was at the height of his glory (he had helped to bring about the conclusion, on March 7, 1573, of the formal peace treaty which ended the Turko-Venetian war), he may indeed have been most instrumental in turning the tide in Henry's favor.[48]

After Henry's flight from Poland, and the ensuing new *interregnum*, Ashkenazi, flushed with his success of 1573, tried to promote a new candidate for the Crown of Poland. Among the contenders was Duke Alphonso II of Ferrara, who was prepared to spend much money to secure his election. It has been estimated that in the first few months of the electoral campaign, his envoys spent the enormous sum of 200,000 florins on douceurs for influential Polish politicians. Moreover, they promised that, if elected, the duke would protect all established liberties, pay off Poland's public debt, recapture all Polish lands lost to Moscow in previous campaigns, establish a durable peace with both the Turks and the Tatars, and pay 200,000 florins to the Polish Treasury. This pledge, though publicly made to the Polish Electoral Convocation, proved insufficient to swing the ballot to the duke. The support of the Ottoman regime was urgently needed, and Ashkenazi, cooperating with the Ferrara Jewish leader Isaac da Fano and a less well-known Venetian Jewish banker, Emanuel (his surname is unknown), entered the ranks. Since the chances of Alphonso's election against the candidacy of the king of Sweden and the Transylvanian prince Báthory appeared less and less favorable, Ashkenazi suggested that the duke immediately dispatch 50,000 ducats as a gift to the sultan, 12,000–15,000 ducats for various court officials, and 10,000 ducats to finance his own efforts. He assured his correspondent Da Fano and the duke himself on October 1, 1574, that if such funds were made available, he could persuade the sultan to support Alphonso's candidacy. In fact, he drafted letters to the sultan and the grand vizier, which Alphonso was to address and which, in Ashkenazi's opinion, were to clinch Turkish support. The Ferrara circles, though generally friendly to Jews, seem to have doubted the extent of Ashkenazi's influence at the Porte or the importance of Turkish support in Warsaw, and were reluctant to follow Ashkenazi's advice. All he obtained, therefore, after sending his nephew with the two draft letters on a costly journey to Ferrara, was an amicable but noncommittal epistle from the duke to Sokolli, but not to the sultan himself. We are not even sure whether the Este Treasury reimbursed Ashkenazi for the 500 ducats he claimed to have expended on his nephew's trip. Possibly, by that time the reports from the duke's partisans in Warsaw were such as to discourage further investments in a lost cause.[49]

Far from discouraged by the failure of this overambitious scheme, Ashkenazi continued to play a significant role in Ottoman foreign relations. Together with the chief interpreter, Horembey, he helped to bring about an informal agreement between Sokolli and the Spanish agent Giovanni Margliani, which was signed on February 7, 1578, and attested by the two intermediaries. In this document, the contracting parties promised that, for the rest of the year, the Turks and the Spaniards would not attack each other's possessions. Yet the Italo-Polish-Turkish Jewish doctor had learned his lesson. Although still a power behind Grand Vizier Sokolli, Ashkenazi lost his zest for promoting a candidate for the Polish

throne after Báthory's death in 1586. However, his disappoint-
ments, even if known to the Italian Jews, did not discourage three
other Jewish entrepreneurs from endeavoring to influence the
choice of the new king of Poland. We recall the contract drawn,
on March 2, 1587, by the distinguished physician, dramatist, and
communal leader Leone de' Sommi Portaleone of Mantua, Jacob b.
Joseph Sorezina, and Lazar b. Joachino Saludore, in which they
vigorously pledged

to see and endeavor with all the power at our disposal that the crown
of Poland be placed on the head of our lord, the duke [Gugliemo of
Mantua], or on the head of his son [Vicenzo] under the firm condition that all the good which God will cause us to receive from this
enterprise shall be shared by each of us equally, just as we shall share
all the expenses incurred by any of us. We have entered a binding
agreement to pursue this enterprise faithfully and righteously and
not to reveal to any person in the world anything about this intervention, except to such individuals as may be helpful in bringing it to a
successful completion.

Unlike Ashkenazi, who had much diplomatic experience as well
as sound knowledge of Polish conditions, these three newcomers
on the diplomatic scene were uninformed amateurs, and their enterprise seems never to have got off the ground.[50]

Remarkably, the leading Jewish diplomat in Constantinople was
not involved in any of these negotiations. Don Joseph Nasi (the
former João Miguez) had made a great career after his arrival in
Turkey, becoming a confidant of Suleiman the Magnificent and
even more so of Suleiman's son and successor, Selim II. He was
elevated to the rank of duke of Naxos by the new sultan, whose
great friendship toward him gave rise to rumors that Selim was not
Suleiman's natural son, but the son of a Jewish lady-in-waiting,
and had been substituted for the great sultan's still-born infant.
Allegedly, Selim even promised Don Joseph the kingdom of
Cyprus after Turkey captured the island from the Venetian Republic during the Turko-Venetian War, which the Jewish duke
had helped to initiate. This promise cannot be verified, however,
and though Turkey retained possession of Cyprus even after her
navy's defeat at Lepanto and the conclusion of a peace treaty between the two countries in 1573, no such semi-independent king-

dom was created. Steadily opposed by Sokolli, Don Joseph was not to earn any of the fruits of that war. It may have been the decline of his influence at the Porte which persuaded him not to participate in the electoral maneuvers in Poland. Moreover, his relations with the French Court and its diplomatic agents in Constantinople had long been very strained because of his claim that Henry II owed him 150,000 ducats. This dispute—which, as we shall see, reached a climax in 1568–69, when the sultan ordered the seizure of French ships arriving in Alexandria, and the confiscation of part of their cargo for the satisfaction of his Jewish favorite's claim—was not conducive to Joseph's amicable relations with France. On the other hand, the duke of Naxos could still less support the candidacy of either a Habsburg or the tsar, both sworn enemies of the Ottoman Empire. Not that he lacked contacts with the Polish government. As early as March 2, 1562, Suleiman had addressed a letter to Sigismund Augustus referring in very flattering terms to Don Joseph, whom he called "a certain Italian Jew and gentleman worthy of all honor, faithful and favored by Us, Our servant and *mutefariq* [courtier]." The sultan simultaneously introduced a former Pole converted to Islam, by the name of Ibrahim, who was then chief interpreter at the Porte. The letter of introduction is not very clear, but its purpose apparently was an exchange of ambassadors between the two countries, an exchange which was to be initiated by Joseph and Ibrahim.[51]

Regardless of the outcome of these negotiations, Joseph utilized the entry thus secured to the royal Court of Poland, primarily for establishing personal commercial contacts. In fact, it was now the turn of the king of Poland to address, on February 25 and March 7, 1570, two cordial letters to the Jewish merchant-diplomat. The tenor of these communications is not quite clear, but they contain allusions to a substantial advance of funds by the Jewish duke to the Polish king; these funds were expected to total, perhaps with interest, 150,000 florins. The honoring salutations, "Excellent Sir and Well-Beloved Friend" and "Illustrious Prince and Beloved Friend" show the high esteem in which the Polish king held his Jewish correspondent. Details of the business relations proposed by the king were to be explained to Don Joseph by one Johannes Vancimulius (Vincentinus), the king remarking, "May God Almighty give Us His aid by means of His servant, so that all that which We have promised may be fulfilled." From Vancimulius Joseph would also learn "how ready is Our desire and inclination towards you both as regards the confirmation of the privileges in due course and as regards any other service." In the second letter, the king referred to his ambassador Andrzej Taranowski, who was shortly to arrive in Constantinople, and added: "We do not wish him to leave without letters from Us to Your Excellency; desiring from Your Excellency that if he may need Your Excellency's assistance, service, or protection in Our business he will know that, by virtue of these letters, he may count upon your support in all things." [52]

It appears that the Polish Court's friendliness toward Joseph was not cooled by hostile rumors such as those reported in the same year, 1570, to Madrid by an unnamed Spanish agent in Constantinople, who described at considerable length Joseph's diplomatic and business operations there. According to this informant, Don Joseph had sworn to his mother-in-law, Donna Gratianisa (Gracia Mendes)—from whom he had allegedly received her daughter's dowry of 700,000 ducats in 1547—that "he would always be an enemy of Christendom," a pledge he supposedly repeated to Suleiman. The most interesting part of this report, which will be more fully analyzed in a later chapter, consists in the enumeration of Don Joseph's Jewish collaborators. They included a number of Polish Jews; among them, one Chesa of Cracow, whom the agent described as "aged 44–45, of fine presence, tall with a long red beard, who directly visits the imperial court under the pretext of selling *zebelini*." Another, named Juda Bensusa, had "recently arrived from Poland." The agent also described how Don Joseph was sending letters "through nonsuspect methods" to Jews in various parts of Poland, particularly to Lwów, Lublin, and Cracow. His messengers allegedly included Abraam Mocia (Abraham Mosso).[53]

Regrettably, the royal letters give us no inkling of the new privileges which were to be conferred upon Don Joseph in return for the loan and the diplomatic assistance to the Polish envoy. But from later documents it appears that they related especially to favored treatment of Don Joseph's business interests in Poland.

Polish-Turkish trade had long been an extremely sensitive issue, particularly in Lwów. Like the German burghers, even the local Jewish merchants of the Red Russian metropolis felt threatened by the competition of the Turkish Jewish businessmen, a competition which became doubly threatening after the occupation of the northern shores of the Black Sea by the Ottoman Turks and their Tatar satellites at the end of the fifteenth century. The Lwów traders feared that the "Portuguese" Jews, having a special entrée to their Sephardic coreligionists on the Balkan Peninsula, might seize full control of that lucrative market. As early as 1502, the Lwów burghers persuaded the authorities to imprison a Turkish Jew, Moses, as an alleged spy. Only after Moses' death in prison did Sultan Bayazid II's direct intervention with the king secure the return of Moses' possessions to his widow. Subsequently, in 1564, when relations between the two countries had been buttressed by several commercial treaties concluded in the years 1519–60, the papal legate, Giovanni Francesco Commendone, complained that the entire trade between Poland and the former Italian Black Sea colonies, as well as Turkey, was in the hands of Jews and Armenians. Even such western Polish Jewish merchants as Jacob Tłusty of Poznań did extensive business with Kaffa and the other Turkish and Tatar emporia. On their part, some Ottoman Jews undertook successful commercial journeys to Poland, despite many difficulties placed in their way by local competitors. Now Don Joseph was granted a virtual monopoly in the importation of southern wines into eastern Poland without having to pay the required customs duties. His agents could also totally disregard the traditional staple rights of the inhabitants of Lwów, which had formerly enabled the local merchants to benefit greatly from their priority in acquiring and selling this much-desired commodity. As early as January 22, 1567, Sigismund Augustus had conferred a pertinent privilege on Don Joseph's Jewish representatives Hayyim Cohen and Abraham Mosso, who had come to Lwów in order to establish there the main outlet for the wine trade. The king justified his extraordinary privilege by Joseph's "services and zeal toward Us." Since, in the interest of the local traders, the Lwów city council tried to sabotage the royal privilege, the king threatened to impose a fine of 2,000 florins and emphasized that this arrangement had been made "to preserve the majesty of Our name among foreigners and to foster Our friendship with the most august emperor of the Turks." In 1568, Joseph further strengthened his dominant position by obtaining from the sultan a decree ordering the Turkish authorities to prevent the duke's competitors from transporting wines from the island of Crete via the Bosporus to Moldavia. Joseph thus secured for himself a near monopoly in the Turkish exports of 1,000 tons of wine annually to that Ottoman dependency and, probably, from there to Poland-Lithuania. Incidentally, he could also give preferential treatment to wines of high quality from his own vineyards on Chios and Cyprus. With the sultan's and the king's support, Joseph thus sought to penetrate even more deeply the vast Polish-Lithuanian market, where good wines were much in demand and fetched high prices.[54]

Nevertheless, the opposition to the commercial activities of the Turkish Jews persisted. Characteristically, the local Jewish merchants joined hands in this matter with their perennial enemies, the Christian burghers. They were animated both by a spirit of commercial rivalry and a measure of xenophobia. The fact that the Turkish merchants were Sephardic Jews, differing in manners, external appearance, and even synagogue rituals from the local Ashkenazic majority, may have sharpened the envy of the Lwów Jewish businessmen. The result was that, after Don Joseph's demise in 1579, his representatives found their business steadily declining, despite the support of both the new king Stephen Báthory and his chancellor Jan Zamoyski. Nor was Zamoyski's effort to attract such Sephardic settlers to his newly enlarged city of Zamość enduringly successful. Typical of the disappointment of the Turkish Jewish agents is a letter written by Moses Cohen and preserved in the Lwów judicial records in connection with the numerous litigations between him and the municipality. Completely resigned after his unlucky deals the agent wrote:

I care for nothing any more, for I trust in the Lord; as long as I have some clothing and bread, I worry about no one [nothing] else, for I know what is going on in the world. I shall be able to earn a living anywhere, and ultimately I shall travel to Jerusalem to live there. . . . If I did not have the sympathy and gracious support of the Lord Chan-

cellor [Jan Zamoyski], who respects me greatly and regards me not as
a merchant but as a friend of the house and hence assigns to me a
place before all others, the Lwów inhabitants would not have calmly
viewed his sympathy for us but would have devoured us alive. . . .
These our dogs [the Lwów Jews] burst from envy and spread many
evil rumors about me, but all these will boomerang against them.

Nor did, it seems, the intervention of another influential Con-
stantinople Jew, David (whom King Sigismund III and Chancellor
Jan Zamoyski in their exchange of letters in 1590 called David
Pasha), bring about more than a temporary relaxation of Turco-
Polish tensions. It was the growing pessimism in Jewish circles, as
well as the objective difficulties which beset all Polish-Turkish
trade relations, that caused the almost total disappearance of the
Turkish Jewish merchants from Poland under the reign of
Sigismund III.[55]

HUMANISM

The generally favorable status of the Jews in Poland and Lithuania to the end of Báthory's regime was owing not only to political
and economic considerations but also to the intellectual upsurge
in Polish society during the sixteenth century. In contrast with the
relatively backward, strictly medieval, culture of the earlier period, that of sixteenth-century Poland reflected the new trends in
European material and intellectual civilization, spearheaded by
the Italian Renaissance. Personalities like Copernicus, Konrad
Celtes (1459–1508), and Klemens Janicki (1516–43), opened up a
new period in Polish science and literature, which was rightly
called the Golden Age of Polish letters. Not until the nineteenth
century could Poland boast again of writers and poets of the
caliber of Mikołaj Rej (1505–1559), Łukasz Górnicki (1527–
1603), and particularly Jan Kochanowski (1530–84). In some respects Poland became the leader of all Slavic nations in the intellectual sphere in this period.

The new intellectual effervescence affected the Jews also. We
shall see that even rabbinic literature received fresh stimuli and
reached new heights of achievement in Poland, heights which
were not again attained for generations thereafter. The novel intergroup relationships, whether friendly or hostile, led to in-

tellectual exchanges between Jews and Christians which could only accrue to the benefit of both parties. To be sure, in Poland and Lithuania the impact of the humanist movement was neither as broad nor as enduring as in many western lands. It was essentially limited to a small, select group of aristocrats, lower gentry, and burghers. Illiteracy still exceeded 75 percent among the adult males, and was much higher among women. Some spokesmen of the older generation actually sang the praises of widespread illiteracy. Lupa Podłodowski, Kochanowski's father-in-law, was quoted as saying: "So long as our Poles did not know how to read, there was more virtue in Poland. Nowadays, together with learning has come a vast increase in cheating and misrepresentation, there is no public order, everyone seeks to reshape the Commonwealth according to his own whim." Yet, with the fervor generated by the Protestant movement, an intellectual élite gradually developed, as was outwardly attested by the increase in the number of Polish printing presses (there were 17 as early as 1500) and in their output. Many books appeared in numerous editions; for instance, Kochanowski's collected works had been published four times by 1600, only sixteen years after his death. If, at the beginning, the new Humanism had largely to be imported into the country by foreigners, particularly Italians and Germans —or, at best, brought back by Polish students from their studies at foreign universities like Padua, Bologna, Paris, and Königsberg— by the end of the sixteenth century, the country could boast of a substantial native intelligentsia.[56]

As far as the Jews were concerned, Polish Humanism did not build intellectual bridges like those which had so greatly facilitated amicable Judeo-Christian relations in the western lands. To begin with, Christian Hebraism played a relatively minor role in Polish culture. Although a number of Polish pilgrims visited the Holy Lands and other territories under Turkish domination, and their reports stimulated their compatriots' interest in the Ottoman Empire (this interest grew in proportion to the conquests of the Turkish armies), many misconceptions still marred Polish views concerning Muslim civilization. It suffices to read Jan Długosz' works to realize how greatly even so eminent an historian and geographer misconstrued conditions in the neighboring Empire, not only because of his anti-Turkish bias but also because of the unreliability of his sources of information. Perhaps the only scholar in Poland who knew a good deal about Turkey was the Italian immigrant Philip Callimach (Callimaco, pen name for Filippo Buonaccorsi, 1437–96), who had spent some years in the Middle East before settling in Poland in 1469 and in 1479 was sent by Casimir IV on a diplomatic mission to the Ottoman capital. So convinced were the diplomatic circles in Constantinople that the Polish Court did not have competent Turkologists in its service, that when in 1558 Suleiman the Magnificent addressed a letter to Sigismund Augustus, his own interpreter, named Strasz, who was a convert from Christianity to Islam, added a transliteration in Latin script to facilitate the task of the Polish chancery officials. Knowledge of Hebrew, too, was brought into Poland's Christian scholarly circles largely by foreigners like Callimach. It was also Callimach who introduced an otherwise unknown Jew, Zul, "Casimir the Jagiellon's favorite," into the humanistic debating society called the *Sodalitas Vistulana,* which, presided over by Callimach, often met in the royal castle to discuss philosophical and cultural problems of mutual interest.[57]

Remarkably, even the University of Cracow, one of the oldest in Europe and the major university in the entire Polish area, long evinced little interest in Hebrew studies. Its theological faculty, which occupied the primary place in the educational structure (as was the case in most other contemporary universities), must have been cognizant of the canon adopted by the Council of Vienne in 1311, which had led to the establishment of Hebrew chairs at the four leading European universities. But it appears that the Polish churchmen, including the enlightened Cracow bishops who controlled the University, were generally satisfied with the study of the Vulgate. Only under the impact of Humanism did the ideal of a *homo trilinguis* gradually penetrate Polish circles. Finally, about 1528, Leonard Dawid, a convert from Judaism, was invited by Bishop Piotr Tomicki, to teach Hebrew at the University of Cracow; he did so until 1533. During that time he published an elementary Hebrew textbook written by Philip Novenianus, and apparently also produced a little Hebrew grammar of his own. After his resignation, instruction in Hebrew was continued, in

1534, by the distinguished Flemish humanist Jan van Campen of the University of Louvain. Introduced to Tomicki by Jan Dantyszek (Joannes Dantiscus), the Flemish scholar greatly impressed the Cracow bishop through his "merits and erudition." However, Van Campen did not stay in Cracow very long. He had a great desire to proceed to Italy, in order to meet the leading Hebrew grammarian, Elijah Levita, and with his aid improve his own knowledge of Hebrew. Yet he spent only nine days with the Jewish savant in Venice. Although on his way to Italy he had picked up in Vienna a recommendation from Bishop Johann Heigerlin Faber to the renowned Italian churchman Girolamo Aleandro (Aleander), this dignitary received him rather coolly and even refused to lend him books from his large library. Van Campen also suffered from lack of funds, was forced to sell his horse to buy food, and had to leave Italy rather hurriedly. But he seems to have secured some valuable hints from Levita, which served him in good stead. He published, among other works, a compilation of grammatical principles and a tract on Hebrew letters and vowels, avowedly culled from the works of Elijah Levita, whom he called "the most learned of all grammarians" and "easily the greatest of the grammarians." After Van Campen's departure from Cracow, a native Pole, Walerian Pernus, assumed the Hebrew lectureship at the University in 1536; but Pernus soon turned to Greek as his major field of interest (this discipline, too, was greatly neglected at the University, as in all other Polish intellectual circles), and ultimately gave up his academic career to become a city clerk. The only learned Hebraist later in the century was another foreigner, the humanist Francesco Stancaro (Franciszek Stankar) of Mantua. But in 1550, only a year after his arrival, Stancaro was arrested because of his heretical teachings. Even the superintendent of the Calvinist Church in the Polish Crown, Felix Cruciger, rejected Stancaro's teachings as those of a "new Nestorius," a charge which may have brought back to many readers Justinian's attack on the ancient heresiarch as "Nestorius the Jew." Helped by friends to be acquitted, Stancaro left Cracow for Königsberg, where he served with distinction as a teacher of Hebrew. Although, through his pupils, especially the Anti-Trinitarians Piotr Giedzek of Goniądz in the Polish Crown and

Szymon Budny in Lithuania, he left a strong imprint on Polish culture in general, he never had a fully qualified successor at the University of Cracow. Thereafter, to the end of the century, instruction in Hebrew was given in a perfunctory manner. By the seventeenth century, it was abandoned entirely.[58]

At the same time, there was no lack of Polish-born talents. Wiktoryn Bitner (Bythner), born in the vicinity of Sandomierz, evidently found Poland an inhospitable area of activity. After studying in Frankfort on the Oder, he was called to Oxford University (about 1635). He taught with distinction for a number of years and published several tracts on the Hebrew language and its grammar.[59]

Nor did the Polish Jews remain unaffected by the Renaissance. Some of them engaged in the study of science, at least in so far as they could from Hebrew books. We have the testimony of such outsiders as the chronicler Maciej of Miechów, who, as early as the beginning of the sixteenth century, admired the Lithuanian Jews for making "use of Hebrew books to study arts and sciences, astronomy and medicine." To be sure, such studies also evoked the opposition of some Jewish leaders. Extremists among the Orthodox even renewed the old controversy about Maimonides' *Guide for the Perplexed,* a controversy which in thirteenth-century Montpellier had resulted in the burning of that classic of medieval Jewish philosophy. The two giants of Polish rabbinic learning in sixteenth-century Poland, Moses b. Israel Isserles and Solomon b. Yeḥiel Luria, became engaged in a lively dispute over the merits of philosophic studies, which as we shall see in a later chapter, ended in the victory of the anti-Maimonist Luria.[60]

Some fanatics went even further. The newly appointed chief rabbi Aaron of Great Poland, a recent arrival from Prague, and his son-in-law, Joseph, fulminated in Poznań against anyone engaging in other than talmudic studies. In a sharp sermon delivered in 1557, Aaron condemned secular studies in a vitriolic fashion. On other occasions he went so far as to contend that too much study of the Bible itself ought to be discouraged, if it interfered with the student's concentration on talmudic lore. His attacks provoked an "enlightened" writer, Abraham b. Shabbetai Horowitz, to reply in kind. Horowitz was an admirer of Maimonides and had written a commentary on the ethical treatise (known as the *Eight Chapters*) by the sage of Fusṭaṭ. In an apologetic pamphlet which he apparently did not dare to publish under his own name, Horowitz argued in favor of intensive study of Scripture, not only because it was the source of divine revelation and the foundation on which the entire system of Oral Law was based, but also because knowledge of Scripture was often needed to defend Judaism against hostile outsiders. He wrote:

This donkey [Aaron] said that one is allowed to study only the Talmud which controverts the biblical injunction, "Observe therefore and do them [the statutes]; for this is your wisdom and your understanding in the sight of the peoples" [Deut. 4:6]. Even if we were most erudite in all the talmudic studies, we would not be considered sages in the eyes of the peoples. On the contrary, all the talmudic speculations, homilies, and methods are subjects of derision among the nations. If we do not learn more than that, how shall we be able to explain the speculations and homilies of the Talmud in a way which would appeal to the nations and which reason would support? Experience has also taught us that no Jewish scholars ever prevailed over [Jewish] sectarians except if they happened to be experts in the Bible and the sciences.

In the sixteenth century, however, such arguments did not sound very plausible to the Jewish masses, inasmuch as their own knowledge of Polish and Latin was very limited. But a few Jewish businessmen and nonrabbinic scholars acquired enough familiarity with Polish to communicate with their Christian counterparts. Practically none read Latin books, long considered by Jews as the exclusive domain of the clergy. Under the circumstances, the interrelations which were usual between Jewish and Christian Renaissance scholars in other lands, were almost totally absent in Poland. Not even the progressive academy founded in Zamość by the enlightened statesman Jan Zamoyski had a Hebraist on its staff. Hence the few Portuguese Jews attracted by Zamoyski to his city, most of whom undoubtedy were deficient in Hebrew learning, had no opportunity to offer intellectual assistance to interested Christian students. Moreover, Humanism was very short-lived in Poland; the country's energies were now channeled into the struggles over the newly spreading Protestant movements.[61]

Another major reason for the relatively weak impact of Hebraism on the Polish intelligentsia was its aloofness from Christian kabbalism. Polish Humanism, unlike that of Italy, France, or Germany, was essentially more rational than emotional. We hear of no Polish mystics—such as those who existed in the country from the fifteenth century on—intensively engaged in the reading of kabbalistic classics like the *Zohar*. There certainly were no Polish counterparts to Pico della Mirandola, Egidio Canisio da Viterbo, or Guillaume Postel. Yet the sixteenth century was the period of the early penetration, into Polish Jewish life and thought, of the classic Jewish Kabbalah (with its reformulation by Isaac Luria and his school in Safed), both in its theoretical speculations and in its practical application. Although alchemy and magic, too, played a certain role in Polish Renaissance culture, they were of a different order than the Kabbalah, which increasingly dominated the minds of the Jewish masses. Unlike neighboring Bohemia, Poland produced but few writers on the magic arts. The most prominent among them, Michał Sędziwój, wrote in Latin, rather than Polish, and found his writings translated into English, French, German, and ultimately Russian, but not Polish. He himself achieved success only after he moved to Prague, where the Court of Emperor Rudolph II was a real haven for alchemists. When in 1583 Olbrycht Łaski introduced two English "experts" in black magic to Báthory, the king's reception was quite cool, and the two Englishmen speedily departed for Prague. The occasional prosecutions of Polish Jews for blasphemy did not lead to trials for necromancy or sorcery; in fact, witch-hunting, in general, came relatively late to Poland. A determined opponent of magic, Stanisław Poklatecki, published in 1595 a sharply critical tract in which he derided all alchemy and black magic, as well as the Jewish Kabbalah. He asked why all alchemists were poor, and why Jewish kabbalists were unable to perform any miracles for either themselves or their downtrodden people. Such an attitude may not have prevented the spread of all sorts of superstitious practices among the masses—such as the use of certain plants for magic healing and amorous purposes; but it was not conducive to the intellectual collaboration of Jewish and Christian kabbalists on a higher level.[62]

Even biblical learning required relatively little consultation with Jews. Most Polish students of biblical writings, including translators and paraphrasts were satisfied with the accepted Latin texts. While interest in the Bible as such greatly increased, and, for the first time, Scripture enjoyed a wide readership among laymen as well as the clergy, the new translations were largely independent of the early Hebrew or Greek texts. The greatest Polish poet of prepartition Poland, Jan Kochanowski, who in his *Psałterz Dawidów* (Davidic Psalter) produced some immortal poetry along biblical lines, was directly inspired by such Latin paraphrases as that published a few years before by George Buchanan, the eminent Scottish humanist. Though Kochanowski's moving *Treny* (Lamentations), written in his bereavement after the death of his daughter Orszula, are deeply indebted to the biblical jeremiads, they betray no direct borrowings from the Hebrew text. True, all translations of the Old Testament unavoidably reflect, to some extent, the Hebraic original. Suffice it to quote Kochanowski's magnificent poem *Czego chcesz od nas, Panie, za Twoje hojne dary?* (What dost Thou demand of us, O Lord, for Thy generous gifts?) which is so deeply permeated with Hebraic motifs that it might as well have been written by a Jew. The same holds true for his *Pieśni o Potopie* (Chants on the Deluge), as well as for many works by another distinguished sixteenth-century writer, Mikołaj Rej, whose biblical studies were greatly stimulated by his Protestant proclivities.[63]

On the more popular level, too, the Polish Renaissance seems to have generated less social rapprochement between Christians and Jews than did similar movements in Italy. True, the great admiration for everything Italian brought about a sudden decline of sexual morality, and there were some Judeo-Christian love affairs. However, they were not frequent enough to arouse much antagonism among the conservatives in either camp nor did they lead, as in many western lands or in Poland during the later Counter Reformation, to the execution of the culprits. At the most, they facilitated intermarriage between new converts and Old Christians. "Mixed" marriages of this type seem to have aroused little opposition, as was demonstrated by the case of Stefan (formerly Ephraim) Fiszel in early sixteenth-century Cracow. Like Abraham Ezofowicz,

Stefan, whose brother was a Jewish communal leader styled "rabbi" and whose brother-in-law was the truly distinguished rabbinic authority Jacob Polak, did not even have to change his family name in order to be admitted to ranks of the high Polish aristocracy. Since his wife and children did not follow him into conversion, he married a noblewoman of the distinguished Łaski family. After her death, he remarried twice, in each case with an aristocratic lady. His numerous progeny injected a considerable amount of Jewish blood into the highest echelons of the Polish nobility. At the same time, his mother and sisters, as well as other Jewish ladies, were frequently seen at the royal court of Sigismund I and Sigismund II Augustus, had very close contacts with such prominent Lithuanian families as the Radziwiłłs, and often appeared publicly in luxurious attire comparable to that of the ruling circles of the nobility and the urban patriciate.[64]

Nonetheless, Jews were often exposed to attacks by urban mobs and by university students. True, we have no evidence that, as was true in Padua, many students of the Jagiellon University obtained loans from Jews on pledges or acquired clothing from them at a reduced rate. Yet such cases doubtless occurred, especially among the numerous foreign students who attended the University of Cracow in the early years of the sixteenth century. According to a recent investigation of the University records, no fewer than 979 students came from foreign countries between 1510 and 1560, for the most part before 1520. Yet, the native students' anti-Jewish feelings and their increasing religious fanaticism, as well as the simple desire to give vent to their exuberance, led them from time to time to make a sport of attacking the Jewish quarter. They exceeded in their zeal the nonacademic youth in Cracow and elsewhere, perhaps because they felt safer from reprisals by the authorities. Owing to the University's autonomy, their crimes could be prosecuted only by the University administration, which proved extremely lenient toward the youthful transgressors under its tutelage. Those numerous students who happened to be of noble origin, moreover, enjoyed the additional protection of the extensive immunities provided by law for the entire noble class. Their parents often felt that their excesses should not be re-

strained, because such discipline might weaken the youths' mas-
culinity.[65]

Only when student attacks upon Cracow Protestants, as well as
Jews, had become an almost annual occurrence (in the 1570s) and
had led to the destruction of Protestant churches specifically privileged by royal decree, the desecration of the Protestant cemetery,
and the burning of Protestant books and other objects, did King
Stephen Báthory issue, in 1577 and 1580, two sharp ordinances
in an effort to stem these abuses. Nevertheless riots continued, and
involved the loss of a number of lives. Ultimately, the Jews found
it most expedient to pay a ransom to the students in order to
achieve a modicum of security. For many years thereafter, a special
Jewish tax called *kozubalec* (a word of uncertain origin, though
probably stemming from the Latin *quassabilis*), the equivalent of
the medieval "dice tax" collected from Jews in certain German
areas, was paid by the Cracow Jewish community. However, the
problem was not limited to Cracow and its University. Students of
provincial colleges, too, often terrorized Jews. In an interesting
responsum, R. Joshua Heschel b. Joseph tells us about the reluctance of the Jewish community of Sandomierz to help out one of
its members, who had fallen behind in his rent for a house belonging to a nobleman. The landowner had forcibly ejected the
tenant, who thereupon appealed to the community to purchase
the house. Otherwise, he asserted, this house located in the middle
of the Jewish street might be sold by the landlord to the "monks,"
that is, to a Jesuit college, and bring a mass of unruly students into
the Jewish quarter.[66]

PROTESTANT SECTARIANISM

Of great importance was the impetus given by Humanism to
the Polish Reformation. The rationalist critique of the classic
Christian sources was greatly reinforced here by the dissatisfaction
of the Polish public with the behavior of much of the clergy, both
higher and lower. Members of various classes, including the large
majority of peasants and noblemen, resented the semienforced
ecclesiastical tithe. They also looked askance at the growth of

Church property, and at the unwillingness of the ecclesiastical establishment to contribute its share to the country's revenues, even though such a refusal weakened Poland's defenses. In 1512 the archbishop of Gniezno owned about 300 villages and 13 towns. About the same time the bishop of Cracow had estates which included some 240 villages, compared with about 30 villages controlled by the greatest lay magnates in Little Poland. Monasteries, too, possessed extensive landholdings. Not even the decrees of 1510 and 1519 outlawing testamentary bequests of landed property to churches and monasteries, stemmed the growth of the mortmain through gifts and purchases. It has been estimated that in the late sixteenth century no less than 20 percent of all the land in the Polish Crown belonged to the Catholic Church. Widespread immorality and corruption among the clergy contributed to the spread of Hussite teachings among the Poles, some of whom actually participated in the Hussite uprisings in Bohemia. Even before Luther, certain rationalist trends persuaded independent thinkers like Jan Ostroróg and Jakub Biernat of Lublin to raise serious questions about some Catholic teachings and practices.[67]

Poland thus had the ground well prepared for the spread of Protestant teachings through the writings of foreign reformers, the numerous visitors from abroad, and the personal contacts of Polish students returning from universities in Germany, Switzerland, and Italy. At first, Lutheranism greatly appealed to Poles in the western provinces, especially in royal and ducal Prussia, as well as in Great Poland and, to a lesser extent, Little Poland. Despite the 1520 prohibition against the importation of Luther's writings, and strenuous objections to Poles visiting Wittenberg, the propaganda emanating from that great center of the Reformation made constant headway in both the Polish cities and the countryside. In time, however, the basically Germanic character of Lutheranism, its considerable Erastianism, and its acceptance of the existing social order discouraged many patriotic Poles.

Lutheran influences were, therefore, soon displaced by those emanating from Calvin's Geneva. Calvinism became an important factor in Lithuania, particularly in Vilna, even more than in the Polish Crown. Sigismund Augustus himself for a while appeared to be a possible proselyte to the new faith. In 1549, on the initia-

tive of a Polish visitor, the Mazovian noble Florian Rozwicz Susliga, Calvin dedicated his Commentary on the Pauline Epistles to
the Hebrews to the king, urging him to assume the role of Heze-
kiah and Josiah and "restore to Poland the pristine doctrine of
Jesus Christ." Five years later the Geneva reformer addressed another letter to the Polish monarch. Although, for reasons which
need not be elaborated here, Sigismund Augustus ultimately
threw in his lot with the Catholic Church (without trying to force
his subjects to follow his example, however), the Calvinist Church
gained ever-new adherents. True, in 1556 the king issued a sharp
decree against the radical reformer Piotr Giedzek of Goniądz for
trying "to propagate the old Arian heresy among the masses." A
year later Sigismund Augustus took issue with the more moderate
activities of Jan Łaski (Joannes a Lasco), nephew and namesake
of the Polish statesman. Łaski's stormy career abroad, during
which he had received a high accolade from the aging Erasmus of
Rotterdam, included the study of Hebrew with Konrad Pellikan
in Switzerland. There he also became friendly with Zwingli, Oeco-
lampadius, and Calvin. After his active cooperation with the
leadership of the Protestant congregations in Frisia and England,
too, this scion of an illustrious Polish family returned to Poland
to engage in reformational work at home. But the king became
apprehensive that such propaganda might interfere with his forthcoming campaign in Livonia, and he withdrew an earlier favorable privilege, lest Łaski's activities result in "spiritual dissensions
and generate internal hatreds among Our subjects." Yet neither
the royal decree aimed at Piotr of Goniądz nor that against Łaski
was implemented in any way. In general, the Crown and many
churchmen had long reacted with considerable detachment, and
even occasional sympathy, to the activities of numerous members
of the high aristocracy, and some royal advisers felt attracted to the
ritualistic simplicity and the deterministic doctrines of the Calvinist gospel. Among its strongest sympathizers was the leader of
the Lithuanian magnates, Mikołaj Radziwiłł, to whom Calvin
dedicated another of his commentaries on the New Testament.[68]

At first, Jews were not directly affected by the spread of the
Protestant movement. Their leaders followed the long-standing
policy of remaining neutral in sectarian controversies among non-

Jews. In fact, with the growingly antagonistic attitude toward Jews and Judaism on the part of Luther and Calvin, Polish Protestants, too, had little incentive to move closer to their Jewish compatriots. Only indirectly could the Jews benefit from the ensuing greater religious diversity, which reduced the monolithic Catholic character of the dominant Polish nationality and, at least for a time, seemed to secure much latitude for individual conscience. We recall that, at a crucial moment during the *interregnum* of 1573, the Warsaw Confederation demanded full freedom of worship for all inhabitants, including Jews and Muslims.

Nevertheless, the few recorded reactions of Polish rabbis to the religious controversies among their Christian neighbors show little elation about the consequent relaxation of pressures on the Jewish minority. The brief and rather obscure reference to the Protestant movement which may be detected in a homiletical work by R. Eliezer b. Elijah Ashkenazi, is not necessarily typical of the feelings of the Polish rabbinate. Born in the Middle East and a student of a Salonican academy, Ashkenazi had subsequently served as a rabbi in Fusṭaṭ, Famagusta, Venice, Prague, and Cremona, before he came to Poland in 1580; he spent only the last five years of his life there. Soon after settling in Poland, he completed his major work *Ma'asei ha-Shem* (The Works of the Lord), which appeared in Venice in 1583. In a passage written in Gniezno in 1580, he obliquely referred to the contemporary interdenominational conflicts by explaining the biblical story of the confusion created among the ancient peoples after they attempted to build the Tower of Babel. In opposition to various earlier speculations, Ashkenazi offered a fantastic reconstruction of the opinions held by the generation of the Tower and of its final downfall. He derived therefrom the lesson that the diversity of faiths among men had had the beneficial effect of contributing to their search for truth and had forestalled the undisputed reign of a single erroneous creed. He expressed the hope that that quest for truth would ultimately lead the nations to the recognition of the true God. Only the Jewish people, he insisted, had always adhered unwaveringly to its ancient traditions, despite its endless suffering from persecution. At the same time, our homilist detected in the contemporary disturbances a confirmation of a messianic computation according to which the coming of the redeemer was to be expected in 1594—that is, but fourteen years from the time of Ashkenazi's writing. In contrast, Eliezer's Polish-born contemporary, Ḥayyim b. Bezalel, served as a rabbi in Prague. His observations clearly reflected the tenser situation in the Bohemian capital, where the Counter Reformation was then making major inroads, which ultimately led to the outbreak of the Thirty Years' War. R. Ḥayyim viewed the raging religious conflict around him as but another incentive for the Jewish people to serve as teachers of the perplexed Christian majority, whom he called the *zera' emet* (the seed of truth), intimating that they, too, were engaged in the quest for truth. He saw in this God-willed situation a confirmation of the old rabbinic saying that the purpose of the Jewish dispersion was to spread the word of God among the nations. However, these few casual homiletical remarks by Polish rabbis, contrasted with the more direct comments of their Mediterranean colleagues, were incidental to the broader ethical teachings they wished to convey to their Jewish audience. On the whole, they testified to the determined effort of the Polish Jewish leaders to preserve their neutrality in the sectarian disputes around them.[69]

More directly involved in the Jewish issue were the smaller Protestant sects, which in Poland attracted many adherents from various classes and became intellectually, if not numerically, a strong factor in the religious fermentation. The Calvinist lay leader in Vilna, Szymon Zacius, a poet and former student of the University of Cracow, complained in 1557 about the presence in his city of "Anabaptists, Libertines, Enthusiasts, Schwenkfeldians, [pupils of] Servetus and [Piotr] De Goniądz, and new Arians who, through their deafening yelps, sadden the minds of the majority of pious and virtuous Christians." The unavoidable result was a growing sectarianism, which weakened the progress of the Reformation against the ever more strenuous Catholic resistance. At times the Protestant sects combated one another with greater vigor than they fought their common enemy. Erasmus was not wrong when he repeatedly warned Jan Łaski that, if the Lutherans came to power in his country, the Poles would suffer a more severe tyranny than under the popes. Remarkably, the outstanding spokesman of the Polish Counter Reformation, Cardinal

Stanisław Hozjusz (Hosius), actually denied the right of the sectarians to prosecute one another. He insisted that only the Church of Rome had the privilege of "separating the chaff from the wheat." [70]

Perhaps the most intriguing of the Polish Protestant sects, which has attracted particular attention in recent years, was that of the Anti-Trinitarians, or Arians, as they were called by their enemies. To be sure, the number of its adherents—for which no statistics are available—was undoubtedly very small. It formed but a minority within the Protestant movement, which itself never achieved a majority status, even among the nobles and the burghers, and most of its teachings were too sophisticated for the masses of illiterate peasants. However, the fermentation generated by the Anti-Trinitarians' radical views, espoused by a number of outstanding writers, poets, and ministers, far transcended their numerical strength. Polish "Arianism," with its various shades of Tritheism, Ditheism, and especially Unitarianism, made its impact felt far beyond the boundaries of Poland-Lithuania, and became a major source of strength for the Unitarian movement in the Anglo-Saxon countries and elsewhere. As has often happened in revolutionary upheavals, there was a proliferation of radical groups, at least until the successful Counter Reformation and reaction under Sigismund III. So long as the Protestant sects were still gaining adherents, Anti-Trinitarianism appealed to certain groups, through both its theological and its social program. It represented a variety of shades and included numerous disciples of Servetus, Lelio Socino (Sozzini), and his nephew Fausto. Lelio visited Poland twice, while Fausto spent the last twenty-five years of his life, 1579–1604, in that country (he was severely beaten in 1598 in the aforementioned anti-Jewish and anti-Protestant student riot in Cracow). Nearer home were such radical reformers as the Silesian Martin Seidel, who publicly argued that Jesus was just a man like any other and that the ancient Jews "justifiedly executed him as a blasphemer and seducer." Naturally, such extremism shocked even Polish, as well as Transylvanian, Anti-Trinitarians, who entertained close relations with one another.[71]

In order to stave off constant charges from all quarters that they were Judaizers, semi-Jews, or followers of Mohammed, the Polish

Anti-Trinitarian groups sought from time to time to achieve a certain harmonization of views and community of action among their adherents. Yet their leaders could not avoid public disagreement (as when Fausto Socino denied any indebtedness to Servetus), although all of them denied having adopted Jewish or Muslim tenets. The frequent references to Islam in the religious controversies may have been owing not only to the presence of many Muslims in Poland but also to Servetus' admission, in his famous trial in Geneva, that he had carefully studied the Qur'an, though he vigorously repudiated the charge that he had espoused its teachings. These suspicions were nurtured by the occasional flight of endangered Protestant radicals (like that of endangered Marranos) to Turkey. But only one such refugee (from a Heidelberg prison), Adam Neusner, in his *De non adorando et invocando Christo,* published in 1562, demanded outright that Jesus not be worshiped.[72]

The Anti-Trinitarian leaders also tried to draw a sharp line of demarcation between their own teachings and those of Judaism. We have an interesting illustration of this attitude in the only extant record of a religious disputation between an "Arian" and a Jew. Marcin Czechowic, a leading Polish Anti-Trinitarian who spent most of his life in Lublin, published in 1575, in beautiful Polish prose, the volume *Rozmowy chrystyańskie* (Christian Talks; the unusual adjective was used by the Anti-Trinitarians to distinguish Christian teachings derived directly from Christ, in contrast with the term *Chrześcijańskie,* which was reminiscent of baptism). In it he devoted five of thirteen chapters to arguments attempting to prove that Jesus was the son of God, as well as of David and Abraham, and that he was the true messiah who had already arrived. He also controverted certain traditional Jewish arguments that the Gospels were full of contradictions. This book drew a reply—first orally, it appears, and then in writing—from the Jewish physician Jacob of Bełżyce, a small town in the vicinity of Lublin. The doctor not only engaged in frequent debates with Czechowic but also attended some sectarian synods, where he witnessed some sharp differences of opinion among the leaders. Explaining to his opponent the choice of a dialogue form for his Talks, Czechowic referred to such synodal debates "in Bełżyce, which you attended yourself, and elsewhere." He undoubtedly alluded to the Synod of 1569 (where, incidentally, the terms Arian and Ebionite were first applied to members of the Anti-Trinitarian group). It is noteworthy that, in his attack on the Talmud, Czechowic refrained from repeating the traditional Christian charge that the work was a compendium of many "follies." He merely emphasized that, were the Talmud really the repository of an Oral Law given to Moses, some reference to it would have been made in Scripture, and Moses would have expressly enjoined his people to teach their children both laws. In this way Czechowic insinuated again, what he and others had often contended, that Catholicism and Judaism had in common an erroneous adherence to a tradition created by men and placed by them almost on a par with the revelation of God.[73]

It appears that Jacob answered many of Czechowic's criticisms calmly and rather effectively. In turn, Czechowic issued in 1581 a rejoinder in which he extensively cited, verbatim, passages from the tract by the Jewish controversialist. To cite only one characteristic example, Jacob was quoted as saying:

I remember the first time when you came to Lublin and you spoke with me in the presence of many important people, you asked me about the Jews' opinion concerning Jesus: whether, according to the Holy Scripture, Jesus was God or only a human being. The people urged me to express my opinion in their presence. It is not pertinent to repeat my answer. You said then that Jesus was only a prophet, greater than other prophets; but afterwards, when you debated with Daniel [Bieliński], I heard you attribute divinity to Jesus and claim that he (i.e. Jesus) is the judge of the living and the dead, and this is evident in your new book.

Jacob may indeed have been right: consistency was not the major virtue either of religious polemists generally or of the Polish Arians specifically. Many of them were men of action, rather than profound theologians who could penetrate the subtleties of the Servetian or Socinian Anti-Trinitarian doctrines. As propagandists they tried to spread whatever truths they perceived, in a simplistic way appealing to the masses. Understandably, they were deeply irked by their lack of missionary success among Jews. Czechowic himself once bitterly complained that it was more difficult to persuade a Jew to adopt Christianity than to induce a wolf to refrain from killing sheep or to train a cat not to catch mice.[74]

Remarkably, Czechowic' controversy with Jacob did not touch on the major problem of social and individual ethics, which was the most important facet of the radical wings of the Reformation. The Jewish apologist apparently did not feel called upon to take issue with Czechowic' extreme pacifism, his advice to adherents not to accept public office (though he recognized the necessity of having a state and government), his insistence upon turning the other cheek, or such ethical injunctions as that proscribing a good Christian from entering into litigation: "If someone wishes to litigate with you and wants to seize your coat, let him also seize your suit." On the other hand, when at the Synod of 1568 Czechowic and the equally influential leader Grzegorz Paweł of Brzeziny suggested that Anti-Trinitarian pastors resign from posts "in which they live off the labor of others, and that they earn their bread with their own hands. They should also give the nobles the brotherly advice that it is unseemly to live off the sweat of poor serfs or to dwell on estates once given to their [the nobles'] ancestors because they had shed blood [in war]," they encountered vigorous opposition. Similarly, many of the radicals admitted, like Calvin, the permissibility of charging interest on loans, which had long been a major issue in Judeo-Christian relations. Even Fausto Socino felt impelled, in his letter of March 8, 1597, to the father of his deceased wife, Krzysztof Morsztyn, to contend that God himself permitted interest, as might be learned from the Mosaic legislation. Yet the anti-Jewish "father of Polish literature," Mikołaj Rej, a Calvinist, lumped together Jews, clerics, and nobles in facetiously explaining that high incomes derived by these groups from their respective pursuits was entirely owing to their small numbers and to the resulting paucity in the supply of their services. In other satires, Rej described how a city's mayor, a sheriff, and a Jew had cooperated in "skinning" the poor, and how judges often delayed the proceedings of empty-handed parties when their Jewish opponents brought gifts of saffron or gold coins.[75]

A major issue in this connection was the debate among the Anti-Trinitarians concerning the continued validity of Old Testament precepts. Here, too, immigrants played a major role. While complaining that many intellectuals believed Thucydides and Sallust more than the New Testament, Fausto Socino taught that biblical revelation can transcend reason and human comprehension but is never contrary to reason or common sense. He also contended that, just as the Old Testament promises do not surpass the limits of human nature, so its precepts, too, remain within those limits. In contrast, the New Testament promises transcend human nature, and hence some of its precepts seem to go largely beyond the natural forces of man. At the same time, he insisted on the careful study of both Testaments, with the aid of good Hebrew and Greek grammars and reliable texts like those prepared by Benito Arias Montano, Xantes Pagninus, Immanuel Tremellius, and Franciscus Junius. Another foreign visitor, Giacomo Massilara, better known under his assumed name of Jacobus (Olympidarius) Palaeologus, was a native of Chios who arrived in Poland after a stormy career in Greece, two arrests by the Inquisition in Rome (he was released from prison the first time in connection with the upheaval following Pope Paul IV's death in 1559), and, ironically, several years of service at the Habsburg court in Vienna. Allegedly, the grand inquisitor Antonio Michele Ghislieri (later Pope Pius V) had assembled 100 witnesses and exposed 2,000 theological errors in Palaeologus' writings, to prove his heterodoxy. While in Poland, Jacobus argued among other matters that the Old Testament had not been abolished by the appearance of Jesus; although he agreed that the Gentiles could attain salvation through faith alone, without observing the Old Testament commandments. He also stated that Muslims and Jews could attain salvation by believing in Jesus as a prophet. He elaborated these views especially in his *Catechesis christianae dies XII,* an extensive imaginary dialogue between two students of Christian theology, a Jew named Samuel, a Mexican Amerindian, and a minister, Telephus, representing the author's views. They were joined on the fifth day by a Papist, a Lutheran, and a Calvinist.[76]

On his part, Szymon Budny, the leading exponent of Anti-Trinitarianism in Lithuania, invoked the Old Testament to justify severe measures against those Anti-Trinitarians who, in his opinion, went too far in rejecting the existing public order and accepted Christian dogmas. He thus sharply controverted what seems to have been the majority opinion, espoused by Jan Niemojewski, Piotr Giedzek of Goniądz, Grzegorz Paweł, Czechowic, and the Raków Congregation, which forbade the acceptance of any public office and the wearing of arms even on journeys "for defense against robbers." At the same time, Czechowic considered the abrogation of Old Testament commandments by the new dispensation as an established historical fact, and sharply condemned the Jews for not seeing Scripture in that light. Grzegorz Paweł of Brzeziny actually assailed the Catholic Church for taking over from the Old Testament its ramified ceremonial system. In one of his most original tracts, he claimed that "Antichrist" (the Papacy) had borrowed from Judaism the practice of infant baptism (in imitation of circumcision), as well as certain holidays, priestly vestments, the idea of churches as holy places, and so forth. He called Church doctrine "the Third Testament of the Antichrists, neither Jewish nor Christian, but Babylonian." [77]

Needless to say, neither Palaeologus nor any of the other leading Anti-Trinitarians became full-fledged converts to Judaism. Szymon Budny may have been quite radical in his Polish translation and interpretation of the New Testament, but this did not make him a Jewish proselyte, as asserted by the hostile Kasper Wilkowski in 1583. Nor was Daniel Bieliński a convert to Judaism because he detected no fewer than 139 "disharmonies" and outright contradictions in the New Testament, a feat which earned him the designation of "uncircumcised Pagano-Yid." (According to Wilkowski, Bieliński had become a Jew before returning to Calvinism.) Bieliński certainly would not have qualified as a Jew at any time, from the standpoint of Jewish law. The same holds true for the followers of the genteel Jan Niemojewski who, in his vivid messianic expectation, sold all his landed property and distributed the yield among the poor. Some of them went so far as to deny the messiahship of Jesus, his resurrection, and his continued reign over the universe. Certainly, the majority would go no further than to subscribe to the declaration adopted on August 26, 1562, at the Synod of Pińczów that (1) every mention of God in the Bible, such as "Hear, O Israel" (Deut. 6:3 ff.), referred to God the Father; (2) He was the Creator of all, including the Son's divinity; (3) the Father is superior to the Son in order *(ordine)* and dignity; and (4) the Holy Spirit is a true God. Even the few Arians who actually switched over to Saturday observance of the Sabbath, but did not undergo circumcision or accept most other Jewish rituals, were no more Jews than are the Seventh-Day Adventists in the United States today. Basically, all these radical dissenters believed in Jesus, if not as equal to God the Father, at least as a supernatural prophetic and messianic personality—a doctrine which no professing Jews were ready to admit. That some of the opponents of the Anti-Trinitarians chose to call them "Jews" was fully in line with the ancient and medieval tradition in sectarian controversies, revived during the Reformation period. Sometimes the Arians were also called Ebionites, in recollection of that ancient Christian sect with a Jewish background which, together with the similar sectarian movement of the Nazarenes, had indeed contributed much to the rise and development of ancient Arianism. But from the Jewish point of view, all these Polish groups were considered full-fledged Christians.[78]

FEW PROSELYTES

In that religiously turbulent age there were a few outright Judaizers. Two such "culprits," Ambrozy of Młowice and Maciej of Swerpiec, appear in the sixteenth-century records of the cathedral chapter of Płock. Others even more determinedly crossed the line from half-hearted to total Judaism. We recall the sensational martyrdom in 1539 of the octogenarian Katarzyna Weiglowa, as well as the story told by Marcin Bielski about a large number of proselytes who were allegedly smuggled out by Jews to the Ottoman Empire, where they were able to profess Judaism openly. Bielski's assertion, repeated by other Polish chroniclers, originated with a hostile Jewish convert to Christianity who had supposedly observed many such new Jews on his travels through the Tatar-dominated Crimea. More remarkably, this otherwise unsubstantiated rumor was given full credence by the government of Poland. In his decree of July 10, 1539, addressed to several bishops and governors in Lithuania, the king wrote:

We announce to your Lordships with this letter that it has been reported to Us that certain persons of the Christian faith living in the city of Cracow and other cities of the Crown of Poland had converted themselves to the Jewish religion and had undergone circumcision. These persons are said to have emigrated from these Our localities into the Grand Duchy of Lithuania; others have been conducted there [by their new coreligionists], live in places under royal, princely, or noble control, profess Judaism, and have intercourse with the local Jews. In order to counteract that aberration and, as is customary, to punish the culprits who dare to do such a thing, We have dispatched there Our courtiers Sila Antonwič and Jan Korčius [to institute an investigation].

These commissioners were to ascertain the facts, imprison not only the proselytes themselves but also those Jews (especially the Jewish leaders) who were responsible for aiding and abetting them, so that all such transgressors might ultimately be tried and convicted. As a result, even the communal leaders of Cracow and Poznań were arrested; they were not discharged until the community of Cracow had paid 20,000, and that of Poznań 10,000 zlotys, while other communities supplied varying lesser amounts to the Treasury.[79]

Evidently, the whole rumor turned out to be fallacious, or at least vastly exaggerated. The king's gullibility was underscored by his repeating the aforementioned canard about Suleiman's reply to Polish-Jewish petitioners that he planned before long to appear in Poland personally and liberate not only the Jews but also many Christians, as he had done in Hungary. It has been suggested that the entire investigation was initiated by greedy Queen Bona, merely to extort from the Jews a substantial ransom, as had been done repeatedly by medieval rulers elsewhere. In any case, the affair had no other untoward consequences for Jews. It did not even permanently envenom the relationship between the Jews and the royal couple.

Some Christians may indeed have been led to accept Judaism and emigrate to Turkey, however. There is no reason to doubt, for example, the report of Hans Dernschwam, an agent of the House of Fugger, who on his journey to Constantinople found some Polish-speaking Jews amidst that cosmopolitan Jewish com-

munity. Since relatively few Jews, even in Poland, had adopted
the Polish language for daily usage, the presence of Polish-speaking individuals suggests that they might have been fairly recent
converts to Judaism. But their number was not very large. Moreover, the rabbinic literature which appeared in an increasing volume in Poland and Lithuania and reflected practically the entire
spectrum of Jewish religious and social life, rarely referred to
any of the legal problems which undoubtedly would have arisen
in marital and family relations had there been a substantial number of proselytes in the country.[80]

There seem to have been equally few Jewish conversions to
Christianity. Jewish converts, moreover, were rarely trusted by
their new Christian coreligionists. A later writer, Stanisław Reszka,
repeated a popular tale about the burial of a Jewish convert to
Calvinism named Lewan, whose gravediggers were unable to re-
fill his grave with earth because of his atheistic convictions. In his
disputation with Czechowic, Jacob of Bełżyce claimed that "no
Jew changes his religion out of conviction. Jews convert to Christianity out of a pursuit of pleasure, [infatuation with] a beautiful
woman, envy, or in order to be released from debts." Of course, no
reliable data concerning conversions to either faith are available.
While we know a good deal about a few outstanding converts, such
as Abraham Ezofowicz or Stefan Fiszel, we hear but occasionally
of one or another neophyte of lower rank. As mere guesswork,
we may perhaps assume that more Jews accepted baptism, because
of external pressures and opportunities, than there were Christian converts to Judaism; this despite the assertions of such
former Jews in Germany as Viktor von Carben, Johann Pfefferkorn, and Antonius Margarita (in writings published in 1504,
1509, 1511, and 1530), that Poland accommodated a great many
Jewish proselytes. These generalizations from individual cases
were doubtless unjustified, even in the second half of the sixteenth
century, when the sharp denominational conflicts among Christians had created a far more hospitable climate for religious conversions to either faith. Needless to say, the official leadership of
all Christian denominations, as well as the rabbis, sharply opposed
any form of apostasy.[81]

EXTRAORDINARY CREATIVE ÉLAN

The sixteenth century, which marked the low point in the history of Ashkenazic Jewry in western and central Europe, witnessed a tremendous upsurge of Jewish energy in the newer settlements of Poland and Lithuania. The vitality of the people, cast out from their old habitats along the Rhine, in southern Germany and France, was demonstrated in an unparalleled way by the swift numerical, economic, and intellectual expansion of the Jews in the Jagiellon lands along the Vistula, the Niemen, and the Dnieper. Within two generations, the communities of Cracow, Poznań, Lwów, and Brest-Litovsk achieved a cultural level which exceeded anything known in Ashkenazic Jewry since the days of the Tosafists. Some Jews even participated in the revival of scientific and philosophic interests characteristic of Renaissance culture, to a degree transcending any activities of this kind in late medieval Germany or northern France. We shall see that the study of Maimonides and, more indirectly, of Aristotelian philosophy began to be cultivated among the Polish Jews to an extent which alarmed the more conservative groups, who feared that it might weaken the study of Torah and perhaps undermine the traditional structure of Jewish life. The two intellectual leaders of the mid-sixteenth century, second to none in the talmudic learning of their day, or even in comparison with the giants of the eleventh to the thirteenth centuries, were sharply divided on this issue. If, as we shall see in the next chapter, the seventeenth century was marked by some retrogression on this matter, the retreat was owing much more to the generally stifling atmosphere of the Catholic Restoration than to any internal developments among the Jewish people.

So long, however, as relative freedom of worship and intellectual exchange continued, to the end of Báthory's reign, some Jews freely associated with Christian scholars and learned a good deal, not only about the secular sciences but also about Christianity as such. Jacob of Bełżyce was not the sole Jewish leader to debate religious issues with the Christian clergy. He was far exceeded therein by Isaac b. Abraham of Troki (1533–94), the famous Karaite polemist, whose *Ḥizzuq Emunah* (Faith Strengthened) became a classic of Jewish controversial literature and even exerted great influence upon major figures of the Enlightenment, especially Voltaire and Lessing, and later on David Friedrich Strauss. Isaac fully realized the great importance to Polish-Lithuanian culture of the extensive religious toleration which still prevailed in the Polish-Lithuanian Commonwealth at the time of his death in 1594. Commenting on the intolerance existing in countries like France, Germany, and Spain—intolerance which had generated the increasingly sanguinary Wars of Religion—he wrote:

All this [the appalling bloodshed among the Christian nations] is a retribution to them for their sins. In the aforementioned three countries [England, France, and Spain] they had shed much Jewish blood through false rumors, evil enactments, and massacres until they finally expelled the Jews from their lands, so that not one Jew remained among them. In contrast, in the other lands in which Jews now live, the authorities punish those who commit wrongs and inflict damage upon the Jews. The governments support the Jews through their privileges, so that they are able to live in their lands peacefully and undisturbedly. The kings and lords of these lands, may He whose Name be blessed increase their welfare, are lovers of grace and justice. . . . That is why He whose name be blessed established peace among them, and even those who believe in different doctrines do not war upon the others, as you witness it today.

Indeed, religious toleration was the keynote of Polish-Lithuanian policy until the onset of the vigorous Counter Reformation under Sigismund III. Even during the brief reign of Henry of Valois, as we have seen, no serious attempt was made to suppress religious dissidence.[82]

It was, indeed, this governmental latitude which enabled the Jewish masses immigrating to Poland to adjust themselves quickly to the new conditions, yet retain the continuity of their historic heritage. Jews residing in Cracow or Grodno, in Brest or Kalisz, continued living the old Ashkenazic way—dwelling in quarters of their own, though not in any enforced ghetto; and speaking a Germanic dialect, now greatly enriched by a growing body of loan words and syntactic borrowings from Hebrew and the Slavonic languages of their neighbors. At the same time they were able to explore ever-new avenues for earning a living, thus increasing their occupational diversity far beyond what it had been in the German-speaking areas from which most of them had come.

It is small wonder, then, that the Polish and Lithuanian Jews now felt much more at ease in their environment. Most Jews would undoubtedly have echoed Moses Isserles' statement advising one of his correspondents to stay in Poland: "Perhaps we ought to prefer a dry piece of bread in peace in these lands . . . where the hatred of Jews has not taken on the dimension of that in German lands. May God allow that this condition continue until the coming of the Messiah." R. Solomon Luria actually likened the position of his coreligionists in Poland to that of the nobles. Although this remark was doubtless borrowed from the observation of the twelfth-century Tosafist Isaac b. Samuel of Dampierre, the rabbi emphasized that the Polish kings had frequently shown kindness to Jews by granting them extensions on overdue tax payments in emergencies. Unfortunately, this Golden Age of Polish and Jewish culture drew to its end under the impact of the ever-sharpening intolerance of the Catholic Restoration, the incipient governmental anarchy, and the diminution of Poland's international influence.[83]

POLAND-LITHUANIA
ON A HIGH PLATEAU

STEPHEN BÁTHORY's sudden demise on December 12, 1586, marked a turning point in the history of the dual Commonwealth of Poland and Lithuania. The ensuing *interregnum,* the third in less than fifteen years, gave a new opportunity for the increasingly unruly gentry to extort from the candidates to the throne further pledges to preserve its "golden liberties." It thus put an end to efforts to strengthen the monarchical power, which, under the conditions of that age, would alone have enabled the country to pursue a consistent long-range foreign policy and establish an enduring reign of law at home.

Even the memory of the great king began to be blackened by many of his self-serving opponents. Foreigners like Michel de Montaigne extolled Báthory as "one of the greatest rulers of the century," and Pope Sixtus V deplored Stephen's passing as "a great loss to the glory of God. Nothing more distressing could have happened to Us, nothing more unfortunate to Poland." Yet at home his denigrators publicly rejoiced over the death of the "tyrant." Even the measure of continuity briefly maintained by the distinguished chancellor and generalissimo Jan Zamoyski, gradually disintegrated under the weak regime of the young, inexperienced Sigismund III (1587–1632), who was more interested in the lifelong pursuit of his dynastic claims to the throne of Sweden (in legal enactments and correspondence, he and his son Wladislaw always called themselves kings of both Poland and Sweden) than in the genuine needs of his adoptive fatherland.[1]

Nevertheless, the process of acculturation of the various ethnic groups inhabiting the vast stretches of Poland and Lithuania proceeded apace. The great flowering of Polish letters during the sixteenth century enhanced the appeal of the Polish language among the intelligentsia, both lay and ecclesiastical, of Lithuania and the

Ukrainian territories in the southeastern parts of the monarchy, as well as among the remaining German-speaking burghers in the cities. The simplification and standardization of Polish spelling, furthered by the ever-increasing output of the country's printing presses—particularly through the publication of a host of politically and religiously controversial pamphlets—brought about the consolidation of a generally accepted literary language. Polish now served as the main medium of communication, not only among the Poles but also in exchanges between the various ethnic groups, with one another and with governmental organs. Before long, large segments of the Lithuanian, Ukrainian, German, and even Tatar and Armenian nobility and burgeoisie became thoroughly Polonized. The Jews of all classes alone effectively resisted assimilation, which they considered a first step to conversion, to such an extent that few of their intellectual leaders possessed an adequate knowledge of the Polish idiom. Although the large majority of the Christian population, especially in the peripheral provinces, were largely illiterate peasants, who continued to adhere to their ancestral customs and modes of expression, their voices, if heard at all, carried little weight in the decision-making bodies of the nation.[2]

This progress of national unification might have been impeded if the dynamic territorial expansion set in motion by Sigismund III's predecessors, had been maintained under his regime. In the first two decades of Sigismund's reign, there was a chance that the crown of powerful Sweden would be united with that of Poland in a personal union; and that, if the war unwisely initiated by him with the Ottoman Empire were brought to a successful conclusion, Poland's boundaries would extend to the Black Sea and possibly include both Moldavia and the Crimea. Most importantly, Báthory's old dream of taking over all of the Muscovite tsardom, and thus unifying the two main branches of the Slavonic world, might have come true. Had that been the case, of course, the ethnic diversity so characteristic of early sixteenth-century Poland, would have been greatly magnified. Instead, there followed an era of national consolidation that was in many ways beneficial to Polish society but at the same time strengthened the growing reactionary trends which became a perennial source of cultural and economic weakness and a real menace to the Jewish people's very survival in the country.

Apart from the general nexus between medieval nationalism and intolerance toward Jews—a nexus which has been analyzed here in an earlier volume (XI)—in Poland, even more than elsewhere, the trend toward the formation of an integrated national state depended on the establishment of a high degree of religious conformity. For a while it appeared that from the religious conflicts developing under Sigismund II Augustus and his successors might emerge a Polish national Church which would pay general obeisance to the Papacy but would be led by bishops appointed by the king, allow priests to marry, introduce vernacular prayers, and make other major changes in the Catholic ritual and organization. However, at a crucial moment in 1564–65, the king refused to cooperate. Although the idea had the backing of such influential leaders as Jakub Uchański, archbishop of Gniezno and primate of Poland, and Mikołaj Sienicki, speaker (*marszałek*) of the Chamber of Deputies of the Diet, the proposed synod in Piotrków which was to promulgate these far-reaching reforms, never met. On the contrary, in 1564 the king solemnly accepted from the papal nuncio Giovanni Francesco Commendone, the newly adopted resolutions of the Council of Trent and promised to adhere to them, although the Polish clergy as a whole waited thirteen years to follow his example. Seemingly more successful was the attempt to wean the masses of Orthodox Christians inhabiting the vast territories of eastern and southeastern Poland and Lithuania from their traditional reliance on the leadership of the Greek Orthodox Church in Constantinople and the more recently established patriarchate in Moscow. Harking back to the efforts of the ecumenical Council of Florence in 1439, the Polish monarchy and hierarchy persuaded many bishops and lay leaders of the Ukrainian and Lithuanian Orthodox populations to conclude with them in 1595–96 the Union of Brest-Litovsk, which laid the foundation for the Uniate Church. While reserving to itself the right to maintain such nonconformist observances as its old Slavonic liturgy and a noncelibatarian priesthood, the new Church recognized the spiritual supremacy of the pope and thus partially healed, on a local level, the theretofore irreconcilable schism between the Eastern

and the Western Church. However, large segments of the Orthodox population rejected the Union and adhered to their traditional faith and folkways. In the end the Union of Brest was as
much a politically divisive as a nationally unifying force. It ultimately served as a major source of political discord, social unrest,
and even national irredentism, which greatly weakened Polish
power on the international scene.[3]

CATHOLIC RESTORATION

In contrast, the Counter Reformation achieved a rapid success.
Under the last two Jagiellon kings the Catholic Church had definitely been on the defensive. To be sure, the large majority of the
Polish people had remained staunchly Catholic. Only a small fraction of the peasant masses, mainly in the western provinces, had
been influenced by their Protestant masters or the ministers employed by them. In the cities, too, most of the confirmed adherents
of Hus, Luther, and Calvin, were recruited from among the
wealthy patricians. Even among the gentry, which rebelled against
the established Church (for socioeconomic even more than for
religious reasons), the number of Protestants never exceeded 20–
25 percent. Yet, with the growing influence of the *szlachta* in all
walks of Polish life, and particularly in the country's domestic and
international politics, even this minority, led by the influential
landowners and at times enjoying the sympathetic cooperation of
numerous members of the Catholic clergy itself, was able to impose a policy of religious toleration on so unwilling a monarch as
Henry of Valois. The aforementioned resolutions of the Warsaw
Confederation of 1573, the tenor of which became part of Polish
public law under Stephen Báthory, not only safeguarded freedom
of worship for all non-Catholics, explicitly including Jews, but
also granted to all a measure of equal rights unparalleled in Europe at that time. According to the Protestant Świętosław Orzelski,
the main contemporary chronicler of the 1573 *interregnum*, the
leaders of the Confederation merely argued that, since Turks,
Armenians, Tatars, Greeks, and Jews not only live in Poland but
also do business and move from place to place in it, profess their
faiths, enjoy liberties, and make use of the same quasi-citizenship

they ought not to be harshly censured while they fulfill the citizen's duties to the Commonwealth. Báthory himself is said to have underscored his adherence to the principle of religious toleration in a pithy epigram: "I am a king of peoples, not of consciences." Even after his death, a convention of knights of the palatinates of Cracow, Sandomierz, and Lublin, held in Cracow in 1586 in order to organize a confederation to fight for their rights during the new *interregnum,* not only adopted a resolution calling for religious toleration but also accepted in their confederation "Jews and all others, no one excluded" who wished to join.[4]

At first the Catholic leadership itself did not oppose a limited degree of religious freedom. True, in its Piotrków synod of 1577 the Catholic clergy pronounced a general excommunication of all promoters of religious dissent. But most ecclesiastical leaders must have realized from the outset the ineffectiveness of such decrees. Others may have shared the paradoxical opinion expressed by Cardinal Stanisław Hozjusz (Hosius), whose influential apologetic tract *Confessio fidei catholicae christianae,* written in 1551 under the stimulus of an earlier Piotrków synod, appeared in 39 editions and several translations in 28 years. This and other works had secured for Hozjusz an international reputation, a cardinal's hat (in 1561), and an important role as one of the papal representatives at the final sessions of the Council of Trent (1562–63). Returning to his episcopal see in Warmia (Ermland), Hozjusz actually argued that religious toleration would promote sectarian dissensions in the Protestant camp and that ultimately the various dissenting groups would devour one another. In his letter of May 20, 1569, to King Sigismund Augustus, he explained: "Either all infidelities [*perfidiae*] are to be ejected [from the country] or all must be tolerated; for if only one sect is proscribed, all the others would appear acceptable and approved." To foster the division among Protestants, he also tried, as we recall, to deny the right of any Protestant denomination to sit in judgment over any other dissident group, and insisted on the Catholic Church's exclusive jurisdiction over all religious transgressions. Nevertheless, the three major, moderately conservative, Protestant sects of Calvinists, Lutherans, and Moravian Brethren eventually found a way to unify their forces. They came to be known as the *Ecclesia major,* which sharply condemned the radical minority of Anti-Trinitarians (the so-called *Ecclesia minor*). Nor was there a paucity of Jew-baiters among all these sects.[5]

Simultaneously, a succession of papal nuncios tried to draw Poland into an alliance of the Catholic powers led by the Austrian and Spanish Habsburgs, and into the Church's anti-Ottoman crusade. Encountering much Protestant opposition, they contended that the inner dissensions aggravated by the religious controversies had become a source of Poland's imperial weakness. This was indeed the tenor of Giovanni Francesco Commendone's historic address to the Polish Diet of 1564. In this context the Jewish issue was not overlooked. For example, in his dispatch of December 21, 1578, to the papal secretary of state, the nuncio Giovanni Andrea Caligari reported that, as soon as he heard that the Jews of Cracow had begun preparing a new edition of the Talmud, he had protested to the Polish chancellor, who "promised me to prevent, in every possible fashion, the work from being printed." Evidently, Caligari had not tried to ascertain whether the talmudic text in the printer's hand had been expurgated by deletion of all purportedly anti-Christian references, as demanded by the Council of Trent. Apparently oblivious of Caligari's report, its recipient, Gregory XIII's secretary of state, Cardinal Tolomeo Galli, but seven months later (July 18, 1579), wrote to Caligari that the nuncio must have heard of the Talmud, "which is so pestiferous, so full of blasphemies and impieties toward our Savior, that it has no equal." While some heretics had been trying to republish it under the excuse that it was an expurgated version, in his opinion its publication in Poland in any form ought to be prevented. Caligari required no such urging. His own anti-Jewish bias came clearly to the fore in his dispatch of June 12, 1579: describing his visit to Lithuania, he casually remarked that "upon entering that country one first finds there Jews, Ruthenians, and other diabolical sects." His like-minded successor, Cardinal Alberto Bolognetti, complained in his report of November 24, 1583, of Catholic laxity in Łuck and the rest of Volhynia. In Łuck, he reported, there "does not even exist a Catholic church, but there is a most beautiful synagogue of the Jews." He also called the city of Brest-Litovsk, from which he wrote, a "conglomeration [*questa concorrenza*] of heretics, schismatics, and Jews." In other dispatches he noted that the Jews defied long-established canon law by building synagogues without prior permission from the ecclesiastical authorities.[6]

In many other ways, too, 1564 marked the beginning of the Catholic counteroffensive. Under the impact of the Trent resolutions, the Polish clergy, however reluctantly at first, embarked upon a program of internal reform. Many corrupt practices, sexual as well as financial, for which priests had been previously censured by their own visitors, were discontinued. As elsewhere, such practices had provided powerful ammunition for anti-Catholic propaganda. In the same year, moreover, the Jesuit Order, after preliminaries reaching back to 1549, was formally introduced into Poland, and the first Jesuit college was established in Braniewo (Braunsberg). This school was followed by an extensive educational network covering the entire country. Education indeed became, for generations, the major Jesuit instrument for indoctrination of the country's youth—a phenomenon which augured badly for all religious dissenters, including Jews. Participating in the general upsurge of monastic orders in seventeenth-century Poland (they increased from 15 in 1600 to 27 in 1700, and the number of male monasteries actually trebled, from 220 to 655), the Jesuits made rapid progress: by 1773, a year for which statistics are available, their membership of 2,341 ranked first in the approximate total of 14,000 monks in the country. Ironically, their educational philosophy and pedagogic methods were deeply indebted to the teachings of a Spanish New Christian, Juan Luis Vives, whose father, we recall, had been executed by the Inquisition in 1521 for judaizing, and whose mother's remains were exhumed and burned eight years later. Vives himself escaped such a summary judgment only by his expatriation to the Spanish Netherlands, where the educational reforms sponsored by him were widely adopted. His reforms later served as guidelines for the Jesuit Order in many lands. We shall see that in Poland-Lithuania, even more than elsewhere, the militant Jesuits, in the vanguard of the Catholic Restoration, proved to be the group most persistently hostile to Jews and Judaism. Often upsetting the traditional balance between toleration and discrimination in the treatment of the Jewish minority, established by the medieval Church, they were often alluded to in Jewish sources as "the black" Jew-baiters.[7]

The Jesuits perceived their great opportunity after the coronation of Sigismund III, himself a former pupil of a Jesuit tutor. Some leading Polish fathers had even supported the Vasa prince's candidacy over that of Archduke Maximilian of Austria, despite the many benefactions their Order had received from the Habsburg dynasty. Upon his arrival in Poland, the twenty-one-year-old king hastened to appoint the Jesuit Piotr Skarga (1536–1612) as his court preacher, and another Jesuit as his father confessor (almost all subsequent Polish kings had Jesuit confessors). Sigismund may not have been any more pious than his predecessor. But unlike Báthory, he often allowed his religious convictions to influence domestic policies. Quite early in his reign the Protestants began to note portents of change. It was widely bruited about, for example, that in 1588, during a prayer assembly to end the plague then raging in the ancient capital, the young king wept inconsolably for an hour and had to be almost forcibly removed from the church. On the other hand (according to the contemporary chronicler, though not an eyewitness to the incident, Konrad Memmius), in 1591, when a mob attacked the Protestant sanctuary in Cracow, the third such destructive action since 1574, Sigismund greeted the news so calmly that he did not cease playing ball, and later sent an inadequate force of 10–12 men to quell the disturbance. Such rumors seemed fully to justify the saying then current among the Protestants that "King Stephen was good for the soldiers, this king will be good for the priests." [8]

One certainly did not hear from Sigismund any declaration like that issued in Psków (Pskov) by Báthory, on the occasion of a similar disturbance in Vilna in 1581. If the news of this outrage proved true, Stephen had written,

We could only receive it with extreme indignation, for in all countries and kingdoms where religion is propagated by force, steel, and fire, and not by teaching and decent behavior, there always follow horrible bloodshed and the plague of civil war. . . . We do indeed desire with Our whole heart that all citizens and inhabitants of Our kingdom, whatever class they belong to, adore the one true God and profess the one and ancient Catholic faith. But as God forewarned us that at the end of the world there would inevitably arise scandals and heresies, We want no one to be compelled to accept the faith. . . . Therefore, leaving the conscience of each to the judgment of God, We tolerate and We protect in this kingdom the *dissidentes de religione,* not only by virtue of the office entrusted to Us by the Orders of the realm so as to ensure religious peace, but also because of the old-established custom.

Although Sigismund, too, had sworn to observe the *pacta conventa* (first formulated after the election of King Henry of Valois in 1573), which included explicit safeguards for liberty of conscience, Skarga and his associates did not let the king forget that, from the outset, the Catholic leaders had sharply condemned the resolutions of the Warsaw Confederation and, in the Synod of Piotrków of 1577, had excommunicated anyone "willing to praise, defend, or sympathize with the said Confederation." In 1593 Skarga himself published a pamphlet blaming the Confederation for the bitter internal conflicts which were tearing the country apart. These conflicts, he predicted, would lead to Poland's total ruination. Pointing especially to some leaders of radical Anti-Trinitarianism, the preacher declared: "There are among the heretical masters some men who believe and teach that there is no need of any king or officials; there suffices the one king crowned in thorns [Jesus]. What will come out of that doctrine? Contempt for the God-ordained [monarchical] office, disobedience, sedition, and the destruction of the Commonwealth." [9]

National unity was indeed the *leitmotif* of Skarga's most influential homilies, the so-called *Kazania sejmowe* (Diet Sermons) which, though never delivered as sermons at any Diet session, were subsequently to inspire generations of Polish patriots. First published in 1597, they appeared in considerably revised editions in 1600 and 1610; until late in the nineteenth century, these revised editions were more readily available to the public than the original version. Among the major revisions in the second and third editions was the deletion of many of the preacher's earlier statements advocating a strong monarchical power. He increasingly acquiesced in the overwhelming control of all political affairs by the gentry, and particularly in the growing concentration of power in the hands of the landowning oligarchy. Constantly referring to biblical examples, he insisted in his Fourth Sermon, devoted to "the third malady of the Commonwealth, being the impact of the heretical plague on the Catholic religion," that the great divine pledges to Israel (in Exod. 19:4–6) "show in the first place that true liberty does not consist only in not serving tyrants like Pharaoh and in escaping their oppression, but also in obeying and submitting to the kingdom's laws and regulations when one lives in the same kingdom, in the same state, under the same king." Simultaneously, he continued, one must wholeheartedly submit to the wishes of the Church. "Just like Moses in the past, the bishops have combined religion with kingdom, and they have simultaneously been priests and kings." All along, Skarga laid special stress on the penalties for disobedience to the divine ordinances.[10]

Generally paying little attention to historical accuracy or to factual details, Skarga claimed that "as long as there were no wretched sects among you, you [the Polish people] were as one man, with one heart and one will, both in your families and in your Diets, where you looked after the interests of the Commonwealth." A typical fire-and-brimstone preacher, he emotionally depicted the dire results of Poland's continued toleration of sectarian diversity. Alluding to the "Turkish menace," which had long been on the minds of listeners throughout Christian Europe, he predicted, in terms of the biblical curses in the *Tokheḥah* (Admonition: Lev. 26:14–43 and Deut. 28:15–68), the ultimate enslavement of his people by its ruthless enemy. These predictions, uttered with great eloquence and a mastery of Polish prose unrivaled in his day (he had already distinguished himself in this field by assisting Jakub Wujek in a new Polish translation of the Bible, which was to become the semiofficial Catholic text for generations of Polish readers), made a tremendous impression, not only on Skarga's contemporaries but even more strongly upon nineteenth-century Poles, who saw in their oppression by foreign masters a realization of the preacher's terrifying warnings.[11]

It was particularly the great poet Adam Mickiewicz who, living in exile in Paris, drew this meaningful parallel. He deeply admired Skarga's "prophetic spirit" and saw in him the embodiment of "the ideal preacher and patriot." But while Mickiewicz viewed the sufferings of the Polish people as a means of a divinely ordained messianic mission similar to that of Israel, the suffering "servant of the Lord," and looked forward to the cooperation of Jews and Poles, the two "brotherly peoples," in the fulfillment of their great supranational tasks, Skarga considered the presence of numerous Jews in Poland to be a source of internal discord and as such a potential cause of the country's ultimate downfall. Not surprisingly, the image of the sixteenth-century court preacher as a great national prophet, which was visually impressed upon the Polish people by Jan Matejko's extraordinarily powerful nine-teenth-century painting of Skarga delivering a sermon, made him the object of a public adulation which brooked no criticism. When in 1897 the Polish historian Stanisław Windakiewicz showed some friends the manuscript of a new, more detached, though quite sympathetic, biography of Skarga, he was warned that the public would greatly resent his dragging the great national hero down from the pedestal on which the preacher had been placed by generations of grateful compatriots. Windakiewicz had no choice but to lock his manuscript away in a drawer. The biography was ultimately published in 1925, in a period of Poland's restored in-dependence, and one in which American and West-European his-torians were far more ruthless in "debunking" their national heroes.[12]

Such a combination of strong royal support and the patriotic appeal to national unity, along with the inherent traditionalism in beliefs and observance of the masses of Catholic peasants and artisans, particularly of the women, proved irresistible. It was rein-forced both by the reforms within the Polish Church, which re-moved many of the grievances that had long been voiced against the Catholic clergy, and by the growing sectarian divisions and in-ternecine animosities in the Protestant camp. True, Poland never developed an institution like the Spanish Inquisition to suppress religious dissent by force in a systematic fashion. Perhaps the country of that period does not quite deserve the designation of "a state without stakes" given it by a modern Polish historian; never-theless, the number of victims sentenced to death by Polish courts, including Jews condemned for alleged offenses against the Cath-olic faith, was always relatively small, compared with the num-bers in the leading West-European nations. There certainly were no large-scale executions like the one under Queen Mary in England in which 273 Protestants were slain, or the later one under Elizabeth which claimed 189 Catholic victims—not to mention the St. Bartholomew's Day Massacre in France. Nor were all of Sigismund III's successors equally intolerant of religious diversity. His own son and heir, Wladislaw IV (1632–48), was much more forbearing and was even willing to contemplate, in 1632, marriage with a Protestant princess as a means of regaining the throne of Sweden. Nonetheless, the climate of opinion among the Catholic majority in Poland had undergone such a change that this project, though warmly supported by Richelieu's France, had to be abandoned in favor of Wladislaw's marriage to the daughter of the Habsburg emperor, Ferdinand II (1637). Neither the posthumous publication in 1637 of the eloquent *Vindiciae pro religionis libertate* by Junius Brutus (a pseudonym of the Anti-Trinitarian Johannes Crell) nor the persistent ecumenical aspirations of some radical reformers, which as late as 1645 found expression in the resolutions of the Anti-Trinitarian Synod of Toruń, won much of a following in Poland, though they were to gain a much more sympathetic hearing in Holland and elsewhere in Protestant Europe. Within little more than a decade (in 1656) the Anti-Trinitarians were formally banished from Poland; only a small minority succeeded in going underground. Even the less radical denominations of Calvinists, Lutherans, and Moravian Brethren now constituted a dwindling minority of the population, and exercised less and less influence on the country's sociopolitical and cultural evolution. In fact, next to the Greek Orthodox and Uniate groups concentrated in the eastern parts of Poland, the Jews remained the principal dissenting minority; and, because of their dispersion throughout the country and their economic vitality, they continued to play a role in Polish and Lithuanian affairs far in excess of their ratio in the population.[13]

IDEOLOGICAL AND FOLKLORISTIC ASSAULTS

Jews were in many ways but a secondary target of the Catholic Restoration, which was aimed principally at Protestants and, to a lesser extent, at the Greek Orthodox schismatics. We recall that even the Council of Trent had paid relatively little attention to the Jewish question. The Catholic Church had long before made its peace with the permanent presence of a Jewish minority and had established a *modus vivendi,* based on a somewhat tenuous balance between toleration on the one hand, and discrimination combined with segregation on the other. As in other periods of Judeo-Christian relations, when a degree of toleration was safeguarded by the state and society at large, the Catholic Restoration in late sixteenth- and seventeenth-century Poland laid primary emphasis upon the elements of discrimination and segregation. Only occasionally did members of the clergy advocate eliminating Jews from a certain locality or region, when it was proposed by one or another of the ever-present anti-Jewish groups in the population.

In general, the Polish hierarchy merely needed to restate the old provisions of canon law, either universal or specifically Polish, in order to support anti-Jewish restrictions. In fact, it had only to cite the resolutions adopted under the leadership of Archbishop Mikołaj Trąba of Gniezno at the national Synod of Kalisz of 1420, which had largely reformulated many earlier canons passed by synods in Poland and elsewhere. Trąba's successors in the Gniezno metropolitan see, serving as primates of Poland, for the most part maintained his anti-Jewish stance. True, despite that persistent antagonism, a sizable Jewish community was established in the archdiocesan capital itself. According to an archival record relating to the local Jewish capitation tax, there were some 500 Jewish residents among the city's total population of about 3,000 in 1579. In 1582–84, the Gniezno Jews erected a synagogue—apparently without any ecclesiastical objections. Destroyed in 1613 by a great fire which burned down a large part of the city, the synagogue was speedily rebuilt. Because of Gniezno's commercial importance, the Poznań Jewish elders had to adopt certain provisions to enable their local traders to deal with the Gniezno merchants. It may also be noted that the distinguished rabbi Eliezer Ashkenazi completed his important work *Ma'asei ha-Shem* (Works of the Lord) in Gniezno in 1580. (According to his colophon, he computed the date for the coming of the Messiah and suggested that the redeemer was due in 1594.) In the 1650s, Jacob b. Naphtali of

Gniezno actually served as a secretary of the Jewish provincial council of Great Poland and was its messenger to Rome.[14]

Nevertheless, under the leadership of the Gniezno archbishops or their archdiocesan colleagues, the bishops of Poznań, a number of provincial synods renewed many traditional regulations, with occasional new emphasis upon certain exigencies of the moment. For instance, the Gniezno Synod of 1580 specifically forbade Jews to bathe with Christians. As late as 1720 the Synod of Łowicz re-echoed the frequently heard complaint that Jews were building new synagogues without having obtained the canonically required authorization from the ecclesiastical authorities (often in addition to permits granted by royal or municipal officials, noble owners of particular plots of land, and the like). More frequently than before, the assembled churchmen referred to alleged Jewish economic abuses. The Synod of Piotrków held in 1542 declared:

We are tired of tolerating the growing audacity of the Jews. Not satisfied with engaging in occupations interfering with the livelihood of Christians, they raise their heads as enemies of the Christian religion. They ridicule all sacred things, they walk and talk on our holidays in all public streets of our city. They also refer to many simple folk and peasants in derogatory terms. They shave them and cut their hair, serve them drinks, keep shops and stores open for them, and perform a variety of tasks desecrating and interfering with our holidays. For this reason, we decree that on holidays no Jew should dare to walk in public places, trade with, serve drinks to, shave, cut hair, let blood, or perform other medical ministrations [for Christians].

In 1642 another synod held in Poznań once more reiterated the prohibition forbidding Jews to trade or do any work on Sundays or Christian holidays; evidently inspired by complaints from competing Christian artisans, the synod again singled out Jewish tavern keepers and barbers for inclusion in that prohibition. The Counter Reformation also embarked upon manifold social welfare activities to alleviate the misery of the lower classes in the city. The Jesuits, especially, established, beginning in 1579, a number of charitable brotherhoods, including low-cost loan banks along the lines of the Italian *monti di pietà*. On the other hand, the Church's own economic interests, especially in its capacity as landlord and investor of surplus funds, caused it frequently to benefit from Jewish tenants, borrowers, and merchants. As its holdings greatly expanded in the early decades of the Counter Reformation through gifts, legacies, and purchases, its administrators, like other landlords, found the presence of Jews quite useful. For example, in the Cracow province alone the Church's possessions increased from 9 towns, 333 entire villages, and 53 portions of villages in 1581, to 13 towns, 12 portions and *jurydyki* in other towns, 489 entire villages, and 70 portions of villages. All of which did not deter some ecclesiastical assemblies from indulging in name calling, as did the synod meeting in Płock in 1733—when the era of European Enlightenment was beginning—by referring to "pernicious, God-detested Judaism." However, none of that was a novelty to Jews, who had long since learned to distinguish between a bark and a bite.[15]

At the same time, the emphasis on religious conformity also accrued to the benefit of Jewish religious observance. Quite apart from the unintentional effects of discrimination on strengthening the solidarity of the Jewish communities, a new stress was laid on the protection of the Sabbath and the Jewish holidays. True, the official Church did not feel obliged to include protective provisions on this score in its synodal resolutions. But it did not object to the kings and royal officials repeating, with renewed vigor, the relevant old safeguards of the royal privileges for Jews, safeguards which in part went back to ancient Roman legislation. Quite early in his reign (May 27, 1592), Sigismund III responded to grievances of Jewish elders by issuing a decree specifically relating to Jewish oaths and other aspects of the Jews' appearance before Polish courts of justice. It included a succinct paragraph (Art. III) stating: "Since it has thus explicitly been provided in the statutes of the realm, Jews, in accordance with the prohibition of their superstitious law, shall be neither summoned nor judged on the days of their Sabbath or other festivals." These general regulations were sometimes expanded by administrative ordinances, such as that enacted in 1659 by Prince Władysław Ostrogski, governor of Cracow, which, among other provisions, clearly stated: "The law has protected Jews against being judged on their holidays, which must be understood to include their fast days [*Bosiny;* literally, days of bare feet], the nine days of mourning [Ab 1–9] and those of the renowned fairs at Jarosław and on Gromnice [the fairs held in Lublin]." These were the stated periods of the semiannual sessions of the Council of Four Lands, which Jewish leaders were not to be prevented from attending by court summonses.[16]

Respect for Jewish religious teachings, as we shall presently see, did not necessarily extend to effective prevention of assaults on synagogues, or of the desecration of Jewish cemeteries. Moreover, in the frenzied era of Counter Reformation and the Wars of Religion, not even purely verbal attacks could be taken lightly. The positions adopted by the clergy became more serious as ecclesiastical influence on secular legislation increased by leaps and bounds. To begin with, all Catholic bishops automatically served as members of the Senate, which shared with the Chamber of Deputies the supreme legislative, and with the king much of the administrative, authority in the country. After 1596, the number of ecclesiastical senators increased by the addition of the Uniate bishops, who often evinced even deeper anti-Jewish hostility than the Roman Catholic episcopate.

More importantly, the impact of the Catholic Restoration on the composition of the Senate, the Diet, and the higher echelons of the bureaucracy became ever more marked as Sigismund III, under papal pressure and against the advice of Jan Zamoyski, appointed only Catholics to any vacant office of importance. This policy persuaded some religiously lukewarm candidates for senatorial or gubernatorial positions (together with the honors and substantial revenues attached to them), to switch over from Protestantism to the favored Catholic side. As a result, the Protestant share in major official posts rapidly declined. While in 1569 the Senate included 58 Protestants, 55 Catholics, and 2 Orthodox lay members and, in 1564, according to Commendone's estimate, two-thirds of all provincial governships were in "heretical" hands, the Protestant proportion in these high positions dwindled rapidly after the first decade of Sigismund's rule. In 1593 when Skarga, with more fervor than accuracy, contended that only one Protestant still sat in the Senate, his was wishful thinking at that moment. But the gradual purge of dissidents proceeded inexorably and at an accelerated pace. Even in Lithuania, where this process was greatly slowed down by the higher ratio of Dissenters among the magnates, the number of Protestant senators, governors, and other high officials constantly declined. At the beginning of the seventeenth century, the total ratio of Protestants in the Polish-Lithuanian Senate had already been reduced to but one-sixth. Jews could not remain unaffected. Of course, they themselves had always been barred by their faith from holding high office, except when they were badly needed as informal advisers in the fiscal administration and on foreign diplomatic missions. But sooner or later all Jews came to feel the impact of the progressive catholicization of Polish-Lithuanian officialdom.[17]

Incidentally, even the transfer of Poland's capital from Cracow to Warsaw, carried through by Sigismund III from 1595 on, because of Warsaw's more central location in the country and greater proximity to Sweden, had an adverse effect on the status of Polish-Lithuanian Jewry. The long-established Jewish community of Cracow, with its influential intellectual and wealthy leadership, had innumerable ties with the royal court and its entourage, as well as with whatever liberal groups remained in the country. In contrast, the 1527 outlawry of Jewish settlement in Warsaw had been reiterated even by the relatively tolerant Sigismund II Augustus in 1570 "as agreed upon by the councilors of Our realm." Ten years later Stephen repeated the prohibition, adding that Jews must not come to Warsaw under the pretense of some service to the king. If they had legitimate business at the Diet or courts, they were first to obtain a city permit for a sojourn of limited duration. In fact, all of Mazovia, culturally perhaps the most backward province of the Polish Crown, had felt relatively few of the changes generated by Humanism and the Reformation, and remained one of the most staunchly Catholic areas in the country. To be sure, Jews had some previous experience in overcoming such handicaps in their negotiations with leaders of the Diet and of the Church synods, when these met in the city of Piotrków, as they frequently did in the fifteenth and sixteenth centuries. Here, too, Jews had been excluded from settlement in the city proper and, according to a decree issued by Sigismund II Augustus on April 20, 1569, were allowed to trade there only during fairs. Not until several decades later do we hear of a "Jewish street" in Piotrków. But quite a few smaller Jewish settlements were close by, and even the great Jewish communities of Cracow and Poznań were not very far away. Moreover, the easy access they had all year to the king and influential nobles in Cracow (the number of courtiers there sometimes reached the staggering total of 1,500) had largely compensated them for the difficulties of maintaining contact with the occasional assemblies of deputies or churchmen in Piotrków. But with the removal of the royal residence to Warsaw, Jewish "lobbying" at court and the Diet was much more difficult; in time it had to be left either to special delegates dispatched to the new capital by the Jewish leaders of various communities or, ultimately, to the so-called Warsaw Committee, maintained on a semipermanent basis by the Council of Four Lands.[18]

Perhaps even more important than the Catholic Church's impact on legislation was its growing influence on public opinion, among all classes but particularly among the rural and urban masses. Apart from the numerous polemical works defending Catholic ideology against Protestant assaults, were writings by churchmen, as well as by lay authors trained or otherwise influenced by the clergy, which promoted the ideas of the Catholic Restoration. A prolific juridical author, Szymon Starowolski, though a layman, wrote in 1634 a major work on jurisprudence, *Accessus ad iuris utriusque cognitionem,* based entirely on the Thomistic-Jesuit view of life. An extreme conservative, Starowolski demanded a vigorous repression of all non-Catholic faiths, and devoted two whole tracts to an attack on the Warsaw Confederation of 1573 and on the very principle of liberty of conscience. The contemporary historical literature was likewise deeply imbued with an antiheretical and anti-Jewish animus. For one example, Józef Bartłomiej Zimorowicz, employed as municipal clerk in Lwów, spent many years, beginning in 1634, in writing an up-to-date chronicle of his city. Using available church records and, for the years 1597–1633, the municipal archives, he assembled much valuable historical material, including some documents since lost. Despite his obvious antischismatic and anti-Jewish bias, his data on the Jewish, Ruthenian, Armenian, and other ethnic groups have served many modern historians of the capital of Red Russia to good advantage. But long before its publication in 1835, his chronicle proved useful to Lwów's municipal administration in its frequent conflicts with Jews. It also helped to disseminate erroneous and one-sided views on the past of the local Jewish community.[19]

More specifically devoted to an attack on Jews and Judaism was Sebastyan Miczyński's *Zwierciadło Korony polskiej* (A Mirror of the Polish Crown), published in Cracow in 1618. A doctor of philosophy (we must remember that, at least in later years, all recipients of that degree at a Jesuit university had to take an oath of fidelity to Thomistic doctrines), Miczyński concentrated on depicting Jewish economic activities, in order to show the extent of the Jews' exploitation of the Polish people and the ensuing ruination of many Christian merchants and artisans. He reviewed in some detail the situation of the various Cracow guilds to demonstrate the damage inflicted upon these pious Catholic folk through unfair Jewish competition. While modern scholars have learned a great deal from Miczyński's ramblings, about specific Jewish occupational activities at the beginning of the seventeenth century, this pamphlet, written in an inflammatory vein, furnished much ammunition to rabble-rousing preachers and to political partisans among the Cracow burghers. It called forth a special decree by Sigismund III, ordering its confiscation and prohibiting its future republication or sale. A similar attack, aimed at Jewish doctors, was published in 1623 by a Catholic priest, Sebastyan Śleszkowski, who presented (according to his title page) "Clear Proof about Jewish Doctors that Those, Who, Contrary to the Prohibitions of the Holy Catholic Church, Use Jews, Tatars, and Other Infidels as Physicians . . . Endanger not only Their Souls but also Their Bodies." Śleszkowski insisted that a sin was also committed by those who advised others to use the medical ministrations of infidels. Most rabid were pamphlets such as Przecław Mojecki's *Żydowskie okrucieństwa* (Jewish Cruelties), which was republished in Cracow in 1606 and again in 1636. We shall see that, by listing a whole array of alleged Jewish desecrations of the host, ritual murders, and other inhuman acts, and providing each story with harsh comments of his own, Mojecki greatly contributed to the popularization of these old folkloristic accusations against Jews and Judaism.[20]

While all these writings were addressed exclusively to a literate audience, public performances of a devotional character often graphically represented to the unlearned masses of peasants and urban proletarians the Jews' alleged inbred hostility toward all Christians. Like the Western *autos sacramentales,* passion plays, and other popular dramas, the devotional performances in Poland and Lithuania greatly contributed to the poisoning of all Judeo-Christian relations, as did many of the representations in the fine arts of scenes from the New Testament and the lives of saints. Not only were all worshipers at church services surrounded by paintings, stained-glass windows, and sculptures portraying a variety of hostile acts by Jews as described in ancient and medieval Catholic literature, but in 1618 a Jew-baiting painter even decorated the walls of the Poznań city hall with murals depicting the exile of the Jews from Jerusalem, a Jewess riding on a pig, and other figures exposing the Jewish people to public contumely. The ensuing attacks on Jews caused the Poznań Jewish community to appeal to the *gród* (court of the castle) for redress.[21]

As a result of that agitation, mob attacks on Christian nonconformists and Jews increased in both number and intensity. Assaults on Jewish streets and synagogues had occasionally taken place in earlier periods as well, but had called forth, as a rule, strong governmental action. Now, however, some officials of the municipalities and the royal administration turned a deaf ear to the complaints of the victims of mob violence. This was particularly true when Protestant churches were attacked, since their elimination by mob action was welcomed, and often actually instigated, by the Catholic clergy. The two Protestant churches in Cracow (permission for their erection, and royal protection, had been pledged by the authorities as late as 1571–72) and others in Poznań, Vilna, Lwów, and a number of other cities were destroyed by arsonists; some of them repeatedly, and in the end never rebuilt. In the sharp Counter-Reformational reaction, the great center of Anti-Trinitarianism the college of Raków (called by a contemporary pamphleteer "the synagogue of gangsters"), which at one time attracted a thousand eager students, was permanently shut down in 1638, to be followed by the total expulsion of the sect from Poland and Lithuania twenty years later. Jews fared somewhat better. While many synagogues, as well as individual Jews, were attacked, they more easily obtained protective royal decrees, not only from Stephen Báthory but also from Sigismund III and his successors, in 1596, 1621, 1622, and frequently thereafter. The constant repetition of these protective decrees, however, betrayed their utter ineffectiveness. From the outset their texts and mode of promulgation showed that they lacked "teeth" for implementation. Even the effort of Sigismund I, in 1530, to place the responsibility for preventing riots upon the Cracow city council, had proved to be a dismal failure. The king's demand that the city deposit a bond of 10,000 marks as a guarantee that it would adopt stringent measures against slayers of Jews, had to be withdrawn within six years, in the face of the city's argument that it could not be held responsible for individual acts of lawlessness. Even less effective proved to be Sigismund III's pertinent decree of 1596, as well as Wladislaw IV's and Michael's confirmations thereof, in 1633 and 1669, respectively. Apparently they were simply disregarded by the city fathers.[22]

Jesuit colleges often became major foci of anti-Jewish disturbances. In Cracow any Jewish pedestrian passing the Jesuit college had to pay 4 groszy; a rider on horseback, 6 groszy; and one traveling by horse and buggy, 12 groszy. As elsewhere, the academic youth frequently let off surplus energy by boisterous behavior toward alleged undesirables. The looting of Jewish shops and homes often proved quite remunerative, especially if it was performed under the guise of religious zeal. Only rarely did the passions thus aroused degenerate into a regular pogrom, such as resulted from the *Schülergeläuf* (student riot) in Lublin in 1646, when 8 Jews were slain, 50 wounded, and 20 houses thoroughly despoiled. More than in earlier periods, the student rioters (often joined by young artisans and apprentices) secured immunity from prosecution by lay authorities, through the intervention of their ecclesiastical superiors, who claimed exclusive jurisdiction over religious personnel. In some cases, miscarriage of justice went so far that Jewish defenders were brought to trial for beating up "innocent" youngsters, particularly if these minors were sons of noblemen, as was often the case. In one instance, the verdict acquitting the students of all guilt (the Jews had already been forced to pay some compensation for alleged injuries) was countersigned by the bishop of Cracow (1628). When in 1613 a Jewish counter-attack proved successful, the rector of the Jesuit college in Lwów accused the "assailants" from the ghetto of a breach of the peace, and of insulting the whole noble class and Christendom. The Jewish communities therefore considered it the better part of wisdom to buy off would-be assailants by paying them a regular annual tribute. Known as *kozubalec*, or *Schüler Geld*, such payments in money or in kind are recorded for most major Polish Jewish communities. So permanent did this institution become throughout the realm, that in 1637 the Lithuanian Council of Provinces actually ordained that thenceforth every Jewish community "calling itself *kahal* shall pay out [*li-sekhor;* literally, hire] *Schüler Geld,* both for its own locality and for the small towns and villages in its vicinity. . . . If it cannot afford to do so, it should be aided by the province, according to the judgment of the provincial elders." At times these expenses became exorbitant. In 1639, when the Vilna community, trying to stave off assaults, overtaxed its resources and appealed to the Lithuanian Council of Provinces for assistance, the latter resolved that thenceforth it would contribute no more than one-fifth, to a maximum of 5,000 zlotys, for such imposts; any excess would require specific authorization by the Council. Nevertheless, these student attacks remained a frequent fact of Jewish life in many Polish cities. Local Lwów records mention assaults in every year from 1572 to 1643; some of them (in 1572, 1618, 1638, and 1641) turned into regular riots with a considerable number of Jewish casualties. They culminated in the "great *Schülergeläuf"* of 1663, which involved 200 casualties and left an indelible imprint on Lwów Jewry for many generations. In Cracow, too, the tensions increased in the seventeenth century, and tumults were recorded in quick succession in 1621, 1622, 1628, 1637, and 1639. That of 1637 cost the lives of 7 Jews, who were thrown by the rioters into the Vistula; 33 others saved themselves from death only by promising conversion to Christianity. In almost all these events the city councils remained passive, or even actively encouraged the assailants, without bringing down upon themselves the wrath of the royal power. The "pogrom" of 1637 apparently evoked merely a verbal reprimand from the Cracow governor.[23]

Occasionally, to be sure, the Jesuit authorities had good reason to restrain their students from looting Jewish homes and shops. By a curious inversion, quite widespread in the Polish-Lithuanian area, it was the Christian clergy who lent money to the Jewish communities; hence it was interested in maintaining their solvency. Of course, this did not prevent individual Jewish moneylenders from extending petty loans to students or clerics in need of cash. Unlike Padua, however, which, as we recall, considered this Jewish function a worthwhile contribution to the life of the city (such loans made it possible for a multitude of foreign students to register at the famed university and to remain there when their funds were short), and thus indirectly as a justification for maintaining Jews in Padua, the Polish university authorities of the Counter Reformation era placed their religious zeal ahead of practical considerations. In general, because of the far greater economic diversification of Polish Jewry, petty moneylending and pawnbroking played a subordinate role in the Jewish economy. Hence even the establishment of Christian charitable loan banks by Skarga and others was not accompanied by an extensive anti-Jewish campaign like those carried on by Bernardino da Feltre and other churchmen in Italy. Moreover, mob attacks on Jews and their institutions, even if inspired by individual clergymen or college administrators, never had the formal sanction of higher Church organs, which only indirectly encouraged such excesses by refusing to censure the assailants. Certainly, there was no such wholesale violent suppression of Judaism or Jewish assemblies of worship as was employed in rooting out Protestant sects from certain regions. For example, the extirpation of "heresy" among the peasant masses in the district of Oświęcim (the city which was to achieve international notoriety under the German name of Auschwitz) by fire and the sword had no parallel in attempts to eliminate Jews from any particular area of Poland and Lithuania. At the most, the Jesuits and other churchmen joined some burghers in agitating for the banishment of Jews from one or another locality. However, even if quite disastrous to Jews in substance, these measures were formally disguised as legitimate, legal actions.[24]

In fact, Skarga himself did not refrain from arousing the populace against the Jews by playing up the theme of alleged Jewish ritual murders. He not only described at length the sufferings of the reputed child martyr Simon of Trent in 1475 but also inserted into this hagiographic sketch a sort of eyewitness account of a similar crime purportedly committed by the Jews in 1574. When a leading churchman, Bernard Maciejowski, bishop of Łuck and later Cracow, compiled an official "report" of a similar blood ritual allegedly performed in 1598 by Jews in the vicinity of Lublin, the Jesuits decided to circulate it in print. (We must note, however, that although, during the last several years before his death in 1608, Maciejowski served as primate of Poland, he was essentially more a political than an ecclesiastical leader.)

In general, the Jesuits, who in Poland even more than in other countries represented the militant arm of the Counter Reformation, were the most effective educational, oratorical, and literary exponents of Polish anti-Judaism of that period. Apart from their theological controversies with Jews, they often plagued the Jewish communities with excessive requisitions for gifts and loans. In a characteristic entry in the communal "Book of Electors" of Poznań in 1632, the elders wrote: "We have noted that the Black Ones [the Jesuits] have the upper hand and are able to do us either harm or good. We have been forced, therefore, to fulfill all their demands and wishes." It should be noted, however, that in Poland, unlike medieval England, France, and Germany, Blood Accusations rarely endangered entire communities. As a rule, only a number of individuals were cited before the courts and, through mendacious testimony (sometimes furnished by the real culprits, who thus tried to escape punishment), as well as "confessions" obtained from the accused under severe torture, were condemned and executed. Only here and there did the ensuing agitation among the masses result in assaults upon other Jews. One of the bloodiest attacks was that in Cracow in 1637, which resulted in the death of seven Jewish outsiders. (For years thereafter, the community commemorated these seven martyrs in an annual day of mourning.) We recall that as early as 1598 Father Przecław Mojecki enumerated 34 ritual murders and 14 host desecrations attributed to Polish Jews up to that time. If, in answer to these allegations, Jewish leaders and their non-Jewish sympathizers, including the kings, referred to the numerous papal bulls and royal declarations in many lands condemning the ritual murder libel as a total lie, Mojecki and his allies argued that those enactments were outright forgeries and that, even if they were authentic, they would attest only the purity of the Jewish faith, not the innocence of particular Jewish criminals.[25]

It is remarkable that a priest like Mojecki should have thus disregarded the early papal bulls outlawing the Blood Accusation which had found their way into the papal *Decretales* and had thereby become part of the main code of canon law, the *Corpus juris canonici.* Less objectionable, from the standpoint of canon law, appeared the belief that fanatical Jews desecrated the host, since this belief was shared by some high churchmen, including the papal nuncio Aloisio Lippomano and the archbishop of Gniezno, Stanisław Golański. After all, the notion that Jews engaged in desecration of the host had long been cherished in many Catholic lands; it found telling expression, for instance, in the annual celebration of the *miracle des billettes* in Paris after 1290 and the *miracle de Sainte-Gudule* in Brussels after 1370. At times even Protestants were accused of aiding and abetting the desecration. Because of the controversy over the doctrine of Transubstantiation, the allegation appeared quite plausible. For example, in Wschowa (Fraustadt) in 1558, a local poet, Fabian Orzechowski, denounced the Lutheran pastor Andrzej Knobloch for allegedly having sold a consecrated wafer to some Jewish visitors at the fair for sacrilegious purposes.[26]

Noting the inefficacy of royal interventions, the Council of Four Lands, it appears, decided in 1640 to send messengers to Rome to implore the Papacy to put a stop to that undying, though totally baseless, accusation. While the details of this intervention are not known, and we do not learn about any new bull issued at that time by the reigning pope, Urban VIII, the character of that embassy may have been quite similar to those of Abraham Szkolny (who in 1540, in behalf of the Poznań community, had secured a brief against the Blood Accusation from Pope Paul III) and Jacob Zelig, who was dispatched by the Council in 1763. Zelig's mission resulted in the famous report of Cardinal Lorenzo Ganganelli to Pope Clement XIII, whom Ganganelli succeeded in 1769 as Pope Clement XIV: the cardinal convincingly argued against the admissibility of the very notion of the Blood Accusation. Another Jewish messenger, Jacob b. Naphtali of Gniezno, apparently sent by the Jewish Provincial Council of Great Poland to Rome in 1654, may have been instrumental in obtaining from the master general of the Dominican Order, Giovanni Battista de Medinis, a letter to the Polish provincial of that Order asking him to protect the Jews against the Blood Accusation (February 9, 1664). Of course, in addition to the purely folkloristic blood allegations, the Church often complained that Jews transgressed the law through their contemptuous behavior toward Catholic institutions and rituals. A very frequent bone of contention was the work performed by Jews in public on Sundays and Christian holidays. Sometimes Christian onlookers were irked by the mere appearance on such days of Jews strolling in public squares and gardens. Even more obnoxious appeared the allegedly widespread practice in which Christian domestics were forced to work in Jewish households on Sundays. Curiously, even Protestants were sometimes accused of similar transgressions. In 1658 a priest, bearing the remarkable name of Krzystof Zygmunt Żydowski, accused five Polish Brethren of "inducing their subordinates to perform work on festival days in contempt of the Catholic faith." In this area Jews could not expect protection from the kings, and often had to resort to extralegal ways of preventing serious prosecution.[27]

One facet of the Judeo-Christian controversy lost much of its acrimony, however. We hear fewer and fewer accusations of Jewish proselytizing. In view of the general intensification of religious polemics and the growing number of Protestant dissenters and Jews in the country, the old accusation that most Christian nonconformists were Judaizers lost much of its verisimilitude. Even Anti-Trinitarians, however close their ideology seemed to come to the Jewish brand of monotheism, were very well distinguished from Jews, whose faith the leading "Arian" controversialists openly combated. True, individuals who sympathized with Jewish views were not lacking. Skarga was not alone in being taken aback by meeting a remarkable lady "heretic." Stopping over in Grodek on his journey to Rome, he became acquainted with Mikołaj Mielecki, governor of Podolia. In vain did he try to reconvert that distinguished Protestant aristocrat to Catholicism.

He found even greater resistance on the part of Mielecki's wife Elżbieta, daughter of the well-known Reform leader Mikołaj Radziwiłł, nicknamed Czarny (Black). A deeply religious and highly educated person, Elżbieta, who had learned Greek, Latin, and Hebrew, had moved from Calvinism to Anti-Trinitarianism and later to so-called Judaizantism, which came quite close to outright Judaism. All the persuasive power of the young would-be Jesuit did not budge her from her point of view. Under Sigismund III, however, individuals like Elżbieta, or the Polish noblewoman in Red Russia who adopted Judaism in 1605, became quite exceptional. If any of them in the secrecy of their hearts were inclined to adopt some Jewish beliefs, they either concealed them successfully or else emigrated to the Ottoman Empire, where they could give free rein to their new religious convictions. In short, Jewish proselytization, a more imaginary than genuine menace to Polish Catholicism even in the religiously turbulent sixteenth century, was no longer a serious issue in Judeo-Christian relations in the era of the Catholic Restoration.[28]

On its part, Jewish leadership became increasingly sensitive about the anti-Jewish accusations. It went to great length in trying to regulate the Jews' behavior so as to offer as little provocation as possible to their neighbors. Among the measures taken was an attempt to persuade the local churches to divert their religious processions from the Jewish quarter. Even individual priests were discouraged from paying visits to the Jewish street. In this way the elders hoped to prevent untoward incidents, actual or imagined, of zealous Jews making derogatory remarks about the Christian faith or rituals. In the economic sphere, too, the communal leaders made strenuous efforts to counteract the ever-recurrent rumors relating to overcharges by Jews to Gentile customers; to malpractices in the collection of taxes or in the handling of coin; and, more generally, to any form of Jewish "domination" over Christian subordinates. Both the Council of Four Lands and the Lithuanian Council of Provinces, as we shall see, forbade Jews to mint coins or to farm taxes to be collected from burghers or peasants, and generally outlawed unfair Jewish dealings with Christian merchants and customers.

Typical of the defensive injunctions is the following resolution adopted at the first session of the Lithuanian Council in 1623:

In all Jewish communities dwelling in the cities and their environs [the elders] should warn their members, the people of the Lord, to be careful neither [to ridicule] nor to assault any Gentile. For we all see that the bitter Exile is getting more and more intense, so that we can no longer sustain the yoke of our trials and tribulations and the divine attribute of justice [and punishment] is threatening [to overwhelm] us because of our sins. And all the people of the land shall know that a man who arbitrarily quarrels with and beats a Gentile and thereby draws prosecution upon himself shall not be assisted financially, even if he should be condemned to a severe penalty. However, he who observes the commandments shall not suffer from any evil.

Local communities frequently adopted parallel resolutions. For example, the community of Poznań issued, in 1628, a proclamation which included the following provision:

The community shall deal extensively with Jewish merchants who publicly desecrate the name of the Lord in their business relations with Gentile merchants. There arises the danger that thereby the livelihood of the children of Israel will be undermined, since there is little room left for Israel's remnant to earn a living. It is very likely that, as a result [of malpractices by a few] Christian merchants will refuse to deal with all Jewish businessmen, God forbid. That is why [the elders] have decided to impose high fines and other penalties [upon such malefactors] and to expose them to public contumely for [their transgressions] which must not be tolerated. Their shame shall also be widely heralded because of the evil deeds they have committed.

Needless to say, like many governmental enactments, such autonomous Jewish regulations often broke down in the face of economic necessity. Jewish leaders were also extremely reticent about allowing the publication of apologetic tracts in defense of Judaism, because some passages in them might be construed by opponents as attacks on the Christian faith. For this reason, the outstanding work of Jewish apologetics, begun by the Karaite Isaac b. Abraham of Troki and completed by Isaac's pupil Józef T. Malinowski in 1595, remained unpublished until its inclusion by the Bavarian Catholic apologist Johann Christoph Wagenseil in his polemical work in 1681. Moreover, the Jewish elders knew that any publication in Latin or Polish might have to pass through the hands of a Catholic censor, who could prevent its appearance, and that, even after publication, it could become the target of attacks by Jew-baiters.[29]

CITIES AND BURGHERS

Jews faced a harsher opposition from their Christian neighbors in the cities than from the Church. Prompted by ethnic, religious, and even more by economic, considerations, large segments of the urban population had few of the traditional restraints of the Church in dealing with the Jewish question, and very frequently went all out in trying to eliminate Jews from their localities. In fact, the unusually sharp antagonism evinced by the Jesuits in Poland toward the Jews may in part be accounted for by the descent of most Jesuits from prejudiced urban families. Even Piotr Skarga originated from the petty gentry in Mazovia, with its deep-rooted anti-Jewish bias and above-average conservatism. The progressive Polonization of the German burghers in the Polish and Lithuanian cities eliminated a major divisive force in the Christian majority. No longer were there anti-German riots like the one which had caused Rodolphus Agricola the Younger to cut short his stay in Cracow and to claim that "there is not a German whom they [the Poles] do not treat worse than a Jew." This process of assimilation, which was practically completed by the onset of the Counter Reformation, made the cityfolk more responsive to patriotic appeals by Catholic preachers and laymen with the explicit or implied goal of achieving ethnic homogeneity at the expense of the Jewish outsiders. A considerable number of cities and towns now succeeded in securing formal decrees *de non tolerandis Judaeis* from the kings, although such privileges were not always observed to the letter.[30]

An extreme illustration of the exclusion of Jews in the sixteenth century are, as we shall see, Duke Albert the Elder's decrees of July 14 and 26, 1567, relating to the privileges of the duchy of Prussia. They stated unequivocally: "Henceforth Jews are not to be tolerated in the duchy." Nevertheless, in Prussia, too, Jewish visitors continued to appear at local fairs and, before long, a few settled especially in ecclesiastical or noble *jurydyki* in the vicinity of cities. Curiously, even Ukrainian Kiev, which had had the oldest recorded Jewish community in the area, now faced, under Sigismund III, rigid residential and communal restrictions for

Jews, while the king favored burghers and frontiersmen. Claiming (contrary to historical truth) that "Jews have never lived in Kiev before," the king ordained in 1619 that no Jew "shall dare to buy, rent, or establish a residence in the city of Kiev under the jurisdiction of the castle, the part of the city belonging to the bishop, or on the grounds of the metropolitan, the archimandrite, monasteries, nobles, Cossacks, or anyone else." Any person acting contrary to this provision was to be condemned to the loss of all his property, half of which was to be turned over to the castle; the other half, to the city hall "without appeal." The small Jewish remnant which defied that decree was soon thereafter overwhelmed by the Cossack rebels and their Tatar allies, who were speedily followed by the intolerant Muscovite regime.[31]

Fortunately for the Jews, their urban opponents were not united. According to Aleksander Brückner, even in the sixteenth century Polish culture was predominantly rural. To be sure, demographically, by 1578 the ratio of the urban population in the entire Commonwealth had risen to some 25 percent. However, economically, large segments of the "urban" population still derived their main livelihood from cultivating the soil, just as many peasants (particularly women) participated in industrial production of textiles, liquors, and the like. In these capacities, the urbanites shared many attitudes with the peasant masses, rather than with the upper bourgeoisie which dominated the cities. Moreover, most of the 1,250 towns estimated to have existed at that time in the Polish Crown (including parts of Silesia and Pomerania controlled by Poland) were very small. Only eight cities had a population exceeding 10,000 souls. They included Gdańsk, with 40,000 inhabitants; Cracow, with 28,000; Poznań and Warsaw, with 20,000 each. While sizable by medieval standards, these cities could not compare with the large Western metropolises, the population of which had risen to more than a hundred thousand each as a result of the population explosion of the sixteenth century. Many Polish towns, moreover, were founded on the private domains of noble lords and were subsequently controlled by these masters and their heirs. This situation was particularly pronounced in the eastern provinces, where many new townships were arising in the magnates' latifundia in the seventeenth century. The distances between the cities, and the difficulties of communication between them, were also sufficiently large to impede the rise of a uniform Polish culture and economy.[32]

All these factors impeded any sustained joint action by the cities against the Jews. True, in an interesting letter of 1521, the city councilors of Lwów urged their confreres in Poznań to join them in an anti-Jewish campaign:

We inform Your Highnesses that the infidel Jews, who for many years have had the license to trade and to purchase certain wares to the prejudice and detriment of the Christian merchants, have [done so] to the ultimate destruction not only of our city but also of all other cities in which they are allowed to live. They take away almost our entire livelihood and that of all our merchants and compatriots, for wherever they can they destroy the trade of Christian merchants. They trade in cities, travel through villages, and do not permit any merchandise to reach Christian hands. . . . For this reason we ask Your Highnesses to indicate to us whether you would be ready at the stated time to join us in opposing such liberties of the Jews and to place before His Holy Royal Majesty such complaints against those Jews on your part.

Similar letters were sent to the municipal councils of Cracow and other cities—evidently bearing little fruit. If concerted efforts of this kind proved but partially successful, the major reason undoubtedly was the general progressive decline of the Polish cities' commercial importance. In arguing for considering the 1530s a critical turning point in the history of Polish civilization, Kazimierz Lepszy has shown that about that time the large Polish banking families of Boner, Kreutzburg, and Krupki, who had theretofore, often in cooperation with the Augsburg Fuggers, performed signal services to the royal court and the local merchant class, and invested considerable capital in Polish mines and industries, were increasingly attracted to the rising economy of the Rhineland. Among those who remained in Poland, many abandoned their banking business and, as often happened in Italy and elsewhere, invested their funds in rural properties and gradually joined the ranks of the landowning nobility. The vacuum created by these departing commercial leaders was filled largely by Jews who at that time had few opportunities to move West and were effectively shut out from the acquisition of land. Nor were the cities adequately represented in the Polish and Lithuanian Diets to form representative bodies entitled to speak in their behalf in a single voice. For a time after 1505 Cracow alone had the right to send deputies to the Diet. Their voices carried little weight, if they were heard at all in the din caused by the overwhelming noble majority. In one turbulent session they were thrown out of the Chamber. If, later in the century, a few other cities were admitted to membership in the Diet, the law restricted their spokesmen to deliberations directly concerning urban affairs. In this respect Jews were somewhat better off. By organizing their provincial councils, and their central Polish Council of Four Lands and the Lithuanian Council of Provinces, both recognized by the government, they possessed semiofficial autonomous organs speaking in behalf of all Polish and Lithuanian Jews.[33]

The inhabitants of the cities were also divided into many groups. The very term "burgher" applied to a Polish urbanite of the time only in the broadest sense. Technically, "citizenship" was enjoyed only by those persons (and their descendants) who were formally admitted to it by the city. These "citizens" were divided between a patriciate of relatively few long-established families of wealth and culture and a majority of craftsmen and petty merchants who eked out a living. It usually was the patrician who was elected to the city council; he often pursued policies helpful to himself and his class. Below the citizens was the large mass of the poor, including those who worked for the master craftsmen; employees of merchants and professionals; servants in the households of the rich; beggars and the underworld. Not surprisingly, students staging riots against Jews found easy allies among the underprivileged, many of whom were envious of the financial success of some of the Jewish businessmen and were particularly eager to partake of the loot from Jewish shops and homes.

Sometimes the *biedota* (the poor) actually accused the town fathers of having sold out to Jews. For instance, when the city of Lwów in 1581 concluded its first commercial "agreement" with its Jews, it strictly delimited their trading rights. Nonetheless, the populace regarded the compact as too favorable to the Jews and spread rumors that they had secured it by bribing some city council members. While in many localities the elders ruled with an iron hand, in others they had to concede some share in the municipal government to the other citizens, especially where the so-called *pospólstwo* (or *communitas*, a general assembly) had to be consulted on major decisions. As in most West-European cities, the patricians tried to maintain public order and, thus, frequently protected Jews against mob assaults, partly because they feared the spread of riots into their own quarters, and partly because they anticipated reprisals from the royal government. At times, some wealthy Christian merchants found it advantageous to co-operate with Jewish businessmen in common undertakings. In contrast, plebeian groups rarely allied themselves with Jews against the ruling families. Such was the case in Lwów in 1651, when both the Jews and the lower classes demanded that the city council adopt a resolution forbidding the elders to go away during emergencies, as had happened in the preceding years when, at the approach of the Cossacks, many Lwów leaders had left the city in a state of near-anarchy.[34]

Other distinctive groups often fared worse than the Jews. Not only did the Protestants living in Catholic cities now suffer severely from the sharply reactionary trends under Sigismund III, but foreigners, including important businessmen settled in Poland for commercial reasons, were often harshly discriminated against. While some leading Polish merchants realized that foreigners, as well as Jews, were of great help in their own mercantile pursuits, the majority of traders and craftsmen saw in them mainly successful competitors. In many cities these foreigners, like the Jews, had to look for shelter in the *jurydyki* under the control of nobles or the Church. In 1562 the Piotrków Diet adopted an extremely xenophobic law, according to which Italian, Scottish, and other foreign merchants not enjoying citizenship in any Polish town were not to live or trade anywhere in Poland. In a seventeenth-century satire, the Polish nobleman Gabriel Krasiński, son of a palatine and himself a castellan of Płock, compared Italian merchants to Jews, not because of their [the Jews'] "detestable" faith but because of their shrewdness, cheating, and misrepresentation. According to Krasiński, foreigners frequently associated with Jews, both economically and socially. Through their far-flung foreign contacts, Jews also established business relations with foreign firms and their agents in Poland. They were thus able to acquire foreign goods on credit and sell them in Poland at substantial profits. According to Sebastyan Miczyński, some Jews had secured such credits from Dutch traders in Gdańsk. Shortly before 1618, other Jewish visitors, at the fairs in Lublin and Jarosław, had purchased from Englishmen cloth on credit for no less than 200,000 zlotys. In short, by their strongly discriminatory policies, the municipal administrations often forced many foreign merchants to share a quarter with Jews in an enclave or a suburb, and thus fostered alliances between the two groups most in competition with the burghers.[35]

Such antiforeign, as well as anti-Jewish, municipal measures often provoked a strong royal reaction. In conferring the privileges of Magdeburg law upon the city of Lwów, Casimir the Great had clearly extended them to all the various groups in the city's population; viz., the "Poles, Rus, Germans, Armenians, Jews, and Saracens." Not only was it possible for King Sigismund I to decree that Jews be treated equally with the Christian merchants in the collection of tolls (1527), and that they be allowed freely to trade throughout the realm (1532), but in additional provisions appended to a renewal of the Jewish privileges at the Diet of Toruń on December 1, 1576, Stephen Báthory bluntly informed the cities that Jews "shall be treated equally with the burghers and be granted the same liberties; except in specific cases [provided by law] they shall remain under exclusive royal jurisdiction." Similar sweeping declarations had previously been inserted by Sigismund Augustus into local privileges; for instance, into that of Przemyśl Jewry in 1559, which read: "Moreover, the said Jews ought to enjoy and use the same liberties . . . which are enjoyed by Our city of Przemyśl." In certain matters, to be sure, Jews remained subject to municipal jurisdiction according to the specific privileges previously granted to particular cities. Typical of that jurisdictional division is the following sentence appearing in a court record of 1603, relating to the litigation between the city of Lwów and a Jewish leader, Nachman Izakowicz. Referring to the divided judicial competences, the writer explained:

(1) in all personal matters they [the Jews] are subject to the lords palatine, which palatines are their absolute and ordinary judges; (2)

in matters relating to real estate, they must, in accordance with the Magdeburg law, accept the city's jurisdiction relating to [the said] real estate. They shall not be subjected to any other jurisdiction from the time when they settle there by agreement with the city.

In other words, only with respect to land belonging in the ultimate sense to the city (evidently with the exception of the noble and clerical enclaves) did the Jews have to turn to the municipal authorities for major decisions.[36]

If antiforeign discrimination thus inadvertently played into the hands of Jewish competitors of the patrician merchants, the same was true also with respect to some members of the Polish lower classes. We shall see that, as in medieval Germany, the artisans and their guilds usually were in the vanguard of the anti-Jewish forces in the Polish cities. Because of ever-narrowing economic opportunities, many craftsmen sought to establish as close a monopoly on production as possible. They often succeeded in securing from city councils, and even from kings and governors, prohibitions barring Jews and foreigners from engaging in a vast array of crafts. Many Catholic Poles were also excluded. Not only was admission to the status of master artisans increasingly restricted, and the way to the top of the profession barred to a great many apprentices by monopolistic laws, but craftsmen or journeymen coming from other localities had to settle in one or another ecclesiastical or noble enclave, or even in the Jewish street, in order to earn a living. These "unfair" competitors, going under the name of *partaczy,* became semioutcasts, similar to Jews not only topographically but also economically and socially. Thus the manifold discriminatory laws, inspired by economic rivalries, whether or not outwardly disguised as religiously or nationalistically motivated, helped bring together Jews, Protestants, foreigners, and nonguild craftsmen into a loose alliance of formidable proportions.[37]

Ironically, some forms of economic discrimination, under whatever ideological guise, ultimately accrued to the benefit of the minority groups, rather than of the recipients of the particular privileges. Such was the case, for instance, when on May 27, 1643, the Polish Diet, evidently under pressure from Christian merchants, enacted a law limiting the profits of their non-Christian and alien competitors. According to the law's provisions, at each sale of imported articles, Christian residents could collect a profit of 7 percent over their costs, and foreign Christians could have a mark-up of 5 percent, whereas Jews had to be satisfied with only 3 percent. When bringing in his goods, every importer was to take an oath that he would charge no more than the allowable maximum. In practice, however, this Diet resolution, whether or not it had a real impact on the general price structure, merely served to publicize the fact, already known to many purchasers, that merchandise sold by Jews was less expensive than that offered by Christians. Long before that decree, Jews had learned to concentrate on increasing their turnover of goods through lower prices. Now this practice received official encouragement and wide publicity. As usual, however, anything done by Jews called forth unfavorable comment on the part of their enemies. Outside observers often noticed that, even in prosperous times, Jews lived modestly in order to accumulate reserves for emergencies—which they faced more frequently than their neighbors. They were particularly abstemious in their drinking habits. In contrast, the fifteenth-century pope Pius II (Enea Silvio Piccolomini) had characterized the average Pole as being "pious in the morning, drunk at noon, and virile in the evening." But rather than drawing praise for their prudent behavior, the Jews were often exposed to public ridicule. The satirist Adam Jarzembski in 1643 described a typical Jew as dressed in rags and eating his radishes, cucumbers, and carrots. "With that the Jew is satisfied, while he accumulates his coins to the satisfaction of his lord, to whom he lends money on pledges. He makes use of his capital, schemes with his brain, sells with small profits, but hardly spends a farthing on food." In all that, one must not forget that when Christian merchants and artisans strove to maintain prices as high as possible, the main sufferers were the Christian consumers. Understandably, therefore, many customers, whether from the poorer classes or from among the patricians and nobles, often defied ideology, as well as city and guild regulations, and sought out the Jewish shopkeeper or artisan in preference to his higher-priced Christian competitor.[38]

Needless to say, in Poland as elsewhere, consumers were unorganized. Whatever mutterings may have been heard among the various classes, they rarely find expression in the existing records.

Only occasionally, when the situation became desperate, did bread riots disturb the public peace, although such "tumults" were usually provoked, in part, by other grievances against the ruling groups. It must be remembered, however, that in a rich agricultural land like Poland-Lithuania widespread famines were quite exceptional. They certainly did not compare in frequency or destructiveness with fires, plagues, or foreign invasions. Hence they left few records behind, and even recent Polish historiography, attuned as it is to any manifestation of class struggle, has not paid much attention to disturbances caused by simple food shortages. Yet whenever they occurred, they must have increased the popular hostility toward Jews.

General price movements likewise may have favored the Jews economically, but adversely affected their sociopolitical relations with their neighbors. This was a period of general inflation in prices, stimulated by governmental policies favoring agricultural producers (principally the oligarchs and other nobles) and by repeated currency devaluations. Moreover, the sixteenth century witnessed a great influx of American silver, which not only changed the traditional relationship between silver and gold from 11:1 to 14:1 but also greatly increased the circulation of coins, which normally tended to inflate the prices of commodities. At the same time the royal treasuries often required more revenue than they collected, in order to defray the high cost of standing armies and protracted wars. Hence they often resorted, as we recall, to debasing the currency with much alloy. This practice increased particularly during the Thirty Years' War, and caused the flooding of Poland with inferior foreign coinage. As usual, Jews served as a convenient scapegoat. In its instruction to the deputies at the Diet, the Cracow dietine meeting in Proszowice on December 13, 1622, referred, in particular, to the Jews' alleged responsibility for the debasement of the Polish currency. The dietine's resolution read:

The statute of the kings Casimirs provides that if one finds six groschen of false currency in the possession of any person of whatever estate, he shall receive capital punishment. Similarly, the constitution of 1620 forbade by perpetual law the circulation of foreign coins under the penalty of the confiscation of all goods and the loss of life; a city neglectful in its supervision of that ordinance was to be punished at the discretion of His Royal Majesty. [The deputies are to] request His Royal Majesty that Jews who, through such egregious defiance of the law, and to the detriment of the Commonwealth, melt good coins of silver or gold should either, following the example of other nations, be expelled from the Crown after the confiscation of their property, or at least be made to contribute a large sum for the benefit of the Commonwealth. They should also deliver twenty leading culprits to the executioner, since they themselves know best who these people are. In memory of this high treason they should also be made to wear yellow caps in accordance with the old statutes, under the penalty of forty marks, at the discretion of the official castellan to whom they were denounced in the first instance, without any possibility of appeal.

As a sort of afterthought, this resolution also demanded that guilty Christian merchants, too, "be penalized by the Diet, in accordance with the statute, by the confiscation of their property and the loss of their lives." This accusation was repeated in other provinces of the Commonwealth as well.[39]

In response, the Lithuanian Jewish Council insisted in 1623 that Jews abstain from participating in the minting of coins in any fashion, because "we see clearly that there is no peace or equanimity in the country in regard to coinage; the hearts of kings and rulers are inscrutable, and one senses obvious portents of danger in this matter. No one can foretell the outcome of the monetary trends until the Diet meets with the king and his dignitaries." The Council evidently had in mind activities like those of the Brest Jewish minter Isaac Brodawka, mentioned in a document of 1571. Half a century later, minting came under such a cloud of suspicion that it was practically suspended in Poland. Nevertheless, not only Jewish moneylenders but also most Jewish traders doubtless were alert to the dangers of debased coins, whereas many of their Christian competitors were far less watchful and hence incurred greater losses.[40]

Partly out of necessity and partly because of their numerous past experiences, Jews were also more prepared to introduce improvements in both production and distribution. Sixteenth-century Poland began participating in the Commercial Revolution then under way in Western Europe, and Jews, whether from Italy, Spain, Holland, or the West-German territories, could enter the new phases of the economy with greater know-how and freedom from traditional shackles. Insofar as some of these methods were introduced by Dutch, English, Scottish, or Italian traders, Jewish businessmen maintained sufficient contacts with these foreign groups to benefit from the innovations. We have Sebastian Miczyński's testimony that Jews distributed textiles, silks, and lumber among numerous home workers, Jewish and non-Jewish, in various localities, and placed many finished products of clothing, furniture, and so forth on the market. Even if they could not participate directly in much maritime shipping, the preponderance of the Dutch on the Baltic Sea (73 percent of all shipping there in 1578, and 85 percent in 1618, was in the hands of Dutch masters) doubtless enabled some Jews to be involved, directly or indirectly, in the land transport of goods to and from Baltic harbors, particularly Gdańsk and Riga.[41]

At times the cities persuaded the Polish Diet to adopt restrictive laws concerning Jewish trade. The Coronation Diet of Sigismund III in 1588 passed a law that "Jews shall not purchase merchandise or victuals, and thereby anticipate Christian purchasers, by going outside the cities to acquire these goods, except at major fairs, under penalty, if convicted, of the loss of their merchandise or victuals." The Cracow city council broadened this provision into a general regulation: "Jews are allowed to acquire victuals at the market only after the Christians have already completed their purchases." If strictly enforced, this ordinance could have made it impossible for the Cracow Jews to acquire sufficient food of any kind. On their complaint, Sigismund III issued an explanatory decree on March 25, 1588, in which he wrote:

We consider it just that Jews, who contribute to Our taxes and to the expenditures of the Commonwealth, should also be admitted to the purchase of victuals and other merchandise. Therefore, based upon the bill adopted by the last Diet, We order your Honors that you should not forbid Jews living anywhere in the Crown, in cities, small towns, and villages, to acquire merchandise and victuals in the customary places. On the contrary, you ought to admit them to the free acquisition of merchandise and the delivery of victuals on a par with Our other subjects. However, in order that Jews not disturb Christians therein, they should not go out of town to make purchases, except at major fairs.

Such royal ordinances were not always obeyed, however, and controversies between Jews and burghers raged almost incessantly in

Cracow and elsewhere over the implementation of detailed municipal regulations. Time and again the Cracow Jewish community sent representatives to Warsaw to appear before the Court of Appeals (the so-called Court of Assessors) in lawsuits against the city council. During one such major litigation in 1601, the city tried to persuade the Diet to adopt a resolution in its favor, but to its chagrin the Diet declared itself incompetent and referred the matter back to the courts.[42]

As a result, many cities often found it more convenient to make formal compacts with the Jewish community circumscribing in many details the rights of Jewish merchants and their limitations. One of the first agreements of this kind was concluded in Cracow in 1485. But interpretation of the individual articles of the Cracow compact often varied greatly on the two sides. Moreover, life proceeded along unpredictable lines. Not only did the number of Jews greatly increase, making their full adherence to the restrictions practically impossible, but new commercial trends automatically rendered many agreed-upon provisions obsolete. In consequence, the entire sixteenth century was filled with claims and counterclaims and, while the 1485 agreement was formally renewed from time to time, the amendments thereto often exceeded in number and importance the items of the original compromise. Under Sigismund III a new agreement was reached in 1597 for an eight-year period. After its expiration the city tried to start afresh, with new prohibitions. Jews protested, and in 1608 the king issued a new ordinance, essentially spelling out the positions previously agreed upon by both sides. This ordinance appeased neither party, and the controversy was renewed time and again, until the catastrophic Swedish occupation of the city in the 1650s. Differences of opinion were still aired on several occasions in the eighteenth century (1744, 1750, 1761). In the meantime the Court of Assessors and other agencies of government were overburdened with the mutual recriminations, while Jews were able to disregard the intended restrictions with the aid of sympathetic royal officials or through douceurs in proper places. Similar agreements, renewals, and breaches, as well as subsequent litigations and royal interventions, occurred in Lwów in 1581, 1592, and 1602; in Poznań in 1549 (confirmed by Sigismund III in 1617, and by King Augustus II in 1697); and many other cities. On the other hand, some Jewish communities managed to procrastinate; Przemyśl succeeded in delaying the Diet's pertinent order from 1567 to 1645.[43]

A major issue in all these negotiations was the extent to which Jews were to be allowed to acquire additional buildings or even to rent new residences or shops in Christian houses. We recall how the maximum number of buildings allotted to Jews by the Poznań city elders had, under the pressure of the Jewish population increase, grown from 49 in 1550, to 83 in 1558, and to 138 in the early seventeenth century. In Cracow the matter was further complicated by the Jews' banishment from the city proper in 1495 and their settlement in neighboring Kazimierz. While in Cracow 55–60 percent of the 146 city council members in the seventeenth century, as examined by Janina Bieniarzówna, were merchants, as against 3 percent who were craftsmen, 60 percent of the Kazimierz elders were artisans and only 3 percent were merchants. Nevertheless, the size, as well as the economic and cultural power, of the Kazimierz Jewish community was so great that in the seventeenth century Kazimierz in effect consisted of two townships, one Jewish and one Christian, living side by side. The main concern of the Cracow elders, therefore, was to keep Jews out of the main city, and particularly out of its major shopping area. With the help of the royal officials, however, Jews were able increasingly to penetrate the center of Cracow itself. About 1600, the city elders complained that "the Jews, even outside the Jewish town [in Kazimierz], have so intermingled with us that it is difficult to recognize whether [Cracow] is a Christian or a Jewish city." According to Sebastyan Miczyński, one Jew, Wolf Bocian (also known as Poper), owned no fewer than seven stores in the city proper. Yet the municipality continued to resist any further Jewish influx, and Miczyński's book was actually written to strengthen that resistance. Nor was the struggle over allowable buildings limited to major centers. Even in a relatively small town like Leszno (Lissa) the rather sympathetic lord, Count Rafał Leszczyński, provided in his privilege of March 10, 1626, that Jews should be permitted to continue owning the 18 buildings then in their possession, plus two more which still were in the planning stage. Clearly, this number compared unfavorably with the 596 buildings owned by the local Christian burghers.[44]

One ought not to deduce from this tale of woe, however, that all relations between Jews and Christians in the Polish cities were of a hostile character. While controversies and litigations left behind much documentation in the archives, and while riots and Blood Accusations were subject to royal interventions and were frequently discussed by contemporary chroniclers, Christian and Jewish, the far less dramatic daily intergroup cooperation becomes known to us only through incidental references in the sources. If a Christian purchaser went to a Jewish shop to acquire merchandise at a better price or of a higher quality than he could secure from a coreligionist; if another Christian pawned an object with a Jewish lender and later returned to pay his instalments on the debt; if a peasant brought some of the fruits of his labor to a Jewish customer and received from him in return either money or some desired industrial objects, these proceedings, though far more frequent, were hardly ever recorded. Only if they gave rise to litigation, which could not be settled amicably between the parties, were such events recorded by the court or the administrative office. Even then, few documents of this kind were considered sufficiently significant to be carefully preserved. For example, a somewhat unusual intervention by a priest is mentioned in one of R. Joel Sirkes' responsa only because it had a bearing on the declaration of death of a Jew so that his wife might remarry. A Christian woman was cited by a witness as having seen that Jew drowning in the Vistula. "I wished to save him," she said, "but I could not, for I feared that he would drag me [into deep water] with him. Some other Christian onlookers likewise refused to help him. A passing priest chastised the brutes and asked: 'Why don't you help the Jew?' In the meantime the unfortunate man drowned." Similarly, the employment by Jews of Christian servants and helpers in various capacities, despite ecclesiastically inspired prohibitions, must have led to some friendly exchanges, not only with the employees themselves but also with their families and friends.[45]

At the same time, Jews performed valuable services for the land-owning nobility. Many newly founded towns were controlled, often privately owned, by magnates and other nobles. There Christian burghers and Jews alike depended on the good will of the lord, who frequently found Jews more pliable and, because of their political helplessness, more anxious to satisfy his extravagant whims. Certainly, the relations between burghers and Jews in such cities differed fundamentally from those in the great urban centers under royal charter. In fact, many of these newly founded towns and hamlets (known in Yiddish as *shtetls*) soon had Jewish majorities, and only the general segregation of Jews from Gentiles prevented outright Jewish domination of the municipal councils. But this story fully evolved only after 1650, in the period of Poland's overall decline, from which both Jews and Christians suffered.[46]

NOBLES' COMMONWEALTH

Although the Jews lived predominantly in cities (the growth of the Jewish rural population in Poland and Lithuania became rapid after the "Deluge"), their position depended much more on the good will of the nobility than on that of the bourgeoisie. In the course of the sixteenth and seventeenth centuries, the entire political and socioeconomic structure of united Poland-Lithuania tended to become a "nobles' commonwealth" which, although headed by a king, had most of its power concentrated in its gentry and high aristocracy. It was decidedly a minority rule. In the mid-sixteenth century, it has been estimated, the total number of persons claiming noble rank did not exceed 500,000, or about 8 percent of the population. Moreover, within that class itself, there emerged a small minority of magnates, which seized much of the economic and political power in the country. It made the middle-class gentry and particularly the lower-class landless nobles (the so-called *gołota* or *hołota*) greatly dependent on it. This political system developed slowly from the mid-fifteenth century on. Some Polish scholars divide the period before the great crisis of the 1650s into one of a "nobles' democracy," from 1454 to 1579; and another of oligarchic control, from 1579 to 1648. To be sure, in legal theory, all nobles remained equal. A popular adage stated: *szlachcic na zagrodzie równy wojewodzie* (a nobleman on his land is equal to the palatine). Even the king himself was supposed to be only *primus inter pares* (first among his peers). But the shifting power constellations, domestic and international, did not quite bear out that legal theory.[47]

In order to safeguard their privileges, the nobles increasingly tried to limit admission to their ranks. According to a statute of 1505, a new-born child acquired noble status only if both his parents were nobles. The royal prerogative of conferring aristocratic rank on deserving persons—which was widely, almost excessively, practiced in West-Central Europe of that period—was subject in Poland, from 1578 on, to the control of the Diet. Only exceptionally could this restriction be waived. Similarly, the process prevalent in the West whereby rich burghers acquired landed estates and thus entered the noble class (a procedure followed in fifteenth-century Poland as well), was greatly impeded by the Diet's prohibition of 1496 against burghers acquiring landed property. This prohibition was renewed in 1538, the Diet setting a deadline of five years for the burghers to dispose of their land. The elevation to noble rank through public service was made extremely difficult by the increasing restrictions on appointments of commoners to governmental posts. These limitations became a general rule in the seventeenth century. At the same time, some nobles could actually lose their noble rank by a judicial sentence of infamy or even by simply marrying a bourgeoise. The attempt to circumvent such prohibitions by the adoption of a child commoner, or even of an illegitimate child of two noble parents, resulted in the loss of noble rank by the adoptive father. True, practice did not wholly conform to these rigid laws, and throughout the early modern period quite a few burghers succeeded in scaling the barriers separating them from the privileged gentry. Yet under these circumstances, it appears very dubious that the Lithuanian system reflected in the aforementioned provision of the Third Lithuanian Statute of 1588, whereby all newly converted Jews were automatically to join the noble class, was effectively applied. (Only near the end of Poland's independence do we learn that, in the short period of eighteen days in December 1764, the newly elected king and grand duke Stanislaus II Augustus, conferred noble titles on no fewer than 48 converts.) It is still less probable that, as some Polish jurists have claimed, after the unification of the two countries through the Union of Lublin this practice was extended to the Polish Crown as well, and that it was formally abolished only by a new Diet ordinance in 1764. In any case, we have no evidence that any professing Jews were ever again allowed to follow the example of Michael Ezofowicz, who was raised to knighthood with the title of De Leliwa. Even the few other known Jewish converts to Christianity never again had a chance to achieve the eminence of Michael's brother Abraham, either as members of the noble class or as high dignitaries in public service. However, Sigismund III and his sons, Wladislaw IV and John Casimir, continued to appoint Jews as "royal servitors" (somewhat resembling the German "court Jews"), who supplied goods to the royal court and were therefore exempted from the payment of tolls and customs duties.[48]

Jews also performed an increasingly important economic function for the nobility in general and for the oligarchy in particular. During the late sixteenth and seventeenth centuries the possessions of the magnates were growing by leaps and bounds. The distinguished generalissimo and chancellor Jan Zamoyski, at his death in 1606, left personal property amounting to 6,445 square kilometers (about 2,460 square miles), which included 11 towns and more than 200 villages; it had been supplemented in his lifetime by the use of royal domains extending over 11,054 square kilometers (about 4,270 square miles) and including 12 towns and 612 villages. Among Zamoyski's own towns was the city of Zamość, which became a major commercial and cultural center soon after he founded it. To enhance its standing, Zamoyski attracted Sephardic merchants and scholars like Chaim Cohen, Abraham Mosso, and their sons, who speedily established Zamość as an emporium in Poland's Levantine trade. After a temporary lull following Zamoyski's death, another wave of Sephardic immigration occurred and again helped keep the city's commerce on a high level, until its decline during the "Deluge" of 1648–60. In general, the possessions of the magnates were scattered over Poland, a characteristic which distinguished them from the mostly contiguous medieval baronies in western Europe. While offering the advantage that crop failures in one region could usually be made up by good crops in another part of the country, such geographic diffusion greatly complicated the tasks of management. In time the expansion of the aristocratic possessions into southeastern Poland created ever-greater latifundia. In Zamoyski's lifetime,

Prince Konstanty Wasyl Ostrogski controlled no fewer than 100 towns and 1,300 villages, with a total annual income of about 1,200,000 zlotys, which about equaled the tax revenue of the country as a whole. Magnates like Ostrogski and Zamoyski needed help in administering their vast estates, supervising the *corvée* labor by the unfree peasants, producing liquor and other goods from the crops, and particularly in marketing surplus grains, lumber, and cattle in the country and abroad. They found that Jews were especially useful as administrators, producers, and agents. As early as 1521, we recall, Justus Ludwig Dietz (Iodocus Ludovicus Decius or Decyusz), Sigismund I's secretary, had observed the general subservience of Christians to Jews, owing to the magnates' predilection for Jewish managers of their possessions: they "thus entrust to Jews dominion over Christians." While a gross exaggeration at the time of its writing, this statement became more and more true in the following generations, with the growth of the magnates' latifundia, the greater complexity of their management, and the increased availability of competent Jewish supervisors.[49]

As usual, enemies overstated the role of Jews in the nobles' economy. In their 1643 protest against Jewish rights in Lwów, the Christian furriers wrote: "Every Crown potentate, every official, every nobleman, every merchant, even without visiting the city . . . secures everything that he needs exclusively through Jews." On its part, the church synod of Warsaw in the same year echoed Dietz' complaint that landlords handed their estates over to Jews, who thus exercised dominion over the peasants. In fact, interested nobles often intervened in favor of Jews. To refer only to the aforementioned magnates, Jan Zamoyski in 1581 interceded with Gdańsk for Jewish traders from Cracow. Similarly, two Poznań Jews seeking to negotiate with Gdańsk's municipal administration about freedom to trade at the city's fairs, sent along three letters of recommendation from leading aristocrats. How necessary such intercessions often were may be learned from what happened to a partnership of four Jewish businessmen from Poznań, Cracow, Lublin, and Lwów who arrived in Gdańsk with merchandise worth 100,000 zlotys. The city nonchalantly forced them to return home with their wares unsold. This drastic step elicited a sharp protest from Sigismund III, who demanded a satisfactory explanation from the city council. On his part, Prince Ostrogski prevailed upon the king in 1589, to extend a privilege granting "all liberties" to the Jews of Biała Cerkiew (Belaya Tserkov). In addition, he himself employed some 4,000 Jews in his far-flung estates, particularly in the manufacture and sale of vodka, beer, and mead.[50]

From the outset the most important aspect of the relationship between the nobility and Jewry concerned the latter's rights of settlement. We recall that many cities had strenuously refused admission to Jews and had thus forced them to secure residential rights from the noble or ecclesiastical owners of the cities' enclaves. These *jurydyki* proliferated in number and size, especially after 1550 when the Diet granted every nobleman the unlimited right to acquire urban real estate and to withdraw it from municipal jurisdiction. Economically, the new settlers performed the valuable function of supplementing the production of, and trade in, goods needed by society—activities gravely hampered by the archconservative, semimonopolistic methods adamantly adhered to by the municipal councils and guilds. By the middle of the seventeenth century, a medium-sized city like Lublin had no fewer than 23 *jurydyki,* some of which accommodated the flourishing Jewish community, still shut out of the city proper. In addition, there were so-called *libertacje;* that is, properties transferred by specific royal privileges from municipal to county jurisdiction, and thus subject to noble control. How serious the breakdown of municipal authority often was, is well demonstrated by Cracow, where in 1667 55 percent of the entire land *within* the city walls belonged to the Church; 16.7 percent, to nobles; and only 28.3 percent was owned by the local burghers. This situation helps to explain the municipality's inability to keep the Jews entirely out of the interior of the city, even at night. Since the Diet, under the *szlachta's* control, voted to subject the purportedly autonomous cities belonging to the royal domain to general "supervision" by royal officials, chosen mostly from among the nobles, the gentry secured considerable authority over both the Jewish and the Christian communities in the major centers of Polish sociopolitical and cultural life.[51]

As early as 1539, Sigismund I transferred to the nobles full authority over the Jews of all localities owned by them. In the approval of that resolution, the bitter overtones of a royal surrender of an important prerogative are clearly audible. The king had stated, as we recall, that "those from whom We receive no benefit shall have none of Our protection." This rather irate exclamation did not necessarily represent a permanent royal policy, however. The kings continued to exercise a measure of overlordship over, and extend some minimal protection to, their Jewish subjects, even within the latifundia of the Polish magnates. But the fate of Jewish residents now depended much more on the good will of their immediate masters than on that of their remote sovereigns in the capital. Much, of course, depended on the convictions, temperament, and even whims of the individual landlords, as well as on the ever-changing climate of opinion. A good illustration of the great diversity of the nobles' attitudes is offered by two small localities belonging to two different lords in the same province. In 1576 the Rus palatine Hieronim Sieniawski founded the new township of Oleszowo, near Lubaczów. In issuing to the new settlers a privilege which included provisions granting Jews equal status with the Christian burghers, he wrote:

The Polish Crown flourishes with people of diverse estates, particularly in regard to their religious allegiance, on the principle that no authority shall exercise power over faith, honor, and conscience. We wish, therefore, to secure a peaceful life especially to those persons, who have suffered persecution not because of any crimes or evil deeds, but for other reasons, so that they may enjoy all the liberties of the laws enacted by us.

In order to assure the permanence of his pledge, Sieniawski stipulated that if any of his descendants "should desire to expel residents because of their type of divine worship," they must compensate them for all their investments in buildings, breweries, gardens, and so forth, and pay 2,000 zlotys to the royal Treasury. In contrast, fifteen years later, the courtier Jan Magier secured from Sigismund III a privilege not to tolerate Jews at all in his newly established town of Magierów (Maheriv, in the district of Rawa Ruska). In his ordinance of January 20, 1591, he stated: "I exclude from residence Jews, a sordid, cunning, underhanded, and anti-Christian tribe because of the principles of their faith. I decree that they should not be tolerated, neither shall the burghers sell or rent them houses, nor shall my successors admit them to the town under any subterfuge whatsoever." At the same time, Magier also excluded from residence all Protestants and other non-Catholics, and provided that "any Catholic deserting the Catholic Church shall immediately be expelled, and his property be either confiscated or compensated for, according to my wish" [52]

In such privately owned towns the lords not only issued basic decrees, collected rents and taxes, and often more or less arbitrarily adjudicated conflicts between the various groups of residents, but also frequently demanded the active participation of all inhabitants in the defense of their localities. This was particularly the case in Lithuania and Belorussia, which were on many occasions exposed to foreign raids and invasions. Here even the Jews, who otherwise were not expected to perform military service, were obliged to help build fortifications, to contribute both money and quarters for the billeting of soldiers (an obligation from which they had often been freed in western countries by paying a fee), and to perform a variety of personal services in emergencies. In December 1648, Prince Janusz Radziwiłł declared that in the town of Birzai (Birż or Birsen) such services must be performed by all houseowners and tenants "of whatever nationality, estate, or condition." Six years later, another Radziwiłł (Michał Kazimierz) explicitly mentioned Jewish owners of buildings in the town of Nieświerz (Nesvizh) as among those who were to stand guard, help fortify the walls, and take part in enlistment for defensive actions. Most interesting were the developments in Slutsk (Słuck), which as a fortress was sometimes styled the "bastion of Lithuania." Its Jewish community, too, was rapidly growing in size, and in economic and cultural standing, so that by 1692 it joined the four previously admitted Lithuanian cities (Brest, Pinsk, Grodno in 1623, and Vilna in 1652) as the fifth major center of the Lithuanian Council of Provinces. From the city's minute book of 1655 we learn that "Jews of this city have their own defense force." This detachment may have been organized during the disturbed period of the Cossack uprising and the Muscovite-Swedish Wars after 1648. In 1681, we are told, the owners and tenants of 173 Jewish houses were joining those of 922 Christian buildings to form three regiments, apparently completely integrated. Clearly, such militias could be used by any aristocratic owner of a town to enforce his will against local opponents, as well as to resist encroachment by outsiders, including royal officials.[53]

Beginning with the resolutions of the Piotrków Diets of 1565 and 1567, which were reconfirmed in 1570, even the royal cities had to submit annual reports about their fiscal administration to the district governor (starosta), who also frequently tried to influence elections to the city council; thus municipal autonomy was greatly reduced. Jews, too, could appeal any sentence by a Jewish court to the provincial palatine (wojewoda), who also appointed the judex Judaeorum, the Christian judge specifically assigned to litigations between Jews and Christians. But the palatine, who was one of the highest officials of the realm and ruled his province almost like an independent prince, often actually favored the Jews, for personal reasons as well as for reasons of state. At times, individual noblemen voluntarily submitted to the jurisdiction of Jewish courts, which enjoyed a reputation for expertise and for a high degree of honor and fairness to all parties concerned. Certainly, no one could claim about the Jewish tribunals what was said about many municipal courts, that many of their arbitrary sentences were pronounced out of sheer ignorance of the law. In some criminal cases, semiliterate judges resorted to torturing the defendants, so as to extract a confession and save themselves the trouble of accumulating more reliable evidence for conviction. Jewish defendants were most frequently subjected to torture, when they were accused of ritual murder or desecration of the host. The very preparation for torture in which the defendant's hair was shaved all over his body—because of the popular superstition that the devil preferred to dwell in a culprit's hair and thence help him to resist confession—must have been especially painful to the conscientious Jew, whose law forbade him to have his beard shaved.[54]

The superiority of Jewish courts of justice, not only over the municipal courts but also over the nobles' tribunals, is easily explainable. The Jewish judiciary consisted of rabbis trained in talmudic law since childhood, who often faced talmudic scholars of equal rank among the lay parties and witnesses. Municipal jurisdiction, on the other hand, was in the hands of elders, some of whom had little, if any, knowledge of law or legal procedure. Moreover, they usually were active businessmen, who could devote little time to careful analysis of the oral and documentary evidence, and had little ability or inclination painstakingly to weigh the merits of the arguments submitted by the lawyers on either side. Many municipal courts functioned more or less like juries today, but generally without the guidance of a professional judge. Their problem was further complicated by the frequent dependence of their cities' legal structure on the Magdeburg law (however modified by Polish enactments and usages), with which they were even less familiar than with local ordinances. No such difficulty existed in many towns owned by nobles, but there the judicial process was even more irregular. Many lords were nearly illiterate; they judged matters according to their personal preferences, without consulting outsiders, and were frequently known to issue completely arbitrary sentences. It is small wonder, then, that both types of lay jurisdiction were subject to frequent criticism like that of the sixteenth-century jurist Bartłomiej Groicki (whose works served as authoritative handbooks in Polish law schools until the partitions of Poland) and Jędrzej Kitowicz, an eighteenth-century rural priest and keen student of local customs and folklore.[55]

As was usual, the lords' excessive power bred much arbitrariness and arrogance toward the Jews, who time and again had to contend with their masters' exorbitant demands. Even royal officials were, as a rule, greatly underpaid; many of them invested considerable sums in securing their appointments, although venality of office, legally approved after 1650, never reached in Poland the dimensions it had in contemporary France. Not surprisingly, quite a few officials sought to secure extralegal revenue in order to maintain the high standard of living expected from their noble rank and public office—a mode of living which increasingly included drinking bouts and the lavish entertainment of friends. Jędrzej Kitowicz' description of eighteenth-century conditions essentially applied to those prevailing before 1650 also. According to him, the greatest drunkards enjoyed a national reputation: "among them one might include every lord and noblemen in differing degrees of drinking perfection." Individual Jews sometimes fell so deeply behind in their payments to local lords that cases were recorded of their handing over their children and/or wives as security. Understandably, such proceedings were sharply condemned by the Jewish leaders. A Jew in Kleck (in the district of Pinsk), who had thus delivered his daughter to the lord, was immediately and most solemnly excommunicated by the community in the synagogue with the blowing of horns, the extinction of lights, and the proclamation that he be treated as an outlaw in the entire province. When, for some unknown reason, the city of Grodno sought an exemption from this ban for its area, its request was rejected by the provincial council.[56]

Among the more famous cases of arbitrary rule by a lord was the procedure of the palatine of Włodzimierz (Vladimir) in Volhynia, who in 1642, apparently because of a single denunciation, banished Yom Ṭob Lipmann Heller, one of the greatest rabbis of his generation, from the province. The efforts of the Jewish communities of the region to dissuade the official from going through with the ban were but temporarily successful. Ultimately, the rabbi was forced to leave Volhynia, though he may well have considered himself fortunate in being "kicked upstairs," for he later served as a rabbi in Cracow (1644–54). There he ended his stormy career, which in 1629–30 had led to his arrest in Prague as an alleged blasphemer against Christianity and his forced departure for Poland. Other "savage" lords, too, are occasionally mentioned in the sources, Jewish and non-Jewish. But, while Jews had to learn to suffer contemptuous treatment silently, physical assaults on them were relatively rare, for even more than in the case of the peasant serfs, most masters exercised self-restraint with them. Just as a serf, if excessively punished, became an inferior worker, a maltreated Jew usually lost whatever loyalty he may have had for that master, and would serve him badly. In fact, unlike the peon, a Jew was legally free at any time to depart for other localities. An attempt made, as late as 1740, by some power-hungry deputies in the Diet, to declare Jews *glaebae adscripti* on a par with large segments of the peasant population, appeared quite senseless to the majority of their colleagues, and the suggestion was not even seriously debated. This suggestion resembled the motion made in 1793, by a Baranów lord at the democratic Quadrennial Diet, to limit the freedom of movement of burghers by forbidding them to leave their towns, under severe penalties.[57]

Nonetheless, the Jews had to be on their guard not to offend nobles, whether serving as royal officials, as lords of their places of residence, or in a private capacity. Time and again the leaders of the two great councils enjoined the communities to remain neutral in conflicts between nobles. In its very first session in 1623, the Lithuanian Council resolved that Jews should not borrow money from Gentiles, and particularly not from noblemen, without special permission from the provincial rabbi or the local communal elder. This provision was further sharpened in 1670, when the Council decided that any loan or purchase on credit from a nobleman should depend on the consent of the entire community, which could limit the amount of the debt according to the financial capability of the borrower. If five members objected to the debt, permission was to be refused outright. The Council further stipulated: "In any case one must never borrow or buy on credit from priests, students, or soldiers, [a prohibition from which] there shall be no dispensation." Evidently, these three groups were considered too dangerously hostile to Jews, out of religious intolerance or greed, to react to a debtor's default in moderation. Similarly, individual Jews were prohibited from proceeding on their own to the lord's castle or the local tribunal, and even from visiting lesser officials, without special permission. The elders were to go so far as to warn any lord or Christian merchant in advance against dealing with a particular Jew of ill repute. In some cases they actually were to indemnify unwary Christians for losses sustained, in order to avoid casting a shadow on the probity of the whole community. In general, a Jewish debtor's simple plea "I have no money" was to be considered a valid excuse only if his insolvency was caused by some emergency, like fire, robbery, or shipwreck. Otherwise the irresponsible or fraudulent debtor was to be left to the untrammeled operation of criminal justice.

At times Jewish leadership took cognizance of the good-will aspects of certain departures from traditional Jewish law. In adopting, in 1603, a series of laws concerning usury, the Council of Four Lands forbade Jews to charge higher prices for merchandise sold to other Jews on credit. They saw in such indirect credit charges a form of usury. In this connection the assembled elders emphasized that the same regulation should apply to sales to dignitaries and nobles, who were accustomed to paying higher prices even for cash purchases. They made it clear, however, that the community should not be held responsible for fugitives' debts owed to nobles or to the royal government itself. Another defensive provision, adopted in 1623 by the Lithuanian Council, concerned the farming of various types of revenue from noble landlords. It read: "If a Jew lost his leasehold because he had not paid his due to the lord and his place was taken by a Christian who performed that task [of collection] for a whole year, [the former Jewish arendator] must not impinge upon the Christian leaseholder's right thus acquired without special permission from the head of the Jewish court." [58]

Most significant were the measures officially taken by the organized gentry, acting through the Polish or Lithuanian Diet. As has been observed, with the death of Sigismund II Augustus, all genuine parliamentary guidance by the monarchy ceased, and legislative power was concentrated in the *szlachta*. Not even the Senate, mainly representing the magnates and the hierarchy, could easily overrule a decision by the Chamber of Deputies, while the king had but a limited veto power, which often did not exceed that of any of the Estates represented in the Diet. In fact, in 1589 the system of *liberum veto* was adopted, whereby a single deputy could, by casting a dissenting vote, nullify any majority decision. To be sure, the exercise of this anarchical right was at first greatly discouraged by the opprobrium it evoked among the majority. But in time more and more hardy individuals were ready to defy public opinion and to insist upon their individual veto power. This generally disruptive procedure, however, did not become a real hindrance to the Sejm's constitutional function until after 1650 and even then a truly determined majority usually found a way to circumvent the disruption.[59]

On the whole, the Diet consistently adhered to the principle that what was good for the gentry was good for the country. On the Jewish question, the Diet legislated in favor of Jews if the laws were likely to promote the *szlachta*'s interests; it legislated against the Jews when its own interests dictated such action or, occasionally, when it could mouth pious phrases in support of the ideological outlook of the Church, without injury to itself. If the Diet rejected anti-Jewish commercial restrictions demanded by burghers, its spokesmen unabashedly argued that such protectionist regulations would necessarily lead to an increase in the prices paid by nobles. It was not until relatively late in the history of prepartition Poland, when the growing anti-Jewish animus in Polish society persuaded the Diet to favor burghers over Jews, as a matter of principle. In 1768 a resolution was adopted which, referring to partial ordinances of the years 1538, 1565, 1567, and 1588, stated:

Considering that Jewry causes intolerable injury to the cities and burghers and takes away their means of livelihood . . . we therefore ordain that the Jews shall engage only in such business and in such localities as are explicitly open to them by their treaties with the cities. . . . They shall not engage in commerce, serve as innkeepers, or pursue a craft without such special treaties . . . under the penalty of [a fine of] 5,000 marks. Only Jews located in Jewish towns may trade there freely and without hindrance according to their privileges.

Although the demand that Jews conclude "agreements" with their municipalities dated back, as we recall, to the Diet's decision of 1567, its original implication was not so outspokenly anti-Jewish. In fact, before 1650 one of the nobles' main preoccupations was to weaken the political power of the bourgeoisie and to gain commercial rights and other economic advantages over it. On the other hand, the gentry consistently demanded that Jews not be allowed to serve as tax farmers, tollmasters, or as lessees of salt mines or other state monopolies, all of which posts the *szlachta* tried to reserve to itself. If some Diets voted that Jews must not employ Christian servants, the reason was not so much the gentry's acceptance of the old canonical prohibition, as its selfish desire to maintain an excess supply of labor for employment in noble households.[60]

At the same time, the Diet ordinance of 1538 (and of the Second Lithuanian Statute of 1566) requiring Jews to wear yellow hats was never implemented. There was indeed no call for it, since in Poland-Lithuania even more than in most West-European lands, each class was distinguished by its own attire, and Jews could for the most part be easily recognized. Occasional antiluxury resolutions, prompted by the nobles' desire not to be surpassed by Jews in luxurious clothing, were readily subscribed to by the Jewish leaders themselves. In fact, the Jewish communal bodies now independently adopted sumptuary laws with increasing frequency, both to avoid evoking envy in Christian neighbors and to preserve Jewish finances for internal use, especially in meeting the Polish government's growing fiscal demands and in supporting their communities' expanding social welfare programs. Moreover, truly hostile legislation by the Diets was not always implemented, Jewish resistance sometimes being abetted by local officials or landlords. In the Diet itself, much anti-Jewish oratory was discounted, because of personal bias. A frequently repeated adage, quoted in an open session in 1746, stated that an official "is either for the Jews when he is bribed, or against them when he expects a bribe." (This situation was, of course, not limited to pre-Emancipation Poland.) In addition there was always Jewish "lobbying" by influential individuals, sent to Warsaw by the two central councils, the provincial councils, or even individual communities. In time, as we recall, a permanent "Warsaw Committee," representing the Council of Four Lands, carefully watched the Diet's deliberations and sought to prevent any antagonistic legislation, and to secure some friendly enactments.[61]

Equally watchful were the Jewish provincial councils and local communities in regard to the sessions of the dietines (*sejmiki*). According to the Polish constitution, such provincial gatherings, often consisting of hundreds of nobles, appearing in person, elected the deputies to the central *Sejm* and provided them with instructions on how to vote on certain issues. Occasionally, the dietines of the whole Polish Crown concerted their instructions. For example, the instructions preliminary to the Diet which met in Piotrków on January 25, 1534, included the following anti-Jewish diatribe:

One should inhibit the Jews' unrestrained license in trading, which is most pernicious for all classes in the realm. For it has come to pass that almost all business is falling into Jewish hands. They [the Jews] adulterate all goods, especially those intended for human consumption, and in doing business with foreign lands—which no Christian is allowed to do—defraud the customs and the Treasury of our most benevolent king. There is no place which the Jews do not penetrate. Traveling to Walachia, they buy up cattle, skins, and other objects of this kind which they export outside Poland, from which arises the great scarcity of all wares here. . . . Nor are they of any use to the Commonwealth and contribute nothing to its defense. Let them display distinguishing marks according to custom. If stolen objects are found in their possession they should restore them to the owners and not enjoy therein any preferential treatment over the Christians, since they themselves are often responsible for the thefts.

(The last statement alluded to the so-called law of concealment, which frequently included a specific Jewish privilege stipulating that a *bona fide* Jewish purchaser of a stolen object be fully indemnified for his outlay before he returned the object to its legitimate owner.) The royal councilors rejected these proposals, however, by referring "to the existing royal charters and the Jews paying all regular and extraordinary taxes." More, with their typical inconsistency, the nobles of the Cracow region assembled in Proszowice in November 1534, but ten months after voting for the anti-Jewish restriction, instructed their delegates to the Sejm to ensure that Jewish merchants not be interfered with, because they sold goods to the impoverished nobles for much less than their Christian competitors did.[62]

Such impulsive and self-serving zigzag policies also characterized many later instructions by the dietines, although the growing power of the gentry should have been accompanied by a greater sense of responsibility for the welfare of the country. For example, the *sejmik* of the Cracow region, meeting in Proszowice on January 22–27, 1597, instructed its deputies to the Diet to vote for using the Jewish capitation tax for defense, especially soldiers' wages. A later meeting in the same locality, on January 2, 1618, adopted a resolution that "Jews should not hold any position relating to the Crown's revenue and taxes. They should not be able to control them either through a lease or in some other way. Anyone who would dare to act against this provision should be punished according to law." On August 9–10 of that year, another *sejmik* meeting in Cracow demanded that each landowner pay a special war tax of 1 zloty per lan (fief of about 40 acres), and that

Jews contribute a lump sum of 3,000 zlotys. "Should they refuse to pay that amount, they ought to deliver their ordinary capitation tax according to the decree of assessment." Most extreme was the aforementioned session in Proszowice of December 13, 1622, which sharply reacted to the contemporary decline of the currency by demanding the expulsion of the Jews from the country. On the other hand, the Red Russian dietine meeting in Wisznia (Vishnaya) in 1590 complained in one of its resolutions (*lauda*) "that the noble people suffer much from the city of Lwów in many other matters, including its prohibitive measures against Jews engaging in various branches of commerce, so that it [its burghers] may raise the prices at will." [63]

Hence it was of considerable interest to the Jewish communities to promote such friendly sentiments and to prevent the adoption of anti-Jewish restrictions. In its first session of 1623, the Lithuanian Council of Provinces passed the following resolution:

In any period of the *sejmiki* meeting before the Diet the heads of each community are to stand guard and carefully investigate lest any innovation be introduced which might prove to be a harmful thorn to us. The necessary expenditure should be defrayed by each community, together with its environs. In addition to the three major communities [Brest, Pinsk, and Grodno] any community in whose locality there is a tribunal and in which the nobles of the district would meet to hold a *sejmik,* that duty of standing guard with respect to the aforementioned question and the expenses of the local community with its environs [relating thereto], devolve upon the heads of that community. Any community which will not stand guard and appoint spokesmen for the *sejmik* shall be fined 100 gold zlotys for charity.

From time to time, both the Lithuanian and the Polish Councils had to regulate the respective contributions by individual communities toward influencing legislation which affected all Lithuanian or Polish Jews. Controversies on this score which arose in 1626 because of divergent claims of the communities of Volhynia, Poznań, and Lwów, had to be settled in the Polish Council's session of 1628. Needless to say, the expenses of the lobbies tended to go up constantly. Whenever the two councils had to cooperate on a single course of action, the Lithuanian group, it may be assumed, contributed only one-seventh of the total sum—its usual share in the general Polish-Lithuanian Jewish taxation. (This ratio was considerably below the contribution of the grand duchy to the general taxation, which usually amounted to about 25 percent.) While we do not have the complete accounts which may have been submitted by the Jewish delegates to their respective councils, since some of these expenditures were definitely confidential, the Lithuanian as well as the Polish costs rose sharply between 1623 and 1670, because "thank God, there is a large Jewish population here and the nobles have set their eyes upon Jewish money." In 1670 the Lithuanian Council voted that the province contribute up to 150 zlotys, while the individual communities were to raise up to 30 *shocks* silver. The contributions of individual Polish communities are also well illustrated by the speedily increasing payments of the community of Poznań: its contribution amounted to 1,500 zlotys in 1646, and skyrocketed to some 50,000 zlotys forty-two years later. Only a part of this rise can be attributed to inflation.[64]

So-called confederations held a peculiar constitutional position, outside the regular parliamentary structure. While in the Middle Ages such assemblies of nobles and burghers were convoked on relatively frequent occasions, the first modern Confederation met in Warsaw in 1573 after an interval of a century. It convened during the first *interregnum*, in order to maintain the regular administration of the country in the absence of a monarch. Another major Confederation of the provinces of Cracow and Sandomierz met in Lublin on December 7, 1586. Both these assemblies went beyond the noble class and were particularly interested in maintaining peace among the contending factions before the election of a new king. The Warsaw Confederation of 1573 has frequently been mentioned here in connection with its declaration of liberty of conscience. Similarly, the Lublin Confederation of 1586 —in which the Cracow city council asked that admission to the Confederation be granted to "all cities, hamlets, and all persons of whatever status and condition; including Jews, and all others, no one excluded"—adopted a resolution stating that its aim was to act "for peace and brotherly love." However, the good intentions of this assembly were brought to nought by the subsequent election of Sigismund III, and the intensification of the Catholic Restoration.[65]

Notwithstanding its obvious ultimate shortcomings, the political hegemony of the gentry soon found ideological defenders among contemporary political thinkers. Gone was the period of the influential theorist Andrzej Frycz Modrzewski, who in the mid-sixteenth century had advocated a certain measure of equality between burghers and nobles, although he did not oppose the control of the Diet by the *szlachta*. In the spirit of the Italian Renaissance and of Roman law, whose impact on Polish legislation he sought to expand, he wished to strengthen the power of the monarchy but restrict that of the clergy. He championed the idea of a Polish national church, combined with general freedom of conscience. While not directly connected with the Jewish question, Modrzewski's fairly liberal approach to Polish constitutional law could only accrue to the benefit of the Jews and other dissenting groups. With the onset of the Catholic Restoration, however, there appeared spokesmen for ecclesiastical-noble control headed by a powerful monarchy. Most important along these lines were the writings of Łukasz Górnicki, who placed before the Polish public the example of the Venetian aristocratic constitution as a desirable model. Piotr Skarga and Krzysztof Warszewicki advocated the supremacy of the Church; though in lay matters, they believed, decisions should rest with the king, assisted by the aristocracy. In his *De optimo statu libertatis,* published in 1598, Warszewicki argued against the Diet's exclusive legislative authority, and declared: "It is more needed and useful for all to obey and execute the laws than to enact them." On the other hand, Stanisław Orzechowski was an extreme spokesman for noble supremacy. In several works published in the 1560s, he saw in the king only a "guardian of the Crown's privileges," on which were based the nobles' dictatorship. While deeply involved in the incipient Counter Reformation, and therefore supporting the hierarchy's claims, he became an eloquent spokesman for the *szlachta*'s exclusive "golden liberty." [66]

Nor were voices lacking which sought to justify the overwhelming power of the noble class by historical arguments relating to its supposed ancestry, considered superior to that of the rest of the Polish population. For some time the so-called Sarmatian school claimed for the aristocracy descent from the ancient Sarmatian tribe, the *Sauromatae* mentioned by Herodotus and other ancient writers as inhabiting parts of eastern Europe outside the Roman Empire. Originally living in the region between the Don and Volga Rivers, these tribesmen later spread to the west and south, reaching the Danube by the beginning of the Christian era. Their reputedly superior qualities and love of freedom were said to have been inherited by their noble Polish descendants. Sometimes one even heard allusions to the biblical genealogy of Noah. According to one theory, the *szlachta* descended in direct line from Noah's eldest son, Shem; the burghers, from Japheth; while the peasant masses allegedly were the descendants of Ham, and the heirs to all the vices attributed to him by the Bible and early postbiblical legends. The proud nobles never hesitated to use the designation Ham for any peasant; few seem to have realized that Shem was the acknowledged biblical ancestor of the Jews. Possibly the more thoughtful adherents of that genealogical fantasy proudly claimed in this fashion a certain kinship with Jesus and his apostles, but rejected that branch of Jewish Shemites who had repudiated his messiahship.[67]

Apart from the general works of political and legal theory, which only incidentally referred to the Jewish question, there was, for the first time in Polish history, a sudden outpouring of a series of specifically Jew-baiting books and pamphlets. Even if written by priests, this literature did not have the chief characteristic of medieval polemics, their emphasis on the theological differences between Judaism and Christianity. The medieval authors often unconsciously pursued the aim of strengthening the faith of the Christian public, rather than combating the Jews, who were no longer present in many of the European countries. The new Polish anti-Jewish literature instead emphasized the purported misdeeds and crimes of contemporary Jews in their relations with Christians. The most important targets were the alleged Jewish blood ritual and host desecration, side by side with the Jews' supposed economic exploitation of the Christian population.

Reference has already been made to the harsh accusations leveled at Jews by Przecław Mojecki, Sebastyan Miczyński, and Sebastyan Śleszkowski in the years 1598 to 1622. Other writers of this genre included Szymon Aleksander Hubicki, who was stimulated by the Blood Accusation of Świniarów near Łosice (in 1598 the subject of a lengthy trial at the Lublin tribunal) to republish Mojecki's anti-Jewish polemic and append to it his own pamphlet entitled *The [Jewish] Traitors' Crime Committed in Świniarów Near Łosice* (1602). Alleged desecrations of the host, on the other hand, which, among other complications for Jews, had brought about the trial of some Jews in Bochnia, inspired Jan Achazy Kmita, clerk for the local salt mine, to describe, in a lengthy poem, the events leading up to the expulsion of the whole Bochnia community. Another writer, Tomasz Treter, devoted a number of pamphlets to the same subject; while the poet Fabian Sebastyan Klonowicz, in his *Victoria Deorum,* compared the Jewish usurer to a wolf who infiltrated a herd of sheep and destroyed his victims. Of course, not all anti-Jewish writings were published. One unpublished Latin tract, *Manifestatio crudelitatis gentis perfidiae et sanguinariae Judaeorum,* written by a royal pensioner, Hieronim Baliński, advocated the total expulsion of the Jews from Poland. The work was, in part, plagiarized by Mojecki. Remarkably, though the Church through its censorship exercised rather effective control over all publications, it did not interfere with this literary poisoning of Judeo-Christian relations—not even with allegations, like the Blood Accusation, which were repeatedly denied by the Papacy. Miczyński's *Zwierciadło,* though written by a priest, was suppressed by royal, rather than ecclesiastical, action. In some cases, the clergy was actually responsible for inflaming passions. For example, in 1620, when a table on which Jews had allegedly pierced the host was discovered in a house located in the Poznań Jewish quarter, the local clergy, without any further trial, staged a solemn procession through the city streets to the Church of Corpus Christi. On that day and the following, no Jew dared as much as show his face at the window of his dwelling. Equally pernicious were the brief references to episodes like that at Bochnia, and the general characterizations of Jews as usurers, exploiters, and enemies of all Christians—characterizations which were interspersed in many widely read political pamphlets and parliamentary addresses, particularly during the stormy debates preceding and accompanying the civil war known as the Zebrzydowski Rebellion (1606–1608).[68]

MONARCHY

Like their medieval and sixteenth-century predecessors, the Counter Reformation kings of Poland and grand dukes of Lithuania stood out as the main protectors of the Jewish people. Even the Vasa kings as a rule maintained the traditional royal policy of admitting Jews from abroad and protecting them against their numerous foes whenever it did not too sharply conflict with the monarchy's other commitments. Of course, the kings were acting from utilitarian motives, according to what they considered most beneficial to themselves or their country. In part, they were guided by the same economic considerations which made many magnates employ Jews as administrators and agents on their estates. Since the recapture of most royal domains from private hands in the mid-sixteenth century, the monarchs directly controlled about one-sixth of Poland-Lithuania's cultivable area, and thus were much the largest landowners in the country. There, as elsewhere in Europe, moreover, the kings found the Jews to be their most reliable servants, because of the Jewish dependence on royal protection. At a time when the gentry claimed for itself the *ius resistendi* or *de non praestanda oboedientia* (that is, the right to refuse obedience to a king who, in its opinion, broke the law) and, in 1606–1608, under the leadership of Mikołaj Zebrzydowski, staged a powerful rebellion against the monarchy, the Jews usually proved to be pliable instruments for carrying out the royal will. The ensuing favorable legal status of Polish-Lithuanian Jewry often impressed foreigners. The Englishman Sir George Carew wrote in 1598 in his *Relation of the State of Polonia:*

They [the Jews] make a greate part of the inhabitants, that be coming to passe for 3 causes: Fyrst allmost all trade is in their hands, the Poles estimate it sordide. Secondly, their usury is not limited. Thirdly, the Princes Sufferance for the greate benefit of the Crowne by theire extraordinary payments. At one tyme they were charged with 40,000 crownes for a present sent to the Emperor of Constantinople for the king maye at his pleasure impose upon them extraordinary tribute.

The mutual interest of the monarchy and the Jews became even more pronounced in the following century, when the kings' legislative powers in most areas of public life were being delimited by the growing prerogatives of the *szlachta*. Though the Diets, general and provincial, could issue regulations concerning Jews, implementation was almost exclusively in the hands of the king and his officials. In fact, according to historians of Polish public law, immediate control over Jews remained one of the few aspects of public law outside the gentry's hegemony. That is why Sigismund III, despite the Catholic Restoration which he actively sponsored, and despite his general affinity for Habsburg policies— through his successive marriages to the archduchesses Anne and Constance, he became a relative of both Emperor Rudolph II and King Philip III of Spain—maintained his predecessors' basically tolerant policy. (In this connection, we also recall Mendel Sax's 1592 mission to Gratz to arrange the details of the marriage contract between Princess Anna, one of the surviving members of the Jagiellon dynasty, and the Habsburg archduke of Styria.) [69]

Mutuality of interest between the Polish kings and Polish Jewry came most clearly to the fore in the successive royal renewals of the basic Charter. Although never using the Western designation of Jews as "serfs of the Chamber," the Polish kings well understood the underlying nexus between the royal protection and the economic and fiscal benefits accruing to the Crown from its Jewish subjects. The palatines and district governors were forbidden to take from Jews "other taxes and contributions," except if voluntarily offered, "because We [the king] reserve them for Our Treasury" (*quia nos eos reservamus pro nostro thesauro*). Similarly, the Charter's provision freeing Jews, even those in possession of hereditary estates, from participation in military expeditions either personally or financially, is explained by the concept "the Jews themselves belong to Our Treasury" (*qui ipsi judei nostri sunt thezauri* [sic]). This fiscal nexus was made doubly clear in the regulation that minor heirs of debtors must not delay paying their debts to Jewish lenders, "for these Jews as Our subjects [*subditi*] shall be prepared to provide Us with their funds for Our necessities." In general, the Polish charters reflect the early stage of the imperial or royal serfdom as it developed in Germany, England, and Spain between 1000 and 1300 C.E. But because the Polish monarchs never called the Jews their "serfs" (as indeed had not been done by their early predecessors in Austria, Hungary, or

Bohemia), there was less opportunity for misinterpretations through equating the Jews with the other "serfs," who were in real bondage. From the outset, moreover, the Crown's authority over Jews was limited by the part assigned to the nobility. The Boleslas-Casimir privilege itself emphasized that it was promulgated with the "knowledge of Our native-born lords and nobles" (*nostrorumque dominorum ac nobilium terrigenarum providencia*). Royal control over Jews might have been strengthened if the "protoabsolutist" tendencies manifest during the regime of Casimir the Great had materialized. However, the difficulties of succession after his death and, for a time, the equivocal status of Wladislaw Jagiello as prince consort or king, made the sharing of legislative authority with the higher and lower nobility increasingly imperative. Ultimately, even the administrative officers, including the palatines or provincial governors, though not the district chiefs, the royal *starostas,* had to be appointed from among the landowning nobility of each particular region. One certainly cannot conceive of a Polish prince offering a juridical formulation for the Jews' status in Poland-Lithuania comparable to that put forth by Marquess Albert Achilles of Brandenburg with respect to fifteenth-century imperial German Jewry. Not that instances of the curtailment of these Jewish freedoms by powerful lords or city councils were lacking, but very frequently these were only the arbitrary acts of magnates, patricians, or urban mobs, who felt few restraints against violating the existing laws.[70]

In general, Sigismund III's relatively friendly policies seem to have amazed the Jews themselves, who must have been greatly alarmed when this pupil of Jesuits was elected to the Polish throne. They tried to explain the new king's unexpectedly benevolent state of mind in a traditionally anecdotal fashion. According to an entry in the minute book of the Cracow community:

On a Sunday [night], the 19th of Shebaṭ, 5355 [January 30, 1595] an intense fire raged in the castle of Cracow [the Wawel]; it destroyed a large part of the castle including the inner chambers of His Royal Majesty. The king and the queen themselves had to escape from their palace into the street of the cathedral and abandon their home. No one was able to extinguish the conflagration except the Jews, who succeeded in saving all the chests containing the king's and queen's treasures and in removing them to the large church near the castle. His Majesty, the king himself, stood at the gate and personally observed the Jews' arduous labors and unwavering devotion. Many objects, too, which had been taken away during the fire were returned [to their owners] through the help of Jews who reported to the king and his officials the whereabouts of all the objects, small or large, which had fallen into their hands, or about which they had information or hints. This event made a great impression, thanks be to God; the heart of the king turned and he became like a changed person, bent upon doing good to His Jewish subjects. Amen.

Of course, this simplistic explanation can easily be disproved by the king's actions in the years preceding 1595.[71]

After his coronation, Sigismund III received a delegation of the Jews of Wschowa (Fraustadt), "living on royal land near the city," who submitted to him, for confirmation and renewal, a copy of the privilege issued in 1580 by Stephen Báthory for the Jews of Płock. This had been the customary procedure with the earlier monarchs, who by renewing the privileges referring specifically to the Jewries of Great and Little Poland had by implication confirmed the existing privileges for the Jews in the rest of the dual Commonwealth as well. It has been suggested that the reason the Wschowa Jews selected the Płock privilege, rather than the numerous older privileges granted to the Jews of Kalisz, Poznań, or Cracow since the days of Boleslas the Pious in 1264, was that they may have hoped thereby to include the few Jews allowed to live in Mazovia under that protective umbrella. But it is more likely that the Wschowa Jews wished mainly to avert their own impending expulsion, not only from the city but also from the castle area outside the city's immediate jurisdiction. The royal confirmation of the privilege (October 12, 1592), now had some of the characteristics of the constitutional oath to observe the *pacta conventa*, exacted by the *szlachta* from every newly elected king since Báthory. Of course, Jews could not claim, as the gentry did, that a king refusing to take the oath had no right to occupy the throne (*si non jurabis non regnavis*). Nevertheless, king after king unstintingly confirmed the Jewish Charter soon after his coronation. In the formulation signed by Sigismund III the Wschowa statute is extant only in copies, dated 1604 and 1620 (available in a Poznań archive), as well as in its reconfirmation by Sigismund's younger son and second successor, John Casimir. Notwithstanding some minor variations, the substance of these texts is the same. The statute thus was but a link in the long chain of basic charters which guaranteed the fundamental rights of Polish Jewry until the end of the Commonwealth. Despite certain formal flaws, the general privilege was also renewed by Wladislaw IV and John Casimir on March 11, 1633, and February 13, 1649, respectively, soon after coronation. To reinforce his various decrees further, Sigismund III, on April 30, 1592, sent out a circular to the leading city councils, stressing, in particular, their duty to honor Jewish trading and other rights. Six years later (July 10, 1598), he addressed another circular to the royal officials throughout the realm, ordering them scrupulously to observe the privileges granted the Jews in all economic and judicial spheres. More specifically, he confirmed on August 8, 1600, the privilege promulgated by Sigismund I in 1527, whereby Jewish merchants were to pay customs duties at the same rates as Christians.[72]

Of importance to Jews also was the fact that the *szlachta* resisted the wholesale "reception" and incorporation of Roman law into the general legal structure of Poland, although it could not entirely prevent some influence on municipal law or on the relations between the burghers and the gentry. In general, even jurists who had studied Roman law abroad (at home, the priestly professors of law at the University of Cracow subordinated Roman to canon law) could merely adduce some of its provisions as arguments from *ratio scripta,* rather than recommend them for direct imitation. As formulated in the *Corpus Juris Civilis* by Justinian and his advisers, the Roman code of law reflected much of the legal evolution of the late Roman Empire, which favored both royal absolutism and legal discrimination against Jews.[73]

Royal efforts to establish a general law for the Jews of the entire realm were greatly hampered by the kings' enforced respect for diverse local traditions and for the numerous privileges enacted by earlier monarchs or diets in favor of certain localities or regions. R. Moses Isserles did not exaggerate when he contended, in one of his responsa, that in Poland "every city has its own taxes and its own rulers, and even the king cannot exercise full control." (These words were written under the reign of Sigismund II Augustus, before the further erosion of monarchical power.) Quite apart, therefore, from the ruler's personal temperament, temporary exigencies, and the pressures exerted by interested parties, Sigismund III and Wladislaw IV could not pursue a consistent Jewish policy. We recall that as early as March 28, 1589, Sigismund III confirmed his predecessors' favorable edict for the Jewish community of Łuck in Volhynia. In the same year he also conceded to Prince Ostrogski that the Jews of the town of Biała Cerkiew (Belaya Tserkov) should enjoy the rights and liberties of the Jews of the Polish Crown as a whole—clearly an instance of wishful thinking, since there did not exist a universal legal system applicable to all Polish Jews. Two years later (February 21, 1591), Sigismund granted an extensive privilege to the Jews of Przemyśl. This noteworthy document, extant in its Latin text, provided, among other matters: "the Jews should have the freedom to acquire houses and possess them by hereditary rights in the entire area which since early times they have inhabited in the city of Przemyśl." They also were to have the same rights as the burghers to acquire and sell merchandise of whatever kind and whatever fashion. In signing this decree the king must have been aware of Sigismund II Augustus' even more sweeping declaration of 1559, that the Przemyśl Jews "should enjoy and benefit from all the liberties which Our city of Przemyśl enjoys." On the other hand, the same Sigismund III felt bound to confirm on January 26, 1588, the right of the citizens of Opoczno not to tolerate Jews in their town, and more specifically to approve their vote forbidding Jews to acquire houses or to secure residences even in its suburbs. Ironically, the Jewish community of Wschowa (Fraustadt), which was in October 1592 one of the first to secure from the king confirmation of the fundamental royal Charter, had itself been the object of a sharply discriminatory regulation three months earlier (July 3). Here Sigismund, at the request of the city council of Wschowa, for the better defense of that city in the event of a foreign attack, affirmed the city's privilege *de non tolerandis Judaeis* anywhere in its suburbs or other neighboring areas outside its jurisdiction. In the Lithuanian part of the dual Commonwealth, too, the kings often yielded to local pressures. For instance, in Mogilev (Mohilev), where Jewish traders and tax farmers were recorded in a number of sixteenth-century documents, Sigismund III in 1626 and Wladislaw IV in 1633 yielded to the protests of the local burghers, and restricted Jewish residential rights to the vicinity of the synagogue, in order to put an end "to conflicts arising from Jews and Christians living on the same streets." A "Jewish street" is also recorded for Vilna from 1592 on; but a year later Sigismund expressly allowed Jews to acquire houses owned by nobles in other parts of the city as well. Here the burghers' opposition to Jews was dramatized by mob attacks, which on two occasions (in 1592 and 1635) led to the destruction of Jewish sanctuaries. Not surprisingly, Wladislaw's decrees of 1633 and 1643, while intended to protect Jewish rights, also included serious limitations on Jewish ownership of real estate. Such inconsistencies characterized all subsequent royal legislation concerning Polish and Lithuanian Jews.[74]

STABILIZED LEGAL STATUS

Nevertheless, one may deduce from the available, relatively rich documentation certain generalizations concerning the status of the Jews in the Commonwealth under the first two Vasas and, *mutatis mutandis*, also under the earlier and later kings. In the first place, the general privilege as restated by Sigismund III not only included, but in some details enlarged, the protective provisions for Jewish life and limb which had originally been taken over from other Central European laws by Boleslas the Pious and his immediate successors. According to the privilege of 1592 (in its extant copies of 1604 and 1620), any Christian murderer of a Jew was to be condemned if his guilt was sworn to by the closest relative of the victim, by an oath on the Scroll of Law. Such a killer was to be executed: "a head for a head, and no other procedure should be applied." Should the murderer succeed in fleeing the court's reach, his entire property was to be confiscated and turned over in part to the nearest relatives of the slain Jew and in part to the royal Chamber. Nor was such a fugitive to secure a safe-conduct for his return to the country, without the consent of the victim's relatives. These provisions marked a considerable modernization of criminal law by replacing the medieval fine (*wergeld*) with the execution of the culprit. Practice, however, often differed widely from these theoretical regulations. A sixteenth-century rabbinic responsum mentions that when a Pinsk widow cited her husband's Christian murderer before the courts, the slayer's punishment was limited to a fine, a clear reversion to the *wergeld*. Similar cases doubtless occurred quite frequently; the Pinsk judgment was recorded only because the victim's creditors wished to seize the fine, whereas the rabbi decided that it must be given to his orphans. On the other hand, a remarkable provision of the Charter extended even greater safeguards to Jewish assailants of Christians. The law prescribed that, if a Jew wounded a Christian —some texts intimate that such contingencies were very rare—the victim had to produce two Jewish and two Christian witnesses, whereupon the assailant was to be punished according to local custom. So radical a discrimination in favor of Jews could be justified only by the greater need for protection on the part of the Crown's Jewish wards.[75]

Clearly, the basic Jewish privilege attempted to discourage accusations of Jewish ritual murder. In this connection, Boleslas the Pious and his successors followed the example set by Bohemian king Přemysl Ottakar II, who in 1254 had promulgated Innocent IV's 1247 bull outlawing such accusations, and had added a pertinent clause to his Jewish statute. One article in the Polish Charter stated that, if a Christian accused a Jew of having kidnaped a child or a youth "without the knowledge of the [generality of the] Jews themselves," the accuser must prove it, as he would any other theft. Moreover, the king stated bluntly,

We ordain that no Jew in such cases may be accused by a Christian claiming that the Jews are every year obliged to use the blood of Christians and the Host of the Christian Church. The statutes of Pope Innocent and the [imperial] constitutions teach us that they [the Jews] are not guilty of such matters which are against their law. Should a Christian in his temerity [persist] . . . he must prove his accusation with [the testimony of] three honest Jews owning property in Our realm who live an unimpeachable life and are steadfast in their belief, as well as with [that of] four Christians who likewise own much property in Our realm, lead an irreproachable life, and are firm in their belief.

If the Christian proved his charge, the Jew was to be executed. If he failed, however, the accuser himself was to suffer death. Nobles and burghers who maltreated mere suspects were to lose all their property to the Treasury, and their lives were to depend on royal grace. The vehemence of these provisions indicates how badly the Polish Jews were in need of protection against the ritual murder libel, which was spreading like wildfire in the Slavonic lands as well. That libel was to be one of the tragic keynotes in all Polish-Jewish relations down to the twentieth century.[76]

On the other hand, fines rather than capital punishment were the penalties imposed upon Jews for cohabitation with Christians —an act treated as a capital offense in most Western countries. Even the churchmen assembled in Wrocław (Breslau) in 1267, who included in their synodal resolutions the first comprehensive canonical program for anti-Jewish segregation and discrimination in the Polish area, demanded only that a fine of ten marks be imposed on those culprits. Not surprisingly, sometimes the threat of denouncement was used to extort substantial bribes from the accused individual, his family or friends, or else to persuade the alleged culprit to save himself by conversion to Christianity. Such a case occurred, for instance, in Opatów (*ca.* 1600). A responsum by R. Meir b. Gedaliah of Lublin records an inquiry from the Jewish elders of that town as to whether they should view such baksheesh as a legitimate form of the "ransom of captives" pre-scribed by Jewish law. In his answer the rabbi pointed out that "even according to their [the Gentiles'] laws, the young man was not subject to capital punishment" and that, hence, the threat was but an attempt to extort money from them. On the other hand, there was indeed the danger that the accused might accept con-version and perhaps turn informer against his erstwhile coreli-gionists. Meir left it, therefore, to the elders' discretion to decide how far they wished to go in appeasing the prosecutor. To under-stand the rabbi's indecisiveness, one must remember that Jewish leaders also were adamantly opposed to interfaith sex relations.[77]

Similarly, the oath *more judaico* in its degrading forms, never became universally accepted in Poland, as it had in many western countries toward the end of the Middle Ages. Efforts to institute such an oath had apparently been made quite early. In reaction, the Boleslas-Casimir statute specifically provided, in its very first article, that Jews should merely swear on the Torah scroll, with its Ten Commandments, whenever the fine involved exceeded 50 silver marks, or by placing their hands on a chain at the synagogue gate in lesser cases, and recite: "So help me God, who illumines and observes, as well as the Books of Moses." This formula was but a variant of that used by most Christians: "So help me God and the Holy Cross." For greater emphasis the statute added: "Such and none other ought to be the Jewish oath in whatever cause, be it small or large." This formula—which is indeed recorded in the litigation between a Cracow Jew named Musscha (Moses) and a noble lady in 1423—is the more remarkable as even some Christians were adding curses against themselves in the event of perjury, curses like those usually associated with the Jewish oath. In 1503, King Alexander himself, while promising the Turkish envoy that he would continue to observe the five-year armistice previously concluded by his deceased brother John Albert, included in his oath the curse that, should he violate his pledge, he "take part with Judas and share the leprosy of Gehazi and the tremor of Cain." This may have been a Byzantine formula recently brought to Poland by some Italians. It was understandable, therefore, that King Alexander also decreed, in 1505, that "the Jew should turn toward the rising sun, stand barefoot upon a stool, be clad in a mantle or cloak, and wear the horned Jewish hat," and in this posture recite a lengthy formula including the customary West-European references to the biblical blessings for truthfulness and the maledictions for perjury. It was considered a sign of the swearer's sincerity if he repeated the oath without stammering; otherwise he appeared suspect and, under special circumstances, his oath might be rejected by the judge and his case lost. Some local officials even tried to emulate the West by insisting that the Jew stand on a three-legged stool, whose shakiness was to undermine the self-confidence of a potential perjurer, or else on the skin of a swine, as the term *rodale* in the royal privileges was sometimes translated. The Jews, however, strenuously objected to these dishonoring innovations, and induced several successive kings to clarify the original intent of the law. In two decrees of 1551 and 1553, in favor of the Jews of Poznań and Lwów respectively, Sigismund Augustus made it perfectly clear that *rodale* referred merely to the biblical Decalogue. Even more emphatic was Stephen Báthory in his decree of 1576 in favor of the Jews of

Łuck. He peremptorily renewed the regulation that, in disputes involving more than fifty pieces of silver, Jews be made to swear "in the synagogue on God's Ten Commandments as delivered by Moses." In lesser cases they were only to hold the chain in front of the synagogue, "according to Jewish law." In another decree, that of 1580 for the Jews of Poznań, the king dismissed as ridiculous the equation of *rodale* with the skin of a pig. He adhered to this point of view in still another decree, in 1585, addressed to "all whom it may concern, collectively or individually." Báthory's interpretation was upheld in 1592–93 by Sigismund III, who specifically outlawed the "superstitions and unneeded ceremonies" sometimes employed in administering oaths to Jews.[78]

Jews were to enjoy also complete freedom of movement throughout the realm. The pertinent article in the Charter is quite explicit:

Every Jew may freely and securely go and travel from one city to another and from one province to another in Our realm without any impediment or hindrance. . . . Every Jew in Our realm may freely and securely and without any impediment transport with him his goods and any kind of merchandise he may wish; he may sell them and buy others, or exchange them for his own benefit. He may freely and securely stay . . . in all cities, villages, and other places of Our realm under Our royal security and safe-conduct, paying only such tolls as are paid by Christians.

There were, of course, limitations, imposed by a number of contradictory local privileges and regulations. Certainly, the cities which enjoyed the privilege *de non tolerandis Judaeis* did not have to admit Jews to residence, despite this sweeping royal declaration. However, the kings tried to prevail upon the local city councils and burghers to give Jews access to their localities during fairs or, as in the case of Warsaw and Piotrków, during Diet sessions. This basic right of freedom of movement for the Jews contrasted sharply with the enforced attachment to the soil of a large segment of the peasant population. We recall that not until the late decades of Poland's independence were any efforts made by the gentry-controlled Diet to curtail that right of the Jews (as well as that of Christian burghers)—efforts which proved utterly futile.[79]

Curiously, the personal freedom of individual Jews was de-limited more by Jewish communal regulations than by those issued by the royal government or local powers. We have seen that, through the so-called *ḥezqat* (or *ḥerem*) *ha-yishub* (acquired right, or ban, of settlement), residence permits were strictly con-trolled by the Jewish communal organs, which enjoyed a wide area of discretion in admitting newcomers. They could also forbid the departure of members who had not paid up the arrears of their communal taxes or, in some cases, who had not contributed their share of the communal indebtedness. Typical of that autonomous Jewish regulation of residence rights was the aforementioned resolution of the Lithuanian Council in 1623, which had also added a specific protective provision for the community of Minsk, even with respect to Jews arriving from the Polish Crown. Native Lithuanian Jews were later (in 1628) included in this prohibition, if they had previously lived for ten years in another province and had failed to pay up all taxes due their community. In these matters the Jewish communal organs thus enjoyed untrammeled self-determination. In contrast, the cities were unable to regulate the admission of Jews to local residence on an individual basis, but rather had to resort to restricting the amount of housing available to the Jewish community as a whole. Of course, such a situation was conducive to overcrowding in the limited space available. However, as we recall in the case of Poznań, Cracow, and other cities, Jews usually found ways to enlarge the permissible area by renting dwellings belonging to the Church or noblemen outside the city's jurisdiction. Much also depended on the so-called "agreements" made by the cities with their Jewish communities, which time and again were subject to violation by either side, and to frequent modification.[80]

Next to the Jews' personal freedoms, those of their religious worship loomed very large. Whatever ethnic characteristics were attributed to Jews by their neighbors, their legal status was defined primarily as that of a tolerated religious minority: the law pro-vided specific safeguards for the practice of their religion and for the safety of their religious institutions. Apart from shielding Jews against being summoned to court or administrative offices on their Sabbath or holidays, the law recognized their right to have their own houses of worship and burial grounds. True, from ancient times, the Church—and following it, the Christian states—required special permits for the construction of new synagogues; prohibited the buildings from being taller than local churches (or, sometimes, even than the private dwellings of Christians); and decreed that synagogues not offend pious Christians by their appearance or their proximity to Christian sanctuaries. Yet as a predominantly immigrant population, spreading out to ever-new localities, the Jews considered synagogues and cemeteries indispensable for the normal pursuit of their religious life. Remarkably, the granting of the necessary permits in Poland rarely led to extended debates, either between the Jews and the Gentile authorities or between ecclesiastical and secular officials. Most Polish synagogues through the centuries—including the beautiful wooden synagogues which, in some respects, marked a Jewish innovation in architectural design—seem to have been built without any formal permits. Attempts by some priests to gain exclusive control over both the granting of licenses and the receipt of the pertinent fees often were disregarded by the secular officials. In fact, in his decree of 1638, Wladislaw IV explicitly provided that only a royal permit be required. But even that requirement seems to have been observed largely in its breach.

From time to time the kings had to deal with exceptional cases, however. As we recall, in permitting on May 5, 1626, and again on August 5, 1628, the rebuilding of a burned-out Łuck synagogue, Sigismund III not only emphasized its importance as a fortress against Tatar attacks but also insisted that the new structure must not exceed the dimensions of the former one. Nor was it to overshadow the neighboring Catholic church. This provision was doubly significant, since almost half a century earlier, as we recall, the papal nuncio had complained of the total absence of a Catholic church in the city, contrasted with the presence there of a beautiful synagogue. More, in an apparently impulsive reaction, Sigismund III handed over to a favorite Christian notary two wooden synagogues (belonging to Rabbanite and Karaite worshipers, respectively) in Łuck, because they had been erected on royal land without a license (April 29, 1629). It was partially to forestall ecclesiastical protests against synagogues exceeding in height or external splendor the local churches, that many Jewish communities built synagogues with their main floor below street level, so that their external height would not appear excessive. To justify this somewhat inconvenient architectural design, the rabbis often quoted the psalmist's exclamation "Out of the depths have I called Thee, O Lord." On the whole, however, few Polish Jewish communities evinced great interest in contructing very elaborate synagogues, even if they could afford them.[81]

Protection of cemeteries had, from time immemorial, two major aspects: the prevention of vandalism or despoliation of graves for mercenary reasons; and the securing of free access to the burial grounds, especially if they were situated at a distance from the locality from which corpses had to be transported. In Poland, as elsewhere, smaller communities could not afford cemeteries of their own, and often had to bury their dead in regional "houses of eternity." Such a situation gave rise not only to assaults on funeral corteges by hostile groups but also to attempts by local landowners to impose tolls on the funeral processions. It was against both these forms of "molestation" that a special article in the general Polish Charter had bluntly declared: "We wish that any collector of a toll [from Jewish funerals] be considered a thief, predator, and robber, whose property is to fall back to Us." The same penalty was to be imposed upon any Christian who desecrated a Jewish cemetery, whereas the defacer of a synagogue had to pay only two pounds of pepper as a fine to "its defender," the palatine. These safeguards were doubtless obtained by Jews anxious to secure protection for their cemeteries and synagogues. In fact, the earliest record relating to Jews in Kalisz, and one of the earliest in all of Poland, refers to a contract signed in 1287 by "the Jewish elders" with a Christian named Ruphinus for the purchase of a knoll "for the purpose of burial" (*pro sepultura*). It must have been a great sacrifice for the Kalisz community to pay for it the large amount of six talents of pepper and saffron. The relatively small Jewish community of Sandomierz in Little Poland, seems quite early to have erected a fine synagogue: one modern investigator has declared it to be the oldest extant synagogue in Polish lands and has plausibly argued for its medieval origin.[82]

Of importance also was the provision that Jewish ritual slaughtering be allowed in all places where Jews were permitted to dwell. The opposition thereto was often reinforced by neighbors' complaints about the stench usually emanating from slaughterhouses. More remarkably, the Charter added that the Jews should be enabled to dispose freely of slaughtered animals in whole or in part. This clause evidently referred to the prevailing practice whereby Jewish butchers sold to Gentile customers those animals whose required examination had revealed some ritualistic flaws and those parts of animals generally proscribed by talmudic law. It was because of this widespread practice in Cracow, Poznań, and Lublin that Sigismund III, in his privilege for the Jews of Przemyśl dated February 21, 1591, permitted the Przemyśl Jews to "engage in the slaughtering and selling of meat to Christians and any other people." This regulation overruled the objections of some zealous Christians, who considered it unseemly that the Christian public should consume meat considered unfit by Jews for their own consumption.[83]

Another area of great concern to Jews was the legislation relating to their self-government. To control the scattered Jewries of their realm, the kings insisted upon the submission of all Jewish individuals to their duly constituted communal authorities. The pertinent article in Sigismund III's Charter read: "If any Jew should not be obedient to his superiors, such a man shall pay a fine of 3 marks to the lord palatine and 3 additional marks to his superiors." At the same time, the succeeding charters also provided that Jews not be subjected to municipal jurisdiction, even in controversies with non-Jews. Mixed litigations were to be adjudicated by the more impartial superior court of the palatine. However, quite apart from the royal *ius evocationis*, whereby the king could on his own initiative assume direct jurisdiction over any case pending in a lower court, the Charter allowed any Jewish litigant to appeal to the king against sentences of the palatinate courts. Even those courts as we recall often had to function in the presence of Jewish elders and hear their advice. Ritual murder trials were to be referred directly to the royal tribunal. Most importantly, matters affecting only Jews were to be adjudicated exclusively by the rabbinical courts, appointed by Jewish communal leaders. There is an intimation in the

Charter, to be sure, that even sentences of the rabbinical courts could be appealed to the king. But there is no evidence that this prerogative was exercised by Jewish parties with any degree of frequency. Undoubtedly the moral pressure exerted by the community and, in extreme cases, the threat of excommunication, persuaded Jewish litigants to submit to rabbinical decisions. How awesome the threat of excommunication was considered, is evidenced by a decision of the Council of Four Lands, which argued against the sanction of excommunication for a certain prohibition because such a penalty would be far more severe than a fine, however large; physical chastisement; banishment from the realm; or commitment to the Gentile authorities. On the other hand, the Jewish communal elders were held collectively responsible for delivering indicted or suspected criminals to the authorities. One such case is discussed in a lengthy responsum by R. Joel Sirkes: A communal sexton, implicated by a defendant tried and subsequently executed for alleged desecration of the host, had gone into hiding. Thereupon the elders were ordered to deliver the sexton; if they failed to do so, they themselves would be liable to be sentenced to the penalty imposed on him by the king. Autonomous control over such other areas as Jewish education and social welfare, was even less under dispute.[84]

Very interesting material, for the most part from the fifteenth and sixteenth centuries, has recently been assembled by Witold Maisel and analyzed in a series of archival studies about the judicial system in Poznań. To be sure, the "Jewish court" (Sąd żydowski), mostly called judicium bannitum generale judaicum in contemporary Latin documents, appears to have been related more to the municipal judicial structure than to the regular Jewish tribunal, which Maisel calls "the court of the Jewish community." The judicium . . . judaicum was basically intended for real estate transactions in the Jewish quarter. That is why its proceedings included not only cases where the parties were Jewish and Christian, like those usually treated by the judex Judaeorum, but also cases where they were exclusively Christian or exclusively Jewish. Probably anything affecting housing in the Jewish quarter was of interest to the municipality, which probably maintained real estate records for the whole city and also enacted for it certain zoining regulations. If, on occasion, some Christians voluntarily submitted their claims to the "Jewish court" in matters unrelated to Jewish real estate, the reason may have been not only, as suggested by Maisel, the plaintiff's convenience (if that court met on a day when other courts were closed) but perhaps also a greater confidence in the operations of that court. Of course, on some occasions the "court of the Jewish community" was called upon to collaborate in a litigation, particularly when a Jewish party or witness was required to take an oath which was usually taken in the synagogue. In one case such collaboration was made necessary because a Christian defendant was accused, by both the victim's father and the Jewish elders, of murdering a young Jew named Philip Sloma. This limitation of the range of the "Jewish court's" competence may also explain the relative paucity of references to it in the plethora of archival documents (references to the "Jewish court" date only from the periods 1430–32, 1453–54, and 1459–60), which so puzzled Maisel. Undoubtedly few Jewish parties felt inclined to repair to that court. Moreover, in the fifteenth century, as we recall, the Jewish quarter in Poznań was still very small. Thereafter, as a result of the growing jurisdictional controversies between the city and the Jews, the monarchy increasingly curtailed the city's authority over the local Jews, which doubtless also diminished the role of the *judicium . . . judaicum*. We know that by 1557 King Sigismund II Augustus, on the complaint of the palatine of Poznań, Janusz Latalski, forbade the city elders ever to incarcerate Jews. In his decree of January 13, the king made it clear that the Jews were subject only to the palatine's jurisdiction and that, hence, for any attempt to molest them the city elders would incur the royal displeasure and a fine of 100 marks.[85]

As was the case in other matters, the government's support of the Jewish communal structure was not quite disinterested. From the outset, Jews were considered an accretion of strength for the monarchy and the country because of their fiscal contributions. We shall see that the totals levied on the Jewish population were constantly increasing, particularly after the introduction of the *pogłówne* (capitation tax) in 1549. But under the existing conditions the government possessed no effective machinery for collecting such a tax from scores of thousands of persons living in widely dispersed areas. Furthermore, Jewish taxpayers residing in noble or ecclesiastical enclaves could often expect their lords to support them in evading the tax. It was, therefore, expedient for the government to delegate the responsibility for collecting the tax to the Jewish communities. To simplify matters further, the communities delivered certain lump sums based on agreed estimates of the number of prospective taxpayers, leaving it to the discretion of the communal elders either to collect the prescribed tax from each family according to its size or to resort to progressive taxation by requiring higher payments from wealthy individuals, and collecting less than the due tax, or none at all, from impecunious groups. Most convenient for the Treasury was to arrange with some central Jewish agency or agencies to assume responsibility for the total sum to be raised in the Polish Crown and Lithuania.

Royal fiscal needs thus met half-way the wishes of the Jewish community itself to have central organs in the two parts of the country which could in addition perform major services for the Jewish community, both through concerted guidance in internal affairs and through representation before external bodies. We remember that Sigismund I's attempt to establish such central leadership by appointing individual chief rabbis for Poland and Lithuania had been rejected by the Jews, unwilling to submit to the will of royally appointed communal officials. However, the stalemate then reached gave way to a compromise, out of which emerged the Council of Four Lands about 1580, and the Council of Provinces in Lithuania about 1623. These organs added greatly to the Jewish community's prestige in foreign lands, and functioned to the satisfaction of both the public authorities and the Jews for several generations, until their abolition in 1764. The ramified problems of Jewish taxation will be considered more fully in the next chapters, but suffice it to say that we hardly hear of forced loans to the government. Even voluntary loans by Jewish bankers became less frequent, partly because even the wealthiest Polish and Lithaunian Jews had relatively limited resources for loans and found it more profitable to invest their capital in commercial undertakings. Certainly, there was no Jew in the Commonwealth who could advance Wladislaw IV (who, in contrast to his parsimonious father, was a lavish spender) credits totaling 1,079,411 zlotys, as was done in 1637 by the Christian plutocrat Jerzy Hewl of Gdańsk. In comparison, the 20,000 zlotys loaned to the king four years earlier by the Jewish brothers Samuel and Lazar Mojżeszowicz for the building of a Polish navy, indispensable to the monarch's Baltic ambitions, almost paled into insignificance. This amount certainly was a small part of the 800,000 or 900,000 zlotys needed to acquire the essential minimum of twenty-five ships. Furthermore, large additional sums had to be raised to equip these men-of-war and to pay their crews. The rapid growth of royal indebtedness, which necessarily impeded all Treasury operations, may easily be gauged by comparison with the preceding century (even discounting the intervening inflation), when Sigismund I's debts totaled only 675,000 zlotys. By spending half that sum the king was able to redeem most of the public domain frittered away by his predecessors.[86]

In some ways more important than royal legislation, which often fell on deaf ears, was the protection extended to Jews by the kings through their appointed officials. While the king played a diminishing role in the legislative area, he remained in control of appointments to all higher and many lower offices. This prerogative gave him much leverage within the power constellation of Polish society, although by an unusual quirk of legislation the king could not remove palatines or district governors without parliamentary approval, except when they had committed ordinary crimes. As a rule, the *wojewoda*s (palatines), even after their power was greatly curtailed; their subordinates, the *podwojewoda*s (subpalatines); and the *judices Judaeorum* were loyal executives of the royal will. True, in 1534 a powerful palatine, like Otto Chodecki of Cracow (he also served as district governor of Halicz, Lwów, Śniatyn, and Kołomyja) could claim exclusive and direct jurisdiction over Jews. In his letter of February 18, 1534, to Peter Kmita, marshal of the realm, Sigismund I had to delay his decision with respect to Chodecki's claim until his return to Poland. He asked only that, for the sake of justice, Chodecki *provisionally* try —in the capacity of a royal commissioner—Jews accused of theft, sacrilege, or counterfeiting. On his return, the king undoubtedly reasserted his own prerogative; but, in the face of the ever-growing

Jewish population, he and his successors were forced to delegate the actual exercise of their judicial authority to the palatines and subpalatines. Yet, whether by personal intervention or through direct orders to their officials in the capital and provinces, the kings continued greatly to influence local situations and helped to adjust conflicts, particularly between the cities and the Jewish communities, in fairly equitable ways.[87]

There also existed since 1578 the Crown Tribunal, or the royal supreme court, to which Jews and others could appeal, and which had the final say, though it could not always assure its execution. To be sure, the extent to which Jews resorted to appeals against their own courts has not been ascertained, since the records of the Crown Tribunal have not yet been examined from the standpoint of Jewish history. Such an undertaking would be extremely difficult today, in view of the tremendous losses sustained by the Central Archive in Warsaw during the Second World War, particularly in this domain. But we know a little more about litigations between Jews and non-Jews which found their way to the supreme court. A telling example is offered by the protracted lawsuit between the Jesuits and the Jews in Lwów in which the Church exceptionally confronted an alliance of the Jews and the city council. In many mixed litigations the presence of the Jewish central organizations, and their provincial subdivisions, proved very helpful in influencing administrative practice on national, regional, and even local levels.[88]

Obviously, not all palatines were friends of the Jews. One of them, Hieronim Gostomski, palatine of Poznań, though a staunch royalist, became an ardent Jew-baiter. Member of a Protestant family, he had been converted by Piotr Skarga to Catholicism, while his father and brother continued to live as confirmed Protestants. He now supported Sigismund III's Catholic policies with the zeal of a neophyte, and often deviated from the king's protective attitude toward Jews. At the crucial session of the Diet in January 1605 (shortly before the Zebrzydowski Rebellion), he delivered a lengthy address which included a sharply anti-Jewish tirade. Gostomski did not limit himself to supporting the motion then under debate, that an impost on Jewish taxpayers should be levied to cover the necessary "presents" for the Tatar rulers so as to forestall their military intervention. He denounced the Jews as "magpies preying on Christians" (*sroki skubiące chrześcijanin*), who commit horrendous crimes, which he had heard of and in part had personally (!) witnessed (without being more specific, he doubtless referred to some blood and host libels). The Poznań palatine now demanded that all Jews be summarily expelled from Poland. Understandably, he also opposed the general idea of liberty of conscience as proclaimed by the Warsaw Confederation of 1573, and contended that "confederations" as such should be eliminated. However, his was decidedly a minority view in the Diet. He was soon vigorously controverted by a colleague, Jędrzej Leszczyński, palatine of Brześć Kujawski and a Protestant, who also argued that a diversion of Jewish funds for gifts to the Tatars would subsequently diminish the royal revenue needed to pay the wages of soldiers in the forthcoming war.[89]

Jews reciprocated the royal protection not only by their fiscal contributions, and their commercial and other services, but also by great personal loyalty to the kings. Apart from reciting in synagogue services the long-established prayers for the welfare of their rulers, some Polish communities inserted into their liturgy such occasional *seliḥot* (penitential prayers) as those composed by R. Eliezer b. Elijah Ashkenazi, which included a supplication for the king's victory in a forthcoming battle (1614). Even Sigismund III is praised by a Jewish chronicler of the early seventeenth century as a "king who was gracious and just, a lover of the law, and a friend of the people of Israel." Sigismund's son, Wladislaw, also earned high praise from contemporary Jewish leaders. The distinguished halakhist, Shabbetai b. Meir ha-Kohen, described him as "a worthy king, entitled to be counted among the righteous men, for he always acted graciously toward the Jews and kept his promises to them." Some Jews even participated in Polish military expeditions to Muscovy and elsewhere. We hear about Jewish combatants indirectly from rabbinical decisions concerning the freedom of women to remarry if their husbands were missing and presumed dead. One case, which came to the attention of R. Joel Sirkes, concerned a soldier named Beracha, who was reported to have performed heroic acts in the Muscovite campaign before he vanished. More frequently, Jews accompanied armies as sutlers, and occasionally as major contractors. However, even these services are but sporadically recorded in the contemporary sources. We hear more often of Jewish personal and financial contributions to the building of local fortifications and the defense of their cities against foreign invaders.[90]

ON AN EVEN KEEL

In the six decades of the reign of the first two Vasa kings (1588–1648), the political and legal status of the Jews in Poland-Lithuania underwent few basic changes. True, there was considerable legislation in detail; quite apart from the kings, the Diets, the lords, and the municipalities issued numerous ordinances of their own which often greatly affected Jewish daily life. At times the new enactments were so contradictory that they required the intervention of the courts or royal officials to establish a *modus vivendi* between the parties concerned. Yet the fundamental royal charters as formulated in the two centuries from Casimir the Great to Sigismund I, together with some major edicts issued in the sixteenth century by Sigismund I, Sigismund II, and Stephen Báthory, remained part and parcel of the country's statutory law and were largely upheld, and sometimes formally confirmed, by Sigismund III and Wladislaw IV.

Needless to say, like the other inhabitants of the dual Commonwealth, the Jews felt the progressive impact of the Counter Reformation. Yet, at least until the 1650s, the country's vaunted sixteenth-century religious toleration was not completely abandoned. Not even the much-hated Anti-Trinitarianism was outlawed before 1658. Judaism as such remained a tolerated religion; its institutions, laws, and mores were largely respected by the ruling classes, although the restrictions the Catholic Church had long imposed on certain religious practices, especially on the building of new synagogues, were now somewhat more strictly enforced. However, under the slowly spreading anarchy in Polish public life, violations were apt to be frequently overlooked by the enforcers, or the Jews found other ways to circumvent them. If the recorded number of privileges *de non tolerandis Judaeis* newly granted to cities during that period was larger than in any preceding sixty-year period, this increase must be contrasted with the vastly larger number of new Jewish settlements which were springing up under the Vasa kings. We shall see that, while immigration from other countries diminished during that period, internal migration and geographic diffusion was greatly accelerated. Regrettably, we have no possibility of determining the exact number of Jewish settlements in the dual Commonwealth at the death of Báthory in 1586, or of those existing in 1647. In any case, the number of towns which shut their gates to Jewish residence was always but a small fraction of all the urban settlements in the country. Moreover, almost all the great metropolitan centers— with the exception of the largest (Gdańsk) and the new capital (Warsaw)—now embraced vibrant and flourishing Jewish communities.

Not even the great conversionist efforts set in motion by Jesuits and other exponents of the Counter Reformation seem to have seriously affected the Jews. The number of converts to Christianity among the Polish-Lithuanian Jews was always minimal and, as we shall see, had little effect on Jewish demographic growth. More serious were the riots, whether stemming from religious or socioeconomic motives, particularly those staged by students and other youthful ruffians. The increased intensity of Blood Accusations and the proliferating anti-Jewish literature likewise were evil portents of coming dangers. But their practical impact before 1648 was still relatively slight.

However, as a result of the ambiguity in the attitude of the dominant class of the Polish gentry, Jews found themselves ever more dependent on the good will of the monarchs, the magnates, and their officials. At the same time, the declining power of the burghers as a class, and the diminution of the political influence of the cities, despite their progressive Polonization, greatly weakened the group which was most consistently anti-Jewish. On the whole, the various checks and balances operating in the so-called *demokracja szlachecka* (nobles' democracy) which characterized Poland before 1650, enabled Jewish leaders in a variety of ways to play one social force against another, and, with the aid of a still largely benevolent monarchy and aristocracy, to maintain their people's upward mobility in the country. In any case, Moses

Isserles' aforementioned statement that Jews lived far more peacefully in Poland than in any other [Christian] country, was still true in the first half of the seventeenth century, with the sole exception of the burgeoning Jewish settlement in Holland.

Most significant during that period was the development of the great central organs of Jewish self-government. Beginning in the 1580s, the Council of Three (later Four) Lands and, after its separation in 1623, the Council of Provinces in Lithuania furnished the Jewish communities throughout the land with powerful weapons for their self-defense, as well as for the advancement of their internal moral and intellectual resources.

In sum, the Jewish community of the dual Commonwealth could now assume the communal and cultural leadership of Ashkenazic, and in some respects of all world, Jewry. Little did the leaders realize that, because of the lopsided social evolution of the country as a whole, over which they had no control, they were living on a volcano which could at any moment erupt and endanger the very survival of the Jewish people in East-Central Europe.

LXIX

TERRITORIAL AND
NUMERICAL EXPANSION

IN CONTRAST to the relative stability in the legal status of Polish-Lithuanian Jewry, the quantitative and qualitative changes in the Jews' socioeconomic structure during the reign of the first two Vasas were enormous. True, tendencies in this direction had become visible in the Jagiellon period, and were strengthened under the short but dynamic leadership of Báthory. But the rapid development and expansion of the settlement area, the great adjustments to a changing economy, and the vast progress in population size and popular education under Sigismund III and Wladislaw IV made that sixty-year span one of the most fertile periods in the history of East-European Jewry. Although not quite reaching the heights of intellectual achievement represented by the outstanding sixteenth-century savants Solomon Luria and Moses Isserles, Polish-Jewish culture now witnessed a considerable broadening of its intellectual base among the masses, and the numerical growth of its leadership through an array of high-ranking jurists and teachers.

Of great significance was the expansion of the territory under the control of the Commonwealth. The Polish regime increasingly realized the importance of its access to the Baltic Sea. Invoking historical precedents going back to the tenth century, it tried to achieve full control not only over the Prussian territories, both royal and ducal, but also over Pomerania to the west and Livonia (Courland, Latvia, and Estonia) to the northeast. In this endeavor to secure the *dominium maris Baltici,* the Commonwealth encountered the powerful rivalry of Denmark, Sweden, and Muscovy, and its early military successes proved very short-lived. But it thus helped to open new areas to some enterprising Jews. Their number was never large, and in most places they met the bitter hostility of native burghers and churchmen, whether Lutheran or Catholic. Yet they were gradually able to establish footholds which survived the retreat of the Polish armies from most of these territories. In one of the occupied areas, that of Courland, the new settlements proved relatively durable.

More important was the military expansion under Báthory and Sigismund III into the eastern and southeastern areas, previously occupied by the Muscovite Empire. Those areas included vast open spaces once governed by the medieval Kievan state but subsequently greatly depopulated as a result of the Mongolian and Tatar invasions. There great new opportunities opened up, not only to individual colonists of various ethnic origins, from all parts of Poland-Lithuania and other neighboring lands, but particularly to the Polish aristocracy, which took over large territories and converted them into vast latifundia. These estates often resembled moderate-sized feudal baronies from which the lords pursued independent military and foreign policies. Magnates like Prince Konstanty Wasyl Ostrogski, Jeremi Wiśniowiecki, and Stanisław Koniecpolski ruled over subject populations of up to 200,000 souls each; commanded private armies of up to 15,000 men (equal in size to Báthory's expeditionary force against Moscow and comparable to Poland's total army of some 25,000 men during most of Sigismund III's reign); established and built up scores of new towns; and engaged in mass production of grain and lumber for export to foreign lands.

These developments were further stimulated by the population explosion in western and southern Europe, which created a tremendous need for imports of grain, cattle, skins, furs, and a variety of lumber products. To satisfy that hunger for raw materials the Polish aristocrats, together with their counterparts in other areas of East-Central Europe, became exporters on a large scale. To a great extent the task of organizing and increasing agricultural production, and of channeling surplus materials to the western markets, was entrusted to Jews. Thus was opened a road toward new economic activities on a scale theretofore undreamed of by the downtrodden Ashkenazic communities of Germany and other western lands in the Late Middle Ages. It was this dynamic evolution which ultimately determined the socioeconomic structure and evolving modern image of East-European Jewry.

INTENSIFICATION OF JEWISH SETTLEMENT

Begun by the last two Jagiellons and Stephen Báthory, Poland-Lithuania's geographic expansion continued unabated under Sigismund III and Wladislaw IV. Before the great crisis of 1648–60, the Polish kings reigned over a territory larger than any state in Europe other than Muscovy. Although their conquests were of but short duration—twice after reaching Moscow, the Polish armies were forced to retreat to the original borders—Poland-Lithuania's expansion immediately opened the gates for Jewish soldiers, artisans, and particularly army contractors. These individuals were often followed by permanent settlers, who ultimately established new Jewish communities, some of which shared the fate of the Polish conquerors, however, and disappeared when the Poles were forced out of a particular region.

In the western direction the Poles largely reclaimed territories over which at one time or another they had exercised a measure of sovereignty. Apart from the duchy of Prussia, which, though its actual administration was entrusted to the electors of Brandenburg, remained a feudal possession of Poland, with its elector-duke obliged to pay homage to the Polish king, Poland also established an overlordship over Pomerania, including the city and district of Szczecin (Stettin). The duchy, which had once belonged to the kingdom of Mieszko I, the founder of the Piast dynasty of tenth-century Poland, was allowed to be increasingly Germanized under its own originally Slavonic dukes, who now came under the sway of Poland. (This situation was in contrast to the case of Silesia, which, because of the pro-Habsburg orientation of Sigismund III, was left under the control of the Habsburg emperors, despite the presence there of a large Polish-speaking population.) Jews may have lived in parts of Pomerania before 1261, but the first authentic record of them there dates only from that year. Various laws affecting Jews attest their presence in Pomerania in the fourteenth century, but for the most part they were too few in number to form regular communities. In 1481, for example, Bogislav (Bogislaus) X (under whose reign Pomerania was reunited after a break of two centuries), in his general charter of Jewish rights, enumer-

ated by name only 9 Jews living in Damm near Szczecin, 5 in
Pyritz (Pyrzyce), 5 in Gartz, and 3 in Greifenhagen (Gryfino), but
was silent about Stargard and Szczecin itself. In this decree, written in quaint German, the Jews were not only admitted to the
country for an initial six-year period, against the payment of unspecified taxes, but were also allowed to lend money on pledges,
except on objects obviously secured by the borrower through robbery or sacrilege. The duke also provided that litigations between
Christians and Jews should be adjudicated exclusively by him or
one of his representatives, and that admissible evidence against a
Jewish defendant could be derived only from the testimony of two
Christians and two Jews. Most importantly, despite the continued
drive of the Pomeranian burghers to secure exclusive staple rights
over all goods arriving in their cities, the Jews living under ducal
protection were given express permission to sell their merchandise freely to any buyer. Of importance also was the provision that
Jews could not be sued in any locality except their own, a provision which was modified in 1490 only by including the Jews of
Pyritz among those whom one could summon to appear before a
court in Szczecin. According to Leopold Donath, a considerable
number of Jews lived at that time in numerous smaller towns
throughout Pomerania. However, this contention is not supported
by the extant documentary evidence.[1]

In 1492–93, to be sure, Jews were accused of desecrating the
host and were banished from the country by the same Duke Bogislav X who, in 1491, had married the Jagiellon princess Anna to
reinforce his Polish allegiance. However, here as elsewhere, the decree of expulsion was not completely implemented, and individual
Jews soon reappeared in the local documents. Yet, despite the impact of Polish suzerainty, the Jewish settlement in Pomerania appears to have remained very small, owing to the continued resistance of the local, largely Germanized population. Even the
adoption of Protestantism by the majority of the inhabitants did
not reduce anti-Jewish feeling. As we recall, a Jewess who came
to Szczecin in 1558 to collect her loans was rather harshly treated
by the local authorities at the bidding of the Protestant clergy.
A truly new chapter of Jewish life in Pomerania began only after
1637 (more effectively, after 1653), following the death of Bogis-

lav XIV, the last native duke, when West Pomerania came under
the full domination of the electors of Brandenburg.[2]

This generally intolerant policy also extended to ducal Prussia.
Although still recognizing Polish suzerainty (the last public homage to the Polish king was paid by Elector-Duke Frederick William to Wladislaw IV in 1641), the duchy maintained its more or
less negative attitude toward all strangers, particularly Jews. Economically, the Prussian cities were greatly dependent on their
trade with Gdańsk. Nevertheless, in contrast to Gdańsk, which admitted foreigners to residence—especially English, Scottish, and
above all Dutch, traders—and at least allowed Jews to visit the
city for fairs and on other occasions, the Prussian towns, led by
Königsberg (Królewiec, in 1946 renamed Kaliningrad), for a long
time tried to keep foreign visitors to a minimum. Many municipal
statutes specifically provided that foreigners could trade exclusively with local merchants. There were, of course, good reasons
for this difference between Gdańsk and the Prussian cities. The
economy of Gdańsk depended to a major extent on the sale and
shipment of grain, handled by the Dutch. It has been estimated
that in most years 80 percent of all grain exported from Gdańsk
landed in Amsterdam; 23 percent was needed for the provision of
that city alone, while the rest was shipped to other parts of the
Low Countries, Spain, England, and other lands. Yet, as we recall,
even Gdańsk, along with Toruń and Elbląg, though parts of the
Polish Crown, managed to secure royal privileges *de non tolerandis Judaeis*. True, ducal Prussia's wall of total intolerance was
breached in 1538 and 1541 by special ducal privileges for the admission to Königsberg of two Jewish doctors, Isaac May and
Michel Abraham. The privilege for Isaac was issued at the request
of a royal councilor, who hoped that the Polish Jewish physician
might cure his ailing wife. In admitting Isaac to residence, the
duke made it clear that the new arrival must neither engage in
moneylending nor be invoked as a precedent for the settlement of
other Jews. In contrast, the 1541 privilege for Michel Abraham
was issued because the duke himself wished to employ the doctor
as his court physician; he even expected the Königsberg elders to
grant formal burghers' rights to the new settler. This decree contributed to the general relaxation of municipal restrictions in the

following years. An edict of Königsberg's three cities (that division arose from special internal conflicts in the past), dated October 25, 1566, merely provided: "Jews are forbidden to store their merchandise in the city. They also should pay a toll on their persons, as is practiced in the royal port of Gdańsk." Evidently, visits by Jews for commercial purposes were to be encouraged so long as the visitors did not infringe on the staple rights of the local burghers.[3]

However, only a year later the duke had to yield to the burghers' pressure, and in his countrywide privilege of July 14, 1567, he provided: "Henceforth Jews are not to be tolerated in the duchy. They shall not be allowed to traverse the country, beginning four weeks from this date. If found here thereafter, they shall be considered legitimate prizes and not be protected by any special letter or seal." In another ordinance, issued twelve days later, the duke emphasized that his outlawry of Jewish settlement was enacted "with the consent of His Royal Majesty of Poland, Our gracious lord and friendly uncle." This xenophobic attitude also found expression in the resolution adopted by the Diet three months later (October 21, 1567), which repeated the prohibition forbidding Jews to trade in the country, notwithstanding the anticipated interventions in their behalf by foreign powers (the resolution mistakenly refers to such an expected intervention as by the "king of Ireland") interested in securing a share in the commercial exchanges with the Lublin merchants and other Polish subjects of the Jewish and Muslim faiths. It probably was some such foreign pressure which induced the Diet to reverse itself in 1569 and to allow Jews to pass through the country. Remarkably, the intolerance of the now predominantly Lutheran burghers extended to would-be settlers belonging to the Calvinist or other Protestant sects. However, the whole area soon became the scene of many battles during the Thirty Years' War, and the trade with the Prussian cities lost much of its allure for Polish Jewish merchants. We hear, therefore, very little about Jews in that region until after ducal Prussia attained total independence from Poland in the peace treaty of Wehlau (Znamenek) in 1657. Thenceforth, Prussian Jewry shared the destiny of the Jews of the electorate of Brandenburg, then under the reign of the mercantilisticminded Great Elector, Frederick William. His regime marked a turning point for the Jewries of Berlin and Frankfort on the Oder, as well as Königsberg and the Pomeranian cities under the rapidly rising star of the electorate, which was soon to become the kingdom of Prussia.[4]

Of far greater importance were the new opportunities for Jewish settlement opened up by the Commonwealth's eastward expansion. As early as the first half of the sixteenth century, Jews were recorded in Winnica (Vinnitsa; 1532), Bar (1541), and Między-bórz (1547); soon thereafter also in Bratslav (Bracław; 1551). But under the regime of Sigismund II Augustus and Stephen Báthory the possibilities for the expansion of the Polish dominion seemed almost unlimited. As a candidate Báthory, through his representative Giorgio Blandrata, promised the Polish gentry, on November 15, 1574, to protect all its liberties and to recapture all occupied lands from Moscow. In some respects, these promises were contradictory. Later observers often blamed the Polish "liberties" for the country's failure to realize its great imperial dreams. Even the foreigner Adam Contzen, father confessor to Elector Maximilian of Bavaria and himself a respected Jesuit political thinker, contended in 1620 that, if Poland had had a hereditary monarchy, it might have been able to conquer Istanbul and penetrate Asia. A similiar assertion was made by the Frenchman Jean de Laboureur de Bleranval, who in 1647, after his return from a lengthy stay at the court of the queen in Poland, published a three-volume travelogue. He claimed that Poland, with an absolute monarchy, could have become the foremost European power, which no one would have been able to resist. Even Emperor Ferdinand II, to whom Contzen's volume was dedicated, feared that an alliance between Poland and Muscovy might create a major imbalance in the European power structure. Rather than combining their forces, however, the two Slavic powers were more or less permanent enemies and, from the long-range view of history, the only question was which country would ultimately prevail. At first it looked as if Poland-Lithuania had the edge. Not only did Polish troops reach Moscow on two occasions, but Poland was able to support for a while the first false Dmitri as tsar of Muscovy (1604–1606). There was even a chance that Wladislaw IV would occupy the Muscovite throne and thus create a triple monarchy of Poland, Lithuania, and Russia, However, all these opportunities were missed, and from the mid-seventeenth century on, Moscow's ascendancy proved irresistible. A century later, Russia would take over the largest slice of partitioned Poland.[5]

Polish-Muscovite rivalry extended over the entire eastern border. One of the immediate problems was which power would succeed in inheriting the Baltic possessions long occupied by the Livonian Order of the Knights of the Cross, a counterpart and ally of the Teutonic Order. Its dissolution in 1561 gave rise to protracted wars among the four neighbors—Poland, Muscovy, Sweden, and Denmark. Under the regnant conception of the age, which did not recognize the general principle of freedom of the seas, the Baltic area could be converted into a *mare clausum* under the exclusive control of the most powerful country of the region. For a long time, Denmark exercised that control, through the tolls it collected at the main passageway through the Sund. Subsequently, Poland and Sweden began replacing Denmark, especially after Poland held on to her control over Courland (Latvian Kurzeme), while Sweden succeeded in occupying Estonia and Latvia. But ultimately they all had to give way to Russian domination of the entire eastern shore.[6]

For the Jews these were almost entirely new lands of settlement. The Livonian Order generally had been extremely intolerant. Typical of its attitude was a decree issued by Grand Master Siegfried (Zeyfridt) von Feuchtwangen in 1309. It read, in part: "For the glory of God and the honor of the Virgin, whose servants We are, We ordain . . . that no Jew, necromancer, magician, or *waydeler* [pagan priest] shall be allowed to live in this country. Anyone sheltering a person of this kind shall suffer with him." To be sure, according to later chroniclers (especially Caspar Hennenberger) and somewhat questionable tombstone inscriptions found in Jelgava (Mitau), individual Jews found their way into the area, but more as visitors and temporary residents, than as permanent settlers. Even the opportunity presented by the dissolution of the Order in 1561 was greatly restricted by the xenophobic attitude of most burghers in the cities and by the religious intolerance of the predominantly Lutheran clergy. In fact, the last grand master, Gotthard Kettler, in secularizing the Order's properties and submitting them to the overlordship of Poland, exacted on November 28, 1561 from Sigismund Augustus the promise that no Jews would be allowed either to trade or to supervise the collection of taxes and customs duties in Livonia. However, so long as Poland held sway in the region, individual Jews entered the successor provinces, often aided and abetted by the local gentry, which followed the Polish nobles' example. This was particularly the case in the duchy of Courland, of which Kettler and his successors served as dukes for several generations under Polish overlordship. The country was subdivided, however, into several autonomous regions. Bishop Johann von Münchhausen of Pilten collected substantial revenue from a residence tax he imposed upon Jewish settlers and traders. In return, as early as 1570 he granted them rights of citizenship and real estate ownership in the area. The city of Hasenpoth (Aizputen) likewise accommodated a considerable number of Jews, while Polangen (Palanga), which joined Courland rather late, brought with it a number of older Jewish settlers from the time it had been part of Lithuania.[7]

Courland's ducal government became less intolerant in the course of time. Especially under the distinguished Duke Jacob (James, sole ruler 1642–82), when Courland temporarily played an internationally significant role, Jewish commercial opportunities and rights of settlement greatly increased. Jacob pursued an ambitious mercantilistic policy and even ventured into the noteworthy colonial enterprise of acquiring possession of the island of Tobago in the West Indies in 1645, and of a district in West-African Gambia in 1651. (Both colonies were lost by his successor Frederick Casimir's treaty with Charles II of England in 1684.) During his reign, Jacob had many dealings with the Dutch, particularly their West India Company, and with the newly created Companha Geral do Comércio do Brasil, which, as we recall, was to a large extent founded by Dutch Jews and Portuguese New Christians. However, these extraordinary undertakings exceeded the human and natural resources of the duchy. As a contemporary observer noted, Jacob "was too wealthy and powerful to be a duke, but not sufficiently wealthy and powerful to be a king." After his death in 1682, the mercantilistic policies of the government continued for a while, and in 1688 a Hamburg Jew, Jacob Abensur, then twenty-seven years old, was appointed by Duke Frederick Casimir as Director of Commerce and Marine of Courland. This was but one of many empty titles achieved by Abensur in his stormy career, which culminated in his conversion to Catholicism in 1706. In Courland, imperial ambitions gradually gave way to all sorts of compromises with the existing power structure, in which the gentry, the cities, and the Church fought one another with growing bitterness. On the whole, here as in Poland, Jews had more friends among the nobles than among the other classes and, for the most part, had a hard struggle to maintain themselves in the cities. Under varying pressures, Duke Ferdinand, whose political weakness did not afford him sufficient security in his own duchy and for a long time forced him to rule from a safe distance in Gdańsk, was persuaded in 1714 to issue a decree ordering the Jews to leave the country within six weeks, under severe sanctions. This decree was not fully carried out, however. Yet Jews played a minor role in various parts of the duchy until it was taken over by Russia during the partitions of Poland.[8]

Even less enduring were the Jews' efforts to establish themselves in what was to become Latvia and Estonia. Here Polish rule lasted a very short time. Despite recurrent efforts to regain the area, the Polish kings were forced to surrender control to Sweden and Moscow. Later the entire Baltic coast northeast of Courland came under Muscovite control. In 1561, when most of Livonia was occupied by Poland, the local authorities exacted from Sigismund Augustus the promise that even the provisioning of the Polish troops would not be entrusted to the "malicious Jewish people." Subsequently, in 1581, the region's most important city, Riga, demanded from the Polish rulers that they not "contaminate or injure the citizens with their [the Jews'] unchristian usury and business transactions." Riga also shared with the rest of Livonia the original Polish pledge that Jews would not be allowed to trade or to control the collection of customs duties. Even after Riga's formal annexation by Poland in 1581, the opposition to trading by foreigners—not only by the Jews but also by the Scots, the English, and particularly the Dutch—was persistently voiced. Although the city secured, in 1596, a royal decree forbidding Jews and other foreigners to trade in it, the municipality later had many occasions to protest against Poland's failure to live up to these enactments. Between 1592 and 1598, and again in 1611, it even sent special delegations to submit its grievances to the Polish royal Council and the Diet.[9]

Like other formerly Livonian municipalities, Riga was supported by the ecclesiastical establishment, both Lutheran and Catholic. The Livonian bishop Otto Schenking, in particular, made frequent use of his official membership in the Polish Senate (for instance, in his aforementioned address at the crucial session of 1605) to speak up against the Jews. True, at times Jews found special protectors among the Polish officials; for example, Prince Krzysztof Radziwiłł (1585–1640). Radziwiłł served as Polish high commissioner and commanding general in the area, and his prestige was to rise greatly after his victory over the Swedes at Jeglava in 1615. Yet when he tried to intervene with the city of Riga in favor of some Jews from his private town of Birzai (Birż), the city council of Riga invoked its established liberties, which included the following provision:

No Jew shall have the right to trade here. They [the Jews] are in general a blasphemous, pernicious, and prevaricating people which in many lands in Christendom is not tolerated at all or else is segregated and restricted by certain distinguishing marks. Hence, if some Birzai Jews should secure certain rights [here], all Jews throughout Lithuania and Poland would appear under a single name and pretend to be Birzai residents. For this reason Your Princely Grace ought to allow the city of Riga to maintain its liberties.

In short, the persistent opposition of the burghers and the Church made any long-term residence for Jews sufficiently unpleasant to keep the Jewish population to a minimum. Native intolerance soon combined with the generally exclusive policies of the Swedish regime to bring about a fairly effective enforcement of the decree of expulsion of Jews issued by the Swedish conquerors after they took over the city in 1621. In fact, Gustavus Adolphus, in his treaty with the surrendering Livonians, stated explicitly that "no Jews or foreigners shall be permitted to live in the country to the burghers' detriment." Hence Joseph Solomon Delmedigo, who spent, on one of his numerous journeys, a short time in Riga before settling for a while as court physician of the Radziwiłł family in Troki, was certainly justified in complaining, in 1623, that he was living "in a country totally devoid of Jewish learning." The Swedish regime on the eastern Baltic shore generally reflected, from 1621 to 1710, the home country's intolerant attitude, which barred any Jewish settlement there until the middle of the eighteenth century. Only occasional Jewish visitors were admitted to Riga for business reasons. In order to control them more effectively, the city established a special "Jewish inn" (first recorded in 1645), where all such visitors had to reside. They could trade only with local merchants. A simple accusation that some of them had acquired furs directly from Muscovite traders led to the incarceration of twenty Jews in 1645. They were released only after it was proved that they had used local intermediaries.[10]

No less intolerant were the Muscovites in those parts of Livonia which they occupied. Ivan the Terrible, who in 1558 first conquered Narva and thus opened a line of communication to the Western lands, revealed his hatred of Jews when he conquered Polotsk five years later. According to contemporary reports, he forced all Jewish inhabitants of the city to embrace the Greek Orthodox faith; 300 staunch resisters were simply drowned in the Dvina. (All captured Catholic churchmen were beheaded.) To be sure, Poland reconquered the city in 1579 and enabled many Jews to come out of hiding; many forced converts were permitted to return to Judaism. But in the formerly Livonian possessions, the Russian authorities had little difficulty in barring Jews from settlement. It was really not until the few surviving Jewish individuals were joined by many immigrants from the Polish-Lithuanian provinces occupied by Russia during the partitions of Poland that flourishing Jewish communities sprang up in Riga and other Latvian cities, as well as in the countryside.[11]

POLAND'S EASTERN DRIVE

The struggle over Livonia was essentially a side issue in Poland's imperial designs. Only the Pomeranian and Prussian harbors on the Baltic, particularly Gdańsk, were of vital importance to Poland's trade with the Western nations. The declaration by the Lithuanian chancellor Albrycht Stanisław Radziwiłł to the French mediator during the Swedish-Polish hostilities in 1656 well reflected Poland's deep national interest in the occupied Prussian territories. "No one," declared the Polish statesman, "can allow his throat to be cut." But the area from Courland to Estonia was of greater relevance for Poland's attempt to stem the Muscovite expansion than for the actual needs of the Polish economy or the country's general strategic position.

Of far greater direct significance was the forestalling of Moscow's occupation of the vast Rus territories (what is now Belorussia and the Ukraine) long incorporated in the Grand Duchy of Lithuania. Ever since January 1547, when Ivan IV was crowned tsar of all Russia, Moscow's drive to conquer these territories was a fundamental feature of the foreign policy of the growing Muscovite Empire. This westward expansion threatened the very existence of Lithuania and, indirectly, of Poland. Hence, the menace of the eastern neighbor overshadowed all other concerns of the dual Commonwealth throughout the sixteenth and seventeenth centuries. To be sure, after Ivan's death the sharp internal divisions in the Muscovite realm made possible repeated Polish efforts to regain all lost territories, a pledge exacted by the gentry from the three successful candidates to the Polish throne after the death of Sigismund Augustus: Henry of Valois, Stephen Báthory, and Sigismund III. During the Muscovite "Time of Troubles" (1603–1613) Dmitri the Pretender, placed on the tsarist throne by ambitious Polish magnates, almost turned the empire into a Polish satellite. After continued warfare in the subsequent years, the hostilities were suspended in 1619 through the fourteen-year armistice of Deulina, though Sigismund III recognized its temporary nature. With good insight, he contrasted the conditions under Russian autocracy with those under the Polish nobles' "Golden Liberty," which frequently resulted in the Diet's refusal to vote funds for the pursuit of the Muscovite Wars. He declared: "The Russians undoubtedly hope to recover their strength in a short time, which should not be too difficult for a country like theirs where discipline is very great. After having got rid of our troops, they can then turn against our country and take back everything they have now surrendered." In fact, even before the expiration of the armistice, hostilities were resumed. During this long conflict there were moments when it looked as if Sigismund's son, the future Wladislaw IV, would be crowned tsar. He was, in fact, offered the throne by a Muscovite delegation in 1610—a plan thwarted mainly by his father's egotism. Later moves in this direction were frustrated by the Vasa prince's inability to adopt the Orthodox faith. In the final, so-called Smolensk War (1632–34), Wladislaw's army had more successes than serious reverses, yet in the peace treaty of Polanowo of 1634 he renounced all claims to the Muscovite throne. However, the dispute over many borderlands, especially in the districts of Smolensk, Seversk, and Chernigov, continued unabated until the catastrophic period of 1648–60.[12]

Any eastward expansion of the dual Commonwealth added directly to the Lithuanian possessions. Most of them were inhabited by a Rus-speaking population which developed the dialects now known as Belorussian or Ukrainian. The ratio of ethnic Lithuanians to ethnic Ruthenians in the Grand Duchy of Lithuania has long been under a debate which has often reflected the nationalist biases of the respective investigators. While Jan Jakubowski, writing before the First World War, estimated that before the Union of Lublin of 1569 the two nationalities were about equal in size, though he considered that the Ruthenians were linguistically and culturally superior, the more recent Polish writer M. Łowmiański admitted that the Lithuanian proportion may not have exceeded 20 percent, while some scholars further lowered that ratio to 10 percent. Modern Soviet historians, on the other hand, have evinced a strong nationalist and imperialist bias in claiming that practically the entire lower class of peasants and urban proletarians in the Lithuanian grand duchy throughout its independence consisted of Rus peoples yearning to be united with their eastern conationals.[13]

Be this as it may, the Union of Lublin brought about fundamental changes in the make-up of Lithuania. On the one hand, large areas of the Grand Duchy were separated from Lithuania and incorporated into the Polish Crown. At the same time, the progressive Polonization of the Lithuanian nobles and burghers

was further accelerated after the Union of Brest (Brześć) and the
establishment of the Uniate Church (1596), as well as the general
Catholic Restoration, though the peasant masses still adhered to
their ancestral language and culture, Lithuanian or Ruthenian.
All this had a strong effect on the position of Jews. While even
before 1569 certain Lithuanian Jewish communities began playing an important role in the entire Commonwealth, none of them,
except perhaps that of Brest, compared in size, affluence, or intellectual vigor, with the major Jewish communities of the Polish
Crown. The break occasioned by the expulsion of all Jews from
Lithuania by Grand Duke Alexander in 1495, though lasting only
eight years, doubtless put a damper on the expansion of Jewish
settlements in the country. Even Vilna, as we recall, was slow to
develop into a major center of Jewish life and thought. Whether
we join the school of "federalists," who consider the status of the
two parts of the Commonwealth as practically equal; or go along
with the "annexationists," for whom the Union of Lublin was
but a camouflaged take-over of Lithuania by the Polish Crown,
there is little doubt that it was after 1569 that the largest influx of
Jews into Lithuania took place.[14]

However, there was a difference between the areas which remained Lithuanian after the Union and included the older Jewries of Brest, Pinsk, Grodno, Vilna, and Slutsk, and those located
along the embattled eastern border, where Jewish communities
were for the most part established only after the occupation by
Polish troops. Remarkably, most of these areas attracted many
Jews, not only to the major cities but also to numerous small towns
and hamlets, although their hold upon their new abodes was often
rather tenuous. Border cities like Smolensk were apt to change
hands from time to time. From the outset the Jews must have
realized that if the Muscovites were to return, as they did sooner
or later, they would suffer even more severely than the rest of the
population. Suffice it to mention that in 1656, when the Muscovite
armies occupied Mstislav, they virtually destroyed the city and all
its inhabitants. The development of Jewish settlements was also
long impeded by the prevalence of dense forests in most of the
eastern districts. While gradually developing into a major source
of raw materials for the export trade, in which Jews actively par-

ticipated, these forests usually reduced the available means of transportation to the few existing waterways. The relative lack of communication accounted for the great local divergences in legal practice and, more broadly, for the preservation of local languages, legal customs, and social mores. For this reason, even the Lithuanian statutes had only limited validity in parts of the country; they were often replaced by the customary laws prevailing in each region and locality.[15]

A telling example of the vicissitudes of the Jewish communities in the eastern areas is offered by the city and district of Mogilev (or Mohilev). Jews were first mentioned in the city in 1522 in connection with Sigismund I's three-year tax farming concession to Michael Ezofowicz. In 1583, Affras Rachmaelovich is recorded as having conducted a large import and export business there, through Lublin and Riga. Yet the Jewish settlement in Mogilev still was so precarious that two years later the burghers formally petitioned Stephen Báthory to prohibit the admission of Jews to their city. Not before the end of the sixteenth century did Jews begin to settle in the area in increasing numbers, giving rise to a series of legal enactments, both favorable and unfavorable, by successive kings. For instance, in 1611 and 1617 (and probably also in the intervening years) a Jew, Eliasz, and a nobleman, Maciej Suchodolski, held a lease on the entire revenue from customs duties. They were informed by a high official that only persons bringing in goods from foreign lands—especially from the Muscovite Empire, "where the roads are open to all"—were subject to the payment of import duties, but that goods purchased within the Commonwealth were to be duty-free. In 1613, on orders from the military, the city had to erect new fortifications, which involved the destruction of many houses belonging to Jews and nobles. Of interest also is that the local butchers' guild forbade Jewish and Christian butchers alike to acquire cattle outside the city limits. The main object of contention between Jews and burghers, however, was the fact that some Jews established residence in the *rynek* (the market square in the center of town), the burghers consistently agitating for the removal of all Jews to the main Jewish quarter, in an outlying section of the city. They attained that objective in 1626.[16]

In a remarkable document of February 4, 1676, King John III Sobieski referred to earlier enactments dated 1605, 1619, 1633, 1634, 1637, 1661, 1664, 1666, 1669, and 1672. Although some of these were intrinsically contradictory, he decided:

In the city of Mogilev there exist many *jurydyki* to the prejudice of the Magdeburg law which serves the city. Hence, with this Our letter We wish to declare all of these separate jurisdictions null and void—with the exception of the areas subject to the castle and the Church—and to submit them all to the municipal jurisdiction. We add the houses of nobles and Jews situated on city land to the municipal jurisdiction, subject to all the burdens of the city of Mogilev, on a par with the other burghers. They [nobles and Jews] have to submit themselves to the city officials with respect to these plots and houses, contravention to be punished according to Our discretion. As to the Jews residing in the city of Mogilev the older laws and privileges issued by the illustrious kings, Our predecessors, in favor of the city of Mogilev clearly provided that the Jews ought not to establish shops and trade in the city itself. Yet, they have in no small measure purchased plots of land and built upon them houses in which they not only dwell but also conduct all sorts of business. We, therefore, ordain with this Our letter that the municipal council of Mogilev, acting in agreement with the [Jewish] community and not through orders of the commissioners, should assign it lands in the suburb in exchange for those held by Jews living inside the wall.

Since before the catastrophe of 1648 Mogilev had developed into a major urban center, rivaling with its 7,000 to 8,000 inhabitants the other major Lithuanian cities (except Vilna), the numerous restrictions heaped upon Jews there greatly served to impede the growth of their settlement, not only in the city proper but also in the entire Mogilev district. Hence, they could not fully participate in the relatively speedy recovery which followed the city's destruction by the invading Muscovite armies in 1654–56. The same held doubly true for incipient settlements like that of Bobrujsk, where the beginnings of Jewish community life were cut short by the catastrophic years, so aptly designated by the popular equation with the "Deluge." [17]

Even worse was the fate of Jews in the important city of Vitebsk. Apart from leaseholds granted here, too, to Michael Ezofowicz in 1522, we hear of individual Jews sporadically appearing in the city from the 1550s on. True, in his approval of the city's privilege in 1597, Sigismund III stated that the Vitebsk burghers should live under the provisions of the Magdeburg law, and that no Jews should be admitted to permanent residence. Yet some Jewish residents and long-term visitors appear in subsequent records. In 1627 the palatine Szymon Sanguszko even permitted the Jews to erect a synagogue in the city or its outskirts. He invoked precedents from earlier decrees of palatines, and vaguely claimed that Jews had had their own houses of worship there in earlier times. More broadly, in 1636 Wladislaw IV expressly approved the Jews' right to settle and trade in Vitebsk, at the request of "the royal servants" Samuel and Lazar Mojżeszowicz (Moiseievich). But before the Jewish community was able to strike deep roots in the city, most of its members (some of whom had actively participated in the defense against the Muscovite invaders in 1654) were deported to the interior of the empire (Kazan, Moscow, and so forth) and their property was presented to various Vitebsk churches.[18]

IN THE SOUTHEAST

In contrast, the provinces severed from the Lithuanian grand duchy by the Union of Lublin benefited immediately from subjection to Polish law and administration. In Volhynia, western Podolia, and Podlasie some of the older communities grew in number, affluence, and cultural strength, so that they speedily rivaled the long-established communities of Great Poland, Little Poland, and Red Russia. At the same time, smaller settlements mushroomed all over the provinces. This growth was soon acknowledged by Jewish leadership, when Volhynia was admitted to the Polish Council as the fourth "land," on a par with the original three. As early as the sixteenth century, Volhynia could boast of such great rabbis as Solomon Luria, who resided for a while in Ostrog; while Vladimir (Włodzimierz), Dubno, Rovno, and above all Łuck, assumed great national and international importance. Running contrary to the general evolution of the region, the leading city of Podolia, Kamenets (Kamieniec), managed to secure privileges denying admission to Jews, but the municipality had to concede their right to settle in suburban territories.[19]

The Polish-Lithuanian conquests on the southeastern borders

quickly opened up vast territories for Jewish settlement, particularly in the districts of Bratslav and Kiev. As early as 1596, Piotr
Grabowski advocated large-scale colonization of the eastern lands.
He was certain that, prompted by *zelus Dei,* greed, or the quest for
adventure, many people would be ready to emigrate to the underpopulated new areas. Grabowski did not mention Jews, and his
emphasis on zeal for God reflected the missionary objective of
converting the Orthodox masses to the Catholic or Uniate Church,
in the spirit of the Union of Brest concluded in that year. But
the general tenor of his argument indicated that he wished to see
all segments of the Polish population participate in his grandiose
colonizing scheme. Numerous Jews, too, realized the novel economic opportunities of going east. Though it is possible that small
groups of Jews had survived the general destruction of Kievan
Russia, the seventeenth-century Jewish settlements were essentially recruited from new arrivals. To be sure, the long-accepted
assumption that, because of frequent Tatar raids, the countryside
around Kiev and Bratslav was almost totally depopulated, and
that even the castles dotting the landscape were largely abandoned,
has had to be revised in the light of more recent exploration. Yet
there is no question that few Jews lived in that area before 1569.
The intensive colonization after that date is well illustrated by the
proliferation of recorded Jewish settlements, the contrast between
the southeastern provinces and Volhynia-Podolia being quite
pronounced. According to Samuel Ettinger's careful computation, Podolia's 9 known Jewish communities in 1569 doubled in
number in the following eight decades. In Volhynia, the 13 communities of 1569 increased to 46 by 1648, or by some 250 percent.
In contrast, the Bratslav district seems to have had but 2 communities in 1569; they increased to 18, or by 800 percent, before
1648. In the district of Kiev, where no organized Jewish community is known to have existed after the fall of Kievan Russia,
the 32 communities recorded by 1648 marked a new beginning.
Writing in 1651, the well-informed Frenchman Guillaume Le
Vasseur le Sieur de Beauplan could even mention "Manupo, a
pitiful castle, upon a mountain called *Baba.* All the inhabitants
are *Jews,* and there cannot be above sixty houses." This sudden
upsurge is the more noteworthy as the later trend in these four

provinces was somewhat reversed—undoubtedly as a result of the catastrophic years 1648–60, from which the southeastern Jewries did not completely recover before the partitions of Poland. As estimated by Ettinger, the percentages of increase for the period 1648–1765 were for Podolia, 81; Volhynia, 94; Bratslav, 48; Kiev (in a smaller area), 67.[20]

Perhaps in anticipation of this upsurge, the government seems to have ordered a minor, yet characteristic, distinction in the treatment of the oath of fealty rendered by local Jews in the respective areas. To force the hand of the magnates and nobles in the Lithuanian grand duchy, Sigismund Augustus, after preliminaries extending over seven years, convoked the grand Sejm of 1569 and ordered all dignitaries and deputies of the grand duchy to appear in person. Though many refused to attend, and were prepared to face the threatened penalties, the Sejm adopted the resolution proclaiming the union of the two countries. Subsequently, Volhynia, Podolia, and Podlasie, as well as the districts of Bratslav and Kiev, were declared integral parts of the Polish Crown; the nobles being invited personally to take an oath of allegiance to the Polish Crown, rather than as hitherto to the grand duchy. In addition the burghers, Jews, and Tatars were ordered to appear at local castles and take a similar oath of loyalty. While in Łuck the official record of June 23, 1569, briefly listed "the Jews of Łuck; [of] the Rabbanite community, Pczolka, Jeeło, Moszko, Szenko, Morduchaj have declared in behalf of themselves and their whole community; [of] the Karaite community, Bat'ko, Hoszwa, Misan, Szanko, Wołczko have declared in behalf of themselves and their whole community," in the case of the more recently annexed communities of Bratslav and Winnica, it appears that all Jews had to appear in person to take that oath. As far as the Winnica ceremony was concerned, the official document dated June 16, 1569, mentions first the leader (*naprzod*) Habram Juryczyn, and follows it with the fully spelled-out names of 14 additional oath-taking Jews (Izrael Strilin, Habram Marduchowicz, Habram Slomicz, Jachim Judicz, Chanan Jakowowicz, Smoil Harchonowicz, Habram Izaczkowicz, Chaczkil Isaczkowicz, Mair Morduchajowicz, Mosko Jakowowicz, Dawid Judicz, Sloma Dziwlik, Jessiman [probably Joselman] Jessimanowicz, Diran Majerowicz).[21]

The rapid territorial expansion of Jews into Poland's southeastern areas was the result of both the new economic opportunities opened to all settlers and of the relative stability of the Jews' political status. We shall see how much this colonization contributed to the economic restratification of Polish and Lithuanian Jewry during the eight decades from 1569 to 1648, and beyond. Legally and politically the Polish Crown made a strenuous effort to secure approval of the annexation from the various classes of the Lithuanian-Rus population (except the largely inarticulate peasant masses), by placing them on a par with their respective compatriots in the Polish Crown. The nobility, in particular, was greatly attracted by the vast "liberties" enjoyed by their Polish counterparts. Even the magnates, who stood to lose some of their political hegemony to the lower gentry, were more than indemnified by the enormous economic potential of their newly acquired latifundia, where ultimately they would also be able to reassert their political supremacy. We recall the vast landholdings accumulated by Prince Konstanty Wasyl Ostrogski, whose possessions covered almost one-third of the entire Volhynian area, while Aleksander Wiśniowiecki before long accumulated landed property, including townships, hamlets, and castles, with a population of some 200,000 souls. On their part, most burghers were pacified by the maintenance of their traditional liberties and extensive self-government under the Magdeburg law. Jews, too, were from the outset promised equality with their coreligionists in the Polish Crown. In fact, legally, Volhynian and Podolian Jews had even earlier begun to be assimilated to those of neighboring Red Russia. Now a sweeping decree issued by Báthory, on December 1, 1576, for both the Rabbanites and Karaites in Łuck and the rest of Volhynia, provided that all Jews residing in royal or private cities be judged in accordance with Polish (not Magdeburg) law, and that the palatinate courts be conducted close to the synagogue and with the participation of Jewish elders. Jews were also to be allowed to engage in all crafts, as well as in retail and wholesale trade, against the payment of the usual tolls. "If any Jew should turn out to be a transgressor and fail to conduct himself according to their law, they [the Jewish elders] should be permitted to banish him from their midst with the aid of Our officials, with the exception only of a Jew willing to accept the Christian faith." [22]

It may be appropriate in this context to consider briefly the position of the Karaite sect in Poland-Lithuania. The origins of its settlement in the Commonwealth are shrouded in the mist of legend, which many nineteenth-century Karaite historians, especially Mordecai b. Joseph Sultański and Abraham b. Samuel Firkovitch, accepted as historical fact and adorned with additional details, including some palpably inaccurate chronological data. More critical scholars have assumed that Karaites first came to Lithuania and its Rus provinces late in the fourteenth century, at the invitation of the grand dukes. It is indeed quite likely that Vitovt, in granting in 1388 his well-known privilege to the Jews of Lithuania, had included the Karaites in that designation. He referred particularly to the community in the city of Troki near Vilna, which at that time served as the grand ducal residence. There the Karaites were more or less permanently to outnumber the Rabbanites. In fact, according to Sigismund I's decree of 1507, which referred to three older privileges granted to Jews (of both denominations), the Troki Karaites enjoyed the rights of burghers under Magdeburg law, and as such regarded their settlement as independent of the city of Troki. It appears that the Rabbanites lived together with other ethnic groups in the Christian section. Before long, however, the Karaite community of Łuck, claiming similar early origins, exceeded in importance the Troki community, which in its early years may have derived much strength from many small Karaite settlements along the Lithuanian boundary with the territories of the Teutonic Order, settlements possibly established by the grand duke in order to fortify the border against the Knights' incursions. These attacks diminished in importance, however, after the Polish victory at the Battle of Grunwald (Grünfelde, 1410). Now it was Łuck's turn to play a great role in Poland's military history. There the Rabbanites and Karaites long lived in harmony and often jointly confronted the enmity of the Christian burghers. Yet at Volhynia's incorporation in the Polish Crown in 1569, their squabbles had to be adjusted by commissioners sent out by the famous Lublin Sejm. Soon thereafter (April 24, 1570), Sigismund Augustus issued a privilege for both groups of Jews of Łuck which included the following statements:

We were shown the privilege of the Jews of Łuck. . . . While still under the suzerainty of the Grand Duchy of Lithuania they enjoyed the same liberties as the Łuck burghers, including the exemption from Lithuanian tolls, because they carried the same burdens on a par with the burghers. . . . We maintain these privileges in force. Since at the recent Lublin Sejm We have also extended that liberty to the burghers in the Polish Crown . . . it appears appropriate that We should grant the same liberty to the Jews of Łuck who carry all the duties together with the burghers. . . . We herewith enact this privilege for both the Rabbanites and the Karaites.

The rights and duties of the two groups of Łuck Jews were spelled out in greater detail in Báthory's decree of December 1, 1576, which remained the fundamental law of the local community to the end of the Commonwealth. Before the final partitions of Poland the Karaites could indeed boast in a memorandum they submitted to the Quadrennial Diet in 1790 that

having been brought to Lithuania in the reign of Vitold [Vitovt], and to Poland in the reign of Jagiello, we have stayed these few hundred years in the capital of Volhynia, Łuck (Lutsk), and in Troki, Poniewież, and Nowe Miasto (New Town) in the Grand Duchy of Lithuania. We are proud of the fact that through all this long time of our stay in Poland—albeit our *fortune* is *scanty* and many of us live from the work of our hands—nobody has been able to prove us guilty of ruffianism or larceny. Our fidelity and friendship to the Polish nation have long been known.[23]

Similar arguments were advanced in the privileges granted to the Jews of the smaller city of Bar, which in 1622 had a burghers' population of some 300 families, or 1,500 souls. In 1615–16 Jews were granted equal rights with the burghers and enjoyed the same exemption from various imposts, in return for performing military services. In 1646 Wladislaw IV confirmed the old privileges of the Bar Jews, including their right to trade freely—also in open shops and cattle markets—to manage inns, to distill and sell liquor, and so forth. The king also specified that they were allowed to maintain a synagogue, a cemetery, a bathhouse, and a fountain. In another decree, of 1647, the king also explicitly permitted a Bar

Jew to purchase a dwelling for himself and his offspring, subject only to the payment of the usual imposts. At the other extreme, the ancient city of Kiev, whose Jewish community antedated any other in the region, now like Kamenets, kept Jews out of the city proper, though not of its environs.[24]

Perhaps the greatest change brought about in the Jews' status by the incorporation of the southeastern provinces, was in the realm of their judicial authority. Before 1569 we have few records of the exercise of such authority even in Volhynia, where most Jews seem to have taken their litigations to Gentile courts. Nor do we hear of any *judices Judaeorum* there before the Union of Lublin. Now, in the very year 1569, the Volhynian palatine Prince Aleksander Czartoryski secured from Sigismund Augustus a special decree (dated August 9) submitting all Jews of the province to the palatine's jurisdiction. While addressed principally to the officials of Łuck, Vladimir (Włodzimierz), and Kremenets (Krzemieniec), the royal emphasis on equal treatment with the older provinces of the Crown as a rule applied to the Jews of all newly annexed provinces. Thenceforth, in their internal controversies Jewish parties were to repair to Jewish courts, while litigations involving non-Jews were to be adjudicated by the subpalatinate courts, as in Lwów and other older Polish areas. Remarkably, in one of the younger cities, Pereyaslav (on the more exposed left bank of the Dnieper), Jews continued to live under the Magdeburg law on a par with the burghers, according to an agreement between the two groups made in 1621 and confirmed by Sigismund III on March 27, 1623. This seems to have been regarded as a concession to the Jews, who for this reason had to extend a sizable loan to the city—although elsewhere they usually preferred to be judged, like the nobles, under the provisions of Polish law. In general, the traditional animosity of the burgher class toward Jews was at first mitigated in these upsurging territories by the vast economic opportunities open to all, the shortage of manpower, and the need of both groups to work together in developing the long-neglected economy of the region. However, in the seventeenth century the fissures between the two classes began to widen, in part for religious reasons. Numerous non-Polonized burghers there shared with the majority of peasants the profession of the Greek Orthodox faith, while many Jews were supposedly helping the nobles and clergy in promoting the Uniate religion, if not outright Catholicism, among their Gentile neighbors.[25]

Unceasing turbulence in the Rus provinces induced the Polish regime from time to time to grant to the Jews, as to other inhabitants, some tax alleviations. For example, in 1547 the Jewish community of Międzyboż (Podolia) was freed by Sigismund I from the payment of all customs duties and tolls, in view of the losses it had sustained from Tatar raiders. The same concession was repeated in 1557 by Sigismund Augustus and, once again, by Stephen Báthory in 1576. After the Union of Lublin, Sigismund Augustus went even further. In order to win over the Volhynian burghers, the Polish Diet and the king freed the Łuck Christian merchants from all tolls, including those collected domestically. The same right was extended immediately to the Jews of Łuck, "since they carry all burdens on a par with the burghers." The only exception was made for some newly introduced duties, collected at the frontiers, which the king reserved for himself and his successors. A similar decree was issued in favor of the Jewish community of Vladimir in the same year. Here an exception was made only in regard to taxes imposed upon salt and wax; but otherwise this concession was to last "forever." [26]

Needless to say, the farther away they lived from the central organs of government, the more arbitrary became the landlords' exercise of power over their possessions. A telling example was offered even before 1569, by the administration of the vast estates allotted to a renegade Muscovite general, Andrei Mikhailovich Kurbskii, who had left the court of Ivan IV and had gone over to the Polish-Lithuanian enemy. Instigated by a converted Jew named Lavrin, the Kovel (Kowel) *starosta* imprisoned Jews assembled in the local synagogue for Sabbath services, under the pretext that they were all guarantors for a guilty coreligionist. "He put them into a prison of indescribable cruelty, into a hole full of water, sealed all the rooms and cellars of their houses, and those of other Jews, and sequestered all their possessions and merchandise." When the Jews of neighboring Vladimir inquired by what right he kept the Jews in prison, the castle's official answered, "Is not a lord permitted to punish his subjects by prison terms and other penalties and even by execution? . . . Since the Jews rely upon the king, let the king come and protect them!" At first all the interventions by high officials proved unavailing. Prince Kurbskii refused to set the Jews free, even after he appeared at the Lublin Sejm of 1569 and no lesser dignitaries than the chancellor of the realm and the marshal (speaker) of the Sejm interceded in their behalf. Only a direct order from the king finally forced his hand, and he had to release the Jews, who had firmly refused to pay the ransom of 500 shock groschen demanded by Lavrin. Such excesses by high-handed aristocrats occurred from time to time in later years as well. However, their abuse of power, quite frequent with regard to their Christian serfs, was mitigated in the case of Jews because of the great benefits the landlords de-rived from the services of their Jewish administrators, tax farmers, and leaseholders of liquor distilleries and inns. We shall see how much this intricate alliance of many leading Jews, and their nu-merous underlings, with the often absentee landlords, helped to antagonize the serf masses against both. At times a self-seeking landlord, or one of his officials, actually appeared in the defense of "his" Jew in either a criminal prosecution or a civil litigation.[27]

Obviously, in Lithuania as in Poland proper, Jews were some-times accused of ritual murder or other offenses against the Chris-tian religion. The extent to which even the head of the Rus dio-cese of Lwów, long under the Polish Crown, was swayed by the folkloristic belief in the blood libel, is attested by Archbishop Joannes Demetrius Solikowski's letter dated July 27, 1583, to the papal nuncio Alberto Bolognetti, in which the churchman matter-of-factly stated that he had freed a Hungarian youth from prison and deadly peril, "which had been prepared for him [the boy] by Jews." Nor could the Jews escape the impact of the religious con-troversies which, in a way different from that in most of the Polish Crown, colored the public life of the newly annexed southeastern provinces. Here, before the Union of Lublin, the large Greek Orthodox majority of the population, particularly in the rural dis-tricts, depended on the religious guidance of the metropolitans of Moscow and the patriarchs of Constantinople. To counteract this dependence, the Polish government, quite early in Sigismund III's regime (1595–1596), persuaded some Greek Orthodox leaders in the Polish areas to join in the Union of Brest and the establishment of the Uniate, or Greek Catholic, Church—which recognized the spiritual supremacy of the popes, and collaborated with the Catholic hierarchy of Poland. The politically inspired Union encountered considerable resistance among the Rus masses, however, and ultimately led to the breakup of the "Ukrainian" provinces, some of which permanently joined the Muscovite Empire. The ensuing controversies made their impact felt even before the Union of Brest. For example, in his report of November 24, 1583, to the papal secretary of state, Cardinal Bolognetti not only complained, as we recall, of the low state of Catholicism in Łuck, but also mentioned his protest to the Vilna castellan Eustachius Wołłowicz, that in some Lithuanian provinces other sects, including Protestants and Jews, had found a quiet retreat, while Catholics were often totally deprived of divine services. Wołłowicz merely promised to try to remedy the situation on his next visit to those areas.[28]

Of course, the appearance of Jesuits in Volhynia in 1569, the very year of the Union of Lublin, and the spread of their overtly propagandistic schools and colleges, might have created an alliance between Greek Orthodox and Jews, since both were subjected to strong Catholic conversionist efforts. (In 1604 the Society of Jesus reported that its members had succeeded in persuading 32 Protestants, 28 Greek Orthodox, 2 Jews, 4 Scythians (Tatars), and 1 Turk to join the Catholic Church.) Indeed, such a defensive alliance later united the Protestants and the Greek Orthodox. On July 1, 1632, during the *interregnum* after the death of Sigismund III, they formed the "Confederation of Schismatics and Heretics," which demanded, among other matters, that the wounding or killing of their ministers of plebeian origin be subject to the death penalty, on a par with that for the injury of nobles, especially since "Jews and Tatars enjoyed the same liberties." Yet the anti-Jewish feeling among the Greek Orthodox, both in Poland and Muscovy, prevented any Judeo-Rus cooperation. A noteworthy example of that feeling was the letter addressed by the patriarchs Jeremias II of Constantinople and Sylvester of Alexandria, on November 20 (30), 1582, to the powerful Orthodox magnate Prince Konstantyn Wasyl Ostrogski, concerning the adherence of their Church to the old Julian calendar and the traditional celebration of Easter. Jeremias, whose position at home was as insecure as his character was vacillating, could not bring himself to accept the new Gregorian reform of the calendar, which Stephen Báthory was enthusiastically introducing into Poland and Lithuania. Hence he and his Alexandrian colleague emphasized, apart from the obvious requirement that the Pascha be celebrated during the spring equinox, the second condition that "it not be observed on the same day on which the Jews celebrate it." Later on, during a two-year visit in Smolensk and the adjoining Polish-dominated areas (1588–90), Jeremias must have frequently given vent to his anti-Jewish sentiments. After the Union of Brest, the numerous Jews employed by the magnates in administering their estates, found themselves in the awkward position of having, as the landlords' representatives, to make recommendations for the appointment of Orthodox or Uniate parish priests. This practice seems to have given rise to hostile rumors alleging that some Jews themselves served as parish priests—a situation equally intolerable to the Jewish community and the Uniate or Orthodox churches. These tensions, deepened by antagonisms of a socioeconomic origin, were constantly building up until the catastrophe of 1648.[29]

Compared with the growing estrangement of the Jews from the Rus masses, both rural and urban, the animosities generated by bigoted Catholic preachers and teachers were, in the long run, less menacing. True, the Jesuit colleges brought with them the western Polish practice of student assaults on Jews. But these apparently were far less frequent and sanguinary in the southeastern cities than in Cracow or Lwów. Being part of a pioneering society and from the outset expected to help defend their cities against raiders, Jews often reacted with force against force and thus helped cut down the frequency of assaults. As we shall see, a number of Jews were attracted to the "Wild Steppes" (*Dzikie Pola*), the open spaces close to the Black Sea, parts of which served as Cossack settlements. It required a law forbidding Jews, as well as burghers, to join the Cossacks in their expeditions against the Tatars or the Turks. At the same time, easy coexistence with Christians led to more intergroup social relations than in other areas of Poland and Lithuania. For example, we learn of cases of Jews and burghers borrowing each others' clothing, which show

that at least part of the costume of the two classes was interchange-
able. In short, in those sparsely settled territories a new type of
Jew began evolving, different in both socioeconomic and cultural
make-up from the majority of his coreligionists living in the older
centers of the dual Commonwealth.[30]

DEMOGRAPHIC TRANSFORMATIONS

With the intensification of Jewish settlement in both the older
and the newer territories under Polish sovereignty, went a steady
growth in the Jewish population. Regrettably, the source materials
for more exact demographic estimates are extremely scanty and
unreliable. Even records relating to revenue from capitation taxes
—a mainstay of Jewish population research in other countries—
are few and far between. No general Jewish head tax was introduced into Poland until 1549, and its collection proved so burdensome and inefficient that the government increasingly tried to
delegate that task to the Jewish communal leaders. After the formation of a central organ for all Polish-Lithuanian Jewry in the
1580s, Jewish taxes were computed not on the basis of actual collections from individual households or of any detailed censuses,
but rather through negotiations between the Treasury and the
Jewish representatives. Naturally, it was to the best interest of the
government to claim as large a number of Jewish taxpayers as
possible, while the Jewish elders invariably sought to minimize it.
The outcome usually was some sort of compromise estimate of the
expected yield which may not even have approximated reality. In
their address to the Warsaw Diet of 1639 the Volhynian nobles not
unjustifiedly complained that the Jewish capitation tax had not
fulfilled its original purpose of greatly alleviating the Treasury's
financial burdens. They claimed that this purpose would have
been better served if Jews had really paid one-half a zloty per
capita, in lieu of the required one zloty or more; and that, by
accepting a lump sum settlement, the royal officials had thwarted
the original intent of the law.[31]

Nor do we possess dependable demographic data relating to the
general population in the dual Commonwealth before the partitions of 1772–95. Polish scholars have long since come to the con-

clusion that the medieval data derived largely from the extant records of the collection of Peter's pence for the Papacy, and those of the sixteenth and seventeenth centuries, for the most part based upon the fiscal *lustracje* (government censuses of property and families, conducted in various regions at various times), reveal so many deficiencies as to make them highly unsatisfactory tools for population research. The most promising source material for the demography of the Catholic majority became available when, under the prompting of the canons adopted at the Council of Trent, Catholic parishes throughout the country began keeping registers of births, marriages, and deaths. However, this was a slow process, which required persistent effort on the part of the ecclesiastical leaders, and as late as 1648 many parishes had not yet adopted the system. Nor did those which had introduced it cover the entire population. Moreover, the necessarily painstaking and time-consuming research in these parish records is still in its infancy. The few investigations hitherto published reveal great discrepancies and have led to very debatable conclusions. Moreover, except for occasional references to Jews in the *lustracje,* the available sources have little direct bearing on the Jewish population; and the Polish-Lithuanian rabbinate never maintained registers corresponding to those for the Catholic parishes in independent Poland. Even for the prevention of bigamy, Jewish communal organs still had to depend on the testimony of witnesses concerning a suspect person's earlier marriage. Nothwithstanding all these legitimate reservations, one must admit that the early parish records, if very carefully examined, would at least shed some light on the number, age, and social composition of the Jewish converts to Christianity in various periods. Indirectly, too, they would offer some comparative material against which to evaluate the size of, and changes within, the Jewish communities of the respective areas, particularly in regard to the victims of certain destructive factors, about which more anon. The same is true, to a lesser extent, of the few extant reports by Church inspectors about their visitation tours through various parts of the country and their impact on ecclesiastical discipline.[32]

Somewhat more reliable, though still quite unsatisfactory, are the population estimates based upon the number of houses occupied by Jews in certain localities. If unable to obtain royal permission to eliminate Jews entirely, municipal councils often tried to limit the size of the Jewish population by locking all Jews into a small Jewish quarter or by expressly stating how many houses the Jews were allowed to occupy. To be sure, life often proved stronger than the desires of the city elders, and the Jewish population frequently expanded beyond the expected numbers. Partially this overflow was accommodated by acquiring houses in the noble and ecclesiastical enclaves outside the city's jurisdiction. But from time to time, Jews persuaded individual burghers to rent them more houses than the prescribed quota, subsequently obtaining approval from the council of that *fait accompli*. We recall how the number of dwellings allotted to Jews in Poznań grew from 49 to 83 according to the treaty concluded between the Jews and the city in 1558. Moreover, despite the city's generally strict zoning regulations, Jews frequently entered "forbidden" houses and remained there. By 1590 the Poznań Jews seem to have inhabited some 115, and soon thereafter 138, buildings. Moreover, even the original houses could be enlarged with additional floors, or otherwise accommodate a much larger number of inhabitants simply by overcrowding. That this situation was unhealthy goes without saying. Among other calamities, it gave rise to fires, which endangered the whole city. Major conflagrations in the Poznań Jewish quarter are indeed recorded for 1447, 1464, 1533, 1590, 1653, 1717, and 1764. In Cracow there were nine major fires within the shorter period of 115 years (1528, 1536, 1551, 1557, 1571, 1585, 1597, 1604, 1643). In other cities, where Jews were less frequently forced to "agree" to such limitations, the number of houses could increase as need arose. For example, in Lithuanian Brest, where in 1566 there were 85 Jewish houses (as against 746 Christian houses recorded there two years earlier), the Jewish dwellings later increased to 136. However, as we shall see, the computation of the number of Jewish residents per house is extremely difficult, since some houses accommodated many more persons per room than others. Hence only a combination of housing totals and other demographic data may yield some approximations of the total number of Jews living in a particular locality—still leaving many other vital statistics open to doubt.[33]

Despite these serious shortcomings, demographic research concerning Jewish life in prepartition Poland must go ahead. Of course, some pessimists consider this type of research utterly hopeless; they often repeat Armand Brett's dictum that to ascertain the number of people living in France or in any other country before 1789 is like estimating the number of animals in Noah's ark. But even in France, which has a venerable tradition of historical demography, Jacques Duparquier has correctly observed that "one must not apply to old statistical computations the same critical methods which one employs with respect to the traditional historical documents. They merit specific treatment. It is as unreasonable to reject them totally as it is to lend them total faith." Certainly, here as in some other fields of Jewish history, throwing up one's hands in despair is an all-too-facile way of disposing of a fundamental historical problem which is likely to shed light on all other social, economic, cultural, and political aspects of life. Facing this important challenge, modern scholarship will simply have to refine the existing methods and devise new ones to deal with this particular line of research.[34]

Under these circumstances, demographic studies on Polish-Lithuanian Jewry before the partitions (with the sole exception of the censuses of 1764–65, discussed below), still depend largely on very fragmentary direct evidence, which must be supplemented by some general considerations of what was likely to have happened, rather than what actually did happen. Unfortunately, the destruction of Polish Jewry during the Nazi Holocaust has left few native Jewish scholars to collaborate with the Polish investigators specializing in this discipline. This is doubly regrettable, since general Polish historical demography, which has a fine tradition going back to Tadeusz Czacki's essays and Wawrzyniec Surowiecki's lectures of the early nineteenth century, and more particularly to Adolf Pawiński's and Aleksander Jabłonowski's indefatigably detailed work in the 1880s and 1890s, has made its greatest advances during the last quarter century. If all Polish specialists have been hampered by the tremendous losses sustained during the Second World War by the state and municipal archives, the few postwar students of Polish Jewish demography have suffered even more severely from the wholesale destruction of Jewish communal records, along with the Jewish population itself, by the Nazi invaders.[35]

On general grounds, we may assume that the Jewish population grew faster than its neighbors. True, the great wave of immigration which had contributed so much to the fantastic expansion of Jewish settlement during the Jagiellon era, seems to have greatly declined in the period of the Polish Counter Reformation. Quite apart from the growing religious intolerance in the country, which might have discouraged a number of non-Catholic would-be immigrants from other lands, the Holy Roman Empire—the main place of origin of the Polish and Lithuanian Jews in the fifteenth century and the first three quarters of the sixteenth—had by 1576, when both Rudolph II and Báthory ascended their thrones, largely completed the series of expulsions of Jewish communities after the Black Death. In fact, after 1550 Germany witnessed a partial resettlement of Jews in areas from which they had been banished. New communities were springing up, not only owing to the immigration of former Marranos, as in Hamburg and Glückstadt, but also as a result of internal movements in parts of western and southern Germany. A number of German Jews, too, found entry into Hamburg through neighboring Altona, beginning with a privilege granted them in 1584 by the relatively tolerant counts of Schaumburg. Frankfort on the Main, which had had a tiny Jewish community in the early 1500s, embraced a settlement of more than 2,200 Jews in 1624; despite the storms of the Thirty Years' War, it temporarily lost less than 20 percent of that number by 1648. The Habsburg possessions likewise began readmitting Jews to Bohemia, Austria, and other provinces, Rudolph II solemnly announcing, as we recall, that "they would never be expelled from Prague or the Bohemian Crown." This pledge may not have been kept to the letter, yet Prague and some Moravian communities were now able to absorb Jewish immigrants, rather than send out hosts of émigrés to other lands. In fact, Prague is said to have accommodated 7,815 Jewish inhabitants in 1638, far more than any Jewish community in Poland or Lithuania of that time. The presence of Jews in the Bohemian capital made itself so strongly felt that, as early as the beginning of the sixteenth century, when the Prague Jewish community was far smaller, Joannes

Pileatorius, a pupil of the well-known anti-Jewish and anti-humanist writer, Ortuinus Gratius (Ortuin de Graes), alluded to it in the *Salutes* he sent to his teacher. Indulging in the then popular search for religioethnic characteristics, he wrote: *In Bohemia haeretici. . . . In Praga Judaei, Coloniae Pharisaei.* Of course, the great disturbances of the Thirty Years' War, which at one time or another ravaged most parts of the Holy Roman Empire, set in motion mass flights of Jews as well as non-Jews. It doubtless was the spectacle of such refugees settling in various parts of Poland which induced Krzysztof Słupecki, in his aforementioned letter to Gerhard Johann Vos (Joannes Vossius) of July 31, 1637, to claim that "the Jewish people has spread widely over the entire Polish Crown and its provinces. It has insinuated itself [*insederit*] into almost all cities, towns, and villages, particularly during the warlike storms in neighboring Germany." But many other German exiles found refuge in western Europe, especially in dynamic Holland. As we recall, enough German Jews had entered Amsterdam in the 1530s to form the first German Jewish community in the Dutch metropolis, followed soon thereafter by a Polish Jewish community.[36]

Moreover, those German Jews who emigrated to Poland around 1600 were not always as welcome to either the royal authorities or their own coreligionists as their predecessors had been. Manifestations of local xenophobia toward these penniless arrivals were not infrequent, and some Jewish communities, such as that of Poznań, often extended to the newcomers residence permits of but short duration. They seem to have been induced to do so not only by the residential restrictions placed upon them by hostile burghers, but also by their own reluctance to assume the additional financial burden of maintaining numerous refugees in a stagnating economy. Typical of the antialien resolutions adopted by the Poznań elders in that period was one issued on Menaḥem Ab 21, 5370 (August 10, 1610), which ordered Gumprecht Naumburg "in the name of the entire community" to remove his brother-in-law Nathan, together with wife and children, from his home, under the fine of 100 Hungarian florins. Another decision of Tishre 27, 5405 (October 27, 1644), banished a widow from Swarzędz (Schwersenz), located some nine miles from Poznań. Only under her and her relatives' insistent representations did the community allow her to stay through the winter "until the month of Iyar during the Gniezno fair [April 1, 1645]. But thereafter she must give up her residence there." Her relatives had to place a bond of 300 zlotys, which was to be forfeited in the case of her failure to depart, "no excuse being accepted." Nonetheless, despite the sound and fury, the traditional Jewish charitable instincts often prevailed. The same Poznań elders, for instance, meeting in mid-January 1642 with their colleagues in a provincial council of Great Poland, had issued the following appeal:

As to the poor refugees coming from Germany and other lands ravaged by roving armies who are now wandering in search of a place of rest and peace, any compassionate person who encounters any of these refugees, man or woman, boy or girl, ought to welcome them with bread and food, and offer them shelter for many nights. This matter will be on the agenda of our meeting at the Gniezno fair in the coming Iyar [April]. At that time, the leaders of the city of Poznań, together with the provincial elders, will decide whether to extend to them financial aid or not. Should there be no unanimous vote on it at that fair, the communities of Poznań and other localities shall allot a sum for that purpose, which the Poznań elders will distribute in their discretion to these indigent people, who will come and settle among us.

Now as in other periods of their migratory history, Jewish wanderers ultimately found places where they could settle, and thus added to the size of the local Jewish population. Among the new immigrants were outstanding citizens like Dr. Isaac May, who settled in Poland after spending a few years in Königsberg, where he served as court physician of the Prussian duke. Another important arrival was Moses Montalto, son of the famous doctor Elijah Montalto, whom we encountered as the exceptionally privileged Jewish physician to the French Queen Marie de Médicis and, for a while, to her son Louis XIII. For unknown reasons, Moses decided to settle in Lublin. However, the total number of new permanent settlers, as compared with the masses of already established residents, was by no means demographically significant; it seems to have contributed relatively little to the astonishing growth of the Jewish settlements in the dual Commonwealth between 1576 and 1648. On the other hand, very few Jews left Poland before

1648. Even the so-called fugitives (*borehim*), some of whom, usually for economic reasons, suddenly vanished from their homes, and often created serious legal and financial problems for their communities, seem for the most part to have remained within the Commonwealth.[37]

However, the process of forming new Jewish communities, even in the older Polish provinces, never stopped. The situation in Swarzędz, though in many details quite unusual, is a case in point. On the one hand, the local lord, Zygmunt Grudziński, opened the town to Jewish settlement before he admitted Protestants, despite his personal sympathy for the Christian religious dissidents. In his agreement of June 3, 1621, with the Jewish elders of Poznań, he not only granted a favorable privilege to prospective Jewish settlers but also obligated himself to erect 32 of the planned 40 Jewish houses, and to subsidize the construction of a synagogue and other Jewish communal institutions, while the Poznań Jewish community was to build 8 houses and share the cost of the public buildings. The new settlers were obliged merely to pay a moderate rental on the houses they occupied. In subsequent years Grudziński welcomed further Jewish arrivals. On the other hand, the financial burdens of the Poznań community had grown in those years by leaps and bounds, and the leaders had reason to fear that any major involvement in refugee relief would push the community to the brink of disaster.[38]

Unquestionably, Jewish population growth now depended more on internal factors than on immigration. It appears that the Jews had a larger rate of natural growth than their neighbors. When Stanisław Hoszowski estimated, with evident exaggeration, that the general population of some 20,000 in Cracow in 1642 had an annual birth rate of 62.1 per 1,000 inhabitants, he added that if Jews were included that rate would have been over 70, although at that time the Jews still constituted but a small minority of the city's population. Under independent Poland and long thereafter, most Jews strongly believed in early marriages, for moral and religious reasons. To make these possible, they had introduced the so-called *kest* system, whereby the parents (for the most part those of the bride) maintained the newlyweds for a period of time, usually until they could start earning a living on their own. So convinced were the Jewish masses of the worth of such arrangements that, when the Russian government in 1835 forbade Jews to marry below the age of eighteen, for men, or sixteen, for women, many Jewish parents rushed their children into marriage ahead of the deadline. Because of their more or less strict adherence to what they considered the first biblical commandment, "Be fruitful, and multiply, and replenish the earth" (Gen. 1:28), there was little birth control, and families usually proliferated. If among the Polish, Lithuanian, and Rus villagers the average life expectancy of a new-born child was at best 26 years, and very likely closer to the 20 years and 10 months computed as the average for the area of Beauvais in France at that time, men usually had to enter into several successive marriages to attain large families of 10 children or more. Even among the late medieval English aristocracy, the life expectancy of a new-born child averaged only 23.78 years in 1400–1425, although it seems to have risen considerably in the following quarter century. Jews, as we shall presently see, doubtless had a longer life expectancy; and by starting their reproductive processes earlier in life, they averaged a relatively larger number of children.[39]

Whatever the difference between Jewish and non-Jewish birth rates may have been, even more important was the seemingly lower Jewish mortality. Neither Poles nor Jews suffered much from civilian war casualties before the great invasions of the 1650s, except in the southeastern borderlands, which were open to frequent Tatar raids. Deaths on the battlefield were not of prime demographic significance even among the Poles and the Lithuanians, since the armies recruited by the Polish kings included numerous Hungarian, German, and other foreign mercenaries; and they were numerically quite insignificant among Jews. But both Christians and Jews sustained great losses as a result of contagious diseases and famines. Poland, to be sure, had escaped the great ravages of the Black Death period. But sporadically it, too, suffered from pestilences, though as a rule they did not last very long, and affected only parts of the country at a time. With a keen perception sharpened by hatred, Sebastyan Miczyński noted some of the demographic factors which favored a larger increase in the Jewish population. Claiming that the Jews so grossly underpaid their capitation tax that it amounted to a grosz rather than a zloty a person, he insisted that they "hide their total number, even though they multiply enormously, for they do not die in wars, they run away before the 'air' [pest], and marry very early." Remarkably, neither friend nor enemy in Poland pointed out another rather important factor, once stressed by the New Christian Felipe de Najera at his aforementioned inquisitorial trial; namely, the absence among Jews of a celibatarian clergy which contributed nothing to population growth. Even if the clergy's ratio in the Polish, Rus, and Lithuanian populations did not equal that in contemporary Spain, the presence of one priest per 550 inhabitants, in addition to many monks and nuns, must have played a certain role in retarding the natural increase among Catholics. Of course, here, too, regional differences prevailed, since the Greek Orthodox, Uniate, and Protestant clergy were allowed to marry. Famines, too, were usually local phenomena, occasioned not by total failure of crops but rather by difficulties in transportation. It has been shown, for example, that grain shipped by land from Little Poland to Vilna increased in price by some 200 percent, whereas the same quantity of grain transported from Cracow to Gdańsk by barges on the Vistula increased in price by little over 16 percent. But it stands to reason that Jews, as both traders and agents for the producing landlords, may have been able better to supply their own coreligionists, especially those living in the larger cities, than the Christian suppliers did the penurious peasant masses, especially those living in an outlying district affected by a severe local crop failure.[40]

The Jewish communities revealed certain peculiar variants in population losses. Because of ritualistic ablutions, the consumption of relatively fresh meats, and adherence to other requirements of Jewish law, they may have been somewhat less affected by contagious diseases. On the other hand, we learn that many Jews, like their non-Jewish compatriots, tried to escape the plague by fleeing to the countryside. (We recall one such occurrence in Cracow in 1588.) These incidents may, or may not, indicate that, on the whole, the villagers, who constituted the large majority of the non-Jewish population, suffered less than city-dwellers from plagues. It is also debatable whether Jewish civilians sustained

fewer casualties than their neighbors in wartime in Poland, as
they very likely did during the Thirty Years' War in Germany.
Since the Polish wars had few of the characteristics of the fanatical
wars of religion, Jews were not necessarily spared by the contending armies because of their noninvolvement in Christian sectarian
struggles. On the contrary, Jews may have been disproportionately
victimized out of religious intolerance aimed specifically at them,
the aforementioned drowning of Jews in Polotsk by Ivan the
Terrible being a case in point. Some Jews also suffered losses of
life and limb in sporadic anti-Jewish riots. Miscarriage of justice,
particularly if connected with blood and host libels, likewise
contributed slightly to the diminution of the Jewish population.
Somewhat more important undoubtedly were the effects of Christian missionary activity among the Jews. While we have no precise
figures, or even approximations, of Jewish conversions to Christianity before the Frankist movement of the eighteenth century,
we do hear of baptized Jews, mentioned incidentally in connection with some specific event, like the imprisonment of the Jews
of Kovel instigated by the convert Lavrin. We also occasionally
hear of forced conversions of Jewish minors. On the other hand,
the few Jewish proselytes as a rule left the country and sought
refuge in a Muslim land. In any case, neither the losses nor the
still smaller gains generated by religious conversions, were numerous enough to have significant demographic effects.[41]

Equally important was the availability for most Jews of both
medical services and communal support in case of illness. Their
majority resided in urban centers, where doctors were generally
more readily available, whereas the peasant masses, particularly in
the less densely populated eastern provinces, often lived scores of
miles away from any trained physician. They had even less access
to the few, usually overcrowded and none-too-sanitary hospitals.
In contrast, Jews frequently had a considerable proportion of well-
trained doctors in their midst. Quite a few Polish Jewish students
went to Padua, one of the most renowned medical schools of the
period; most of them returned to exercise their profession in Poland. At the same time there existed many charitable Jewish organizations especially dedicated to the care of the sick. The community at large, too, and certainly the traditionally tight-knit

families, considered it one of their major obligations to help heal
the indigent sick. As a result, the mortality of infants and little
children, in particular, was doubtless much lower among the Jews
than among their Christian neighbors.[42]

Regrettably, we possess no adequate source material to venture
more precise estimates of the differences in infant and child mortality among the various ethnic groups inhabiting Poland and
Lithuania in early modern times. But even in the nineteenth and
early twentieth centuries a major difference between East-European Jews and non-Jews is well attested. A very telling example
is offered by Russia in 1896. In the case of Russian boys, the death
rate below one month of age was 8.1 percent; from one to three
months, 6.8 percent; from three to six months, 6.6 percent; from
six to twelve months, 8.4 percent. The figures for Russian girls
were 2.7, 6.4, 5.9, and 7.8 respectively. Among Jews, on the other
hand, the percentages were much smaller. They were 2.63, 2.4,
2.9, and 5.7 for boys; and 2.62, 2.2, 2.3, and 5.0 for girls. In other
words, of 1,000 new-born Russian boys, 299 died during the first
year; for Russian girls, the losses amounted to 228 per 1,000. On
the other hand, for every 1,000 Jewish infants, an average of only
136.3 boys or 121.2 girls died during the first year. According to
Egon Vielrose's computations, even in the three most advanced
and prosperous western provinces of the Polish Crown (Great Poland, Little Poland, and Mazovia), of 1,000 new-born children, on
the average only 788 survived to age one, 606 to age two, 545 to
age five, and, with the greatly diminished mortality in the following decade, 500 to age fifteen. In other words, no more than
one out of two new-born children could be expected to live to
the age of reproduction. Similarly, in his study of conditions in
Poznań, Stanisław Waszak came to the conclusion that 45 percent
of all new-born children died before reaching the age of five, and
20 percent more failed to survive beyond the age of twenty-five.
In the Jewish case, early mortality was so much lower that as
many as two out of three children may have survived to the age
of fifteen and may soon thereafter have begun to reproduce themselves. These factors, combined with the apparently smaller mortality among adults, too, could grow in geometric progression and,
at the end of a few generations, produce a tremendous divergence

between the population growth rate of the Jewish minority and that of the Christian majority.[43]

STEADY POPULATION GROWTH

How do these largely theoretical considerations about the *likely* trends in Jewish migrations, natality, and mortality in the dual Commonwealth before 1650 compare with the rather scarce data preserved in the extant documents, and with the conclusions drawn therefrom by the students of Polish historical demography? Unfortunately, the few censuses taken of Polish and Lithuanian Jews in that period were neither complete nor thorough; nor have their records been adequately preserved in the archives. The fairly sustained effort of the Jewish census made in 1550 (a year after the introduction of the special Jewish head tax) proved sufficiently disappointing to be only partially repeated in the following years, and to be totally abandoned in 1578. Even the general *lustracje* conducted in various palatinates in the sixteenth and seventeenth centuries not only differed in time and method but were often restricted to the so-called royal cities; whereas the private towns under the control of nobles and churches, which even in the Lublin palatinate embraced about 70 percent of the whole urban population, were not included. In fact, some landlords cooperated with the Jewish elders in trying to sabotage any census which would result in larger tax payments by "their" Jews and thus imperil their own revenue from the Jewish community.

On their part, the Jews had an age-old phobia with regard to being counted. Apart from their self-interest in minimizing the number of prospective poll tax payers, they vividly remembered the scriptural description of the census conducted by King David: "And again the anger of the Lord was kindled against Israel, and He moved David against them saying: 'Go number Israel and Judah.'" As a result of that census, we are told, a pestilence raged in Israel which cost the lives of 70,000 Israelites from Dan to Beersheba. Ber (Birkenthal) of Bolechów was later to boast that, even in 1765, he had influenced the elders of his community, in their report to the census takers, to underestimate the Jewish population of his community by about one-third (883 instead of 1,300

persons). This despite the fact that the Polish legislators, anticipating resistance and fearing that the landlords might temporarily
remove the entire Jewish population from each locality before the
arrival of the enumerators, had provided:

Should all the Jews and Karaites of one or another town down to the
last person depart or die out, in such a case the lord of that town or
his administrator shall take an oath before the Economic Commission
that these Jews had departed not because of any court-connected cause
but because of their own impertinence or temerity, or that they had
died out because of a plague. [The lord was also to swear] that he had
not appropriated their [the Jews'] possessions except possibly for the
payment of debts owed either to himself or to other creditors but not
as a result of an acquisition at any regular price. When the time comes
for the payment of the head tax, all available funds shall be freed for
that purpose and all Jewish houses and other properties in that town
shall be disposed of by the municipal office and used for defraying the
tax.

No exodus of an entire community is recorded in connection with
the census of 1765, but omissions of varying magnitude were undoubtedly quite frequent.[44]

At the same time, another age-old deterrent causing people to
resist governmental censuses—namely, the fear of being drafted
into the army—played but a minor role among the Jews of the
dual Commonwealth. We recall that Jews, unlike the peasants,
were as a rule not subject to military service, except in some places
for local defense against an enemy attack. No sooner did Austria
institute obligatory military service in its newly occupied Galicia,
however, than potential draftees, Jewish and non-Jewish, began
using all means of evasion, from concealment of names and inaccurate reporting of the age of male family members to census
enumerators, to actual flight.[45]

Nonetheless, we may regard the enumeration of 1765 as the first
real census of Polish Jewry. At that time the government, bent
upon substantially increasing its revenue from the Jewish head
tax, abolished the two central councils of the Jewish communities,
theretofore the main agents for gathering taxes from the Jews. As
we shall see in a later context, the operations of both the Councils
and the individual communities were by then in great disarray,
occasioned by a growing debt burden, the servicing of which had

to be defrayed from the yield of the tax collection, and by the growing despotic regime of a self-perpetuating communal élite. The Polish government now ordered that all Jewish inhabitants over the age of one be listed, with the aid of the local communities, so that the Treasury would be furnished with a new basis for computing the tax. In each community the rabbi, a Jewish lay leader, and the sexton, accompanied by a nobleman specifically designated for this task, had to visit each Jewish household and jointly compile complete lists of every Jewish family in town by name, sex, and age, as well as occupation. Jews located in villages were ordered, under the sanction of excommunication, to appear in the neighboring towns and submit the required lists. Most of these records have been preserved (at least until the ravages of the Second World War) and subjected to careful reviews by a number of scholars, particularly Raphael Mahler. Needless to say, these data, though painstakingly accumulated, were by no means complete—Mahler was obliged to raise the resulting figures by some 20 percent—but they are infinitely superior to any other record pertaining to the Jews of Poland-Lithuania before the partitions.[46]

The figures thus obtained could be further checked against subsequent partial censuses, especially those conducted with somewhat more refined methods in both the Austrian and the Prussian territories taken over from Poland in 1772–95, as well as the censuses of 1808 and 1810 in the short-lived Duchy of Warsaw. However, the much larger territories incorporated into the Tsarist Empire had no really satisfactory population estimates until 1897. Furthermore, any demographic computation looking backward from the more reliable statistical data compiled in the nineteenth and twentieth centuries—a method often effectively used in various West-European areas—is impeded in Poland by the great devastation of the period 1648–60. This break in continuity, aggravated by the general deficiencies of the earlier computations, has doubly hampered demographic studies of Polish and Lithuanian Jews and, because of their large number, those of world Jewry as a whole.[47]

With all these limitations, one must venture some tentative estimates of Jewish population and other demographic factors as best one can in the light of extant sources. Polish demographic research has made considerable progress in the last quarter century, and can furnish a better background for Jewish studies in this field than was previously available. The best estimates that can be advanced here for the period from 1500 on are as follows: As mentioned above, in 1500 the Jewish population in the dual Commonwealth did not exceed 30,000, in a total population of about 5,000,000. By 1576, at the advent of Báthory, the number of Jews had rapidly grown to some 150,000, representing an increase of some 400 percent in an area which (by 1582) had expanded to about 815,000 square kilometers, or about 315,000 square miles, and accommodated a total population of about 7,500,000 (without ducal Prussia and Silesia). In the subsequent seventy-two years (1576–1648), the number of Jews had trebled again, to approximately 450,000. Interveningly, the area of the Commonwealth had increased to about 990,000 square kilometers, or some 382,000 square miles, by 1634, and accommodated a population of about 10,000,000 (the loss of most of Livonia in 1635 but slightly diminished the general population of the Commonwealth in the following decade, and was essentially made up by natural growth elsewhere). In other words, the ratio of the Jewish population rose from 0.6 percent in 1500, to 2 percent in 1576, and 4.5 percent in 1648. As a result of the great catastrophes of the Cossack uprising and the Swedish-Muscovite invasions, the Jewish population dwindled by more than 100,000, owing to deaths, emigration, and the increased mortality of the suffering survivors; and amounted to less than 350,000 in 1660. Soon thereafter a period of slow recovery set in, and by 1764 the total number reached some 750,000, in a total population of 11,400,000 on the country's diminished territory—or about 6.6 percent.[48]

The Jews' rapid population growth between 1500 and 1576 is not surprising, since this was the period of greatest Jewish immigration from central Europe, of a substantial upsurge in the Polish economy, and of the general welcome extended to the Jewish settlers by the Polish monarchy and important segments of the dominant nobility. An immigrant population usually includes a higher than average ratio of persons of reproductive age (15 to 45)—this is partially true also in the case of Jewish migrations, which were often characterized by whole families, including children and aged persons, moving from one area to another—and hence its birth rate is as a rule higher than average. If the Polish peasantry, as reputed, averaged as many as 45–50 births per 1,000 persons a year, it stands to reason that that ratio was at least equaled, and probably exceeded, by the Jews in prepartition Poland, and more so in the dynamic first three-quarters of the sixteenth century. The slowdown of Jewish immigration in 1576–1630, followed by a new wave of Central-European refugees from the Thirty Years' War, did not substantially reduce the natural Jewish increase, stimulated as it was by Poland's great geographic expansion and the accelerated internal migrations which took place after the Union of Lublin in 1569. We recall the speedy increase in Jewish settlements in the palatinates of Volhynia, Podolia, Kiev, and Bratslav. According to S. Ettinger's estimates, between 1569 and 1648 the Jewish population of Volhynia increased from 3,000 to 15,000, or by 400 percent; and that of Podolia, from 750 to 4,000, or by 430 percent; while the Kiev and Bratslav palatinates, both of which had but an insignificant number of Jews in 1569, by 1648 included a Jewish population of 18,825 and 13,500, respectively. At the same time, there were considerable increases in the number of Jewish inhabitants in the older provinces of the Polish Crown, and an even greater growth in the areas that remained under the suzerainty of the Grand Duchy of Lithuania.[49]

In order to comprehend this amazing increase more fully, we must here refer briefly to its catastrophic reversal during the 1648–60 "Deluge." For one example, it has long been accepted that the Muscovite army, on conquering Vilna in 1655, slaughtered 25,000 persons. This figure is decidedly exaggerated; it exceeds the total number of Vilna inhabitants before 1655, put at about 20,000, although one must not overlook the possibility that, before the Muscovite occupation, Vilna had attracted thousands of refugees from the provinces, seeking shelter in what they considered the relative safety of the Lithuanian capital. On the other hand, immediately before the occupation of the city by the Muscovites, there was a mass flight of both soldiers and civilians. We have the graphic description of that flight by one of the refugees themselves, R. Moses b. Naphtali Hirsch Rivkes:

On Wednesday, the 24th [23rd?] of Tammuz, 5415 [July 28, 1655] al-most the whole Jewish community ran for their lives like one man; those who had horses and carts went forth with their wives, sons and daughters, and some of their belongings, and others went on foot, carrying their children on their shoulders. I went forth with my stick in my right hand, after seizing my bag of phylacteries.

In any case, the number of victims was enormous, the Jews prob-ably figuring disproportionately among those who suffered from Muscovite intolerance. It has been shown that forty-nine dwellings in Vilna which were located on three streets of the Jewish quarter and on a street where Jews lived without authorization, accommo-dated 1,360 persons in 1645, but only 415 in 1662, representing a loss of nearly 70 percent. If, according to a recent estimate, even the three western provinces of the Polish Crown, whose inhabi-tants had numbered 3,830,000 in 1650, embraced a population of but 2,900,000 in 1660, this loss of 25 percent or more was in-dubitably exceeded in the case of Jews, who suffered both from religious animosity and as a predominantly urban population. Some scholars have actually claimed that during those catastrophic years certain regions sustained population losses ranging from 49 percent in rural districts to 62½ percent in the cities.[50]

Before the "Deluge," however, the founding of ever-new cities was still in full swing. It is estimated that to the 1,000 townships which existed in the Polish Crown (without Silesia or western Pomerania) in 1578 no fewer than 100 more were added before 1650. The Jews doubtless constituted an ever-increasing segment of the urban inhabitants, who in 1650 amounted to some 23 per-cent of the Commonwealth's total population. We have seen that Jews played a great role in the new towns and hamlets, particularly in the newly colonized southeastern districts. With the general in-crease of the Jewish population, and the simultaneous restrictions on the number of dwellings Jews were allowed to occupy, as we recall, fires often had a doubly damaging effect upon the Jewish quarters. As elsewhere in central Europe, major conflagrations, which sometimes devastated entire cities, were often blamed on Jews, especially if the fires happened to have started in the Jewish quarter. Quite apart from the adverse psychological effects of such fires, the number of Jewish victims must have been appalling. Many Jewish houses had to shelter several families each, including numerous children, while non-Jewish buildings averaged two hearths for a total of only 10–11 persons. According to Stanisław Lipnicki's aforementioned description of the 1550 Jewish census in the royal cities of several palatinates, some houses in the Jewish quarters had 13–22 tax-paying inhabitants. In Poznań, where the housing situation has been carefully examined, one Jewish house seems to have accommodated 38 persons in three rooms. On the other hand, general climatic changes, which often had a detrimental effect on grain production in various areas in the sixteenth and seventeenth centuries, probably affected Jews more as traders, agents, and consumers than as producers.[51]

Even less informative are the data relating to the number of Jewish victims of the recurrent plagues in Poland and Lithuania. One wishes we possessed more computations like those relating to the mortality of Cracow Jewry in the period here under review. Based upon the records of the local burial society, beginning in 1543, Feiwel Hirsch Wettstein found that in the first forty-seven years of the society's existence 1,750 Cracow Jews died, while in the following fifty years 2,850 Jews passed away, the increased figure undoubtedly owing in the main to the intervening growth of the Jewish population. To be sure, these figures are incomplete, since they record only adult deaths; small children, the most vulnerable segment of the population, were not included in these lists. At any rate, random samples taken from the 1550s and 1560s show that, in ordinary years, between 20 and 50 persons died per year; while during the period of a plague lasting 13 months and 6 days in 1551–52, a total of 220 persons passed away. During a longer but less deadly plague lasting 39 months and 19 days, apparently only 75 persons died, which did not exceed the normal range.[52]

If we may judge from the better-known data of the 1765 census, Polish and Lithuanian Jewry had in general a fairly even balance between the sexes. This was important in so far as there were relatively few old bachelors and spinsters, although the number of widows considerably exceeded that of widowers. On the whole, the life expectancy of Jews was a bit longer than that of non-Jews;

thus most unmarried children doubtless still had their original set of parents. Second marriages following divorces because of the first wife's alleged sterility, though encouraged by the rabbis on theoretical grounds, seem to have been quite rare. Early remarriages after the loss of a mate were widely accepted, however, especially because propagation was extolled as a religious obligation. Probably even more than their non-Jewish counterparts, Jews seem to have been able to maintain large families and nurture their children into adulthood, with the aid of the extensive communal welfare system when needed. The pressure generated by the resulting population explosion, on the means of subsistence in the Polish-Lituanian Jewish settlement, was indeed a major factor in forcing Jews to utilize all available avenues for earning a living.[53]

DEEPENING ROOTS

During the six decades of the regime of the first two Vasas, the Jews of the dual Commonwealth not only held their own politically and legally but also sank deeper roots into their new environment. True, the great dynamism of the first three-quarters of the sixteenth century, when intellectual and religious ferment, combined with rapid population growth and economic advances, lent extraordinary vitality to the entire Polish civilization, was dampened by the Counter Reformation. Yet the Jews suffered less than their neighbors from the immediate impact of that reaction; legally and culturally they were allowed to pursue their communal and intellectual activities more or less undisturbed. The forces of disintegration set in motion at that time for the country at large, were not yet manifest to the Jewish masses or even their leaders. Only with the shock of the Cossack massacres and the Swedish-Muscovite Wars did Polish-Lithuanian Jewry awaken to the perils of their country's decline.

At the same time, Jews were hesitant to settle in large numbers in the northwestern and northeastern territories occupied by Polish troops under the reigns of Stephen Báthory and Sigismund III. From the outset they must have sensed the unfriendliness of the largely German-speaking municipal administrations dominant in Prussia (both ducal and royal), Pomerania, and the various parts of Livonia. While the German burghers in Polish cities, too, had long been averse to the admission of Jews and, even where they had to reconcile themselves to the *fait accompli* of Jewish settlement, tried to curtail the size and rights of the Jewish population, they could easily be overruled by the monarchy and the growingly powerful gentry. In the newly conquered northern territories, however, the Polish regime was too shaky, and its hold on these provinces too unstable because of the competing expansionist designs of Denmark, Sweden, and Muscovy, for the central government sharply to defy the established ruling classes in behalf of its Jewish subjects. The generally hostile merchant and artisan groups were effectively supported by remnants of the Teutonic Order, with its long-standing tradition of refusing toleration to Jews, and by the preponderant ecclesiastical establishment. Unlike Poland-Lithuania, where the rise of various Protestant sects greatly contributed to mutual religious toleration, the new northern provinces were dominated by the Lutheran clergy, which here, as in the Holy Roman Empire, often maintained a determinedly anti-Jewish stance.

On their part, the Jews themselves apparently felt rather uncomfortable in these areas. The record of their persecutions throughout Germany and of their recurrent expulsions from one German city after another must have been too fresh in their minds for them to seek admission there in large numbers. Only a few adventurous spirits succeeded in overcoming the various legal and economic barriers, and settled in cities like Königsberg or Szczecin in the west and Jelgava (Mitau) or Riga in the east. A number of them were physicians, invited by leading personalities for their greatly valued medical services; others were accomplished businessmen, appreciated for their help in expanding international trade. But these were small beginnings. While laying a foundation for future growth of the Jewish communities in Königsberg and Riga, and particularly throughout the province of Courland, these settlers played a very minor role in the economy of the entire area before 1648.

In contrast, Poland's expansion into the southeastern areas proved to be a great boon for the Jewish people. For the most part underpopulated, these vast territories urgently needed colonizers, with whatever skills they possessed for agriculture, industry, or trade. Development also depended in large measure on capital investment, as well as on effective organization and management. Joining hands with other new arrivals—recruited not only from various ethnic groups in the older provinces of Poland-Lithuania but also from neighboring countries—enterprising Jews flocked into these large territories in ever-increasing numbers. Supported, in particular, by the magnates, who badly needed both personnel and capital for the large-scale cultivation of their vast latifundia, Jews established a number of communities in the rapidly growing larger towns, as well as in the hamlets and villages. This opening of a vast frontier transformed many former Jewish petty traders and artisans from the western provinces into tillers of the soil, innkeepers, liquor distillers, and leaseholders in their own right, or into agents, administrators, and officials for the landlords—all helping vastly to expand the population and its productive capacity in these areas, which had become, under prolonged Mongolian domination, almost virgin land again.

This process came to full fruition only in the century of reconstruction after 1660. At that time nearly one-third of the entire Jewish population of the dual Commonwealth lived in the new territories. But firm foundations for this development had been laid from the days of Báthory on.

Remarkably, the Counter Reformation but slightly impeded this evolution. Though the general religious intolerance it generated threatened to affect the Jews, the Catholic leaders concentrated on converting the predominantly Orthodox peasant masses to Roman Catholicism, or at least to attract them to the newly formed Uniate churches, and the local clergy had little energy to spare for converting the "obstinate" Jews. Moreover, the Jews themselves, often dependent on, and allied with, the landlords, could be utilized by them as helpers in their Polonizing efforts.

Of course, this situation was explosive, and the Jews had to pay a high price for their cooperation with the ruling class. But for the immediate future and, after the tragic interlude of 1648–60, under the newly reestablished, more or less peaceful, Polish regime, this expanding frontier area held out much greater promise to the Jews than the increasingly overcrowded and economically declining provinces of the old Polish Crown.

LXX

SOCIOECONOMIC RESTRATIFICATION

POPULATION GROWTH of the dimensions experienced by Polish-Lithuanian Jewry during the crucial century and a half before the Cossack uprising of 1648 also helped to give rise to a revolutionary transformation in the general social and economic structure of Ashkenazic Jewry. The people which, even after the second fall of Jerusalem, had in its majority lived from agriculture, had, under the pressure of external and internal forces, become almost exclusively a people of traders and moneylenders in Europe north of the Alps. Its craftsmanship, formerly highly diversified, was increasingly restricted by hostile Christian guilds to a few crafts and an almost entirely Jewish clientele. Now, in Poland and Lithuania, trade and (partly in connection with it) banking still occupied an important place in the Jewish economy; but at the same time growing new opportunities stimulated many Jews to enter industry and certain branches of agriculture, as well as the professions. While this process was temporarily retarded by the "Deluge" of 1648–60, its momentum resumed after relative peace was restored to the country, and the Jewish communities started rebuilding their shattered fortunes. This progress was accelerated through the gradual shift of the Jewish population from the commercially more advanced western provinces, to the chiefly agricultural eastern regions, particularly the Rus areas, which by 1764 seem to have embraced nearly 40 percent of the Jewish inhabitants of the dual Commonwealth.[1]

The causes of this epochal transformation are manifold. To begin with, there was the perennial pressure of the growing Jewish population, which forced it to broaden its economic base for subsistence. The approximately 450,000 Jews who inhabited the Commonwealth in the 1640s, simply could not make a living from the narrow range of occupations to which their ancestors in central and western Europe north of the Alps had been confined by law, custom, and the interplay of various political and economic forces. Just as in the Muslim lands and medieval Christian Spain or Sicily, the Jewish masses in Poland had to find many new occupational outlets, for sheer survival. Yet the speed with which the predominantly German Jewish immigrants adjusted to the less hostile, if still rather strange, environment, and made early use of their economic opportunities, is truly amazing.[2]

Great transformations in the European economy at large reinforced these demographic stimuli. The sixteenth century witnessed, as we recall, an unparalleled population explosion in several West-European countries. The discovery of America, and the ensuing expansion of European civilization into the New World, as well as into African and Asian lands, generated a new wave of prosperity. With it arose a growing demand for food, clothing, and shelter, a demand intensified by the spreading quest for a higher standard of life. It was soon discovered that Poland and Lithuania with their vast, fertile, and as yet sparsely populated, lands could supply much grain, cattle, lumber, and other agricultural products to the metropolises of the Western world. Export of these goods was facilitated by the availability of navigable rivers, particularly the Vistula, which could transport bulky and heavy staples at a relatively low price. These advantages were increased when Poland occupied much of the Baltic shore of Pomerania and, later, of Livonia, whence ample shipping, particularly under Dutch registry, could relay produce to the hungry Western cities. Contemporaries quickly realized this advantage; for example, Giovanni Botero (J. B. Benesius) in 1603 adduced several illustrations of Poland's ability to save distant countries from starvation. Another contemporary writer compared Poland, as a granary for Western Europe, to ancient Egypt, which performed a similar function within the framework of the Roman Empire. The vast forests of northeastern Poland and Lithuania supplied much-needed lumber, from which, it is said, Philip II's "Invincible Armada" was built. The further geographic expansion of the Commonwealth, especially its occupation of the extremely fertile southeastern Ukrainian areas, vastly extended Poland's productive area. On their part, Poland and Lithuania benefited greatly from the importation of Western textiles, precious jewels and metals, colonial wares, and other commodities. After 1569 the strengthened cohesion of the Polish-Lithuanian provinces under one regime, which, however weak internally, still commanded considerable military and diplomatic power, made these West-East exchanges even more mutually advantageous. By eagerly entering the stream of both production and reciprocal exports, the Jews were now in a position to contribute significantly to the rapid expansion of international trade.[3]

In the long run, to be sure, Poland paid a high price for its temporary prosperity. By concentrating on agriculture while neglecting industrial development, and by pursuing a one-sided commercial policy favoring the politically powerful but economically rather unproductive gentry, the country began lagging behind the rest of Europe during the Commercial and Industrial Revolutions. This backwardness began to be strongly felt in the seventeenth century, when Western Europe's dynamic progress suffered setbacks lasting several decades. Whether or not we agree with the scholars who claim that that century witnessed an economic crisis of major proportions (admittedly it was neither simultaneous nor equally severe in the different regions), there is no question that the relative economic and political power of East-Central and Western Europe was constantly shifting in favor of the West. Even before the "Deluge," symptoms of an economic depression manifested themselves in many Polish-Lithuanian areas. With the Cossack uprising, and the Muscovite-Swedish Wars, which did not cease after the peace treaty of Andruszów (Andrusovo) of 1667 (it has been found that of the 68 years between 1648 and 1716 no fewer than 55 were war years), the dual Commonwealth not only sustained a catastrophic decline in population, and a resultant diminution of its labor force, but also suffered from intensified economic dislocation and a growing political anarchy. In 1752 the keen observer David Hume was not guilty of gross exaggeration when he wrote:

Of all European kingdoms Poland seems the most defective in the arts of war as well as peace, mechanical as well as liberal; yet it is there that venality and corruption do most prevail. The nobles seem to have preserved their crown elective for no other purpose, than regularly to sell it to the highest bidder. This is the only species of commerce with which that people are acquainted.[4]

BANKING

We need not expatiate here on the importance of the economic activities of Polish and Lithuanian Jewry in the early modern period. These activities were a vital element of Jewish life in the Commonwealth; they frequently were the main *raison d'être* for the Jews' entire sociopolitical and legal status, and have often been mentioned in our earlier chapters. We need concern ourselves now, therefore, mainly with some major trends in the East-European Jewish economy, and particularly with the great changes which occurred in the period here under review.

At first, to be sure, the Jewish arrivals, for the most part from the Holy Roman Empire, continued to earn their livelihood by their traditional occupations, especially moneylending and trade. The Polish rulers expected that, by adhering to their accustomed ways of life, the Jews would help to develop the country's backward economy. For this reason, Boleslas the Pious and his early successors stressed, in the general Jewish privileges, these occupational activities as needing protection. The basic charter issued by Casimir the Great begins with seven articles dealing with the treatment of pledges held by Jews as security for loans, and adds six more similar provisions in the remaining thirty articles. While some scholars explain this discrepancy as due to the complicated nature of loans and other monetary transactions, we need but recall that the medieval Polish charters were deeply indebted, both in their overall formulation and in their detailed provisions, to similar earlier enactments by Frederick II of Austria and other Central-European monarchs, who in turn had followed in the footsteps of the imperial legislators from Charlemagne and Louis the Pious to Frederick II, the last of the Hohenstaufen. To the end of the fifteenth century, money trade was indeed a dominant feature in the economic relations between Jews and Gentiles in the newly developing areas along the Vistula, the Dnieper, and the Niemen (Neman). Of course, facing fewer legal barriers, many moneylenders extended their activities into the related areas of tax farming and collecting customs duties and tolls, which often led them into still other branches of commerce, and even into direct landownership. This varied combination of economic enterprises also characterized the settlers of the first half of the sixteenth century and beyond. Such wealthy businessmen as the elder Moses Fiszel (followed by his grandson and namesake) and Salomon Calahora in Cracow, Izak Nachmanowicz in Lwów, and Michael Ezofowicz in Brest-Litovsk often appeared in their diverse capacities as "royal servitors," and as leaders of their respective Jewish communities as well. The younger Fiszel and Calahora even added to the various branches of business and public service a very active medical practice.[5]

However, moneylending constantly receded in proportion to other business activities, not only among the affluent leaders but also among the middle-class Jews. This transformation was reflected in the later royal charters. In the privilege issued by Casimir IV—which, as confirmed by Sigismund I and his successors, became the fundamental law for Polish Jewry to the end of the Commonwealth—the last two paragraphs took cognizance of the changed situation. While the original privilege, issued by Boleslas and expanded by Casimir the Great, had but briefly provided, in Article 12, that no one should interfere with any Jewish traveler or his merchandise, and that no tollmaster should collect from such travelers a higher toll than was paid by burghers of the same place of residence, the expanded charter promulgated by Casimir IV was much more explicit:

We further ordain that all Jews residing in Our realm shall be able freely and securely to purchase and acquire, without any hindrance or confiscation, all merchandise and other salable goods, however they may be called. They shall be able to trade in them in whatever fashion is employed by the Christians living in Our realm. Should any Christian deny these Jews the right to act in this manner or hinder them in any way in their business he would do it contrary to all Our royal ordinances and incur Our grave displeasure [Art. 45].

We ordain in addition that every merchant and whoever else he may be who exhibits his goods at an annual or weekly fair, shall sell them to the Jew on a par with the Christian. Should anyone act contrariwise and should the Jew submit a complaint against it, these salable goods shall be taken over for Our and the palatine's benefit [Art. 46].

Needless to say, in many Jewish communities some petty moneylenders still continued to extend loans to non-Jews on pledges. But their economic and social importance constantly declined, as did their percentage in the Jewish population. In many areas their places were actually taken by Jewish agents, who did not extend loans on their own, but merely found willing lenders among both Jews and Gentiles; they were satisfied with receiving moderate commissions for their services. According to Sebastyan Miczyński: "Jews not only engage in usurious transactions by themselves but have also infected some unfortunate citizens of this Crown. . . . A few [Christians] publicly lend money on usury; others—which is more cruel—hand the money over to Jews for usury." [6]

Although the canonical prohibition of "usury" (referring to interest of any size) still loomed large in the sixteenth-century debates in Poland, the facts of life induced many Christians, both native and foreign, to secure substantial revenues from loans. True, the contemporary theologians Stanisław Sokołowski and Marcin Śmiglecki published, in 1589 and 1596 respectively, antiusury pamphlets sharply attacking this practice of Christian lenders, whom they equated with Jews. Some churchmen, including Piotr Skarga, promoted the idea of charitable loan banks for needy Christians. Beginning in 1579, this idea, which had spread from fifteenth-century Italy through many European countries, led to the establishment in Poland, too, of a series of *montes pietatis*. Yet, at least one brotherhood, established in Warsaw in 1636, saw itself forced to charge 7 percent on its charitable loans to defray its expenses. This local inconsistency was of little importance to Jews, since but a few of them were able to live for any length of time in the new Polish capital. On the other hand, with the growing prosperity in sixteenth-century Poland and the rising prices of grain and other victuals in both domestic and international trade, the Polish landowners were able to accumulate much capital from sales of agricultural produce. This was also true of many churches and monasteries, whose landholdings were increasing by leaps and bounds and whose business administration was, on the whole, even more efficient than that of the lay landowners. Since direct investment of surplus funds in mercantile undertakings required much commercial know-how, many magnates and churchmen found it easier to place their capital at the disposal of experienced merchants, especially Jews, against the payment of interest, which varied according to the risks involved. Because of the inflationary trends in the country and the growing scarcity of capital, the rate of interest often rose from decade to decade, at times reaching 100 percent. These tendencies, and their acceleration after the "Deluge," are well illustrated by the developments in Zamość, although because of the settlement there of numerous Sephardic Jews, its Jewish community was not entirely typical. During the seventeenth century, Jews borrowed from nobles four times as much, and from the clergy fifty-six times as much, as they lent to them. Even in their relations with burghers after 1650, the Zamość Jews appeared in the records as borrowers as frequently as in their capacity of lenders.[7]

Ironically, the Jewish communities themselves were among the most favored borrowers. As public bodies endowed with the right of taxation, and as institutions enduring through generations, despite business cycles, the kahals seemed to offer greater financial security than individual debtors. Because of their ability to obtain long-term loans at lower rates of interest, some Jewish communities (like the municipalities) found it profitable to borrow money for reinvestment, particularly in loans to members. They were, of course, restrained by the possibility that some borrowers might default on their debts. But, even when they had taken no part in the original loans, Jewish communities often found to their chagrin that powerful creditors held them responsible for their members' debts—a collective responsibility readily taken over from the medieval practice of holding cities and even fellow-burghers responsible for debts of other burghers in international trade. Some communal elders felt themselves obliged to warn prospective noble creditors against extending loans to certain unreliable Jewish debtors, or to those who had suffered reverses and were likely to end in bankruptcy. Other loans were negotiated by the individual Jewish businessmen directly with the nobles, the community merely guaranteeing repayment. In return, the kahals frequently imposed on all such borrowers a special tax, which sometimes amounted to one-fifth of the interest payments to the lender. In time, many communities, increasingly forced to resort to deficit financing in their own communal budgets, had to borrow money in order to defray communal expenses. The result was that the communal debts grew rapidly; but many nobles and local churches, finding investments elsewhere less attractive, continued to lend their surplus capital to Jewish communities. Such communal loans were constantly renewable, the lending institutions often being more interested in the regular interest yield than in the repayment of the capital, which might have to be reinvested at greater potential risks. With the growing fiscal pressure of the government on the communities, especially in the period after 1648, the imbalance between indebtedness and running expenses took on unprecedented dimensions. For example, the community of Cracow found in 1724 that its total budgetary revenue of 39,075 zlotys easily covered its operating expenses of 23,356 zlotys. But it could not even approach covering the communal debt, the annual interest on which already exceeded 45,000 zlotys. The much smaller community of Leszno (Lissa) had in 1703 a public debt of but 3,345 zlotys. But within seven years that debt increased elevenfold; and it reached the staggering total of 535,493 zlotys in 1764, when the central organs of Polish and Lithuanian Jewry were suppressed. The enormous size of that debt burden may be gauged from the fact that the Cracow Jewish community's indebtedness in 1765 had risen to 135 Polish zlotys per capita. This was the equivalent of a debt of 810 zlotys per average family of six persons. A similar situation prevailed in Vilna; while the two other leading Lithuanian communities, Brest and Grodno, had an indebtedness of 70 and 160 zlotys per capita, respectively.[8]

The ever-worsening situation of the Jewish communities is placed into bolder relief by comparison with the generally more satisfactory financial operations of the Christian municipalities. On the whole, the cities were controlled by a minority of wealthy businessmen, pursuing rather self-serving policies. Their administrators were but partially restrained by the postulates of Judeo-Christian ethics, of which they were reminded from time to time by their preachers. They encountered, as a rule, even greater antagonism on the part of the szlachta than did the Jews, though of course the Church and the masses were much less hostile toward them. Yet, being burdened by fewer taxes, they were able at times to borrow funds at the nominal rate of 2–3 percent and lend them to their constituents at 18 percent or more. They also collected

large rents from city-owned housing and other municipal enterprises and services. In Poznań, for example, such revenue more
than quadrupled between 1500 and 1650; its share of the total
municipal budget rose from 31 percent in the 1580s to 45 percent
in the 1640s. While these factors varied from city to city, almost
all of them had a far better fiscal structure than the Jewish communities even before the "Deluge," the gap widening further in
the generally depressed eighteenth century.[9]

To a large extent this deterioration was owing to a rapid inflation: the value of the Polish zloty declined, over a century and a
quarter, by about 1,600 percent (the original gold zloty was now
worth 16–17 zlotys in currency). However, some devaluation had
already become quite pronounced under the first two Vasas. Before 1580, in Poland as in the rest of Europe, the old relationship
between gold and silver had, as a result of the influx of American
silver, changed from the medieval ratio of 11:1 to 14:1. More, the
silver content of a grosz, which by 1580 had gradually declined to
0.69 grams, fell to but 0.29 grams, according to an ordinance of
1623. The Jewish communities' impoverishment also came about
through a misguided fiscal policy, dictated partly by the interests
of the plutocracy which increasingly dominated communal management and partly by changing commercial constellations, which
obliged it to honor the loans and accumulated interest of many
defaulting debtors. Moreover, even without any legal justification,
mighty officials and lords often disregarded contractual agreements
and forced the community to pay debts long before the due date.
An interesting placard posted on all Poznań synagogues on Thurs-
day, Marḥeshvan 16, 5407 (October 25, 1646), and written in a
typical mixture of Hebrew and Yiddish, stated in part:

The community announces that, in a session of the entire communal
assembly, no one missing, careful consideration was given to the very
large amount it owes to the magnates and which it must provide for
the war, may God give us peace! In addition our community has realized that the magnates often come in the middle of the term and demand repayment of their loans, and that, in any case, we will have to
pay them at the time due. It is very difficult even in an ordinary year
to collect enough money to pay up the amounts owed to the magnates
on the due date; how much more so in an unusually difficult year.
Everyone is well aware, moreover, that the magnates are violent, and

no one dares to tell them what to do. This may, God forbid, result in bloodshed. That is why it was decided, from today on to collect forty assessments, the yield of which is to be used to pay the magnates 40,000 zlotys and the rest to defray [the ordinary] communal expenses.[10]

Clearly, there also were Jews who lent money to nobles. However, their number constantly diminished, and not many of them were found even in the rapidly expanding southeastern areas. An interesting case, recorded in Łuck in 1565, referred to a Jewish (Karaite) moneylender, Betko, son of Nisan (Misanowicz), from whom Prince Lew Sanguszko borrowed 716 shock groszy under the condition that, if he did not repay that amount within one year, the debt would be doubled. Characteristically, in 1583, when Betko adopted Christianity, he immediately turned over all his deeds to his son, Moses, who had remained Jewish. Even Prince Kurbskii, who, as we recall, once decided to expel the Jews from his township of Kovel, in 1565 borrowed 100 zlotys from a Kovel Jew (this amount seems to have increased to 125 through the addition of some interest). Yet, especially after the incorporation in 1569 of Volhynia and Podolia—together with the newly added provinces of Kiev and Bratslav—into the Polish Crown, we find more borrowings by Jews from the princes and other nobles of that area, than vice versa. Many of these loans were relatively small; but the loan of 20,000 reichstaler extended by the nobleman Tuczyński to a Jew in Poznań in 1637 was sufficiently large for the lender to ask for a guarantee from the community. Nevertheless, complications followed.[11]

Some communities in both parts of the dual Commonwealth early realized the danger of borrowing from powerful, often arbitrary, magnates, as was clearly stated in the Poznań announcement of 1646. On one occasion in 1688, the elders at first refused, then ultimately approved, a guarantee for a Poznań Jewish borrower of but 600 zlotys from a nobleman named Tomicki or Tomanicki, "for that nobleman has already written that we are responsible for our members." As early as 1671, the community had noted that many members had been "caught in the net of the noble Tomanicki, and were submerged in deep waters of indebtedness to him." The elders therefore warned every debtor to prepare the sum needed for the repayment of a loan to that creditor four weeks before the due date. For similar reasons the Lithuanian Council, in its first session of 1623, had adopted a resolution "that no community shall assume any [permanent] debts. Should a temporary shortage occur, forcing the communal elders to borrow money, they may do so, provided they pay back the loan within a year, under the sanction of a penalty and fine at the discretion of the provincial chiefs." Nevertheless, both in Lithuania and in the Polish Crown, caution was frequently thrown to the winds. After the emergencies of the 1640s and 1650s, even the Council of Four Lands itself had to incur, in 1666, a debt of 26,000 zlotys to Kazimierz Kowalkowski, secretary of the Treasury. This debt, repayable in four yearly instalments, apparently originated from tax arrears which the Council was unable to meet. The sanctions included in the deed of indebtedness show how low the Council's credit had sunk. If the instalments were not paid on time, the creditor was "to seize all Jews, both the provincial chiefs and the common Jews, in their respective localities—at fairs, markets, on the roads, as well as in private dwellings—and imprison them. . . . In that case our merchandise as well as the possessions of all Jews of the Crown may be taken away, the academies may be closed, and the houses of Jews in cities and hamlets may be confiscated and handed over to Christians or to anybody else." True, such drastic foreclosures seem never to have been applied in practice. But their mere statement highlighted the dangers involved when the communities at large and, particularly, the central organs of Polish-Lithuanian Jewry, incurred indebtedness directly or even guaranteed loans for coreligionists.[12]

Nonetheless, communal indebtedness generally grew by leaps and bounds. Apart from expending large amounts on welfare, particularly in periods of emergency, communal leaders had to continue lending money to, or guaranteeing loans for, members in distress, regardless of the inherent risks. Only occasionally did they resort to pressure on relatives to provide such loans. A characteristic entry in the Poznań minute book reads:

It is public knowledge that the community carries a tremendous burden nowadays in providing for the maintenance of the poor receiving regular financial aid. . . . In addition, it spends money on poor refugees who have recently arrived and who [cannot borrow money because they] have neither pledges nor land. . . . There also are persons temporarily impoverished because of lack of cash, though they own places [synagogue seats] and other real estate on which they wish to borrow from the community, loans which the communal chest is unable to provide. . . . It therefore was decided that such persons asking for a loan on any kind of real estate shall come and present their problems to the assembled community which will decide whether some wealthy member of the family should be obligated to extend such a loan for a certain amount publicly known to the community [Sunday, Sivan, 15, 5390 = May 26, 1630].[13]

Remarkably, there was relatively little governmental regulation of interest rates on Jewish loans. Originally, Jews were allowed to charge 100 percent; in 1367 the rate was reduced to 53 percent. But later charters mentioned no rates. Ecclesiastical bodies and most nobles were chiefly concerned with the security of their investments, which they preferred to entrust to Jewish communities on a long-term basis. Sometimes monasteries charged as little as 7 percent for such loans, a rate considered permissible by the managers of the Warsaw *mons pietatis* as well. On the other hand, businessmen as a rule sought higher revenue through short-term loans. Among Jews the community often drew a line between borrowings of very short duration (usually by traders wishing to purchase merchandise momentarily available at a low price in order to sell it with considerable profit at a forthcoming fair) and those which were to be repaid at a much later date. The Poznań community tried to hold rates on long-term loans to between 22 and 25 percent annually. However, on credit extended during a fair and repayable immediately thereafter, interest was chargeable at an annual rate of up to 50 percent. Loans granted three weeks before the fair could be subject to a charge of 33⅓ percent in 1639, and up to 50 percent when credit tightened in 1646. But for the subsequent three weeks the allowable range was only up to 22 percent in 1639, and up to 25 percent in 1646. These rates varied, however, from area to area and period to period. The Cracow communal ordinance of 1595 limited the interest rate to 20 percent; for some time this rate seems to have been adhered to in practice. At the same time the prevailing rate in Lithuania was one percent per week, or some 50 percent during the usual Jewish lunar year. While mainly intended to ensure the availability of short-term loans, such a system often led to the impoverishment of borrowers who could not meet their obligations at an early date. By 1670 the Lithuanian Council resolved that high interest "devours the borrowers to such an extent that they cannot carry it," and ordered the communities under its jurisdiction to set rates sustainable by their membership.[14]

Interest could easily be concealed under various guises through special contractual arrangements. For example, in 1630, the Poznań community bought 10,000 zlotys' worth of gold jewelry from one of its leaders, Zvi Hirsch b. Isaac, and subsequently received these 10,000 zlotys as a loan with a moderate 10 percent interest charge, renewable after five years for another ten years. However, in another stipulation Zvi Hirsch was exempted from any tax on that income. Since taxes were quite high, the creditor's gain from the loan was substantially increased. There may also have been a hidden discount at the time of the loan, if the value of the jewelry was less than the amount lent. More overt was a transaction some fifteen years later between another communal leader, Zvi Hirsch b. Mendel, who had lent the community 15,000 zlotys which he had borrowed from a Christian merchant, Adam Busch of Gdańsk. It was arranged that, in repayment, the community should disburse 3,000 zlotys annually over a period of twelve years. The payment of 36,000 for a loan of 15,000 was explained by the lender's obligation simultaneously to satisfy a loan of 22,000 zlotys owed by the community to Busch, the community merely pledging itself to return to Zvi Hirsch that amount plus all costs incurred by him in that connection. At times the reverse was true, and even rich individuals, like Joseph Mendel in Poznań, occasionally needed a guarantee from the community for large loans from Christian traders. In a transaction recorded in 1637, Joseph Mendel borrowed from the nobleman Tuczyński 20,000 reichstalers. In 1645–46 we still hear of that debt, though in one place it is mentioned as amounting to 130,000 zlotys, and in another as 100,000 zlotys. Basically this represented the same original amount, perhaps supplemented by different interest accruals and reduced by intervening payments. Moreover, as late as 1667, that is, thirty years after the date of borrowing, the loan of 100,000 zlotys was still outstanding.[15]

In general, there were relatively few "teeth" for the enforcement of the credit regulations by the central councils. To begin with, the very business conducted by the individual communities in lending to or borrowing from its members with interest was in violation of the general antiusury legislation of the Bible and the Talmud. In fact, when the Council of Four Lands in 1607 adopted its summation of existing laws on usury, its spokesman, Joshua b. Alexander Falk ha-Kohen, explicitly stated: "As to the custom of heads of communities borrowing money from Jews for communal purposes and paying them specific interest, I have found no support for it by any legal precedent or any reliable [scholarly] authority." Yet no community seems to have hesitated to continue in its accustomed ways. Similarly, in 1674 when the Council of Four Lands limited all interest charges to 18 groszy weekly for every 100 zlotys (an annual rate of about 30 percent), the Poznań community decided to submit the matter to its officiating rabbi and his academy to decide whether the resolution "applies to us and obliges us to observe the ordinance of the Council of Four Lands." Evidently, the Council had failed to provide this resolution with appropriate sanctions. Nor was it apparently recorded in any other extant communal source, most likely because the local elders felt that the Council had not taken cognizance of the continual depreciation of money and the other risks involved in loans. Much more important was the long-range impact of the Council's extensive 1624 ordinance against "fugitives" (borehim) —a term which often applied also to insolvent debtors who remained in their old residences. Among its thirty-eight articles, two provided that no court should grant an extension to debtors, other than those who were the victims of fire or burglary, unless the extension accrued to the creditor's benefit. The Council also imposed a penalty of excommunication for fraudulent bankruptcies. At the same time, various communities adopted preventive measures, such as forbidding men under twenty years of age, and newlyweds during the first three years of marriage, to contract business loans. Experience had taught them that young persons often fell prey to ruthless speculators. However, the necessity for credit transactions was so overwhelming that the same communal authorities who enacted such regulations also had to look for subterfuges to circumvent the old biblical-talmudic antiusury laws. It was under the impact of those economic necessities that the Polish Council itself, while adopting, in 1607, its comprehensive "Statute regarding Usury," had to make a most significant concession. Prepared by one of the Council's outstanding rabbinic leaders, Joshua Falk ha-Kohen of Lwów—author of the well-known commentary on the Karo-Isserles code of laws, entitled *Sefer Me'irat 'eynaim* (Book of Enlightening the Eyes), from which he became generally known under the acronym SM'A—this compilation, approved by the rabbinic and lay members of the Council, sanctioned the standardized legal fiction that the lenders merely participated in the borrower's business profits.[16]

Connected with this relationship between creditor and borrower was the growingly important activity of agents and brokers. An entire class of middlemen developed who knew of persons, particularly non-Jews, having ample funds which they wished to invest profitably. On the other hand, the middlemen were also aware of prospective borrowers, and of their credit standing, much beyond the ken of the would-be creditors. Arranging transactions between such persons became a profitable business. It soon called forth a number of communal regulations concerning the legitimate rate of commissions. At first the communal elders, generally unfavorably disposed to that entire professional class, tried to limit the brokers' rewards to 0.25 or 0.5 percent of the borrowed capital. In practice, the commissions often were much higher, especially if the borrower was in dire need, or if the lender had been unable to place an advantageous loan elsewhere. Regrettably, we have far less information about the actual credit operations than about the regulations which the government occasionally, or the Jewish communal organs more frequently, tried to impose upon every phase of that trade. The elders often insisted that the lender pay the amount of the loan directly to the borrower and not transmit it through the broker. For Christian capitalists, Jewish mediators could also be used for loans to other Christians, whereby the lender eliminated the onus of charging "usury" to a coreligionist.

Of course, there were professional moneylenders and others who borrowed money for the purpose of relending it. At times, inexperienced young men saw in such double transactions an easy opportunity to make a profit through the spread between the interest rates they paid and charged. However, they were frequently victimized by speculators or unscrupulous agents. Hence came the aforementioned communal prohibition forbidding newlyweds to borrow in the first three years of their marriage. But in all these matters Polish authorities, including Jews, could invoke innumerable precedents set for earlier generations of Jews in West-European and Mediterranean societies.[17]

In order to facilitate credit transactions, Polish Jewry expanded the use of negotiable instruments. We recall that under the rule of early medieval Islam, Jewish bankers had already made use of the *suftaja* to transfer funds without resorting to cash payments. Somewhat similar drafts were used by medieval Ashkenazic Jewry, especially in connection with fairs, when any transfer of coins was exposed to the perils of the road. We shall see that even in eighteenth-century Poland a group of Jews returning from a fair was despoiled both of its merchandise and its cash. For such reasons, as well as to facilitate transfers of funds from one person to another without repeated certification of signatures, Polish Jewish businessmen began extensively using the so-called *mamran* (doubtless a corruption of the Latin *membrana,* or parchment). First recorded in Poland by the distinguished jurist Mordecai b. Abraham Yaphe, in a book published in 1598–99, this type of document contained on one side only the signature of the issuer and on the reverse side in exactly the same position the amount payable and the due date. Later on the text was amplified in various ways, but it retained the original system of having the debtor's signature and the amount and date due written in the same position on the two sides of the document. As late as 1770, for example, one *mamran* read:

The meaning of this deed is that the signatory on the reverse side is obliged to pay the amount of 13 ducats in cash, God willing, in the middle of Adar 5530 [approximately March 8, 1770]. The holder of this deed is entitled to require payment of this indebtedness from the debtor or his representative, wherever he may be, particularly in Breslau [Wrocław] or Frankfort [on the Oder]. This bond shall carry with it all the rights possessed by a bill of exchange before the state courts. Done with a handclasp and with all possible assurance of the validity of this indubitable writ of indebtedness, with the provision that the holder of this deed shall enjoy full faith with respect to all matters pertaining to this indebtedness.

For a specific reason, however, Polish lenders preferred to issue several *mamran*s for smaller amounts, rather than a single *mamran* for the total amount of indebtedness. According to Jewish practice, all creditors of a defaulting debtor had to share equally in the proceeds from the liquidation of his property, *regardless* of the size of their respective claims. Each *mamran,* therefore, was entitled only to the same percentage of the debtor's assets; whereby a creditor with a large claim attested by a single *mamran* stood to lose much more than if he presented several *mamran*s. In other words, in such cases each *mamran* was treated as if it had an identical value on a par with scrip—of which it was, in some respects, but an interesting variant.[18]

GENERAL COMMERCE

In the course of the sixteenth century, the Jewish money trade often became but a handmaiden of general commerce. Like non-Jewish merchants, Jews often extended credit to purchasers, for which, if it was of some duration, they usually charged interest. Safeguards for repayment, security for the loan, and all other aspects of moneylending, played a considerable role in such transactions. On the other hand, local shopkeepers selling merchandise to farmers frequently had to be satisfied with payments in kind. In smaller localities, goods acquired in this way probably formed an important part of a retail merchant's inventory, so that he benefited from the sales of both the original and the derivative wares. Occasionally, payments in kind also figured prominently in the revenue of small-town doctors and other professionals.

Most prominent, if not most numerous, was the class of merchants engaged in international trade. With the upsurge of the Polish economy in the sixteenth century, the old trade routes from East to West assumed new significance. The "Tatar" route, leading from the Caspian Sea via the northern shores of the Black Sea to southern Poland, and the "Moldavian" route connecting the Balkans with the same southern provinces of Poland-Lithuania, led to Lwów, from which the trade radiated westward to such emporia as Lublin, Cracow, Warsaw, Poznań, Toruń, and Gdańsk. At the same time, the land routes from Muscovy led through Lithuania to Vilna and Gdańsk, and often branched out into Warsaw, Lublin, or Poznań, all of which, together with Cracow, served as the main connecting links with the Holy Roman Empire. Despite the availability of improved highways made possible by greater utilization of the large mass of serf labor, waterways, particularly those leading to and through the Vistula to the Baltic and, to a lesser extent, through the Dnieper to the Black Sea, played an enormous role in the transportation of bulky and heavy staple goods, such as grain, and lumber and other forestry products. These were the most important articles of export from Poland and Lithuania. Only for cattle, the third large component of the export trade, did land transportation remain the least expensive method, inasmuch as hundreds or thousands of heads of oxen, sheep, horses, and other animals could be driven from Moldavia and the Ukraine, whence many of them originated, to the western provinces of Poland, and thence to Germany and other lands. So lucrative was cattle export that the Moldavian authorities, in response to complaints that Jewish purchasers were bringing about the ruin of local merchants, forbade Jews to travel deep into their country—a prohibition which apparently went largely unheeded.[19]

Reference has already been made to the great need for Polish grain and lumber in the large western metropolises. The appetite for beef was also quite staggering. According to some nineteenth-century studies, in the Late Middle Ages some German workers' families consumed an average of four pounds of meat and eight quarts of butter daily. An amazing entry in the account book of a Dominican monastery in Strasbourg of 1523 tells us that every outside worker received daily, at noon and evening, an allotment of 6–7 kilograms (13–15 pounds) of meat. (It stands to reason that any surplus, not consumed on the spot, was to be taken home for the worker's family.) Hence the local production in central and western Europe required much supplementation from Polish and other exporters. Also transported overland as a rule were such important products as animal pelts, furs, and wax. Furs, largely imported into Poland from Muscovy, were reexported to the West, especially from Poznań. It has been calculated, for instance, that Poznań's annual export of the high-priced sable furs rose from 2,400 pieces in 1519–20 to 3,800 in 1585; weasel (ermine, marten, or mink), from 1,000 pieces to 19,120; and the most popular fur, dormouse, from about 500,000 to over a million units. Several other kinds of furs were also sold in thousands of pieces each. In comparison, direct shipments of all furs from Muscovy via the four Baltic ports of Narva, Riga, Gdańsk, and Königsberg, totaled only a little over 500,000 pieces in the eight years of 1562–69. Wax, too, was an important article of Polish-Lithuanian export. It was widely used, not only in the manufacture of candles for churches and private homes but also, because of its durability and light weight, in barter trade and other forms of payment. It is estimated that between 1537 and 1553 Poland shipped 12,000–23,000 stones (of ca. 29 pounds each) westward annually; in the second half of the century the shipments rose to some 30,000 stones a year. In return, the dual Commonwealth received major supplies of textiles, cosmetics, and oriental products, as well as metals, precious stones, and other luxury goods to supply the demand of the growingly wealthy landowners and urban patricians.[20]

Of the commodities for human consumption, only wine was imported in substantial quantity, principally from Hungary and Turkey, despite its relatively high price. Jews had the usual difficulties in handling wine of Gentile provenance, because of the talmudic prohibition against "wine of libation" used for idolatrous purposes. Although medieval rabbis living among Christians and Muslims had long before greatly modified that prohibition by pointing out that their monotheistic neighbors rarely thought of consecrating any but a small percentage of the wine in their possession for ritualistic purposes, pious Jews still refrained from drinking wine handled by non-Jews. But the majority of Polish rabbis, led by Moses Isserles, tolerated the widespread Jewish trade in wine, even if it was originally cultivated, processed, and transported by Gentiles. More serious, Jewish wine merchants faced such curious Jew-baiting accusations as were voiced by Sebastyan Miczyński, who wrote: "[They] buy not only in barrels but entire wine cellars in Hungary, and this is the sole reason why only small barrels arrive in Poland nowadays, and contain wine so diluted as never was the case." Nonetheless, Jews continued to play a significant role in the importation of wine, and possibly in the reexport trade as well.[21]

An interesting illustration of the far-ranging activities of Jews residing even in smaller localities is offered by a 1541 document recording the vicissitudes of one Iliya Moiseievich Doktorovich of Tykocin, then part of Lithuania. On a visit to Leipzig, this Lithuanian merchant acquired some precious jewelry from a Nuremberg trader for 1,900 zlotys. In return, he promised to deliver 400 hundredweights of flax in Vilna. As security he left 80 pieces of sable. At home he encountered difficulties with his promised shipment, however. After partial delivery he was arrested; and the representative of the Nuremberg merchant seems to have absconded with both the jewels and the objects he and his employer had received from Doktorovich, who had in the meantime been released. The final outcome of that affair is unknown.[22]

Jews thus found manifold openings in the various fields of international trade. Quite a few were engaged in the transport of goods. A whole class of Jewish wagoners and coachmen (in Latin *vectores;* also known under their Yiddish-Hebrew designation of *baalagoles*), often portrayed in modern Yiddish literature, moved merchandise from city to city and over short or long distances. We do not have sufficient information about the fees charged by them; but it stands to reason that, as in the case of non-Jewish wagoners, the remuneration was scaled according to distance and the weight of the transported goods. Fees doubtless also varied from locality to locality, and increased with the risks involved, since at least the major haulers had to assume the responsibility for objects lost. Curiously, in 1637 the Lithuanian Council of Provinces ordained that Jewish drivers must not wear the garb called *furmanki,* the usual attire of Polish coachmen—either because they were afraid that with this attire they might violate the prohibition against *sha'atnez* (wool mixed with linen; Lev. 19:19, Deut. 22:11) or, as the resolution intimates, in order to separate the Jewish drivers more effectively from their non-Jewish confreres. At times, however, Jewish entrepreneurs hired Christian carters, and vice versa. The general insecurity of travel and transport on the roads must have discouraged many wagoners from carrying expensive cargo great distances, particularly in the eastern provinces. Jewish wagoners were exposed to special dangers because of their "strange" religious observances. On occasion, when forwarding agents registered at toll gates and customs houses they did not give the names of the goods' owners, but rather their own, as payers of tolls or duties—a circumstance which complicates statistical computations of the Jewish part in the export-import trade. On the other hand, many Jewish exporters, acting as agents for nobles or churchmen whose estates they administered and whose surplus produce they, either personally or through subagents, sold to purchasers abroad, had every incentive to name the real or purported noble or clerical owners because of the extensive privileges enjoyed by those classes.[23]

In general, the export-import trade could be very lucrative for well-connected and experienced businessmen. Since the magnates and the gentry supplied some 75 percent of all the grain exported via Gdańsk, they and their Jewish agents enjoyed the benefits of the Sejm's class legislation which freed all agricultural exports from taxes and allowed for duty-free importation of much foreign merchandise for the nobles' own use. Jewish agents claiming such exemptions sometimes came into conflict with Jewish tax farmers who demanded payment of the usual duties. However, in one such controversy brought to his attention, R. Joel Sirkes sided with the agent. True, international traders had to watch the rapidly changing supply and demand situation very closely. According to a recent estimate, the prices of rye exported from Gdańsk to Amsterdam in 1631–40 yielded profits of as little as 0.3 percent in 1632 and 1.6 percent in 1633, but as high as 73.0 percent in 1640 —as compared with 91.1 percent in 1606. This instability may actually have played into the hands of Jewish merchants or agents, whose much-needed alertness and business know-how was thus often demonstrated to the original noble or ecclesiastical producers. A farsighted businessman not in need of immediate cash returns could, with fuller information about conditions prevailing in the harbor city and the recipient countries, time his sales more profitably. At an early stage of that quickly developing trade, to be sure, direct Jewish participation was threatened by a royal prohibition forbidding the Lublin Jews to deal in grain. This decree, dated December 30, 1521, though issued in response to a litigation between the local Jews and the burghers which was followed by the appointment of a royal commission to investigate the merits of the parties' contentions, could easily be extended to other Jews as well. But this royal decision seems not to have been carried into effect, since Sigismund I himself nine years later (April 16, 1530) stipulated that the Lublin Jews, like the burghers, should be obliged to pay only the "old customs duties." In 1550 they were expressly placed on a footing of equality with the burghers with respect to weights, measures, duties, and royal taxes.[24]

Another important medium for both international and domestic trade was the fair. From time immemorial, towns held frequent meetings of sellers and buyers on stated days. Locally they often held weekly markets, which attracted peasants from the neighboring villages who brought their produce for sale and acquired from the merchants industrial products needed at home. These local markets were overshadowed in importance by large national and international fairs. In the seventeenth century the most important foreign fair extensively used by Polish and Lithuanian merchants was that held at Frankfort on the Oder. "The flowering of the Frankfort fairs," observes Selma Stern, "coincides with the settlement of Jews in the Prussian state." However, Polish Jews cultivated those fairs long before their official resettlement in Prussia in the mid-seventeenth century. Of growing influence also were the fairs held in Wrocław (Breslau) and Leipzig. We recall that all these cities had at different times expelled their Jews and, by the end of the sixteenth century, no longer had any local Jewish communities. Nevertheless, they opened their gates to Jewish traders, either because of the expected financial benefits or, as in the case of Wrocław, under Polish pressure. For Frankfort, too, Sigismund III intervened with the elector of Brandenburg to secure a significant concession for prospective Jewish visitors.[25]

On the other hand, the domestic fairs in Gdańsk, Toruń, Poznań, Cracow, Jarosław, and Lublin attracted numerous foreigners, many of whom transacted important business with Jewish merchants. Lublin's annual February fairs, in particular, attracted large crowds of exhibitors and would-be purchasers. As early as 1517, even before the organization of a full-fledged Jewish community in the city, the Austrian envoy Siegmund von Herberstein referred to the important role played by Jewish merchants at the Lublin fairs. There Jewish traders from all over the Commonwealth had a chance of direct contact with one another, as well as with a motley of foreign traders and agents. According to the Cracow patrician Andreas (Andrzej) Cellarius, Lublin in the mid-seventeenth century was visited by "merchants from most distant lands, Germans, Greeks, Armenians, Arabs, Muscovites, Turks, Frenchmen, Italians, and Englishmen." Curiously, as late as 1641, the Lublin burghers sued some Jewish merchants before the royal Court of Assessors. They claimed that Jewish competition, both in crafts and commerce during the fairs and while the Crown Tribunal was in session, seriously undermined their livelihood. Thereupon the judges sentenced the Jewish merchants of Lublin to pay an indemnity of 50,000 zlotys to the burghers, and forbade them to interfere with the privileges of the Christian municipality. In general, however, local merchants benefited from the presence of Jewish exhibitors at the fairs, and even those Polish cities which excluded Jews from permanent residence (for example, Gdańsk and Toruń), were fairly hospitable to Jewish traders during fairs. They usually extended their welcome to visitors to include several days before the opening of the markets, for the preparation of their displays, and about two weeks thereafter for winding up their affairs. Some exhibitors found it to their advantage to reduce the pressure of having to dispose of all goods within the limited time or of having to seal and store them until the following fair, and entrusted any remaining merchandise to local agents, under the guise of a fictitious sale, for later disposal. Domestic fairs became so important that many contemporary contracts, Jewish and non-Jewish, used their names as substitutes for calendar dates in designating time limits for payments or deliveries.[26]

Jewish communities as such often had to play an active role at these large gatherings. In 1617, for instance, the Council of Four Lands directly requested the city council of Wrocław to admit the wives of Polish Jewish merchants to its fairs, a request which, after some hesitation, was complied with at least for one year. Exceptionally, representatives of the communities themselves engaged in selling and buying. More frequently, the communal elders delegated one of their members to serve as a "market judge," in order to settle disputes among Jewish participants. Occasionally, he also acted to prevent overpricing or shady deals by Jewish businessmen which might blacken the name of the community at large. This office, the appointment to which seems at times to have required the approval of one of the central councils, not only gave its holder a sense of power but also produced revenue from fees at the judicial proceedings. It loomed so large in importance that in 1644 the Lithuanian Council of Provinces decided that the Brest community's monopoly in naming one of its members for this post at the Lublin fair be replaced by an annual rotation of delegates from Brest, Grodno, and Pinsk. Almost immediately, however, Brest was granted a postponement of that change for six years. In contrast, according to a resolution of 1647, the more provincial fair of Kopyl (?) was to be supervised permanently by a Brest delegate, together with a second delegate alternately designated by the two other communities. Sometimes the communal representative had to defend the rights of a coreligionist before the local authorities, particularly against unfair treatment by a Gentile seller or buyer, or against seizure of goods by a foreign creditor to satisfy claims on him or one of his compatriots. The two fairs of Lublin and Jarosław, in particular, became so important for Jewish businessmen throughout the country that they became the regular meeting places of the Council of Four Lands, since many of its members wished to attend the fairs. As a result, some of the most distinguished rabbis of the country also met in Lublin or Jarosław, in order to advise the Council on matters of law and morals. In time such rabbinical gatherings resembled little synods and, in cooperation with the lay members, adopted formal resolutions which became binding enactments for all Polish communities. They also indirectly influenced the Lithuanian Council and had an impact on the evolution of Jewish law in other countries as well. We shall see that these sessions gave the Jewish communal elders the opportunity to settle a variety of communal and private affairs.[27]

Understandably, trade at fairs usually required much capital investment. At times, therefore, Jews of various localities formed partnerships to raise the necessary funds. For example, after 1550, four Lithuanian Jews (Isaac Brodawka of Brest-Litovsk, Eliezer Abramowicz of Tykocin, Izaak Lamowicz of Śledzew, and Aron Izraelowicz of Grodno) jointly raised 100,000 zlotys for their trade with Gdańsk. Their case was unusual only because, after they had brought their valuable merchandise to the Baltic city, they were turned back by the local burghers. Their complaint to the king brought about a royal intervention, which, however, at best indemnified them for direct losses but not for the profits they might have obtained from selling their goods at the fair. Needless to say, international trade was also conducted by Jewish and non-Jewish businessmen outside the fairs. For example, the extensive exchanges between Cracow and Prague, each of which embraced a major Jewish community, were almost entirely in Jewish hands. Sebastyan Miczyński complained that, whereas in the past several Poznań Jews had imported, from Leipzig, Frankfort [on the Oder], and other foreign and domestic localities, goods worth only several scores of thousands of zlotys, in 1618 Mojżesz Fekus and Lewek Bogacz (the Rich) were each bringing in wares valued at several hundred thousand zlotys. Another rich Poznań merchant, Jeleń, allegedly invested 150,000 zlotys "to bring in all sorts of merchandise from Nuremberg, Leipzig, and Frankfort and to import others from France, the Netherlands, Lübeck, Hamburg, Szczecin, Amsterdam [!], Sweden, Norway, and Moscow by sea to Gdańsk. He has an understanding with overseas merchants; he receives and buys from them goods which he then transports to various markets and sells to Christians for two or three times their cost." Jeleń's coreligionist Wolf Bocian (Poper) not only owned seven retail stores in Cracow but, with a capital of 300,000–400,000 zlotys, employed agents all over Poland, "for there is no merchandise which he fails to handle." [28]

Some Jewish merchants also operated with borrowed capital. If we discount Miczyński's anti-Jewish bias, we find his description of such transactions fairly representative of what actually happened, from time to time:

Under the leadership of a Cracow Jew Feivel, they [the Jews] fraudulently borrowed 300,000 zlotys from merchants in Gdańsk, especially

Dutchmen. In Elbląg [Elbing] they likewise caused the local merchants losses of 100,000 zlotys. More recently in Lublin and Jarosław they received various textiles on credit from honorable Englishmen for 200,000 zlotys; by cheating them out of that amount they reduced these aliens to poverty. An Elbląg merchant, Akraga . . . started his textile business with 100,000 zlotys. Not long thereafter Jews got [goods] from him. . . . Enjoying a good credit standing, he obtained more merchandise from other traders and added it to his deliveries to his Jewish customers. In this way he not only lost his own investment but also misled other merchants to the tune of 600,000 zlotys.

The amounts are undoubtedly exaggerated, and the more or less simultaneous occurrence of these incidents is highly suspect; but they do illustrate the risky nature of all trade among perfect strangers meeting at fairs. Jewish elders were understandably concerned about the aspersions cast on the entire Jewish community as a result of shady deals by individual Jews. In 1646 the Poznań Jewish communal council adopted a resolution reading: "Regarding unreliable men who acquire merchandise on credit while they notoriously never pay their debts, it was unanimously decided that none of them should be allowed to travel to Gdańsk without the elders' knowledge. The officials present at the fairs of Toruń and Gdańsk should check on them and warn merchants not to extend any credit to them. The community shall also punish, at its discretion, all sinful agents engaged in mediating shady deals." [29]

Honest traders had to be cognizant, moreover, of such misfortunes as had beset Iliya Doktorovich of Tykocin in 1541. Nor were the fairs themselves safe places for exhibitors. The gathering of a multitude of strangers and their wares in relatively small towns like Lublin, naturally increased the ever-present danger of a fire. One conflagration in 1624 destroyed much of the merchandise on display and, by a chain reaction, caused numerous insolvencies among the merchants of Lwów and other cities. Great variations in the demand for goods, especially grain, added to the uncertainties of the markets. For example, Polish grain exports to the Netherlands varied sharply from one year to another in both price and quantity. In the single decade of 1622–31, we find swings in the pendulum of sales from as high as 62,528 lasts (of 60 bushels each) in 1622, to but 43,281 and 25,226 lasts in the following two

years, respectively. By 1629 and 1630 the exports dropped cata-
strophically to 8,985 and 8,941, though they recovered in 1631 to
31,797 lasts. One may easily see how risky an enterprise it was to ship
grain from a great distance and at large expense to the harbor and
then fail to sell it. We understand, therefore, why in 1567 the
mighty Prince Lew Sanguszko, in borrowing 2,750 zlotys from a
Grodno Jew, Marek, to be repaid upon the arrival of the prince's
grain shipment in Gdańsk, had to promise in the contract that, if
the debt was not repaid by the due date, the creditor could temporarily take over the prince's vast landholdings and keep them
until he was reimbursed.[30]

While Jewish trade with Western lands was promoted by the
fairs and continued on a fairly high level into the seventeenth century (except for the dislocations created by the Thirty Years' War
and subsequently by the Muscovite-Swedish invasions of Poland),
that with the East greatly diminished. Lwów, which had competed
on almost equal terms with Venice in the trade with the Middle
East in the fifteenth century, began losing ground after the Portuguese expansion opened the Orient to the West and many goods
could be shipped directly to Lisbon for distribution in western
and central Europe. Even Lwów's once flourishing exchanges with
Jewish traders in Constantinople, as we recall, greatly declined in
the latter part of the sixteenth century. Manifold reasons accounted
for this decline: the general weakening of Turkish power, economic as well as political, at the end of the century; the simultaneous diminution of Jewish influence in Constantinople; the
general drop in European trade with the Black Sea area after the
displacement of Italian commercial and political influence there;
and, finally, the gradual deterioration of Polish-Turkish political
relations, which soon led to outright war and the great Polish defeat at Cecora in 1620. These great transformations in the pattern
of trade between the Ottoman Empire and Poland found a telling
expression in the important exchanges of Polish grain for Greek
wines. The demand for Polish grain on the part of the rapidly
growing population of the North-Italian metropolises was increasingly satisfied by imports from Gdańsk to Genoa and Venice on
Dutch and Italian ships. On their return journeys the Western
masters loaded their ships with wines from Crete and other Vene-

tian and Genoese colonies in the eastern Mediterranean. The much shorter land route from Turkey lost its allure after a Turkish (Tatar) raid across Poland's southeastern frontier in 1589. When the raiders struck the important city of Śniatyn, it was in the midst of its annual fair, which had attracted many merchants from far and wide; and the assailants carried home a rich loot. Early in 1590 the sultan formally canceled the existing Turko-Polish treaty of "perpetual peace." Three years later the Zaporogian Cossacks retaliated by thoroughly plundering the Moldavian city of Giurgiu during its fair. A Moldavian uprising against Turkish overlordship in 1595, and a successful attack on a large mercantile caravan by mercenaries in the service of the Walachian hospodar in 1599, further emphasized the great hazards of shipping goods to and from the Balkans. These difficulties in overland transport were seriously aggravated by local commercial rivalries and appetites.

Despite his good relations with King Sigismund II Augustus, Don Joseph Nasi was accused, while paying a brief visit to Lwów in August 1570, of having acquired forbidden merchandise (probably tin used for armaments) for export to Turkey in defiance of a Polish embargo. Although speedily exonerated, he and his associates must have become doubly aware of the risks involved in dealing with the Polish authorities. Finally, more and more of the Red Russian lords sought to enrich themselves by imposing tolls on all merchandise passing through their lands on its way to Lwów. The payment of such tolls greatly reduced the importers' profits. It doubtless also contributed to recurrent liquidity crises. Don Joseph's agents had to borrow money at such high rates of interest that the situation ultimately led to their financial ruin. Thus ended the meteoric rise of the Sephardic traders from Constantinople in Lwów. They were but partially replaced by another group of Sephardim, who came from Italy and settled in Zamość.[31]

Whatever trade with the Balkan peninsula was still carried on in Red Russia, increasingly fell into the hands of the Armenians, though a few Polish Jews still held on to their diminishing share, particularly through purchases of cattle in Moldavia for resale in Poland and beyond. Remarkably, though themselves an ethnic-religious minority struggling for commercial rights, the Armenians had long since joined Lwów's plebeian groups, represented by the Committee of Forty in the city administration, in fighting Jewish competitors. In 1597, for example, they helped arouse that Committee to accuse the municipal council of having made a commercial agreement with the local Jews,

as a result of which all merchandise and victuals, not only in Lwów but also in the entire Rus land, have been handed over to Jews. This measure has caused grave damage and detriment to the city's commerce and the impoverishment of its burghers to such an extent that the artisans cannot purchase anything from other Catholics in the face of Jewish competition.

All this sound and fury was about an agreement dating back to 1581, which was more restrictive than permissive in regard to Jewish commerce. Trade with Turkey was generally freer, but Jews were excluded from purchasing any beverages, victuals, or medicines there and were forced to make all acquisitions in the presence of a special city "interpreter." In exporting to Turkey, on the other hand, the Jewish shippers had to pay exorbitant sums for transport. In 1585, for example, a Turkish Jew, Abraham Gambai, hired three Christian wagoners to carry an unspecified cargo to Constantinople at a cost of 528 zlotys. The resistance of the petty shopkeepers, too, made trade with Turkey very difficult. When four Lwów Jews acquired 1,400 stone of raisins from a Greek in Constantinople, the shipment was intercepted for "examination" by officials of the Committee of Forty before it reached its destination. Among the arguments advanced for the seizure was one that the Jewish purchasers might divert the shipment to Śniatyn and Walachia, disregarding the city's staple rights.[32]

In contrast, Muscovy remained consistently antagonistic toward Jewish traders. Hence, the most important article of Muscovite export to Poland and the West, namely furs, had to be acquired by Jewish merchants in Smolensk (as long as it was in Polish hands) or in Mogilev (Mohilev) and other Lithuanian cities, and transported from there to the various Polish fairs. Moreover, the Muscovite drive to the sea for direct exchanges with Western Europe was crowned with partial success by the occupation of Narva on the Baltic (definitively in 1704) and the founding of Archangel (1583), on the northern Dvina, close to the White Sea.

Subsequently, the acquisition of Riga (1710) fully opened up the famous "window to the West," of which Peter the Great made so extensive a use in the early eighteenth century. On the Lithuanian side, however, Jews remained quite active in importing goods from Muscovy and sending them to the Polish Crown and further west. In the sixteenth century Brest and Slutsk, in the seventeenth Vilna and particularly Mogilev, the main centers of that East-West exchange, embraced substantial Jewish communities. They included such Jewish merchants with far-flung business interests as Michael Ezofowicz and Saul Judycz Wahl of Brest and Affras (Ephraim) Rachmaelovich of Mogilev.[33]

The diplomatic and military vicissitudes in the relations between Poland and Muscovy, as well as the general Muscovite xenophobia, often led to extremely protectionist trade policies. While in 1550 Ivan IV strictly prohibited any entry by Jews into Muscovite possessions, twenty years later he also excluded Armenian and Greek envoys, under the excuse that they were hostile Ottoman subjects. Conversely, in 1597 Sigismund III closed his country's frontiers to Muscovite visitors, and forbade his own subjects to visit Muscovy. (But he had to revoke this order in the following year, as he stated, because of the hardships this prohibition inflicted upon his subjects.) In contrast, not only Dmitri the Pretender, whose occupation of the tsarist throne depended entirely on the military aid of Polish magnates, but also Tsar Feodor I, Ivan's successor and a candidate for the Polish crown after Báthory's death, opened to the Poles vistas of free trade and unimpeded travel even beyond the Muscovite boundaries, into Persia, Bukhara, and Khiva. When Wladislaw IV, as crown prince and later king of Poland, aspired to the Muscovite throne, he made similar pledges to Muscovite merchants for freedom of trade with Poland and the West. But these ventures proved quite futile, and had little bearing on the actual commercial relations between the two countries. In any case, Jews remained excluded from direct participation in the Russo-Polish trade, which was maintained on a modest scale, weathering all political and military storms, even during the hostilities between Muscovy and Poland-Lithuania.[34]

DOMESTIC MARKETS

International trade, though quite lucrative and prestigious, furnished a livelihood to far fewer entrepreneurs and employees than domestic commerce did. Moreover, most international merchants also engaged in domestic trade, whether wholesale or retail, or both. Only some 20 percent of Polish-Lithuanian grains were exported to other lands. Most of the agricultural produce not consumed on the spot by the farmers, landlords, and their retinue, found its way into the domestic trade, particularly in the larger cities. Here, too, Jewish traders began playing an ever more conspicuous role. Some foreign visitors were greatly impressed by this difference between the Jews in Poland and those residing in their home countries. The wife of the French marshal De Guébriant, who in 1645 spent some time in Cracow, wrote with amazement that the Jews of Kazimierz "have as their occupation not usurious moneylending as elsewhere, but rather physical labor, commerce, and the farming of revenues and taxes." A Catholic abbot who visited Poland in 1688–89, reported with abandon that "without the Jews, who constitute one-third of the realm's population, the Poles would surely die of hunger, for they are lazy, while the Jews are industrious." [35]

In contrast to these obvious exaggerations or vague generalities, some details are offered in Sebastyan Miczyński's reports, however biased. Apart from making a sweeping statement that Jews "appear in droves at fairs, especially the principal ones, such as at Łęczyca, Łowicz, Poznań, Gniezno, Toruń, Lublin, Lwów, Jarosław, and Cracow, so that one can hardly distinguish any Christians among them," Miczyński enumerates a considerable number of local Jewish businesses in various cities. With respect to Cracow, especially, he goes into considerable minutiae in describing the location of Jewish shops like those owned by Wolf Bocian (Poper), one of the richest local Jews. Bocian also conducted a wholesale business, particularly in cloth and saltpeter, while his son, Marek, dealt in herring and spices bought in Gdańsk. Other Cracow wholesalers included Mojżesz Szakowicz, who in 1643 acquired at the Lublin fair for 6,500 zlotys dormouse skins for resale at home.

Another, Jakob Eberle, is recorded as having delivered sable skins to the royal court for 1,700 zlotys. Samuel Jakubowicz conducted a large-scale business in silver, while Izak Jakubowicz brought merchandise with him to Warsaw for sale during the Diet sessions. A very interesting "Brief listing of goods, brought by both urban and suburban Jews to Lwów from Germany, and those shipped by them abroad, that is to Śniatyn," over the years 1577–78, was prepared for the courts by Konstanty Korniakt, a tax farmer; it covers a wide variety of objects. In general, there was hardly any article of commerce which was not sold by Jews to Jews and, to the extent permitted by the restrictive laws and the competition of Christian merchants, to non-Jews. In the ever more numerous townships controlled by private lords, in particular, Jews were given a much wider latitude. For instance, in Tarnów a decree of 1637 specified that the Jews could trade at home, in markets and shops, "on a par with the [Christian] merchants." Regrettably, not even the careers of the most successful businessmen can be described in any detail on the basis of extant records. Certainly, satisfactory institutional or individual biographies like those written about the English Eastland Company and Samuel Edwards have not been, and are not likely to be, produced with respect to Polish Jewish firms or merchants.[36]

Equally regrettable is our lack of information about Jewish activities in the real estate business, which must have grown considerably in that period of the great Polish urban expansion. Of course, we may learn a good deal indirectly from the laws limiting the number of Jewish houses in a particular locality and such privileges as were issued by the Grudziński family in favor of Jewish settlers in Swarzędz (Schwersenz). But we have very few records of Jews' purchases (or sales) of real estate, such as came into their possession from defaulting debtors, for example. Certainly, studies like those made possible by the municipal records in medieval Cologne and Vienna, would greatly enrich our knowledge of the socioeconomic status of the Polish and Lithuanian Jews. More detailed data about the architectural and social aspects of Jewish housing, whether or not it substantially differed from that of Christians in the various regions of the country, would also be highly welcome.[37]

Data concerning the local retail trade, which furnished a livelihood for a multitude of Jewish shopkeepers and employees, are
even scarcer and less satisfactory. By and large, retail transactions
were conducted on a cash basis between merchant and customer;
and either these transactions were never recorded at all, or the
records which were kept were not considered worthy of preservation. It was, indeed, a rare find when Janina Morgensztern discovered in the Zamość Archive the record of an inventory of the
possessions of a local Jewish merchant, Lejb Józefowicz, who in
1675 was robbed and slain with his wife. We cannot even tell
whether his relatively small assets and liabilities were typical of
the majority of Jewish merchants in his day or before the "Deluge." Much is left to speculation from the few available documents. This is, indeed, the major shortcoming of Roman Rybarski's succinct treatment of the Jewish role in Polish commerce of
the sixteenth century. Because he relies mainly on records of customs duties paid at a few regional collecting points, this leading
authority on the history of sixteenth-century Polish commerce
sweepingly asserts as "two indubitable facts: that (1) at the time
of the full flowering of Polish trade, that is, in the middle of the
sixteenth century, Jewish participation in it was generally very
weak; and (2) this participation grows, as the economic conditions
of the urban population deteriorate, and the cities decline." Yet
even Rybarski indirectly admits the insufficiency of the pertinent
sources when he refers, for instance, to the city of Kalisz, which
happened to embrace one of the oldest Jewish communities in
Poland. He asserts that, while names of Jews are almost totally
absent from the local customs records for 1547–48, thirty-three
years later the records indicate that Jews "dominated" certain
branches of commerce. Rybarski also concedes that in the following decades Jews played an increasing role in Polish international,
as well as domestic, trade, and that, by the late eighteenth century,
they were the predominant group in almost every aspect of Polish
business. On the whole, we must be content with the particles of
information preserved in records of Jewish tax payments, tolls and
customs duties, and occasional litigations before general courts,
and in brief references in rabbinic responsa, private letters, and
the like.[38]

This paucity of source materials interferes even more gravely with any investigation of the pursuits of Jewish peddlers in hamlets and villages. We hear, for example, that a Poznań communal resolution forbade peddlers "to trade in the city's market or in houses near the market; only in the suburbs or in the rear of houses in small lanes behind the market" were they to pursue their business (1670). On the surface, it appears that peddling was not a major Jewish occupation, except perhaps in some larger towns. Security of the roads was none too good in the sixteenth and seventeenth centuries; if anything, the situation deteriorated in the early post-"Deluge" period. Jews traveling to fairs could journey in groups. Even then, we recall, highway robbery was quite frequent. A Poznań resolution in 1640 urged group journeys to all fairs, forbade members to leave the group before it reached its destination, and ordered the travelers to defend themselves jointly against attacking peasants or highwaymen. Individual peddling must have been an extremely precarious undertaking for Jews, in view of the growing hostility toward them on the part of both the urban and the rural proletariat, particularly in the southeastern regions. Otherwise the sparse and scattered population, for which purchases at weekly fairs were a more arduous undertaking, might have promoted extensive peddling. At the same time, the presence of a growing number of Jewish arendators (see below) who supplied necessary goods to the peasants, and the general lack of cash among the peasant serfs, must have discouraged it. At any rate, Jewish peddlers are rarely recorded in the extant sources on prepartition Poland.[39]

The Jews' gradual progress in Polish-Lithuanian commerce, which was to reach its apogee in the last decades before the partitions of the country, was owing to both their spirit of enterprise and their strong motivation. Generally stimulated to find ever-new openings as an inescapable condition for sheer survival, they found their task facilitated by the local Christian merchants' excessive conservatism and unwillingness to work hard along unaccustomed paths. On their part, Jewish businessmen undertook long and arduous journeys, not only to the West but also to Hungary, Moldavia, Greece, and Turkey—the hazards of these trips being but slightly mitigated by the brotherly reception they could expect from coreligionists at their destinations. In their uphill struggle for commercial and other rights, they received much encouragement from the *szlachta,* which, though resentful of the occasional interference with their own trade by the Jews, disliked the Christian burghers even more, as potential rivals in the exercise of political as well as economic power. From the fifteenth to the seventeenth century, therefore, we hear of numerous enactments by the gentry-dominated diets and dietines against the burghers and their trade (many such examples have been noted, especially in Chapter LXVIII), and also of hostile references to the burghers in the sociopolitical literature of the age, written for the most part by noblemen.

As early as the fifteenth century, the leading political thinker Jan Ostroróg had stressed that the cities were unproductive because they usually embraced a large number of beggars and monks. He also opposed the brotherhoods of merchants or artisans as conducive to higher prices for the consumers. Later on, Marcin Kromer, himself a former burgher raised to the nobility and engaged in various diplomatic missions, prepared a general survey of conditions in Poland, for the benefit of the newly elected king Henry of Valois (this report was handed to the king, on his arrival at the frontier, by the Polish primate, Archbishop Stanisław Karnkowski). Kromer spoke out vehemently against the burghers' love of luxury, dislike of work, and their preference to delegate all tasks to employees. He also blamed them for slavishly adopting foreign inventions and for engaging in usurious transactions. (These attacks gave him the opportunity to vent his ire at usury by the Jews as well.) Andrzej Frycz Modrzewski complained of the burghers' widespread dishonesty, and blamed the high cost of products on the presence of too many middlemen and on the merchants' excessive profits without work. "I should call them robbers rather than merchants." It was indeed the prices usually charged by Jewish merchants that proved to be the major weapon in the struggle against the burghers. Even the generally unfriendly lower gentry, assembled at the Dietine of Halicz in 1632, instructed its deputies to the forthcoming Diet session seriously to consider "during the present tight situation" the opening to Jews of various avenues of commerce so that "everything should become less expensive." Remarkably, in his *Worek Judaszów* (The Pouch of the Judases) Sebastyan Fabian Klonowicz combined attacks on Jews with those on all merchants, and preached a kind of basic work ethic alien to most patricians and other hidebound urban conservatives. Of course, even more important was the nobles' self-interest in selling the products of their landholdings at the highest possible prices, and obtaining the manufactured goods at the lowest. Jews readily responded to this drive of the *szlachta*, supported by the monarchs, by helping it to dispose of their agricultural produce advantageously and by offering it desirable merchandise at much smaller markups. We recall, for example, the diet's decree of 1643 limiting the profits of Jewish traders to 3 percent, as against the 5–7 percent markup allowed to Christian merchants. Whenever necessary, Jews also delivered a variety of goods to the gentry on credit and supplied them with all sorts of novelties to satisfy their craving for foreign luxuries. In this endeavor the Jewish businessmen were aided by the presence of an ever-growing and more diversified class of Jewish craftsmen.[40]

Some of the psychological difficulties of Poland's upper classes in many ways resembled those of the aristocracy in Spain during the rapid decline after her Golden Age. Of course, there were important differences between Spain's strong, and Poland's weak, monarchy. Moreover, Spain's total intolerance toward professing Jews contrasted with Poland's toleration of religious dissidents even during the period of the Counter Reformation, which made possible a constant enhancement of the Jewish population in the dual Commonwealth in numbers, affluence, and cultural power. True, minor progress was temporarily achieved in Spain by a small circle of Marranos under Philip IV. But a long-term Marrano settlement was seriously impeded by both the Inquisition and the doctrine of *limpieza*. In any case, as we recall, the Polish public mixed a certain admiration for the great military power and staunch Catholicism of the Spanish people with a sharp condemnation of the atrocities committed by the Inquisition, the rumors of which, connected with the "Black Legend," obtained a considerable circulation in Poland-Lithuania as well.[41]

URBAN INDUSTRY AND GUILDS

Despite the antagonistic attitude of the gentry and, to a lesser extent, of the Church to the burghers, Poland's industrial development proceeded apace, and only gradually slowed down, along with the country's mercantile and financial activities, in the first half of the seventeenth century. For Jews, however, that century marked the beginning of their large-scale entry into industrial pursuits—a movement which, after its tragic interruption in mid-century, continued with great vigor, and reached its culmination in the decades before the partitions of Poland.

As a rule, it was only through commerce and banking that Jews were able to accumulate sufficient capital to invest in sizable manufacturing enterprises. Frequently, it was indeed the merchant or the banker who also financed, and even initiated and organized, a particular industrial undertaking. While an increasing number of individual Jewish artisans produced a variety of goods in both the major and the smaller communities, the impetus to large-scale production usually came from the leaders.

Among the early pioneers in this field was Lewko, who in 1368 leased from the government the production of the Wieliczka and Bochnia salt mines. We also recall Saul Judycz Wahl of Brest-Litovsk, whose manifold business activities included the exploitation of the royal salines. In 1580 Prince Lew Sapieha, the distinguished Lithuanian chancellor, had three Jewish partners in the mining and sale of salt, which was an important commodity in Poland and also was exported in large quantity, especially to Hungary, Silesia, and Moravia. Officially a royal monopoly, salt production and distribution was often entrusted to private entrepreneurs under a royal license. The chief salt mines in Poland were located in Wieliczka and Bochnia in the palatinate of Cracow. The growth of the salt industry in Wieliczka, which, as a rule, accounted for over two-thirds of the national output, is well illustrated by the rapid increase of production from 4,565 bałwans (of about 10 barrels each) in 1503 to 6,435 in 1537, and 15,899 in 1564. Bochnia's smaller output showed less acceleration: from 2,269 bałwans in 1535 to 2,783 in 1560, and 4,010 in 1576. A parallel growth was also witnessed by the production of another type called the hundredweight salt (*sól centnarowa*). At one time, the Wieliczka mines alone employed more than a thousand workers. It has been shown that in the years 1532–71 the net income from Wieliczka mining ranged from a low of 29,812 zlotys in 1541–42 to a high of 46,512 zlotys in 1563. Bochnia's net revenue declined from a high of 25,725 zlotys in 1525 to a low of 8,654 zlotys in 1553–54, to increase but slightly to 9,692 zlotys in 1570–71. Thereafter the gross revenue kept on increasing; it reached about 120,000 zlotys in the two mining areas in the early 1600s and rose further to 160,000 in the 1640s. But this rise was partly the result of currency inflation, and the accompanying expenses went up even faster.

Like Wahl, Dr. Salomon Calahora included salines among his ramified business ventures. On one occasion, the physician-businessman secured from King Stephen a license for himself, his son Abraham, and another Cracow Jew, Hadidah (or Nadidah), to explore a smaller private saline in Felsztyn near Halicz (or Telatyn, probably Delatyn near Kołomyja) for a period of six years, free of all imposts (January 24, 1580). To be sure, the smaller Red Russian salines, particularly around Drohobycz, had been developed largely by a Warsaw burgher, Melchior Walbach, who was the first to employ more advanced, semicapitalistic technology. But before long the wealthy Nachmanowicz family in Lwów secured, among other privileges, royal concessions to exploit the mines in Drohobycz, Bolechów, and elsewhere. The yield of even these less important mines may be gauged from the contract concluded in 1634 by two Jews, Jacob Kopel of Kałusz and Jacob Gombrycht of Lwów, with the Christian businessman Marcin Drużycki, for the delivery of salt to Jarosław in payment of a loan of 20,000 zlotys. Thirteen years earlier, a partnership of six Lwów Jews is recorded as having sold 4,000 barrels of Bolechów salt (probably worth some 20,000 zlotys) in the course of one month. In 1564 a Halicz Jew, David, was said to have secured an annual income of 1,100 zlotys through farming the revenue from the salt tax in the Halicz province. Because of the high cost of overland transportation, as well as the allocation of certain quotas of the production to neighboring areas (according to a royal ordinance of 1493 supported by custom for generations), the northern and northeastern provinces of Poland-Lithuania found it less expensive to import salt from other countries across the Baltic, partly in return for exports of grain or lumber. In this trade, too, Jews played a prominent role.[42]

Because of the large income often yielded by mines, this industry attracted not only leading capitalists among burghers and Jews but also some high state dignitaries. In 1525, for example, several Cracow burghers led by Paweł Kaufman formed a partnership with the palatine of Cracow Krzysztof Szydłowiecki, the future generalissimo Jan Tarnowski, and other aristocrats to secure the concession to explore for gold and silver in the Tatra and other Polish mountains. Even the famous Fugger firm of Augsburg evinced some interest in the Polish copper mines. The production of iron ore and its refining into iron in various forms (steel was produced in Poland somewhat later than in western Europe), and the rather limited mining of silver and copper, seem to have attracted less Jewish interest, except in the conversion of these raw materials into finished products. Incidentally, the prominence of Jewish businessmen in salt mining doubtless irked the local population. It may not be too venturesome to suggest that the hatred of Jewish entrepreneurs, and of their Jewish representatives, contributed something to the anti-Jewish host libel in Bochnia, and to its bloodthirsty description by Jan Achazy Kmita, a clerk in the Bochnia saline administration.[43]

Mercantile capital also contributed to the development of other Jewish industrial pursuits. For example, the Jewish "guild of furriers" in Cracow in 1613 was really as much a merchant guild of traders who sold furs as an association of artisans who manufactured them. However, many dealers, Jewish and non-Jewish, found it advantageous not merely to import Muscovite raw skins from Smolensk for export to western Europe via Gdańsk, or to the German fairs via Poznań and Toruń or Wrocław, but also to finish some of them into higher-priced furs and even to trim garments with them for the use of local aristocrats. In such cases the merchants frequently engaged skilled furriers, tailors, or dyers. The dealers thus helped to create a diversified Jewish artisan class, which was to play a considerable role in the Polish Jewish economy.[44]

By and large, craftsmen required little capital investment. Very frequently it was the customer who came to the artisan and ordered some clothing or other product, often supplying the materials and paying only for the work. Even in crafts which used a moderate number of tools, each artisan could as a rule supply his own equipment. Only at a later date, when Jews began to organize their own guilds, as we shall see, were these organizations able to establish collective workshops, or advance funds to enable individual masters to purchase more costly equipment. Such was the case especially with tanneries. Among the Jews, certain specialized societies, like those in charge of loan banks, or the community at large, also performed these functions. Newcomers from other cities or countries who sought to establish themselves in one or another craft, after securing residence rights from the generally reluctant communal organs, often received support from both the community and individual coreligionists. But, in the main, artisans had to rely on their own initiative and resources in overcoming the numerous difficulties placed in their way by non-Jewish, as well as Jewish, competitors.[45]

All along, Jewish artisans had to fight their way upward against the staunch resistance of the Christian burghers. Time and again, their Christian compeers, whether organized in guilds or working as individuals, tried with all the means at their disposal to prevent Jewish competition. They often secured pertinent privileges from the government, even if these conflicted with the general royal charters granted to Jews. As a result, there were endless litigations before the courts. Under the pressure of both royal officials and city councils, certain agreements were made between the municipalities and the Jewish communities, which usually resulted in the curtailment of Jewish rights. Independently, some city councils issued regulations against individual Jewish crafts, either outlawing them entirely or restricting them to work for an exclusively Jewish clientele.

At the same time, Jews acquired many allies among the non-Jewish population, since many restrictions, particularly if relating to the admission of new members, affected other ethnic and religious groups as well. Even Poles professing one or another Protestant faith were often excluded from the predominantly Catholic guilds. Greek Orthodox or Uniate Ruthenians and Lithuanians, Muslim Tatars or Turks, and Armenians were as a rule placed outside the fold. Of course, some guilds discriminated against Jews more sharply than against the other groups, and enjoyed fuller support from their city councils. On the other hand, under the legal situation existing in Poland at the time, many Jews were able to practice their industrial specialties in the *jurydyki,* where the decisive power rested with the landlords. The nobles as well as the masses often favored Jews and other low-wage "interlopers." Some Christian *partaczy* actually settled in the Jewish quarter.[46]

As the literal meaning of the term *partaczy* (blunderers) indicates, these "unauthorized" craftsmen were supposed to perform work of inferior quality. To prevent competition, many guilds, with the support of their city councils, actually forbade their members to teach their skills to outsiders other than those formally admitted as apprentices or journeymen. However, such restrictions were circumvented by illicit instruction from a guild member or a *partacz.* Even in Poznań, where the guild monopolies were rather strictly enforced, we find the case of a "Ruthenian" artisan taking an oath (in 1578) that he had taught two Poznań Jews the art of dyeing beaver furs, for which he claimed that they owed him 10 zlotys. Needless to say, some Jewish immigrants to Poland had brought with them certain skills from the Holy Roman Empire, particularly from the lands of the Bohemian Crown, Italy, or the Muslim states, all of which had a growing number of Jewish artisans. We need but recall the Prague census of 1546, which listed (among approximately 200 Jewish families) 8 glaziers, 8 butchers, 6 dice makers, 3 makers of musical instruments, and 9 others plying a variety of crafts. As the number of workmen in various categories increased in Poland, the opportunities for training grew to such an extent that the "unlicensed" master artisans themselves, out of self-interest, likewise restricted the number of their apprentices. As soon as the Jews began organizing their own guilds, moreover, these organizations often included in their statutes training restrictions similar to those enacted by their Christian counterparts.[47]

The status of apprentices and journeymen was far from enviable. Yet Jewish parents were often prepared to pay substantial amounts for the training of their children. One such early agreement, concluded in Cracow about 1650, read as follows:

The honorable Judah Fikseles Katz articles his son Moses Eliah Fikseles Katz to the master tailor, the honorable Kopel Moses Keplish who undertakes to train [the youth] in sewing and cutting of every kind of garment. He shall not conceal anything from him, important or unimportant, and shall provide him board. The boy shall serve the full legal term of apprenticeship as it is established for all artisans in our community. When he shall have completed his term of apprenticeship he may take up mending and patching. The said Judah shall pay Kopel [the master] 10 Polish zlotys as fee for his son before the 1st day of Kislev 411 [1650] and 10 zlotys on the 1st day of Heshvan 412 [1651]. In the 4th year Kopel shall have the option of employing the youth at half the wages [offered him] by any [other] master tailor.

This contract, as well as the first payment of 10 zlotys by the father, was attested by the communal secretary, Moses Abraham Mattatias Delakrut. Contracts of this kind generally differed from locality to locality. There was a major disparity, in particular, between apprentices who lived with their masters, in which case the parents had to pay for room and board as well, and those who lived at home. Generally, the hours of work were extremely long, often from sunrise to sunset, and in winter as many as five hours beyond sunset. Nor was the status of those who advanced to the rank of journeyman altogether satisfactory. Their wages probably were no larger than those paid by guild members to their Christian counterparts—ranging, in the sixteenth century, from 8 to 15 groszy a week, or a total of approximately 14–26 zlotys per annum. It is small wonder, then, that in the eighteenth century, when the Jewish guilds were flowering, Jewish journeymen often organized their own associations to fight for better wages and working conditions.[48]

As in the case of other restrictive laws, the Polish-Lithuanian cities had to make allowances for certain crafts connected with the Jewish religion. We recall that even the narrow-minded medieval German guilds had had to accommodate some Jewish slaughterers and, to a lesser extent, Jewish butchers to provide ritually acceptable meats. Slaughterers, to be sure, belonged more to the category of professionals, or communal civil servants, rather than to the artisan class. They had to be persons of known piety and talmudic learning, and usually had to pass an examination on the pertinent laws and practices and receive a certificate from an established rabbi, in order to qualify for their job. Only thus could the communities be assured that they would not only kill cattle and fowl according to the minute requirements of Jewish law but also be competent to examine the slaughtered animal's lungs and otherwise ascertain that it did not have any crucial physical defect which would disqualify it for Jewish consumption. Some of the slaughterers were also skilled deveiners (*wyżylacze,* in Polish; or *noqrim,* in Hebrew), able to remove the femoral nerve (*nervus ischiadicus*) from the thigh of the slaughtered animal and thus make sure that other parts of the animal would be ritually permissible. More remarkably, the Polish Jewish butchers, too, had more than the average education, and enjoyed a fairly high social standing. The following observation by an Italian rabbi at the end of the sixteenth century has often been quoted: "It is generally known to any visitor of that community [of Cracow] that all butchers and deveiners there are rabbinically trained wise men, bookish, and experienced in learned debates, for it is still a custom in all the lands of Germany, Bohemia, Poland, and the Rus not to appoint slaughterers, examiners, and butchers, except scholarly and God-fearing men." Not surprisingly, despite such precautions, many controversies arose from time to time about the qualifications or the morals of individuals performing these tasks.[49]

At the same time, being used to the sanguinary trade of cutting up animal carcasses, many butchers also developed fighting qualities, and offered vigorous resistance to rioters and violent intruders. An interesting episode occurred in Lwów in 1607, when, at the instigation of Christian butchers, two young nobles, together with more than a dozen rowdies, entered the Jewish quarter and attacked and gravely wounded two Jewish butchers. Thereupon other Jewish butchers counterattacked, severely manhandled the young men, and dragged them to the *gród* (the court of the castle). In addition, the wives of the wounded men instituted a criminal suit against the two leading malefactors. However, the affair seems to have bogged down because of a jurisdictional dispute as to whether the *gród* or the municipal court was to adjudicate it. The butchers' self-assertiveness also accounts for the ultimate failure of all attempts by the cities of Lwów, Cracow, and others to limit the number of Jewish butcher shops or to prohibit Jewish butchers from selling meat to non-Jews. In two decrees of 1580 and 1585, even the generally friendly King Stephen, in response to a controversy between Christian and Jewish butchers in Lwów, upheld that prohibition, but without effect. On the other hand, the original compact imposed in 1485 by the city council of Cracow upon the local Jewish community, allowed the Jews to maintain only four butcher shops. This number was later increased to eight, employing two butchers each. However, a contemporary source mentions the presence of no fewer than twenty-seven Jewish butchers in the city.[50]

Another more or less universal Jewish occupation was that of tailoring. This craft, too, was connected with a religious requirement, in so far as only Jewish artisans were likely strictly to observe the prohibition against mixing wool and linen in any garment (sha'aṭnez). On their part, the Christian guilds and city councils often tried at least to prevent Jewish tailors from selling their wares to Christians. These efforts proved futile against the lure of lower prices and occasional credit offered by Jews to their customers. Nor did Jewish tailors always wait for purchasers to come to them for suits or coats; instead, they sometimes took the initiative and, with the help of agents and "runners," attracted customers to their homes or shops. To the oft-voiced complaint that Jews were buying up incoming victuals and other merchandise before they reached the interior of the city, Miczyński added the grievance that, "not contented with sales in their stores, Jews send out other Jews to the markets, homes, and shops with satchels filled with goods, and lure away customers [from the legitimate merchants and artisans]." This antagonist also blamed the Jewish tailors for exhibiting ready-made clothing in anticipation of future demand. In addition, Jewish artisans, as well as merchants, often coming from other countries and maintaining contacts with coreligionists abroad, were able to offer the latest Western fashions, or some previously unknown materials suitable for human wear. At times, to be sure, Jewish tailors were involved in disputes with their own coreligionists. There were, for example, jurisdictional disputes between tailors and furriers as to who was to complete a fur-lined coat after the furrier had prepared the skins and the tailor the cloth. But here, too, residence in a privately owned town or in one of the *jurydyki* within the royal cities helped the tailors to circumvent whatever restrictions were enacted by the municipal organs and to expand their trade, in sharp competition with the existing guilds. Connected with tailoring also were such crafts as cap- and collar making, which were specifically mentioned in the Cracow agreement of 1485 as occupations open to "the poor Jews." [51]

We must remember, however, that, just as the Jewish religion favored the establishment of independent Jewish trades in tailoring and meat processing, it also imposed considerable limitations on Jewish artisans. The very taboo on mixing wool and linen required some communal supervision over tailors. In issuing, in 1607, regulations aimed primarily at curtailment of undesirable luxury in clothing, the Council of Four Lands added the provision that the community should "investigate with extreme care [the ramifications of] the prohibition of *sha'atnez* over which many persons stumble." The local elders were also instructed to exercise care in allowing tailors to use hemp thread. The Lithuanian Council was more specific. In its resolution of 1639, it ordered the tailors to sew only with thread bought from Jews (who would clearly distinguish thread made from linen or hemp), and seven years later likewise turned the tailors' attention to both hemp thread and entire garments made of hemp in lieu of wool. Similar provisions were included in various local statutes and were discussed in some detail in the contemporary rabbinic literature. Above all loomed the prohibition against work on the Sabbath. True, with the usual concentration of Jewish artisans in the Jewish quarter of Polish-Lithuanian cities, the governmental outlawry of work on Sundays and Christian holidays affected the Jews there much less than it did their coreligionists in the more sparsely populated West-European ghettos. Doubtless for this reason we hear of relatively few ecclesiastical demands that the Jews abstain from work on these days within the confines of their own dwellings and workshops. Yet abstention from work from Friday sundown to Saturday sunset must have entailed considerable difficulty for many individuals, such as Jewish apprentices of Christian masters and Jewish masters employing Christian help. That is possibly one of the reasons why many Polish rabbis felt that the biblical-rabbinic laws regarding the Sabbath rest commandment should be elaborated in greater detail and even sharpened by some additional regulations, so as to secure total observance. This general concern led to the rigorous "Ordinances Pertaining to the Prohibitions Arising from the Sabbath and Holidays," submitted to the Polish Council in 1590. Attributed to R. Meshullam Feivish of Cracow, these regulations were formulated, it is likely, by this savant while he was still living in an eastern territory, probably Brest-Litovsk. The enforcement of such strict regulations carried with it many social and economic implications for the Jewish society of the entire dual Commonwealth. Hence they were formally adopted by the central Polish Council, in which the then provincial Lithuanian Council was still actively represented.[52]

Jewish participation in most other arts and crafts likewise proceeded apace in an ever-accelerating fashion. In his careful study of the Jewish artisans in the province of Red Russia, Maurycy Horn found that they were represented in no fewer than 40 different trades. In a major city like Lwów, Jews were recorded in no fewer than 32 trades, while in the somewhat smaller localities of Przemyśl and Bełz, they were active in 24 and 12 trades, respectively. In another study, Horn calculated that Tatar and Cossack raids immediately reduced the industrial output of temporarily occupied Bełz by some 10 percent; but that in five cities where there were no such incursions, industrial production grew by between 40 and 214 percent. Other scholars identified 20 or more crafts plied by Jews in each of the major communities of Cracow, Lwów, Lublin, and Poznań. There were, of course, varying degrees of participation. For example, the building trades, very active during Poland's population explosion in the sixteenth century, continued to flourish in the following half a century, owing to the foundation of some 100 new towns and the expansion of the 1,000 older cities. Yet Jews were seriously hampered by the numerous residential restrictions the municipal councils imposed upon them, and by the ensuing overcrowding of their quarters. Echoing contemporary observers, some modern scholars have rightly stressed the unsatisfactory condition of most ghetto buildings, and have even ascribed to it the frequency of fires arising there. But under the existing legal limitations, aggravated by the ever-present danger that the municipality might suddenly secure a royal privilege *de non tolerandis Judaeis,* solidity and esthetics of construction had to be neglected in favor of the utilitarian consideration of providing as much dwelling space as possible within the permitted area. Undoubtedly, the Jewish share in the building trades in the privately owned towns, where Jews enjoyed broader industrial and commercial liberties, assumed somewhat greater dimensions. But even the more extensive data flowing from the eighteenth century are none too informative. At the same time, however, a considerable number of unnamed Jewish artists, architects, and builders lavished their energies on building small but beautiful wooden synagogues and decorating them with exquisite taste. We shall see, in another context, that they made a significant contribution to the history of Jewish art.[53]

It would take us too far afield to try to enumerate all the arts and crafts in which Polish-Lithuanian Jewry was represented. Temporary exigencies or some purely accidental reasons may have caused individual Jews to favor one occupation over another. For example, at first we hear of relatively few Jewish goldsmiths—traditionally a Jewish occupation in many lands—as compared with the numerous Jewish silversmiths, who in some areas almost monopolized that occupation. This is the more remarkable as some work in gold had been performed in Poland as early as the Piast period, according to modern archaeologists. Such work could hardly have escaped the attention of the much-discussed Jewish minters of that period. It appears that in later years the Polish aristocrats and their wives regarded imported jewelry as more prestigious. The lady described in 1650 by the Polish satirist Krzysztof Opaliński, himself a former Poznań palatine and member of the Diet, was very likely typical of her class in exclaiming: "Jews have for sale these jewels from Germany; they must all be bought for me!" Similarly, Jewish glaziers, who in some German areas were the only Jewish craftsmen allowed to carry on their trade, seem not to have been particularly active in Poland or Lithuania.[54]

More Jews took up such borderline trades as that of the barber-surgeons or that of printing. While barbers earned much of their income through haircutting and other cosmetic operations, they were also semiprofessionals who performed the medical services of bloodletting, cupping, and the like. These ministrations required some paramedical training, and barbers often enjoyed high standing among other craftsmen and tradesmen. Even more highly esteemed was printing, which not only required the mechanical skill for composition and presswork but also presupposed a good education and an ability to understand the texts set to type. As a rule, compositors—and still more, proofreaders—were learned individuals, who occasionally improved upon the readings in the manuscripts submitted to them. With slow beginnings in Cracow and Lublin, this craft spread through most of Poland and Lithuania and became a source of income for an important segment of the artisan population. Although never attaining the dimensions of the Venetian and Amsterdam firms, some Polish and Lithuanian presses played a significant role in both the economic and the cultural life of the Jewish communities. There also were rare professionals like one Michał b. Joseph, who was engaged by King Sigismund II Augustus to build a bridge over the river Bug. In short, Jews entered an increasing number of occupations which happened to be open at a given moment, and they continued to work in them unless they were forced out by external pressures.[55]

With the constant numerical increase and diversification of Jewish craftsmen, their relations with the Christian guilds underwent major changes. Here and there, under the pressure of circumstances, individual Jews were even admitted to the Christian guilds as regular members, although they could not exercise all rights of membership. Such was the case, for instance, in the younger community of Ukrainian Belaya Tserkov (Biała Cerkiew), where two Jewish master tailors and two butchers joined the appropriate local guilds, although other Jews very likely engaged in these crafts without guild membership. In Płock, no fewer than nine of the numerous Jewish tailors were members of the Christian guild. Generally, however, as of old, the guilds remained not only professional organizations but also religious brotherhoods, with special religiously colored oaths of admission and loyalty, individual patron saints, observance of denominational religious festivals, and so forth. No conscientious Jew would participate in such activities even if the Christian majority had let him do it. Similarly, it appeared incongruous for a Jew to be elected an officer in a Christian guild, which would thus be officially sanctioning his control over Christian fellow members. But he could enjoy equality of economic opportunity. In most cases, though, Jewish craftsmen were merely made to contribute financially to the upkeep of the guild, in return for certain limited privileges. Even more frequently, Jewish and non-Jewish artisans lived side by side, with alternating phases of cooperation and conflict.[56]

Before long the number of Jewish craftsmen increased sufficiently for them to organize guilds of their own. A population of about 450,000 by 1648, though widely dispersed over most of the 1,100 townships and many villages throughout the dual Commonwealth, often embraced, at least in the major cities, a number of members of the same craft. Some Jewish guilds at first represented several related crafts, and later split up into independent organizations. The full development of Jewish guilds, to be sure, was to come only after the Jewish communities' recovery from the sanguinary Cossack uprising. By the mid-eighteenth century Jews became a dominant industrial factor in many Polish and Lithuanian cities; in some areas they actually constituted a majority of all craftsmen. At that time even the medium-sized town of Leszno (Lissa), with a relatively young Jewish community, possessed Jewish guilds of tailors, haberdashers, locksmiths, leather workers, barbers, goldsmiths and gold embroiderers. Simultaneously, the ratio of craftsmen in the Jewish population increased to about one-third. Incidentally, the provision, frequently inserted into the statutes of Jewish guilds, that only married men could qualify for full membership as master artisans, did not so much reflect religious and moral attitudes to marriage, or a wish to promote Jewish population growth, as the fear that bachelors, unburdened by family obligations, might underbid their older, married confreres. Incipient manifestations of all these trends were noticeable before 1648, when a few Jewish guilds began to be organized. One of the earliest, the statutes of which have been preserved, was the guild of Jewish barbers and surgeons established in Cracow in 1639. While pursuing the usual monopolistic practices and pledging its members to prevent outsiders from doing their work, the guild demanded that members not raise prices "for bloodletting, cupping, haircutting, and the healing of bruises and wounds" beyond what the people were accustomed to pay. To prevent competition among members, the statute also provided that, if a patient wished to engage a different surgeon, no colleague should accept the call until the first surgeon was fully paid for his services. There also were provisions for the treatment of apprentices and for other matters of common concern. Yet remarkably, fines for breaking the rules were not to be imposed by the officers of the guild, but by those of the community at large.[57]

For a long time, Christian guilds refused to recognize the legitimacy of any Jewish guild. It appears, though we do not have direct evidence, that even after the formation of the first Jewish guilds, the Christian craftsmen preferred to regard all Jewish competitors as "interlopers." Regrettably, the pertinent registers are preserved only for the years 1598 and 1600, before the formation of any Polish Jewish guild. The Christian craftsmen were more lenient only in cases where no competition existed. For instance, in 1616 the Lwów city council insisted that Jews be barred from all handicrafts, "with the exception of melting silver, for there are none of this kind among us now." [58]

However, even the relationship between the Jews' own communal organization and their artisan guilds was often quite ambivalent. On the one hand, the craftsmen required the assistance of the Jewish community in safeguarding their rights against outsiders; sometimes they needed financial assistance in order to acquire tools or to enforce some of their own guild ordinances against fellow Jews of the same or another locality. The communal elders also mediated from time to time in jurisdictional disputes between guilds, and served as more-or-less impartial judges in controversies between artisans and customers. On the other hand, they had to bear in mind the interests of the entire community, rather than those of any of its segments. For instance, they tried to prevent the bitterness that often prevailed between Jewish and Christian craftsmen from too greatly ruffling the waters of Judeo-Christian relations in general.

In two characteristic proclamations of 1600, the Poznań *kahal* had to take cognizance of the Christian guilds' repeated complaints

[that] the Jews run after carriages of nobles visiting the city, asking what they wish to buy, so that the arrivals never see any [local] merchants. It is particularly against the furriers, tailors, and *petlicarzy* [scarf makers] that they [the Christian artisans] have raised their voices, which may accrue to the injury of the whole community. Despite numerous warnings on our part there are many recalcitrant members and evil-doers who refuse to listen, so that the danger has become immediate.

The community denounced three Jews by name for having served as "runners" offering furs, clothing, jewels, and the like to visitors; and ordered them to suspend these activities for a year under the sanction of the loss of their residential rights. Unavoidably, there was some discrimination on the part of the elders, who were recruited mostly from among the upper merchant classes and the intellectuals (in Poznań, for instance, each of three Jewish merchant associations delegated five representatives to the communal board) and often looked down upon the poorer, less educated artisans and petty agents. Wherever the interests of merchants clashed with those of the craftsmen, the elders were likely to side with their own group. This situation gave rise to occasional conflicts, which became more frequent in the eighteenth century, as a result of the general deterioration of Poland's economic life, including that of its Jewish population. Consequently, some recent historians, especially among those inclined toward a Marxist interpretation of history, have emphasized this class struggle within the Jewish communities. However, it can hardly be denied that before 1648, and to a large extent even to the end of the dual Commonwealth, these conflicts were far exceeded in importance by the solidarity imposed upon all Jews, regardless of wealth and class, by the persistent struggle for survival against a generally hostile urban and rural environment. Certainly, the internal Jewish conflicts were far less serious than the controversies often raging between the cities' *pospólstwo* (commoners) and the patrician city councils. Even these altercations among members of the Christian majority did not quite resemble the sharp inner conflicts in medieval German and other Western cities, where the artisans often succeeded in seizing control of the city councils. There certainly was no Polish city in which the artisan groups could simultaneously combat the city council and the Jewish community, replace the patricians on the council with their own members, and expel the Jews from the city, as did the Fettmilch rebellion in Frankfort on the Main in 1614.[59]

With respect to Poznań, we must also bear in mind that it was primarily a mercantile, rather than a manufacturing center. Its Jewish artisans, however diversified, probably were greatly outnumbered, not only by shopkeepers but also by a great variety of agents. Before 1648, this situation doubtless existed in most larger Jewish communities. The whole class of intermediaries found it very hard to eke out a living, because of the constant increase in their number and variety (they were recruited largely from what later came to be called the *Luftmenschen;* that is, persons without a known occupation). On one occasion, when the Lwów city council tried to force the Jewish agents to deliver half of their earnings to the official "interpreter," who served as an appointed mediator between foreign and local merchants, the affected Jews appealed directly to the king, claiming that this decree would lead to their death by starvation. In his decree of June 22, 1640, Wladislaw IV sharply censured the council for its procedure—"inequitable, unChristian, and deserving of every condemnation." The king ordered the council to see to it that no damage would be inflicted on the agents, whom he referred to as "citizens of Our city"; and he threatened the municipality with a severe fine in the case of disobedience.[60]

ARENDAS AND VILLAGE INDUSTRIES

Quite different was the situation in rural districts. At first only a few wealthy Jewish financiers like Wołczko were led, through their financial dealings with the king, into pioneering in the development of agricultural settlements. But during the sixteenth century a number of Jewish businessmen were engaged in buying up grain and lumber for export or domestic consumption; in this connection they doubtless had to supervise deliveries at either end. Some Jews also began playing an active role in organizing and promoting village industries and in distributing the products. It has been estimated that, during that period, no less than 80 percent of ethnographic Poland's population derived its livelihood from agriculture and allied endeavors. The ratio was still higher in the Rus and Lithuanian provinces.[61]

Rural industries were divided between the peasants' production, largely for their own or other local needs, and that on the larger or medium-sized estates, which manufactured both for internal consumption and for the market. Villages usually had some craftsmen, such as smiths or carpenters. But since these workers rarely found enough customers in a single village, there was only one artisan per three villages, on the average. Many farmers had to learn to perform certain chores by themselves. Certainly, much clothing was produced by women weaving and sewing for their own families, while all sorts of repair jobs were done by men and women at home.

However, there also developed an incipient putting-out system, in which an urban entrepreneur hired a number of village workers, particularly women, to prepare semifinished or finished products, which he then placed on the market. Polish Jews seem to have pioneered along these lines. Arriving in the country with some previous technical experience from other lands, some of them also began distributing work among their less skilled or less venturesome coreligionists, who were rejected by the organized local craftsmen at "interlopers." This system was greatly hampered by the nobles' growing power, which resulted in the so-called second serfdom of the peasantry and preempted most of the working time of the village population. Nevertheless, Jews found considerable use for their talents as administrators or agents for the landlords, or else as leaseholders, taking over entire villages and employing serfs on their own account. The growing concentration of landholdings in relatively few hands greatly facilitated this delegation of power. It is estimated that in 1581 0.7 percent of all the landlords owned 8.7 percent of all the villages, while in 1629 2.1 percent of landlords had mastery over 29.8 percent of the villages. Even within the village areas, moreover, the portions under direct seignorial or substitute management were generally much more productive than the parts cultivated by more independent peasants paying the lords through both dues (in money or in kind) and free labor. According to the figures adduced by Andrzej Wyczański, in 1551–80 the lands under manorial administration in the more advanced western provinces yielded between 88.3 percent in Mazovia and 94 percent in parts of Great Poland, or an average of 91.9 percent of the total revenue. The reasons why the aristocrats left any land at all under independent peasant cultivation, Wyczański explains, were the general insufficiency and unreliability of hired labor and the considerable cash investment needed for wages before one could expect any return from crops, the size and price of which could not be predicted. This situation, incidentally, furnished an additional incentive to the lords to entrust the actual management of their entire estates—or certain parts thereof, like mills or distilleries—to wealthy arendators. A detailed investigation concerning a single village owned by the Cracow episcopal chapter showed that in the years 1573–84 it yielded an average annual revenue of 7,000 zlotys, whereas in 1585, when the property was leased to an outsider, the income suddenly increased to 10,000 zlotys. These factors operated even more strongly in the following decades, particularly in the east.[62]

Among the village industries which lent themselves to rapid expansion were the flour mills. Very frequently millers were engaged by the landlords (or their noble or Jewish substitutes) on a product-sharing basis. Mills (driven by water, wind, or horses), utensils, and grain, were supplied by the landlord, while the peasant-miller did the actual work. In return, most contracts required the miller to deliver two-thirds of the flour to the landlord, and to provide certain personal services. Only at a later date (in the 1690s) do we hear of a miller in the Cracow palatinate who merely paid his landlord a cash rent of 65 zlotys annually. But even he had to dispose of all his flour through a. Jew acting in the landlord's behalf. On a somewhat larger scale was the ramified lumber industry, which cut timber into logs and planks and sometimes turned them into barges; upon arrival in Gdańsk, these barges were unloaded and occasionally dismantled into lumber again. Many workers also dug large pits for burning wood to make ash or charcoal; others produced tar and other forestry products, all of which subsequently became important items of both domestic and export trade.[63]

Of growing importance, too, was the third major rural industry: the production of beer, mead, and liquor, particularly vodka. First introduced into Poland in the sixteenth century, vodka quickly developed into a national beverage and led to the aforementioned excesses among the eighteenth-century *szlachta*, who lionized a man surpassing his peers in his ability to drink. As early as 1650 the liberal satirist Krzysztof Opaliński exclaimed with abandon: "They all drink, bishops and senators/ They drink themselves to death. Prelates also drink/ Soldiers, nobles drink in cities, manors, and villages." In short, imbibing alcohol was speedily becoming a national pastime and disease. To be sure, some cities, such as Trembowla in the Halicz district in 1578, secured royal privileges forbidding Jews to distill liquor of any kind or to maintain taverns. But such decrees did not affect Jewish arendators of private estates or even of entire royal districts. In the same area, the Jew Wulf, who held the lease over the district (*starostwo*) of Śniatyn, even had under his control a force of several hundred dragoons. Not surprisingly, liquor sales skyrocketed. Quite early the liquor industry was monopolized by either landlords or towns; but, particularly in the Rus regions, production and distribution was often left to Jewish leaseholders. Much liquor was sold in taverns, likewise controlled by the landlords and their Jewish associates. In many areas the peasants were required to drink their liquor only in the landlord's (or his Jewish tenant's) inn, and to buy a certain prescribed quantity of it on all festive occasions, such as weddings. Frequently unable to fulfill these requirements without borrowing, the peasants fell ever more deeply into debt. True, an ordinance of 1567 (?) for the royal possessions provided that

it shall be forbidden to Jews to extend any loans on interest to Our farmers without the knowledge of the official in charge, for many simple people are ruined by the impious usury caused by the Jews' cunning. Henceforth any Jew giving cash to one of Our farmer-serfs without official knowledge, shall lose his money. This provision shall be announced in all their synagogues (*szkołach*) or through their elders, wherever Jews live in Our cities.

Yet, for the most part, official approval was not too difficult to obtain. More importantly, if carried into effect at all, this ordinance affected only the royal domain, and not the ever-expanding latifundia or other possessions of private landlords. Not surprisingly, therefore, the number of Jewish taverns increased by leaps and bounds. In Belaya Tserkov (Biała Cerkiew), for example, there were no fewer than 17 Jewish taverns next to 100 Jewish residential houses. Tavern keeping was not limited to Jews, however. According to a report submitted to Catherine II in 1765, in the relatively small Ukrainian town of Głochów, 166 taverns distributed intoxicating drinks to all comers, long before any Jews were allowed to settle in that region.[64]

Among village industries of special interest to Jews was dairy production, which required ritual supervision. The central councils of Polish and Lithuanian Jewry felt obliged to issue a series of pertinent regulations. A characteristic resolution adopted by the Council of Four Lands in 1607 read:

Let it be announced in all communities that no man shall make cheese and butter in a village for sale to Jews except after appearing before his rabbi. The rabbi should investigate his conduct and, if it proves to be honorable, shall hand him a written and signed certificate. To a man unknown to him personally, no rabbi should give such a license. Nor shall anyone make [such products] alone, for it is impossible that he would not step out [for a moment] and leave [the products] unguarded. Similarly, at every market and fair they [the elders] should carefully investigate whether the sellers possess such written licenses from the rabbis of their districts.

The Lithuanian Council more succinctly decreed, in one of its early sessions (in 1628) that "he who makes cheese and butter in a noble's court or in a village shall not be permitted [to sell them] unless he is well known as a pious person and is not a bachelor. Whenever he has to go away, he shall lock the room [in which he leaves the products] with his own lock and place his seal on it." It is easy to see that such strictness encouraged some pious Jews to settle in villages and devote themselves to the butter and cheese business. They thus became involved in related agricultural pursuits, such as feeding and milking cows; and, by observing the peasants at work, they learned something about agriculture in general.[65]

In the Polish Crown, to be sure, this industry was controlled largely by the nobility. Apart from the western latifundia, in which the magnates employed impoverished nobles in most of the administrative and supervisory posts, many medium-sized landholdings were likewise reserved for the gentry. In the eastern latifundia, however, the owners often had to go into debt before their widely scattered properties were assembled. There, Jewish moneylenders, who extended credit to both the magnates and the lesser landlords, received much rural property as security for their loans. By the end of the sixteenth century this system gave way to a form of lease (arenda), Jews assuming the management of an entire village, or even of a number of villages, in return for a stipulated annual payment, sometimes a lump sum given to the owner in advance. At times there was a sort of lend-lease combination, as when the leading Jewish entrepreneur of the region, Abraham Szmoiłowicz (son of Samuel) of Turzysk (Turisk), Volhynia, first paid off a debt owed by Prince Fiodor Sanguszko to another magnate, and subsequently leased the prince's properties. These arrangements frequently extended to the possessions administered by *starostas* (district governors) and other managers of royal domains. According to a census of 1616, of ten Ukrainian districts (*starostwa*), four had all their landed properties under the control of arendators, one had 99 percent; and in four the land under such control ranged from 68.6 to 85.4 percent of the total. Only one had but 34.2 percent encumbered by an arenda. And this happened *after* the tremendous effort made, in the preceding century and a quarter, to recapture most of the royal domains, previously lavishly given away to "deserving" dignitaries! Evidently, the district governors felt that they, or the Treasury, would derive greater financial benefits if Jewish leaseholders managed these lands than if they themselves, or their subordinates, tried to do so.[66]

Jewish arendators took over practically all the landlord's authority over the inhabitants of villages and hamlets alike, collected dues from mills and other establishments, exacted the required days of labor from the serfs, and even administered justice to them all. They often had the right to condemn a criminal to death, although we do not hear of any executions ordered by Jews. They also were the licensed liquor distillers, brewers, and owners of taverns and other facilities. Naturally, they employed numerous subordinates, primarily Jews. It was for them that the Lithuanian Jewish Council made an exception from its general prohibition forbidding Jews to employ more than one Christian servant per household. (Less wealthy Jews annually contributing only 4 groszy to the communal taxes, were forbidden to employ even a single Gentile servant without the elders' authorization; while publicly supported families were not to have any servants at all.) In general, the tenancy system gave the arendator an advantage in that the title to the property remained with the landlord, who assumed a major responsibility for protecting both the land and the tenant's personal security. To be sure, rarely did a landlord specify, as did Prince Wroński in 1594, that in the event of a conflict between him and his tenants (Abraham Szmoiłowicz and his Christian partner)

concerning the land, the burning of produce, or any other damage caused by neighbors which requires the intervention of other people—all that will go on our account. . . . Similarly, if by chance, which God forbid, there should arise some enemy destruction of the property or any other damage from fire, plague, or if the produce should be destroyed by hail, we shall, on notice from the gentlemen leaseholders, dispatch two of our representatives, while they [the leaseholders] shall add two representatives of their own. Whatever [damage] these men will assess, we shall be obliged to pay.

Many contracts at least provided that the rent need not be paid in the case of fire, plague, raids by Cossacks or Tatars, or some other force majeure.[67]

Clearly, the entire arenda system was built upon the growing servitude of the Polish and Lithuanian peasantry. In ethnographic Poland, which principally embraced Great Poland, Little Poland, and Mazovia, Jews long played a relatively minor role in farm leaseholds. Even in the latifundia of the aristocracy and the Church (such as those of Jan Zamoyski, the archbishopric of Gniezno, and others mentioned above), most of the administration was handled by the landlords themselves or by impoverished nobles who formed their permanent retinue, sometimes even by a few talented peasants. Only after 1650 do Jewish arendators of breweries and taverns appear in the records of the Cracow palatinate; for instance, in the leases of two villages in 1692–93—one for the relatively high annual rent of 500 zlotys. In contrast, in Volhynia, Podolia, and some neighboring districts Jewish tenancy took hold quite early, while in the newly developing, extremely fertile, provinces of Bratslav and Kiev tenancy was hampered by the area's underpopulation and the need to attract peasant settlers to cultivate what was sometimes virgin soil. The new settlers were often given extensive privileges, which protected them from excessive exploitation by the landlords, at least until the expiration or cancellation of their "liberties." Nevertheless, in time, the system of serfdom and arendas spread into those districts, too, especially into the areas which remained under the Polish regime after the Peace of Andruszów of 1667.[68]

Volhynia and Podolia remained major centers of arenda enterprises. Abraham Szmoiłowicz (his patronymic varies in the documents) was particularly active in accumulating vast tenancies, some of which extended over hundreds of square miles. In 1601, for example, Prince Grzegorz Sanguszko farmed out to him and another Jew the two towns of Horochów (Gorokhov) except the castle therein, and Przemil, together with all the neighboring villages, for three years for the huge rent of 40,000 zlotys. In a contract of 1594, Prince Piotr Zabrzeski had more explicitly leased all his possessions

located in the district of Krzemieniec, including the new and old city of Krzemieniec, the new Zbaraż, and Kolsec, with all the villages and settlements appertaining to these estates, together with the noble boyars, the burghers, and the serfs of those cities and villages, . . . all their debts, obligations, and privileges, with the arendas, taverns, tolls, ponds, the mills and their revenues, with the manors [folwarki], the various tithes paid by the boyars, burghers, and serfs of those districts, and all the other revenues, to Mr. Mikołaj Wransowicz and to Efraim the Jew of Międzyboż for the amount of 9,000 zlotys of the Polish currency for three years.

According to an inventory of 1620, no fewer than 4,000 Jews were employed in various capacities by Prince Konstanty Wasyl Ostrogski, then palatine of Kiev, in his vast estates, including the city of Ostrog. This may be an exaggeration, but there is no doubt that Ostrog developed into a major Jewish cultural center boasting a long line of distinguished rabbis. To some extent it was "almost a new Jerusalem," as it was styled by a seventeenth-century Polish writer. Most remarkably, even the churches often mortgaged some of their revenues with Jewish leaseholders. For example, the bishop of Włodzimierz (Vladimir), Volhynia, leased to a Jew his "tenth week"; that is, the payments from bridge tolls, carriages, and measures, which were customarily paid to the church every tenth week.[69]

In this line of business, which employed many Jews and contributed much to relieving the Jewish communal tax burden and also, indirectly, to the maintenance of the Jewish communities themselves, there was a great temptation to engage in competitive bidding and even to attempt to displace existing leaseholders. To prevent Jews from outbidding one another ad infinitum, the Lithuanian Council insisted on preservation of the "acquired right" (ḥazaqah) of each particular tenant. The rule was that if a Jew held a lease for three years and met all his obligations to the landlord, no outsider was to interfere with his continuing the leasehold to the end of his life. After his death, his heirs were to carry on to the end of the contracted period; but thereafter any other Jew was free to secure the lease. A Jew might also bid for the lease if the original Jewish tenant failed to meet his obligations to the landlord; or if he had already been replaced by a Christian tenant for at least one year. Some tenants established close personal relations with the landlords: one tenant boasted that, no matter how high a rent another would-be tenant offered, the master would never accept it. Certainly, many a Jew became a sort of major-domo and relieved his landlord of all administrative responsibilities, so that the owner could spend more time in government service, politics, or sheer amusement in Warsaw or Paris. Absentee landlordism was indeed quite common; and the chances are that, without the Jews' enterprising spirit, alertness, and tireless labor, large stretches of the underdeveloped southeastern provinces would not have achieved so soon the state of civilization which they reached before 1648 and even surpassed in the later prepartition period.[70]

Clearly, the sweeping regulations adopted between 1623 and 1628 in the early sessions of the Lithuanian Council were subject to many subsequent modifications. To begin with, the Lithuanian

Jews were bent upon favoring local residents. That is why they provided in 1626 that no one interfere with the acquired rights of an arendator in his place of residence. At the same time, the leaders were careful to emphasize the supreme importance of the common good. They reserved to themselves the right to override existing *hazaqot* in emergencies. Early in the Thirty Years' War, for example, they outlawed arendas in minting coins, because the rapid depreciation of currency cast a pall on everyone connected with the circulation of money, and the Jewish elders legitimately feared a reaction by the suffering masses. They were less anxious to interfere with the established order in response to members' complaints that their livelihood was endangered by certain arendas. In 1634 the Council decided to postpone deliberation on that subject. But three years later it specifically authorized local courts in communities embracing 15 Jewish families or more, at their discretions, to provide a living for some individuals by nullifying the acquired rights of others with respect to the production and distribution of vodka. However, all such proceedings, bordering on expropriation, had to be conducted in a spirit of justice and mutual accommodation. Certainly, no one was to lose his privilege for the entire duration of his contract. The elders also realized that problems connected with leaseholds were much too complicated to be subject to general provisions; they preferred to decide controversies according to the merits of each individual case. They were further aware that any action required discretion and secrecy, and that it might greatly affect the good will of non-Jewish neighbors. They provided, therefore, that major decisions in matters concerning leaseholds should be made by lay elders rather than courts, since active communal leaders could more adequately gauge the temper of the non-Jewish public and the political impact of any decisive action. Finally, they resolved that all records pertaining to leaseholds be kept in special minute books apart from the general protocols of the communal board, so that they would be accessible to a very limited circle of trustworthy persons. As a further precaution against "leaks," they demanded that all entries be couched in terms understandable only to a few initiates.[71]

Evidently, arendas were fraught with perils. Jewish tenants were fully aware that, as a rule, they dealt with powerful nobles, some of whom served as high royal officials, liable to break contracts or otherwise proceed arbitrarily when the spirit moved them. An interesting case was reported in Lwów in 1595. One of the leaders of the Jewish community, Israel Eideles (son of Edel or Adela), better known as Israel Złoczowski, arranged with the nobles Aleksander and Samuel Zborowski for the lease of a large area in the Złoczów district. It included four large fish ponds, pastures, market and road tolls, mills, breweries, malt houses, distilleries, and taverns, together with the revenues from serf labor in the entire district of Złoczów, for the annual rent of 4,000 zlotys payable in advance. Characteristically, the contract also provided that the landlord would keep pigs away from the mills during the entire period of the lease—evidently a precaution against the then widespread practice whereby the miller would feed a prescribed number of the landlord's swine free of charge. Another clause pledged the owner to indemnify Israel in case, "God forbid, an enemy, Tatar, or soldier, the plague, fire, or water should damage the ponds and mills." All these safeguards proved in vain the following year, however, when a Lwów official Jan Swoszowski invaded the property with an armed force, expelled Israel and his aides, occupied the buildings, and started selling the fish to Lwów merchants. Thereupon Israel sued both the two landlords and the invader. We do not know how he fared against Swoszowski, though the court issued a judgment against the Zborowskis entitling Israel to take over one of their villages. But on the arrival of the bailiff (*woźny*) to execute the sentence, Aleksander Zborowski chased him with dogs, and expelled him from the estate. Israel's motion to the court that a ban be imposed upon the violent landlord had no effect, and the lease amounted to a total loss for him.[72]

Nevertheless, there was much envy and resentment of Jewish arendas on the part of Polish writers, particularly of the Jew-baiting variety. A poem published in Cracow in 1648 complained that many an impoverished noble was being ousted from his native village and forced to move to the city. "They do not wish to lease him land, for the Jew offers more money. . . . Who is the greater cause of the *szlachta*'s decline? Impious lords or [their] Jewish benefactors?" With his usual penchant for exaggeration, Przecław Mojecki declared: "Travel to Lithuania and the Rus [areas], you will find Jews controlling customs, serving as arendators, tollmasters, saline managers; they hold monopolies on inns, so that you cannot obtain your necessities anywhere else." His complaint was echoed by another notorious Jew-baiter, Sebastyan Miczyński. On the other hand, some Jewish contemporaries rather rashly gloated over the fact that in Poland, in contrast to other countries, Jews were actually able to exercise control over Christian serfs. This glorification of Jewish power was used particularly to support the argument that Jews should the more strictly observe the law, out of gratitude for God's benefactions. In his aforementioned "Ordinances," expatiating on the legal safeguards for Sabbath observance, R. Meshullam Feivish stated:

When we lived in Exile under Egyptian oppression our forefathers chose to observe the Sabbath day for rest, even though they had not yet been ordered to do so [before the revelation of the Torah]; they were therefore aided from Heaven to establish this as a day of rest for the generations to come. How much more should we fulfill this commandment of the Torah and the sages in a place where Gentiles live under the control of these men [Jewish tenants]!

But whatever the evaluation of these conditions was in Jewish or Christian public opinion, the landlords merely followed the advice of one of their leading agricultural experts, Anzelm Gostomski, whose work on husbandry enjoyed wide acceptance. In 1588 Gostomski, himself a landlord and palatine of Rawa, advised magnates to follow the adage: "Expenses shall not exceed income." He also advocated that they enforce strict discipline among their peons and impose severe penalties for any infraction of rules, however slight. Needless to say, the serfs resented the Jew, their direct oppressor, more than the landlord whose orders the Jew executed.[73]

Remarkably, however, we hear relatively little from the peasants themselves. Even the various petitions they submitted to their masters or the royal authorities rarely refer to abuses by Jews. To be sure, with the aid of government officials, the lords and their Jewish leaseholders were often able to intercept such petitions before they reached the proper authorities. When in

1634 the peasants of two villages in the district of Drohobycz heard of a forthcoming royal visit to Lwów, they decided to send a delegation to the king to submit grievances against the extortionist practices of Izak Nachmanowicz the Younger. But the deputy governor arrested the delegates, had them flogged, and kept them in prison for four days. In 1637 a peasant rebellion against Nachmanowicz was crushed by Izak's henchmen, and the rebels' leader, Jan, was slain. Yet the paucity of peasant petitions against Jewish leaseholders is striking, since the voicing of grievances had become one of the milder forms of peasant resistance. Compared to armed uprisings, which were rare, or flight from the village, the submission of petitions was an innocuous way of asking for redress of specific abuses. And it certainly would have been easier for the peasants to protest against alleged misdeeds by Jewish leaseholders than against the conduct of the landlords themselves or their Christian subordinates.[74]

An important side effect of Jewish land leases was that many tenants (particularly of smaller properties) and their Jewish employees settled on the land, to be close to the scene of action. This undoubtedly was a major factor in the substantial migration of Jews from the West to the newly developed areas. We recall that the final census of 1764 covering all prepartition Poland and Lithuania showed that some 40 percent of the Jewish population then inhabited the eastern provinces. With that geographic transfer went an occupational redistribution, since about one-third of the total gainfully employed Jewish population now resided in rural districts. Very likely the majority of these settlers in villages and hamlets cultivated vegetable gardens and orchards on the side, raised fowl, and kept goats and even cows, primarily to satisfy the needs of their own families, but also in some cases to supply produce for sale or barter. In this way many Jews learned anew the long-neglected skills of cultivating the soil and the art of animal husbandry. In addition, stimulated by the religious requirements concerning dairy products and meats, many a village Jew doubtless produced his own milk, butter, and cheese, and sold his surplus to Jews in neighboring towns. Even in Great Poland we occasionally come across such astonishing data as those recorded in later years in some provincial towns belonging to noblemen. According to the census figures of 1775–76, the town of Kórnik, with a population of 1,150 persons, embraced 144 agricultural families, 62 of them Jewish. Another township, Zaniemyśl, with a population of 482 souls, included 11 such families, all of them Jewish. It stands to reason, however, that many of these Jewish "farmers" also engaged in some handicrafts and/or commerce. In other words, a substantial number of Jews almost imperceptibly found their way back to the soil, from which Ashkenazic Jewry had long been almost totally alienated.[75]

Like the story of the small shopkeepers, that of the petty Jewish farmers, working the land full or part time, found few interested reporters. Except for occasional references to participants in litigations or intercommunal disputes, our documents are almost totally silent on the daily activities and behavior of rural Jews. Here and there we read words of derision written in contempt of the "unlearned" Jews living on the land. Sometimes they were censured by moralists for their neglect of one or another Jewish legal requirement or for their maintaining too close contacts with the Gentile population. It was, indeed, primarily for them that the aforementioned Sabbath ordinances were issued, in 1590, at a time when the agrarianization of the East European Jews was only beginning. Ironically, unexpected by the sixteenth-century leaders, these very "backward" Jews living in the southeastern Rus regions several generations later were to set in motion the hasidic movement, one of the most significant religious movements in modern Jewish life.

TOLLS AND TAXES

Related to the leases of farmlands and rural industries were the various forms of tax and toll collection. In the aforementioned Sabbath ordinances, emphasis was laid upon the possible violations of the Sabbath rest commandment in connection with the farming of tolls. The ordinances provided that the Jewish leaseholder

should contractually sublease to a Gentile the collection [of the toll] so that the Gentile should receive a share of a grosz or more from every zloty, whereupon he would perform the work on his own account. This procedure was permitted to avoid heavy losses [for the Jewish contractor]. If it is possible to arrange that the Gentile collect the tolls outside the Jew's house it would be better; the Jew might look on from a distance and supervise the Gentile so that he would not conceal his receipts. Supervision over matters is permitted on the Sabbath, provided only that the Jew shall not assist the Gentile in the collection of the toll, in accounting for it, or in giving change, over which matters many now stumble.

In fact, Jewish leaseholders often employed Gentile collectors for other reasons as well: when Jewish agents were unavailable or, because of legal difficulties, were unable to sign contracts in certain areas. Some tollmasters merely wished to escape the frequent controversies with toll payers about the amounts due. Abuses on the part of collectors alternated with attempts by shippers of goods to conceal dutiable objects or to claim that they had already paid the duty at another station. Cheating on both sides was greatly facilitated by the confusing variety of tolls imposed by diets and dietines, palatines, cities, and private lords, as well as by the intrinsically contradictory overall legal situation involving royal, municipal, and private regulations and customs.[76]

Tax and toll farming by Jews was honored by long tradition. We recall the services rendered by Wołczko the toll farmer, "in whose industry, circumspection, and foresight" Wladislaw Jagiello had "placed his fullest confidence," according to his statements of 1423 and 1425. In 1452–54 another Jewish tax farmer, Natko, served King Casimir IV in the towns of Lwów and Gródek. The king himself attested that Natko "commended himself to Us with his extraordinary solicitude and industry; We hope to receive many increments for Our Treasury through his diligence and ingenuity." Other Jewish tax collectors of the period, Schachno and Schaynko, were also mentioned at that time. In 1504 it was the turn of another Lwów Jew, Jossko, to serve King Alexander. According to several decrees issued by the king in 1502–1504, Jossko held, because of "Our certain knowledge and deliberation," contracts as toll collector in the lands of Podolia, Halicz, Lwów, Sanok, Przemyśl, Bełz, and Chełm. In 1504 Alexander exempted Jossko and his family for three years from all taxes usually paid by Jews, because of the losses the Jewish entrepreneur had sustained from warlike disturbances in Red Russia. When Jossko passed away in 1507, not only did Sigismund I confirm Jossko's testament, which left all his possessions to his widow Golda, but as late as 1518 the king renewed Golda's residential rights in Lublin and freed her from all taxes paid by Jews in the realm, except for an annual contribution of 10 marks. The system of tax farming by Jews continued later in the sixteenth and seventeenth centuries, notwithstanding the sharp opposition of the *szlachta*, which tried to reserve this remunerative activity to members of its own class. The matter was taken up at several sessions of the Diet. In 1538 the Sejm adopted a formal resolution, reading in part:

We herewith prescribe and ordain that henceforth and for all future times those in charge of the collection of our revenues must without exception be members of the landed nobility professing the Christian faith. . . . We decree that it be unconditionally observed that no Jew be entrusted with the collection of state revenues of any kind, for it is unseeming and runs counter to the divine law that such persons be allowed to occupy any position of honor and to exercise any public function among the Christian people.

The Diet unequivocally repeated that prohibition in 1562 and 1565.[77]

Since these enactments proved unavailing (their ineffectiveness was demonstrated by their repetition in quick succession), the *szlachta* tried to enlist the assistance of Jewish communal authorities in upholding this ban. It succeeded at least in persuading the newly formed Polish Council, in its first session of 1580, to declare: "Conditions in these lands require strengthening, especially with reference to men so greedy to secure profits and get rich from large and vast arendas that we fear that they will cause immense danger to the majority. Therefore, we have unanimously agreed that anyone calling himself a Jew shall have no dealing with the leasing of *czopowe* [liquor tax] in Great Poland, Little Poland, and Mazovia either from the king, may His Majesty be exalted, or through officials, or under any subterfuge whatsoever." This prohibition was strictly enforced by such rabbis as Joel b. Samuel Zvi Sirkes; in one of his responsa, he explained that the Jews would otherwise be "in great jeopardy because of the Gentiles' outcry in many localities that Jews dominate them and behave toward them like kings and lords." Yet from the outset the other

Polish provinces, including Red Russia, evidently were exempted from that ban because the *szlachta* itself realized that Jewish leaseholders had become too entrenched there for any action against them to be effective. Cases such as that recorded in Lwów in 1636 may well have occurred frequently elsewhere, too. A Polish official appointed by the dietine of Wisznia wished to secure a higher income from the liquor tax, but his offer to renew the lease under terms more advantageous to himself was rejected by the well-known Lwów businesswoman Róża Nachmanowicz (for generations thereafter known in local Jewish folklore as the Goldene Roize), who had held that lease for a number of years. In vain did the official try to secure bids from other Jews, who remembered the sharp communal regulation against unfair competition. Admitting failure, the nobleman restored Róża's lease on its old terms. Her son, Izak Nachmanowicz the Younger, succeeded, in the 1630s and 1640s, in securing a similar lease in the city of Lwów, from the hostile municipal administration; while Samuel Borowicz of Złoczów contracted in 1633 to collect that revenue for the entire Lwów district.[78]

The Polish Council's wide-ranging prohibition included other leaseholds by Jews, whenever they were obtained in competition with Christians, particularly nobles. The chief leaders of Polish Jewry specified that Jews should not lease any mints or salines or any customs duties at the frontiers: "They shall not deal in this type of business at all . . . and anyone who will dare to arrange for such an activity shall be excommunicated from the two worlds [this world and the hereafter], and segregated from any of the Jewish sacra." Such a culprit was generally to be treated as an outlaw and an accursed individual. The prohibition seems to have been effective, however, only in regard to the *czopowe* in the three major Polish provinces. Even Mazovia, which had not tolerated Jews for more than half a century, had nevertheless made an exception for one Moses Celnik (the tax farmer), and allowed him to operate successfully in this field to the middle of the century. Evidently because the liquor tax had become an important source of revenue for both the state and the tax farmer (it yielded, at times, as much as 25 percent of all state revenue from indirect taxes), its lease was widely coveted by the landless nobles. More over, with its collection often went the equally remunerative production and sale of liquor. Hence, competition was much sharper in this area than, for example, in leaseholds for salines or mints. Exploitation of salines, as we recall, was largely limited to a few localities in Little Poland and Red Russia; it also required considerable technical know-how, and the investment of much capital. Mints, too, presupposed the application of a more advanced technology, as well as large investments in materials, tools, and wages; and minting often embroiled leaseholders in disputes and perils.[79]

Difficulties in collecting tolls were aggravated by the complex and intrinsically inconsistent administration. Only at Włocławek, a crucial junction on the Vistula navigation route and hence particularly important for the export of grain via Gdańsk, was toll collection directly managed by royal officials. All other toll and duty stations had to be leased out for agreed-upon lump-sum payments. Furthermore, ever since the law passed by the Diet of 1496, the nobles exported grain and other agricultural produce duty free; they similarly imported duty-free machinery, clothing, and other goods for their own needs. Hence there was no end of disputes between the toll collectors and the wagoners, frequently peasants, with respect to such claims of immunity from duties. Some coachmen, allegedly acting in behalf of nobles, were unable to produce certificates to that effect; or else produced attestations which the collectors, rightly or wrongly, considered forged. At the same time, many Jewish collectors were none too familiar with the languages of the transport workers, generally Poles, Ukrainians, or Lithuanians. Some local archives have preserved receipts for the payment of tolls which were written in Hebrew or Yiddish because the collectors were unable to fill them out in the language of the local majority. With tempers often flaring up, there was much violence and bloodshed. Very frequently courts were busy for years with litigations concerning the merits of tolls which were collected, or over related disputes ending in assault and battery. A Poznań Jewish partner of Izak Nachmanowicz the Younger was accused of having, at a toll station near Śniatyn, torn up a legitimate receipt for an earlier payment of the toll submitted to him by some Lwów merchants and of having, with the assistance of the local burgomaster, illegally seized their goods.[80]

Reciprocally, as agents and leaseholders of noble possessions, Jews were often the victims of maladministration at the toll gates. Of course, they claimed that, since the transported property ultimately belonged to the landlord, they were entitled to his toll immunity. This claim was recognized as legally valid by such rabbis as Joel Sirkes. Yet the collectors, Jewish and non-Jewish, often disputed it, particularly if the shipper could not prove that every item exported came from his master's property or that every object imported was to serve the lord's own needs. Sometimes the Jewish plutocrats secured specific immunities from the king. On his visit to Lwów early in his reign in October 1634, Wladislaw IV received Izak Nachmanowicz the Younger and his less-known partner Izak Abrahamowicz. The king had learned about the advances of funds and other services the two Jews rendered in 1626, to the Polish army, which had unsuccessfully fought the Swedes under Gustavus Adolphus in Prussia. In recognition, Wladislaw issued a diploma, mentioning the help "given by them to the Treasury and the Commonwealth with greatest diligence and dexterity and which they have hitherto not ceased rendering," and appointing them royal servitors. As such they were subject only to direct royal jurisdiction, and enjoyed full freedom of trade throughout the Commonwealth, with complete immunity from taxes, duties, and tolls, both royal and private. This decree may have encouraged Izak to deal harshly with peasants and recklessly borrow money from nobles, burghers, and Armenians—practices which ultimately led to his total ruin. Finally, tollmasters were not always secure with their own employees. One of them, Jacob Doktorowicz, was actually assaulted and robbed by his own coachman and servant (1607). The culprits fled, and apparently were never brought to justice.[81]

Conflicts of this kind proved to be a double-edged sword whenever a Jewish tollmaster also administered a magnate's vast latifundia and had to secure for himself exemptions from tolls collected by others. Evasion of tolls, under one excuse or another, was quite common. Long after the event, the newly elected king Sigismund III ordered, on April 23, 1588, the Rus palatine to investigate rumors that "during the recent *interregnum* some Jews of Lwów, Śniatyn and other localities" had imported goods from Walachia without paying the required duties. We do not know the outcome of that investigation. In general, because of the enormous complications in these crisscross relationships, it is almost impossible to reconstruct today the entire story of the administration of customs duties and tolls in prepartition Poland, or of the Jewish share therein, on both the collecting and the paying sides. Nor has the vastly scattered source material yet been subjected to the careful detailed investigation by modern scholars that it indubitably deserves.[82]

In one area, however, the combined prohibition of the state and the Polish and Lithuanian Councils was truly effective. After 1581 we hear of fewer and fewer Jews holding leases of minting rights or connected in any other way with minting. We recall the great confusion into which the entire process of manufacturing coins had fallen in the dual Commonwealth in the course of the sixteenth and early seventeenth centuries. From the outset, like many other European governments, that of Poland considered minting primarily a revenue-producing activity—a premise which the great savant Nicholas Copernicus specifically criticized in his famous treatise *De moneta cudenda ratio* (About the Coining of Currency, which incidentally, alluded to what would later be called Gresham's law; that is, the general tendency of bad currency to displace good currency). It is small wonder, then, that most governments were tempted to manipulate coinage by reducing the silver and gold content of their coins, so that the difference between metallic and nominal values would accrue to the benefit of the Treasury. Polish finances were often in serious disarray (at one time in 1509 the *podskarbi* Andrzej Kostelecki found that the Treasury's cash had dwindled to 67 zlotys), and the temptation to tamper with coinage was correspondingly greater. The effects on the economy, however, were disastrous, and the ensuing sufferings of the population at large caused minters and their agents to be objects of public opprobrium. That is why not only the Polish Council in its resolution of 1581 but also the Lithuanian Council at its first session of 1623, sharply forbade Jews to seek arendas in minting; all transgressors were threatened by both councils with the most severe excommunication. Purely economic considerations reinforced these prohibitions. We remember how greatly the economy of the entire Commonwealth was undermined during the Thirty Years' War by the influx of debased coins from neighboring lands. Between 1616 and 1623 the silver content of the typical 3-groszy coin declined from 1.53 to 0.90 grams. Ultimately, the local minting of coins proved completely unrewarding, and under Wladislaw IV most Polish-Lithuanian regions discontinued that practice altogether. This situation helps to explain why the Polish-Jewish plutocracy of the seventeenth century had no counterpart to the Prague Jewish banker Jacob b. Samuel Bassevi, who was raised by Ferdinand II to the rank of nobility for his services to the imperial government along these very lines. Yet even Bassevi, after his inevitable downfall, was saved from total ruin only by the intervention of his famous collaborator, General Albrecht von Wallenstein.[83]

While the collection of tolls, duties, and other imposts had become an important source of revenue for many Jewish entrepreneurs and their employees, the reverse was also true; that is, the taxes paid by Jews became an increasing burden on both individuals and communities. True, Polish taxation generally was not quite so ruinous before the "Deluge" as it was to become in the eighteenth century. Under Sigismund III and Wladislaw IV, Poland suffered more from fiscal anarchy than from legitimate imposts. Although no exact data can be presented as to what portion of the national income went into meeting the great variety of levies by the two states, the provinces, and the municipalities, it appears that Poland-Lithuania was in this respect no worse off than most neighboring countries, or, for that matter, most Western countries today. We have approximate estimates of the revenue collected by the central Treasury in certain years, but (except in a few special instances) the income from local and regional taxes has yet to be ascertained from the widely scattered and, regrettably since World War II, greatly depleted archives.[84]

Early in the sixteenth century the king's private property was not yet clearly separated from property belonging to the state. Most state expenses were still carried by the royal domain. Whenever kings were short of funds, they borrowed by mortgaging some of their landed property; the failure to redeem it usually converted it to the lender's private possession. Often Sigismund I gave such estates to military or civilian dignitaries as a reward for special services. Occasionally, Jews were among the beneficiaries of such gifts; for instance, in 1463 Casimir IV gave land to Liva Lewin of Brest-Litovsk. It took, as we recall, a major effort for the Polish statesmen and the Diet to recapture much of that royal domain. First suggested by Wojciech Żychliński as early as 1465, these proceedings did not fully start before 1536, and reached fruition only in 1562–69. In 1590, long after the end of the Jagiellon dynasty, and the succession of kings from various families and countries, measures were taken to separate the outlay for the royal court (which included expenses for foreign missions and the reception of foreign envoys) from those devoted to the administration of the country. Both sets of expenses increased constantly. About 1600 the "court" (*nadworny*) budget amounted to 386,000 zlotys (including Lithuania's share of 150,000), of which the revenue from the royal domain and from mining royalties yielded 74,000 and 90,000 zlotys, respectively. At that time the "public" Treasury collected about 580,000 zlotys annually. In the 1650s that revenue rose to 2,600,000 zlotys, partly in response to the country's growing needs and partly as a result of growing inflation and an informal devaluation of the currency. In fact, 580,000 zlotys in 1600 were equivalent to 290,000 gold ducats, whereas half a century later the 2,600,000 zlotys were valued at no more than 466,000 ducats, since the relationship between the zloty and the ducat had declined from about 1:2 to less than 1:5.5. In addition to the state revenue, there were separate taxes and other imposts collected by palatinates, district governorships, municipal bodies, churches, and private lords; special payments to the king and high officials of the central, regional, and local governments; fees and "gifts" to public employees for services rendered, generally considered perfectly legitimate, as well as less overt bribes. Only exceptionally do we hear of any governmental interference with bureaucratic corruption, as in a case reported by R. Solomon Luria where the king forced the dignitary concerned to return the bribe to the donor.[85]

Beyond all these regular taxes there were extraordinary contributions for emergencies. For example, on June 27, 1643, Wladislaw IV ordered the communities of Cracow, Lwów, Lublin, and Poznań to collect from their own members and other Jewish communities 60,000 zlotys, to be handed over to the royal secretary, Jan Wisemberg, by January 6 (7), 1644. This amount was to be used to pay of some Commonwealth debts as voted by the Diet. The cities had already promised to contribute their share, and it was resolved that the Jews should do the same out of "due gratitude" to the country. The general fiscal disarray was much aggravated by the fact that the two wealthiest classes, the nobility and the clergy, were officially tax exempt. Members of the *szlachta* often found themselves in a quandary. Their tax exemption was ideologically justified in Poland, as in Europe's other feudal countries, by their carrying the burden of the country's defense. This medieval rationale became rather obsolete in the early modern period, when professionally trained mercenary armies proved far superior in battle to the noble part-time soldiers, who in civilian life were for the most part either landlords or officials. While clamoring for tax exemption, the *szlachta* was at the same time reluctant to vote substantial amounts for the maintenance of a permanent mercenary force, because it feared that, once in control of a standing army, the king might become too powerful and curtail its "liberties." The medieval justification for the clergy's tax-exempt status—namely, that it served as the bearer of culture and education in the country—was also greatly weakened in the Renaissance era, when the speedy growth of a lay intelligentsia and Reform sectarianism actually rendered the Catholic establishment a culturally retarding factor. Yet tradition persisted, and the churches, monasteries, and other ecclesiastical institutions, together with their vast landholdings and urban real estate, continued to be almost totally tax exempt. Only exceptionally did the Church, spontaneously or under pressure, contribute something to state revenues, but the voluntary character of these contributions was emphasized by their designation as a *donum* or *subsidium charitativum* (charitable donation).[86]

Characteristically, rabbis, too, and often such synagogue officials as cantors and sextons, as well as the synagogue and the Jewish cemetery, were as a rule freed from taxation. In the Jewish case, to be sure, ordination did not necessarily lead to service in the religious sphere. Many young Jews ordained by the heads of their academies or by other scholars, never had any intention of accepting rabbinical office, but rather went into business or some other occupation. If we are to believe the romanticizing chronicler Nathan Neṭa Hannover, a community embracing 50 Jewish families as a rule included no fewer than 30 ordained men. Hence this criterion for tax exemption became quite vague. Seeking to clarify the issue, the Lithuanian Council in 1628 adopted the general rule that "scholars who continually and diligently study the Torah and do not engage in business, should be given concessions in regard to taxes." It further resolved, in 1631, that

students of the Law, living at home and studying with utmost diligence and not engaging in business, shall be given relief from taxation in the following manner: a scholar diligently applying himself to study in his own domicile and owning property of up to 4,000 zlotys shall be granted, at the assessors' discretion, a discount of no less than one-quarter and no more than one-third from the usual assessment of other members; a scholar studying in another locality and owning property of up to 1,500 zlotys, shall be granted a discount of one-half the usual assessment.

These provisions were further liberalized in 1679–83, when both resident and nonresident scholars were granted a blanket deduction of 50 percent. On the other hand, general tax exemptions were often granted by kings to their servitors and other favorites. Naturally, when the communities assumed the responsibility for lump sum payments, the tax exemption of any individual—usually granted to those belonging to the wealthiest group—increased the burden of the other Jewish taxpayers. Nevertheless, few kings followed the example of Sigismund I, who in 1527 revoked, under pressure from Jewish representatives, his previous tax exemptions of certain Jewish individuals, except for that of his friend Doctor Izaak, who was to pay no more than 8 zlotys annually to the end of his life.[87]

If we analyze the major sources of direct and indirect taxation, we find that, fundamentally, Jews were treated no differently from other groups, except the nobility and clergy, in regard to direct revenues stemming from the following (in Kazimierz Lepszy's classification): (1) the royal domain; (2) the salines in Wieliczka, Bochnia, and Red Russia; (3) the Olkusz mines; (4) duties and tolls collected at the frontiers or at Włocławek; (5) export and import taxes in Gdańsk and Elbląg; (6) land taxes paid by farmers, initially at 2 groszy from land belonging to nobles and bishops, and 4 groszy from land belonging to monasteries (it was later raised to 30 groszy, or 1 zloty, per lan); (7) revenue from mints; (8) *podwodne* (transport tax), paid by the royal cities; and a billeting tax (*stacyjne*) paid by all cities, monasteries, and Jews; and (9) a number of lesser imposts. Among the more extraordinary revenues were the following: (1) *pobór* (land tax), specially voted to be collected from lands, both cultivated and fallow, leased by peasants and others—which included flour mills, smitheries, and so forth; (2) *szos* (property tax), paid by burghers on crafts and real as well as movable property; (3) *pogłówne* (capitation tax), particularly from Jews (see below); (4) *czopowe* (liquor tax); and (5) the *subsidium charitativum* of the clergy. As may be seen from the above listing, each category was uniformly paid by Jews as members of their particular taxpaying group. When the Diet imposed a tax on urban real estate in 1557, the Jews, like the burghers, had to pay 30 groszy for each of their holdings in the cities, royal, private, or ecclesiastical. This was apparently intended as the counterpart of the land tax per lan in the same amount. Practice differed greatly from theory, to be sure, Jews often paying more than their share. This was particularly true regarding the numerous additional imposts voted by the provincial dietines or levied by palatines, district governors, or private lords. On the other hand, generally forming independently taxed corporate groups, the Jewish communities were on the whole freed from municipal taxation, except for specific contributions to jointly maintained facilities.[88]

The sum total of these regional and local taxes frequently exceeded the state revenue, though there is no way of estimating the total amounts collected. We are still less able to guess the share of the Jewish revenue in the bewildering array of local and provincial imposts. We are a little better informed about the over-all revenue of the state, which rose during the regime of Sigismund I (1507–1548) from about 50,000 zlotys to 100,000 zlotys annually in the Polish Crown (without Lithuania). Within less than two decades it rose further, to over 185,000 zlotys in 1564; and five years later, after the Union of Lublin and the incorporation of the southeastern provinces, to 360,000 zlotys. This rise was somewhat illusory because of the decline in the value of the zloty and also because of the prevailing system of delayed payments. In 1564 only 47 percent of the tax came in on time; the arrears amounted to 40 percent in the following year, to fully 87 percent in 1566, and still more in the following year.

From the Jewish point of view, the progressive decentralization of Polish tax collection in the years 1587–1613 had both favorable and unfavorable features. It was more favorable in so far as negotiations with palatines and lesser officials, as well as with private lords, were conducted on a more personal level than the bargaining with high royal dignitaries in remote Warsaw or, what was worse, discussions with an unruly Sejm in an attempt to dissuade it from imposing insupportable levies upon the Jewish communities. Obviously, negotiations with provincial dietines, often attended by mobs of undisciplined nobles, were even more difficult. It required both subtleness and the playing of one group against another for Jewish representatives to prevent hostile legislation, fiscal or otherwise. Fortunately for all taxpayers, the dietine resolutions were frequently not fully executed.

Apart from contributing to general imposts, Jews had to pay special taxes, particularly the "Jewish poll tax." Capitation taxes were no novelty in either Jewish or Polish fiscal history. They had played a preeminent role in the relations between Jews and the Gentile states since the ancient Roman emperors, the Sassanian "kings of kings" in Persia, and the medieval caliphs. In Poland, too, attempts to impose a poll tax on the whole population had been made in 1498 and 1520, though with little immediate success. Renewed efforts from time to time likewise broke down, mainly because the population censuses, which were to be made every year to furnish reliable data for tax assessment, demanded too much money, time, and energy. In 1549 the government tried its luck with the Jews, probably because they still were relatively few in number, formed an easily distinguishable group, and were concentrated in a few major cities. This first special Jewish poll tax was to be collected only in the royal cities, because the lords owning private towns were still trying to stave off any interference by royal tax collectors with "their" Jews. By 1552, however, the tax was extended to all Jews in Poland and Lithuania. Yet, here, too, the problem of regular censuses became a stumbling block. Especially after 1569, when the Polish Crown embraced Podlasie, Volhynia, and the Ukrainian provinces, the *lustracje* of the greatly increased Jewish population became quite sporadic. Thus was conceived the idea that, just as cities had been delivering negotiated lump sums on the basis of their estimated taxable population, the Jewish communities, too, could be organized so as to pay amounts agreed upon from year to year. Still more advantageous and convenient to the Treasury, it appeared, would be for these communities to establish a central body of representatives with which it could negotiate about the size of the annual tax. Since efforts to unify Polish-Lithuanian Jewry had, for other reasons, been initiated in the preceding decades, the pertinent discussions were brought to a successful conclusion in 1579. This was an epochal event in Polish Jewish history. It led immediately to the establishment of the Council of Three Lands, later changed to Four and then Five Lands. Finally, after Lithuania's separation in 1623, there emerged the permanently functioning Polish Council of Four Lands and Lithuanian Council of Three, later Four, and still later Five, Provinces.[89]

Understandably, the revenue from the tax grew in proportion to the rise in the Jewish population. Beginning in 1579 with an impost of 10,000 zlotys for the Polish Crown and 3,000 zlotys for Lithuania, the amounts were doubled by 1590. (In return, the Jews were assured by the *podskarbi* Jan Firlej, in 1603, that they would be free from any other poll tax and from the *pobór*, or land tax.) In 1649 the Polish contribution was still 20,000 zlotys, but Lithuania's was doubled again, to 12,000 zlotys, doubtless reflecting the progressive eastward diffusion of Jewish settlements, as illustrated by Vilna's intervening rise to leadership within Lithuanian Jewry. Remarkably, despite the ruin of Polish-Lithuanian communities in the subsequent seven years, and the tremendous losses in both manpower and wealth owing to massacres and emigration—losses which the government conceded—the poll tax in 1656 rose to 70,000 zlotys. It held at that level for three years, but increased in 1660 to 100,000 zlotys. This was more than would have been accounted for by the rise in the Jewish population (we recall our estimates of a Jewish total of 150,000 persons in 1578 and 450,000 in 1648 before the pogroms and the flights) and the intervening inflation. The documents pertaining to the tax collections of the 1650s shed characteristic light on the methods of payment. Rather than delivering the total amount due to the *podskarbi,* as had been the practice in earlier years—in 1589, for example, Izak Nachmanowicz the Elder delivered the full amount due from all Jews in the dual Commonwealth, in two instalments to Jan Dulski—the Council paid differing amounts to specially designated recipients, such as generals fighting the enemies in particular regions, provincial leaders, or palatines. The few extant documents also reveal that the total Jewish payments did not quite equal the assessed sums, and the gaps grew from year to year. But this had long been a regular feature of all recorded Polish tax receipts.[90]

Curiously, in the early years, neither the Diet nor the Council was sure of the wisdom of the innovation concerning direct payments by the Council rather than through experienced and financially responsible tax farmers. Even after some fifteen years of the new system's more or less successful operation, the Diet still reserved the right to revert to tax farming. In its *Uniwersał poborowy* (tax collection circular) of March 20, 1595, it renewed the demand that each Jew pay a poll tax of one zloty, but added the clause: "in any case, should a more advantageous way be found, we shall be in a position to farm out [that tax]." However, by that time the Council, perhaps out of vested interest, now thoroughly disapproved this procedure. In its session of Sivan 5355 (May–June 1595), it resolved:

The leaders of the people here assembled have unanimously agreed concerning the emergency which may arise if, God forbid, the king, may His Majesty be exalted, and the lords should wish to collect the head tax from the Jews [through tax farmers], that no Jew should endeavor to lease it from the king and the lords. Rather the matter should rest with the present poll tax procedure. The only exception should be if all the elders and leaders of all the lands should jointly decide to secure the tax leaseholds. If even one of them dissents, they should not be able to overrule him under any circumstance except by a unanimous vote.

Evidently, neither side tried to alter the existing system during the seventeenth century. Despite its ever more glaring deficiencies, it even outlasted several attempts made in the 1700s to revert to direct collections, until 1764, when both Councils ended their remarkable careers.[91]

Far more irksome were the sudden extraordinary taxes, such as the aforementioned large contribution of 60,000 zlotys, demanded by Wladislaw IV in 1643 toward the payment of royal debts. The cost to Jewish taxpayers of the notoriously venal fiscal bureaucracy was also very high. Zdzisław Kaczmarczyk and Bogusław Leśnodorski rightly observed that "the *podskarbi*s and tax collectors usually amassed great fortunes during their terms in office." Though helpful to some Jewish communities, who secured lower assessments through bribes, in the long run this unsavory procedure proved very expensive, because the recipients were often insatiable. Apart from bribes, Jews were expected to pay salaries to palatines and subpalatines (in Poznań, the amounts were 4,000 and 1,000 zlotys annually), district governors, and many other officials, including churchmen. Such Jewish contributions to institutions of another faith were rationalized by the time-honored argument that, through the acquisition of land for their own settlement, Jews had taken over properties which would have been subject to an ecclesiastical tithe; hence they were making up for the losses incurred by the local clergy. Equally disturbing was the *kozubalec* (the regular impost to keep unruly students from attacking the Jewish quarter), as well as direct payments for the maintenance of local Christian schools. In sixteenth-century Lwów, annual Jewish payments to the Christian school included 16 pounds of pepper, 16 lots (about 10 grams each) of saffron, 30 zlotys for the rector of the school, 30 zlotys for the students, and 20 zlotys for the father confessor. Before each Christmas and Easter the community of Cracow had to deliver 189 pounds of sugar, 86 pounds each of pepper and ginger, 68 pounds each of rice and raisins, 188 lots of cinnamon, 152 lots of saffron, 182 lots of cloves, 56 pounds of almonds, and a variety of other products, as well as cash, to a number of officials of the Jagiellon University. In a curious practice reminiscent of a similar one in medieval Spain, Jews also had to maintain the lions and the tigers kept in the royal palace; later that obligation too, was commuted into a cash payment.[92]

At the same time, Jews paid considerable amounts to city treasuries, although the very principle of their being taxed by the cities was a permanent bone of contention. If unable to secure a royal privilege *de non tolerandis Judaeis,* the burghers generally tried to impose many local taxes upon the Jews. For example, in 1631 and again in 1635 the Lwów municipality sued the Jews before Sigismund III and then Wladislaw IV for nonpayment of their share in the municipal expenses, demanding from them a contribution of 10,000 zlotys in 1631 and probably an even larger sum four years later. Many such imposts went under the heading of "rents" paid by Jews for the use of the land on which they were allowed to erect their dwellings or for their houses, too, if these also belonged to the municipality or to city lords. Jews had to pay "rent" for their cemeteries; contribute funds toward the building of fortifications; donate prescribed "gifts" to mayors and other city elders; pay license fees for the exercise of many occupations, and so forth. The story of the fiscal administration of the city of Poznań offers some illuminating illustrations. After 1550 the municipal income from houses in the Jewish quarter rose from 8 zlotys to 160 zlotys in 1601 and to 256 zlotys in 1631. A special tax derived from the Jewish slaughterhouse located outside the wall averaged 29 zlotys annually in the 1540s; but it rose quickly to 43 zlotys in mid-century, and to 55 zlotys by the beginning of the seventeenth century. According to their agreement with the burghers, the Poznań Jews also had to pay 40 zlotys a year for their commercial rights in the period 1539–47; over 50 zlotys annually from 1547 to 1564; and finally 72.66 zlotys in the first half of the seventeenth century. In addition, both the cities and the Jewish communities had to spend considerable amounts in opposing each other. Their delegations to the dietines, and their appearances before the royal tribunals to defend their respective points of view, were costly in money and effort on both sides, despite frequently inconclusive results.[93]

Other interesting illustrations are offered by the fiscal provisions included in the compacts between the Jews and the municipality of Cracow in 1553–54, 1608–1609, and 1615. In the first of these agreements, the Jews had to promise to pay 35 zlotys, one stone of pepper, and one pound of saffron annually for permission to live in the municipal area, in addition to 2 groszy per head for their cattle to graze in the municipal pasture. They also had to pay the fees for the royal approval of that agreement. In 1583 they had to promise again to adhere to the arrangements of 1553, and also to pledge themselves to build the so-called Bochnia rampart, to pay up all arrears, and not to sell any liquor to non-Jews.

The compact of 1608–1609 increased the annual payment to the city council to 80 zlotys, the Jews being forced to post a bond of another 80 zlotys, which was to be forfeited if they violated a single article in the agreement. In 1615 this compact was amended by the expansion of several articles and the inclusion of a fine of 24 groszy for each infraction by an individual Jew. In such cases the fine was actually to be divided between the city and the Jewish community. If the Jewish elders were in any way involved in a violation, however, the community was to forfeit its bond of 1,000 marks to the Kazimierz city council. Remarkably, thirty years later (March 20, 1645), when the Jewish community concluded, under municipal sponsorship, an agreement with the Christian guild of innkeepers (the curious terminology here used spoke of negotiations between the council of the "Kazimierz Commonwealth" and the "Jewish Commonwealth"), the council added a special Article xiii, reading: "If the Jewish elders will not keep this agreement or help in its enforcement, they shall pay a penalty of 2,000 zlotys." [94]

Reviewing the vast variety of Jewish imposts recorded in the sources, however, we must always remember that most of them were neither universal nor synchronous. They were recorded in one locality or another, or in the same locality at different times. Nor were the amounts mentioned in the normative sources necessarily reflective of what was actually collected. Suffice it to note the numerous instances of arrears mentioned above, which effectively reduced the collected totals for even some of the major state imposts. Nonetheless, the ever-growing fiscal burden upon the Jewish communities was extremely heavy before 1648; and it became quite crushing in the eighteenth century.

In addition, the Jewish communities had ever-larger expenditures for their own needs. As the population grew, the elders' responsibilities in maintaining synagogues, cemeteries, schools, slaughterhouses, and baths increased in geometric proportion. "Parkinson's law" of the unceasing growth of bureaucracies operated in the Jewish establishment as elsewhere, especially in the later period of ever-greater concentration of power in the small plutocratic-rabbinic minority and narrowing employment opportunities in the "private" sector, concomitant with Poland's general economic decline and the Jewish population's growing geographic diffusion. The expenses for welfare alone, whether disbursed by the communal treasuries, various charitable societies, or philanthropic-minded individuals, grew by leaps and bounds, and greatly exceeded the parallel expenditures by churches and other Christian institutions. Nevertheless, beggars on the streets and from door to door became a permanent sorrowful reminder of the ramified biblical-talmudic injunctions concerning the charitable obligations of every Jewish individual and communal body toward less fortunate coreligionists. In short, Jews kept on paying overtly and clandestinely an enormous part of their own income. It is impossible to gauge precisely the total amounts thus spent annually, even before 1648, and doubly so after the "Deluge." A list compiled by Majer Bałaban from the local archives, almost certainly incomplete, showed that in the six years of 1642–47 the Cracow Jewish community alone paid the huge sum of 70,649 zlotys to a number of Christian lenders, both burghers and Jesuits. It also acknowledged additional balances on its debts totaling 101,339 zlotys. It is small wonder that the Jewish communities in general sank deeper and deeper into debt, or that this debt became insupportable by the end of the dual Commonwealth.[95]

RUMBLINGS OF DISCONTENT

The geographic, numerical, and economic expansion of Polish and Lithuanian Jewry before 1648 often blinded the Jewish leaders, as well as the masses, to the instability inherent in the Jewish position in a society which generally favored the small minority of nobles and clergy, excluding the vast majority of burghers and peasants, along with the numerous ethnic minorities. Jews and other ethnic groups owed their relative well-being to the protection extended them by the kings, whose power was constantly declining. Protection by the aristocracy, on the other hand, depended entirely on the exigencies of the moment and the profitability to the magnates of maintaining the Jews. To increase that profitability, Jews, like the lower gentry in the great landlords' service, often had to tighten the screws on the subject population, in order to obtain the greatest revenues possible for both the masters and themselves.

This situation could not last. Time and again the Polish peasantry, even in the western provinces, staged uprisings against their lords, though these rebellions never assumed the proportions of the Peasants' War which raged in Germany in 1525. Some waves of that revolt flowed over into Poland, but they were diverted by the simultaneous penetration of the Protestant Reformation, whose radical wings, at least, promised a betterment of the status of the masses. Instead, the condition of the peasants worsened, developing into the "second servitude." Generally, too, the Protestant movement, with its contribution to religious toleration, lost its influence under the Counter Reformation during Sigismund III's regime. The religious reaction thus initiated did not stop with a counteroffensive against Protestantism, but tried to reduce all dissenters—including the Greek Orthodox population inhabiting vast stretches of Lithuania and southeastern Poland—to total impotence, so as to prepare the ground for ultimate religious conformity with either Roman Catholicism or the Uniate Church.[96]

Unrelenting pressure by the Polish ruling class eventually succeeded in Polonizing and Catholicizing a considerable majority of the upper Lithuanian and Rus nobility, including the powerful Sapieha, Wiśniowiecki, and Sanguszko families. Many lower nobles and burghers, too, were converted to either Catholicism or the Uniate Church. At the same time, Catholic propaganda generated a reaction among the staunch Greek Orthodox majorities in the eastern part of the dual Commonwealth. As a result of these and other conflicts the great Cossack rebellion erupted in 1648, setting most of the eastern provinces aflame; together with the subsequent Muscovite and Swedish invasions, it brought about Poland's cataclysmic decline, and spelled the beginning of the end of the country's independence.

Jews were caught in the middle of this struggle. The situation in southeastern Poland did not resemble that during the Thirty Years' War in the West. In the Holy Roman Empire the conflicting sectarian armies frequently considered the Jews a fairly neutral "third force," which could advantageously be left alone to maintain some socioeconomic continuity in the areas occupied by the belligerent forces. In contrast, many Polish and Lithuanian Jews had been too obviously employed by the Polish-Catholic magnates and their officials to be considered anything but allies and tools of the enemy by the rebellious Ukrainian peasants and their Cossack instigators. From the point of view of proximity and daily contact, the Jewish arendators and their Jewish subordinates were actually the more conspicuous representatives of that oppressive regime, since they frequently supervised the serfs' work and collected the prescribed taxes and tolls in behalf of the masters. Since Jews held leases on liquor production and sales, the peasants, who often incurred heavy debts on account of their drinking, held the Jews doubly responsible for the ills of that system, which neither side could remedy even if it wished to do so. Equally irksome was the Jewish leaseholders' involvement with the farmers' religious practices, through the collection of charges due the Greek Orthodox churches in the landlords' domains. Among the most grievous complaints heard from the peasants was that ecclesiastical fees were exacted for each baptism of a child and each wedding of a daughter. According to some accusers, the Jewish collectors were not always satisfied with the legitimate fees but, under one subterfuge or another, extorted larger payments from even the most impecunious peasants at those events of great family celebration—events which often brooked no delay. Undoubtedly some greedy collectors, whether Jews or nobles, were responsible for such extortions. With respect to Jews, easy generalization led to the condemnation of the entire Jewish people. A later Ukrainian folk song popularized the contention that Jews kept the keys to all Ukrainian Greek Orthodox churches in their possession and opened the sanctuaries only after payment of the fees demanded.[97]

However, many of the socioeconomic arguments pointing to excessive Jewish collaboration with the landlords as one of the primary causes for the great Cossack uprising were *vaticinia ex eventu*. Horrified by the gruesome spectacle of the Cossacks' genocide of Jews, many observers, including some of the Cossack leaders and their sympathetic later historians, were inclined to place the onus of guilt on the Jews themselves. But in the local literature written before 1648 the complaints against Jews are neither very frequent nor harsh; they are, if anything, less vehement and detailed than those heard at that time from Jew-baiters in ethnographic Poland.[98]

Even Bohdan Chmielnicki himself, archenemy of Jews and chief architect of the massacres, did not give vent in his early utterances to his venomous hatred of Jews on either economic or religious grounds. In the letters he addressed in the first half of 1648 to King Wladislaw IV, the Polish generalissimo Mikołaj Potocki, and other dignitaries, as well as in the instructions he gave to the Cossack delegates sent to Warsaw, he recited a whole array of grievances relating to sufferings he himself or his Cossack confreres had sustained at the hands of Polish officials, not Jews. The more comprehensive demands the Cossack envoys were to submit to the king included the moderately worded passage: "On behalf of our clergy of the ancient Greek religion we instantly request that its rights not be infringed upon. The holy Orthodox churches which were forcibly taken over under the terms of the Union [of Brest], such as those of Lublin, Krasnystaw, Sokal, and elsewhere, shall be restored to their old liberties." Only in his long list of personal complaints (which included a reference to an attempt on his life which had forced him to escape to the Zaporozhe), Chmielnicki added, almost parenthetically, the remark that his people "suffer even from Jews intolerable injuries and insults of a kind no Christians sustain in Turkish lands, although we are the servants of His Majesty our King." The heading of the letter he allegedly addressed to Oliver Cromwell some time after the massacres, referred to his persecution of Jews last in the enumeration of his achievements: "Theodatus [Latin for Bohdan] Chmielnicki, by God's grace hetman of the Greek Church, emperor of all Zaporogian Cossacks, terror and extirpator of Poland's nobility, destroyer of their fortresses, exterminator of Roman priests, persecutor of ethnic adherents of Antichrist and Jews." Since the authenticity of this letter is subject to doubt, one ought not derive from it any far-reaching conclusions. In any case, his deeds spoke louder than his words. But it is quite possible that his wholesale destruction of Jewish life, like many other facets of his campaigns and diplomatic maneuvers, were not premeditated before he was drawn into the whirlpool of his grand political action. A fuller analysis of these and other aspects of the Cossack uprising of 1648 must be relegated to a later volume.[99]

A major complicating factor in the relations between the Ukrainian peasantry and the Polish regime was the growth of the Cossack settlement in the Zaporozhe. Its presence was increasingly felt in the destiny of the entire area, in fact of the dual Commonwealth as a whole. The name Cossack was apparently derived from the Turkish term *quzaq*, translatable as "free warrior" or "freebooter." Many of the Cossacks indeed fit both descriptions. From the outset the Zaporogian settlers were refugees from other parts of Poland-Lithuania and neighboring lands. The majority of them had been oppressed peasants, who chose escape into this free area. Others were refugees from religious persecution, who sought a domicile where they could profess the Greek Orthodox faith without interference. Still others were fugitives from justice who had committed serious crimes, including homicide. Quite a few looked for a life of adventure, cherishing the excitement in the unstable and perilous, but highly satisfying life of pioneers and fighters. In fact, many burghers, nobles, and Jews found the romantic descriptions of the Cossacks' warlike expeditions irresistible. In their "heroic" period of the early seventeenth century, the Cossacks reached Trebizond on the northern shore of Asia Minor (never occupied by enemy forces since the Turkish conquest), and the very gates of Constantinople—setting fire to cities, killing a multitude of local residents, and returning with enormous booty. Life in the Zaporozhe has often been compared to that of the American Wild West, with its lights and shadows. In the nineteenth century, especially, in the period of European romanticism, the Cossacks and their *czajki* (small, makeshift, often defective, but battle-proved and extremely swift, ships) became the subject of numerous exalting ballads written by the great Russian and Polish poets of the period. In their glorification of Cossack exploits even the Poles were prone to forget the deep wounds inflicted upon their fatherland by these piratical free lances. The increasingly severe laws enacted by the Polish Diet between 1590 and 1638 somewhat to restrict the Cossacks' movements, which greatly complicated Poland's international relations, were in many cases "too little and too late." In other instances they went too far and provoked several Cossack uprisings, culminating in the catastrophe of 1648.[100]

Such a combination of religious, economic, and social grievances also led to anti-Jewish pogroms, which had all the earmarks of genocide, on a scale theretofore unprecedented in eastern Europe. This explanation of the sudden tragic turn of events in 1648, and particularly of the Zaporogian Cossacks' massacres of Jews, was offered by contemporaries soon after the events, and has been readily accepted by most modern historians. Understandably, some writers have followed their particular national and religious biases and traditions. Poles like Aleksander Jabłonowski have emphasized above all the great historic achievements of the Polish pioneers in the southeastern provinces, while blaming all shortcomings on the Jewish middlemen, who allegedly estranged the Rus masses from their Polish lords. Ukrainian historians, on the other hand, have stressed the religious and national steadfastness of the Ukrainian peasants, and have glorified the Cossacks as fighters for national liberation and freedom of religion. In a petition submitted as early as 1620–21 to the Diet, the Kiev Metropolitan Ion Boretsky and other Orthodox churchmen wrote:

As for Cossacks, we know that these brave men are our kinsmen, brothers, and Christians of the Orthodox faith. . . . They are the tribe of the glorious Rus lineage which sprang from Japhet and fought valiantly against the Greek Empire alike on the Black Sea and on land. . . . It is certain that, with the exception of God himself, nobody else in the world does so much good for the enslaved Christians as the Greeks who buy the freedom of the slaves, or the King of Spain with his mighty fleet, and the Zaporozhian Cossacks with their courage and victories. What other people gain by words and treatises, the Cossacks win by actual deeds.

In contrast, many Poles in the seventeenth and eighteenth centuries viewed the Cossacks, to quote a Polish priest and encyclo-

pedist, Benedykt Chmielowski, "not as a distinct national group
in Poland, but rather as a gathering of a dishonest company of
rascals, fugitives, good-for-nothings, scamps, Greek Orthodox sectarians, drunkards, and Polish peasants enamored of anarchy and
loot." Russian historians of this tsarist period were in a greater
quandary. They could not present the Cossacks as national freedom fighters, because they generally considered Ukrainians to be
"Little Russians," and not a nationality apart. But they could emphasize the religious and economic wrongs committed on the Cossacks by both the Polish nobles and the Jews. On their part, Soviet
historians have preferred to gloss over the religious issues, and
have laid greatest stress on the class struggle.[101]

Foreigners like the contemporary French engineer Guillaume
Le Vasseur le Sieur de Beauplan, or the Italian Geronimo (Hier-
onymus) Pinocci, King John Casimir's secretary, writing in 1651
and 1664, respectively, took a somewhat more balanced view. Yet
they still referred to the Jewish agents of the magnates in derogatory terms. Beauplan, who had spent seventeen years in the
Ukrainian area and was a keen and usually accurate observer,
voiced few independent judgments concerning Jews. For example,
he describes life in Kiev in considerable detail and refers to its
5,000 or 6,000 inhabitants, but he does not mention that Jews
came into the city despite its privilege de non tolerandis Judaeis,
secured in 1619. Pinocci, on the other hand, sweepingly states:

Jews have lived in the Ukraine from ancient times, just as they have
in other cities of the Polish Crown, dwelling there on the basis of the
same laws. But they have been mightier and quite domineering there.
So long as the lords, serving as district governors, resided in the Ukraine,
the Jews behaved in a modest fashion. But some thirty years ago [in
the early 1630s] when these governorships were handed over to playful
youngsters and their administration was entrusted to the lords' servants who began listening to Jews, the latter were given the opportunity to expand. They promised large revenues from places which
had theretofore brought no income at all; they offered arendas of
20,000 zlotys if the lord would order that no one be allowed to produce or sell liquor except themselves. This circumstance imposed
many burdens on the Cossacks, especially since, at the Jews' request,
the district governors were sending officials out to suppress the [un-
licensed] vodka distilleries wherever they could find them. They [the
Jews] also leased mills, ponds, and even entire estates, paying the lords
large rents but in turn collecting much money.

Evidently, this foreign resident of Warsaw had little personal knowledge of what was happening in the southeastern provinces, and merely served as a mouthpiece of the court circles around John Casimir, who tried to exonerate the royal administration from all responsibility for the catastrophic events of the preceding years. Remarkably, even Jewish leaders, with their age-old penchant for self-accusation, censured the injustices wrought by Jewish arendators upon the Ukrainian peasants. In a noteworthy passage discussing the ethical implications of the doctrine of individual rewards and punishments, R. Moses b. Naphtali Hirsch Rivkes emphasized: "I have recorded for the generations to come that I have seen a great many persons who became rich by misleading non-Jews; they were unlucky, lost their fortunes, and left nothing for their heirs. In contrast, many who sanctified the name of the Lord and returned every important erroneous payment to the non-Jew, have grown and prospered; they have left their estates intact for their children." A Jewish dirge of 1648 more succinctly explained: "Wherefore has the catastrophe befallen us? Because the wealthy did not take care of the poor." [102]

Without minimizing the partial validity of these statements, we must not forget the great achievements of the Polish colonization of the southeastern territories, and the Jewish role therein. Of course, there were some of the drawbacks common to all colonizing movements. But unlike the West-European colonizers of the Western Hemisphere, especially the Spaniards, who directly or indirectly contributed to the steady decline of the native populations (we recall with particular horror the sudden diminution in numbers of Mexico's Indian population in the first decades after Cortés' conquests), the Poles and the Jews not only preserved whatever remnants of the old Rus population they found in the vast southeastern provinces but also opened the new frontier to the mass immigration of Rus, as well as Polish and Jewish, settlers and even attracted a great many foreigners, including refugees from Tatar and Muscovite oppression. For one example, a city like Stary Konstantinov, which in 1603 had a population of no more than 4 hearths or families, embraced 130 hearths a quarter of a century later. We also recall the above-mentioned figures pertaining to the tremendous population growth throughout the Ukrainian area. In the eight decades between 1569 and 1648, it

gained more than 400 percent in the two older provinces of Volhynia and Podolia and far more in the provinces of Bratslav and
Kiev, previously almost deserted. According to Beauplan's doubtless exaggerated figures, the Zaporozhe embraced in the 1640s a
population of 120,000. All these territories permanently retained
their strong Rus majorities.[103]

The influx of a mass of sturdy immigrants into that more or
less deserted area was in many ways similar to the settlement of
the American West. The major difference was that, while the
American frontiersmen were free and independent individuals
whose westward movement encountered only weak and scattered
native Indian tribes, often eliminated in armed combat, the
Polish nobles and their subordinates, including the Jews, welcomed the presence of the limited manpower they found on the
spot, and encouraged the settlement of new arrivals who came
into the area of their own volition. The adverse feature of that
type of pioneering was that the Polish landlords, to whom large
tracts of land were donated by the government, converted most of
the working population into rural serfs along the patterns of much
of the Polish and Muscovite peasantry of the time. On the whole,
these masters tried to attract farmers from the older provinces of
Poland and Lithuania, often defying the Polish laws which prohibited peasant-serfs to leave their lords' properties. Some of the
powerful Lithuanian landlords, such as the Sapiehas or the Radziwiłłs, made military expeditions to recapture their fugitive serfs
from the new masters. But the Polish landlords in the Ukraine
fiercely resisted these "encroachments" and kept as many newcomers as possible on their estates. New settlers who were unwilling to accept the harsh conditions of serfdom could of course run
away again; very frequently to the Zaporozhe, where they could
enjoy the free, though perilous, life of the Cossacks. In general,
the new settlers brought with them more advanced methods of
cultivating the soil, and revived the early medieval traditions of
the Kievan state, with its far-flung commercial relations. They
also more successfully defended both the rural and the urban
population against the interminable raids by Tatars, and thus obtained a measure of security for the peaceful pursuit of agriculture, the crafts, and commerce throughout the land. The draw-

backs that existed in the socioeconomic system there were largely characteristic of most early phases of modern capitalism and were the price which had to be paid for progress. As elsewhere, Jews were highly welcome so long as they were instruments of that advance, but were resented more than anyone else if they played a role on its seamy side.[104]

Relations between the Jews and the Cossacks were quite ambivalent. On the whole, the Zaporozhe was a military frontier, established mainly for the defense of the underpopulated provinces which had long been under attack by Tatar raiders. At the same time, the Cossack settlements served as a sort of safety valve for Poland, inasmuch as the most activist, discontented elements from all over the dual Commonwealth, unable or unwilling to withstand the repression at home, could escape to the more libertarian Zaporozhe. Among the ethnically heterogeneous Cossack settlers were some Jews, many of whom sooner or later found their way to the baptismal font. After all, they had for so long been cut off from the main body of Jewry, and their Jewish education had been so sadly neglected, that they probably saw no point in maintaining their allegiance to Judaism or their observance of Jewish ritual, which was extremely burdensome in that strange environment. However, enough professing Jews remained within the Cossack group for them to form in 1612 a small Jewish detachment of 11 soldiers, within the Cossack force accompanying the Polish military expedition against Moscow. It was particularly the Karaites, most of whose ancestors had come to Lithuania and Poland from the Crimea, as well as the native tribe of Rabbanite Jews called Krymchaki, who were prone to join the Cossacks. The Krymchaki, speaking a Turkic dialect, may well have been a part of the considerable influx of Crimean refugees into the Zaporozhe. In fact, in 1637 we hear of a Cossack colonel, Iljasz Karaimowicz, who was supposedly of Rabbanite or Karaite origin. After the surrender, in a document signed by the future hetman Bohdan Chmielnicki, of the rebellious Cossack forces under Paweł Pawluk Michnowicz (later executed together with his lieutenant Tomilenko), Karaimowicz temporarily took over the leadership of the entire Zaporozhe.[105]

Such a motley of peoples was not likely to develop strong anti-

Jewish feelings. It included other religious minorities, especially Muslims and Catholics, as well as Russian sectarians. Hence the Greek Orthodox majority, itself under the oppressive regime of the Polish aristocracy, did not develop those special traits of religious intolerance which characterized the Polish Counter Reformation. True, Jews suffered, along with Poles and others, from the Cossack uprisings beginning in 1590 under General Krzysztof Kosiński. When aroused by the attempts of the Polish magnates to infringe upon their liberties, the Cossacks attacked provincial cities as far as Volhynia and Belorussia. Certainly, in November 1593, when Semen Nalevaiko besieged Slutsk and allegedly forced the city to pay him a ransom of 10,000 gold pieces, the Jews, who had long actively participated in the city's defense, must have suffered both physically and financially. Yet in most of these uprisings the Cossacks revealed no specifically anti-Jewish animus. Only in 1637—that is, a mere eleven years before the "Deluge"—did widespread Jew-baiting become manifest. Nevertheless, during the great crisis the Cossacks turned out to be the most ruthless killers of Jewish men, women, and children in almost all the Ukrainian communities they occupied. Evidently, the aforementioned socioeconomic grievances against Jewish arendators and tax farmers made themselves less strongly felt in the Zaporozgian area. On many occasions the Cossack leadership may merely have responded to the expectations of the Ukrainian peasantry, whose aid they had enlisted in their campaigns against the Polish authorities. However, we must not forget that in their expeditions into Tatar and Moldavian or Turkish territories the Cossacks evinced no more regard for human life. After attacking Black Sea towns as far as Trebizond—once the capital of an independent Greek empire (1204–1461), but since September 1461 an Ottoman possession—and the suburbs of Constantinople, they burned and sacked the cities, took as much loot as they could carry away, and, as a rule, massacred most of the population. Their small boats, *czajki*, had no room for numerous captives. Unlike the Tatars, the Cossacks had no use for prisoners, since they were not engaged in supplying slaves to the Near-Eastern markets, and would only have had to feed and care for such human cargo until they reached home. In attacks on Turkish or Tatar territories, they could justify their actions on the ground that they were killing infidels in the name of religion, but this excuse did not apply to the suburbs of Constantinople, inhabited largely by Greeks and other Christians. It certainly had no bearing on Varna or Jassy (Iași), both of which were razed and most of whose inhabitants were killed by the Cossacks, though they were Bulgarian and Moldavian coreligionists. Because of the religious disparity, the Cossacks had even less reason to spare Jews, unless they expected almost immediate ransom.[106]

International complications converted the 1648 uprising into a severe disturbance. By a curious turnabout, the Tatars, theretofore hereditary enemies of the Cossacks, now became their allies. In the Tatar case socioeconomic grievances and religious animosities played a minor role; their soldiers were simply bent upon pillage and the taking of captives whom they could sell as slaves in the Ottoman Empire. They had probably also heard that Jewish captives were a particularly precious commodity because Turkish Jewry, if need be with the aid of coreligionists in other lands, always paid a high ransom for these "slaves." Otherwise Tatar-Jewish relations in the past had often been quite friendly. In the sixteenth century we even find that Jewish envoys of the Crimean khans conducted diplomatic negotiations with the kings of Poland and other neighboring lands. Nor were the members of the Tatar minority living in Lithuania, most of them émigrés from the Tatar states, deeply hostile to Jews, with whom they shared the golden age under King Stephen Báthory. During the Counter Reformation, to be sure, many Muslims were persecuted; some of them left the Vilna-Troki region and settled in more hospitable Volhynia. Of course, those who became farmers on land belonging to the Polish aristocracy, which covered more than half of the Volhynian area, may have been adversely affected by the oppressive practices developed by the magnate-Jewish alliance. But there is no evidence that Poland's Tatar subjects collaborated directly with the invaders from the Crimea, who were often restrained from assaults on Poland by their Ottoman overlords.[107]

These relations were but a part of international power politics. In the period of the Kosiński and Nalevaiko uprisings, there was even the curious experiment of Emperor Rudolph II, in 1594, to enlist Cossack support against the Ottoman Empire. Persuaded by a Polish nobleman, Stanisław Chłopicki, in cooperation with a Jew, Moses, the Habsburg court in Prague negotiated with the Cossacks for a diversionary invasion of Hungary so as to relieve the pressure of the Turkish armies fighting there against the Austrian and imperial troops. These early negotiations resulted in a mission to the Zaporozhe of an Austrian diplomat, Erich Lassota von Steblau, who had previously served Archduke Maximilian, the defeated candidate for the Polish throne. Lassota carried with him imperial letters authorizing him to enlist the services of some Cossack detachments; they were to bear their own flags and to be amply provided for with funds brought along by the envoy. Although this undertaking had no tangible results, it gave the Cossacks increased self-confidence, and lent them a measure of international recognition. It but slightly affected relations between Poland and Turkey, which were at peace through most of the sixteenth century. But when Polish-Turkish relations deteriorated, ultimately leading to open warfare, the Tatars utilized the new opportunity for self-enrichment. Nevertheless, this hostile constellation would not have had catastrophic results for Poland, were it not for the intervening recovery of both Muscovite and Swedish power. Moscow had by that time overcome its "Time of Troubles" and, under the Romanov dynasty, resumed its imperial expansion on a large scale. Sweden, after the conclusion of the Thirty Years' War (in which it had at first played a preeminent role but later suffered considerable reverses), could now concentrate on its long-time enemy, the dual Commonwealth. This concatenation of international conflicts, combined with the inner weaknesses resulting from Polish economic mismanagement and political near-anarchy, gave the Cossack-Tatar alliance an unprecedented opportunity, of which the Jews were to become major victims. Before 1648, however, this threatening situation was not fully realized by contemporaries, Jewish or non-Jewish, who continued to live under the delusion of security. Apparently no influential Jewish homilist, fulminating against the moral decay of contemporary Jewish society, railed against the risky exploitation of the Ukrainian peasantry.[109]

OCCUPATIONAL DIVERSITY

In retrospect, the century and a half under the reign of the three Sigismunds, Stephen, and Wladislaw IV appear as the happiest period Polish-Lithuanian Jewry ever had. At first, it was the dynamism of sixteenth-century Poland which opened the country's gates to large-scale Jewish immigration and established the formerly small and struggling Jewish communities on a firm legal and economic basis. Because of the spread of the Reformation and the rise of numerous new sects, as well as the influx of various new ethnic groups, including Scots, Italians, Armenians, and Tatars, there was an upsurge of activity on all fronts. With the Italian Renaissance spreading its influence into Poland, and the considerable amount of religious toleration which the growing sectarian diversity and the modern humanist approach to life promoted, there was room for the Jewish newcomers to build up a semiindependent social and communal structure under royal protection.

Even during the Counter Reformation, Jews continued to expand and strike ever-firmer roots in the country. True, religious toleration greatly declined. But, while the main attack of the spokesmen for the Catholic Restoration was directed against the Protestant Churches and was gradually extended to Greek Orthodoxy (which was undermined by the formation of the Uniate Church), the Jews were left largely to their own devices in building up their communal organization. To some extent the growing control of the Catholic Church over the minds of its adherents contributed to the steady increase in power of the Jewish leadership over the communities both locally and nationally. In the 1580s the originally sporadic attempts to form provincial councils culminated in the establishment of the central Jewish organization, the Council of (Three or) Four Lands, soon paralleled by the separate Lithuanian Council. If anything, Jewish communal solidarity was strengthened by the Counter Reformation, which generated anti-Jewish forces of considerable magnitude. While most Polish publicists of the preceding generations had been satisfied with occasional anti-Jewish tirades, a fairly large and ramified Jew-baiting literature now spread its venom among all literate classes, and even many persons unable to read learned at second hand about the facts and rumors thus disseminated. Led by Catholic priests like Przecław Mojecki and Sebastyan Miczyński, the chorus of accusations against Jews, including the revived blood and host libels, filled the air and inspired many public debates in both the central and the provincial diets. From the pulpits, too, the clergy, led by that generation's outstanding preacher, Piotr Skarga, fulminated against Jews, not only as religious dissidents but also as enemies of all Christians in the socioeconomic sphere. As of old, the burghers joined the clergy in demanding curtailment of the Jews' rights, if not their total elimination from the country. From time to time, indeed, many a city secured for itself a royal privilege *de non tolerandis Judaeis*.

As a result of these and other internal frictions, there was a growth of obscurantism and a general decline of Polish culture. No longer did the University of Cracow boast of great scholars— there certainly was no second Nicholas Copernicus to adorn Polish science before the end of the Commonwealth. Nor did poets of the rank of Jan Kochanowski reappear on the firmament of Polish letters until the nineteenth century. What was worse, the masses and the lesser intelligentsia held ever less enlightened views in public and private life alike.[109]

Jews could not remain unaffected. By the end of the sixteenth century the most glorious chapters of Polish Jewish learning had already been written. No longer were there halakhic giants like the rabbis Solomon Luria, Moses Isserles, and Mordecai Yaphe, who revived the glory of rabbinic scholarship for all of Ashkenazic, indeed of world Jewry. Yet the continued growth of rabbinic studies on the broad plateau of mass education, combined with the work of a larger number of fine scholars, compensated, by the quantitative spread of Jewish learning, for the lack of some of its earlier profundities. We shall see in another context how widespread Jewish education had become among all classes of the urban Jewish population and how variegated and rich now became the literature on the Talmud, Kabbalah, moral philosophy, and, on the popular plane, of Yiddish Bible translation and belles-lettres. All these subjects were pursued with passionate intensity by a multitude of professional scholars and lay students.

Even more far-reaching in many ways was the high degree of Jewish biological and socioeconomic vitality. Demographically, the Jewish population continued to increase rapidly, though at a somewhat slackened pace. If our population estimates are at all correct—and no one can be very confident of any figures suggested for the sixteenth and seventeenth centuries, particularly in eastern Europe—the dual Commonwealth's Jewish population, which had grown by some 400 percent between 1500 and 1576, was still able to gain at least 200 percent in the following seventy-two years. This was a substantial increase, much greater, indeed, than that of the Gentile majority of the population. Equally significant was the growing dispersal of Jews into almost all nooks and corners of the Commonwealth. While a number of cities may have closed their gates to Jewish settlers, many others opened them for the first time to a significant influx of these still rather strange, but increasingly useful, arrivals. Literally hundreds of new Jewish communities sprang up all over the land. More, for the first time Jews penetrated deeply into rural districts, and by 1648 a substantial proportion of the Jewish population lived on the soil and, at least partially, from the soil. Not surprisingly, the center of gravity of the Jewish people was constantly moving eastward; the Jews, more numerous and in possession of greater resources, were now able to perform significant pioneering functions, particularly in the underpopulated southeastern provinces.

The economic restratification of the Jewish people, running counter to the developments of the preceding centuries, was not completely stemmed even by the great tragedy of the Cossack uprising. While never completely recovering from the shock of that catastrophe, Polish and Lithuanian Jewry continued in its established ways of the pre-"Deluge" period. Of course, it suffered from the general deterioration of Polish life and the growing political and economic anarchy, which the occasional reform projects advanced by more farsighted statesmen and publicists were unable to prevent. Nonetheless, the Jews continued to increase in number and economic diversification, and progressively deepened their peculiar brand of East-European Jewish culture. Polish-Lithuanian Jewry, and its descendants in the postpartition successor states, became the main reservoir of Jewish manpower and intellectual dynamism for many lands—sending out émigrés first into neighboring territories such as Livonia, Moldavia and Slovakia, and soon to Central and Western Europe and its New World dependencies as well.

All these developments were to emerge after 1648. Unquestionably, no one was able to foresee the horror of the catastrophe before it came. Like the ruling circles in Poland, Jewish leadership lulled itself into a false sense of security. Yet, at the moment of great crisis, the people's inherent vitality, resourcefulness, and vigor reasserted themselves, and before long it resumed the earlier rhythm of life with sufficient élan to face all subsequent adversities with a measure of equanimity.

NOTES

ABBREVIATIONS

AHSI	Archivum historicum Societatis Iesu
APH	Acta Poloniae historica
Baer Jub. Vol.	Sefer Yobel le-Yitzhak Baer (Yitzhak Baer Jubilee Volume). Jerusalem, 1960.
BZIH	Biuletyn of the Żydowski Instytut Historyczny, Warsaw
CPH	Czasopismo prawno-historyczne
ES	Evreiskaya Starina
Gelber Jub. Vol.	Sefer ha-yobel mugash li-khebod N. M. Gelber (N. M. G. Jubilee Volume). Tel Aviv, 1963.
HUCA	Hebrew Union College Annual
HZ	Historische Zeitschrift
JC	Salo Wittmayer Baron, The Jewish Community: Its History and Structure to the American Revolution. 3 vols., Philadelphia, 1942. The Morris Loeb Series. Reprinted Westport, Connecticut, 1972.
JJLG	Jahrbuch der Jüdisch-Literarischen Gesellschaft. Frankfurt a. M.
JNOS	Jahrbücher für Nationalökonomie und Statistik
KH	Kwartalnik historyczny
KHKM	Kwartalnik historii kultury materialnej
MGWJ	Monatsschrift für Geschichte und Wissenschaft des Judentums
MZ	Miesięcznik żydowski
ORP	Odrodzenie i Reformacja w Polsce
PAAJR	Proceedings of the American Academy for Jewish Research
PAN	Polska Akademia Nauk
PAU	Polska Akademia Umiejętności
PH	Przewodnik historyczny
Philippson Festschrift	Beiträge zur Geschichte der deutschen Juden. Festschrift . . . Martin Philippson. Leipzig, 1916.

RDSG	Roczniki dziejów społecznych i gospodarczych
REA	Russko-Evreiskii Arkhiv. Compiled by Sergei A. Barshadskii *et al.* St. Petersburg, 1882–1903.
REJ	Revue des études juives
VL	Volumina Legum
VSW	Vierteljahrsschrift für Sozial- und Wirtschaftsgeschichte
YB	Yivo Bleter
ZGJD	Zeitschrift für Geschichte der Juden in Deutschland (new series unless otherwise stated).
ZOF	Zeitschrift für Ostforschung

NOTES

CHAPTER LXVII: POLAND'S GOLDEN AGE

1. A. Brückner, *Dzieje kultury polskiej* (History of Polish Culture), II, 10. The beginning of the sixteenth century clearly marked the turning point in the history of Poland–Lithuania. While some scholars prefer dating that moment to the year 1500, others consider 1520 or 1530 more appropriate. No one questions, however, that the mid-seventeenth century, the period of the Cossack uprising and the Muscovite-Swedish Wars, marked the beginning of the country's sharp decline, both economically and politically—a decline from which, despite ups and downs, Poland was not to recover until the debacle of the Partition Era. See, for example, the discussion at the *Pierwsza Konferencja Metodologiczna Historyków Polskich* (First Methodological Conference of Polish Historians), published in 1952; esp. K. Lepszy, "The Break of the 1530s," I, 314–19; and Władysław Czapliński, "The Pivotal Importance of the Mid-Seventeenth Century in the History of Poland," *ibid.*, pp. 331–33. Scholars have also long realized that during the first half of the seventeenth century the dynamic evolution of the country's economic, political, and cultural life of the preceding century had considerably slowed down. But while historians mainly interested in Poland's internal developments have preferred 1572 as the dividing line, those viewing the continued rise of Polish power in international affairs and economic prosperity have viewed the reign of Stephen Báthory (Batory; 1576–86) as the high point of Polish grandeur.

From the Jewish point of view the year 1503, in which Jews were readmitted to Lithuania, may be chosen as the starting point for the new evolution, this being the period of the great acceleration of Jewish immigration into Poland as well. On the other hand, 1586, the year of Báthory's death, was also of crucial importance to the Jews, since under the reigns of his successors, Sigismund III (1587–1632) and Wladislaw IV (1632–48), the Counter Reformation became a dominant factor in Polish public life. Needless to say, the Cossack massacres of 1648, and the chaos generated by the Muscovite-Swedish Wars, affected Polish Jewry more than Poland as a whole. I therefore believe that, despite the continued numerical growth and geographic expansion of Polish-Lithuanian Jewry during the six decades of 1586–1648, the two regimes of the Vasa monarchs represented a period of relative stagnation in contrast with the dynamism of the preceding eighty years.

2. See Ananaiasz Zajączkowski, "On Khazar Culture and Its Heirs" (Polish), *Myśl karaimska*, n.s. I, 5–34; *supra*, Vols. III, pp. 196 ff., 323 ff. nn. 30–43; X, pp. 31 ff., 313 ff. nn. 36 ff.; M. Balaban, "Der Gang der jüdischen Kulturelemente vom Rhein bis an die Weichsel und den Dnieper (XI.–XVII. Jahrhundert)," *La Pologne au VIIᵉ Congrès international des sciences historiques, Varsovie, 1933*, III, 191–216, esp. pp. 196 ff.; idem, *Dzieje Żydów w Krakowie i na Kazimierzu* (A History of the Jews in Cracow and Kazimierz, 1304–1868), I, 57 ff. Balaban also compiled a list of

localities in Bohemia from which Jews were expelled in the period from 1499 to 1518. See J. Bondy and F. Dworský, *Zur Geschichte der Juden in Böhmen*, I, 187 No. 298; 199 f. No. 313; 205 ff. Nos. 322–23, 326, 330–31 and 333–34; 220 f. No. 345; 226 f. No. 350; 230 f. No. 356; *supra*, Vol. XI, pp. 262 ff., 274 ff. and the notes thereon.

3. S. A. Bershadskii *et al.*, eds., *REA*, III, 104 f. No. 81, 128 ff. No. 104; M. Bersohn, *Dyplomataryusz dotyczący Żydów w dawnej Polsce* (Documents Relating to Jews in Old Poland: Derived from Archival Sources, 1388–1782), pp. 238 f. Nos. 451, 454–55; and *supra*, Vols. IX, pp. 199 f., 334 n. 6; XI, pp. 279, 421 f. n. 103; XIII, pp. 262 f., 446 f. nn. 63–64. Sigismund's intervention with Sternbergk almost gives one the impression that the emigration of some Jews from Bohemia to Poland was pre-arranged by the two governments. If this was done at all, it was probably through a gentlemen's agreement between Sigismund and Vladislav or his son Louis, rather than in a formal treaty, of which there is no record. Such an understanding was not impossible, even with the later Habsburg rulers of Bohemia, in view of the often cordial relations between Maximilian and the Jagiellons, and the fact that the emperor rather reluctantly agreed to the departure of Jews from his realm—we recall his frustrating the wish of the Ratisbon burghers to expel their Jews—and he may well have been willing to see them find refuge in a friendly neighboring country. See *supra*, Vols. XI, pp. 234, 349 f. n. 43; XIII, pp. 243 f. n. 42; the observations by S. Arnold *et al.* in their "The Problem of Rounding Out the National Territory and the Direction of Its Expansion to the Middle of the Sixteenth Century" (Polish), in the collective *Historia Polski* (A History of Poland), ed. by T. Manteuffel *et al.*, published under the auspices of the Historical Institute of the Polish Academy of Science, Warsaw, I, Part 2, pp. 174–212, esp. pp. 199 ff.

4. The assimilation of the German burghers with the Polish majority had been under way since the Middle Ages. Nonetheless, most major Polish cities retained their strongly German character until the influx, in the sixteenth and seventeenth centuries, of many landless Polish nobles seeking new economic opportunities in the growingly prosperous urban centers. Although not quite typical of the rest of the country—it included a much larger ratio of Dutch, English, and other western merchants than other cities—the population of Gdańsk (Danzig) revealed the persistence of the German element. See the careful archival study by H. Penners-Elwart, *Die Danziger Bürgerschaft nach Herkunft und Beruf 1537–1709*.

5. See M. Bersohn, *Dyplomataryusz*, pp. 26 f. No. 11, 226 ff. Nos. 411–13; M. Bałaban, *Dzieje*, I, 220 ff.; J. Tazbir, "Old Polish Opinions about Spaniards" (Polish), *PH*, LVIII, 605–623, with Russian and French summaries; *supra*, Vols. III, pp. 155 f., 305 f. n. 40; X, pp. 40, 319 n. 48; XIII, pp. 89 f., 355 n. 30. The dispatch, on Tammuz 16, 5327 (June 23, 1567), of a Jewish envoy to Poland by one of the Tatar khans, is mentioned incidentally in a reply by Moses b. Joseph of Trani, in his *Resp.*, II, No. 78. A resident of the Black Sea city of Kaffa, the envoy, Meir Ashkenazi, is said to have told of his mission for the khan to one Elijah b. Nehemiah, when they met in Goa, India, where Meir had brought a consignment of pagan slaves from Egypt. This world traveler further explained that he had had earlier contacts with Lithuanian Jews and that one of his brothers had actually been a student at the academy of Brest–Litovsk. See B. Z. Katz, *Le-Qorot ha-Yehudim be-Rusiah, Polin, ve-Lita* (Excerpts Relating to the History of the Jews in Russia, Poland, and

Lithuania in the Sixteenth and Seventeenth Centuries), p. 52. Although entirely derived from hearsay, this story has all the earmarks of authenticity.

Of interest also is the 1554 correspondence between the Slovakian city of Bardejov (Bartfa, Bartfeld) and the Jewish physician Jacobus de Anselmis of Cracow, "doctor of philosophy and medicine who with his wife and family had come from Italy to Poland." The Jewish doctor was invited by the stricken city to come and stem the spreading pestilence. He was granted the necessary travel papers. Similarly, when Stephen Bocskay, the Transylvanian leader of an anti-Habsburg insurrection, suffered from an angina pectoris in 1605, he appealed to Sigismund III to send him the physician Eleazar, "a Jew by descent, education, and religion." Eleazar spent three months with the duke, but his ministration proved of no avail, and Bocskay died in 1606. See M. Atlas, "Two Physicians in Poland in the Sixteenth and Seventeenth Centuries" (Hebrew), *Gelber Jub. Vol.*, pp. 9–12; and *supra*, Vol. X, pp. 182, 373 f. n. 37.

Of course, some of these Iberian and Italian Jews may have reached Poland-Lithuania in a circuitous way via the Ottoman Empire or Germany. For example, Abraham b. Yeḥiel of Cologne, buried in Lwów in 1522, was a descendant of Portuguese and Provençal Jews; his father, Yeḥiel, served as "high judge" in either the Cologne electorate or in Lwów. See his epitaph, reproduced by J. Caro in his *Geschichte der Juden in Lemberg von den ältesten Zeiten bis zur Theilung Polens im Jahre 1792*, pp. 178 f. See also, more generally, M. Balaban, "Die Portugiesen in Lemberg und Zamość" in his *Skizzen und Studien zur Geschichte der Juden in Polen*, pp. 11–19; idem, *Juedische Aerzte und Apotheker aus Italien und Spanien im XVI. und XVII. Jahrhundert in Krakau* (reprinted from *Heimkehr*, Berlin, 1912); and N. M. Gelber, "On the History of the Sephardim in Poland" (Hebrew), *Oṣar Yehude Sefarad* (Tesoro de los Judíos Sefardíes), VI, 88–98; and *infra*, nn. 7 and 40.

6. S. M. Dubnow, "The Spoken Language and Popular Literature of the Polish and Lithuanian Jews during the Sixteenth and the First Half of the Seventeenth Century" (Russian), *ES*, I, 7–40 (showing the relative paucity of Slavonic loan words in the rabbinic or popular literature, as well as in the communal records of the period); J. Fischer's Heidelberg dissertation, *Das Jiddische und sein Verhältnis zu den deutschen Mundarten*, I, Part 1 (Allgemeiner Teil und Saltzlehre); and the interesting contrast drawn by U. Weinreich between "Yiddish and Colonial German in Eastern Europe: the Differential Impact of Slavic," *American Contributions to the Fourth International Congress of Slavicists, Moscow, September 1958*, pp. 369–421, reaching the conclusion that "in German, the Slavic elements formed a lexical veneer, whereas in Yiddish they became a 'constructive force' that transformed the language and gave it a 'new quality'" (p. 407). See also I. Trunk, "Hebrew-Yiddish Entries in Polish Documents of the Seventeenth and Eighteenth Centuries" (Hebrew), *Gelber Jub. Vol.*, pp. 79–84; R. Mahler, "Yiddish and Hebrew Documents Concerning the Jewish Censuses in Poland in the Second Half of the Eighteenth Century" (Yiddish), *YB*, III, 208–222, 477–79; and idem, "Jewish Names of Localities in Old Poland (On the Basis of Archival Sources)" (Hebrew), *Reshumot*, V, 146–61 (includes a list of cities in which the census was conducted). On the ancient Persian loan words in the Talmud, see *supra*, Vol. II, pp. 206, 405 n. 38. A fuller analysis of the Yiddish, Ladino, and other Jewish languages and literatures will be offered in a later chapter. Socially and politically the development of a separate Yiddish lan-

guage was facilitated by the presence in Poland-Lithuania of many spoken languages. Even the Polish intelligentsia, both clerical and lay, cultivated a sort of bilingualism, first in Polish and Latin, and then in Polish and French. See C. Backvis, *Quelques remarques sur le bilinguisme latino-polonais dans la Pologne du seizième siècle;* and, from another angle, M. R. Mayenowa, *Walka o język w życiu i literaturze staropolskiej* (The Struggle for Language in the Life and Letters of Old Poland), 2d ed.

7. A. Zajączkowski, *Karaims in Poland: History, Language, Folklore, Science;* A. Szyszman, *Osadnictwo karaimskie na ziemiach Wielkiego Księstwa Litewskiego* (The Karaite Settlement in the Lands of the Grand Duchy of Lithuania); J. Talko-Hryncie-wicz, *Karaimi i Karaici litewscy* (Lithuanian Karaim and Karaites). See also such monographic studies as Y. Hessen, "The Conflict between the Karaites of the City of Troki and the [Rabbanite] Jews" (Russian), *ES,* III, 569–79; I. A. Kleinman, "Civil Dissension among the Karaites in the City of Troki. From Unpublished Documents of the Seventeenth Century" (Russian), *ibid.,* XIII, 38–49; I. Kruglevitch, "Family Names and Proper Names of the Karaites" (Russian), *ibid.,* IX, 317–19; A. M. Pulyanov, "Toward an Anthropology of the Karaim in Lithuania and the Crimea" (Russian), *Voprosy Antropologii,* XIII, 116–33; and *infra,* Chaps. LXIX, n. 23; and LXX, n. 105. On the Krymchaki, see I. Kaia, "The Krymchaki (Native Crimean Jews): an Ethnographic Sketch. On the Basis of Numerous Observations" (Russian), *ES,* IX, 398–407; S. Weissenberg, "Family Names of the Karaites and the Krymchaki" (Russian), *ibid.,* VI, 384–99. See also *infra,* Chap. LXX, nn. 104–105. Although both groups were numerically weak, their importance in the history of East-European Jewry must not be minimized. They will reappear in many contexts in forthcoming chapters.

8. The text of the canon adopted by the Piotrków Synod of 1542 is reproduced by B. Ulanowski *et al.* in their *Studia i materyały do historyi ustawodawstwa synodalnego w Polsce* (Studies and Sources for the History of the Synodal Legislation in Poland during the Sixteenth Century), IX, 67 f.; *infra,* Chap. LXVIII, n. 15; L. Gumplowicz, *Prawodawstwo polskie względem Żydów* (The Polish Legislation Relating to Jews), pp. 50 ff.; M. Schorr, *Żydzi w Przemyślu do końca XVIII wieku* (Jews in Przemyśl to the End of the Eighteenth Century), pp. 138 ff. No. 68. An example of how the Counter Reformation clergy treated requests for permits to build new synagogues is offered by Archbishop Jan Andrzej Prochnicki, who on August 10, 1624, made the following reservation: "the infidel Jews should not construct a sumptuous and expensive synagogue, but only a modest one and of small dimensions." Cited by M. Bałaban in his *Żydzi lwowscy na przełomie XVI i XVII wieku* (The Jews of Lwów at the Turn of the Sixteenth to the Seventeenth Century), pp. 52 ff., 218 ff. Prochnicki's predecessor, Archbishop Dymitri Solikowski, actually boasted in a letter to the pope on July 27, 1583, that he refused to give his approval for a synagogue built in Lwów several years before, despite the Jews' "insistent petitions and gifts." See A. Theiner, *Annales ecclesiastici, quos . . . ab anno MDLXXII ad nostra usque tempora continuat,* III, 431 f. No. 42; Bałaban, *Żydzi lwowscy,* p. 58. Several other ecclesiastical interventions (in Cracow, Łuck, Przemyśl, and other localities) are mentioned by Bałaban in his *Zabytki historyczne Żydów w Polsce* (Jewish Historical Remains in Poland), pp. 54 ff. See also D. B. Teimanas, *L'Autonomie des communautés juives en Pologne aux XVIe et XVIIe siècles,* pp. 145 ff.

Even synagogues already functioning for some time were not completely safe. If the clergy holding services in a neighboring church felt disturbed by the sight or sound of Jewish worshipers, they often found means to force the Jews to give up congregational meetings in that building. Such occurrences, earlier noted for other countries in Gregory I's decision regarding the Jews' vox psallentium, and frequently thereafter, led to an interesting inquiry from the Jewish elders of Łuków to R. Meir b. Gedaliah of Lublin. Having been forced to abandon their house of worship, the elders wanted to know whether they could dispose of the land to private individuals, who might build a bathhouse or other structure there which would profane the sacred character of the previous building. They also expressed the apprehension that the local clergy might appropriate the land for Christian religious uses. R. Meir decided that the Jewish elders had the right to sell the land and use the money for a new house of worship in another location. See his Resp., Warsaw, 1881 ed., fols. 24d (46b) f. No. 69. In general, however, not only the Polish government but also the Polish clergy applied the old canonical provisions concerning Jewish houses of worship with greater moderation than did their counterparts in other countries. See supra, Vols. II, pp. 181, 192, 282, 398; III, 9 f., 134 ff., 188, 230; VII, 283 ff. n. 88; IX, 10 ff., etc.; and infra, Chap. LXVIII, n. 80.

9. J. Łukaszewicz, Obraz historyczno-statystyczny miasta Poznania w dawniejszych czasach (The Historical-Statistical Image of the City of Poznań in Times Past), I, 75, or German trans. by J. Königk and Tiessler, Historisch-statistisches Bild der Stadt Posen, I, 56 ff., 58 n. 1; J. Caro, Geschichte der Juden in Lemberg, p. 20; I. (Y.) Schipper, Studya nad stosunkami gospadarczymi Żydów w Polsce podczas sredniowiecza (Studies in the Economic Conditions of the Jews in Poland during the Middle Ages), pp. 152 ff.; and the revised Yiddish trans. entitled Virtshaftsgeshikhte fun di Yidn in Poiln be'esn mitelalter, pp. 153 ff., 172 f. An example of a Jewish community established in a city possessing a royal privilege de non tolerandis Judaeis was offered by J. Morgensztern in her "From the History of the Jews in Kraśnik to the Middle of the Seventeenth Century" (Polish), BZIH, no. 34, pp. 71–96, with an English summary, pp. 172 f. See also J. Goldberg's more general review, "De non tolerandis Judaeis. On the Introduction of the Anti-Jewish Laws into Polish Towns and the Struggle against Them" in Sefer Rafael Mahler (Studies in Jewish History Presented to R. M.), pp. 39–52.

The major bone of contention among the Polish cities was the so-called staple rights. Each city tried to force all merchants bringing wares within its confines, even if only in transit, to place them on display in the local warehouse or market, and to give local merchants the opportunity of bidding first for this merchandise. During the sixteenth century there was a protracted conflict between the cities of Cracow and Lwów concerning these rights. The government often ineffectually tried to settle such conflicts amicably. See S. Górzyński, Polityka składowa Polski do roku 1565 (Poland's Policy regarding Staple Rights to 1565). Needless to say, Jewish traders, too, had to overcome the difficulty of transporting their merchandise to the proper destination in the face of the various local restrictions.

10. M. Bałaban, Dzieje Żydów w Krakowie, I, 55 ff.; B. Baranowski and S. Herbst, "The Deterioration in the Conditions of the Development of Cities, Industrial Production, and Mining" (Polish) in T. Manteuffel, ed., Historia Polski, I, Part 2, pp. 450–80, esp. p. 472; J. Łukaszewicz, Obraz, I, 75 ff.; J. Meisl, Geschichte der

Juden in Polen und Russland, I, 150 f.; *infra,* n. 13; and Chap. LXVIII, n. 72. Although not an all-Jewish city—for quite a while Jews constituted only a minority of the population—Kazimierz accommodated an increasing number of Jews who, ultimately, so dominated it that, aided by their extensive self-government, they seemed to live in a city of their own. This development, an augury for many smaller Jewish settlements all over Poland and Lithuania, lent a specific character to Jewish life in the area. These internal facets of the East-European communities will be more fully discussed in later chapters.

11. See M. Balaban, "Die Krakauer Judengemeinde-Ordnung von 1595 und ihre Nachträge," *JJLG,* X, 296–360; XI, 88–114, esp. XI, 90; S. M. Dubnow, *Pinqas ha-Medinah* (The Minutes of the Lithuanian Council of Provinces: a Collection of Enactments and Decisions from 1623 to 1761), ed. with intro. and notes, esp. p. 10 Nos. 46–47; and other sources cited in my *JC,* II, 6 ff., 234; III, 98 f. nn. 2–3. Although these decisions of the Lithuanian Council are dated in 1623, they undoubtedly reflect cumulative resentments of several decades. Harking back to old medieval traditions, this isolationist attitude must have existed earlier in the sixteenth century to some extent; it found expression particularly in Cracow's communal conflicts between the new Jewish immigrants from the Bohemian realm and the older settlers. The internal Jewish aspects of this lack of hospitality will be more fully discussed in connection with the Jewish self-government in a later chapter.

12. S. M. Dubnow, *Pinqas ha-Medinah,* p. 10, and numerous other entries listed in the Index, p. 345 *s.v.* Ḥezqat Yishub; my *JC,* in the entries listed in the Index, III, 354 *s.v.* Ban of Settlement, 517 *s.v.* Residence Rights, etc.; and F. H. Wettstein, *Debarim 'attiqim* (Ancient Subjects: Materials for the History of the Jews in Poland, Especially in Cracow), pp. 7 No. 7, 10 f. No. 14; J. Caro, *Geschichte der Juden in Lemberg,* pp. 19 f. See also *infra,* Chaps. LXVIII, n. 8; LXX, nn. 70–71. Withdrawal of residence rights, tantamount to deportation from a city or region, was an extremely severe penalty. Ancient Roman law did not exaggerate when it styled a sentence of this kind as *capitis diminutio.* We shall see in another context that this sanction was rarely applied by the Jewish judiciary. The mere threat of it must have sufficed to keep out undesirables who might have succeeded in securing residence rights by some subterfuge.

13. S. A. Bershadskii, ed., *REA,* III, 58 ff. No. 36, 158 ff. No. 127; M. Balaban, *Die Judenstadt von Lublin,* with drawings by Karl Richard Henker; B. Mandelsberg-Schildkraut, *Meḥqarim le-toledot Yehude Lublin* (On the History of Lublin Jewry), with introductions on the authoress and her work by Nachman Blumenthal *et al.;* various other articles in Yiddish and Polish by her, listed *ibid.,* pp. 53 ff.; N. Shemen, *Lublin, shtot fun torah* (L., City of Torah, Rabbinic Lore, and Ḥasidism); J. Mazurkiewicz, *Jurydiki lubelskie* (Juridical Enclaves in Lublin); Moses b. Israel Isserles, *Resp.,* Warsaw, 1883 ed., fol. 97a No. 120. While Solomon Luria formally served only as head of the Lublin academy, his great eminence as a talmudic scholar secured him wide recognition. The admiration extended to him by his community during his lifetime found a telling expression in the inscription placed upon his tombstone by his contemporaries. See the eloquent text reproduced

by S. B. Nisenbaum in his ed. of *Evreiskie nadgrobnyie pamiatniki goroda Liublina* (Jewish Tombstones of the City of Lublin in the Sixteenth through Nineteenth Centuries: Photographs and Texts with Notes), pp. 10 f. No. 7.

Lublin's importance as an emporium often led it into conflicts with other cities, such as Lwów, with respect to staple rights. Nonetheless, its three major annual fairs attracted many merchants, including Jews, from Lwów and other unfriendly cities. These fairs took place at stated periods and lasted over two weeks each (see *infra*, Chap. LXX, n. 26). The ample data preserved in Lublin's municipal records for the years 1528–31 show that visitors from Cracow, mentioned in 229 entries, were the most numerous. Although Kazimierz was listed separately, with 41 entries, it is likely that some of the Cracow transactions also involved Jews, directly or indirectly. Brest-Litovsk, with 33 entries, doubtless had a contingent of Jewish merchants who at that time played a considerable role in the business life of that Lithuanian center, particularly in its trade with the Polish Crown and foreign lands. See the fine archival study by H. Samsonowicz, "Lublin's Commerce about the Year 1600" (Polish), *PH*, LIX, 612–28, with Russian and French summaries. An interesting record of such visits from Lithuania was published by R. Mahler in "A Contribution to the History of the Economic Relations of Lithuanian Jews with Poland in the Sixteenth Century (Hebrew-Yiddish Customhouse Registers from Bielsk Podlaski and Łuków, Written in 1580)" (Yiddish), *Yivo Historishe Shriftn* (Studies in History), II, 180–205, with an English summary.

14. T. Wierzbowski, *Przywileje królewskiego miasta stołecznego Starej Warszawy* (Privileges of the Old Royal Capital Warsaw, 1376–1772), pp. 75 f. No. 33, 86 f. No. 76, 101 f. No. 85, 120 ff. No. 100; E. Ringelblum, *Żydzi w Warszawie* (Jews in Warsaw), Vol. I: From the Origins to the Last Expulsion in 1527; I. Trunk, *Shtudies in yidisher geshikhte in Poiln* (Studies of Jewish History in Poland), pp. 25 ff.; J. Shatzky, *Geshikhte fun Yidn in Varshe* (The History of the Jews in Warsaw), I, 19 ff., 45 ff.; I. Schipper, "The 'Warsaw Committee': a Contribution to the History of Jewish Autonomy in Old Poland" (Polish), *Sefer ha-Yobel (Ksiega jubileuszowa;* Jub. Vol. in Honor of) *Mordecai Ze'ev (Markus) Braude*, pp. 145–57; *supra*, Vol. X, pp. 36 f., 317 f. n. 45. See also T. Chudoba, "Problems of Warsaw's Vistula Trade in the Sixteenth Century" (Polish), *PH*, L, 297–321. On the other hand, the four documents reproduced by S. M. Szacherska (in collaboration with E. Koczorowska) in her "Unknown Warsaw Privileges of the Fifteenth and Early Sixteenth Centuries" (Polish), *PH*, LI, 368–84, have no reference to Jews.

As pointed out by Shatzky, Stephen Báthory's decree of March 14, 1580, allowing Jews to serve as tax farmers for the nobility, specifically mentioned only Warsaw as the place where they must not establish residence. From this decree one may actually deduce that some Jews lived in other parts of Mazovia, even in one or another Warsaw suburb, and that a few may have secretly settled in the city itself. On the other hand, when the royal privilege of 1576 for the Jews of Łuck allowed them to trade in any locality of the Polish Crown, and thus seemingly opened the gates of Warsaw to Jewish traders, the king himself soon "clarified" the situation by his renewal in 1580 of the decree excluding Jews from Warsaw. Nevertheless, it appears that Jews of Brest-Litovsk played a considerable role in the commerce of Warsaw, which was an important way station in Brest's export trade via Gdańsk. See A. Wawrzyńczyk, "Warsaw's Role in the Trade with the Grand Duchy of

Lithuania and with Russia in the Sixteenth Century" (Polish), *KH*, LXIII, No. 2, pp. 3–26. On the general situation after Warsaw became Poland's capital in 1595 see, more fully, *infra*, Chap. LXVIII, nn. 18 and 38.

15. I. Klauzner, *Toledot ha-qehillah ha-'ibrit be-Vilna* (A History of the Jewish Community in Vilna), Vol. I: Environment and Communal Organization, pp. 3 ff.; Israel Cohen, *Vilna;* both based largely on the researches by S. A. Bershadskii. See also, more generally, M. Łowmiańska, *Wilno przed najazdem moskiewskim 1655 roku* (Vilna before the Muscovite Invasion of 1655), esp. pp. 55, 91. On the history of the Jews of Lithuania, one must still rely heavily on the documentation and analysis produced by Bershadskii in his *Litovskie Evrei* (Lithuanian Jews: a History of their Legal and Social Status in Lithuania from Vitovt to the Union of Lublin, 1388–1569); and his ed. of *REA*. A general review of the relations between Jews and the Polish bourgeoisie is offered, though with sparse documentation, by A. N. Frenk in his *Ha-'Ironim ve-ha-Yehudim be-Polin* (The Burghers and the Jews in Poland: an Historical Study). See also *infra*, Chap. LXVIII, nn. 30 ff.

16. I. Schiper, "The Development of the Jewish Population in the Territories of the Old Commonwealth" (Polish). *Żydzi w Polsce Odrodzonej* (Jews in Resurrected Poland), ed. by him *et al.*, I, 21–36; R. Mahler, *Toledot ha-Yehudim be-Polin*, pp. 92 f.; *supra*, Vol. X, pp. 36, 317 n. 44.

17. See S. M. Dubnow, *Pinqas ha-Medinah*, pp. 4 f. Arts. 6–8; M. Bałaban, *Żydzi lwowscy*, pp. 252 ff.; Z. Pazdro, *Organizacya i praktyka żydowskich sądów podwo-jewodzińskich* (Organization and Practice of the Jewish Palatinate Courts in the Years 1740–1772), pp. 176 ff. No. 11, 188 ff. No. 15; Moses b. Isaac Menz (Minz *or* Mainz), *Resp.*, Lwów, 1751 ed., fols. 49 f. No. 63; and other sources pertaining to Poland, as well as other countries, in my *JC*, I, 23 ff.; III, 105 ff. nn. 12 ff. While these sources for the most part reflect seventeenth-century conditions, some prece-dents were established by the earlier, though less well organized, sixteenth-century communities. See also B. Cohen's Hebrew study of "The Palatinate Jurisdiction con-cerning Jews in Old Poland," *Sefer Rafael Mahler* (Jewish Studies Presented to R. M.), pp. 47–66. The discriminatory treatment of the minor settlements was but a facet of the inner struggles within the Polish Jewish communities, which will be more fully analyzed in a later chapter. See also I. Sosis, "Social Conflicts in the Jewish Communities of the Sixteenth and Seventeenth Centuries according to the Rab-binic Responsa" (Hebrew texts with Yiddish translations), *Zeitshrift* (Minsk), I, 225–38.

18. S. Arnold and A. Wyczański, "The Socioeconomic Development of the Village" (Polish) in T. Manteuffel's ed. of *Historia Polski*, I, Part 2, pp. 78–107; *Akta grodzkie i ziemskie* (District and Estate Records from the Days of the Polish Com-monwealth), ed. by O. Pietruski *et al.*, II, 76 ff. Nos. 46 and 49; I. Schipper, *Studya nad stosunkami gospodarczymi Żydów w Polsce*, pp. 157 ff.; in the Yiddish trans., *Virtshaftsgeshikhte*, pp. 163 ff. In general, we are better informed about the few prominent Jews—like Wołczko, Isaac Hispanus, or Michael Ezofowicz, who received grants from the Polish kings or Lithuanian grand dukes—than about the real tillers of the soil. Moreover, like their wealthier coreligionists, many ordinary farmers engaged on the side in a variety of occupations, such as collecting governmental

tolls or peasant dues for the landlords, keeping taverns, and lending money. The economic aspects of the Jewish role in Polish and Lithuanian agriculture will be discussed *infra*, Chap. LXX. The complexities and differences of opinion in studies of rural Poland in the sixteenth century are well illustrated by the controversy between Tadeusz Ładogórski and Władysław Pałucki concerning the methods of preparing an historical atlas for Poland. See *KH*, LXXIV, 89-97, 99-110, 559-61, 911-13.

19. See H. Jolowicz, *Geschichte der Juden in Königsberg in Preussen*, pp. 6 ff.; H.-J. Krüger, *Die Judenschaft von Königsberg in Preussen 1700–1812;* [A. Stein], "Zur Geschichte der Juden in Danzig," *MGWJ*, VI, 205-214, 241-50, 321-31, 401-411, esp. pp. 210 ff.; J. Kirszbaum, *Geshikhte fun di Yidn in Danzig* (A History of the Jews in Gdańsk). See also H. Penners-Ellwart, *Die Danziger Bürgerschaft nach Herkunft und Beruf, 1537–1709*, which shows, on the basis of careful archival research, the presence of many West-Europeans among Gdańsk's inhabitants, but furnishes no data on the Jewish settlers in the city, probably because of their small number and often unauthorized sojourn. Typical of the business relations between the Polish Jewish merchants and the Gdańsk burghers was a contract concluded by one Jacob Beer of Cracow with Jerzy Klefild, a citizen of Gdańsk, in which the Jew promised to ship to Gdańsk 200 *łaszty* (some 12,000 bushels) of flour. See M. Bersohn, *Dyplomataryusz*, p. 67 No. 84.

20. See A. Kłodzinski, "On the Archive of the Crown Treasury in the Cracow Castle" (Polish), *Archiwum Komisji Historycznej* of PAN, 2d ser. II, 124–578, esp. p. 542. Recent investigations of some sixteenth-century censuses include A. Tomczak *et al.*, eds., *Lustracje województw wielkopolskich i kujawskich* (Censuses of the Great Polish and Kuyavian Provinces in 1564-65); S. Hoszowski, ed., *Lustracje województw malborskiego i chełmskiego* (Censuses of the Provinces of Marienburg and Chełmno in 1565); idem, *Lustracje województwa pomorskiego* (Censuses of the Pomeranian Province in 1565); J. Topolski, ed., *Lustracje województwa podlaskiego* (Censuses of the Province of Podlasie in 1570 and 1576). Other extant lists may also prove very useful in reconstructing the Jewish and general populations. See, for instance, J. Morgensztern, "Information on the Jewish Population of Kraśnik on the Basis of an Inventory of 1631" (Polish), *BZIH*, no. 32, pp. 27-42, 85–86. Less detailed materials are available for Lithuania; they were analyzed more than half a century ago by B. Rubshtein in "About the Number of Jews in the Grand Duchy of Lithuania in the Mid-Sixteenth Century" (Russian), *ES*, VIII, 20-28. See also the general data supplied by J. Jakubowski in his *Studya nad stosunkami narodowościowemi na Litwie przed Unią Lubelską* (Studies about the National Relations of Lithuania before the Union of Lublin) arguing that Obrazm Ciołek, King Alexander I's envoy to Rome, rightly asserted in 1501: ". . . the Lithuanians speak their own language. Since, however, the Ruthenians occupy almost half of the duchy, they [the Lithuanians] more commonly use the latter's language which is more graceful and easier" (A. Theiner, ed., *Vetera Monumenta Poloniae et Lithuaniae . . . historiam illustrantia*, II, 278); K. Pakštas, "Earliest Statistics of Nationalities and Religions in the Territories of Old Lithuania, 1861," *Commentationes balticae*, IV-V, 169-211 (this first serious attempt, made under tsarist domination, sheds little light on prepartition Lithuania).

We must warn, however, that the frequently available rolls of citizens (or of those newly admitted to citizenship) which are extant for many Polish cities, are of limited use in estimating the Jewish population in those cities. Because of their extensive autonomy and largely separate form of existence, few Jews applied for admission to the status of burghers. For one example, the records available for Lwów concerning the new citizens in the years 1405–1426 and 1461–1514 mention only three Jews, as contrasted with 679 Germans, 394 Poles, and lesser numbers of other nationalities. Possibly some Jews were included in the large category of 359 burghers unidentified as to nationality. See H. Weczerka, "Herkunft und Volks-zugehörigkeit der Lemberger Neubürger im 15. Jahrhundert," *ZOF*, IV, 506–530, esp. p. 515. See also K. Górski's pertinent remarks (despite a bit of special pleading) in his "On the Problem of Statistics of Nationalities in the Late Middle Ages" (Polish), *Przegląd Zachodni*, X, Part 2, pp. 445–54; *supra*, n. 4; and, more generally, my fuller analysis of the demographic evolution of Polish-Lithuanian Jewry, *infra*, Chap. LXIX.

21. See the generally justified observations by Z. P. Mombert, "Ueber die geringe Zuverlässigkeit älterer Volkszählungen," *JNOS*, CXXXIX, 744–51; and *supra*, Vol. XIV, pp. 4 ff., 243 ff. The widespread assumption, borne out by the records, that the growth of Polish-Lithuanian Jewry was very slow during the Middle Ages proper and but slightly accelerated in the early decades of the sixteenth century, clearly controverts the even more widely held opinion that the main source of the increase was the forced emigration from the Holy Roman Empire during the era of the great expulsions in the fifteenth and early sixteenth centuries. Certainly, the largest growth came later in the sixteenth century and at the beginning of the seventeenth, at a time when the forced migrations had largely ceased, giving way to voluntary movement, out of economic rather than political motivations. It appears, indeed, that after 1550 it was natural growth which primarily accounted for the rapid proliferation of Polish-Lithuanian Jewry. These demographic and occupational trends will be more fully analyzed *infra*, Chaps. LXIX–LXX.

22. *Ad quaerelam mercatorum Cracoviensium responsum Judaeorum de mercatura*, first cited by T. Czacki in his *Rozprawa o Żydach i Karaitach* (Discourse on Jews and Karaites), ed. by K. J. Turowski, pp. 46 f.; J. Perles, "Geschichte der Juden in Posen," *MGWJ*, XIII, 325 f. The authenticity of the Cracow apologetic pamphlet, still known to both Czacki and Joachim Lelewel, has often been questioned. Despite the apparent loss of all copies since their time, the pamphlet was defended by I. Schipper in his *Studya*, pp. 311 ff., and in the Yiddish edition, pp. 232 ff. In any case, the figures quoted by the Jewish apologist of 1539 were a clear exaggeration, even if we interpret, with Balaban, the statement referring to the Polish traders as relating to non-German Polish burghers alone. See M. Bałaban, *Dzieje Żydów w Krakowie*, I, 107 f. On the situation in Poznań, see also S. Waszak, "Population and Residential Housing in Poznań during the Sixteenth and Seventeenth Centuries" (Polish), *Przegląd Zachodni*, IX, Part 3, pp. 64–136, esp. pp. 78, 81, 83 ff., 100 f., 105, 113, 118 f. This careful investigator was evidently unable to consult any Jewish archival sources (see pp. 72 ff.), and hence he readily underestimated the number of Jews in 1590 as about 1,550, and the buildings inhabited by them as about 115. See also *infra*, Chap. LXIX, n. 33.

23. See B. (D. B.) Weinryb, "Private Letters in Yiddish of 1588" (Yiddish), *Yivo*

Historishe Shriften (Studies in History), II, 43–67; David b. Solomon Gans' chronicle *Ṣemaḥ David*, Prague, 1592 ed., I, fols. 636 f.; Frankfort, 1692 ed., I, fol. 45b (to be read together with the story of the great drought and earthquake in eastern and central Europe, *ibid.*, II, fols. 116 and 67b, respectively); the graphic description of the Poznań riot of 1580 in the "Chronicle from the Days of King Stephen Báthory of 1575–1582," ed. with an intro. by H. Barycz in *Archiwum Komisji Historycznej* of the Polish Academy, XV, No. 81, 349–440, esp. pp. 416 f.; *supra*, Vols. X, pp. 35 f., 316 nn. 42–43; XI, 163 f., 367 n. 53. See also, more generally, A. Walawender, *Kronika klęsk elementarnych w Polsce i w krajach sąsiednich w latach 1450–1605* (A Chronicle of Elemental Catastrophes in Poland and Its Neighboring Countries in the Years 1450–1605); Vol. I, dealing with "Meteorological Phenomena and Plagues," found a continuation in S. Namaczyńska's *Kronika klęsk elementarnych w Polsce . . . 1648–1696.*

24. M. Bałaban, *Dzieje Żydów w Krakowie*, I, 47 ff.; J. Łukaszewicz, *Obraz historyczno-statystyczny miasta Poznania*, II, 271 f.; J. Perles, "Geschichte der Juden in Posen," *MGWJ*, XIII, 323 f., 361 f., 451; XIV, 165. See A. Walawander's *Kronika klęsk*, Vol. II, which treats of "The Warlike Destructions and Fires." The curious comment by Mikołaj Rej of Nagłowice about Jewish obesity is found in his *Zwierciadło* (A Mirror in Which Every Estate May View Its Affairs), ed., by J. Czubek and J. Łoś, with an Intro. by I. Chrzanowski, II, 94.

25. Some Polish scholars prefer to call the new governmental form the "Nobles' Republic" or the "Nobles' Democracy," which merely adds to the perennial confusion in the employment of these much-abused terms. The dating, too, is controversial. While Stanisław Kutrzeba, the last generation's outstanding historian of the Polish constitutional system, considered the country a fairly typical medieval state run by an hereditary king with the aid of "estates" until 1572, many recent scholars have preferred to use the Nieszawa Statute of 1454 as the starting point for this epochal transformation. See S. Kutrzeba's *Historia ustroju Polski w zarysie* (A History of the Polish Constitutional System in Outline), as against A. Wyczański's *Polska Rzeczą Pospolitą Szlachecką* (Poland as a Nobles' Commonwealth, 1454–1764) and W. Czapliński's comments thereon in his review in *KH*, LXXIII, 369–80. The 1454 date is accepted also by Z. Kaczmarczyk in his Polish paper on "The Type and Form of the Polish State in the Period of the Nobles' Democracy" and the discussants thereof in *Odrodzenie w Polsce* (The Renaissance in Poland: Materials Submitted at the Scholarly Session of the Polish Academy of Science on October 25–30, 1953), Vol. I: Historia, pp. 479–528, 529–39. Chronologically, this rise and decline of the Polish gentry coincided with the upsurge and subsequent stagnation of Jewish life in the country. Needless to say, however, this constitutional evolution was but one of many factors, internal and external, which affected the destinies of Polish-Lithuanian Jewry in the fifteenth to the eighteenth century.

26. M. Bersohn, *Dyplomataryusz*, pp. 23 ff. Nos. 5–9, 226 ff. Nos. 411 ff. The range of Casimir IV's "protoabsolutism" and its implications are clarified in K. Górski's "The Internal Administration of Casimir the Jagiellon in the Polish Crown" (Polish), *KH*, LXVI, 726–59. However, there emerged other forces which brought about a considerable weakening of the monarchical power. See W. Knoppek's "Changes in

the Composition of the Political Forces in Poland in the Second Half of the
Fifteenth Century and Their Connection with the Formation of the Two-Chamber
Diet" (Polish), *CPH*, VII, Part 2, pp. 55–95, with a French summary.

27. F. Papée, ed., *Akta Aleksandra króla polskiego* (Documents from the Reign of
Alexander, King of Poland, 1501–1506), esp. pp. 111 ff. No. 91, 175 ff. No. 121,
299 ff. No. 176, 474 No. 283, 527 f. No. 314. The remarkable clause in Jan Łaski's
(Joannes de Lasco's) compilation *Commune incliti Polonie regni privilegium consti-
tutionum et indultum*, Cracow, 1506 (a code of law considered, along with the
eighteenth-century *VL*, superior to any other contemporary European compilation,
by O. Balzer in the Intro. to his ed. of *Corpus iuris Polonici*, III, pp. xi f.), need
not be taken at face value. Perhaps, like his many other policies, Alexander's treatment of Jews was in part intended to captivate the benevolence of the powerful
Church. Yet, Łaski's pious declaration by no means impinged upon the validity of
the major Jewish Charter, the story of which in the period 1500–1650 will be told
in the next chapter. See also *supra*, Vol. X, pp. 41 ff., 319 ff. nn. 50 ff.

28. Contemporary opinions about the respective merits and demerits of the
reigns of John Albert, Alexander, and Sigismund I greatly varied. Modern historians, too, have sharply disagreed on their evaluation. Perhaps the most judicious
overall survey has been presented by M. Bobrzyński in his *Dzieje Polski w zarysie*
(A History of Poland in Outline). But new data and insights have been made available by special monographs relating to the three kings. See esp. F. Papée, *Jan
Olbracht;* idem, ed., *Akta Aleksandra: S.* Górski, *et al.*, eds., *Epistolae, legationes,
responsa, actiones et res gestae Serenissimi principis Sigismundi, ejus nominis primi
regis Poloniae . . . collectae:* A. Dembińska, *Zygmunt I* (Sigismund I: an Outline of
the Internal Political History in the Years 1540–1548).

29. See P. Bloch, *Die General-Privilegien der polnischen Judenschaft* (an enlarged
and revised reprint from the *Zeitschrift der Historischen Gesellschaft für die Provinz
Posen*, VI), pp. 107, 115; L. Gumplowicz, *Prawodastwo polskie względem Żydów;*
M. Schorr, *Rechtsstellung und innere Verfassung der Juden in Polen*, pp. 6 ff.; and
infra, Chap. LXVIII, n. 70. Authors searching for references to Jewish "serfdom"
in the Polish charters started from the premise that in the Western countries the
term *servi camerae* had a derogatory intent. Certainly, such an interpretation as
given to it by Margrave Albert III Achilles of Brandenburg in 1462, with respect to
the unlimited powers of the Holy Roman Emperor over Jews, would have been
impossible in Poland. But, as we recall, even in the Empire, and still more so in
other countries, the main purpose of this designation, at the outset, was to indicate
the protective and mutually advantageous relationship between the ruler and his
Jewish subjects. See *supra*, Vol. XI, pp. 4 ff., 289 ff.

30. A. Brückner, *Dzieje kultury polskiej*, II, 332; M. Bałaban, *Dzieje Żydów w
Krakowie*, I, 66 n. 1, etc.; W. Pociecha, *Królowa Bona (1494–1557): Czasy i ludzie
Odrodzenia* (Queen Bona, 1494–1557: Times and People of the Renaissance), Vols.
I–IV (Vols. III–IV were posthumously ed. by H. Łowmiański, Ł. Dworzaczek *et al.*;
Vols. V–VI were to appear later), see esp. III, 112 f., 205 ff. Nos. 5–6 (reproducing
the deeds of sale of 1533 and 1536), 285 n. 65; D. Quirini-Popławska, *Działalność
Włochów w Polsce w I połowie XVI wieku* (The Activities of Italians in Poland in

the First Half of the Sixteenth Century at the Royal Court, in Diplomacy and the Ecclesiastical Hierarchy); S. A. Bershadskii, *REA*, I, 334 ff. Nos. 333–34; S. Friedenstein, *'Ir gibborim* (A City of Heroes: a History of the Jews in Grodno); M. Bersohn, *Dyplomataryusz*, p. 41 No. 41; and *infra*, n. 31. In the decree of 1537 Sigismund also emphasized that the Jews of Cracow were under the supervision of the palatine (*wojewoda*) and of no one else.

31. L. Lewin, *Die Landessynode der grosspolnischen Judenschaft*, pp. 22 ff.; M. Bałaban, *Dzieje Żydów w Krakowie*, I, 61 ff.; P. Bloch, "Der Streit um den Moreh des Maimonides in der Gemeinde Posen um die Mitte des 16. Jahrhunderts," *MGWJ*, XLVII, 153–69, 263–79, 346–56, esp. pp. 349 ff. The privilege of 1527 was repeated with some variations for other provincial rabbis in decrees of 1541 and 1551, reproduced in full by M. Bersohn, *Dyplomataryusz*, pp. 47 ff. Nos. 46 and 57. On the Ezofowicz family and Abraham's descendants, who assumed the name Abrahamowicz, see the monographs by J. Wolff, *Żyd ministrem Króla Zygmunta* (A Jew, Minister of King Sigismund), esp. I, 31 ff.; M. Balaban's brief sketch, "Die Brüder Abraham und Michael Esophowicz, Ritter von Leliwa (Finanzminister und Judenmeister)" in his *Skizzen und Studien zur Geschichte der Juden in Polen*, pp. 77–96; W. Pociecha, *Abraham i Michał Ezofowicze, działacze gospodarczy XVI wieku* (Abraham and Michael Ezofowicz, Business Leaders of the Sixteenth Century); idem, *Królowa Bona*, II, 120; III, 55, 100 f., 140 f., 217 n. 31, 244 n. 82; and *infra*, Chap. LXX, n. 36. The important role of Abraham of Bohemia, Michael Ezofowicz, and other leaders in the history of Jewish self-government in Poland and Lithuania will be more fully described in the context of the development of Jewish communal autonomy, in a later chapter.

32. Justus Ludwig Decius (Decyusz, Dietz), *De Sigismundi I. temporibus liber; VL* (Polish Statutes; reprint of a collection of laws published in Warsaw in 1732–92), I, 270 (550); M. Schorr, *Rechtsstellung*, pp. 9 f.; Meir b. Gedaliah of Lublin, *Resp.* No. L. That Dietz wrote as a competitor rather than as an impartial witness was evident from his own large-scale financial operations. Through the numerous loans *auf Wiederkauf* he extended to noble landowners, some of whom were unable to repay them on time, he acquired vast estates by ruthless foreclosures. It stands to reason that one or another Jewish business manager of such a noble debtor may have frustrated Dietz' manipulations. See A. Hirschberg, *O życiu i pismach Josta Ludwika Decjusza (1485–1545)* (On the Life and Works of J. L. Dietz [1485–1545]), pp. 51 f.; and *infra*, Chap. LXVIII, n. 49.

On the general approach of the editors of the *Volumina*, see the introduction to Vol. I, published in Warsaw, 1732; and S. Grodziński's analysis thereof in his "Stanisław Konarski's Views on the Development of Polish Law in the Light of His Introduction to the *Volumina Legum*" (Polish), *CPH*, V, 109–123. The "lord" of Rymanów mentioned in Meir's responsum may have been but a despotic government official in the township, which in the sixteenth century still had a strong German element in its population. See A. Fastnacht, *Osadnictwo ziemi sanockiej w latach 1340–1650* (The Settlements of the Sanok District in the Years 1340–1650), pp. 205 f.

33. The era of Sigismund II Augustus has often been treated in the Polish historical literature. The older contributions are well reviewed by M. Bobrzyński in

his *Dzieje Polski w zarysie,* II, 49 f. Of interest also are such biographical sketches as E. Gołębiowski's *Zygmunt August. Żywot ostatniego z Jagiellonów* (Sigismund Augustus: the Life of the Last of the Jagiellons); S. Orzechowski's *Żywot i śmierć Jana Tarnowskiego* (The Life and Death of Jan Tarnowski, Commander-in-Chief of the Polish Crown), ed. by K. J. Turowski; J. Jasnowski, *Mikołay Czarny Radziwiłł* (M. C. R., 1515–1565: Chancellor and Land Marshal of the Grand Duchy of Lithuania and Palatine of Vilna). Noteworthy sidelights on the personality of the king and on his environment—though not on his attitude toward Jews or even toward Hebrew culture, so popular among contemporary humanists in other lands —are shed by such monographs as K. Hartleb's *Biblioteka Zygmunta Augusta* (Sigismund Augustus' Library: a Study in the History of the Royal Court); and K. Morawski's "From the Social Life of the Period of Sigismund Augustus" (Polish), reproduced in his *Czasy Zygmuntowskie na tle prądów Odrodzenia* (The Times of the Sigismunds against the Background of Renaissance Trends), ed. with an Intro. by J. Tazbir, pp. 78 ff.

34. See P. Bloch, *Die General-Privilegien der polnischen Judenschaft,* pp. 6 ff.; M. Schorr, *Żydzi w Premyślu,* pp. 73 ff. App. i; M. Bałaban, *Dzieje Żydów w Krakowie,* I, 110 ff. For fuller analysis of the legal status of Polish-Lithuanian Jewry in the sixteenth and seventeenth centuries, see *infra,* Chap. LXVIII.

35. See A. Mączak, "Export of Grain and the Problem of Distribution of National Income in Poland in the Years 1550–1650," *APH,* XVIII, 75–98. The ability of the nobles to keep the prices of their agricultural produce very high was facilitated by the general inflation in Europe during the sixteenth century. Moderate before 1550, the inflation rapidly accelerated in the second half of the century. It has been estimated that during the sixteenth century, the price of grain increased by 150 percent in England; 300 percent in France, Saxony, and Muscovy; and 500 percent in Spain. In Poland there were numerous local price variations even in individual grain products, but on the whole the western Polish cities paid more for produce than those in the eastern provinces. In general, food prices went up by some 300 percent, whereas clothing prices increased on the average only 60–100 percent. See S. Arnold and M. Bogucka, "The Economic Prosperity of the Cities" (Polish) in T. Manteuffel *et al.,* eds., *Historia Polski,* I, Part 2, pp. 107–146, esp. pp. 135 ff.

36. See S. Kutrzeba and W. Semkowicz, eds., *Akta Unji Polski z Litwą* (Documents pertaining to the Polish Union with Lithuania, 1385–1791), pp. 207 ff. No. 98, 319 ff. Nos. 139–40; and *infra,* Chap. LXIX, n. 21. The impact of the Union of Lublin on the position of the Jews, especially in Lithuania, has never been fully explored. Only one aspect, that of "The Jurisdiction of the Jews in Lithuania after the Union of Lublin," has been described by Z. Honik in his Yiddish essay in *YB,* XIV, 316–34. More generally, Honik contends that, before 1569, the Lithuanian Jews "enjoyed all the rights of the non-Jewish population" and hence were also subject to the same regulations in the jurisdictional area. According to Honik, such equality contrasted with the status of their Polish coreligionists, who were "serfs of the Polish king" and were therefore under the control of the royal palatine (*wojewoda*). This theory must be modified in the light of the observations offered *supra,* n. 29. Yet, there is no question that the rise of the Lithuanian gentry, and

its growing political and cultural Polonization, had a profound influence on the position of the Jews in the Grand Duchy—a phenomenon which is yet to be analyzed in detail. On the earlier ambivalence of the gentry in the perennial conflict between pro-Muscovite and pro-Polish orientations, see O. P. Backus, *Motives of West-Russian Nobles in Deserting Lithuania for Moscow, 1377–1514*. Also of great importance to the Jewish communities was the incorporation of Volhynia, Podlasie, and parts of the Ukraine into the Polish Crown under the terms of the new treaty. See the original documents of the Union of Lublin and the respective acts of incorporation, reproduced in facsimile by J. Siemieński in his compilation, *Dyplomacja dawnej Polski ilustracja archiwalna* (Diplomatie de l'ancienne Pologne présentée en reproductions des actes des archives exposées dans . . . l'Exposition Générale Polonaise à Poznań en 1929), pp. 19 ff.

Among the numerous problems awaiting further elucidation is whether all Jewish converts in Lithuania were indeed automatically elevated to noble rank. See M. Janecki's negative reply to his own query, *Erhielten die Juden in Polen durch die Taufe den Adelstand?* (Reprint from the *Vierteljahrsschrift für Heraldik, Sphragistik und Genealogie*, XV); and the succinct juridical analysis of the problem by O. Balzer in his Polish review of Janecki's essay in *KH*, II, 433–38, affirming the statutes' legal validity. In the Polish Crown, too, especially in Red Russia, some would-be converts seem to have been raised to the ranks of the nobility. On July 27, 1696, the Wisznia dietine instructed the deputies to the Diet to take measures against Jews who "had recently been admitted, according to law, to the jewel of nobility under the condition of accepting the holy Catholic faith, but have usurped the noble title without fulfilling that condition." See A. Prochaska, ed., *Lauda wiszeńskie* (Resolutions of the Dietines of Wisznia, 1572–1732), III (Akta grodzkie, XXII), 287 ff. No. 101, item 9. In any case, we have few actual records of Jewish converts being raised to the nobility in either Lithuania or the Polish Crown. This paucity of evidence did not deter the anti-Jewish scholar Teodor Jeske Choiński from claiming that such converts injected much Jewish blood into Poland's noble families. See his *Neofici polscy* (Polish Neofites). However, neither Choiński nor M. Balaban was able to adduce definite proof for such immediate change in status of converts during the sixteenth century. See Balaban's *Skizzen und Studien*, pp. 77 ff. Certainly, the record of only 12 Jews baptized over a period of 67 years (1583–1650) in the main church in Lublin, a major center of Jewish life with a rapidly expanding Jewish population, seems to confirm the general impression that the Catholic mission among the Polish Jews was relatively ineffective. At any rate, none of these converts is recorded as having joined the ranks of the nobles, although, true to an old Catholic practice in many lands, some of these baptismal ceremonies were performed by high ecclesiastics, and the new converts were sponsored by godparents recruited from among the dignitaries of state and Church. These new Christians are not even mentioned in the town records as full-fledged burghers. See R. Szewczyk, *Ludność Lublina w latach 1583–1650* (Lublin's Population in the Years 1583–1650), pp. 107 ff.

It is very likely, therefore, that despite the repetition of the questionable provision in the Third Lithuanian Statute of 1588, the new influence obtained by the Lithuanian gentry through the Union of Lublin had made it more conscious of the resulting possible entry of Jews into its ranks. The general ambiguities concerning the operation of the respective Lithuanian statutes have given rise to great differences of opinion among modern scholars. See S. Ehrenkreutz's older, but still useful, review "The State of Investigations Relating to the Lithuanian Statutes" (Polish), *Ateneum wileńskie*, II, 289–341; S. Ptaszycki's "Something about the Third Lithuanian Statute and the Subsequent Legal Norms in Lithuania" (Polish), *Księga pamiątkowa* (Memorial Volume in Honor of) *Oswald Balzer*, II, 297–313, esp. p. 300; and *infra*, Chap. LXVIII, n. 48.

37. S. A. Bershadskii, *REA*, II, 127 ff. Nos. 188 ff.; M. Balaban, "Episodes from the History of Ritual Murder Trials and the Anti-Jewish Literature in Poland in the Sixteenth–Eighteenth Centuries" (Russian), *ES*, VII, 163–81, 318–27; idem, *Dzieje Żydów w Krakowie*, I, 112; David Gans, *Ṣemaḥ David* (Chronicle), Prague, 1592 ed., II, fol, 112a; Frankfort, 1692 ed., II, fol. 75a. On the blood and host accusations and other manifestations of popular and literary Jew-baiting in early modern Poland and Lithuania, see *infra*, Chap. LXVIII.

38. *VL*, II, 859. The death of the last Jagiellon, and the following two *interregna* (interrupted only by Henry of Valois' brief sojourn in Poland), marked a watershed in Polish constitutional history. It is not surprising, therefore, that the four years from 1572 to 1576 are widely commented on by both contemporaries and modern historians. Among the contemporary chroniclers, see especially Ś. Orzelski's *Interregni Poloniae libri*, ed. by E. Kuntze, which, among other matters, cited the resolution of the Warsaw Confederation on May 3, 1573 (pp. 94 f.), and the king's attendance at the baptism of the impoverished Jewish woman (p. 162). This ambivalence generated by the largely liberal mood in the country and the election of an intolerant king, underscored the difference between conditions in Poland and France. See also J. Librach's pertinent observations on "La Paix religieuse en Pologne au temps de la Saint-Barthélemy," *Bulletin* of the Société de l'histoire du protestantisme français, CXIV, 507–520; and S. Gruszecki's succinct analysis "The Social Image of the Warsaw Confederation of 1573" (Polish), *ORP*, XIII, 145–57.

The general conditions which led up to the wholly elective nature of the royal office, and the specific negotiations preliminary to the election of King Henry, are treated by Z. Wojciechowski in "Les Conditions intérieures et extérieures de l'établissement du trône électif en Pologne. Les éléments mediévaux dans l'organisation de l'état polonais du XVIe au XVIIIe siècle," *CPH*, I, 5–24; P. Skwarczyński in "Les Tractations autour de l'élection d'Henri de Valois comme roi de Pologne (1573)," *Revue internationale d'histoire politique et constitutionelle*, V, 215–23; W. Sobociński in his *Pakta Konwenta. Studium z historii prawa polskiego* (Pacta Conventa: a Study in the History of Polish Law); and J. Czubek, ed., *Pisma polityczne z czasów pierwszego bezkrólewia* (Political Writings of the Days of the First Interregnum).

39. Solomon Ashkenazi's favorable attitude toward the candidacy of Henry of Valois may appear less surprising when we recall that in 1572–73 he played a prominent role at the Porte in Constantinople, and was particularly instrumental in helping to secure a peace treaty between the Ottoman Empire and Venice. See *supra*, Vol. XIV, pp. 78 f., 335 n. 6. From the standpoint of Ottoman policy, the election of a Habsburg or the Russian tsar to the Polish throne would have enhanced the power of Muscovy or Austria, both considered the hereditary enemies of the sultan. In fact, this possibility may have induced some Polish patriots to

promote the election of Ivan IV, in the hope of creating an imposing East-European empire in which the economically and culturally more advanced and westernized Poles would become the senior partners.

On Wahl, see P. Bloch, "Die Sage von Saul Wahl, dem Eintagskönig von Polen," *Zeitschrift der Historischen Gesellschaft für die Provinz Posen*, IV, 233–58; Z. Edelman, *Gedulat Sha'ul* (Saul's Greatness: a History of Saul Wahl and His Descendants); M. Bałaban, *Dzieje Żydów w Krakowie*, I, 112; idem, "Dichtung und Wahrheit über den Eintagskönig von Polen Saul Wahl," *Skizzen und Studien*, pp. 24–44; and A. S. Feinstein, *'Ir tehillah* (The Renowned City: a History of the Jewish Community of Brest from Its Foundation to the Present Day), pp. 16 ff. "The Jews during the First [Polish] *Interregnum*, 1572–1574" are briefly treated by I. A. Kleinman in his Russian study in *ES*, XI, 110–28. See also, more generally, the two comprehensive biographies of H. de Noailles, *Henri de Valois et la Pologne en 1572*, 2d ed.; P. Champion, *Henri III roi de Pologne*, Vol. I: 1573–74. On the involvement of Ashkenazi and other Jewish leaders in the international intrigues and negotiations during the two Polish *interregna*, see also *infra*, nn. 47–48.

40. I. Schwarz, "Ein Wiener (Donau) Brückenprojekt aus dem XVI. Jahrhundert," *Jahrbuch für Landeskunde von Niederösterreich*, n.s. XII, 79–100, esp. pp. 80, 86 ff. App. i (on F. H. Wettstein's suggestion, Schwarz identifies the builder with the Mendel Sax who appears in a 1583 document as one of the Jewish elders obligating the community not to build houses outside Kazimierz); N. M. Gelber, "An Unknown Letter by Mendel Isack of Cracow to Emperor Rudolph II" (Yiddish), *YB*, XI, 401–405 (reproducing that epistle, dated January 16, 1589); M. Bałaban, *Dzieje Żydów w Krakowie*, I, 143 ff.; M. Bersohn, *Dyplomataryusz*, pp. 105 ff. No. 165; A. Pawiński, ed., *Skarbowość w Polsce i jej dzieje za Stefana Batorego* (The Polish Fiscal System and Its History under Stephen Báthory), in *Źródła dziejowe*, VIII, 129; and *supra*, Vol. XIV, pp. 181 f., 373 n. 36. That the king paid his Jewish lender interest at the relatively low rate of 6-1/2 or 7 percent is less surprising than the fact that he had to pledge 2 boxes of silverware weighing 750 marks for the relatively modest loan of 5,000 zlotys; also that Báthory had still not repaid the loan more than two years later. But lending money to one's king was always risky, in view of the power disparity between the royal borrower and his creditor-subject. Stephen must have been in financial straits after his marriage to Anna, the Jagiellon princess, to whom he gave a wedding present said to be valued at 60,000 ducats. After his coronation, on May 1, 1576, he also had to keep the promise, made in his behalf by his ambassador before the election, to pay 200,000 florins to the Polish Treasury for the country's defense.

On the king's last illness and the extended debate on its nature, see esp. A. Knot, "La Cour, la vie privée et la mort d'Étienne Batory" in the collective volume, *Étienne Batory roi de Pologne, prince de Transylvanie* [ed. by E. Lukinich and J. Dąbrowski for the Hungarian and Polish Academies of Science], pp. 404–424, esp. pp. 416 ff. and the literature listed there. Remarkably, Calahora is not mentioned here among the numerous court physicians, perhaps because he had already left royal service and had embarked upon an independent business career. If so, he, and the Jews of Poland, may have been spared becoming the scapegoats for the king's mysterious malady by the ever-present rumor mongers. See also H. Z. Schering, *Czy królobójstwo?* (Was It Regicide? A Critical Study concerning the Death of King Stephen the Great Báthory).

41. See M. Bersohn, *Dyplomataryusz*, pp. 98 ff. Nos. 146, 148–50, 152–53, 157, 159, 161–64, 166, 177, 179, 180–82, 184; 263 ff. Nos. 540 ff., esp. No. 543 (this privilege refers to Scots as well as Jews in Prussia); Báthory's decree of February 10, 1577, reproduced, from an archival transcript of its confirmation by Wladislaw IV on May 2, 1633, by J. Perles in his "Geschichte der Juden in Posen," *MGWJ*, XIII, 330 ff. n. 10; and J. Łukaszewicz, *Obraz historyczno-statystyczny miasta Poznania*, II, 89, 297 f. The other version mentioned in the text is supplied by H. Barycz's edition of *Kronika z czesów króla Stefana Batorego* (A Chronicle from the Days of King Stephen Báthory, 1575–1582), ed. with an Intro. (reprinted from the *Archiwum* of the Historical Commission of *PAN*, XV, pp. 349–440). See esp. the graphic description of the anti-Jewish riot in Poznań, pp. 70 f. (416 f.). In his Introduction, pp. 10 ff. Barycz plausibly argues for Leonard Gorecki's authorship of that chronicle. Gorecki, known as the writer of other historical works, lived and wrote in Great Poland and was very close to the events he described. That he was rather free in his criticism of the otherwise much-admired king and managed to maintain, even in that stormy period of religious controversy, a measure of sang-froid, makes his narrative doubly reliable.

42. See M. Bersohn, *Dyplomataryusz*, pp. 98 ff., esp. Nos. 147, 160, 169, 185, 192; E. Rykaczewski, ed., *Relacye nuncyuszów apostolskich i innych osób o Polsce od roku 1548 do 1690* (Reports of Apostolic Nuncios and Other Persons about Poland in the Years 1548 to 1690), I, 59 f.; A. Bolognetti, *Epistolae et acta 1581–1585*, ed. by E. Kuntze and C. Nanke (Monumenta Poloniae Vaticana, V–VI), II, 16 ff. No. 11. Quite relevant also is the contemporary biography of the leading statesman Jan Zamoyski by R. Heidenstein, *De vita Joannis Zamoyscii*, reproduced together with other biographical data in Count Tytus Adam de Kościelec Działyński's *Collectanea vitam resque gestas Joannis Zamoyscii . . . illustrantia* (see also Bersohn, p. 104 No. 163); and other sources of Jewish interest summarized by J. Morgensztern in her Polish study of "Regesta from the Crown Registry Relating to the History of Jews in Poland (1574–1586)," *BZIH*, nos. 47–48, pp. 113–29. See also such monographs as H. Jablonowski's Wrocław dissertation, *Die Aussenpolitik Stephan Báthorys (1576–1586)*; J. Siemieński's "King Stephen's Policies Relating to the Diet" (Polish), *PH*, XXXIV, 31–53; and the aforementioned collection of essays *Étienne Batory, roi de Pologne, prince de Transylvanie* [ed. by E. Lukinich and J. Dąbrowski], which includes an extensive bibliography of both primary and secondary sources.

43. See Giovanni Andrea Caligari, *Epistolae et acta, 1578–1581*, ed. by L. Boratyński (Monumenta Poloniae Vaticana, IV), esp. pp. 320 ff. No. 175, 363 ff. No. 196, 553 ff. No. 309; and *infra*, Chap. LXVIII, n. 25. On Stephen's general ambivalence toward sectarian controversies, see also K. Völker's "Stefan Bathorys Kirchenpolitik in Polen, 1574–1586," *Zeitschrift für Kirchengeschichte*, LVI (1937), 59–86.

44. M. Bersohn, *Dyplomataryusz*, pp. 104 ff. Nos. 160, 162, 185, 190; S. Kutrzeba, ed., *Akta sejmowe województwa krakowskiego* (Records of the Dietine of Cracow). I, 113 ff. No. 36, 119 Art. 12. Of interest also is the royal privilege granted in 1578 at the Diet session in Warsaw to one Calman b. Mordecai of Lublin to establish a new Hebrew printing press in that city and to issue "all kinds of books in the Hebrew language." The king mentioned in this connection that theretofore the

Jews had had to import Hebrew books from abroad, at great cost and inconvenience to themselves, and to the detriment of the Polish economy. To protect Calman's investments, the king forbade the importation of those books from abroad, or their domestic reproduction for sale, under the sanction of a huge fine of 1,000 Hungarian florins, half of which was to go to the Treasury. See Bersohn, pp. 109 f. No. 178; and J. C. Albertrandi's earlier Polish rendition in his *Panowanie Henryka Walezego i Stefana Batorego* (The Reigns of Henry of Valois and Stephen Báthory), ed. by K. J. Turowski, pp. 457 f. Doc. No. 2. The general history of Hebrew printing in Poland and elsewhere will be treated in a later chapter.

45. See W. Pociecha, ed., *Acta Tomiciana* (in W. Górski *et al.*, collection), XVII, 238 No. 167, 424 No. 323, 485 f. No. 381; *supra*, nn. 3 and 5; Vol. X, pp. 40 f., 319 n. 49. On the impact of the "Turkish menace" on other Central European countries, see *supra*, Vol. XIII, pp. 444 f. n. 59; and *infra*, n. 55.

46. See, for instance, O. Balzer, *Sądownictwo ormiańskie w średniowiecznym Lwowie* (The Armenian Administration of Justice in Medieval Lwów); idem, *Statut ormiański w zatwierdzeniu Zygmunta I z r. 1519* (The Armenian Statute in Sigismund I's Confirmation of 1519) in his *Studya nad historyą prawa polskiego* (Studies in the History of Polish Law), IV, Parts 1 and 2. Polish pilgrimages to the Holy Land started much later than those from other western countries, because Poland did not convert to Christianity until the tenth century. The earliest record of a Polish pilgrimage dates from 1154. Subsequently, it appears, there was a long hiatus in these journeys until the fifteenth and sixteenth centuries, when they became quite popular. See the literature listed by J. Czubek in the introduction to his *Mikołaja Krzysztofa Radziwiłła peregrynacja do Ziemi Świętej (1582–1584)* (The Journey of M. K. R. to the Holy Land, 1582–1584). It may be noted that, before his departure Radziwiłł (surnamed Sierotka) consulted King Stephen, who, as a Transylvanian prince, had long lived under Turkish overlordship and was naturally much better informed about conditions in the Ottoman Empire than most of his Polish-Lithuanian subjects. Other journeys by Poles, including that of the later eminent generalissimo (*hetman*) Jan Tarnowski, are described by K. Hartleb in his *Polskie dzienniki podróży w XVI wieku* (Polish Travelogues of the Sixteenth Century as a Source of Contemporary History); his ed. of Tarnowski's "The Oldest Travelogue to the Holy Land and Syria" (Polish) in *KH*, XLIV, Part 1, pp. 26–44; Marcin Bielski's *Kronika* (Chronicle), Cracow, 1597 ed., p. 580, cited *supra*, Vol. XIII, pp. 223, 425 f. n. 20. Nonetheless, knowledge of conditions in Turkey was still very meager, especially in Poland's western provinces. See B. Baranowski, *Znajomość Wschodu w dawnej Polsce do XVIII wieku* (The Knowledge of the Middle East in Old Poland to the Eighteenth Century). All this did not prevent amicable relations between the two powers. See the older, but still very useful, study of J. Bartoszewicz, *Poglądy na stosunki Polski z Turcją i Tatarami* (Aspects of Poland's Relations with Turkey and the Tatars, the History of Tatars Settled in Poland, the Privileges Granted Them, and Mention of Some Eminent Polish Tatars).

47. See A. Dembińska, *Zygmunt I. Zarys dziejów wewnętrzno-politycznych w latach 1540–1548* (Sigismund I: an Outline of the Internal Political History in the Years 1540–1548), esp. pp. 207 f., 233 ff.

48. See P. Skwarczyński, "Les Tractations autour de l'élection d'Henri de Valois comme roi de Pologne (1573)," *Revue internationale d'histoire politique et constitutionelle*, V, 215-23; idem, "The *Decretum electionis* of Henry of Valois," *Slavonic and Eastern European Review*, XXXVII, 113-30; P. Champion, comp., *Lettres de Henri III roi de France*, ed. with an Intro. and Notes by M. François, I, 292 f. No. 837; V. Meysztowicz, ed., *Documenta Polonica ex archivo generali Hispaniae in Simancas*, Vol. I (Elementa ad fontium editiones, VIII), pp. 157 f. No. 116; Ashkenazi's and the new French ambassador Jacques de Germiny's statements in E. Charrière, ed., *Négociations de la France dans le Levant*, III, 883 n. 1, 932 n.; C. Roth, "Dr. Solomon Ashkenazi and the Election to the Throne of Poland, 1574-5," *Oxford Slavonic Papers*, IX, 8-20.

In evaluating the conflicting claims of Ashkenazi and the French ambassador, we must bear in mind that the French had, ever since 1566, covetously prepared for the possible succession of a French prince to the throne occupied by the childless Sigismund II Augustus. See M. Serwański, "French Aspirations for the Polish Throne during the Reign of Sigismund Augustus" (Polish), *KH*, LXXXI, 251-66, with a French summary. On the Ottoman policies during the first *interregnum*, see also J. Pajewski, *Turcja wobec elekcji Walezego* (Turkey's Attitude toward De Valois' Election); and the literature listed *supra*, n. 39; and Vol. XIV, pp. 78 f., 335 n. 6.

It may be noted that, notwithstanding Ashkenazi's inability to persuade the French of the services he had rendered them during the election campaign, Henry, as king of France, continued to enlist the aid of Jews and Marranos in his negotiations with England and the Porte. When in 1581 he visited Alvaro Mendes in Paris, "accompanied by the dukes of Lorraine and Guise and the minions," he may not have known that many years before, Mendes had gained entry to Constantinople for his father and family, owing to Suleiman the Magnificent's personal intercession in their behalf with the Venetian authorities. See my "Solomon ibn Ya'ish and Sultan Suleiman the Magnificent" in *Joshua Finkel Festschrift*, ed. by S. B. Hoenig and L. D. Stitskin, pp. 29-36. But he must have realized, as did the English ambassador who reported this royal visit, that Mendes was a New Christian, and thus was suspect in the eyes of the ultraorthodox Frenchmen, as well as the Spaniards. Henry was also probably informed by his agents in Turkey about some of the moves Mendes had already made at the Porte to pave the way for his later settlement in Constantinople and his brilliant career there as a professing Jew, Solomon ibn Ya'ish, the duke of Mytilene. See *supra*, Vol. XV, pp. 83 f., 415 f. n. 13. The role of the Papacy during the election campaign has not been fully clarified, despite P. de Cenival's analysis of "La Politique du Saint-Siège et l'élection de Pologne (1572-1573)," *Mélanges d'archéologie et d'histoire* of the École française de Rome, XXXVI, 109-203. Its leanings toward the Habsburgs, the staunchest supporters at the time of the incipient Counter Reformation, and joint enmity toward the Turks, doubtless persuaded it to favor Archduke Ernest's candidacy, rather than that of the French prince, whose backing by the French nation itself was rather questionable. See also L. von Pastor, *The History of the Popes*, English trans., ed. by R. F. Kerr, XX, 385 ff.

49. See L. Szádeczky, "L'Élection d'Étienne Báthory au trône de Pologne," *Étienne Batory roi de Pologne prince de Transylvanie*, [ed. by Lukinich and Dąbrowski], pp. 82-104, esp. pp. 88, 93 f., 96; other relevant literature cited *supra*,

LXVII: POLAND'S GOLDEN AGE

n. 42; and particularly the documents published by C. Roth in his "Dr. Solomon Ashkenazi," *Oxford Slavonic Papers*, IX, 8–20. Isaac da Fano's role in this undertaking may be explained by the familiarity he had acquired with conditions in Poland after his arrival in Cracow on November 2, 1545, as an envoy from the Court of Ferrara to take part in the negotiations regarding the marriage of Sigismund Augustus with a Ferrara princess. Certainly, his identity with the Ferrara envoy Isaac mentioned in a Polish archival document, is highly probable. See D. Quirini-Popławska, *Działalność Włochów w Polsce* (The Activities of Italians in Poland), p. 86. Da Fano probably also was the financier, Isaac son of Benjamin, whose eight-year banking concession of May 1573 was extended for an indefinite period in 1576, "lest that bank cease operations to the disadvantage [*incomodo*] of the people." See A. Balletti, *Gli Ebrei e gli Estensi*, p. 68.

Most remarkable was Ashkenazi's draft of a letter which the duke of Ferrara was to write to the sultan. Alphonso was to argue that his election would be "beneficial [to Turkey] inasmuch as I am a relative of Your Highness because a lady of My House was the wife of one of the emperors, your predecessors," a contention which Suleiman had allegedly recognized. Moreover, the duke was also to claim some relationship to Sigismund Augustus, the deceased king of Poland (*ibid.*, pp. 17 f. App. No. 4). It is evident that Alphonso, at whose court no one seemed to recall any such dynastic relationships, made no use of Ashkenazi's proposal, but preferred instead to address to Sokolli a far more balanced letter, with less extravagant claims. It appears that no influential circles in Poland ever arrayed themselves on the side of the Ferrara duke.

50. On the informal Turco-Spanish truce of 1578 and Ashkenazi's role therein, see F. Braudel, *La Méditerranée et le Monde Méditerranéen à l'époque de Philippe II*, 2d ed., rev. and enlarged, II, 441 (citing two Simancas archival documents). The strange diplomatic interlude of 1587, and the lack of perspicacity of the persons involved, were revealed by the Italian and Hebrew documents published by B. (C.) Roth in "Dr. Solomon Ashkenazi," *Oxford Slavonic Papers*, IX, 19 f. No. 8; and in "A Mantuan Jewish Consortium and the Election to the Throne of Poland in 1587" (Hebrew), *Baer Jub. Vol.*, pp. 291–96. Poorly preserved, the text had to be partly reconstructed from a semiofficial Italian translation which undoubtedly had been prepared for the ducal chancery, whence it found its way into the Modena archive. Roth's entire article was translated into Polish by D. Dąbrowska in *BZIH*, no. 30, pp. 3–11. See *supra*, Vol. XIV, pp. 87 f., 339 n. 16. Leone de' Sommi, as an author and communal leader, will be cited here in various contexts in later chapters.

51. See A. de Lamartine, *Histoire de Turquie*, V, 36; E. Charrière, ed., *Négociations*, IV, 747; A. Galante, *Don Joseph Nassi Duc de Naxos d'après de nouveaux documents*, pp. 24 f., 31 f. App. ix (French), 38 f. (Turkish); J. W. Hirschberg, "Joseph Nasi's Participation in the Polish-Turkish Negotiations of 1562" (Polish), *MZ*, IV, 426–39, esp, pp. 434, 436. On Joseph's relations with France and the ensuing Turkish action in Alexandria, see esp. P. Grunebaum-Ballin's *Joseph Naci duc de Naxos*, pp. 99 ff., 119 ff. But this otherwise well-documented study furnishes few data about Don Joseph's relations with Poland. Though we have no direct information about the sultan's alienation from Joseph after the Turkish defeat at Lepanto, it appears that Sokolli's rising influence turned Selim's ever-hesitant mind

against the Jewish favorite. The decline in Joseph's standing at the Court was accelerated after Selim's death in 1574 and the succession of Murad III, with his generally less favorable attitude toward his Jewish subjects. The spectacular career of this Jewish duke and other Jewish grandees will be discussed more fully in connection with the general history of the Jews in the Ottoman Empire, in Vol. XVII.

52. Sigismund Augustus' letters of February 25 and March 7, 1570, were first published by A. Kraushar in his *Historya Żydów w Polsce* (A History of the Jews in Poland), II, 318; and again by M. Bersohn in "Einige Worte Don Joseph Nasi, Herzog von Naxos betreffend," *MGWJ*, XVIII, 422–24. They were once more reproduced by H. Graetz in his interesting Note 6 of his *Geschichte der Juden*, 4th ed., IX, 536 f.; and are now available in an English translation by C. Roth in his biography *The House of Nasi: the Duke of Naxos*, pp. 55 ff. Roth also quotes more fully than Graetz a passage by an unnamed Italian rabbi included in a Halberstamm MS, No. 390, now in the Jews' College Library, London. The rabbi reported a rumor circulating in his country that "Joseph Nasi (may his might increase!) sent a special envoy to the king of Poland, with various princes and servants accompanying him. Great honor was done to him [the envoy] and to all his attendants, and the king showed him his treasure-house and his gold and silver and precious vessels and everything else he had in his deposits, withholding nothing. . . . But the purpose of the envoy's coming is not known."

53. This interesting report was published from a Simancas archival document by V. Meysztowicz, ed., in *Documenta Polonica*, I (Elementa, VIII), 169 ff. No. 133. See *supra*, n. 48; and *infra*, Vol. XVII.

54. F. Papée, ed., *Akta Aleksandra*, pp. 194 No. 128, 233 No. 150; D. Goldberg-Feldman, "The Commerce of Poznań Jews in the First Half of the Sixteenth Century" (Yiddish), *Bleter far Geshikhte*, I, 51–57; Giovanni Francesco Commendone's letter of March 25, 1564, reproduced in a Polish trans. in J. C. Albertrandi's *Pamiętniki o dawnej Polsce*, I, 99–102; A. Galante, *Don Joseph Nassi*, pp. 13 f., 29 f. No. v (French), 36 No. v (Turkish); idem, "Nouveaux documents sur Joseph Nassy, Duc de Naxos," *REJ*, LXIV, 236–43, esp. p. 240 No. iv; M. Schorr, "Zur Geschichte des Don Josef Nasi," *MGWJ*, XLI, 169–77, 228–37; M. Bałaban, *Żydzi lwowscy*, p. 459 ff., App. pp. 9 fl. No. 9, 25 No. 23. It should be noted that wine, which was the main commodity in the privileged position enjoyed by Joseph and his agents, was very costly in Poland—in contrast to other victuals—and, hence, its duty-free importation there promised to be extremely lucrative. See F. Braudel, *La Méditerranée*, 2d ed., I, 173. Lamartine's statement that Don Joseph also owned vineyards in Sicily appears questionable, however, inasmuch as that island was under the domination of his enemy Philip II—unless we assume that he camouflaged his ownership under the name of some Christian agent. See *supra*, n. 51. The negotiations and vicissitudes of these and other Turkish Jewish businessmen in Lwów are of greater interest to the economic than to the legal and political history of Polish Jewry; they will be better understood in the context of the other aspects of Jewish commerce in Poland-Lithuania, which will be treated *infra*, Chap. LXX.

55. M. Schorr, "Zur Geschichte," *MGWJ*, XLI, 169 ff., 176 f., 228 ff.; M. Bałaban, *Żydzi lwowscy*, pp. 462 ff.; W. Łoziński, *Patrycyat i mieszczaństwo lwowskie w*

XVI i XVII wieku (Patricians and Burghers in Lwów in the Sixteenth and Seventeenth Centuries), pp. 49 ff.; S. Kutrzeba, "Poland's Commerce with the East in the Middle Ages" (Polish), *Przegląd Polski*, CXLVIII, 189–219, 462–96; CXLIX, 512–37; CL, 115–45, esp. pp. 137 f.; Z. Świtalski, "The Reasons for the Withdrawal of the Turkish Jews, Refugees from Spain, from the Levant Trade of the Polish Commonwealth in the Last Years of the Sixteenth Century" (Polish), *BZIH*, no. 37, pp. 59–65, with an English summary, pp. 109–110; J. Morgensztern, "Jewish Mediation in Establishing Unofficial Diplomatic Contacts between the Polish and Turkish Sovereigns' Courts in 1590 (In the Light of the Correspondence between King Sigismund III and Jan Zamoyski)" (Polish), *ibid.*, no. 40, pp. 37–49, with an English summary, pp. 89–90; and, more generally, F. Braudel, *La Méditerranée*, 2d ed., I, 178 ff.; and J. M. Malecki's succinct observations on "Die Wandlungen im Krakauer und polnischen Handel zur Zeit der Türkenkriege im 16. und 17. Jahrhundert," in O. Pickl's ed. of *Die Wirtschaftlichen Auswirkungen der Türkenkriege. Die Vorträge des 1. Internationalen Kongresses zur Wirtschafts- und Sozialgeschichte* (5–10 Oktober, 1970), pp. 145–51. Only a few decades later was there some revival of Sephardic settlement and trade in Zamość. See J. Morgensztern's "On the Economic Activity of Jews in Zamość in the Sixteenth and Seventeenth Centuries" (Polish), *BZIH*, no. 53, pp. 3–32, 134, with an English summary; M. Balaban, "Die Portugiesen in Lemberg und Zamość in his *Skizzen und Studien*, pp. 11–19; and M. Pieszko, *Zamość—gród kanclersko-hetmański* (Zamość: the Town of a Chancellor and Generalissimo: an Historical Sketch). See also the additional data yielded by the *Archiwum Jana Zamoyskiego. Kanclerza i hetmana wielkiego koronnego* (The Archive of Jan Zamoyski, Chancellor and Generalissimo of the Polish Crown), ed. by W. Sobieski *et al.*, Vols. I–IV; and *infra*, Chap. LXX, nn. 31 f.

56. A. Brückner, *Dzieje kultury polskiej*, 3d ed., II, 347; A. Wyczański, "The Culture of the Polish Renaissance: an Attempt to Define Its Historical Mentality" (Polish), *ORP*, X, 11–51, esp. pp. 24 ff., 43; H. Barycz, *Historja Uniwersytetu Jagiellońskiego w epoce Humanizmu* (History of the Jagiellon University in Cracow in the Period of Humanism), pp. 84 ff.; A. Kawecka-Gryczowa, *Rola drukarstwa polskiego w dobie Odrodzenia* (The Role of Polish Printing in the Renaissance Period); idem *et al.*, *Drukarze dawnej Polski od XV do XVIII wieku* (Printers of Old Poland from the Fifteenth to the Eighteenth Century), Vols. IV–VI. See also such detailed investigations as *Monumenta Poloniae typographica XV et XVI saeculorum*, ed. by J. Ptaśnik, Vol. I: *Cracoviae impressores XV et XVI saeculorum*; the facsimiles reproduced by K. Piekarski, in his ed. of *Polonia typographica saeculi sedecim zbiór podobizn* (Collection of Facsimiles of the Printing Stock of the Polish Presses of the Sixteenth Century); and, related thereto, J. Dużyk's "From the History of Censorship in Cracow in the Fifteenth through Eighteenth Centuries" (Polish), *Roczniki* of the Library of PAN II, 375–411; and *infra*, Chap. LXX, n. 55.

The printing presses greatly facilitated the propagation of all sorts of teachings among larger groups in the population. They also served such Christian missionary efforts as the translation of the New Testament into Hebrew and Yiddish, although Paweł Halicz's contention (in the Introduction to his publication of the Yiddish version), that "all rabbis possessed copies of the Gospel; they merely hid them before the simple-minded people," is a blatant exaggeration. These aspects, as well as the noteworthy story of Hebrew printing in sixteenth-century Poland, will be discussed here in later chapters.

57. B. Baranowski, *Znajomość Wschodu w dawnej Polsce do XVIII wieku,* esp.
pp. 19 ff., 22 ff., 48 ff.; and, more generally, H. Barycz's aforementioned history of
the University of Cracow (*supra,* n. 56), *passim.* Of great value still is the older,
comprehensive work by K. (C.) Morawski, available in a French translation by
P. Rougier entitled *Histoire de l'Université de Cracovie. Moyen âge et Renaissance;*
and the comments on the latter two works by A. Jobert in "L'Université de
Cracovie et les grands courants de pensée du XVIe siècle," *Revue d'histoire moderne
et contemporaine,* I, 213–25. Among the early Christian Hebraists in Cracow, the
Italian Callimach has aroused considerable interest among modern scholars. As we
recall, he was also politically influential as an adviser to Casimir IV and his son
John Albert, in which capacity he was able in many ways to help their Jewish
subjects. See *supra,* Vol. X, pp. 47 f., 323 n. 59. At the same time, he was one of the
intellectual leaders of the Polish Renaissance. See F. Bujak, "Callimach and the
Knowledge of the Turkish Empire in Poland at the Beginning of the Sixteenth
Century" (Polish) in his *Studia geograficzno-historyczne,* pp. 114–37; J. Garbacik,
"Callimach as a Diplomat and Politician" (Polish), *Rozprawy* of PAN, Hist.-Philos.
Section, LXXI, 371–532; J. Zathey, "Quelques recherches sur l'humaniste Kallimach
(Filippo Buonaccorsi 1437–1496)," *Congresso internazionale di studi umanisti, Ober-
hofen, September 1960,* pp. 123–39; and A. Kempfi, "Une Polémique méconnue de
Callimaque à propos du platonisme de Marsilio Ficino. Quelques pages d'histoire
de la science sur l'homme aux origines de la Renaissance en Pologne," *Archives
internationales d'histoire des sciences,* XVII, 263–72.

So preponderant was Italian influence on the Polish Renaissance that Desiderius
Erasmus of Rotterdam, who had the greatest impact on the new trends in other
European countries, played a much smaller role in Poland. See C. Backvis, "La
Fortune d'Érasme en Pologne," *Colloqium Erasmianum* (Actes du Colloque international réuni à Mons, . . . 1967), pp. 173–202, esp. pp. 174 ff.; and, on the other
hand, the literature analyzed by W. Weintraub in his "Italian-Polish Cultural
Relations: Review Article," *Slavic Review,* XXV, 133–42. See also some new materials
assembled in the *Bibliografia literatury polskiej okresu Odrodzenia* (Bibliography
of Polish Literature in the Renaissance Era: Materials) compiled by K. Budzyk *et al.,*
although Budzyk and his associates, like most other scholars in the field, pay little
attention to the Jewish or Hebraic aspects of that literature. On the special inter-
relations between the universities of Cracow and Padua, see Y. Marchiori, "Scolari
e maestri dell'Università di Cracovia negli 'Acta inclytae Nationis Poloniae,'"
*Relazioni tra Padova e la Polonia. Studi in onore dell'Università di Cracovia nel
VI centenario della sua fondazione;* and J. Warchat, "Polish Jews at the University
of Padua" (Polish), *Kwartalnik poświęcony badaniu przeszłości Żydów w Polsce,* I,
No. 3, pp. 37–72.

58. H. Barycz, *Historia Uniwersytetu,* pp. 88 ff.; Jan (Johann) van Campen, *Ex
variis libellis Eliae Grammaticorum omnium doctissimi huc fere congestum est,* etc.;
idem, *Libellus de natura literarum et punctorum hebraicorum,* both published in
Cracow, 1534, with dedications to Bishop Piotr Tomicki; *Acta Tomiciana,* ed. by
W. Pociecha, XVI, Part 1, p. 132 No. 52; XVII, 102 f. No. 78; M. Bałaban, "The
Intellectual Life and Morality of Polish Jewry in the Sixteenth Century" (Polish),
Kultura Staropolska, Cracow, 1932, pp. 606–639 (also reprint). No modern bibliog-
rapher seems to have seen Dawid's Hebrew grammar, but it apparently still existed
among the manuscripts of Józef Andrzej Załuski. See the article "Dawid, Leonard"

in the *Polski Słownik Biograficzny* (Polish Biographical Dictionary), ed. by W. Konopczyński *et al.*, IV, 461. Van Campen also reissued, in Cracow, his Latin paraphrase of the Psalms, entitled *Psalmorum omnium iuxta hebraicam veritatem paraphrastica interpretatio*, first published in Nuremberg in 1532. Being written in Latin, it appealed to an international audience and, in a relatively short time, appeared in 30 editions. (No such publishing success later greeted even the distinguished Polish Psalter by Jan Kochanowski, which in the poet's lifetime was issued only 12 times.) Thus it was a Polish bestseller, for, we must not forget, it was not until 1548 that a brief Polish liturgical pamphlet was first printed in Poland. See P. Zwoliński, "The First Printed *Polonicum:* Jan Mączyński's Ojczenasz [Paternoster] of 1548 and Its Reimpressions until 1719" (Polish), *Slavia Occidentalis,* XXVII (= Władysław Kuraszkiewicz Jubilee Issue, I), 341–47, with a French summary (the first published Polish trans. of the well-known prayer). It may also be noted that Van Campen was brought to Poland by the influential, humanistically inclined Bishop Jan Dantyszek (Joannes Dantiscus), who played a considerable role in influencing his countrymen to cultivate the new humanistic learning in vogue in the western lands. See I. B. Müller-Blessing, "Johannes Dantiscus von Höfen. Ein Diplomat und Bischof zwischen Humanismus und Reformation (1485–1548)," *Zeitschrift für die Geschichte und Altertumskunde Ermlands,* XXXI–XXXII, 59–238; and *supra,* Vol. XIII, pp. 166 f. n. 9.

59. See the biographical sketches on "Bitner (Bythner), Wiktoryn (Victorinus)" in the *Polski Słownik Biograficzny,* ed. by W. Konopczyński *et al.,* III, 181 ff.; and in the *Dictionary of National Biography,* London, 1921–22 ed., III, 617 f. Among his Hebrew works, the *Lingua eruditorum sive institutio methodica linguae sanctae,* Oxford, 1638; and his *Lyra prophetica Davidis regis sive analysis psalmorum,* London, 1645, are especially worthy of note. In some respects Bythner reminds one of Immanuel Tremellius, except that, being born a Christian, he seems to have encountered less difficulty in teaching at foreign universities than did the Luccan convert from Judaism. See *supra,* Vols. XIII, pp. 166 f., 396 f. n. 9; XV, pp. 445 f. n. 86.

60. Maciej of Miechów, *Tractatus de duabus Sarmatiis, Asiana et Europiana,* Cracow, 1577, II, Part 1, p. 33 (also in contemporary German and Italian translations). See also H. Barycz's biography *Maciej z Miechowa* (M. of M. 1457–1523, Historian, Geographer, Physician, and Organizer of Science); and *supra,* Vol. X, p. 318 n. 46.

61. See P. Bloch, "Der Streit um den Moreh des Maimonides in der Gemeinde Posen um die Mitte des 16. Jahrhunderts," *MGWJ,* XLVII, 153–69, 263–79, 346–56 (also reproducing a long fragment of the anonymous pamphlet written in reply to the Poznań rabbi Aaron and his son-in-law Joseph, esp. p. 263); S. P. Rabbinowitz, "Traces of Liberal Thought in the Polish Rabbinate of the Sixteenth Century" (Russian), *ES,* IV, 1–18 (identifying the author of that pamphlet as Abraham b. Shabbetai Horowitz who refers in the text to his earlier commentary on Maimonides' *Eight Chapters*); and other data discussed by M. Bałaban in "The Intellectual Life," *Kultura Staropolska,* pp. 606 ff. (also reprint, pp. 2 ff.). Not surprisingly, however, even Horowitz was later swayed by the onset of religious reaction among the Poles and the Jews, and retracted his views in 1602.

The unfamiliarity of the Jews with the local languages will become more evident in our later discussions. This was doubly true in the case of new "Portuguese" arrivals from the Balkans, such as those settling in Zamość, who were usually unable to converse with the Polish burghers, even in German. Hence, for instance, the representatives of Don Joseph in Lwów transacted almost all their business in Italian, orally or in writing. See *supra*, n. 57.

62. Stanislaw Poklatecki, *Pogrom czarnoksięskie błędy, latawców zdrady i alchimickie fałsze* (Defeat of Black Magic Errors, Fliers of Treason, and Alchemistic Falsehoods), Cracow, 1595, cited by A. Brückner in *Dzieje kultury polskiej*, pp. 228 ff., 231; M. Bałaban, "The Intellectual Life," *Kultura Staropolska*, pp. 622 f. (reprint, pp. 17 f.); S. A. Horodezky, *Mystisch-religiöse Strömungen unter den Juden in Polen im 16.–18. Jahrhundert;* idem, *Shelosh me'ot shanah shel yahudut Polin* (Three Hundred Years of Polish Judaism); and *supra*, Vol. XIII, pp. 172 ff., 400 ff. nn. 15 ff. The situation changed in the seventeenth century, when mysticism secured a much greater following in Polish society. See Julian Krzyżanowski, *Od religijności do mistyki* (From Religiosity to Mysticism: a Sketch of the History of Internal Life in Poland), Vol. I. By that time, however, the general intellectual climate of Poland had changed, and Judeo-Christian intellectual segregation had increased sufficiently to preclude any genuine cooperation between Polish and Jewish mystics.

63. See K. Górski, "The Bible and Biblical Matters in Rej's Postilla" (Polish), *Reformacja w Polsce*, XII, 62–125, esp. pp. 120 f. (using the Old Testament mainly for its messianic predictions; incidentally also confusing Ecclesiastes with Ecclesiasticus); Julian Krzyżanowski, *Mikołaj Rej i rodzima kultura literacka jego czasów, z wypisami* (M. R. and the Native Literary Culture of His Time, with Notes); idem, *Jan Kochanowski i humanizm w Polsce* (J. K. and Humanism in Poland); idem, *W wieku Reja i Stańczyka* (In the Century of Rej and Stańczyk: Sketches from the History of the Renaissance in Poland). A number of other distinguished writers of the sixteenth and seventeenth centuries who reveal clear traces of the impact of biblical language and imagery are mentioned by W. Fallek in "The Influence of the Bible on Polish Poetry" (Polish), *MZ*, III, Part 2, pp. 287–88. Needless to say, indebtedness to biblical prototypes did not necessarily lead to a better understanding of Judaism or Jewish life. We shall see (*infra*, Chap. LXVIII) that Rej, Sebastjan Fabian Klonowicz, and others were not at all hampered by it in unperturbedly repeating the popular accusations against Jews. This important subject in its manifold aspects deserves a comprehensive scholarly monograph.

64. M. Bałaban, "The Intellectual Life," *Kultura Staropolska*, pp. 615 f. (reprint, pp. 10 f.); idem, *Dzieje Żydów w Krakowie*, I, 40 ff.; idem, "Jakob Polak, der Baal Chillukim in Krakau, und seine Zeit," *MGWJ*, LVII, 59–73, 196–210, esp. pp. 201 ff.; and *supra*, n. 30. On the general relationships between the Jews and the Polish aristocracy, both higher and lower, see *infra*, Chap. LXVIII.

65. See I. Kaniewska. *Młodzież Uniwersytetu Krakowskiego w latach 1510–1560* (The Youth of the Cracow University in the Years 1510–1560; Studies in the History of Cracow's University Youth in the Period of the Renaissance); idem, "On the Question of the Origin of the Cracow Students in the Sixteenth Century"

(Polish), *KH,* LXXIII, 115–17 (a defense of her position against strictures by Władysław Dworzaczek); idem *et al., Studja z dziejów młodzierzy Uniwersytetu Krakowskiego* (Studies in the History of the Youth at the University of Cracow in the Renaissance Period), ed. by K. Lepszy; and H. Barycz, *Historya Uniwersytetu Jagiellońskiego,* pp. 309 ff., 639 ff., 646 ff., 652 f. On the relations between Jews and students in other countries, see *supra,* esp. Vol. XI, p. 185.

66. See Fausto Socino's own description of the attack on him by the Cracow students in 1598, in his *Listy* (Letters), trans. into Polish by T. Bienkowski *et al.,* and ed. by L. Szcucki, I, 23 f. The reformer resented, most of all, the loss of his papers; he declared that he would give his life to regain them. See also M. Martini's admiring biography, *Fausto Socino et la pensée socinienne. Un maître de la pensée religieuse, 1539–1604;* and, more broadly, R. Żelewski's analysis "Denominational Disturbances in Cracow during the Period of the Dissidents' Preponderance in 1551–1573" (Polish), *ORP,* VI, 91–111, with a French summary; and his additional *Materjały do dziejów Reformacyi w Krakowie* (Sources for the History of the Reformation in Cracow: Denominational Disturbances in the Years 1551–1598). On the events in Sandomierz, we have merely the oblique reference by R. Joshua Heschel b. Joseph of Cracow in his *She'elot u-teshubot Pene Yehoshu'a* (Responsa), Vol. II on Ḥ. M. No. 97, Lwów, 1860 ed., fols. 8 f. As usual this responsum is undated, but the event probably took place early in the seventeenth century. The impact of the Jesuits and their schools on Jewish life in Poland and Lithuania will be more fully discussed in the next chapter. Despite outward similarity, the German "dice tax" differed from the *kozubalec* in that it was not intended to serve as a pay-off against riots. See I. Rivkind, "Dice Tax in Connection with the Tax of Disgrace" (Hebrew), *Zion,* I, 37–48; and my *JC,* II, 316 f.; III, 207 f. n. 30. See also *infra,* Chap. LXVIII, nn. 22–23.

67. See J. Topolski, *Rozwój latyfundium arcybiskupstwa gnieźnieńskiego od XVI do XVIII wieku* (Development of the Latifundium of the Archbishopric of Gniezno from the Sixteenth to the Eighteenth Century; with over one hundred statistical tables and a French summary, pp. 371–79); W. Sobociński, "Jan Ostroróg's *Monumentum* and the Early Reformation in Poland" (Polish), *ORP,* III, 9–52; IV, 35–80, with English summaries (wishes Poland free from papal controls); other relevant data cited by K. Lepszy in his "Reformation in Poland" (Polish), *Historia Polski,* ed. by T. Manteuffel *et al.,* I, Part 2, pp. 261–91, esp. 262 f.; idem, "Die Sozialen Hauptprobleme der Reformation in Polen in den Werken polnischer Historiker aus den Jahren 1945–1960," in *La Renaissance et la Réformation en Pologne et en Hongrie (1450–1650), (Studia Historica,* LIII), pp. 183–209; and *infra,* nn. 68 and 74. On the Polish part in the Hussite movement, see E. Maleczyńska, *Ruch husycki w Czechach i w Polsce* (The Hussite Movement in Bohemia and Poland). See also J. Midulka, "Poles in Bohemia and Their Role in the Development of Hussitism" (Polish), *ORP,* XI, 5–27, with a German summary; W. Dziewulski's attitude study "Silesian Society and the Hussites" (Polish), *ibid.,* V, 5–45, with a French summary (because of the author's thesis that the masses, angry over the frequent military forays of the Hussite armies, opposed the movement, the editors felt constrained to publish a reservation that the article was intended merely as a subject for future discussion); *supra,* Vol. XIII, pp. 210 ff., 417 ff. nn. 6–11; and *infra,* Chap. LXVIII,

n. 3. On the important work of Jakub Biernat of Lublin as a forerunner of the Polish Reform movement, see his *Wybór Pism* (Selected Writings), ed. with an informative intro. by J. Ziomek.

68. See K. Hartleb's biographical sketch of *Floryan Rozwicz Susliga*, esp. p. 88; J. Jasnowski's ed. from an archival source of "Sigismund Augustus' Two Edicts against Piotr of Goniądz and Jan Łaski," *Reformacja w Polsce*, IX–X, 442–43; other sources quoted by O. Bartel in his "Zwingli, Calvin, and Poland" (Polish), *PH*, LVI, 144–50; and *supra*, Vol. XIII, pp. 291, 462 n. 100. On the remarkable personality of Jan Łaski, see his *Opera, tam edita quam inedita;* and the biographical studies by H. Dalton, *Johannes a Lasco;* and by O. Bartel, *Jan Łaski*, Vol. I: 1499–1556. While we do not know much about his attitude toward Jews and Judaism, Łaski's "ecumenicity" apparently did not extend to the Jewish people nor, for that matter, to Catholics or to radical reformers. See H. Kowalska-Kossobudzka's analysis of "Jan Łaski's Conception of the Church. From the History of Ecumenical Thought in the Polish Reformation" (Polish), *ORP*, X, 81–101. See also *infra*, n. 69.

Partly because of its peculiar features, the history of the Polish Reformation has attracted much interest, not only among Polish historians. For example, in the comprehensive study *Der Polnische Adel und die Reformation 1548–1607*, G. Schramm has devoted much space to a well-documented analysis of the unusual type of Reformation which spread in Poland "against the will of the reigning prince." See also the comparative studies in *La Renaissance et la Réformation en Pologne et en Hongrie (1450–1650)*, ed. by G. Székely and E. Fügedi (papers originally submitted to a joint Conference held in Budapest and Eger, October 10–14, 1961); O. Bartel's "Martin Luther in Poland," *ORP*, VII, 27–50, with a German summary; E. W. Zeeden, "Calvins Einwirken auf die Reformation in Polen-Litauen. Eine Studie über den Reformator Calvin im Spiegel seiner polnischen Korrespondenz," *Syntagma friburgense. Historische Studien Herman Aubin . . . dargebracht*, pp. 323–59; A. Schwarzenberg, "Besonderheiten der Reformation in Polen," *Kirche im Osten*, I, 52–64, emphasizing the lack of a decisive leadership and the excessive attempts to adapt to Catholic ways of worship and organization (pp. 56 ff.); G. Rhode, "Die Reformation in Osteuropa. Ihre Stellung in der Weltgeschichte und ihre Darstellung in den 'Weltgeschichten,' " *ZOF*, VII, 481–500. Of special interest to Jews was, understandably, the impact of the Reformation on the cities. See such monographs as J. Dworzaczkowa, "The Introduction of the Reformation in the Royal Cities of Great Poland" (Polish), *ORP*, X, 53–80; G. Schramm, "Lemberg und die Reformation," *Jahrbücher für Geschichte Osteuropas*, n.s. XI, 343–50. On Lublin, see *supra*, n. 67; and *infra*, n. 73. Needless to say, the general literature on the Polish Reformation is very vast. See, for instance, A. Kotarska's "Bibliography of the Reformation for the Years 1945–1960" (Polish), *Archiwum historii filozofii*, IX = L. Kołakowski *et al.*, eds., *Religie racjonalne* (Rational Religions: Studies in the History of Religion in the Fifteenth and Sixteenth Centuries), pp. 169–202, with a German summary; and the more recent *Bibliographie de la Réforme 1450–1648*, Fascicle 5, ed. for the International Committee of Historical Sciences by A. Kawecka *et al.*, esp. pp. 1–35 (covers the publications of 1940–55).

69. Eliezer b. Elijah Ashkenazi, *Ma'asei ha-Shem* (The Works of the Lord; homilies), Parts I (Works of Creation), xxxi; II (Works of Patriarchs), i; IV, colophon, Żółkiew, 1802 ed., I, fols. 63a–64b; II, 59b; Ḥayyim b. Bezalel, *Sefer ha-Ḥayyim*

(The Book of Life; on ethics), Cracow, 1593, both cited by H. H. Ben Sasson in "The Reformation in Contemporary Jewish Eyes," *Proceedings* of the Israel Academy of Sciences and Humanities, IV, 2, esp. pp. 21 f.; and other sources cited *supra*, Vol. XIII, pp. 219, 423 n. 15.

70. Szymon Zacius, cited by S. Kot in "L'Influence de Michel Servet sur le mouvement antitrinitarien en Pologne et en Transylvanie," in the collection of essays, *Autour de Michel Servet et Sébastien Castellion*, ed. by B. Becker, pp. 72–135, esp. p. 78; Erasmus' warnings to Jan Łaski, cited by A. Brückner in his biographical sketch of the younger Łaski in his *Różnowiercy polscy. Szkice obyczajowe i literackie* (Polish Dissidents: Behavioral and Literary Sketches) in the annotated edition by L. Szczucki, p. 47; and Cardinal Hosius' reservations cited by J. Tazbir in his "Polish Religious Controversialists in the Face of the Persecution of Anti-Trinitarianism in the Sixteenth Century" (Polish), *PH*, LIII, 717–29, with Russian and French summaries, esp. p. 723. Although far less pronounced than in Germany, France, or Spain, the Erasmian influence on the Polish intelligentsia had some significance with respect to the Reformation, since Polish Protestantism was even more deeply indebted to Renaissance rationalism than were similar movements in neighboring lands. See also C. Backvis, "La Fortune d'Érasme en Pologne," *Colloquium Erasmianum*, pp. 173–202, esp. pp. 174 f., 199 f.; and *supra*, n. 57.

71. J. F. A. Gillet, *Crato von Crafftheim und seine Freunde*, II, 539 No. 71; L. Szczucki in his *Marcin Czechowic (1532–1613): Studyum z dziejów antitrynytaryzma polskiego XVI wieku* (M. C., 1532–1613: a Study in the History of the Polish Anti-Trinitarianism of the Sixteenth Century), p. 259 n. 10. See *infra*, n. 73. On the part played by the peasantry in the Polish Reformation, see W. Urban, *Chłopi wobec reformacji w Małopolsce w drugiej połowie XVI wieku* (The Peasants' Attitude toward the Reformation in Little Poland in the Second Half of the Sixteenth Century). Although Urban draws a distinction between the economically backward areas, where (as in England and Holland) few peasants were attracted to the early Reform movements, and the more advanced Little Poland, where the share of peasants among the adherents of the new faiths was much larger, he cannot deny that even in the district of Lublin (next to Vilna the main citadel of Anti-Trinitarianism) the sect's appeal to the peasant masses was neither deep nor enduring. Remarkably, in Urban's documentation there appear three Christians who apparently bore without compunction the surname Żydowski (Jewish). One, a landlord, allowed his farmers to hold Calvinist services in a barn; another, a burgher of Pinczów, "the Polish Athens," was haled before an ecclesiastical court for obstructing payment to a Catholic convent (1683); the third was a Catholic priest who denounced five Polish Brethren for inciting farmers to work on certain Catholic holidays. See *ibid.*, pp. 218, 225, 262.

72. The literature on Polish Anti-Trinitarianism is enormous. For our purposes it may suffice to cite the following recent publications: S. Kot's aforementioned (n. 70) "L'Influence de Michel Servet"; idem, *Socinianism in Poland. The Social and Political Ideas of the Polish Antitrinitarians in the Sixteenth and Seventeenth Centuries*; J. A. Tedeschi, ed., *Italian Reformation Studies in Honor of Laelius Socinus* (Faustus' uncle and chief teacher); M. Martini, *Fausto Socino et la penseé socinienne. Un maître de la pensée religieuse (1539–1604)*, esp. pp. 80 ff.; A. Jobert,

"Quelques impies du XVIᵉ s. Fauste Socin et les non-adorants," *Cahiers d'histoire*, XIII (= Mélanges d'histoire André Fugier), 143–54; Z. Ogonowski, *Socynianizm polski* (Polish Socinianism); and, more generally, D. Caccamo, *Eretici italiani in Moravia, Polonia, Transilvania (1558–1611)*. *Studi e documenti; infra*, Chap. LXVIII, n. 20; L. Chmaj, *Bracia polscy: ludzie, idee, wpływy* (Polish Brethren: Men, Ideas, Influences), which includes his essays of 1924 and 1926, considerably revised, on the impact of Polish Anti-Trinitarianism on Baruch Spinoza and Hugo Grotius (pp. 209–262, 263–98); and the collection of essays, ed. by Chmaj under the title *Studia nad Arianizmem* (Studies in Arianism; with English summaries), with G. Schramm's comments thereon in his "Neue Ergebnisse der Antitrinitarier Forschung," *Jahrbücher für Geschichte Osteuropas*, n.s. VIII, 421–36; and his comprehensive review article "Antitrinitarier in Polen, 1556–1658. Ein Literaturbericht," *BHR*, XXI, 473–511. Among others, G. H. Williams has pointed out the importance of "Anabaptism and Spiritualism in the Kingdom of Poland and the Grand Duchy of Lithuania: an Obscure Phase of the Pre-History of Socinianism" (in *Studia*, ed. by L. Chmaj, pp. 215–62). See also his more comprehensive study *The Radical Reformation;* and *supra*, Vol. XIII, pp. 437 f. n. 43. We shall see that even the distinguished Polish political thinker Andrzej Frycz Modrzewski (Andreas Fricius Modrevius), although generally unaffiliated with any Protestant sect, received many stimuli from the radical wing of the Reformation. See also the various monographs, cited in the following notes, relating to individual leaders and to other aspects of Protestant-Jewish relations in Poland and Lithuania during the sixteenth and seventeenth centuries.

73. Marcin Czechowic, *Rozmowy chrystyańskie* (Christian Talks, Called in Greek Dialogues, Which You May Call a Great Catechism; Includes Various Discourses on the Foremost Articles of the Christian Faith, and a Separate Discourse on Jewish Sayings Whereby They Wish to Destroy Our Lord Jesus Christ and the Gospels), n.p., 1575. Czechowic, a major figure in Polish Arianism, has often been treated in Polish historiography. See especially the biographical sketch and numerous other references to this heresiarch in A. Brückner's *Różnowiercy polscy*, with the revisions by L. Szczucki, *passim;* Szczucki's full-length biography, *Marcin Czechowic*, esp. pp. 89 ff., 126 ff., 260 ff.; and, on the locale of many of these debates, see S. Tworek's *Zbór lubelski i jego rola w ruchu ariańskim w Polsce w XVI–XVII wieku* (The Lublin Congregation and Its Role in the Arian Movement of Poland in the Sixteenth and Seventeenth Centuries). On the various Anti-Trinitarian synods of 1561–69, including that of Bełżyce of 1569, see S. Zachorowski, "The Oldest Synods of the Polish Arians" (Polish), *Reformacja w Polsce*, I, 208 ff.

74. Marcin Czechowic, *Odpis Jakoba Żyda z Bełżyc na Dyalogi Marcina Czechowica: na który zaś odpowiada Jakobowi Żydowi tenże Marcin Czechowic* (The Reply of the Jew Jacob of Bełżyce to Marcin Czechowic' Talks; with the Same Czechowic' Rejoinder to the Jew Jacob), Raków, 1581; and the analysis of that debate by J. M. Rosenthal in his "Marcin Czechowic and Jacob of Bełżyce. Arian-Jewish Encounters in 16th Century Poland," *PAAJR*, XXXIV, 77–97, esp. p. 88 (here slightly varied). Needless to say, the reconstruction of Jacob's views from a few random quotations in an opponent's reply is extremely hazardous. True, Czechowic seems to have made an effort to reproduce his interlocutor's ideas without falsification; the very Polish style of Jacob's utterances greatly differs from the polished prose of the excellent

stylist Czechowic. However, we can not tell how much the Anti-Trinitarian author simply failed to mention or deliberately suppressed part of his opponent's argument, in order that his own rejoinder might sound more plausible. In one of his replies, he blames Jacob for jumping from one subject to another before completing his argument, but this reproach (as is often the case) may represent his own short-coming more than his opponent's. This was indeed, the objection raised by Jacob in the passage quoted in the text. In any case, Jacob did not dare to publish his strictures, nor was his debate mentioned anywhere in the Jewish literature of the period. The reasons for this restraint are obvious, and they essentially hold true for the work by Jacob's greater contemporary, Isaac of Troki, as well. See *infra*, n. 82. The two sides in these perennial Judeo-Christian exchanges have been discussed here in various contexts, esp. *supra*, Vol. IX, Chap XXXIX; some novel characteristics of the sixteenth- and seventeenth-century debates will be analyzed in a later chapter.

75. M. Czechowic, *Rozmowy chrystyańskie, passim;* S. Zachorowski, "The Oldest Synods," *Reformacja w Polsce*, I, 208 ff.; Faustus Socino (Sozzini), *Listy*, ed. by L. Szczucki, II, 193 ff. No. LXXIX; Mikołaj Rej of Nagłowice, *Zwierciadło* (A Mirror in Which Every Estate May View Its Affairs), ed. by J. Czubek and J. Łoś with an Intro. by I. Chrzanowski, esp. I, 128, 167, 176; II, 94, 214 ff., 297; idem, *Facecje albo śmieszne powieści* (Facetious or Funny Stories), excerpted in his *Pisma prozą i wierszem* (Writings in Prose and Verse), ed. and commented on by A. Brückner, p. 233; and, more generally, K. Lepszy and A. Kamińska, "The Genesis and Social Program of the Radical Trend Among the Polish Brethren" (Polish), *ORP*, I, 33–70; and other publications listed by L. Hajdukiewicz in his "Survey of Investigations on the History of the Reformation and Counter Reformation in Poland in the Years 1939–1952" (Polish), *Reformacja w Polsce*, X, 150–214, esp. pp. 169 ff.; and by J. Tazbir in "Recherches sur l'histoire de la Réforme en Pologne (1945–1958)," *APH*, II, 133–53, esp. pp. 143 f. On Rej and Grzegorz Paweł, see *supra*, n. 63; and *infra*, n. 77.

It is difficult, however, to generalize about the social program of the Polish Anti-Trinitarian movement. As in the dogmatic sphere, so also in their attitudes toward social programs, the leading "Arians" widely diverged. The most extreme spokesmen for a radical overthrow of the existing order were foreigners such as Maciej Vehe-Glirius. It was in part for this reason that contemporaries accused this German reformer of judaizing. As the Lublin physician Kasper Wilkowski observed in 1583, "so long as he traveled up and down Poland, he cheated the ministry, the congregations, and the lords out of the remnants of their Christianity, although he did not circumcise them. It is known how many persons this unworthy fellow (together with his disciple Franciczek Dawidowicz [Franz David, a Transylvanian]) had seduced into direct Judaism in Poland and Transylvania." See Wilkowski's *Przyczyny nawrócenia do wiary powszecznej* (Causes of the Return to the Faith Universal from the Satanic Anabaptist Sects), Book I (Vilna, 1583), pp. 87–88, cited by A. Brückner in *Różnowiercy*, p. 149; and *supra*, Vol. XIV, pp. 181 ff., 373 nn. 36–38.

76. See Fausto Socino, *De sacrae scripturae auctoritate libellus*, Rabów, 1611, in the excerpts reproduced by M. Martini in her *Fausto Socino*, pp. 104, 396; his Latin letter of February 24, 1602, to Walenty Radecki, published by L. Chmaj in his

348 LXVII: POLAND'S GOLDEN AGE

"Two Unknown Letters by Fausto Socino" (Polish), in his ed. of *Studia nad arianizmem*, pp. 527-30; G. Pioli, *Fausto Socino; supra*, Vol. XIII, pp. 325 f. n. 53, 329 f. n. 60, 355 n. 64; Jacobus Palaeologus, *De discrimene Veteris et Novi Testamenti*, completed in Cracow, 1572; idem, *De tribus gentibus*, likewise written in Cracow, 1572; idem, *Catechesis christianae dies XII*, completed in Cluj, 1574, all cited from MSS by A. Pirnát in his German essay on "Jacobus Palaeologus," *Studia nad arianizmem*, pp. 73-129, esp. pp. 79 ff., 86 ff., 103 ff., 108; A. Brückner, *Różnowiercy*, pp. 149 ff. See also G. Rill, "Jacobus Palaeologus (*ca.* 1520-1585). Ein Antitrinitarier als Schützling der Habsburger," *Mitteilungen* of the Österreichiches Staatsarchiv, XVI, 28-86; other studies quoted by L. Szczucki in "Jacob of Chios-Palaeologus: a Biographical Sketch" (Polish), *ORP*, XI, 63-91; and his *W kręgu myślicieli heretyckich* (In the Circle of Heretical Thinkers), pp. 11-121. It may be noted that, for some reason, Palaeologus left Poland and was later extradited by Emperor Rudolph II to Rome. Although on February 13, 1583, he marched in an auto-da-fé with two Portuguese and two Spanish Marranos and eleven other condemned, he was granted a reprieve after promising to write repentant letters to his former followers. Yet, ultimately, he was beheaded on orders of the Roman Inquisition in 1585. See L. von Pastor, *The History of the Popes*, XVI, 319; XIX, 302 ff., with an extensive bibliograpy (p. 303 n. 2).

77. Szymon Budny, *O urzędzie miecza używającym* (On the Office Using the Sword: a Confession of the Congregation of Lord Jesus), published in 1583, now available in a critical ed. by S. Kot (see esp, p. 37); A. Brückner, *Różnowiercy*, pp. 117 f.; Kot's biography of "Szymon Budny, der grösste Häretiker Litauens im 16. Jahrhundert," *Wiener Archiv für Geschichte des Slawentums und Osteuropas*, XI (1956 = Festschrift Felix Schmid, II), 63-118, esp. pp. 96 ff.; H. Merczyng, *Szymon Budny jako krytyk tekstów biblijnych* (S. B. as Critic of Biblical Texts), which reproduces many excerpts from Budny's trans. of the New Testament, as well as the methodologically significant dedicatory Preface. Budny was less critical of Old Testament passages, probably because he was less familar with Hebrew: on his translation he worked with a young assistant, probably a convert, since other Christian Hebraists refused to help him. But his restrained criticism made him doubly suspicious in the eyes of his opponents (pp. 46 ff.). Less controversial was the issue of resurrection and the immortality of the soul, although in his teachings on that subject, which included a denial not only of immortality but of the very existence of a soul, Grzegorz Paweł doubtless went beyond anything he may have learned from Jewish discussions thereon; see his *O prawdziwej śmierci, zmartwychstaniu i żywocie wiecznym Krystusa* (On True Death, Resurrection, and Immortality of Christ), in a facsimile of the first ed. reissued by K. Górski and W. Kuraszkiewicz; and, more generally, Górski's biography of *Grzegorz Paweł z Brzezin: monografja z dziejów polskiej literatury arjańskiej XVI wieku* (G. P. of B.: a Monograph on the History of the Polish Arian Literature of the Sixteenth Century), esp. pp. 230 ff. and 234 n. 2, which offer cogent arguments for Grzegorz Paweł's authorship of that tract. Certainly, Rej's generalization (in his *Zwierciadło*, II, 342) that all Unitarians denied the immortality of the soul, was unjustified.

78. K. Wilkowski, *Przyczyny nawrócenia*, extensively cited by A. Brückner in his *Różnowiercy*, pp. 158 ff., 164 f.; J. Płokarz, "Jan Niemojewski" (Polish), *Reformacja w Polsce*, II, 71-117, esp. p. 85 (also referring to the Russian "Judaizers" in 1567-

70 as to "the new Judaism, that is, the doctrine teaching not to invoke God's Son, [to observe] the Sabbath, and so forth; the wealthy Lublin merchant, Walenty Krawec, infected with Judaism in Hungary and Lithuania, and the Muscovite Esajaz, one of the seven Orthodox priests who had accepted 'the light of the Gospel' and therefore had to leave Moscow. In this fashion these two men have wrought much harm to the Lublin congregation"); the Pinczów declaration of 1562, reproduced by J. Domański and L. Szczucki in their "Miscellanea Arianica" in L. Chmaj *et al., Studia z dziejów ideologii religijnej XVI i XVII wieku* (Studies from the History of the Religious Ideology of the Sixteenth and Seventeenth Centuries = *Archiwum historii filozofii*, VI), with an English summary, pp. 199–288, esp. p. 214; L. Chmaj, *Bracia polscy*, pp. 25 ff. (a succinct summary of Bieliński's life, including the story of his ultimate return to the Calvinist mainstream and of his death, as a broken man, in 1591); E. M. Wilbur, *A History of Unitarianism*, Vol. I: Socinianism and Its Antecedents, pp. 265–482. On the impact of Polish exiles on other European countries, particularly Holland, see *ibid.,* pp. 483 ff., 535 ff.

Even if we were to believe the assertion of an unscrupulous Jesuit polemist about Budny's last moments, we could not consider this outstanding leader of the Vilna Anti-Trinitarians a full-fledged Jew. According to the Jesuit Szczęsny Zebrowski (M. Łaszcz) in his *Recepta na Plastr Czechowica* (Rejoinder to Czechowic' *Plaster* [a Critique of Jakub Wujek]), "when on his deathbed Budny was asked what he thought of Christ, he replied that just as in his lifetime he had thought very little of him, he now held him in even less esteem. He thus died a Jew." Extensively cited by Brückner, pp. 118 f., 192 f. Quite apart from the general tendency among warring Christian factions to accuse each other of judaizing, this situation somewhat resembled that of the Iberian Marranos. From the point of view of the Church, anyone secretly observing certain Jewish rituals or cherishing specific Jewish beliefs was considered a judaizing heretic, or even an apostate. But for the Jews the fulfillment of several requirements of Jewish law was a precondition for any proselyte's admission to the Jewish community. See *supra*, Vol. XIII, pp. 348 ff. n. 19. Despite these essential differences, many pious Catholics felt free to dismiss the Protestant churches by simply calling them "synagogues." See the reiterated use of this term by Count Albrycht Stanisław Radziwiłł in his important Memoirs, although some members of that leading family still openly professed a Protestant faith. See his *Memoriale rerum gestarum in Polonia, 1632–1656*, ed. by A. Przyboś and R. Żelewski, III, 27, 37, etc.

79. B. Ulanowski, ed., *Acta Capituli Plocensis, 1514–1577*, ad 1539, 1550–51, etc.; the full documentation of the governmental correspondence in E. Zivier's "Jüdische Bekehrungsversuche im 16. Jahrhundert," *Philippson Festschrift*, pp. 96–113; and Marcin Bielski's *Chronicle* cited *supra*, n. 46; and Vol. XIII, pp. 223, 425 n. 20. See also W. Sobieski, "Jewish Propaganda in the 1530s and 1540s" (Polish), *Przegląd Narodowy*, XXI, 24–42; M. Mieses, "Judaizers in Eastern Europe I–VI" (Polish), *MZ*, III, Part 2, 41–62, 169–85; IV, Part 1, 147–59, 241–60, 342–58, 566–76. Anti-Trinitarians, too, were often accused of harboring treasonable pro-Turkish sentiments. In his 1597 attack on Czechowic, the Jesuit Szczęsny Zebrowski recklessly stated: "Your Arian elders formerly delivered Greece and Constantinople to the Turks. Now you pursue the same goal . . . and wish to deliver the Polish Kingdom to them." Cited by A. Brückner in *Różnowiercy*, p. 118.

That there were indeed various degrees of conversion was also demonstrated by a lady of high social standing, Elżbieta Mielecka. Daughter of the outstanding Polish magnate of Lithuania Mikołaj Radziwiłł, she was married to a general of the Crown and palatine of Podole. Yet, because of her association with various Protestant groups, we are told, "she fell into such confusion that she did not know what to believe. She moved from Calvinism to the Arian confession, and finally adopted even the errors of Judaism." She allegedly learned to recite the entire Old Testament by heart. Only the persuasive powers of the Catholic father Benedykt Herbest brought her back to her ancestral faith. See M. J. A. Rychcicki (M. Dzieduszycki), *Piotr Skarga i jego wiek* (P. S. and His Period), I, 178; Mieses, IV, 256. See also J. Juszczyk's judicious analysis "On Studies about Judaizantism" (Polish), *KH*, LXXVI, 141–51. While mainly concerned with developments in Muscovy, and rightly rejecting the skepticism voiced by some Russian scholars, about the judaizing movement there, Juszczyk mentions certain Polish ramifications of that movement, particularly those introduced by the sectarian Feodozy (Theodosius) Kosy after his arrival in Volhynia in 1575.

In many cases, however, the individuals concerned did not even pretend to be formal Judaizers. In 1471 one Stanisław Gandek of Pultusk (northeast of Warsaw) was cited by an ecclesiastical court for having uttered the heretical views that "the priest does not prepare the true body of Christ [the host] but rather a demon, . . . that the Blessed Virgin Mary had conceived and borne a child like any other woman . . . and that the faith of the Jews was superior to that of the Christians." Despite Gandek's vigorous denials, he was sentenced to imprisonment and penance. But no one seems to have accused him of having gone beyond such verbal "blasphemies," by undergoing circumcision or practicing any Jewish rituals. See the text reproduced by Louis Lewin in his brief note, bearing the somewhat misleading title "Judaisieren im mittelalterlichen Polen und Russland," *MGWJ*, XLIX, 744–45.

80. Hans (Johann) Dernschwam, *Tagebuch einer Reise nach Konstantinopel und Kleinasien 1553–55*, ed. with notes by F. Babinger (Studien zur Fuggergeschichte, VII), p. 106; M. Mieses in *MZ*, IV, 157 f.; Stanisław Reszka (Rescius), *De atheismis et phalarismis evangelicorum*, Naples, 1596, cited by A. Brückner in his *Różnowiercy*, p. 146. Clearly, as a pupil of Stanisław Hosius, the leader of the Polish Counter Reformation, Reszka is a biased reporter. Yet his anecdote concerning Lewan's burial (cited in the next paragraph of the text) may indeed have been a genuine product of Polish folklore. We recall the persistent rabbinic advice regarding proselytism, summarized in the pithy talmudic epigram that "the right hand should repel, while the left hand should attract" all would-be candidates for conversion. Polish Jewry generally adhered to this principle. The two Councils and individual rabbis alike often counseled extreme caution in admitting proselytes, lest the Jewish community at large be embroiled in serious conflicts with the Polish government and society. Some later rabbis went so far as to require proof of Jewish origin, especially in certain marital cases. See, for instance, Hillel b. Naphtali Herz in his *Beth Hillel* (The House of Hillel; a commentary on Joseph Karo's *Shulḥan 'Arukh*), on E.'E. This subject will be more fully elucidated in a later chapter.

81. M. Czechowic, *Odpis*, p. 31, cited by J. Rosenthal in his "Marcin Czechowic," *PAAJR*, XXXIV, 87; Viktor von Carben, *De vita et moribus Judaeorum*, Cologne,

1504 (?); 2d ed., 1509; also appended to his *Opus aureum et nouum et a doctis viris diu expectatum*, with an Intro. by Ortuinus Gratius, Cologne, 1509; Johann Pfefferkorn, *Der Handspiegel gegen Reuchlin's Gutachten zugunsten des Talmud*, Cologne, 1511; Antonius Margarita, *Der Gantz Jüdisch Glaub*, Augsburg, 1530. The three inveterate polemists against Judaism were, of course, special pleaders. So was Ortuinus Gratius (Ortuin de Graes), who had a major share in the composition of Carben's and Pfefferkorn's pamphlets. See H. Graetz's *Geschichte*, 4th ed., IX, 65 ff., 477 ff. Note 2; and *supra*, Vol. XIII, pp. 182 ff., 223 ff., 407 f. n. 28, 426 f. n. 21. Undeniably, some secret proselytes may have escaped detection in Poland-Lithuania. This country had no effective inquisitorial court to investigate rumors and denunciations, and before the onset of the Counter Reformation even the bishops were more imbued with greed than with religious zeal (according to the irate report by the papal nuncio Giovanni Francesco Commendone in 1564). Nevertheless, the number of full-fledged proselytes apparently was never very large.

82. Isaac b. Abraham of Troki, *Ḥizzuq Emunah* (Faith Strengthened), I, xlvi, in Johann Christoph Wagenseil's ed. of *Tela Ignea Satanae*, Altdorf, 1681, Part III, pp. 61–480, esp. pp. 375 f. (Hebrew and Latin); also in later editions and translations into German by D. Deutsch, and into English by M. Mocatta. Remarkably, according to a leading Protestant pastor, Johann Müller of Hamburg, manuscripts of Troki's apologetic work were circulating in Hebrew, as well as in Spanish and German translations, within half a century after the author's death in 1594. A German translation prepared by a convert, Michael Gelling, in 1631, is still extant in the Hamburg Municipal Library today. It was on the basis of such manuscripts that Müller undertook to answer, in 1644, some of the Karaite controversialist's strictures against the New Testament. His reply, however, entitled *Judaeismus und Judenthumb, das ist ausführlicher Bericht von des jüdischen Volcks Unglauben, Blindheit und Verstockung*, Hamburg, 1644 (2d ed., Hamburg, 1707), merely brought the work of the Karaite apologist to the attention of Christian intellectuals. See G. Müller, "Christlich-jüdisches Religionsgespräch im Zeitalter der protestantischen Orthodoxie. Die Auseinandersetzung Johann Müllers mit Isaak Trokis *Ḥizzuk Emuna*," *Glaube, Geist, Geschichte. Festschrift für Ernst Benz*, pp. 513–24. See also *supra*, n. 7. The work of this influential defender of Judaism, his courageous assault on the Christian Gospels, as well as his familiarity with the writings of such radical Christian reformers as Szymon Budny and Marcin Czechowic, will be more fully analyzed here in the context of the Jewish apologetical literature of the period.

83. Moses b. Israel Isserles, *Resp.*, Jerusalem, 1970 ed., p. 417 No. 95; Solomon b. Yeḥiel Luria, *Yam shel Shelomoh* (Solomon's Sea: Novellae on the Talmud) on Baba batra, x, 21; *supra*, Vol. XI, pp. 18 f., 294 f. n. 19. See also the similar contrast, between the attitudes of an average Pole and an ordinary German, drawn by Ḥayyim b. Bezalel in his *Viqquaḥ mayim ḥayyim* (Lively Debate: a commentary on Moses Isserles' *Torat ḥaṭat* [Law of the Sin Offering: a theological tract]), with additions by Elijah b. Israel, Amsterdam, 1711, V, 4. It is not surprising that the religious toleration in Poland in the second half of the seventeenth century amazed many contemporary observers. It has also been the subject of many investigations in modern times. See, for instance, J. Librach's aforementioned (n. 38) essay; J. Tazbir, "La Tolérance religieuse en Pologne au XVIe et XVIIe siècle," *La*

Pologne au XIIe Congrès internationale des Sciences Historiques, Warsaw, 1965, pp. 39-40; and, in the general European context, J. Lecler's chapter on "Poland, 'Refuge of Heretics' in the Sixteenth Century," in his *Histoire de la tolérance au siècle de la Réforme,* Vol. I; or in the English translation by T. L. Westow entitled *Toleration and the Reformation,* I, 407-423. To be sure, the Jews' status in medieval and early modern Europe could be affected as adversely by nationalist intolerance as it was by religious exclusiveness. In the sixteenth century, Polish national feeling made great strides. See J. Tazbir, "From Studies on Xenophobia in Poland in the Period of the Late Renaissance" (Polish), *PH,* XLVIII, 655-82, with Russian and French summaries; and other publications cited in his "Recherches sur la conscience nationale en Pologne au XVIe et XVIIe siècle," *APH,* XIV, 5-22. However, at least in sixteenth-century Poland-Lithuania, Jews, like Tatars, were treated primarily as religious rather than ethnic minorities, and as yet felt little of the impact of intolerant nationalism. See P. Dąbkowski, "National Tolerance in Old Poland" (Polish), *Studia lwowskie,* ed. by K. Badecki *et al.,* pp. 183-94.

CHAPTER LXVIII: POLAND-LITHUANIA ON A HIGH PLATEAU

1. See A. Śliwiński, *Jan Zamoyski, kanclerz i hetman wielki koronny* (J. Z., Chancellor and Generalissimo of the Polish Crown), also citing Montaigne's and Sixtus V's high evaluation of Stephen Báthory's reign (pp. 212 f.); H. Biaudet, *Sixte Quint et la candidature de Sigismond de Suède au trône de Pologne en 1587 d'après des documents inédits des archives secrètes du Saint-Siège;* K. Lepszy, *Walka stronnictw w pierwszych latach panowania Zygmunta III* (Partisan Struggles in the First Years of Sigismund III's Reign); and the literature listed *supra,* Chap. LXVII, esp. n. 40.

2. See A Brückner's *Dzieje kultury polskiej* (A History of Polish Culture), II, *passim.* The growth of Polish national consciousness was promoted, rather than impeded, by the prevailing toleration of ethnic diversity in the sixteenth century, although the masses of the Rus peasantry, as well as the majority of Lithuanians, generally resisted even the adoption of the Polish language as a medium of daily communication. See *supra,* Chap. LXVII, nn. 80 and 83. See also, more generally, J. Katz's extensive documentation, from contemporary Hebrew sources, in his *Exclusiveness and Tolerance: Studies in Jewish-Gentile Relations in Medieval and Modern Times.*

3. See E. Bałakier, *Sprawa kościoła narodowego w Polsce XVI wieku* (The Question of a National Church in Sixteenth-Century Poland); and some earlier studies, cited by G. Schramm in *Der Polnische Adel und die Reformation,* p. 200 n. 44. On the progress of the interchurch negotiations, and their partially successful conclusion in the Union of Brest, which ultimately was greatly to affect the fate of the Jewish communities in the Ukrainian areas, see the older, but still very informative, study by J. Pelesz, *Geschichte der Union ruthenischer Kirche mit Rom von den ältesten Anfängen bis auf die Gegenwart;* and O. Halecki's more recent review in his *From Florence to Brest (1439–1596).* See also W. Czermak, "The Problem of Equality of Rights of Schismatics and Catholics in Lithuania, 1432–1563" (Polish), *Rozprawy* of PAU Hist.-Phil. Section, XLIV, 349–405. On the early stirrings of Polish nationalism, a subject still insufficiently explored by modern historians, see, for instance, E. Maleczyńska, "From Studies in Nationalist Slogans in the Sources of the Hussite Period" (Polish), *PH,* XLIII, 60–82; J. Tazbir, "Recherches sur la conscience nationale en Pologne au XVIᵉ et XVIIᵉ siècle," *APH,* XIV, 5–22; and *supra,* Chap. LXVII, nn. 66 and 83.

4. See W. Urban, *Chłopi wobec reformacji w Małopolsce* (The Peasants' Attitude toward the Reformation in Little Poland in the Second Half of the Sixteenth Century), esp, pp. 130 ff., 209 ff., 265 f.; Świętosław Orzelski, *Interregni Poloniae libri* [octo], ed. by E. Kuntze, pp. 94 f., 384; J. Lecler, *Toleration and the Reformation,* II, 403; S. Kutrzeba and A. Przyboś, eds., *Akta sejmikowe,* I, 113 ff. No. xxviii (esp. pp. 118 f. Arts. 11–12), 207 ff., 211 Art. 7, 213 Art. 17, 386 ff.; *supra,* Chap. LXVII,

n. 38; and *infra*, n. 6. Regrettably, the numerical strength of the Protestant denominations in the various classes of the population under the reign of the respective monarchs has not yet been carefully investigated. Even with respect to the *szlachta*, the most active and articulate group in the population, we possess only unreliable estimates. Janusz Tazbir, one of the best-informed students of the Polish Reformation and Counter Reformation, mentions in passing ratios as diverse as 16 and 20–25 percent. See his popular biography of *Piotr Skarga*, p. 10. However, there is little doubt that even at the height of their religious propagandizing late in the sixteenth century, the Reform groups constituted a relatively small minority of the population. On the religion of the peasant masses, who constituted the majority of inhabitants in both parts of the monarchy, see also the more comprehensive picture presented by S. Czarnowski's "The Religious Culture of the Polish Rural Population" (Polish), reprinted in his *Dzieła* (Works), ed. by N. Assorodobraj and S. Ossowski, I, 88–107. Incidentally, Czarnowski, a lifelong progressive, also courageously raised his voice, in 1936, against the then frequent "Antisemitic Incidents in Schools of Higher Learning " (Polish), *ibid.*, V, 55–59.

5. See Stanisław Hozjusz (Hosius), *Opera omnia*, ed. by S. Reszka, II, 266 (also *ibid.*, pp. 247, 255); the comments thereon and on other passages by J. Lortz in his *Kardinal Stanislaus Hosius, Beiträge zur Erkenntnis der Persönlichkeit und des Werks*, esp. pp. 99 ff., 122 f.; J. Tazbir, "Polish Religious Controversialists in the Face of the Persecution of Anti-Trinitarianism in the Sixteenth Century" (Polish), *PH*, LIII, 717–29, with Russian and French summaries; and *infra*, n. 6. See also J. Lecler, *Toleration and the Reformation*, II, 392; Hozjusz' correspondence with Duke Albert of Prussia, ed. by E. M. Werniter in his *Kardinal Stanislaus Hosius, Bischof von Ermland und Herzog Albrecht von Preussen. Ihr Briefwechsel über das Konzil von Trient (1560–1562);* and the large additional bibliography listed by R. Pollak *et al.* in their *Piśmiennictwo polskie*, I (= *Bibliografia literatury polskiej. Nowy Korbut*, ed. by K. Budzyk *et al.*, II), pp. 266–73.

6. See Giovanni Andrea Caligari, *Epistolae et acta, 1578–1581*, ed. by L. Boratyński (Monumenta Poloniae Vaticana, IV), pp. 95 ff. No. 61, 209 ff. No. 115, 255 No. 133; Alberto Bolognetti, *Epistolae et acta 1581–1585*, compiled by Boratyński and ed. by E. Kuntze and C. Nanke (Monumenta Poloniae Vaticana, V–VII), esp. II (VI), 666 ff. No. 382. See also Bolognetti's request that King Stephen intervene to prevent the erection of a beautiful synagogue "in defiance of canonical prohibitions," *ibid.*, p. 451; C. Cesis's *Il Cardinale Alberto Bolognetti e la sua nunziatura di Polonia;* and, more generally, E. Rykaczewski, ed., *Relacye nuncjuszów apostolskisch* (The Reports of Apostolic Nuncios and Other Persons about Poland in the Years 1548–1690); and J. Brzeziński, "About the Concordates of the Holy See with Poland in the Sixteenth Century" (Polish), *Rozprawy* of PAU, Hist.-Phil. Section, XXX, 262–92 (with a documentary appendix, mainly dealing with the first decades of the 1500s), esp. pp. 271 ff., 284 ff.

The complicated story of the ecclesiastical censorship of the Babylonian Talmud from the thirteenth century on, its impact on the printing and preservation of that voluminous work, and the concession granted by the Council of Trent as expressed in the pertinent 1564 bull by Pope Pius IV have been discussed here in various connections. See esp. *supra*, Vols. IX, pp. 63 ff., 270 ff. nn. 11–16; XIV, pp. 19 ff., 310 ff. nn. 18–22; Chap. LXVII, n. 43; "The Council of Trent and Rab-

binic Literature" in my *Ancient and Medieval Jewish History: Essays,* ed. by
L. A. Feldman, pp. 353–71, 555–64. On the early editions of various talmudic
tractates in Cracow and Lublin, see Ḥ. D. Friedberg, *Ha-Defus ha-ʿibri be-Qraqa*
(Hebrew Printing in Cracow: Its Development from 1530 to Our Days), pp. 5 ff.;
idem, *Toledot ha-Defus ha-ʿibri be-Polaniah* (History of Hebrew Typography in
Poland), 2d ed. enlarged, esp. pp. 10 ff. The broader aspects of this phase of Polish
Jewry's cultural endeavor, and its peculiar implications for communal action, will
be analyzed in later chapters.

7. See J. Korewa, "Les Débuts de la Compagnie de Jésus en Pologne, 1549–1564,"
AHSI, XXXIV, 3–35; L. Piechnik, "The College of Braniewo in the Sixteenth
Century: a Study of the Beginnings of the Jesuit School System in Poland" (Polish),
Nasza Przeszłość, VII, 5–72, with a French summary; the various essays included in
that journal's four-hundredth anniversay issue commemorating the establishment
of the Jesuit Order in Poland, Vol. XX; A. Chruszczewski, "Les Ordres religieux
en Pologne au XVIIᵉ et au XVIIIᵉ s.," *Le Millénaire de catholicisme ·en Pologne—
Poland's Millennium of Catholicism,* pp. 119–25; A. Wojtkowski, "Données historiques sur l'enseignement catholique pour laïques," *ibid.,* pp. 461–97, esp. 466 ff.;
supra, Vol. XIII, pp. 76 f., 343 n. 14; the comprehensive history of the Polish Order
by S. Załęski entitled *Jezuici w Polsce* (Jesuits in Poland; also in an abridged one-
volume edition under the same title).

It is noteworthy that the aggressive drive of these newcomers evoked much resentment not only among the non-Catholics, who became its victims (we shall have
frequent occasions to refer to hostile encounters between Jews and Polish Jesuits),
but even among the Catholic clergy. See esp. J. Tazbir, *Literatura antyjezuicka w
Polsce* (Anti-Jesuit Literature in Poland, 1578–1625: an Anthology); and, from
another angle, idem, "The Sociopolitical Role of the Jesuits in Poland (1565–1660)"
(Polish) in his *Szkice z dziejów papiectwa* (Sketches from the History of the Papacy),
pp. 99–144.
It may also be noted that the Jesuits did not limit their activities to the nobles
and burghers, but often extended their work of indoctrination to the peasantry.
With respect to Little Poland, see the data marshaled by W. Urban in his *Chłopi
wobec reformacyi,* pp. 239 ff. See also S. Czarnowski's "The Catholic Reaction in
Poland at the End of the Sixteenth and the Beginning of the Seventeenth Century"
(Polish), reprinted in his *Dzieła,* II, 147–66; and W. Czapliński's "Grandeurs and
Miseries of the Catholic Church in Poland after the Council of Trent" (Polish),
ORP, XIV, 5–26 (pointing out that, through its vast landholdings, its seats in the
Senate, and so forth, the Polish hierarchy became deeply involved in economics and
politics and gradually lost its great spiritual élan of the early days of the Catholic
Restoration; however, these manifestations of spiritual weakness really came to the
fore only after 1650); the essays, ed. by J. Kłoczowski, *Kościół w Polsce* (The Church
in Poland), Vol II: Fifteenth through Eighteenth Centuries; with J. Tazbir's pertinent critical remarks in his "On the History of the Church in Poland" (Polish),
KH, LXXVIII, 647–56.

8. Jan Wielewicki, *Dziennik spraw Domu Zakonnego OO. Jezuitów u Św. Barbary
w Krakowie* (Diary relating to the Affairs of the Monastic House of the Jesuit
Fathers at the Church of St. Barbara in Cracow [from 1579 to 1629]), Vols. I–IV ed.
by J. Szujski *et al. (Scriptores rerum Polonicarum,* VII, X, XIV, XVII), I, 118;

Konrad Memmius (Jacobus Francus), *Relatio historica quinquennalis,* Wahrhaftige Besschreibung fuernehmer, denkwürdigen Geschichten, so sich innerhalb fünf Jahren, nemlich anno [15]90 bis auf [15]95 verlauffen sich zugetragen haben, Frankfort, 1599, pp. 46 ff., reproduced by R. Żelewski in his ed. of *Materjały do dziejów Reformacyi w Krakowie: Zaburzenia wyznaniowe* (Sources for the History of the Reformation in Cracow: Denominational Disturbances in the Years 1551–1598), pp. 181 ff. No. 250; the dispatch of the Nuncio Hannibal of Capua of January 1, 1587, cited by G. Schramm in *Der Polnische Adel und die Reformation,* pp. 284 ff. See also the older, but still valuable, study by A. Brückner, "Denominational Hatred under Sigismund III: a Behavioral and Literary Sketch" (Polish), *Przewodnik naukowy i literacki,* XXX, 403–418, 499–509, 595–610; and other publications reviewed by L. Hajdukiewicz in his "Survey of Investigations on the History of the Reformation and Counter Reformation in Poland in the Years 1939–1952" (Polish), *Reformacja w Polsce,* X, 150–214; *supra,* Chap. LXVII, n. 66.

9. Stephen's Psków (Pskov) decree of 1581, here cited from the English translation in J. Lecler's *Toleration and the Reformation,* II, 403 f.; Piotr Skarga, *Upominanie do Ewangelików* (Admonition to the Evangelicals and Other Non-Catholics), first published in 1592; idem, *Proces Konfoederaciey* (The Trial of the [Warsaw] Confederation), published in 1595; revised and enlarged in 1596 and called *Proces na Konfoederacyia* (on these titles see Skarga's *Dzieła. Spis bibliograficzny* [Works: a Bibliographical Listing], ed. by K. Otwinowski, pp. 18 f., 21 ff.); numerous other data cited by R. Pollak *et al.* in their compilation, *Piśmiennictwo polskie,* II (= K. Budzyk *et al., Bibliografia,* III; see *supra,* n. 5), pp. 236–45; J. Tazbir, *Piotr Skarga,* pp. 60 f., 66; T. Grabowski, *Piotr Skarga na tle katolickiej lieratury religijnej w Polsce wieku XVI* (P. S. Against the Background of the Catholic Religious Literature in Sixteenth-Century Poland, 1536–1612), p. 370. Needless to say, the Church tried to strengthen the force of its bans by various sanctions. See W. Wójcik, "The Prosecution of Those Who Disdain the Commandments and Remain under Ecclesiastical Penalties, as Practiced in Poland until 1565" (Polish), *Nasza Przeszłość,* XXV, 33–68. These provisions were further sharpened at the onset of the Catholic Restoration. But even then their implementation often left much to be desired.

10. Piotr Skarga, *Kazania sejmowe* (Diet Sermons), Sermon IV (see K. Otwinowski's remarks on Skarga's *Dzieła,* p. 25); A. Berga's French trans. entitled *Les Sermons politiques (Sermons de Diète, 1597),* pp. 104 ff., 109. The preacher certainly stirred the imaginaton of his patriotic listeners when he described Poland's greatness in the past, a greatness which, he contended, was entirely owing to the whole nation being united in its Catholic faith. He pointed, in particular, to the example set by Zbigniew Oleśnicki, who had suppressed the rebellious Confederation of Korczyn and had put to flight the Hussite dissenters. (Some readers of the published sermons undoubtedly also recalled Oleśnicki's strongly anti-Jewish stance; see *supra,* Vol. X, pp. 46 f., 323 n. 58.) It was such unity in thought and action, he also insisted, that had made possible the country's imperial expansion (at its height, under Báthory, Poland-Lithuania indeed covered an area twice that of France). Going further, Skarga claimed that Poland "had extended its boundaries from one sea to another [from the Baltic to the Black Sea]. It has made you so redoubtable to your neighbors that they dare not rise up against you." See Skarga's Second Sermon, devoted to "the love of one's fatherland" (in Berga's French trans., pp. 68 f.). Few of

his compatriots were inclined to challenge his confusing an unattainable national dream wth an accomplished reality.

11. Skarga, *Proces Konfoederaciey, passim;* idem, *Kazania sejmowe,* Sermon I (in Berga's French trans., pp. 50 f. and *passim*); J. Lecler, *Toleration and the Reformation,* p. 408. See also Skarga's uncritical acceptance of the anti-Jewish blood libel, cited *infra,* n. 25; and, more generally A. Berga, *Un Prédicateur de la Cour de Pologne sous Sigismond III, Pierre Skarga (1536-1612). Étude sur la Pologne du XVIᵉ siècle et le Protestantisme polonais,* which forms, together with Berga's very informative introduction to his trans. of *Les Sermons politiques,* a most significant contribution to Skarga research by a foreigner.

12. Adam Mickiewicz' famous Paris lectures of 1841–42, curiously published in the French original *after* their Polish and German versions, under the title *Les Slaves, cours professé au Collège de France (1841-1842),* esp. Lecture xl (II, 65 ff.; also largely reproduced by Berga in the Introduction to his trans. of Skarga's *Les Sermons politiques,* pp. 1 ff.; and in the Polish trans, by F. Wrotnowski, entitled *Literatura słowiańska wykładana w Kolegium Francuzkiem* [Slavic Literature Expounded in Lectures at the Collège de France], I, 503 ff., 577 f.); S. Windakiewicz, *Piotr Skarga,* Intro.; Tazbir, *Piotr Skarga,* pp. 192 ff. On Mickiewicz in Paris and his attitude toward Jews and Judaism at that time, see A. G. Duker, "The Mystery of the Jews in Mickiewicz's Towianist Lectures on Slav Literature," *The Polish Review,* VII, no. 3, pp. 40–66 (also reprint); idem, "Mickiewicz in Hebrew Translation" in W. Lednicki, ed., *Adam Mickiewicz in World Literature: a Symposium,* pp. 561–68; idem, "Adam Mickiewicz's Anti-Jewish Period: Studies in 'The Books of the Polish Nation and of the Polish Pilgrimage,' " in *Salo Wittmayer Baron Jubilee Volume,* ed. by S. Lieberman in association with A. Hyman, I, 311–43; A. Walicki, "Two Polish Messianists: Adam Mickiewicz and August Cieszkowski," *Oxford Slavonic Papers,* n.s. II, 77–105; and the literature listed therein. An example of the widespread adulation of the famed preacher, which persisted into the twentieth century, is offered by the essays ed. by J. Pawelski (like Skarga, a member of the Society of Jesus) in *Duch Skargi w Polsce Współczesnej* (Skarga's Spirit in Contemporary Poland: a Memorial Volume at the Celebration of the Four-Hundredth Anniversary of the Birth of Father Piotr Skarga in Warsaw, 1536–1936).

In his political sermons, the preacher referred to the Old Testament far more frequently than the New. Certainly, the fulminations of the ancient Israelitic prophets, especially Isaiah and Jeremiah, against their compatriots, and their desperate warnings about Israel's forthcoming downfall because of its religious transgressions, lent effective parallels to the conditions in Poland. In his patriotic admonitions, Skarga could also eloquently quote passages from the intertestamentary Apocrypha and Pseudepigrapha, particularly the Books of Maccabees. On his part in Wujek's Polish translation of the Bible and, more generally, on the impact of the Bible on the Polish letters of that period, see M. Kossowska, *Biblia w języku polskim* (The Bible in the Polish Language); W. Fallek, "The Influence of the Bible on Polish Poetry" (Polish), *MZ,* III, Part 2, pp. 287–88; and *supra,* Chap. LXVII, n. 63.

13. See J. Tazbir, *Państwo bez stosów* (A State without Stakes: Sketches from the History of Toleration in Sixteenth- to Eighteenth-Century Poland); Z. Tawicka, "A Projected Calvinist Marriage of Wladislaw IV" (Polish), *ORP,* XI, 93–100 (with a French summary); Johannes Crell (under the pseudonym Junius Brutus), *Vindiciae*

pro religionis libertate, 1637, reed. in Latin with a Polish trans. by I. Lechońska, and an Intro. and Notes by Z. Ogonowski (invoking among other precedents, the toleration of Sadducean and other sectarians by the ancient Jews; pp. 20 f.); J. Lecler, *Toleration and the Reformation*, pp. 418 ff.; K. E. J. Jorgensen, *Ökumenische Bestrebungen unter den polnischen Protestanten bis zum Jahre 1645; supra*, Chap. LXVII, n. 71. On the underground survival of small remnants of Anti-Trinitarians after 1658, see J. Tazbir, "Polish Crypto-Arianism" (Polish), *ORP*, X, 187–211.

To be sure, at the height of the Reformation, the Diets of 1562 and 1564 demanded the abolition of the time-honored exemption of the clergy from military service. But this agitation quickly abated, and even under Sigismund III, when Polish armies were fighting on many fronts, the gentry no longer demanded that priests participate in military expeditions, but only that they send substitutes with full equipment. See S. Grzeszczuk, "The Clergy's Participation in Military Campaigns in the Sixteenth and Seventeenth Centuries" (Polish), *ORP*, XIV, 26–57, with a French summary. However, many soldiers appreciated the spiritual consolation of religious services which were rendered to them in illness (and also after death) by local priests, if not yet by regular army chaplains. See G. Schramm's succinct observations on the "Nationale und soziale Aspekte des wiedererstarkenden Katholizismus in Posen (1564–1617)," *Festschrift . . . Percy Ernst Schramm*, II, 61–71, which, with minor variations, apply to other Polish provinces as well.

Quite different was the situation in Lithuania, with its relatively large and deeply entrenched Greek Orthodox population. See R. Krasauskas, "The Catholic Church in Lithuania in the Sixteenth and Seventeenth Centuries: the Causes of Its Decline and the Factors in Its Resurgence" (Lithuanian), *Suvažiavimo Darbal* (Rome) VI, 189–241; *supra*, n. 3; and some other studies briefly surveyed by J. Tazbir in his review article "Post-War Investigations on Religious Tolerance in Poland" (Polish), *PH*, LX, 554–61.

14. See *supra*, Chap. LXVII, n. 69; and Vol. X, pp. 33 f., 315 f. n. 40; *infra*, n. 15; Z. Chodyński, ed., *Synodus archidiocense gnenensis*, pp. 45 ff.; L. Lewin, *Die Landessynode der grosspolnishen Judenschaft*, pp. 38 f.; D. Avron, ed., *Pinqas ha-Ksherim shel Qehillat Pozna* (Acta electorum communitatis Judaeorum posnaniensium [1621–1835]), p. 9 No. 37; Eliezer b. Elijah Ashkenazi, *Ma'asei ha-Shem* (The Works of the Lord), The Hague, 1776, end; J. Perles, "Geschichte der Juden in Posen," *MGWJ*, XIII, 361 n. 1; A. Warschauer, *Geschichte der Stadt Gnesen*, esp. pp. 131 f., 172 ff.; J. Topolski, ed., *Dzieje Gniezna* (A History of Gniezno), esp. pp. 67 ff., 282. Topolski's computation that there were some 500 Jews in Gniezno in 1579 was based on the assumption that the capitation tax was paid by 110 heads of families, rather than individuals. See *infra*, n. 63; and Chap. LXX, nn. 88 ff. This assumption is somewhat controverted by the fact that there were only 30 Jewish houses in the city. Nor can we deduce such a figure from the size of the Jewish population (some 600–700 souls) two centuries later, any more than we can claim that, because in the late eighteenth century there were 53 Jewish and only 4 Christian tailors in the city, Jews formed a large segment of the local artisan class in 1579—a fallacious argument which Topolski himself rejects (pp. 271, 281 ff., 342, etc.).

15. See B. Baranowski and S. Herbst, "The Multinational Nobles' Commonwealth" (Polish) in T. Manteuffel, ed., *Historia Polski*, I, Part 2, pp. 416–565, esp. pp. 446 f.

It may be noted, however, that the crucial national Synod of Piotrków of 1589, which sharply denounced the tolerant provisions of the Warsaw Confederation of 1573 and thereby contributed to the Counter-Reformational campaign under Sigismund III, had little to say on the Jewish question as such. See M. Morawski's detailed analysis in his *Synod piotrkowski w roku 1589* (The Piotrków Synod in the Year 1589). Regrettably, the material pertaining to Jews in the Polish synodal legislation has never been fully assembled or carefully analyzed. J. Sawicki's comprehensive *Concilia Poloniae; żródła i stulya krytyczne* (The Polish Synods: Sources and Critical Studies), Vols. I–X of which appeared in 1945–63 (Vol. I in a 2d ed. revised in 1961), devotes each volume to a specific area and thus far has dealt only with certain Church provinces. See, for instance, V, 182 ff. (on the Gniezno Synod of 1580).

For a fuller understanding of the ecclesiastical attitudes, one should also consider whatever records are still preserved of the deliberations at the diocesan synods. According to an archiepiscopal ruling of 1406, such assemblies were to take place once a year. They also were to prepare data and formulate motions for the provincial synods. Yet little has been done about an investigation of these "grass-roots" convocations, despite a call to action sounded almost half a century ago by W. Abraham in his "From the History of Synodal Legislation of the Płock Diocese" (Polish) in *Księga pamiątkowa* (Memorial Volume . . .) *Oswald Balzer*, ed. by him *et al.*, I, 1–11. See also J. T. Sawicki's fine survey, "Geschichte und heutiger Stand der Vorarbeiten zur Gesamtausgabe der polnischen Synodal-Statuten," *Zeitschrift der Savigny-Stiftung für Rechtsgeschichte*, Kanonistische Abteilung, XLVI, 395–429. Except for Sawicki's own work, little progress has been made in this field in the years since the publication of this essay. We must still rely, therefore, on such older collections as B. Ulanowski *et al., Studia i materiały do historii ustawodawstwa synodalnego w Polsce* (Studies and Sources for the History of the Synodal Legislation in Poland), pertaining to the sixteenth and seventeenth centuries. See also other records listed in J. T. Sawicki's *Bibliographia synodorum particularium* (Monumenta iuris canonici, Ser. C: Subsidia, II), and the "Supplementum" thereto in *Traditio*, XXIV, 508–511. Of limited use also are the more specialized surveys by W. Padacz, "Jews in the Polish Synodal Legislation" (Polish) *Przegląd Katolicki*, LXXIV, 649–50, 666–67; and M. Morawski, "The Attitude of the Church toward the Jewish Peril in Old Poland" (Polish), *Ateneum kapłańskie*, XLI, 1–22, 115–36, esp. pp. 115 ff. Apart from their brevity, these essays have the disadvantage of having been written with the anti-Jewish bias characteristic of many Polish publications in the years preceding the outbreak of the Second World War. By way of contrast, as well as complementary information, we may also mention the *Akta synodów różnowierczych w Polsce* (Records of the Dissident Synods in Poland), of which Vol. I, covering the period 1550–59, ed. by M. Supałło, appeared in 1966. Needless to say, in other legislative activities concerning Jews, the Polish churchmen were restricted by the general principles regarding the treatment of the Jewish minority which had long before been laid down by the Papacy, ecumenical councils, leading theologians, and other organs of the Church Universal. However, as other provinces of the Church, the Polish and Lithuanian branches were able to adjust many requirements of general canon law to specific local conditions. On the Polish Church's general economic attitude, see also C. Bauer, "Rigoristische Tendenzen in der katholischen Wirtschaftsethik unter dem Einfluss der Gegenreformation," *Adel und Kirche. Festschrift für Gerd Tellenbach*, pp. 552–79.

16. Sigismund III's decree of 1592, reproduced by Z. Pazdro in his *Organizacya i praktyka żydowskich sądów podwojewodzińskich* (Organization and Practice of the Jewish Palatinate Courts), pp. 159 ff. No. 8 Art. iii; and again by M. Bałaban in his *Żydzi lwowscy*, Part II, pp. 34 ff. No. 33 Art. iii; Prince Władysław Ostrogski's ordinance of 1659 in L. Gumplowicz's *Prawodawstwo polskie względem Żydów* (The Polish Legislation Relating to Jews), pp. 113 ff. Art. V. See also other data reviewed by I. Lewin in *The Protection of Jewish Religious Rights by Royal Edicts in Ancient Poland* (reprinted from the *Quarterly Bulletin of the Polish Institute of Arts and Sciences*, April, 1943), esp. pp. 4 ff.

17. J. Szujski *et al.*, eds., *Dyarusze sejmów koronnych, 1548, 1553 i 1570* [roku] (Diaries of the Crown Diets of 1548, 1553, and 1570) (*Scriptores rerum polonicarum*, published by PAU, I), pp. 154 f.; H. Merczyng, *Zbory i senatorowie w dawnej Rzeczpospolitej* (Protestant Communities and Senators in the Old Polish Commonwealth), pp. 19, 138 f.; E. Barwiński, "Sigismund III and the Dissidents" (Polish), *Reformacja w Polsce*, I, 51–57; and other sources cited by G. Schramm in *Der Polnische Adel und die Reformation*, pp. 176 f., 300 ff. Apart from their activities within the Church and as legislators or administrators in public bodies, some churchmen also distinguished themselves as authors of juridical tracts. See E. Jarra's general survey of "The Juridical Creativity of the Polish Clergy (966–1800)" (Polish), *Sacrum Poloniae Millennium*, I, 253–390; and W. Sawicki, "Rôle de l'Église dans l'organisation et l'administration de l'État polonais avant les partages (966–1795)," *Le Millénaire du catholicisme en Pologne—Poland's Millennium of Catholicism*, pp. 555–88 (the expanded monograph on this subject, here promised, appeared in Polish, *ibid.*, III, 167–260).

Understandably, the great ecclesiastical influence on the country's legal enactments and practices aroused considerable opposition, not only among non-Catholics but also among such learned Catholic lay jurists as Kasper Siemek of Cracow, who wrote in 1632: "If men trained in priestly lore turn to public affairs, misfortune follows, and dishonesty as well as infidelity stem directly from it. . . . Seeking to ruin Poland and its liberty, the monks have assumed the guise of sanctity in order to instill greater fear among their neighbors." Cited in J. Bardach, ed., *Historia państwa i prawa Polski do roku 1795* (The History of the State and Law in Poland to the Year 1795), Vol. II: From the Middle of the Fifteenth Century to 1795, by Z. Kaczmarczyk and B. Leśnodorski, p. 275.

18. T. Wierzbowski, *Przywileje królewskiego miasta stołecznego Starej Warszawy* (Privileges of the Old Royal Capital Warsaw), pp. 86 ff. No. 76, 101 f. No. 85 (these privileges were reconfirmed by Wladislaw IV in 1633; *ibid.*, pp. 120 ff. No. 100); J. Shatzky, *Geshikhte fun Yidn in Varshe* (A History of the Jews in Warsaw), I, 45 ff.; J. Tazbir, *Piotr Skarga*, pp. 9 ff.; *supra*, Chap. LXVII, n. 14; I. Halperin, ed., *Pinqas Va'ad 'Arba Araṣot* (Acta Congressus Generalis Judaeorum Regni Poloniae (1580–1764) quae supersunt omnia cum deperditorum fragmentis et testimoniis), pp. 75 No. 196 (1640), etc.; S. M. Dubnow, ed., *Pinqas ha-Medinah* (The Minutes of the Lithuanian Council of Provinces: a Collection of Enactments and Decisions from 1623 to 1761, Published from a Grodno Manuscript, with Additions and Variants from Copies in Brest and Vilna, Ed. with an Intro. and Notes), pp. 3 No. 2 (1623), etc.; I. Schipper, "The 'Warsaw Committee': a Contribution to the History of Jewish Autonomy in Old Poland" (Polish), *Sefer ha-Yobel . . . Mordecai Ze'ev (Markus)*

Braude (Jubilee Volume in Honor of M. Z. B.), pp. 145–57. On Piotrków, see M. Feinkind's brief summary in his *Dzieje Żydów w Piotrkowie i okolicy* (A History of the Jews in Piotrków and Its Environs from the Earliest Period to the Present), pp. 3 ff.

Understandably, the Jewish leaders tried to prevent individual Jews acting in private capacity from negotiating with influential persons in Warsaw without consulting their official representatives. As early as 1623, the Lithuanian Council adopted a resolution that "no one shall go to the Warsaw Diet without the knowledge and written authorization of his local court," under severe physical and financial penalties. Dubnow, *Pinqas*, p. 9 No. 39. The workings of the Jewish "lobby" in Warsaw will be more fully discussed in a later volume.

19. Szymon Starowolski, *Accessus ad iuris utriusque cognitionem*, Cracow, 1633; idem, *Reformacja obyczajów polskich* (The Reform of Polish Customs), Cracow, 1636, new ed., Cracow, 1859; the remarks thereon by Z. Kaczmarczyk and B. Leśnodorski in J. Bardach's ed. of *Historia państwa i prawa Polski*, II, 279 f.; Józef Bartłomiej Zimorowicz, *Leopolis triplex* or *Kronika miasta Lwowa* (A Chronicle of the City of Lwów), first published in M. Piwocki's Polish trans.; and then in the Latin original in *Pisma do dziejów Lwowa* (Writings relating to the History of Lwów), ed. by K. J. Heck. Heck also published "Sources for a Biography of Józef Bartłomiej Zimorowicz (Ozimek)," Part I (Polish), *Archiwum do dziejów literatury i oświaty w Polsce*, VIII, 161–240; and a general biography of *Józef Bartłomiej Zimorowicz* (J. B. Z., Burgomaster, Poet, and Chronicler of Lwów). Zimorowicz's work was continued by the equally anti-Jewish Catholic priest Jan Tomasz Józefowicz. See L. Charewiczowa, *Historiografia i miłośnictwo Lwowa* (Lwów's Historiography and Amateur Writings). Clearly, the contribution of Polish Historiography, local and general, to the shaping of the public's attitude toward Jews and Judaism in prepartition Poland merits detailed monographic treatment.

20. Sebastyan Miczyński, *Zwierciadło Korony polskiej. Urazy ciężkie i utrapienia wielkie, które ponosi od Żydów* (A Mirror of the Polish Crown. Suffering Heavy Insults and Great Mortification from Jews), Cracow, 1618; Sebastyan Śleszkowski, *Jasne dowody* (Clear Proof that Those Who, Contrary to the Prohibitions of the Holy Catholic Church, Use Jews, Tatars, and Other Infidels as Physicians . . . Endanger not only Their Souls, but also Their Bodies), Cracow, 1623; Przecław Mojecki, *Żydowskie okrucieństwa, mordy i zabobony* (Jewish Cruelties, Murders, and Superstitions), Cracow, 1589, 1598, etc.: Sigismund III's order to confiscate Miczyński's book reproduced in M. Bersohn's *Dyplomataryusz dotyczący Żydów w dawnej Polsce* (Documents Relating to Jews in Old Poland), pp. 124 ff. No. 219 (recognizing the legitimacy of the complaint by the Jewish community that Miczyński's work was liable to incite the people to violence against the Jews, "so that they are no longer secure with respect to their lives and possessions"); the observations on all these works by M. Bałaban in his *Dzieje Żydów w Krakowie*, pp. 124 ff., 288 f.; *supra*, Vol. X, pp. 35 f., 316 f. n. 43; and, more generally, K. Bartoszewicz, *Antysemityzm w literaturze polskiej XV–XVII w.* (Antisemitism in Polish Literature in the Fifteenth through Seventeenth Centuries).

These blatantly Jew-baiting works were but a part of the large polemical and apologetic literature published by Catholic spokesmen in defense of their own faith. More frequently, anti-Jewish polemics were incidentally inserted into attacks on infidels in general or on Anti-Trinitarians in particular, because of their alleged Judaistic leanings. See, for instance, J. Tazbir, "Polish Religious Controversialists" (Polish), *PH*, LIII, 717–29; and, more generally, the essays assembled by L. Chmaj *et al.* in *Studia z dziejów ideologii religijnej XVI i XVII wieku; supra*, Chap. LXVII, n. 78.

21. See, for instance, the brief sixteenth-century *Dialog o męce Pana naszego* (Dialogus de passione Domini nostri), reproduced in J. Lewański's *Dramaty staro-polskie, antologia* (Old Polish Dramas: an Anthology), II, 269–84, in which Judas and the archisynagogus play prominent roles. See also *ibid.*, IV, 137 ff., 169 ff., 269 ff., 296 ff.; VI, 9 ff., 59 ff., 90 ff., 175 ff.; and, more generally, S. Windakiewicz's brief surveys of "Le Drame dévotieux en Pologne," *Bulletin international* of PAU, 1893, pp. 190–91; idem, "Le Théâtre populaire dans l'ancienne Pologne," *ibid.*, 1901, pp. 157–63; idem, "Le Drame liturgique en Pologne au moyen âge," *ibid.*, 1902, pp. 62–64; and, more fully, J. Lewański's various other publications, esp. his *Średniowieczne gatunki dramatyczno-teatralne* (Medieval Genres of Theatrical Dramas), under the editorship of M. R. Mayenowa, Parts 1: The Liturgical Drama; and 3: Misterium; and his *Studia nad dramatem polskiego Odrodzenia* (Studies in the Drama of the Polish Renaissance), esp. pp. 104 ff., 114, 171 ff., 175 f., 202 ff., 205 f., 216 ff.; W. Schenk, "Aus der Geschichte der Liturgie in Polen," *Le Millénaire du catholi-cisme en Pologne—Poland's Millennium of Catholicism*, pp. 145–221. On the painter of the Poznań murals, and the community's protest against this public incitation to Jew-hatred, see J. Łukaszewicz, *Obraz historyczno-statystyczny miasta Poznania* (The Historical-Statistical Image of the City of Poznań in Times Past), I, 86 ff.; J. Perles, "Geschichte der Juden in Posen," *MGWJ*, XIII, 417 f.

Characteristically, we hear of no similar protests by Jews against the public liturgical performances, which were imbued with an equally strong anti-Jewish bias. Possibly because the Jews respected anything connected with the religious services of other faiths, they raised no objection to these likely sources of public disturbance. At the same time, none of the extant records suggest that attacks on Jews resulted directly from these dramatic performances in Poland. Nor do we hear, on the other hand, of sympathetic chords struck in the hearts of worshipers during the annual recitation of the traditional Catholic prayer *Pro perfidis Judaeis*. See *supra*, Vol. V, pp. 351 f. n. 68. This entire subject, and particularly its connection with the rising tide of religious intolerance in the seventeenth century, merit a more detailed and dispassionate examination.

We must bear in mind, however, that not all early modern Polish plays exhibited anti-Jewish sentiment. In Piotr Baryka's secular drama *Z chłopa król, komedyja dworska* (A Peasant Turned King: a Court Comedy), Cracow, 1637, and in the religious *Dialogus na święto Narodzenia* (Dialogus pro festo Nativitatis) of the mid-seventeenth century, the Jew actually appears as a pitiable victim of blackmail—in one case, by an official; in the other, by a student. See the texts in J. Lewański's *Dramaty*, IV, 137 ff., 169 ff., 269 ff., 296 ff. Even in the play *Świat na opak wywrócony* (The World Turned Upside Down), written by the priest Deodat Nersesowicz in 1663, the Jew is depicted only as taking a *kozubales* (*kozubalec*), or ransom money, from a student, rather than vice versa. *Ibid.*, VI, 417 ff., 422 f. In contrast, a popular anonymous pamphlet, *Kozubales abo Obrona wszystkich żydów* (K., or, The Defense of All Jews), first published in 1626, and republished in 1630, 1641, and 1683, served, through both its bold red and black title page and its general content, to whip up anti-Jewish feeling. See the reproduction in K. Badecki's *Literatura mieszczańska w Polsce XVII wieku* (Poland's Bourgeois Literature in the Seventeenth Century: a Bibliographical Monograph). With a Foreword by A. Brückner, pp. 169–75 (includes an extensive bibliography). At the same time, the burgeoning Polish novel of the sixteenth and seventeenth centuries concentrated on daily human relations, particularly of an amorous nature, but seems to have been little used for propagandistic purposes. Perhaps the impact of Giovanni Boccaccio's *Decameron* and the contemporary French novel made the authors of fiction avoid dealing with controversial political and religious problems. See, for instance, T. Kruszewska-Michałowska's analysis in *"Różne Historyje"* (Various Stories: a Study in the History of the Old Polish Novel), esp. pp. 63 ff., showing its generally moralistic, rather than denominationally oriented, content.

22. B. Baranowski and S. Herbst, "The Achievement of Supremacy by the Oligarchy and the Struggle for Livonia (1576–1609)" (Polish), in T. Manteuffel's ed. of *Historia Polski* (A History of Poland), I, Part 2, pp. 495–525, esp. pp. 521 f.; M. Bałaban, *Dzieje Żydów w Krakowie*, I, 82 ff., 104, 125 f., 132 f.; R. Żelewski, "Denominational Disturbances," *ORP*, VI, 91 ff.: J. Perles, "Geschichte der Juden in Posen," *MGWJ*, XIII, 416 ff., 449 f., etc.; *supra*, Chap. LXVII, n. 66.

23. M. Bałaban, *Dzieje*, I, 122 ff., and 132; idem, *Die Judenstadt von Lublin*, p. 12; idem, *Żydzi lwowscy*, pp. 492 ff.; Part 2, p. 135 No. 104 (reproducing the text of Wladislaw IV's decree of 1638 ordering the detection and punishment of the instigators of the Lwów disturbances of that year); S. M. Dubnow, ed., *Pinqas ha-Medinah*, pp. 70 No. 335, 79 No. 390; J. Ptaśnik, *Obrazki z życia żaków krakowskich w XV i XVI wieku* (Sketches from the Life of Cracow's Students in the Fifteenth and Sixteenth Centuries), esp. pp. 10 ff., 46 ff.; and other literature listed *supra*, Chap. LXVII, n. 65. According to Ptaśnik, riots against Jews and Protestants recurred annually from 1574 on. The government tried to stem such excesses by prohibiting the unauthorized bearing of arms. But these prohibitions proved ineffectual; they could not even prevent attacks of students upon one another, or upon Catholic burghers. The tribute to stem student violence was often paid to the teachers. For example, in Wschowa (Fraustadt), the Jewish community gave 20 thalers and two expensive pieces of clothing to the local priest Grabowski. See L. Lewin, *Die Landessynode*, p. 85 No. 41.

Despite—or perhaps because of—the strangeness of the term, the *kozubalec* became the subject of the aforementioned "best-selling" pamphlet, *Kożubales abo Obrona wszystkich Żydów* (in its 1641 edition more explicitly reading: To Whom the Kozubales Is To Be Paid and to Whom Not). See K. Badecki, *Literatura mieszczańska w Polsce*, pp. 169 ff.; with some additional bibliografical data in his *Nieodszukane pierwodruki literatury mieszczańskiej w Polsce XVII wieku* (Undetected First Prints of the Bourgeois Literature of the Seventeenth Century; reprinted from *Pamiętnik literacki*, XXII–XXIII), pp. 21 f. No. 27. See also the pertinent responsum by R. Joshua Heschel b. Joseph cited *supra*, Chap. LXVII, n. 66. The frequency of attacks on Jews in various cities in Poland is well illustrated by the brief summary in R. Mahler's *Toledot ha-Yehudim be-Polin*, pp. 181 f.

24. See *supra*, Vol. X, pp. 290 ff., 430 nn. 84–85; XIV, pp. 76 f., 104 f., 334 f. n. 5, 344 f. n. 34; W. Urban, *Chłopi wobec reformacji w Małopolsce*, pp. 209 ff. On Raków,

its role in the Anti-Trinitarian movement, and its destruction after the death of Sigismund, who had repeatedly resisted its violent suppression, see the essays ed. by S. Cynarski, *Raków ognisko arianizmu* (R. the Focus of Arianism), esp. pp. 49 ff. and 195 ff.; J. Tazbir, "The Destruction of the Arian Capital" (Polish), *ORP*, VI, 113–38; and *supra*, Chap. LXVII, nn. 72 ff.

25. Piotr Skarga, *Żywoty świętych* (The Lives of the Saints), Vilna, 1579; D. Avron, ed. *Pinqas ha-Ksherim*, p. 40 No. 199; M. Bałaban, *Dzieje*, I, 82, 123, 132 ff., 137 ff., etc.; idem, *Die Judenstadt von Lublin*, pp. 33 f. (Maciejowski's printed "report," mentioned by Bałaban without a source reference, appears dubious; it apparently was not seen by K. Estreicher [see his *Bibliografia polska*, XXII, 11 f.], nor is it alluded to by his biographers, J. Dziegelski and J. Maciszewski, in their brief sketch, "Maciejowski, Bernard," in *Polski Słownik Biograficzny*, XIX, 48–52); Bałaban, "Episodes from the History of Ritual Murder Trials and the Anti-Jewish Literature in Poland in the Sixteenth–Eighteenth Centuries" (Russian), *ES*, VII, 163–81, 318–27; P. Mojecki, *Żydowskie okrucieństwa, passim*; L. Lewin, *Die Landessynode*, p. 44; *supra*, Vols. X, pp. 35 f., 316 f. n. 43; XI, pp. 146 ff., 358 ff.; Chap. LXVII, n. 43; and in many other contexts.

26. See Aloisio Lippomano's aforementioned letter to Stanisław Golański of 1556, reproduced by E. Rykazewski in his ed. of *Relacye nuncyuszów apostolskich*, I, 59 f. (*supra*, Chap. LXVII, n. 42); J. Dworzaczkowa, "Counter Reformation in Wschowa [Fraustadt] in the Years 1577 to 1632" (Polish), *Roczniki historyczne*, XXXVI, esp. p. 9. See also, more generally, *supra*, Vol. XI, pp. 164 ff., 367 ff. nn. 54–60. Nor is it surprising that these churchmen were so prone to believe confessions obtained under torture. We must not forget that the confessions of alleged culprits had long played a decisive role in inquisitorial trials and the Church's other judicial proceedings. To the literature cited *supra*, Vol. XIII, pp. 39 ff., 324 ff. nn. 41 ff., add J. Uhrmann's recent study, *Das Geständnis im kanonischen Prozess*.

Curiously, even the Polish Protestants were not completely immune from the belief in Jewish ritual murders. In 1637, in the period of greatest danger from Counter-Reformational repression, Krzysztof Słupecki de Conary, a prominent Protestant lay dignitary, asked Gerhard Johann Vos (Vossius) what he thought about alleged Jewish murders of Christian children, and added: "I do not know whether it ever was sufficiently proved." However, shaken by the Lublin affair of the preceding year (in which a Jewish surgeon, Mordecai b. Meir, was accused by a monk of having drawn too much blood for ritual use when administering a bloodletting, and was executed), the Polish aristocrat sought advice from Vos. We recall that the Amsterdam humanist, though expressing the wish that all Jews be converted to Christianity, discounted the likelihood of ritual murder, as did his friend Hugo Grotius. See Gerhard Johann Vos (Vossius), *Epistolae et clarorum virorum ad eum epistolae*, comp. by P. Colomesius, Augsburg, 1691, I, 229 No. 185; II, 181 f. No. 250; M. Bałaban, "Hugo Grotius und die Ritualmordprozesse in Lublin (1636)," *Festschrift Simon Dubnow*, pp. 87–112, esp. pp. 110 ff. App. i–ii; *supra*, Vol. XV, pp. 62, 406 n. 73; and, on the Lublin Blood Accusation, see Bałaban, *Die Judenstadt von Lublin*, pp. 34, 105 n. 3 on Chap. IV.

27. See the literature cited *supra*, n. 25; I. Halperin, *Pinqas Va'ad*, pp. 71 f. No. 193; [Moritz Stern,] comp., *Die Päpstlichen Bullen über die Blutbeschuldigung*, 2d

ed., pp. 123, 134 ff.; C. Roth, ed., *The Ritual Murder Libel and the Jews. The Report of Cardinal Lorenzo Ganganelli (Pope Clement XIV)*; L. Lewin, *Die Landessynode*, pp. 45, 57; J. Dworzaczkowa, "Counter Reformation in Wschowa" (Polish), *Roczniki historyczne*, XXXVI, 1–42, with a French summary. Small as the Wschowa Jewish community was—the city as a whole was then the third largest in Great Poland—it played a considerable role in the western trade of Poznań Jewry. It therefore appears rather frequently in the Poznań community's minute book. See D. Avron, ed., *Pinqas ha-Ksherim, passim*. See also Hugo Moritz, "Die Älteste jüdische Niederlassung in Fraustadt," *Historische Monatsblätter für die Provinz Posen*, II, 179–84; idem, *Reformation und Gegenreformation in Fraustadt*.

28. See M. J. A. Rychcicki (M. Dzieduszycki), *Piotr Skarga i jego wiek* (P. S. and His Period; listing biographical studies of Skarga by his contemporaries and early successors), I, 179; J. Tazbir, *Piotr Skarga*, pp. 25 f.; and, more generally, M. Mieses, "Judaizers in Eastern Europe I–VI" (Polish), *MZ*, III–IV, esp. IV, 255 ff.; E. Zivier, "Jüdische Bekehrungsversuche im 16. Jahrhundert," *Philippson Festschrift*, pp. 96–113; *supra*, Chap. LXVII, n. 79. A case similar to that of Elżbieta Mielecka was recorded by the Muscovite sectarian Feodozy Kosy after his arrival in Volhynia in 1575. There he met Princes Anna Korecka who, in her religious quest, gradually moved from Calvinism to Anabaptism, then to Judaizantism, and finally embraced the Rusian Orthodox faith. See J. Juszczyk, "In Studies about Judaizantism" (Polish), *KH*, LXXVI, 147. In contrast to some other historians, Juszczyk clearly distinguishes between "Judaizantism" (that is, the adoption of certain Jewish beliefs and practices) and full-fledged Judaism. Such half-Jews remind one of the ancient *sebomenoi* or *metuentes* (God-fearing Gentiles), about whom see *supra*, Vols. I, 284, 415 n. 41; II, 149 f., 388 n. 29; and Chap. LXVII, n. 79.

29. See *supra*, Chap. LXVII, n. 82; S. M. Dubnow, *Pinqas ha-Medinah*, p. 13 No. 69; D. Avron, *Pinqas ha-Ksherim*, p. 16 No. 81. See also, more generally, I. Sosis, "Social Conflicts in the Jewish Communities of the Sixteenth and Seventeenth Centuries according to the Rabbinic Responsa" (Yiddish), *Zeitschrift* (Minsk), I, 225–38; idem, "The Jewish Council in Lithuania and Belorussia in Its Legislative Activity" (Yiddish), *ibid.*, II–III, 1–72 (consisting largely of excerpts from long-known sources); and *infra*, n. 86. On the Christian censorship of all books published in Polish or Latin, see J. Dużyk, "From the History of Censorship in Cracow in the Fifteenth through Eighteenth Centuries" (Polish), *Roczniki* of the Library of the Polish Academy, II, 375–411. The various aspects of Jewish communal and literary defenses against anti-Jewish attacks, as well as of the self-discipline imposed by Jewish communities upon its members, will be dealt with in the context of other Jewish communal and intellectual activities in later volumes.

30. See Rodolphus Agricola the Younger's letter to the Viennese humanist Vadian, cited by Z. Wojciechowski in his *Zygmunt Stary*, p. 116; and *supra*, Chap. LXVII, n. 4. The process of Polonization proceeded most rapidly in Little Poland, Red Russia, and Lithuania. The farther east a city was located, the more the original German colonizers were confronted by an influx of other ethnic elements, from the Eastern lands, as well as from the Polish-Lithuanian countryside. The greater distances from Germany likewise tended to reduce the impact of German culture.

31. See *infra*, Chap. LXIX, nn. 3–4 and *passim; supra*, Chap. LXVII, n. 9; A. Jabłonowski, *Źródła dziejowe* (Historical Sources), XII, 379; P. A. Mukhanov, *Sbornik* (Documentary Collection), 2d ed., pp. 112 ff. Doc. No. 115. According to an obscure reference by the Kiev bishop Józef Wereszczyński, Jews had been expelled from Kiev at one time because of a Blood Accusation, although he admitted that in his day (he served as bishop in 1581–98) there were many Jews in the Ukrainian capital. See his *Sposób osady nowego Kijowa* (The Method of Settlement in New Kiev and the Defense of the Former Capital of the Duchy of Kiev), Cracow, 1595; reproduced in his *Pisma polityczne* (Political Writings), ed. by K. J. Turowski, p. 38; F. Rawita-Gawroński, *Żydzi w historji i literaturze ludowej na Rusi* (Jews in the History and Popular Literature of the Ukraine), pp. 62 ff. See also J. Brutzkus, "Der Handel der westeuropäischen Juden mit dem alten Kiew," *ZGJD*, III, 97–110; I. N. Darewski, *Le-Qorot ha-Yehudim be-Kiev* (Contribution to the History of the Jews in Kiev); *supra*, Vol. III, pp. 213 ff., 217, 337 f. n. 56.

32. B. Baranowski and S. Herbst, "The Multinational Nobles' Commonwealth" (Polish) in T. Manteuffel, ed., *Historia Polski*, I, Part 2, pp. 450 ff.; A. Brückner, *Dzieje kultury polskiej* (A History of Polish Culture), 3d ed., II, 343 f.; J. Bardach, ed., *Historia państwa*, II, 61. See also, more generally, J. Ptaśnik, *Miasta i mieszczaństwo w dawnej Polsce* (Cities and Burghers in Old Poland); S. Herbst's succinct observations on "The Burghers' Culture in Poland around 1600" (Polish), *Studia renesansowe*, I, 9–24; S. Kutrzeba, "Municipal Autonomy and the Legislative Power of the City Lords in the Old Polish Commonwealth" (Polish), *Księga pamiątkowa* (Memorial Volume . . .) *Owsald Balzer*, II, 93–101; and numerous other monographs, such as were reviewed by A. Gieysztor in "Les Recherches sur l'histoire urbaine en Pologne, 1960–1962," *APH*, VIII, 79–90 (dealing much too briefly with the period of 1500–1650).

33. I. Schipper, *Studya*, pp. 350 f. App. viii; K. Lepszy, "The Break of the 1530s" (Polish) in *Pierwsza Konferencja Metodologiczna Historyków Polskich* (The First Methodological Conference of Polish Historians Held in Warsaw on December 28, 1951 – January 12, 1952), I, 314–79; L. Rymar, "Cracow's Participation in the Diets and Dietines of the Commonwealth" (Polish), *Rocznik krakowski*, VII, 187–258, esp. pp. 241 f., 258, showing that such attendance was quite expensive for the city. The author estimates the total cost during the sixteenth century at the equivalent of some $400,000 in gold, one-eighth of which was to pay for drinks for the assembled, often turbulent, nobles.

The social appreciation of the burghers' class also was constantly sinking. As in contemporary Spain, the Polish nobles looked down upon all commercial and industrial occupations. If a member of their class entered trade or joined an artisan guild, he quickly lost, to all intents and purposes, his noble status. Even holding a municipal office was considered a low-status occupation among the *szlachta*. It is small wonder, then, that many patrician families tried, through marriage and the acquisition of rural property, to join the ruling class of nobles. We shall see that the gentry tried to prevent the dilution of its ranks by erecting all sorts of legal obstacles. Yet these were not insurmountable. More remarkably, there were also cases of nobles entering the burgher class, when such a metamorphosis accrued to their financial advantage. See the examples of that two-way social mobility presented by W. Dworzaczek in "The Infiltration into the Burgers' Estate by Nobles in Great Poland to the Sixteenth and Seventeenth Centuries" (Polish), *PH*, XLVII, 656–84, with a French summary, pp. 831–32; and his "Perméabilité des barrières sociales dans la Pologne au XVIe siècle," *APH*, XXIV, 22–50, esp. pp. 27 ff., 29 n. 21, 32 (referring to ennobled Jewish converts, beginning with the fifteenth-century Lithuanian bishop of Samogitia, Marcin); and *infra*, n. 48.

34. See J. Bieniarzówna, *Mieszczaństwo krakowskie XVII wieku. Z badań nad strukturą społeczną miasta* (The Cracow Burghers of the Seventeenth Century: From Studies on the City's Social Structure), esp. Chaps. II (on the conflict between the city council and the *communitas* in the years 1623–26), and III (on the social and financial structure of Cracow in the middle of the seventeenth century); J. Bardach, ed., *Historia państwa*, I, 409 ff.; II, 63 ff. Characteristic of the lower bourgeoisie's complaints against the local oligarchies is the letter addressed in 1576 by the Lwów burghers to the king, arguing that the patricians "choose their sons and relatives for various offices and committees so that these may follow them is their rule over the city and thus conceal their transgressions against the city laws . . . . Also in order to maintain the council's rule over the city, they try to sow dissension and controversy among the populace." Cited by J. Ptaśnik in his *Miasta*, p. 162. The text of the Lwów agreement of 1581 is reproduced and analyzed in M. Bałaban's *Żydzi lwowscy*, pp. 408 ff.; Part 2, pp. 17 ff. No. 16. See also Ł. Charewiczowa, "The Economic Restrictions of Schismatics and Jews in Lwów in the Fifteenth and Sixteenth Centuries" (Polish), *KH*, XXXIX, 193–227, esp. p. 226; and, more generally, I. Schiper, *Dzieje handlu żydowskiego na ziemiach polskich* (A History of Jewish Commerce in Polish Lands), esp. pp. 60, 68.

35. Gabriel Krasiński (died 1676), *Taniec Rzeczypospolitej Polskiej* (The Dance of the Polish Commonwealth), excerpted from an extensive Dzików MS and ed. by A. Brückner in his "Taniec R. P.: an Historical Sketch" (Polish), *Przegląd Polski*, CXXXIII, 189–240, esp. pp. 215 f., 223 f.; *infra*, Chap. LXX, n. 29. Compared with Protestants, Jews were far less frequently the targets of satirical barbs, though in attacking heterodox Christians some satirists were prone to refer to their affinity with Judaism. See, in general, Z. Nowak, *Kontreformacyjna satyra obyczajowa w Polsce XVII wieku* (The Counter-Reformation Satire on Mores in Poland of the Seventeenth Century), esp. pp. 200 vv. 51 ff. (*Synod ministrów heretyckich*: a parody on a Protestant synod, published in 1611), and 358 f. (Jan Zrzenczycki's dedication of his Polish trans. of the German satire *Anatomia Martyna Lutra*, published in 1619); M. Małowist, "Le Commerce de la Baltique et le problème des luttes sociales en Pologne au XVe–XVIe siècles," *La Pologne au Xe Congrès International des sciences historiques à Rome*, pp. 125–64.

Jews may also have been preferred as contracting parties because of the still-operative medieval custom of holding foreigners responsible for the debts of their compatriots. See *supra*, Vol. XII, p. 109 f., 295 n. 45. To be sure, the distinguished sixteenth-century jurist Bartłomiej Groicki advised his compatriots to appeal first to the home authorities of alleged debtors, if necessary through the Polish king, before seizing the goods of an innocent alien. See his *Tytuły prawa magdeburskiego* (Titles of the Magdeburg Law), Cracow, 1567, newly reed. by K. Koranyi (see *infra*, n. 55), p. 151, cited in J. Bardach's ed. of *Historia państwa*, II, 201 f. Yet many Polish claimants doubtless used the more drastic method because it was the easier way to secure satisfaction. Foreign traders probably felt more confident that Jews would employ such tactics only as a last resort, since their coreligionists in other lands could help them to reach the responsible party. Various other aspects of Jewish commercial enterprise will be discussed in Chap. LXX.

36. J. Caro, *Geschichte der Juden in Lemberg*, pp. 3 f.; Stephen Báthory's privilege of 1586, reproduced in "A Cracow Compilation of Jewish Statutes and Privileges (*Sumaryusz przywilejów*)" (Russian), ed. by M. Schorr from the Cracow archives in *ES*, I, 247–64; II, 76-100, 223–45, esp. II, 97 Art. xxix; M. Schorr, *Żydzi w Przemyślu*, pp. 73 ff. App. i; idem, *Rechtsstellung und innere Verfassung der Juden in Polen*, p. 7.

37. Z. Kaczmarczyk and B. Leśnodorski in J. Bardach, ed., *Historia państwa*, II, 66 f., 69 ff.; R. Rybarski, *Handel i polityka handlowa Polski w XVI stuleciu* (Poland's Commerce and Commercial Policies in the Sixteenth Century); M. Bogucka, "The Struggle of the Burghers with the Patricians of Gdańsk in the Second Half of the Sixteenth Century" (Polish), *PH*, XLV, 408–459, 546–48, 564–66, with Russian and French summaries; idem, "Merchants' Profits in Gdańsk Foreign Trade in the First Half of the 17th Century," *APH*, XXIII, 73–90 (includes references to her own and other recent well-documented writings); A. Mączak, "La Compagnie orientale anglaise (Eastland Company) et le commerce dans la Baltique dans la seconde moitié du XVIe siècle," *ibid.*, pp. 91–104; and, more generally, D. Krannhals, *Danzig und der Weichselhandel in seiner Blütezeit vom 16. zum 17. Jahrhundert;* and A. Attman, *The Russian and Polish Markets in International Trade, 1500–1650.* See also *infra*, nn. 41, 46, and 83; and Chap. LXX, nn. 24, 30, and 46.

For the most part, to be sure, these legally underprivileged groups fought one another even more harshly than their common enemies. But the mere fact that the municipal administration often had to contend with many opposing non-Jewish forces, diverted much of its attention from the Jews. On occasion, the municipal elders actually sided with Jews. Not only did many of them consider it their duty to suppress anti-Jewish riots, but they sometimes joined with Jews in protracted court litigations. We recall such an alliance over the Lwów Jesuit attempt to appropriate a synagogue and adjacent land in the Jewish quarter. See the detailed and fully documented description of the ensuing litigation in M. Bałaban's *Żydzi lwowscy*, pp. 89 ff, and 572 ff. App. iii. These varying constellations, which depended largely on the self-interest of the respective parties, and their effect upon the Jews, merit detailed monographic treatment.

38. The Diet resolution of 1643, in *VL*, 1737 ed. IV, 76 f., also cited from a Lwów archival source by M. Bałaban in *Żydzi lwowscy*, p. 458; A. Brückner, *Dzieje kultury polskiej*, p. 348; Adam Jarzembski, *Gościniec albo opisanie Warszawy* (An Inn or A Description of Warsaw), Warsaw, 1643; new ed., p. 10 (also cited in a Yiddish translation by J. Shatzky in his *Geshikhte fun Yidn in Varshe*, p. 50). On the generally rising prices, see *infra*, n. 40.

39. S. Kutrzeba and A. Przyboś, eds. *Akta sejmikowe województwa krakowskiego* (Records of the Dietine of the Cracow Province, 1572–1680), II, 12 Art. 12; B. Baranowski and S. Herbst in T. Manteuffel, ed., *Historia Polski*, I, Part 2, pp. 466 ff.; M. Bersohn, *Dyplomataryusz*, p. 89 n. 135. Needless to say, no class was immune from the great temptation to engage in coin clipping and other currency abuses.

As early as October 31, 1502, Stanisław of Chodecz, the district governor (*starosta*) of Lwów, asked the king that he be empowered to take a variety of strong actions against these practices. He pointed, in particular, to the need to stop Prince Wiśniowiecki from flooding the country with forged Polish and Lithuanian currency. He also reported his difficulties in supervising Jews who were smuggling wax from Lithuania without paying customs duties, gratuitously adding: "Through it the Jews are of great detriment to the reign of Your Majesty, none being worse than they." F. Papée, ed., *Akta Aleksandra*, pp. 175 ff. No. 121. Even before that time, in 1406, a Jew named Peter was executed in Cracow for circulating forged money. According to Jan Długosz, before the culprit ascended the stake, he was marched through the market place, wearing a crown decorated with false coins. In 1455, three Cracow Jews found themselves obliged to deliver to the authorities a female forger, named Złota. See Długosz, *Historia*, book x, ad 1407, Leipzig, 1711–12 ed., Part 2, col. 186; M. Bałaban, *Dzieje Żydów w Krakowie*, I, 23.

40. S. M. Dubnow, *Pinqas ha-Medinah*, p. 15 n. 81; I. Halperin, ed., *Pinqas Va'ad 'Arba Araṣot*, pp. 42 ff. No. 110 citing a noteworthy reply by R. Joel Sirkes in his *Resp.*, n.s. (*ha-ḥadashot*), Korzec, 1785 ed., fols. 22c f. No. 43, which also stressed the often irresistible temptation offered by money-exchange, on account of both greed and necessity.

Another Sirkes responsum (in his *Resp.*, ed. by E. F. Eisenberg, Frankfort, 1697 ed., fols. 11 f. No. 16) well illustrates the confusion created in Poland by the *Kipper und Wipper* (clippers and counterfeiters) in Germany in the early 1620s. In the summer of 1624, a Jewish lender refused the prepayment of a three-year loan of 5,000 imperial florins extended on Sivan 1, 5383 (May 30, 1623), because of a rumor that the imperial currency would be revalued. See *supra*, Vol. XIV, pp. 231, 388 f. n. 6. R. Sirkes argued that the poor quality of the imperial coins, "consisting of copper with little silver added . . . because the emperor has had to pay his soldiers, multiplying like the locusts, to fight the wars around him," justified the rumor. He decided, therefore, in favor of the lender. See also, more generally, I. Unna, "Historisches aus den Responsen des R. Joël Serkes," *JJLG*, II, 203–211, esp. p. 209; and S. K. Mirsky, *R. Joel Sirkes ba'al ha-Bakh* (R. J. S., Author of the *Bayit ḥadash;* His Life and Works, reprinted from *Ḥoreb*, VI, 41–75), esp. p. 33.

The movement of prices in the sixteenth and seventeenth centuries, which has produced a vast literature in West-European countries, has also been of considerable interest to Polish historians in recent decades. See such monographs on the major Polish cities as S. Hoszowski, *Ceny we Lwowie w XVI i XVII wieku* (Prices in Lwów in the Sixteenth and Seventeenth Centuries), with a Foreword by F. Bujak, or in the French trans. entitled, *Les Prix à Lwów (XVI–XVII siècles);* J. Pelc, *Ceny w Gdańsku w XVI i XVII wieku* (Prices in Gdańsk in the Sixteenth and Seventeenth Centuries); idem, *Ceny w Krakowie w latach 1369–1600* (Prices in Cracow in the Years 1369–1600), preceded by E. Tomaszewski's *Ceny w Krakowie w latach 1601–1795* (Prices in Cracow in the Years 1601–1795); W. Adamczyk, *Ceny w Lublinie od XVI do końca XVIII wieku* (Prices in Lublin from the Sixteenth to the End of the Eighteenth Century); idem, *Ceny w Warszawie w XVI i XVII wieku* (Prices in Warsaw in the Sixteenth and Seventeenth Centuries); and, more generally, the pioneering work, still of considerable merit, by A. Szelągowski, *Pieniądz i przewrót cen w XVI i XVII wieku w Polsce* (Money and Price Fluctuations in Sixteenth- and Seventeenth-Century Poland). On conditions in other countries, see *supra*, Vol. XII, pp. 121 ff., 301 nn. 59 ff.; S. Hoszowski, "The Price Revolution in Central Europe in the Sixteenth and Seventeenth Centuries" (Polish), with the comment thereon by M. Małowist in his "Poland and the Price Changes in Europe in the Sixteenth and Seventeenth Centuries" (Polish), *KH,* LXVIII, 297–314, with Russian and French summaries; and 315–19, respectively.

The very fact that price rises and declines often differed widely in Polish cities shows how much they depended on varying local conditions and the ensuing differences in supply and demand. One can understand that such great variations played into the hands not only of speculators but also of alert businessmen who were in early possession of pertinent information. It is clear that in many phases of trade, Jewish merchants, with their far-flung connections in and outside the country, had a considerable edge over their numerous Christian competitors, whose horizons often did not extend beyond the boundaries of their particular province. If, as a result, Jews were able to import lower-priced merchandise from another locality, and easily underbid their competitors, this was viewed as "unfair" competition by the injured parties, and added to the existing animosities. At the same time, Jews suffered as consumers from the sudden rises in prices. In view of the rising cost of woolens, the Jewish community of Poznań, in cooperation with Great Poland's Jewish provincial council, in 1633 appointed special "commissioners for woolens" to monitor price trends before the coming Gniezno fair. See L. Lewin, *Die Landessynode,* pp. 76 No. 23, 78 No. 29. The nexus between prices and group relations has yet to be investigated in detail.

41. Sebastyan Miczyński, *Zwierciadło Korony polskiej, passim,* cited by I. Schiper in his *Dzieje handlu,* p. 74; B. Baranowski and S. Herbst in T. Manteuffel, ed., *Historia Polski,* I, Part 2, p. 464. See also *supra,* n. 37; and *infra,* Chap. LXX, nn. 28 ff.

42. See *VL,* II, 1243; M. Schorr, ed., "A Cracow Compilation of Jewish Statutes" (Russian), *ES,* II, 228 f. Art. v; M. Bałaban, *Dzieje,* I, 114 ff., 118. The Court of Assessors, presided over by the chancellor of the realm and consisting of other high officials and four senators, without any municipal representatives, could more impartially perform its main function of serving as a court of appeals against measures adopted by the cities. See J. Bardach, ed., *Historia państwa,* II, 156 f. Controversies about priority in acquiring victuals had been quite frequent in German-Jewish relations during the Middle Ages. In Poland, however, there was as a rule a sufficient supply of food, so that the Cracow regulations were but a chicanery or, if successful, a roundabout method of ousting Jews.

In contrast to the discriminatory laws promulgated by the councils of "royal" cities, the enactments of the lords in their "private" urban settlements often favored Jews. For one example, the lords of the later rather important city of Tarnów, located about 50 miles east of Cracow, often regulated the behavior of the city's population in considerable detail. In the 1560s, Jan Tarnowski issued no fewer than five statutes prescribing how the inhabitants were to extinguish fires, weigh meat, erect and maintain buildings, defend the city against enemies, and so forth. One of his successors, Władysław Dominik, in his ordinance of 1637, provided bluntly that the Tarnów Jews "may trade in all kinds of merchandise in their homes, in the market, and in their shops, undisturbedly and on a par with the burghers. They may also distill liquor and serve it in their inns." Soon thereafter, however, the city suffered from a severe plague, which is said to have killed more than half of the population. This catastrophe was followed by the destruction of the city by the invading Swedish army. Yet the Jewish community recovered rather quickly and resumed a fairly normal life, on the basis of a new privilege issued in 1670 by Władysław Dominik's son, Aleksander Janusz, and, on his prompting, of an "agreement" it signed with the city council in the same year. See I. Schipper, "Jews in Tarnów to the End of the Eighteenth Century" (Polish), *KH*, XIX, 228–39, esp. pp. 229 ff. See also, more generally, T. Opas's succinct analysis of the relations between "The Private Towns and the Commonwealth" (Polish), *KH*, LXXVIII, 28–48, with a Russian summary; further illustrated by a number of statistical tables relating to the lands of the Crown by A. Wyrobisz in "The Role of Private Towns in Poland in the Sixteenth and Seventeenth Centuries" (Polish), *PH*, LXV, 19–46, with Russian and French summaries; and *infra*, n. 51.

43. See *supra*, Vol. X, pp. 38 f., 318 n. 46; and Chap. LXVII, nn. 20 ff.; M. Bałaban, *Dzieje*, I, 120 ff.; idem, *Żydzi lwowscy*, pp. 395 ff.; J. Perles, "Geschichte der Juden in Posen," *MGWJ*, XIII, 325 f. The centuries-long Cracow controversy was replete with interesting constitutional and procedural issues, often resolved politically, rather than on juridical grounds. In 1606, for example, Sigismund III appointed two commissioners (his secretary and a canon of the Cracow church) to examine the arguments presented by the two sides and report back to him. But when the commissioners summoned representatives of the city to a hearing, the elders refused to appear. After repeatedly denouncing the city council's insubordination to royal commands, the commissioners submitted a report on the basis of the Jewish testimony alone. See F. K. Piekosiński, ed. *Kodeks dyplomatyczny miasta Krakowa* (Collection of Documents Pertaining to the City of Cracow), II, 868; idem and S. Krzyżanowski, eds., *Prawa, przywileje i statuty miasta Krakowa* (Laws, Privileges, and Statutes of the City of Cracow, 1507–1795), II, Part 2, p. 1659; Bałaban, *Dzieje*, I, 118. See also K. Bąkowski, *Dzieje Krakowa* (A History of Cracow), pp. 122 f.

44. See M. Bałaban, *Dzieje*, I, 88 f.; *supra*, Chap. LXVII, n. 22; J. Bieniarzówna, *Mieszczaństwo krakowskie*, pp. 156 ff.; S. Miczyński, *Zwierciadło*, p. 97; L. Lewin, *Geschichte der Juden in Lissa* [*Leszno*], pp. 4 f., 350 f. No. 1; M. Schorr, *Żydzi w Przemyślu*, pp. 15 f., 26 ff. In places like Wschowa (Fraustadt), where Jews were no longer allowed to reside, the inhabitants were even enjoined not to let a Jew spend a night in their homes. See J. Perles, "Geschichte der Juden in Posen," *MGWJ*, XIII, 450. Bocian (Poper), who was considered the wealthiest Jew in Cracow, Miczyński estimating his fortune at 300,000 zlotys, is discussed at some length in Bałaban's *Dzieje*, I, 176 ff. and *passim*, offering a profile of Bocian's far-flung business activities; his communal activities, which included the building of his synagogue in 1620 (it was still known as the *Poper shil* in the twentieth century); and his testament, opened at his death in 1625.

45. See Joel Sirkes, *Resp.*, Frankfort, 1697 ed., fol. 44c f. No. 69. Occasionally, we even hear of formal cooperation between city councils and Jewish communities. For example, both segments of the population of Krosno in the Sanok district submitted in 1608 a petition to the lord against the neighboring nobles' unruly behavior, which endangered all peaceful inhabitants. In 1620 they even filed a joint lawsuit against such violent neighbors, and took similar action in 1623 and 1625. See

M. Horn, "Jews in the Sanok Region up to 1650" (Polish), *BZIH*, no. 74, pp. 3–30, with an English summary, pp. 141 f., esp. pp. 26 ff. We also recall the Lwów city council's support of Jews in their litigation with the Jesuits, mentioned *supra*, n. 37.

The data on the social interrelations between the various ethnic groups inhabiting Poland and Lithuania are relatively meager. Contemporary writers and legislators were more interested in preventing social intercourse, particularly between Jews and Gentiles, than in recording the numerous instances of mutual understanding. This was indeed the characteristic attitude of the leaders on both sides. If Christian burghers endeavored to exclude Jewish houseowners and tenants from their quarters, mainly for economic reasons, Jews had even more compelling motives to try to keep Gentile inhabitants out of the Jewish street. From ancient times they viewed such residents as potential security risks during anti-Jewish riots. These suspicions went so far as to prompt certain Jewish communities to secure governmental privileges implicitly providing for their right *de non tolerandis Christianis*. See *supra*, Vol. X, pp. 38 f., 318 n. 46; and, for the earlier periods, the numerous entries listed in the *Index* to Vols. I–VIII, p. 137 *s.v.* Segregation. The general problem of Polish-Jewish social relations will engage our attention in various contexts in later chapters.

46. We certainly must not overlook the great regional and local variations among the cities and Jewish communities of Poland and Lithuania—variations which make sweeping generalizations quite perilous. Much primary and secondary material has become available over the years in the numerous histories of individual communities, written in Hebrew, Yiddish, Polish, Russian, and German. Some of the older publications pertaining to cities in Great Poland, other than Poznań, are listed in M. Bałaban's *Bibliografia historii Żydów w Polsce* (A Bibliography of the History of the Jews in Poland and Neighboring Countries for the Years 1900–1930), pp. 108 ff. Nos. 2781–2948. Unfortunately, the continuation of this important handbook, published shortly before the Second World War, fell victim, together with its author, to the Nazi regime. See I. Trunk, "Meir Balaban, Student of Jewish Communal Organization and Autonomy in Old-Poland" (Yiddish), *YB*, XLIV, 198–206. On the other hand, the great Holocaust has stimulated the publication of a host of nostalgic monographs on the history of communities destroyed by the Nazis. One of the earliest such collections, ed. by J. L. Fishman (Maimon), bears the provocative title (borrowed from a talmudic phrase) *'Arim ve-Immahot be-Yisrael* (Cities and Mothers in Israel: a Holy Memorial for Jewish Communities Destroyed by Impious Sadists in the Last World War), Jerusalem, 1946 ff. A great many other publications have been listed by J. Robinson and P. Friedman, eds., in their *Guide to Jewish History under Nazi Impact*, with Forewords by B. Dinur and S. W. Baron (Joint Documentary Projects of Yad Washem and Yivo Institute for Jewish Research, Bibliographical Series, I); and the bibliographies of the Holocaust literature in Hebrew, Yiddish, and Western languages, likewise edited by them. See P. Friedman, comp., *Bibliografiah shel ha-sefarim be-'ivrit 'al ha-sho'ah ve-'al ha-geburah* (Bibliography of Books in Hebrew on the Jewish Catastrophe and Heroism in Europe); idem and J. Gar, comps., *Bibliografie fun yidishe bicher vegn ḥurban un gevure* (Bibliography of Yiddish Books on the Catastrophe and Heroism). While concentrating on the recent periods, the authors of many of these monographs assembled interesting data on the history of the Jews in Polish and Lithuanian cities before 1650 as well.

Regrettably, further research in this field has been impeded by the Nazis' large-scale destruction of Poland's archival collections. For example, it appears that the very rich Central Archive in Warsaw sustained a loss of some 90 percent of its older collections. See I. Sulkowska, "Les Archives Centrales des Actes Anciens à Varsovie," *APH*, IX, 115–27; and, more fully, idem, *Straty archiwów i bibliotek warszawskich* (Losses of the Warsaw Archives and Libraries in the Area of Historical Manuscript Sources); and A. Stebelski, *The Fate of Polish Archives during World War II*, English trans. from the Polish by B. Przestepska. Even more damaging to the prospect of fruitful Jewish historical research in Poland and Lithuania is the survival of but a tiny Jewish community in the area, with only a few members able and willing to devote themselves to the study of their ancestral communities. Against great odds the Jewish Historical Institute in Warsaw has been able to issue a number of publications, including its *Biuletyn*. But only a few studies pertaining to the period before 1650 appeared, even in the more favorable climate of the first two decades of reconstituted Poland. Although the situation has somewhat improved in recent years, A. Sawczyński's complaint to the Twelfth International Congress of Historical Sciences, Vienna, 1965, that the period of the three Vasa kings and their successor, King Michael, had suffered from greater neglect by modern scholars than either the medieval or the Enlightenment period, is still essentially true today. See his "Das XVII. Jahrhundert in der polnischen Geschichte und Geschichtsschreibung," *Teki historyczne*, XIV, 97–106.

Nonetheless, there is enough source material available for a series of comprehensive works concerning the old Jewish communities of the area, including the relations between the Jews and their neighbors in various periods. Such a wide-ranging investigation would replace the only monograph now available, A. N. Frenk, *Ha-'Ironim ve-ha-Yehudim be-Polin* (The Burghers and the Jews in Poland), which even in its day (1921) was too general and undocumented to be quite satisfactory.

47. See Z. Kaczmarczyk and B. Leśnodorski's estimates of the size of the noble class in Poland in the mid-sixteenth century in J. Bardach, ed., *Historia państwa*, II, 75 f.; the periodization suggested by J. Maciszewski in *Szlachta polska i jej państwo* (Polish Nobility and Its State), p. 49; other views expressed by J. Senkowski in his "Periodization of the Era of the Nobles' Democracy" (Polish), *Odrodzenie w Polsce* (The Polish Renaissance), I, 535–39, and in the discussion thereon, pp. 540 ff.; B. Baranowski and S. Herbst in their chapters concerning "The Multinational Nobles' Commonwealth" in T. Manteuffel, ed., *Historia Polski*, I, Part 2, pp. 416–565, esp. pp. 448 ff. See also A. Wyczański's popular survey, *Polska Rzeczą Pospolitą szlachecką* (Poland, a Nobles' Commonwealth, 1454–1764).

At the beginning, to be sure, the gentry, in their rise to power, to some extent displaced the magnates who had been chief advisers of the Jagiellon dynasty. In time, however, the oligarchy reasserted its supremacy, and even in the elections to the Chamber of Deputies conducted by the regional dietines (*sejmiki*) of nobles appearing in person, many magnates succeeded in winning seats for themselves or their favorites. According to W. Dworzaczek's computation, in the years 1572–1655 the magnates and wealthy nobles constituted 47 percent of the deputies from Great Poland, although their share diminished to 23 percent among the representatives from Little Poland. See "The Social Composition of the Diet Representation from Great Poland in the Years 1572–1655" (Polish), *Roczniki historyczne*, XXIII, 281–310, with a French summary. As pointed out by that author, the clergy, especially the large majority of bishops, who occupied seats in the Senate *ex officio*, were likewise recruited from the noble class, particularly from its higher echelons.

48. See *VL*, I, 97: "We decree that commoners should not be raised to the rank of nobility except at a Diet session"; the text of the 1538 Diet ordinance forbidding burghers to acquire landed property, reproduced by J. Sawicki in his compilation of *Wybór tekstów źródłowych z historii państwa i prawa polskiego* (A Selection of Texts from the Sources for the History of the Polish State and Law), p. 122 No. 51; N. M. Gelber, "Die Taufbewegung unter den polnischen Juden im XVIII. Jahrhundert," *MGWJ*, LXVIII, 225–41, esp. p. 239 n. 1; and *supra*, n. 33. The few Cracow elders who, in the seventeenth century, were raised to the ranks of the nobility, either by serving as royal secretaries or by acquiring landed estates in defiance of the existing laws, were but exceptions confirming the rule of the gentry's exclusiveness. See J. Bieniarzówna, *Mieszczaństwo krakowskie XVII wieku*. On the automatic noble status of Lithuanian converts, see the aforementioned debate between M. Janecki and O. Balzer, and other publications cited *supra*, Chap. LXVII, n. 36. One may agree with S. Ptaszycki's arguments (against S. Bershadskii) and assume that the official text of the Lithuanian statute was not that translated into the Rus language (no longer extant), but rather its Polish formulation, and that its provisions were generally applied for several generations. See his aforementioned essay in the *Księga pamiątkowa . . . Oswald Balzer*, II, 297–313. Yet one must admit that there really is very little evidence that the article referring to Jewish converts to Christianity was actually applied.

Among the "royal servitors" under Sigismund III and Wladislaw IV, we need but mention Salomon Włochowicz, his sons Joseph and Baruch Lewek Włoch, and other members of his family in Cracow, and Izak Nachmanowicz and his family in Lwów. On the other hand, Jan Zajączkowski and Jakób Bielski, the two merchants appointed by Sigismund as servitors, particularly in charge of supplying furs to the royal court, achieved that honor only after their baptism. See M. Bersohn, *Dyplomatarusz*, pp. 124 No. 218, 140 ff. Nos. 250–52; M. Bałaban, *Dzieje*, I, 210 ff.; idem, *Żydzi lwowscy, passim;* I. Schiper, *Dzieje handlu*, pp. 63 f. (not all persons mentioned here were official "servitors").

49. Justus Ludwig Dietz (Iodocus Ludovicus Decius or Decyusz), *De Sigismundi I. temporibus liber* (1521), in the collective Polish trans. entitled *Księga o czasach króla Zygmunta* (A Book on the Period of King Sigismund), p. 123; *supra*, Chap. LXVII, n. 32; J. Morgensztern, "On the Jewish Settlement in Zamość around 1600" (Polish), *BZIH*, nos. 43–44, pp. 3–17, 134; idem, "Notes on the Sephardim in Zamość in 1588–1650" (Polish), *ibid.*, no. 38, pp. 69–82, 121; idem, "On the Economic Activity of the Jews in Zamość in the Sixteenth and Seventeenth Centuries" (Polish), *ibid.*, no. 53, pp. 3–32, 134; idem, "Jewish Credit Operations in Zamość in the Seventeenth Century: Credit Given and Taken" (Polish), *ibid.*, no. 64, pp. 3–32; idem, "Taxes Paid by the Zamość Fee Tail Jews in the Sixteenth and Seventeenth Centuries" (Polish), *ibid.*, nos. 71–72, pp. 9–38, all with English summaries; N. M. Gelber, "On the History of the Sephardim in Poland" (Hebrew), *Oṣar Yehude Sefarad* (Tesoro de los Judíos Sefardíes), VI, 88–98 (also listing the 39 Sephardic houseowners recorded in Zamość for the years 1588–1650); and, more generally, B. Baranowski and S. Herbst, "Multinational Nobles' Commonwealth" in T. Manteuffel, ed., *Historia Polski*, I, Part 2, pp. 440 ff. Not surprisingly, Dietz (Decyusz), whose hostile remark on Jewish power is cited in the text, did not hesitate to use the services of a Cracow Jew, Lazar, in acquiring jewels in Venice for the king. See the royal privilege in favor of Lazar, reproduced in S. A. Bershadskii's *REA*, III, 162 ff. No. 130; Bałaban, *Dzieje*, p. 84; and *supra*, Chap. LXVII, n. 32.

It may be noted that Ostrogski's princely title was entirely owing to his descent from Ukrainian feudal princes who had retained their titles after the Union of Lublin, despite the aversion of the generally egalitarian Polish gentry to such distinctions between one nobleman and another. The king's right to confer a title was strictly delimited, even in the case of foreigners. On the two magnates mentioned here who played some role in Jewish affairs, see A. Tarnawski, *Działalność gospodarcza Jana Zamoyskiego, kanclerza i hetmana* (Economic Activity of J. Z., Chancellor and Generalissimo of the Polish Crown 1572–1605); the biography by A. Śliwiński cited *supra*, n. 1. Ostrogski's Ukrainian antecedents, in part, may have induced him to become the most powerful opponent of the Union of Brest, a position which may also have contributed to his generally more tolerant outlook on religious diversity. See K. Lewicki, *Książę Konstanty Ostrogski a Unja Brzeska 1596 roku* (Prince K. O. and the Union of Brest of 1596); and *supra*, n. 3.

50. See M. Bałaban, *Żydzi lwowscy*, p. 452; Jan Zamoyski's intervention of 1581 recorded by W. Siemieński in W. Sobieski's and his *Archiwum Jana Zamoyskiego, kanclerza i hetmana wielkiego koronnego* (The Archive of J. Z., Chancellor and Generalissimo of the Polish Crown), II, 43 No. 414; I. Schiper, *Dzieje handlu*, pp. 64, 79; M. Bersohn, *Dyplomataryusz*, p. 114 No. 193; S. Kardaszewicz, *Dzieje dawniejsze miasta Ostroga* (The Older History of the City of Ostrog), p. 118; *supra*, nn. 34, 38; and Chap. LXVII, n. 32. The ever-increasing collaboration of the Jews with the Polish magnates reached its peak after 1650. However, even earlier it accrued to the benefit of both parties and was a perennial source of grievance for competing Christian merchants and artisans.

51. *VL*, II, 597; J. Mazurkiewicz, *Jurydyki lubelskie* (The Lublin *Jurydyki*); M. Niwiński, "The Class Division in Cracow Real Estate Ownership in the Sixteenth and Seventeenth Centuries" (Polish), *Studia historyczne ku czci Stanisława Kutrzeby* (Historical Studies in Honor of Stanisław Kutrzeba), II, 549–84, esp. p. 559; J. Bardach, ed., *Historia państwa*, II, 62 f., 259 f.; *supra*, Chap. LXVII, n. 13. See also W. Sobisiak, *Rozwój latyfundium biskupstwa poznańskiego w XVI doXVIII wieku* (The Development of the Poznań Bishopric's Latifundium in the Sixteenth through Eighteenth Centuries), with an English summary; also listing the earlier literature, including that relating to the archbishopric of Gniezno, of which Poznań formed a part. The author estimates the total area of Poznań's episcopal domain at some 75,000 hectares, or over 180,000 acres.

Of course, the authority of the nobles was greatest in towns established on their own land, in some of which the Jews ultimately formed a majority of the population. To all intents and purposes, these were Jewish towns, run largely by the Jewish community, whose authority was limited only by the lord's will, or whim. One such town was Opatów (bearing the abridged name Apta in Hebrew). Starting as a small Jewish settlement dependent on the major regional center, Cracow, the Opatów community became in the course of time sufficiently large and independent to try to throw off Cracow's control. See H. Horowitz, "Die Jüdische Gemeinde Opatow und ihre Rabbiner," *MGWJ*, LXXIV, 10–23; *infra*, n. 80. However, one cannot quite generalize, from the developments in Opatów, about the evolution of Jewish settlement and self-government in other communities of similar size, as is done by A. N. Frenk in his *Ha-'Ironim ve-ha-Yehudim, passim*. There were, indeed, a great many local variations. For instance, in the town of Ostrog, which speedily grew into a major center of Volhynian Jewish culture, the ruler Anna Chodkiewiczowa, doubtless under the influence of a local priest, decreed in 1627 that, while the Jews were generally to retain their rights, they were not to build a synagogue taller than the church, perform public burial rites in the daytime, or sell liquor to Christians on holidays until after the church services. See S. Kardaszewicz, *Dzieje*, p. 118 n. 1. See also S. Kutrzeba's aforementioned *(supra,* n. 32) essay in the *Księga pamiątkowa . . . Oswald Balzer*, II, 93–101.

52. *VL*, I, 270, cited *supra*, Chap. LXVII, n. 32; M. Horn, "Jews in the Voivodship of Bełz in the First Half of the Seventeenth Century: a Statistical Assessment" (Polish), *BZIH*, no. 27, pp. 22–61, with an English summary, pp. 115–16, esp. pp. 32 f.; *Słownik geograficzny Królestwa Polskiego* (Geographical Dictionary of the Kingdom of Poland), ed. by F. Sulimierski *et al.,* V, 895–97; VII, 477–79. Some examples of individual decrees issued by sixteenth-century Polish kings in favor of local or provincial Jewish communities were published from Kiev and St. Petersburg archives by A. E. Harkavy in his *Meassef niddaḥim* (Collection of Stray Items), pp. 64, 84–89, 109–110, 128–29. Stanisław Kutrzeba exaggerated, however, in contending that the entire royal legislation served as but a theoretical framework, against which legal practice could be measured from time to time, but that, by itself, it possessed little compulsory force. See his remarks on "The Legal Status of the Jews in Poland in the Fifteenth Century" (Polish), *Przewodnik naukowy i literacki*, XXIX, 1155. In fact, wherever royal power was strong, the Jewish privileges carried great weight, indeed. It was only later that the general curtailment of the rights of the Crown affected the status of its Jewish subjects.

53. See the interesting data submitted, on the basis of extensive archival research, by A. P. Hryckiewicz in his twin essays, "The Militias of the Magnates' Towns in Belorussia and Lithuania in the Sixteenth through Eighteenth Centuries" (Polish), *KH*, LXXVII, 47–62, with a Russian summary; and "The Magnates' Fortified Cities in Belorussia and Lithuania" (Polish), *PH*, LXI, 428–44, with Russian and French summaries. In the latter study, the author discusses particularly the cities of Słutsk (429 ff.), Bychów (437 f.), and Nieświerz (454 ff.). A Bychów document of 1758 mentions Belorussians, Poles, Tatars, and Jews as serving in the local militia. Even more cosmopolitan was the contingent in Birzai, where in 1673 Jews enlisted in the militia, alongside Lithuanians, Poles, Belorussians, Germans, and Scots. See Hryckiewicz in *KH*, LXXVII, 57. Independently, Jews often had to fight in self-defense, not only against foreign enemies but also against their internal foes. On these occasions, their well-built stone or brick synagogues could be used to good advantage, for gathering in large numbers of potential victims and holding out against besiegers for some time. Such fortified synagogues existed in Łuck, Tarnopol, and other localities. See *infra*, n. 81; and E. Horn, "Legal and Economic Situation of the Jews in the Towns of the Halicz Province around 1600" (Polish), *BZIH*, no. 40, pp. 3–36, with an English summary, p. 89, esp. p. 28. These aspects of Jewish military service in seventeenth- and eighteenth-century Poland and Lithuania, as well as their likely antecedents, merit further detailed study.

54. *VL*, II, 694, 726, 809; Z. Pazdro, *Organizacya i praktyka żydowskich sądów podwojewodzińskich* (Organization and Practice of the Jewish Courts of the Deputy Palatines in the Period 1740–1772; on the Basis of Lwów Archival Materials), pp. 8 f.,

159 ff., 176 ff. No. xi, Art. 4; L. Lewin, *Die Landessynode*, p. 39. To be sure, the provision in the Lwów ordinance issued by Palatine Marek Matczyński on March 21, 1692, which obligated the courts adjudicating litigations between Jews and Christians to meet in the synagogue yard in the presence of Jewish elders, who "should vote according to their understanding of the cases under review and the judicial process, and thus adjust the matter according to the ancient custom and law of that synagogue," did not meet with the approval of Matczyński's eighteenth-century successor, August Czartoryski. The new palatine particularly objected to the synagogue locale as impinging on the dignity of a court representing the highest provincial office. See his ordinance of December 31, 1771, reproduced by Pazdro, pp. 188 f. No. xv. See also S. Kutrzeba's aforementioned study "Municipal Autonomy," *Księga pamiątkowa . . . Oswald Balzer*, II, 93–101. The broader aspects of the Jewish judicial administration will be analyzed here in a later chapter. For the time being, reference may be made to my *JC*, II, 69 ff., 207 ff.; III, 123 ff., 172 ff., and the numerous other passages listed in its Index, III, 447 ff., *s.v.* Judiciary and judges; and M. Lisser's brief review "Jewish Courts of Justice in Poland to the End of the Eighteenth Century: Their Structure and Peculiarity" (Polish), *BZIH*, no. 34, pp. 97–130, with an English summary, p. 173 (from a Master's essay written in the 1930s).

55. See Bartłomiej Groicki's *Porządek sądów i spraw miejskich prawa magdeburskiego w Koronie Polskiej* (The Order of Municipal Courts and Functions According to Magdeburg Law in the Polish Crown), Cracow, 1559; idem, *Artykuły prawa magdeburskiego które zwą speculum saxonum* (Articles of Magdeburg Law, a Rendition of Eike of Repgow's *Sachsenspiegel*—Judicial Proceedings in Cases of Capital Punishment—The Law of Judicial Fines according to Magdeburg Law), Cracow, 1558, together with several other of his works newly reedited by K. Koranyi (all these tracts include frequent citations from the Old Testament); and J. Kitowicz's *Opis obyczajów za panowania Augusta III* (A Description of Customs during the Reign of Augustus III), ed. by R. Pollak, esp, pp. 180 ff., 227 ff., 237. Although Kitowicz describes early eighteenth-century conditions, his observations doubtless reflect long-established usages and their underlying superstitions. The nobles' judiciary was little restrained by the regional royal officials, particularly since many magnates had military forces of their own which could defy royal orders. See, for instance, A. Hryckiewicz's aforementioned "The Militias of the Magnates' Towns," *KH*, LXXVII, 47–62. See also the brief, but illuminating, data cited by A. Brückner in his *Dzieje kultury polskiej*, 3d ed., II, 49 ff.

56. See the mutually complementary studies by A. Błoński (W. Pałucki), *Studia nad uposażeniem urzędników ziemskich w Koronie do schyłku XVI wieku* (Studies of the Financial Provisions for the County Officials in the Polish Crown to the End of the Sixteenth Century), with a French summary, pp. 309–310; W. Czapliński, "The Sale of Offices in Poland in the Middle of the Seventeenth Century" (Polish), *PH*, L, 51–61; E. Cieślak, "The Venality of Municipal Offices in Gdańsk in the Seventeenth and Eighteenth Centuries" (Polish), *CPH*, XXI, Part 2, pp. 69–100, with a French summary, pp. 99–100; and, on the Jewish reaction, S. M. Dubnow, *Pinqas ha-Medinah*, pp. 9 Nos. 44–45, 17 f. No. 89. Despite the solemnity and severity of the excommunication of the Jew from Kleck, cases in which other Jewish debtors pledged close relatives seem to have occurred with sufficient frequency for the Lithuanian Council, in its 1670 session, to repeat that "he who mortgages his wife

and children to Gentiles shall be excommunicated from the two [this and the future] worlds." *Ibid.,* pp. 155 f. No. 637.

57. Yom Ṭob Lipmann b. Nathan Heller, *Megillat Ebah* (Scroll of Hostility; a record of personal sufferings), [ed. by M. Körner with a German trans. by J. H. Miro]; or in a slightly different version reprinted in A. Kahana's *Sifrut ha-historiah ha-yisraelit* (An Anthology of Jewish Historical Literature), II, 277–99; I. Halperin, *Pinqas Va'ad 'Arba Araṣot,* p. 69 No. 186 with the editor's note thereon; B. Z. Katz, *Le-Qorot ha-Yehudim,* p. 12; A. N. Frenk, *Ha-'Ironim ve-ha-Yehudim,* p. 55; J. Bardach, ed., *Historia państwa,* II, 281; T. Opas, "The Personal Liberty of Burghers of Towns Belonging to Nobles in the Province of Lublin in the Second Half of the Seventeenth and in the Eighteenth Centuries" (Polish), *PH,* LXI, 609–629, with Russian and French summaries; idem, "Private Towns and the Commonwealth" (Polish), *KH,* LXXVIII, 28–68, with a Russian summary; and *infra,* n. 79.

According to Heller, his expulsion was caused by his Jewish enemies, who resented his determined stand against the acquisition of rabbinical posts through money. See M. Brann, "Additions à l'Autobiographie de Lipman Heller," *REJ,* XXI, 270–77; Halperin, pp. 61 ff. Nos. 176, 178–79. It appears that the newly arrived foreigner Heller, whose uncompromising stand on controversial issues had already led to his imprisonment (with the threat of a death penalty) by the Habsburg authorities in Prague and Vienna (see *supra,* Vol. XIV, pp. 220 f., 393 n. 15), must have antagonized not only the persons directly involved in those more-or-less clandestine transactions but also many others who approved of the widespread practice of "simony." They regarded financial aid to a hard-pressed community from its new spiritual chief as no more reprehensible than offers of large sums of money to the Treasury by candidates for election to the throne of Poland, or the aforementioned venality of public office. See *supra,* n. 56; Chap. LXVII, esp. nn. 48–49. These examples can readily be multiplied.

58. S. M. Dubnow, *Pinqas ha-Medinah,* pp. 7 Nos. 21 and 26, 9 No. 39, 16 No. 85, 38 No. 163, etc.; I. Halperin, *Pinqas,* pp. 18 ff., esp. p. 21 No. 65, 45 ff., esp. p. 51; D. Avron, ed., *Pinqas ha-Ksherim,* p. 77 No. 381. Conversely, the communal elders frequently had reason to complain of abuses by nobles or their underlings. While recourse against a noble landlord who owned and despotically ruled a particular town was very limited, there was a better chance of redress when a royal official was the offending party. In 1628 the Jewish community of Poznań adopted a resolution opposing the local burgrave. The elders were instructed "to take an oath that they would do everything possible to have him deposed"; they were allowed to spend up to a certain amount (crossed out in the minute book) for this purpose. See, on this case and a similar one in 1640, Avron, pp. 11 No. 46, 70 No. 387; J. Perles, "Geschichte der Juden in Posen," *MGWJ,* XIII, 449. See also such regional studies as T. Opas's "Jews in Towns Owned by Nobles in the Lublin Region in the Eighteenth Century" (Polish), *BZIH,* no. 67, pp. 3–37 (Jews formed at that time 34 percent of the local population, and took part in municipal elections); and E. Horn's "Legal and Economic Situation of the Jews in the Towns of the Halicz Province" (Polish), *ibid.,* no. 40, pp. 3–36, both with English summaries.

Regrettably, the archives of cities under noble control have not been satisfactorily preserved, nor as yet sufficiently utilized. In some records, moreover, a Jewish party is often given without a name, as happened, for instance, in the four documents reproduced by A. Kamiński *et al.*, eds., in *Inwentarze dóbr ziemskich wojowództwa krakowskiego* (Inventories of Landed Estates in the Cracow Palatinate, 1576–1700: a Selection from the Books of Reports of the Cracow Tribunal), pp. 258, 269, 323, 353; and, more generally, K. Chojnicka, "Archivalia of the Nobles' Cities in Great Poland (Old Polish Period)" (Polish), *Archeion*, LIV, 79–91. On the still rather unsatisfactory state of "Research in the History of Small Towns in Poland," see A. Wyrobisz's pertinent Polish essay in *PH*, LIX, 124–57. He admits, however, that there has been a growing interest in this area, especially with respect to Belorussian towns, and he offers a survey of recent publications in this field, including those by Maurycy Horn and Elżbieta Hornowa, who have also contributed some articles on Jewish economic activities in the prepartition period to *BZIH*.

59. K. Grzybowski, *Teoria reprezentacji w Polsce epoki Odrodzenia* (The Representational Theory in Poland during the Renaissance Period); H. Olszewski, *Sejm Rzeczypospolitej epoki oligarchii 1652–1764* (The Diet of the Polish Commonwealth in the Period of the Oligarchy 1652–1764: Law—Practice—Theory—Programs); and W. Czapliński's critical review of both these and other recent works, some of which were prepared under his guidance, in his "On the Problems Facing the Polish Diet in the First Half of the Seventeenth Century" (Polish), *KH*, LXXVII, 31–45, with a French summary. See also Czapliński's survey of some other writings in this field in his "Polish Seym in the Light of Recent Research," *APH*, XXII, 180–92; and *infra*, n. 60. The supposedly required unanimity in all votes at the Polish Diets, has lent itself to much exaggeration in the popular mind, as well as among historians. In fact, the *liberum veto* not only was very sparingly used in the period here under review but, even during Poland's growing anarchy in the eighteenth century, was often disregarded by the majority. Yet, the threat of a veto by a determined minority or a single individual overhung all the deliberations in the Diet, and frequently prevented the enactment of much-needed reforms. See the fine comparative study by W. Konopczyński, *Le Liberum veto: étude sur le développement du principe majoritaire*.

60. *VL*, VII, 755; W. Smoleński, *Stan i sprawa Żydów polskich w XVIII wieku* (The Status of the Jews and the Jewish Question in Poland in the Eighteenth Century), p. 8 (reprinted in his *Pisma historyczne*, II, 223–93); my *JC*, I, 280 f.; III, 64 f. n. 56. A brief summary of the more important Diet ordinances referring to Jews in the period 1500–1648 is offered by R. Mahler in his *Toledot ha-Yehudim be-Polin*, pp. 169 ff. The deputies' sympathetic attitude toward the burghers in 1768 resulted from the intervening rapid decline of the cities, and the practical elimination of any serious opposition on their part to the *szlachta's* predominance. It was indeed this weakness of the Third Estate—in contrast to the prevailing trends in Western Europe—which helped to undermine Poland's political and military strength and greatly contributed to its annexation by the three partitioning powers.

61. See my *JC*, II, 247; III, 183 n. 2; I. Schipper, "The Financial Ruin of the Central and Provincial Autonomy of the Jews in Poland (1650–1764)" (Yiddish), *Yivo Ekonomishe Shriftn*, II, 1–19, esp. p. 19; idem, "The 'Warsaw Committee'; a Contribution to the History of Jewish Autonomy in Old Poland" (Polish), *Sefer ha-Yobel. . . . Mordecai Ze'ev (Markus) Braude*, pp. 145–57. Understandably, the Jews tried to influence deliberations in both the central and provincial diets. Some ma-

terials along this line have been assembled by I. Lewin in his "The Jews' Participation in Diet Elections in Old Poland" (Polish), *MZ*, II, 46–65. However, a thorough
study of this aspect of Polish-Jewish relations is very difficult, because of the lack
of a comprehensive, Hansard-like corpus of the Diet's deliberations. While some
partial records appeared many years ago in the *Scriptores rerum polonicarum*, ed.
by J. Szujski *et al.*, and a number of detailed editions and analyses have also been
published in more recent years (see below and in the next note), these are too
diverse and sporadic to offer a sufficiently comprehensive picture of the debates on
the Jewish question. They give us still less information about the behind-the-scenes
negotiations with Jewish representatives before and during these debates. See, for
instance, J. Szujski's aforementioned ed. of *Dyaryusze sejmów koronnych 1548, 1553
i 1570 [roku]* (Diaries of the Crown's Diets of 1548, 1553, and 1570); A. Czuczyński,
ed., *Dyaryusze sejmowe roku 1585* (Diet Diaries of 1585); A. Sokołowski, ed.,
Dyaryusze sejmowe z roku 1587 (Diaries of the Diet of 1587); G. Barwiński, ed.,
Dyaryusze sejmowe r. 1597 (Diaries of the Diet of 1597); A. Strzelecki, *Sejm z roku
1605* (The Diet of 1605); also offering a good review of the deliberations of the
various preparatory provincial diets, which reflected the highly charged partisan
atmosphere preceding the outbreak of the Zebrzydowski Rebellion in the following
year. The generally loyalist Diet of Psków, echoing the strongly pro-Catholic orientation of its Mazovian constituency, reiterated its adamant objection to the guarantees
of religious liberty enunciated by the Warsaw Confederation of 1573; pp. 37 ff., 65;
and *infra*, nn. 63 and 79; J. Byliński, *Sejm z roku 1611* (The Diet of 1611);
S. Ochmann, *Sejmy z lat 1615–1616* (The Diets of 1615–1616); J. Seredyka, *Sejm w
Toruniu z 1626 roku* (The Diet in Toruń in 1626), with an English summary. Although ultimately without effect, the deliberations in 1626 were a testimony to the
realization by the gentry, or at least by some of its more thoughtful members, that
the fiscal burdens of the peasants, burghers, and Jews could not continue to increase indefinitely while the nobles contributed very little. See also the further
literature cited in S. Kutrzeba's general analysis *Sejm walny dawnej Rzeczypospolitej
Polskiej* (The Main Diet of the Old Polish Commonwealth); and in J. Bardach, ed.,
Historia państwa, II, 114.

Much can also be learned from the few available studies on the composition of
the respective diets. They especially help to explain the parliamentary situation in
each session, which could affect Jews favorably or adversely. See S. Kutrzeba, "The
Composition of the Polish Diet, 1493–1793" (Polish), *PH*, II, 43–76, 179–202, 309–341;
and W. Dworzaczek's aforementioned study (*supra*, n. 47). Yet such monographic
studies, however valuable, underscore the existing lacunae in our knowledge, which
are the more remarkable as interest in the history of the Polish diets and their
resolutions antedated the partition of Poland. In 1765 Stanisław Burzyński published
the first pertinent compilation, grandiloquently entitled *Zebranie wszystkich seymów
i praw polskich* (A Collection of All the Polish Diet Deliberations and Laws), which
he dedicated to the then new king, Stanislaus II Augustus; it was printed in the
royal press of Warsaw. This auspicious beginning was not followed up for a long
time, however. Of considerable help in identifying the various Diet sessions is
W. Konopczyński's *Chronologia sejmów polskich 1493–1793* (A Chronology of Polish
Diets, 1493–1793). This list embraces 245 assemblies; in his Intro. the author also
analyzes a number of methodologically significant problems. Nevertheless, despite
all these problems, enough data are available even now for a good monograph reviewing in detail the deliberations of various Polish diets, national and provincial,

on Jews and Judaism (see *infra*, nn. 62–63). Such a study would also facilitate, as well as give new impetus to, additional archival research in this field.

62. See the texts of the 1534 resolutions, reproduced in Stanisław Górski's original collection of *Epistolae, legationes, responsa, actiones et res gestae . . . Sigismundi Primi* in the *Acta Tomiciana*, Vol. XVI, ed. by W. Pociecha, Part 1, pp. 100 ff. No. 51 item 3, 111 ff. No. 53 item 3; Part 2, pp. 358 ff. No. 573. On the "law of concealment," and the special Jewish privileges appertaining thereto, which have been the subject of protracted debates over the years, see *supra*, Vol. XII, pp. 120 f., 299 ff. n. 58, and the sources listed there. The reasons for the generally favorable treatment of Jews in Poland's foreign trade are discussed *infra*, Chap. LXX.

63. S. Kutrzeba and A. Przyboś, eds., *Akta sejmikowe województwa krakowskiego* (Records of the Dietine of the Cracow Province 1572–1680), I, 70 ff., 78 ff., 136 ff., 207 ff., 211, 374 ff., 381 n. 44, 386 ff.; II, 12, etc.; A. Prochaska, ed., *Lauda wiszeńskie* (Resolutions of the Dietines of Wisznia, 1572–1732), with S. Sochaniewicz's comments thereon in his "From the History of the Wisznia Dietine (1673–1732)" (Polish), *KH*, XXIX, 17–54; and *supra*, n. 39. On the meetings of the Red Russian dietines, see H. Chodynicki's analysis of *Sejmiki ziem ruskich w wieku XV* (The Dietines of the Rus Lands in the Fifteenth Century), esp. pp. 117 ff., furnishing a list of both general and district assemblies, but also pointing out that the extant sources give us information mainly on their judicial functions; and, from the organizational standpoint, S. Sieniowski, "The Organization of the Halicz Dietine in Old Poland" (Polish), *Sprawozdania* of the Towarzystwo Naukowe in Lwów, XVII, 139–47, revealing the numerous inconsistencies characteristic of these gatherings. The resolutions of the Cracow dietine are further elucidated by W. Urban's study of "Social Composition and Ideology of the Cracow Dietine, 1572–1606" (Polish), *PH*, XLIV, 309–332, with French and Russian summaries. On other regional dietines, see esp. W. Dworzaczek, ed., *Akta sejmikowe województwa poznańskiego i kaliskiego* (Records of the Dietines of the Provinces of Poznań and Kalisz), Vol. I, for instance the debate at the dietine of Środa (December 30, 1602) about the instructions to be given the deputies at the forthcoming Sejm. After complaining about the general burden of taxation and reviewing the unsatisfactory international situation, the members demanded the imposition upon Jews of a tax of a different order from the one under negotiation between them and the government, "which accrues only to the benefit of the Crown Treasurer [*podskarbi* Jan Firlej]" (p. 254 No. 86; cf. *infra*, Chap. LXX, n. 90); and W. Hejnosz's succinct remarks (preliminary to his planned publication of the text of these proceedings from a copy of the original which had been removed from Vilna during the Russian evacuation of 1915 and had not been retrieved) on "The *Lauda* [Resolutions] of the Dietine of Chełm" (Polish), *Sprawozdania* of the Towarzystwo Naukowe in Lwów, XV, 34–38.

These publications offer but a sample of the vast, as yet largely unpublished. materials pertaining to the approximately 70 dietines, which assembled under various names for other than electoral purposes, and performed a variety of legislative functions. Many of them, like the ten regional dietines in the relatively small duchy of Mazovia, had little bearing on the Jewish situation. But others, in both the Crown and Lithuania, deserve a detailed examination of their impact on the situation of Polish-Lithuanian Jewry. Thus far only the dietines of Wisznia have been subjected to a brief analysis by A. Prochaska, the editor of its resolutions, in his essay, "The Attitude of the Dietine of Wisznia toward the Jews" (Polish), *Prze-wodink naukowy i literacki*, 1920, pp. 755–68.

64. S. M. Dubnow, ed., *Pinqas ha-Medinah*, pp. 10 No. 6, 27 No. 111, 157 No. 654; I. Halperin, ed., *Pinqas*, pp. 54 Nos. 153–55, 58 No. 160; L. Lewin, *Die Landessynode*, p. 89 No. 45; idem, "Neue Materialien," *JJLG*, III, 106 No. LII. See also other data analyzed by I. Lewin in his "The Jews' Participation in Diet Elections" (Polish), *MZ*, II, 52 f. Such political activities often led to friction, not only between individual communities but also between the two councils. See, for instance, the compromise achieved in 1681, on an intercommunal conflict, by the representatives of the two central bodies, according to the minutes reproduced by Dubnow in *Pinqas ha-Medinah*, pp. 284 ff.

65. See S. Kutrzeba and A. Przyboś, eds., *Akta sejmikowe województwa krakowskiego*, I, 113 ff. No. xxviii, esp. pp. 118 f. Arts. 11–12. Only the Warsaw Confederation of 1573 has been subjected to careful study. See esp. S. Ptaszycki, "The Warsaw Confederation of 1573: Archaeographic and Linguistic Reflections" (Polish), *Reformacja w Polsce*, V, Part 3, 90–97; idem, "The Fate of the Warsaw Confederation of 1573 in the Light of New Data" (Polish), *ibid.*, VI, 106–121; W. Budka, "Who Signed the Warsaw Confederation of 1573?" (Polish), *ibid.*, I, 314–19 (pointing out that among the 98 signers, 14–17 of the 28 senators, and 52–60 of the 70 deputies of the nobles, were Protestants); S. Gruszecki, "The Social Image of the Warsaw Confederation of 1573" (Polish), *ORP*, XIII, 145–57, with a French summary (contends that the major factors were the magnates and the middle *szlachta*); and *supra*, Chap. LXVII, nn. 38 and 44. While these studies do not refer to the Jewish question as such, they nevertheless very well reflect the temper of the age which produced the memorable resolutions on religious toleration.

Of an entirely different nature was the rather exceptional 1615 meeting of three western Polish cities. Called to pursue the common interests of these cities, this gathering, too, went under the name of a "confederation." See R. Walczak, *Konfederacja Gdańska, Elbląga i Torunia* (The Confederation of G., E. and T., 1615–1623), cited from a MS by Z. Kaczmarczyk and B. Leśnodorski in J. Bardach, ed., *Historia państwa*, II, 296 f. But, unlike the abortive anti-Jewish alliance of Lwów, Poznań, and Cracow in 1521 (see *supra*, Chap. LXVII, n. 9), this interurban collaboration was not aimed at Jews. Certainly, the Jewish population in that entire area was much too small to require concerted action.

66. Andrzej Frycz Modrzewski (Andreas Fricius Modręvius), *Opera omnia*, ed. with Latin introductions and Notes by K. Kumaniecki; A. Luczak, *Die Staats- und Rechtslehre des polnischen Renaissancedenkers Andrzej Frycz Modrzewski (Andreas Fricius Modrevius)*; and, more generally, K. Lepszy's biography *Andrzej Frycz Modrzewski*, 2d ed.; Łukasz Górnicki, *Droga do zupełnej wolności* (A Way to Complete Freedom), first posthumously published by his son in Elbląg, in 1650, and dedicated to King John Casimir); Krzysztof Warszewicki (Varsevitius), *De optimo statu libertatis libri duo*, Cracow, 1598; Piotr Skarga's writings discussed *supra*, nn. 9 ff.; Stanisław Orzechowski, *Rozmowa albo dialog około egzekucyjej Korony Polskiej* (A Dialogue about the Executive Power in the Polish Crown), 1563; and his *Quincunx, to jest wzór Korony Polskiej* (Q., That is an Example for the Polish Crown), 1564; both reed. by J. Łoś, with an Historical Commentary by S. Kot; and his other works.

These and other political writers are analyzed in the older, but still very informative, work by S. Tarnowski, *Studia do historyi literatury polskiej. Pisarze polityczni XVI wieku* (Studies in the History of Polish Literature: Political Writers of the Sixteenth Century); and, briefly, in J. Bardach, ed., *Historia państwa*, II, 89–113.

67. Herodotus, *History*, IV, 21, 37, and 110 ff., ed. in Greek with an English trans. by A. D. Godley (Loeb Classical Library), II, 221, 257, 309 ff.; and in G. Rawlinson's English trans., 3d ed., III, 18, 95 ff., 201 ff. Essay 3; and W. W. Howe and J. Wells, *A Commentary on Herodotus with Introductions and Appendices*, new impression, I, 310, 341, 424 ff. Appendices xi–xii; and, fuller and more up to date, T. Sulimirski, "The Forgotten Sarmatians: A Once Mighty Folk Scattered among the Nations," in E. Bacon, ed., *Vanished Civilisations of the Ancient World*, pp. 279–98. On the alleged "Sarmatian" origins of the *szlachta*, and its bearing on contemporary political theory, see J. Tazbir, "From Studies on Xenophobia in Poland in the Period of the Late Renaissance" (Polish), *PH*, XLVIII, 655–82, with Russian and French summaries, esp. pp. 673 ff.; idem, "Recherches sur la conscience nationale," *APH*, XIV, 15 f.; S. Cynarski, "The Shape of Sarmatian Ideology in Poland," *ibid.*, XIX, 5–17. See also B. Ulanowski, ed., *Sześć broszur politycznych z XVI i początku XVII stulecia* (Six Political Pamphlets of the Sixteenth and Early Seventeenth Centuries), for the most part arguing for Catholic unity and "liberties" for the people, and, more generally, the collection of excerpts from five centuries of Polish political writings, ed. by M. Kridl *et al.*, under the title, *The Democratic Heritage of Poland "For Your Freedom and Ours": an Anthology*, trans. with the editorial assistance of L. Krzyżanowski. These few hints must suffice here, since a thorough exploration of Polish political writings, lay even more than ecclesiastical, and of their authors' varying attitudes, directly or indirectly relating to the contemporary Jewish question, still is a major scholarly desideratum.

68. Przecław Mojecki, *Żydowskie okrucieństwa, mordy y zabobony* (Jewish Cruelties, Murders, and Superstitions), Cracow, 1589 and 1598; reprinted in Cracow, in 1602, by Szymon Aleksander Hubicki under the title *Żydowskie okrucieństwa nad Najświętszym Sakramentem y dziatkami chrześcijańskimi* (Jewish Cruelties on the Most Holy Sacrament and Little Christian Children), to which he appended his pamphlet entitled *Tychże zdrayców [żydowskich] zbrodnia w Świniarowie pod Łosicami popełniona* (The [Jewish] Traitors' Crime Committed in Świniarów Near Łosice, Which Was Tried at the Lublin Tribunal A. D. 1598); Jan Achazy Kmita, *Proces sprawy bocheńskiej z Żydami* (Proceedings of the Bochnia Affair with the Jews concerning the Most Holy Sacrament of the Eucharist Bought by the Jews from Sacrilegious Thieves, Miraculously Revealed), Cracow, 1602. A second impression, Cracow, 1606, had the following supplementary title: *Przytym dekret króla JM* (To Which Is Appended the Decree of His Majesty the King as to How the Infidel Jews Have Been Publicly Convicted and for This Reason Expelled from Bochnia. Necessary for the Chroniclers; idem, *Talmud Abo wiara żydowska. Nie tylko Rabinom, ale i nie-Rabinom potrzebny, a postpulstwu krotofilny* (The Talmud; or, The Jewish Faith. Needed Not Only by Rabbis But Also by Non-Rabbis and Amusing to the Populace), Cracow, 1610, offering the customary anti-Jewish selection of excerpts from the Talmud (Kmita wrote at least four other anti-Jewish pamphlets); Sebastyan Fabian Klonowicz, *Victoria Deorum. In qua continetur veri herois educatio*, n.p., n.d. [1587 or 1600], esp. Chaps. xiv and xxvi; idem, *Worek Judaszów to*

iest złe nabycie maiętności (The Pouch of the Judases; That is, the Evil Acquisition of a Fortune), Cracow, 1600, 1603, and frequently thereafter. More recently a critical edition of the *Worek* has been issued with revisions by K. Budek and A. Obręska-Jabłońska and a juridical commentary by Z. Zdrójkowski by PAN. See the remarks on all these writings in Karol Estreicher's standard *Bibliografia polska*, XIX, 306 f., 326 f.; XXII, 354 f., 510 f.; and K. Bartoszewicz *Antysemityzm w literaturze polskiej, passim.* Of interest also is M. Dembrowska's analysis, *Metoda bibliografii polskiej Karola Estreichera* (The Methods Employed in Karol Estreicher's Polish Bibliography) 2d ed. enlarged, with an English summary.

It may be noted that these Jew-baiting authors not only were themselves persons of some social standing but were undoubtedly sponsored, at least to some extent, by the high officials to whom they dedicated their works. Mojecki was a canon of the Opoczno church; Hubicki served as rector of the bishopric of Cracow. The second edition of Mojecki's tract, which included Hubicki's Appendix, was dedicated to Adam Stadnicki, burgrave of Przemyśl. Kmita served as an official of the Bochnia salt mines, and in this capacity was probably involved in the trial of the local Jews. He emphasized that his description of the trial was *emes* (truth; which he printed in both Latin and Hebrew characters) and took as a motto a little verse beginning: "This book, unpleasant to Jews and Aryans/ Will be a delight to saintly Christians." Klonowicz emphasized on the title page that he was serving as city councilor and Jewish judge (!) in Lublin. He dedicated one edition of his *Victoria Deorum* to Mikołaj Firlej, the palatine of Lublin, and another to General Adam Gorayski.

These and other writings, and their backgrounds, are analyzed, in part, by M. Bałaban in his "Episodes from the History of Ritual Murder Trials" (Russian), *ES*, VII, 163–81, 318–27; and in considerable detail by K. Bartoszewicz in his *Antysemityzm.* The Catholic reaction to the rumors of host desecration in Poznań in 1620 is graphically described by J. Łukaszewicz in his *Obraz historyczno-statystyczny miasta Poznania*, II (also in his *Historisch-statistiches Bild der Stadt Posen*, German trans. by Tiesler, II, 236). On the suppression of Miczyński's *Zwierciadło*, see Sigismund III's decree of August 31, 1618, reproduced by M. Bersohn in his *Dyplomataryusz*, pp. 124 ff. No. 219; *supra*, nn. 23–25; and Chap. LXVII, n. 37. Jew-baiting references to the Bochnia affair, and to other aspects of Judeo-Polish relations of the Zebrzydowski period, are found in J. Czubek's ed. of *Pisma polityczne z czasów rokoszu Zebrzydowskiego* (Political Writings of the Period of the Zebrzydowski Rebellion, 1606–1608), esp. II, 115 f., 133 f., 144, 248 f.; III, 51, 91, 116. See also the anti-Jewish speeches delivered by two bishops and one palatine at the Diet of 1605, cited *infra*, n. 89.

69. *VL*, II, 901, 922 f.; J. Czubek, ed., *Pisma polityczne z czasów rokoszu Zebrzydowskiego;* Sir George Carew, *Relation of the State of Polonia and the United Provinces of that Crown anno 1598*, ed. by C. H. Talbot, p. 68; the comments thereon by S. Mews in *Ein Englischer Gesandschaftsbericht über den polnischen Staat zu Ende des 16. Jahrhunderts*, esp. p. 46; M. Bałaban, *Dzieje*, I, 151; other data briefly analyzed by Z. Kaczmarczyk and B. Leśnodorski in J. Bardach, ed., *Historia państwa*, II, 122 ff.; and *supra*, Chap. LXVII, n. 40. The contrast between the proto-absolutist tendencies of the fifteenth century and the weak elective monarchy of the seventeenth, is well illustrated by J. Bardach's analysis "Le Pouvoir monarchique en Pologne au moyen âge," *Recueil de la Société Jean Bodin*, XXI, Part 2, pp. 563–612.

The author traces here the gradual decline of monarchical power: in the absence from the Chamber of Deputies of representatives of either the burghers (except a few from Cracow) or the clergy (the bishops held seats only in the Senate), the monarchy had to face the increasingly unruly gentry alone. This imbalance had, as early as 1505, produced the constitution *Nihil Novi*, which greatly circumscribed the royal prerogatives.

Understandably, despite its deep involvement in the progress of the Counter Reformation in all Christian countries, Spain was primarily concerned with Sigismund's international relations and military ventures. Not even the role of the Spanish Jewish émigrés or their descendants in eastern Europe seems to have aroused the curiosity of Spanish diplomats. At least this is the impression one gains from the 1613 dispatch transmitted by the Spanish ambassador in Poland to Madrid via Prague, which, in its brevity and rather one-sided approach, contrasts with the wide-ranging contemporary reports by the Venetian ambassadors and papal nuncios. See V. Meysztowicz, ed., "Relatio burgravii Abraham de Dohna, oratoris regis Hispaniae, de missione quam a. 1613 ad regem Poloniae absolvit," *Antemurale*, XII, 77–88; and *supra*, n. 49; and Chap. LXVII, n. 5.

70. See P. Bloch, *Die General-Privilegien*, pp. 103 f. (Preamble), 107 Art. 9, 115 f. Arts. 36–37; and in John Sobieski's confirmation of 1676 in L. Gumplowicz, *Prawodawstwo polskie względem Żydów*, pp. 162, 165 Art. 6, 172 Art. 19. Even in the last confirmation of the Jewish privilege by Stanislaus II Augustus Poniatowski, where this fiscal nexus is slightly toned down, the king still quotes Casimir's statement about the Jews, *quos Nobis et regno specialiter conservamus thesauro*. See *Sumaryusz przywilejów*, ed. by M. Schorr in *ES*, II, 94. Phrases like *Judeus noster*, used in Casimir IV's intervention in behalf of Sloma of Grodno in 1453, are in line with this general notion of a connection between the Jews and the royal power. Yet the unusual formula in the Preamble, and particularly the term *nobilium terrigenarum*, was used by such critics as R. Hube to impugn the authenticity of this entire document. See his careful study of the text and confirmations of "Boleslas' Jewish Privilege" (Polish), *Biblioteka warszawska*, 1880, 426 ff.; and Bloch's reply thereto in *Die General-Privilegien*, esp. pp. 79 f. n. 1. Incidentally, reference to the consent of lords and nobles was not limited to the Jewish privileges; such consent was frequently invoked, for instance, by Casimir the Great in other constitutional enactments. See O. Balzer's ed. of *Statuty Kazimierza Wielkiego* (The Statutes of Casimir the Great), posthumously ed. by Z. Kaczmarczyk *et al*. (*Studia nad historią prawa polskiego*, XIX), pp. 286 ff. Art. xv, 436 ff. Arts. lxxii–lxxiii, 502 ff. Art. xcv. In any case, whatever one thinks about the authenticity of the text, submitted by the Poznań Jews to Casimir IV in 1453 (see *supra*, Vol. X, pp. 46, 322 n. 57), this text subsequently served as the basic royal constitution regulating the status of the Jewish masses of early modern Poland. In our analysis we need but cite, therefore, mainly the provisions of this so-called Boleslas-Casimir statute. See also K. Górski, "The Internal Administration of Casimir the Jagiellon in the Polish Crown" (Polish), *KH*, LXVI, 726–59.

71. F. H. Wettstein, *Debarim 'attiqim* (Ancient Subjects), p. 4. On the 1595 fire in Cracow—one of many which devastated that city, like many others in the early

modern period—see A. Walawender, *Kronika klęsk elementarnych w Polsce* (Chronicle of Elemental Catastrophes in Poland), *passim; supra,* Chap. LXVII, n. 23; and *infra,* Chap. LXIX, nn. 40–41.

72. See P. Bloch, *Die General-Privilegien der polnischen Judenschaft,* pp. 62 ff.; R. Hube, "Boleslas' Jewish Privilege" (Polish), *Biblioteka warszawska,* 1880, p. 433; M. Bersohn, *Dyplomataryusz,* p. 122 No. 206; J. Morgensztern, "Regesta," *BZIH,* no. 51, p. 61 Nos. 2–5. The dates of some of these confirmations differ in the extant records. As entered in the Crown registers (*Metryka Koronna*), Wladislaw confirmed the basic Charter on March 9 (or 16) and April 24, 1633, while John Casimir added his confirmation in January 1649. See M. Bersohn, pp. 131 No. 230, 138 f. No. 247; J. Morgensztern, *BZIH,* no. 58, p. 168 Nos. 1 and 8. On the position of the Jews in Płock, and their legal vicissitudes there since their city's incorporation into the Polish Crown in 1495, see I. Trunk, *Shtudies in yidisher geshikhte in Poiln* (Studies in the History of the Jews in Poland), pp. 25 ff. The implication that Sigismund III wished to maintain the Jewish charters unchanged had already been indicated in 1589 by his privilege for the Jews of Łuck. See *infra,* n. 74. It may be noted that Archbishop Stanisław Karnkowski of Gniezno, the primate of Poland, warned the new king not to hesitate to deny toleration to Protestants, and reminded him that it was he, the archbishop, who had anointed the king. In this connection Karnkowski referred rather bitingly to "*Heli,* the chief elder of the Jews." See V. Meysztowicz, ed., *Documenta Polonica ex archivo generali Hispaniae in Simancas,* V, 77 f. No. 46; and *supra,* nn. 14–15.

The nexus between the mission of the Wschowa (Fraustadt) elders to the king and the local developments in that city is quite apparent in the light of the archival data reviewed by H. Moritz in "Die Älteste jüdische Niederlassung in Fraustadt," *Historische Monatsblätter für die Provinz Posen,* II, 179–84. Wschowa, at that time an important center of commerce, began attracting Jewish traders and moneylenders in the sixteenth century. To circumvent the city's opposition, some Jews settled in the environs of the castle, under the protection of the district governor. On April 13, 1592, the city council dispatched its secretary, Stefan Korczak, to Cracow to secure a royal order that the Jews ("the infidel rabble who insinuated themselves" into the castle area) be banished from the city. Although the king complied and sent two such orders to the governor (on April 27 and July 3), this official was in no hurry to execute them. Three years passed before the expulsion was actually carried out (July 1595). The issuance of the general Charter in October 1592 had at best contributed merely to the *starosta*'s delaying action. See also *supra,* n. 27; and Chap. LXVII, n. 10.

73. See A. Brückner, *Dzieje kultury polskiej,* 3d ed., II, 209; and, more generally, K. Bukowska, "On the Reception of Roman Law in Old Poland's Municipal Law" (Polish), *CPH,* XX, 71–92, with a French summary; idem, "Le Droit romain en Pologne an XVIIᵉ siècle," *Revue historique du droit français et étranger,* XXXIX, 76–89; and her more detailed Warsaw dissertation, *Tomasz Drezner, polski romanista XVII wieku i jego znaczenie dla nauki prawa w Polsce* (T. D., a Polish Romanist of the XVII Century and His Significance for the Study of Law in Poland); and other writings listed in J. Sawicki's regular surveys of "Materials for a Polish Historico-Juridical Bibliography" (Polish) in *CPH* from Vol. VI (1954) covering the publica-

tions of 1944–1953, and for the subsequent years; for instance, *ibid.*, XXII, No. 1, 285–357 (for 1968); XXIII, 275–334 (for 1969).

74. Moses Isserles, *Resp.*, cited by B. Z. Katz in his *Le-Qorot ha-Yehudim*, p. 3; M. Bersohn, *Dyplomataryusz*, pp. 113 ff. Nos. 192, 193, 196; 204 f. Nos. 545, 549; J. Morgensztern, "Regesta" (Polish), *BZIH*, no. 51, pp. 60 f. Nos. 6 and 9; *supra*, n. 69; and Chap. LXVII, nn. 15 and 55. See also Sigismund Augustus' comprehensive privilege for the Jews of Przemyśl, dated June 29, 1559, and reproduced, together with other documents, by M. Schorr in his *Żydzi w Przemyślu*, pp. 73 ff. App. i, 78 App. v, 82 App. vii, 92 App. xv, etc.

75. See the text in P. Bloch, *Die General-Privilegien*, pp. 108 f. Arts. 13–15; 111 f. Art. 26; and in the version later approved by King John Sobieski in 1676, reproduced by L. Gumplowicz in *Prawodawstwo polskie względem Żydow*, pp. 79 f., 166 Arts. 7–8, 168 Art. 17; Meir b. Gedaliah of Lublin, *Resp.*, Metz, 1769 ed., fol. 39c No. 86. Of interest also is the related statutory provision: "If a Jew [uninvited] should enter the house of some Christian, the Christian should not consider it an imposition, grievance, or molestation." Bloch, p. 109 Art. 16; Gumplowicz, p. 166 Art. 9. This evidently was not intended to infringe upon the privacy of Christian homes, although privacy was generally less valued then than it is today, but rather to ensure that any Jew could visit a Christian for business or other reasons without being accused of "molestation." On the other hand, since the days of Boleslas, the same law had provided that a Christian was not to enter the home of his Jewish creditor to seize his pledge unlawfully; that is, without a prior court order (Bloch, p. 112 Art. 28; Gumplowicz, p. 169 Art. 18).

76. See P. Bloch, *Die General-Privilegien*, pp. 116 f. Arts. 38–39; L. Gumplowicz, *Prawodawstwo*, pp. 172 f. Arts. 20–21; Přemysl Ottakar II's decrees of 1254 in G. Bondy and F. Dworský's *Zur Geschichte*, I, 17 ff. Nos. 24–25. Article 39 of the Polish Charter clearly marked a considerable expansion of the protective provisions of Boleslas the Pious' original statute. The requirement of four Christian witnesses of proven honesty and membership in the propertied classes, was new. The original statute either did not specify the number of witnesses or, in the version preserved by Łaski, followed Přemysl Ottakar's requirement of three Christian and three Jewish witnesses, without further qualification. See Bloch, pp. 28 f. Art. 32. Even more noteworthy is the insertion into the Boleslas-Casimir privilege of the same sanction on the accusation of host desecration (*utentur sanguine christianorum annuatim vel sacramentis ecclesaie christianorum*). This addition evidently represented a need which arose in Poland at a later date, perhaps during the Poznań disturbances of 1399. It is quite possible, therefore, that these amplifications stemmed from a later hand than that of Casimir the Great or even Casimir IV, though specific interpolations of this kind, if indeed made, did not impinge on the much-debated authenticity of that statute's basic provisions. True, these provisions did not stem the tide of the Blood Accusations, which not only greatly complicated Jewish life in Poland but also caused many difficulties for the royal administration. In an effort to introduce some clarity into the highly diffuse penal procedure, Wladislaw IV, in his confirmation of the 1633 privileges for Cracow Jewry, provided

that any Jew accused of ritual murder should be imprisoned by the local municipal organs and delivered to the district governor (*starosta*), but that for the trial itself the king would delegate a special judge to join the governor. However, even this decree was subject to many variations, and its effectiveness depended entirely on the energy and good will of the royal officials, who often helplessly faced the vindictive clamor of a frenzied populace. See Bałaban, *Żydzi lwowscy*, pp. 325 ff.

77. J. D. Mansi, *Sacrorum conciliorum collectio*, XXIII, 1178 f., summarized in J. Aronius, *Regesten zur Geschichte der Juden im fränkischen und deutschen Reiche*, pp. 301 ff. No. 724; R. Meir b. Gedaliah of Lublin, *Resp.*, Metz, 1769 ed., fols. 10c f. No. 15. Regrettably, Vol. V (devoted to the synods of the archdiocese of Gniezno) of J. Sawicki's comprehensive *Concilia Poloniae: Żródła i studya krytyczne* (Polish Synods: Sources and Critical Studies) discusses only the assemblies of the years 1407–1720.

78. See the general procedure described by the anonymous German author of the thirteenth-century Polish law book, ed. by A. Z. Helcel in his *Starodawne . . . pomniki*, II, 16 f. Art. v, 279 No. 1922, 281 No. 1935; the Boleslas-Casimir statute, Art. iii, in Bloch, *Die General-Privilegien*, pp. 47 (German), 105 (Latin); Stephen Báthory's statute of 1580, cited in Latin with a German excerpt, *ibid.*, pp. 96 ff.; F. Papée, ed., *Akta Aleksandra*, pp. 231 ff. No. 149; *VL*, I, 337 (giving the lengthy Latin formula of the extensive oath *more judaico*); Bersohn, *Dyplomataryusz*, pp. 100 ff. No. 152; Z. Pazdro, *Organizacya i praktyka żydowskich sądów podwojewodzińskich*, pp. 99 ff., Appendix, pp. 161 f. No. 3, 168 ff. Nos. 7–8; M. Bałaban, *Żydzi lwowscy*, pp. 319 f. (reproduces the lengthy formula of a fiscal oath of 1628–29, with many maledictions for perjurers), Documentary section, pp. 34 ff. Nos. 33 and 35; and, more generally, S. Borowski, *Przysięga dowodowa w procesie polskim późniejszego średniowiecza* (The Oath of Evidence in the Polish Procedure of the Late Middle Ages), esp. pp. 37 ff. The interrelationship between oaths and maledictions is well illustrated by the examples assembled by P. Dąbkowski in his *Litkup: Studyum z prawa polskiego* (Leikauf [Contractual Agreement Confirmed by Drinking]: a Study in Polish Law), esp. the Appendix "On Oaths and Curses" (pp. 56–68).

Perhaps the most remarkable feature of the long formula mentioned in the text is the obligation of the Jew to turn toward the sun. This ritual, doubtless of pagan origin, appeared first in a Polish nobleman's oath late in the fifteenth century, and was later added to oaths taken in the army. See W. Semkowicz, "The Oath to the Sun: a Comparative Legal-Ethnological Study" (Polish), *Księga pamiątkowa* (Memorial Volume in Honor of) *Bolesław Orzechowicz*, II, 304–377, esp. pp. 365 (referring to a Grimm brothers' folk tale about a German tailor whose murder of a Jew was betrayed by the sun) and 375 f. App. ii (reproducing a 1573 text concerning a similar Turkish oath); amplified by Semkowicz in his "More about tthe Oath to the Sun in Poland" (Polish), *Studia historyczne* (Historical Studies: a Memorial Volume in Honor of) *Stanisław Kutrzeba*, I, 429–44. The application of that oath to Jews could actually be interpreted as a testimony to their relatively high status. With the general conservatism prevailing in the treatment of Jews, it appears that this kind of oath was still being administered to some Jews testifying before village courts in the eighteenth century, long after it had gone out of use with respect to the other classes of the population. See S. Szczotka, "The Application of the Oath to the Sun in the Rural Courts of the Eighteenth Century" (Polish), *CPH*, II, 452–58 (citing only a single, somewhat dubious, text of 1767, however); J. Bardach, ed., *Historia państwa*, I, 352 f.; II, 199 f.

79. See P. Bloch, *Die General-Privilegien*, pp. 109 f. Art. 17; L. Gumplowicz, *Prawodawstwo*, pp. 166 f. Art. 10. Apart from the privilege of not tolerating Jews—often granted to cities by those very kings who stressed the Jews' freedom of movement—the independent, semisovereign rights exercised by the noble lords over their private towns could become a grave obstacle. We recall Sigismund I's irate pronouncement that, since he was not collecting revenue from Jewish residents in such towns, he was not obliged to protect them. But in time the royal capitation tax and other imposts were for the most part collected from Jews of the entire realm through their central, regional, or local communities, and the kings had every incentive to enlarge the Jewish rights of travel and trade in as many localities as possible. This prerogative also included foreign countries, from business trips to which Polish and Lithuanian Christian traders were long barred by law. Domestically, too, the kings tried to secure for Jewish businessmen the right to visit all fairs on an equal basis with their nonlocal Christian competitors.

80. S. M. Dubnow, *Pinqas ha-Medinah*, pp. 10 Nos. 46–47, 42 No. 202, etc.; *supra*, Chap. LXVII, nn. 8, 11–12 and the sources cited there. The exercise of controls over the admission of new settlers required extensive knowledge of existing economic and political conditions in the country, as well as of the attitude of Christian neighbors and government officials toward Jews. For this reason the Polish and Lithuanian Councils demanded that every action of this kind by a local community be reviewed by the provincial elders. With the growth in numbers, affluence, and self-assertion of the local communities, however, the Council of Four Lands increasingly had to respect the independent decisions of local leaders; for instance, in the case of Opatów in 1687. See H. Horowitz, "Die Jüdische Gemeinde Opatow und ihre Rabbiner," *MGWJ*, LXXIV, 11.

81. See P. Bloch, *Die General-Privilegien*, p. 111 Art. 122; L. Gumplowicz, *Prawodawstwo*, p. 168 Art. 14 (both referring merely to unlawful attacks on synagogues); Wladislaw IV's decrees of 1633 and 1638, reproduced by M. Bałaban in *Żydzi lwowscy*, App. pp. 113 ff. No. 85; and by M. Schorr in his *Żydzi w Przemyślu*, pp. 138 ff. No. 68; J. Morgensztern, "Regesta," *BZIH*, no. 51, p. 64 Nos. 23–25; Ps. 130:1; L. Lewin, *Die Landessynode*, pp. 10 f., 20 f. The royal charters steered clear, however, of the basic question: By whom (and under what circumstances) were permits to be issued for the erection of a new house of worship or the enlargement of an existing one? This question, which had troubled Jewish communities since the Christian Roman Empire, was left largely unresolved in Poland. Only Wladislaw IV, though outwardly accepting the canonical regulations concerning the construction of synagogues, felt the need to insist that the license be given by the king or his officials. The various aspects of Jewish artistic creativity connected with the Polish synagogues have aroused the interest of many art historians, and will be dealt with here at some length in another chapter. For the time being, suffice it to refer to one of the latest monographs, by M. Piechotkowa and K. Piechotków, *Bóżnice drewniane* (Wooden Synagogues).

Some synagogues, especially in the southeastern provinces, were built of stone, and could serve as part of the fortifications of the respective localities. An outstanding example of such a fortified house of worship is the Łuck synagogue built in 1626. Its photograph has frequently been reproduced; for instance, in I. Halpern *et al.*, eds., *Bet Yisrael be-Polin* (The House of Israel in Poland), pp. 68 f. Others, some of which are no longer extant, were erected in Tarnopol, Żołkiew, Brody, and other cities soon after the tragic events of 1648–49. See esp. M. Bałaban, "Fortified Synagogues in the Eastern Districts of the Commonwealth" (Polish), *Nowe Życie*, I, 197–203; and, more broadly, in his *Zabytki historyczne Żydów w Polsce* (Jewish Historical Remains in Poland), pp. 64 ff.

82. P. Bloch, *Die General-Privilegien*, pp. 110 f. Arts. 18 and 21; L. Gumplowicz, *Prawodawstwo*, pp. 167 f. Arts. 10 and 13; D. Kandel, "Old Synagogues in Poland" (Polish), *Kwartalnik poświęcony badaniu przeszłości Żydów w Polsce*, I, Part 1, App. It is possible, however, that these protective provisions were inserted largely in emulation of other royal statutes, rather than because of actual local difficulties. We do not know of any chicaneries connected with the transport of Jewish corpses or the desecration of Jewish cemeteries in Poland on any scale comparable to the related difficulties encountered by Jews in Western Europe. True, our medieval sources are very sparse and uninformative, and certainly do not warrant any *argumentum a silentio*. By the time rabbinic and other sources began to flow more freely, in the sixteenth and seventeenth centuries, most Polish-Jewish communities had cemeteries of their own, and funeral corteges did not have to travel great distances. Nevertheless, it was quite important for the Jews to have the protective provisions on the statute books. See also I. Lewin's aforementioned essay, *The Protection of Jewish Religious Rights by Royal Edicts in Ancient Poland*, esp. pp. 10 f. Needless to say, some desecrations of Jewish cemeteries by hooligans or thieves occurred from time to time in Poland, too. More remarkably, in his retaliatory gesture of 1629, Sigismund III gave away not only the two "illicit" synagogues in Łuck but also two orchards which had been set aside for conversion into a Jewish burial ground. See J. Morgensztern, "Regesta," *BZIH*, no. 51, p. 64 No. 25.

83. P. Bloch, *Die General-Privilegien*, p. 110 Art. 20; L. Gumplowicz, *Prawodawstwo*, p. 167 Art. 12. Here as in many other cases, protective provisions were also necessary to combat the competitive appetites of the guilds. Christian butchers used all means at their disposal to prevent Jews from selling meat, even to their own coreligionists, and especially to Christian customers. While these contingencies were not foreseen in the basic charters, royal officials repeatedly intervened to frustrate such designs. With their usual inconsistency, however, the kings sometimes respected contradictory rights acquired by the Christian guilds. For example, in his decree of December 10, 1620, Sigismund III granted the Christian butchers' guild in Sandomierz the exclusive right to buy large cattle, whereas Jewish butchers were to be allowed to acquire and sell only sheep and goats. See J. Morgensztern, "Regesta," *BZIH*, no. 51, p. 68 No. 52.

84. P. Bloch, *Die General-Privilegien*, pp. 107 f. Arts. 7–8, 10–11; L. Gumplowicz, *Prawodawstwo*, pp. 164 ff. Arts. 5–7; Joel Sirkes, *Resp.* [n.s.], Korzec, 1785 ed., fols. 22c f. No. 43. Wealthy Jews, functioning as "servitors" at the royal court, sometimes felt free to defy the Jewish communal authorities. They claimed that, just as they were generally exempted from paying customs duties on imported merchandise, they ought also to be freed from their share in communal taxation. Such practices

were, indeed, frequently recorded in Spain and other areas where royal favorites obtained specific royal tax exemptions not only for themselves but for their descendants as well. Needless to say, the struggling Jewish communities in Poland could not afford to allow some of their wealthiest contributors to escape taxes, which were not assessed on an individual basis but were collected in lump-sum payments from the entire community. A conflict on this score arose, for example, between the influential court physician Dr. Salomon Calahora and the community of Cracow. See M. Bałaban, *Kalohorowie* (The Family Calahora: From the History of the Jews in Poland); idem, *Dzieje*, I, 143 ff., 228 ff.

85. See W. Maisel, *Sądownictwo miasta Poznania do końca XVI wieku* (The Judicial Administration of the City of Poznań to the End of the Sixteenth Century; with a German summary, pp. 351–53); C. Krawczak, "The Origin and Development of Building Codes in Poznań to the Year 1838" (Polish), *Studia i materiały do dziejów Wielkopolski i Pomorza* (Studies and Materials for the History of Great Poland and Pomerania), IX, Part 1 (XVII), 31–56; Sigismund II's decree of January 13, 1557, reproduced by A. Sawczyński in "Das XVII. Jahrhundert in der polnischen Geschichte und Geschichtsschreibung," *Teki historyczne*, XIV, 97–106 (presented to the Twelfth International Congress of Historical Sciences, Vienna, 1965), p. 384 No. 13. Evidently, however, much of the Poznań judicial evolution analyzed by Maisel represents earlier stages, which in the late sixteenth and early seventeenth centuries were considerably refined, partly in connection with the more fully recognized Jewish autonomy in judicial affairs.

86. See I. Halperin, *Va'ad*, Intro. pp. xvii ff., and *passim;* W. Czapliński, *Polska a Bałtyk w latach 1632–1648* (Poland and the Baltic in 1632–1648: a History of the Navy and of Maritime Policy), esp. pp. 12, 37 ff., 79 n. 16, 93 ff.; and A. Sucheni-Grabowska, *Odbudowa domeny królewskiej w Polsce, 1504–1548* (The Rebuilding of the Royal Domain in Poland, 1504–1548). Polish kings, without resorting to forced loans, found ways of pressuring their Jewish subjects into making "voluntary" contributions to the Treasury. For example, on April 28, 1578, Stephen "appealed" to the Cracow Jews to deposit 1,000 marks in pure silver at the mint, under the direction of Rafał Leszczyński, as an aid to monetary reform. In 1643, Wladislaw IV demanded from the Jews a contribution of 60,000 zlotys toward the repayment of his debts, burghers likewise being "persuaded" to share in that task. See the summary of Stephen's decree of 1578, and the Latin text of the decree issued by Wladislaw in 1643, in M. Bersohn's *Dyplomataryusz*, pp. 108 No. 170 (also in J. Morgensztern's "Regesta," *BZIH*, nos. 47–48, p. 176 No. 65), 132 f. No. 238; and in the official Polish translation reproduced in M. Bałaban, *Żydzi lwowscy*, App. p. 141 No. 110.

87. See the aforementioned data on the *Straty bibliotek y archiwów warszawskich* and other publications listed *supra*, n. 46; M. Bersohn, *Dyplomataryusz*, p. 121 No. 202; *Acta Tomiciana*, ed. by W. Pociecha, XVI, Part 1, pp. 230 f. No. 114. To be sure, the powers of both the king and the palatine had been considerably whittled down in the course of the sixteenth century. For example, the king could no longer issue pardons or amnesty for convicted defendants. Nor would a palatine now venture to impose a fine of 63 marks and 18 groszy for what he considered to be the illegitimate execution of a Jew by another court, as did one of his prede-

cessors in 1447. See the text in *Akta grodzkie i ziemskie*, XIV, 249 No. 1969. Moreover, all palatines were now subject to occasional inspections by officials designated in Warsaw. See, for instance, Z. Guldon, ed., *Lustracje województw wielkopolskich i kujawskich* (Inspection of the Palatinates of Great Poland and Kujavia, 1628–32). Nevertheless, in practice the palatines, through their subpalatines and the *judices Judaeorum*, exercised effective judicial control over Judeo-Christian litigations.

88. See *supra*, n. 37. Clearly, the ability of almost any Jewish individual to appeal directly to the king or the Crown Tribunal might have led to considerable abuse. That is why the Lithuanian Council, in its constituent session of 1623, provided that any citation of a Gentile by a Jew before the royal tribunal or even a provincial court required prior notification of the Jewish communal elders. They were also to be notified after a Jew was summoned as a defendant. See Dubnow, *Pinqas ha-Medinah*, p. 12 No. 61. On the structure and procedure of royal courts, see Jan Łączyński's treatise prepared in 1596 by royal order and entitled *Kompendium sądów Króla Jegomości* (A Compendium of His Majesty's Courts). This work was ed., from the author's autograph copy and other MSS, with an informative Intro. by Z. Kolankowski in his *Zapomniany prawnik XVI wieku: Jan Łączyński* (A Forgotten Jurist of the Sixteenth Century: Jan Łączyński and his "Compendium of His Majesty's Courts": a Study in the History of the Polish Juridical Literature). Regrettably, though himself an experienced court scribe, Łączyński does not refer to specific practices affecting Jews. See also the succinct remarks by Z. Kaczmarczyk and B. Leśnodorski in J. Bardach's ed. of *Historia państwa*, II, 126; S. Kutrzeba, "The Legal Status of the Jews in Poland in the Fifteenth Century" (Polish), *Przewodnik naukowy i literacki*, XXIX, 1007–1014, 1147–56; idem, *Studya do historyi sądownictwa w Polsce* (Studies in the History of the Judiciary in Poland).

89. Hieronim Gostomski's and Jędrzej Leszczyński's addresses of January 28, 1605, summarized from *Zbiór diaryuszów sejmowych* (Collection of Diet Diaries), XXXI, Part 1, pp. 827–29 and 831–33, and on the basis of a Czartoryski MS, by A. Strzelecki in his *Sejm z roku 1605*, pp. 98 ff., 124 ff. This author also points out (p. 100 n. 1) that in "Ein Wojewode von Posen über die Juden," *Historische Monatsblätter für die Provinz Posen*, III, 125–30, J. Caro was misled by a confused account of that debate in a Gdańsk MS and erroneously attributed the pro-Jewish speech to Gostomski. On the other hand, Strzelecki fails to mention the sharp attacks on Jews included in the speeches of Bishop Maciej Pstrokoński of Przemyśl and Otto Schenking of Livonian Wenden. Their speeches, delivered on January 27, 1605, favored the enactment of a new Jewish tax so as to pay the Tatar khan the "gift" (*upominek*)—a euphemism for the tribute which Poland had earlier been paying to keep the Tatars at peace, but which had not been paid for several years. These "votes" included, according to Caro, such pearls of wisdom as Pstrokoński's contention that it was perfectly legitimate to persecute the Jewish enemies of Christ whom "the Romans had already opposed and on whom they imposed all sorts of burdens, as on other senseless animals." On his part, Schenking, whose anti-Jewish sentiments came clearly to the fore in the negotiations to keep Jews out of Livonia in the 1590s, harped on the theme that severe taxation of Jews was fully justified, since "they neither sow nor build anything, but live exclusively on the blood of the nobles." See *infra*, Chap. LXIX, n. 10.

90. I. Halperin, *Pinqas*, p. 29 No. 89; David Gans, *Ṣemaḥ David* (The Scion of David; a World Chronicle), Part II, Prague, 1592 ed., fols. 115a, 116b; with the continuation, Frankfort, 1692 ed., fols. 67a, 68a, 85b; Shabbetai b. Meir ha-Kohen, *Megillat 'afah* (Flying Scroll, on the Martyrs of the Cossack Uprising of 1648), first published in the Intro. to his *Seliḥot ve-qinnot* (Penitential Poems and Lamentations), Amsterdam, 1651. On the title, see M. Steinschneider's observations in his *Catalogus librorum hebraeorum in Bibliotheca Bodleiana*, II, 2246 f. No. 6870 item 10; M. Schorr, *Żydzi w Przemyślu*, pp. 15, 96 ff. App. xx; Joel Sirkes, *Resp.*, [o.s.] fols. 37 ff. No. 57; other data summarized in S. K. Mirsky's *R. Joel Sirkes*, pp. 27 ff.; in E. J. Schochet's comprehensive biography, *Bach, Rabbi Joel Sirkes, His Life, Works, and Times;* and *supra*, n. 53. It may be noted that at that time Jews were not admitted to Moscow. Jews had to use Smolensk as their center for the Polish-dominated Russian territories; these territories, however, were reconquered by Russia, where, as we shall see in another context, total religious intolerance prevailed during the seventeenth century. On the whole, the war with Muscovy was initiated by Báthory, but was greatly intensifed by Sigismund III and Wladislaw IV, and was far from popular, even with the Polish *szlachta*. See esp. J. Maciszewski, *Polska a Moskwa, 1603–1618* (Poland and Moscow, 1603–1618: Opinions and Attitudes of the Polish Nobility); and his brief French summary "La Noblesse polonaise et la guerre contre Moscou, 1604–1618," *APH*, XVII, 23–48. The situation in Muscovy before 1650, and the difficult position of the Jews there, will be treated more fully in the next two chapters.

LXIX: TERRITORIAL AND NUMERICAL EXPANSION

1. J. Peiser, *Geschichte der Synagogen-Gemeinde zu Stettin. Eine Studie zur Geschichte des pommerschen Judentums*; L. Donath, *Geschichte der Juden in Mecklenburg von den ältesten Zeiten (1266) bis auf die Gegenwart (1874); auch ein Beitrag zur Kulturgeschichte Mecklenburgs. Nach gedruckten und ungedruckten Quellen*, esp. p. 79; and, particularly, U. Grotefend, *Geschichte und rechtliche Stellung der Juden in Pommern von den Anfängen bis zum Tode Friedrich des Grossen*, esp. pp. 54 ff., 115 f. (136 ff., 197 f.); also reproducing the text of Bogislav X's decree of 1481. See also *supra*, Vols. IX, pp. 213, 340 f. n. 19; XI, pp. 14 f., 292 f. n. 13; XII, pp. 111, 295 n. 46; and, more generally, the literature reviewed by E. Keyser in his "Neue polnische Forschungen zur Geschichte Danzigs und Pomerellens bis zum 13. Jahrhundert," *ZOF*, XVI, 676–91; T. Cieślak's succinct observation on "Bogislav X (1474–1523), the Creator of the Modern State [of Pomerania]" (Polish), *Przegląd Zachodni*, VI, Nos. 5–6, pp. 427–34; Z. Boras, *Stosunki polsko-pomorskie w drugiej połowie XVI wieku* (Polish-Pomeranian Relations in the Second Half of the Sixteenth Century: A Political Sketch); with some supplementary materials in the review thereof by E. Bahr in *ZOF*, XVI, 731; and, more generally, the comprehensive *Historia Pomorza* (A History of Pomerania), ed. by G. Labuda *et al.*, Vol. I, Parts 1–2.

2. U. Grotefend, *Geschichte und rechtliche Stellung*, pp. 56 (138 ff.); *supra*, Vol. XIII, pp. 255, 443 n. 55. The backbone of the anti-Jewish Pomeranian burghers was strengthened by the competing interests of neighboring Denmark and Sweden, which offered a permanent threat to the burghers' independence but also counterbalanced Polish influence. The prestige of Poland, moreover, even at the height of its power, must have greatly suffered in 1569 when Sigismund II Augustus had to borrow 100,000 thalers from the Pomeranian duke through the mediation of the leading Szczecin bankers, the Brothers Loitz. It sank further when the Polish Diet refused to recognize that debt, which in fact was never repaid. Fortunately for the Jews, it was a Christian, rather than a Jewish, bank which had thus been impoverished and, in 1572, declared its bankruptcy. Hans Loitz escaped to Poland. See H. Hering, "Die Loytzen," *Baltische Studien*, XI, 80–92; J. Papritz, "Das Handels- und Bankhaus der Loitzer zu Stettin, Danzig und Lüneburg im 16. Jahrhundert," *Forschungen zur brandenburgischen und preussischen Geschichte*, XXXVIII, 1 ff.; and B. Wachowiak, "Preponderance of the Feudal State" (Polish), in G. Labuda, ed., *Dzieje Szczecina* (A History of Szczecin), Vol. II: From the Tenth Century to 1805, pp. 283 ff. See also, more broadly, the comprehensive analysis by W. Czapliński in *Polska a Bałtyk w latach 1632–1648. Dzieje floty i polityki morskiej* (Poland and the Baltic in 1632–1648: a History of the Navy and Maritime Policy).

3. See J. L. Saalschütz, "Zur Geschichte der Synagogen-Gemeinde in Königsberg. Nach meist ungedruckten Quellen," *MGWJ*, VI–VIII, XI; H. Jolowicz, *Geschichte der Juden in Königsberg i. Pr. Ein Beitrag zur Sittengeschichte des preussischen Staates. Nach urkundlichen Quellen bearbeitet*, pp. 5 ff.; and, to a lesser extent, M. Aschkewitz, *Zur Geschichte der Juden in Westpreussen*, mainly concerned with

the more recent period. The importance of the Gdańsk grain exports to Holland was dramatically illustrated in 1591 during a widespread famine in Italy. At that time the Italian public benefited greatly from the supply of Baltic grain by 400 Dutch merchantmen. Gdańsk loomed so large in Dutch eyes that, according to a popular adage, Dutchmen could expect to double their investments there in a single season. Similarly, the trade between Szczecin and the West was handled largely through Dutch shipping. According to statistical data available for the two decades 1620–29 and 1630–39, 266 and 272 Dutch ships passed through the Sound on their way to Szczecin, as against 16 and 21 ships, respectively, of all other nations combined. See B. Wachowiak, "Preponderance of the Feudal State" (Polish), in G. Labuda's ed. of *Dzieje Szczecina*, II, 276.

Not surprisingly, the Amsterdam Stock Exchange assigned a special section on its floor to Muscovite and Baltic traders. In fact, in 1666, it was estimated that three-quarters of the capital handled by that exchange was invested in the Baltic Sea trade. However, because of the restrictions from which they suffered in Gdańsk and other Baltic ports, Amsterdam Jews seem to have played but a small role in that trade, which was often extensively handled on the Polish side, by their coreligionists, as agents for the nobles. It is estimated that the nobles handled 75 percent of all the business conducted over the Vistula River, whereas the burghers' share was less than 25 percent. See H. I. Bloom, *Economic Activities of the Jews of Amsterdam in the Seventeenth and Eighteenth Centuries*, pp. 97, 180, 184; *supra*, Vol. XV, pp. 47 f., 399 n. 56; A. E. Christensen, *Dutch Trade in the Baltic about 1600. Studies in the Sound Toll Register and Dutch Shipping Records*, esp. pp. 213, 216, 385; M. Bogucka, "Amsterdam's Baltic Trade in the First Half of the Seventeenth Century in the Light of Freight Contracts" (Polish), *Zapiski historyczne*, XXXIV, Part 2, pp. 7–33 (based on a fairly large sample of 1784 contracts culled from 124 notarial ledgers; this is an important statistical study, though it does not allow for any computation of the Jewish share in that trade); S. Matysik, "The Relations between Gdańsk and Poland and Gdańsk's Structure in the Years 1454–1793; Present State and Need of [Further] Investigations" (Polish), *Przegląd Zachodni*, X, Nos. 7–8, pp. 390–414; B. Wachowiak, "From Studies on Shipping on the Vistula in the Sixteenth and Seventeenth Centuries" (Polish), *ibid.*, VII, Nos. 1–2, pp. 122–36; M. Małowist, "The Economic and Social Development of the Baltic Countries from the Fifteenth to the Seventeenth Century," *Economic History Review*, 2d ser. XII, 177–89. The new developments in Brandenburg-Prussia under the Great Elector and his successors, briefly alluded to *supra*, Vol. XIV, pp. 285 f., 410 n. 62, will be discussed in a later volume.

4. J. L. Saalschütz, "Zur Geschichte der Synagogen-Gemeinde in Königsberg," *MGWJ*, VI, 440 ff.; VII, 166 f.; H. Jolowicz, *Geschichte der Juden in Königsberg*, pp. 9 ff. These data once again show that the conversion of the Prussian duke and the majority of the population to Protestantism did not diminish their religious intolerance toward Jews. Also of considerable interest to the early stages of Protestant predominance is the aforementioned exchange of letters by Duke Albert and Cardinal Hozjusz (Hosius) during the third and final session of the Council of Trent. See *supra*, Chap. LXVIII, n. 5. On the Prusso-Polish relations of that crucial period, see such monographic studies as S. Delzel, *Das Preussisch-polnische Lehnverhältnis unter Herzog Albrecht von Preussen (1525–1568)*, with the comments thereon by A. Vetulani in his Polish review, "A New Work on the Prussian Vas-

salage in the Years 1525–1568," *Zapiski historyczne*, XXXIV, 139–47; K. Lepszy, "Ducal Prussia and Poland in the Years 1576–78" (Polish), *Księgą pamiątkowa (Mélanges)* . . . *Wacław Sobieski*, I, 149–96; and, more generally, W. Czapliński, "Les Territoires de l'Ouest dans la politique de la Pologne de 1572 à 1784," *APH*, IX, 5–27; idem, *Polska a Prusy i Brandenburgia za Władysława IV* (Poland and Brandenburg-Prussia under Wladislaw IV). See *supra*, n. 3.

5. Z. Wojciechowski, *Zygmunt Stary (1506–1548)*, p. 277; L. Szádeczky, "L'Élection d'Étiénne Báthory au trône de Pologne" in E. Lukinich and J. Dąbrowski, eds., *Étienne Batory, roi de Pologne, prince de Transylvanie*, pp. 82–104, esp. p. 94; Adam Contzen, *Politicorum libri decem in quibus de perfectae reipublicae forma, virtutibus et vitiis* . . . *tractatur*, Mayence, 1620; Jean de Laboureur de Bleranval, *Histoire et relation du voyage de la Royne de Pologne et du retour de Madame la Mle [Maréchale] de Guébriant. Avec un discours historique de tovtes les Villes et Estats*, Vol. II: *Traité du royaume de Pologne*, both cited by Z. Wójcik in his "On the International Position of the [Polish] Commonwealth in the Seventeenth Century" (Polish), *KH*, LXXIX, 632–44, supplementing an earlier chapter by the same author, analyzing "The International Situation of the Commonwealth" (Polish) in J. Tazbir, ed., *Polska XVII wieku. Państwo—społeczeństwo—kultura* (Poland in the Seventeenth Century: the State, Society, Culture), pp. 13–51.

6. See H. Dopkewitsch, "Die Hochmeisterfrage und das Livlandproblem nach der Umwandlung des Ordenslandes Preussen in ein weltliches Herzogtum durch den Krakauer Vertrag vom April 1525," *ZOF*, XVI, 201–255, with an English summary; S. Arnell, *Die Auflösung des livländischen Ordensstaates. Das schwedische Eingreifen und die Heirat Herzog Johans von Finland 1558–1562*; C. Lepszy, "La Pologne et la souveraineté sur la Baltique au milieu du XVIe siècle," *Revue d'histoire économique et sociale*, XL, 32–47, esp. pp. 32 f., 39, 46; E. Tarvel, "Livonia's Relations with the [Dual] Commonwealth in International Law and Its Administrative Structure in the Years 1561–1621" (Polish), *Zapiski historyczne*, XXXIV, no. 1, pp. 49–77, with a German summary (showing how, earlier promises to the contrary, the Polish regime under Báthory, and still more after 1598, tightened its control over Livonia; this factor seems to have been of little consequence for the Jews, however); and, more generally, the numerous histories of the Baltic countries, written not only in the native languages but in German as well, because of the Germans' great interest in the Teutonic settlements along the Baltic. See, for example, G. von Rauch's recent *Geschichte der baltischer Staaten*. Very useful also are the selected annual bibliographies of current publications of the *ZOF* and the *Zapiski historyczne*. The Jewish aspects are rarely discussed, however. The recent reprinting of E. [A.] Winkelmann's *Bibliotheca Livoniae Historica. Systematisches Verzeichniss der Quellen und Hülfsmittel zur Geschichte Estlands, Livlands und Kurlands*, 2d and greatly enlarged ed., which as early as 1878 was able to list sixteen entries relating to Jews (pp. 91 f.), has pointed up the relative neglect of this field of research over the last century.

7. See R. J. Wunderbar, *Geschichte der Juden in den Provinzen Liv- und Kurland, seit ihrer frühesten Niederlassung daselbst bis auf die gegenwärtige Zeit*; J. Joffe, *Regesten und Urkunden zur Geschichte der Juden in Riga und Kurland*, esp. Nos. 3–6; I. (J.) Hessen, "The Jews in Kurland (Sixteenth to Eighteenth Centuries)" (Russian), *ES*, VII, 145–62, 365–84 (mostly concerning the period after

1650); and, based largely on Wunderbar's and Hessen's researches, Levi b. Dober (L. B.) Ovchinskii, *Toledot yeshivat ha-Yehudim be-Kurland* (A History of Jewish Settlement in Courland from 1561 to 1908), 2d ed. enlarged and rev., mainly useful for the data it supplies on the internal developments of the Jewish communities and on their lay and rabbinic leaders.

The somewhat ambiguous clause in Kettler's treaty of surrender to Poland of November 28, 1561: "Judaeis vero nulle per totam Livoniam commercia, vectigalia, teloniave ullo unquam tempore concedamus," reproduced by Joffe, No. 6, has been subjected to diverse interpretations. While Wunderbar and many of his successors saw therein merely a restriction of Jewish trading and toll farming, other scholars, including Anton Buchholtz (see *infra*, n. 9), interpret the clause as a refusal to permit any temporary residence by Jews as well. If this was, indeed, the new duke's intention, it evidently remained unfulfilled, since a fair number of Jews settled in various localities under the protection of Polish officials. That their total remained rather small was probably owing more to the disturbed conditions in the country, occasioned by the constant wars over control of the Baltic coast, than to the legal difficulties of securing settlement rights. The general weakness of both the dukes and their Polish overlords in relations with the burghers and nobles of Courland must also have discouraged any large-scale Jewish immigration.

8. See J. Joffe, *Regesten, passim*. The role of Jews in Jacob's ambitious undertakings and during the reign of his successors has not yet been clarified. Apart from Jacob Abensur, several Hamburg "Portuguese," including Manuel Teixeira, evinced interest in participating in the Curish ventures, despite the existing serious political obstacles. See H. Kellenbenz in his *Sephardim an der unteren Elbe*, pp. 158 f., 400 ff. See also *ibid.*, pp. 247, 286, 421. The dramatic upsurge of Courland under the reign of Duke Jacob attracted considerable attention from both contemporaries and modern historians. See esp. O. H. Matthiesen, *Die Kolonial- und Überseepolitik Herzog Jakobs von Kurland 1640–1660*, esp. pp. 37 ff., 118 ff., 213 ff. Apps. 5a–d, 425 ff.; W. Eckert, *Kurland unter dem Einfluss des Merkantilismus (1561–1682), ein Beitrag zur Verfassungs- Verwaltungs- Finanz- und Wirtschaftsgeschichte Kurlands im 16. und 17. Jahrhundert*, esp. pp. 240, 250; A. V. Berkis, *The Reign of Duke James of Courland, 1638–1682*. See also the interesting observations, though somewhat vitiated by the political biases of the First World War, in D. Schaefer's *Kurland und das Baltikum in Weltgeschichte und Weltwirtschaft*.

9. Our main information about the Jews of Riga in the period here under review is derived from A. Buchholtz's three-quarter-century-old monograph, *Geschichte der Juden in Riga bis zur Begründung der Rigischen Hebräergemeinde im Jahre 1842*. See also J. Joffe's *Regesten, passim;* and A. von Bulmerincq's *Aktenstücke und Urkunden zur Geschichte der Stadt Riga, 1710–1740*, which, though relating to eighteenth-century events, shed some light on the earlier conditions as well. These records were used to good advantage by Buchholtz himself, from whose estate they were culled a few years after the publication of his *Geschichte*.

Few additional data, though considerable new insights, have been furnished by more recent publications. See the pertinent data supplied by G. Hollihn, *Die Stapel- und Gästepolitik Rigas in der Ordenszeit (1201–1562). Ein Beitrag zur Wirtschaftsgeschichte Rigas in der Hansezeit;* H. A. von Ramm-Helmring, *Studien zur Geschichte der Politik der Stadt Riga gegenüber Polen-Litauen im Zeitalter des beginnenden*

Kampfes um das Dominium maris Baltici; W. Küttler, *Patriziat, Bürgeropposition und Volksbewegung in Riga in der zweiten Hälfte des 16. Jahrhunderts;* W. Lenz, Jr., *Riga zwischen dem Römischen Reich und Polen-Litauen in den Jahren 1558–1582.*

10. A. Buchholtz, *Geschichte, passim;* Joseph Solomon Delmedigo, *Sefer Elim* (Elim [Exodus 15:27]; a scientific-philosophical tract), Amsterdam, 1628–29, fol. 30 b; *supra,* Chap. LXVIII, n. 90. The intervention of Prince Krzysztof Radziwiłł, in favor of the Jews of Birzai (his permanent residence), for whom he had previously obtained a privilege from Sigismund III (see *supra,* Chap. LXVIII, n. 43), becomes clearer in the light of the great influence this Polish general and diplomat exerted on the affairs of that area. See H. Wisner's recent study of "Krzysztof Radziwiłł's Livonian Campaign in the Year 1617–1618" (Polish), *Zapiski historyczne,* XXXV, 9–34. Regrettably, we have no information about the discussions on the Jewish question within ecclesiastical circles during the Reformation and Counter Reformation in Livonia. For example, the records of the Catholic synod held under the chairmanship of Bishop Otto Schenking in Riga on March 4, 1611, and of the visitation of that diocese by the papal prothonotary Giovanni Maria Belletto, might yield some clues on this subject. But the two pertinent pamphlets published by Schenking on those occasions, were extremely rare even a century ago, and have been unavailable to me. See E. Winkelmann, *Bibliotheca Livoniae Historica,* p. 99 Nos. 2297–98. On the sporadic contacts of the Hamburg Jews, especially Jacob Abensur, with Riga, see H. Kellenbenz, *Sephardim,* pp. 166, 401 f., etc.

11. S. A. Bershadskii, *Regesti i nadpisi,* Nos. 527–30; [I. Ansey, ed.,] "The Taking of Polack—1579: an Elizabethan Newssheet," *Journal of Byelorussian Studies,* I, 16–22, citing contemporary reports about Ivan's cruelties toward Polotsk's population in 1563, which made a tremendous impression in Western Europe; A. Taube, "Die Livlandpolitik Zar Ivan IV. Groznyj in der sowjetischen Geschichtsschreibung," *Jahrbuch für Geschichte Osteuropas,* XXXI (n.s. XIII), 411–44. Ivan's atrocities in Polotsk gave rise to a Jewish folk tale analyzed by I. Berlin in "A Story about Ivan the Terrible and the Destruction of the Jewish Community in Polotsk" (Russian), *ES,* VIII, 173–75. The Russo-Polish rivalry in the Baltic area, though but a part of a long historical clash between Muscovy and Poland, had peculiar aspects which merit special attention. Regrettably, the generally pertinent observations by R. Wittram in his "Methodologische und geschichtstheoretische Überlegungen zum Problem der baltischen Geschichtsforschung," *ZOF,* XX, 601–640, with an English summary, furnish illustrations almost exclusively from the nineteenth and twentieth centuries, when conditions radically differed from those of the preceding two centuries.

12. Radziwiłł's and Sigismund III's statements cited by Z. Wójcik in his aforementioned essay on the "International Position of the Commonwealth" in *Polska XVII wieku,* ed. by J. Tazbir, pp. 17 and 22. The Polish *szlachta's* lukewarm attitude toward the Muscovite Wars, and its self-seeking reluctance to vote the necessary appropriations at the Diet, are discussed by J. Maciszewski in his *Polska a Moskwa, 1603–1618,* and by other writers. On Poland-Lithuania's earlier role in the southeastern provinces mentioned in the text, see S. M. Kuczyński's analysis, *Ziemie czernihowsko-siewierskie pod rządami Litwy* (The Chernigov-Seversk Lands under

Lithuanian Rule), mainly concerned with the period up to 1502. The general history of the Russo-Polish wars of the period has been treated in an extensive specialized literature and summarized in general histories of Russia, the Ukraine, Lithuania, and Poland.

13. See J. Jakubowski, *Studya nad stosunkami narodowościowemi na Litwie przed Unią Lubelską* (Studies about the National Conditions in Lithuania before the Union of Lublin); H. Łowmiański, "Observations on the Social and Economic Foundations of the Jagiellon Union" (Polish), *Księga pamiątkowa ku uczczeniu wydania I Statuta litewskiego* (Commemorative Volume for the Celebration of the [Anniversary of the] First Lithuanian Statute), pp. 214–326; and J. Bardach's succinct data in his recent *Studia z ustroju i prawa Wielkiego Księstwa Litewskiego* (Studies in the Structure and Law of the Grand Duchy of Lithuania in the Fourteenth through Seventeenth Centuries), p. 48 n. 26. For the general background of the Jewish history of the period, see especially such studies as L. Wasiliewski's *Litwa i Białoruś* (Lithuania and Belorussia: an Historical Sketch of the National Relations), 3d ed.; and V. I. Picheta, *Belorussia i Litva XV–XVI vv.* (Belorussia and Lithuania in the Fifteenth and Sixteenth Centuries: Studies in the History of Their Socioeconomic, Cultural, and Political Development), esp. pp. 281 ff. (on the general legal evolution), 525 ff. (on the Union of Lublin), and 595 ff. (on cultural developments).

Of course, here, too, the authors' nationalist biases, often reflecting the changed political relationships between old rivals before and after the Second World War, are well illustrated by such publications as V. H. Pertsev *et al.*, eds., *Istoriia Belorusskoi SSR* (A History of the Belorussian Soviet Socialist Republic); J. Stankiewicz's sharp critique thereof in "The Soviet Falsification of Belorussian History," *Belorussian Review*, IV, 56–86; and the more moderate review of other writings in the Russian language by A. (or L.) Varonič in "A History of Belorussia in the Works of Russian Historiography," *ibid.*, II, 73–97. From the standpoint of Jewish history, it is noteworthy that all three cities, Brest, Pinsk, and Grodno, which in 1623 founded the "Lithuanian" Council of Provinces, as well as Slutsk, which in 1692 joined them as the representative of the fifth province, have from their incorporation in the Soviet Union been located within the Belorussian Republic, and even now do not belong to Soviet Lithuania. On the historic changes in nomenclature and the ensuing ambiguity in the extant sources, see D. Doroshenko, "Die Namen 'Rus,' 'Russland,' und 'Ukraine' in ihrer historischen und gegenwärtigen Bedeutung," *Abhandlungen* of Das Ukrainische Wissenschaftliche Institut in Berlin, III, 3–23; and N. P. Vakar, "The Name 'White Russia,' " *American Slavic and East-European Review*, VIII, 201–213 (prefers the designation Belorussia for the region in question, and advocates that the political term "White Russians," should be reserved for Soviet exiles fighting the Communists). See also, from another angle, H. Paszkiewicz's paradoxical query, "Are the Russians Slavs?" in *Antemurale*, XIV, 59–84, and his arguments against the generally accepted affirmative view.

14. See *supra*, Chap. LXVII, n. 26; and *infra*, n. 21. The old conflict between the federalists and annexationists over the interpretation of the meaning of the Union of Lublin is briefly analyzed by J. Bardach in his *Studia z ustroju i prawa Wielkiego Księstwa Litewskiego*, esp. pp. 21 ff. See also H. Łowmiański's pertinent observations

in his critique of this work entitled "The Grand Duchy of Lithuania—Problems of Structure and Law" (Polish), *KH*, LXXXIX, 885–96.

The eight-year interlude under Alexander may also have had an adverse effect on those returning Jewish settlers who were unable to prove their earlier residence in the country and hence were treated as foreigners, subject to the xenophobic Lithuanian laws of the period. See P. Dąbkowski, "The Status of Foreigners in Lithuanian Law (1447–1588)" (Polish) in *Studya nad historyą prawa polskiego* (Studies in the History of Polish Law), ed. by O. Balzer, V. This argument may, indeed, have been advanced by those who had acquired the confiscated Jewish property by purchase or government award in 1495–1503, and were now unwilling to restore it to the former owners or their heirs, as ordered by two royal ordinances. Nonetheless, the Jewish exiles staged an astonishingly speedy recovery, and successfully reestablished their shattered communal structure. This amazing vitality was demonstrated by the appearance, on March 21, 1514, before Sigismund I, of a joint Jewish delegation from Troki, Grodno, Brest, Łuck, Vladimir (Włodzimierz), Pinsk, and Kobrin (Kobryn)—a delegation which secured important privileges for Lithuanian Jewry. See A. Gomer's Cologne dissertation *Beiträge zur Kultur- und Sozialgeschichte des litauischen Judentums im 17. und 18. Jahrhundert*, pp. 7 f.

15. Kh. D. Ryvkin, *Evrei v Smolenskie* (Jews in Smolensk: Outlines of the History of Early Jewish Settlements in the District of Smolensk), pp. 34 ff., 51 ff.; R. A. French, "The Historical Geography of the Forests of Byelorussia in the Sixteenth Century," *Journal of Byelorussian Studies*, I, Part 3, pp. 168–83; and *infra*, nn. 17 and 50. On the extent to which local and regional variations are reflected even in the data preserved in the *Litovskaya Metryka* (Lithuanian Registry), see esp. S. Sawicki's succinct analysis and bibliography in "An Historical Conspectus of the Sources of Byelorussian Law," *Journal of Byelorussian Studies*, I, Part 3, pp. 226 ff. Those regional variations, as we shall see in another connection, affected the local Jewish communities there even more than elsewhere.

16. See the extensive documentation assembled in the *Belorusski Arkhiv* (Archivum Alboruthenicum), Vol. I (XVI–XVII Centuries), ed., with a Foreword by Z. Daugiala for the Historical-Archaeological Commission of the Institute of Belorussian Culture, pp. 30–208; and *infra*, n. 17. The cooperation between Eliasz and Suchodolski evoked complaints on the part of the burghers, especially after 1617, when a royal official specified that all merchants should inform the two leaseholders in advance about their travel plans and what kind of merchandise they intended to bring in. *Ibid.*, pp. 92 ff. No. 51, 98 f. No. 56. See also the other data furnished *ibid.*, pp. 69, 104 f., 165 f. On Affras Rachmaelovich, see also A. Buchholtz, *Geschichte der Juden in Riga*, p. 12; and *infra*, Chap. LXX.

17. *Belorusski Arkhiv*, I, 180 ff. No. 115; and R. A. French, "Bobrujsk and Its Neighborood in the Early Seventeenth Century," *Journal of Byelorussian Studies*, II, 29–56. Remarkably, John Sobieski failed to mention the important decree issued on July 23 1626, in behalf of Sigismund III by Leon Sapieha, hetman (commanding general) and palatine of Vilna, in which a controversy between the burghers and the Jews was supposed to be settled by the removal of the Jews from the main city square to similar buildings in another location, preferably to the street where the Jews had already established their synagogue. At the same time, Jewish

houseowners were to be subject to the same taxes and other imposts levied upon the burghers. *Belorusski Arkhiv*, I, 128 ff. No. 77. On the smaller communities of the district, see B. Toporowski, "Information about Jews in the Region of Mogilev (1599–1697)" (Russian), *ES*, IX, 320–21, summarizing a few new data published in a local journal.

18. See *Belorusski Arkhiv*, I, 128 ff. The story of the Jews in Vitebsk and several other important frontier communities under the Polish-Lithuanian regime has never yet been elaborated in detail. We have only brief articles in *Voskhod* and other periodicals. Even these are concerned largely with the period after the partitions of Poland. But some data are incidentally mentioned in local monographs and other specialized studies, such as the aforementioned essay by A. P. Hryckiewicz, "The Magnates' Fortified Cities" (Polish), *PH*, LXI, 428–44. Much information was analyzed some ninety years ago by S. A. Bershadskii in his collections of various sources, as well as in his comprehensive volume *Litovskie Evrei* (Lithuanian Jews: a History of their Legal and Social Status . . . 1388–1569). See also *supra*, Chap. LXVIII, n. 86.

19. See O. Halecki's balanced analysis of *Przyłączenie Podlasia, Wołynia i Kijowsczyzny do Korony* (The Incorporation of Podlasie, Volhynia, and the District of Kiev in the Crown in 1569); and J. Bardach's *Studia z ustroju*, pp. 21 ff. Theoretically, Lithuanian legislation before 1569 was supposed to retain its full validity after the Union. However, the amalgamation of the new provinces with the rest of the Polish Crown made most of the older laws obsolete. Even the provisions of the Second Lithuanian Statute of 1566, often called the "Volhynian Statute" and considered binding in Volhynia to the eighteenth century, were frequently disregarded. For example, Art. 12 No. 4, forbidding Jews "to appear in public in expensive clothing with gold chains," and insisting in general that they and their wives not display gold or silver—probably not strictly applied in Lithuania proper—seems to have carried no weight in Volhynia. Yet, here as elsewhere, the Jewish communal leaders themselves at times rigidly enforced such sumptuary regulations. See M. Bałaban, "Luxuries among the Jews of Poland and Their Suppression" (Polish), *Księga pamiątkowa* (Commemorative Volume on the Fiftieth Anniversary of the Fourth Gymnasium Named after Jan Długosz in Lwów), esp. p. 5.

20. Piotr Grabowski, *Polska niżna albo Osada polska* (The Low Poland or Polish Settlement), n. p., 1596, reproduced in J. Górski and E. Lipiński, comps., *Merkantylistyczna myśl ekonomiczna w Polsce* (The Mercantilist Economic Theory in Poland in the Sixteenth and Seventeenth Centuries), with an Intro. by E. L., pp. 35 ff., esp. pp. 61 ff.; Guillaume Le Vasseur le Sieur de Beauplan, *A Description of Ukraine*, English trans. [of 1774 ed.] with an Intro. by J. T. Petychyn, p. 456; *infra*, Chap. LXX, n. 102. See S. Ettinger's twin Hebrew essays "The Legal and Social Status of Jews in the Ukraine from the Fifteenth to the Seventeenth Century," *Zion*, XX, 128–52; and "Jewish Participation in the Colonization of the Ukraine (1569–1648)," *ibid.*, XXI, 107–142, each with an English summary. Both essays are based on his Hebrew University dissertation, *Ha-Yishub ha-yehudi be-Ukraina* (The Jewish Settlement in the Ukraine from the Union of Lublin to the Tragedy of 1648). See esp. *Zion*, XXI, 113 ff., 124. These statistical computations are supplemented with a map of Jewish settlements of the period 1503–1648, and an alphabetical list of 115

localities, with the dates of their first mention in the extant documentation. It stands to reason that, since many records are no longer available, the list is incomplete. In evaluating the trends in the growth of Jewish communities in the new areas, we must bear in mind that there was a general decline of the economy and of the colonizing élan in the entire Commonwealth after the tragic 1650s; as a result, fewer new towns, even those owned by private landlords, were established in the later period. See T. Opas, "Private Towns and the Commonwealth" (Polish), *KH*, LXXVIII, 28–48, with a Russian summary, esp. pp. 30 ff.

21. S. Kutrzeba and W. Semkowicz, eds., *Akta Unji Polski z Litwą 1385–1791* (Records of the Union between Poland and Lithuania, 1385–1791), pp. 207 ff. No. 98, 319 ff. No. 139, 321 ff. No. 140. It may be noted that in the original invitation addressed to members of the royal Council, Diet deputies, and district governors, the king guaranteed his subjects in Podlasie and Volhynia that he would maintain all their privileges and liberties. "Should you have any grievances or discontent, be they on account of customs duties and tolls, or on account of Jews, or for whatever other reasons, We promise to alleviate all of them and adjust them to the existing liberties of the noble estate in Our Crown." *Ibid.*, p. 209. On occasion the king was prepared to secure the allegiance of the influential gentry by making some minor concessions at Jewish expense. For instance, the Bratslav nobles were told that thenceforth they would be allowed to sell their mead to anybody, rather than, as theretofore, to Jews alone. See O. Halecki, *Przyłączenie*, pp. 217 ff., 221. Of considerable interest also are the preceding debates at the decisive Lublin Diet which called for that great constitutional convention—in so far as they are reflected in *Diaryusz sejmu lubelskiego 1569 r.* (Diaries of the Lublin Sejm of 1569), ed. by Tytus Adam Działyński. In the long run, however, the specific royal pledges, even if seriously meant, seem to have been fully implemented only with respect to maintaining the principle of equal rights of the respective estates in the annexed provinces with those enjoyed by their counterparts in the Polish Crown. But we have no evidence that special grievances against Jews were subsequently adjusted with reference to this pledge. See also J. Bardach in his *Studya z ustroju*, pp. 45 ff.; J. Pelewski's suggestive new approach to "The Incorporation of the Ukrainian Lands of Old Rus into the Polish Crown in 1569: a Tentative New Approach" (Polish), in *PH*, LXV, 243–62, with Russian and French summaries; and *supra*, Chap. LXVII, n. 36.

22. See the list of the landed possessions assembled by Aleksander Wiśniowiecki in W. Tomkiewicz's *Jeremi Wiśniowiecki (1612–1651)*; and S. Ettinger, "The Legal and Social Status" (Hebrew), *Zion*, XX, 134 ff. The Polish text of Báthory's 1576 decree is reproduced by M. Bersohn in his *Dyplomataryusz dotyczący Żydów w dawnej Polsce*, pp. 100 ff. No. 152. See also J. Morgensztern, "Regesta," *BZIH*, no. 47, p. 118 No. 20. Many other privileges extended by the Polish kings to the Jews, both Rabbanite and Karaite, in Łuck and the rest of Volhynia have been mentioned *supra*, n. 19; and Chap. LXVIII, *passim*.

23. See the text of Sigismund Augustus' decree of 1570 in the *Arkhiv Yugo-Zapadnoi Rossii*, Part 7, III, 63 ff.; that of Báthory of 1576, reproduced in Bersohn's *Dyplomataryusz*, pp. 100 ff. No. 152; and other sources analyzed by M. Bałaban in his "Karaites in Poland, an Historical Study" (Polish), reproduced from earlier Polish and Hebrew articles and considerably revised in his *Studja Historyczne* (Historical

Studies), esp. pp. 37 ff.; J. Mann, *Texts and Studies in Jewish History and Literature*, II, 551 ff.; A. Zajączkowski, *Karaims in Poland: History, Language, Folklore, Science* (with an extensive bibliography), esp. p. 65 from which the English translation of the passage in the Karaite memorandum of 1790 is quoted here with minor variations. See also *supra*, Chap. LXVII, n. 7; and *infra*, Chap. LXX, n. 105. The story of the Karaites in Poland-Lithuania will be more fully analyzed in a later volume, in connection with the sectarian Jewish movements of the period.

24. See A. Jabłonowski, *Lustracje Królewszcyzn ziem ruskich Wołynia, Podola i Ukrainy* (Censuses of the Royal Domain in the Rus Lands of Volhynia, Podolia and the Ukraine in the First Half of the Seventeenth Century), pp. 41, 137; Bersohn, *Dyplomataryusz*, p. 138 Nos. 245–46; M. Kulischer, "Jews in Kiev: an Historical Sketch" (Russian), *ES*, VI, 351–66, 417–38, esp. pp. 354 f.; I. N. Darewski, *Le-Qorot ha-Yehudim be-Kiev* (Contribution to the History of the Jews in Kiev, Formerly and Today), I, 58 ff.; and *supra*, Chap. LXVIII, n. 31.

25. M. Bersohn, *Dyplomataryusz*, pp. 83 f. No. 120, 262 No. 535; J. Morgensztern, "Regesta," *BZIH*, nos. 47, p. 118 No. 30; 51, p. 70 No. 62; S. A. Bershadskii, *Dokumenty i Materialy dlia istorii Evreev v Yugozapadnoi Rossii* (Documents and Sources for the History of the Jews in Southwestern Russia), in *Evreiskaia Biblioteka*, VII–VIII; S. Ettinger, "The Legal and Social Status," *Zion*, XX, 140 f., 143.

26. M. Bersohn, *Dyplomataryusz*, p. 104 No. 159; A. Jabłonowski in his *Lustracje . . . Wołynia, Podola i Ukrainy*, p. 147; S. Ettinger in *Zion*, XX, 137. As far as the Jewish community at large was concerned, such exemptions from duties and tolls were a double-edged sword. They certainly benefited all merchants and consumers, including Jews. But they must have greatly reduced the income of Jewish tax farmers and their numerous employees (probably for the most part Jews, too)—a class which, as we shall see, was growing by leaps and bounds precisely in those dynamic southeastern provinces. See *infra* Chap. LXX, nn. 24 and 76 ff.

27. The Kurbskii affair is described at great length in his biography entitled *Zhizn kniazia Andreia Mikhailovicha Kurbskogo v Litve i na Volynie* (The Life of Prince Andrei Mikhailovich Kurbskii in Lithuania and Volhynia), first published by the Kommissiia dlia razbora drevnikh aktov (Commission for the Selection of Old Documents), Kiev, esp. II, 1–5. See also Kurbskii's *Sochineniia* (Works) in the *Russkaia Istoricheskaia Biblioteka*, published by the Arkheograficheskaia Kommissiia, Vol. XXXI; and the summary of the controversy by S. Ettinger in *Zion*, XX, 139 f. Such maltreatment of the subject population was, of course, not a rarity among native Polish landlords either. The fact that we rarely hear of atrocities committed on Jews is probably owing both to absentee landlordism and to the recognition by many masters that their Jewish administrators and leaseholders could not easily be replaced, certainly not on terms favorable to the lords. But temperamental outbreaks against individuals must have been much more frequent than it would seem from the extant sources. On the other hand, out of self-interest many magnates tried to safeguard the property and trading rights of "their" Jewish helpers. At times they probably even shielded their Jews against court sentences which they considered unjustified, although we know of no Jewish case in any way resembling that of the petty nobleman Samuel Łaszcz. A favorite of the Polish generalissimo Stanis-

ław Koniecpolski, Łaszcz publicly ridiculed the court sentences hanging over his head, which included no fewer than 236 decrees of banishment and 37 decrees of infamy. He evidently got away without paying any price for his misdeeds. Moreover, in many instances the intervention of a powerful official may have impeded the courts from issuing any adverse sentence in the first place. See B. Baranowski and S. Herbst in the *Historia Polski,* ed. by T. Manteuffel, I, Part 2, p. 449.

28. Alberto Bolognetti, *Epistolae et acta, 1581-1585,* ed. by E. Kuntze and C. Nanke, II, 447 No. 251; 671 No. 382; and other passages cited *supra,* Chap. LXVIII, n. 6. Intolerance toward the Greek Orthodox made itself felt even in the old Lithuanian capital of Vilna, and penetrated deeply into the burghers' groups. While in 1536 the city council had consisted of an equal number of Catholics and Orthodox, in the seventeenth century the Orthodox were increasingly displaced from all positions of honor in both the city administration and the local guilds. By 1650 the city had only one Orthodox church, as compared with 23 Catholic and 9 Uniate churches, and one each of Calvinists, Lutherans, other dissidents, and Muslims. On his accession to the throne, on November 4, 1632, when Wladislaw IV signed the *pacta conventa* with the Rus Orthodox pledging them freedom of worship, the agreement was repudiated by the Uniates, under the excuse that it required papal approval, which was indeed refused by Pope Urban VIII in a brief to Wladislaw. See A. Theiner, comp., *Vetera monumenta Poloniae et Lithuaniae . . . historiam illustrantia,* III, 402 No. 339; K. Chodynicki, "On the Denominational Relationships in the Vilna Guilds" (Polish), *Księga pamiątkowa* (Memorial Volume) *Oswald Balzer,* I, 117-31; M. Łowmiańska, *Wilno przed najazdem moskiewskim 1655 roku* (Vilna before the Muscovite Invasion of 1655), pp. 47 ff.; and M. Kosman's succinct Polish observations on the "Denominational Conflicts in Vilna around 1600," *KH,* LXXIX, 3-23, with a Russian summary, particularly pp. 7, 9, 12, 18 f., 31 ff. See also, more generally, K. Chodynicki *Kościół prawosławny a Rzeczpospolita* (The Orthodox Church and the Commonwealth: an Historical Sketch, 1370-1632); and J. Pelesz, *Geschichte der Union der ruthenischen Kirche mit Rom,* esp. II, 194 ff. Further information about the ecclesiastical situation in the grand duchy has been forthcoming from P. Rabikauskas in his edition of *Fontes Historiae Lithuaniae,* of which only Vol. I, covering the dioceses of Vilna and Samogitia (Żmudż), has thus far been published. It may be expected that the even more complicated situation in the dioceses of Łuck and Kiev will be illumined by the new data in Vol. II.

29. A. Šeptyckyj, comp., *Monumenta Ukrainae historica,* Vols. I (1075-1623); II (1624-1648), esp. I, 29 ff. No. 52, 243 ff. No. 379; II, 135 ff. No. 85; E. J. Harrison, *Lithuania Past and Present,* p. 50; I. Galant, "Were the Jews Concessionaires of Greek Orthodox Churches in the Ukraine?" (Russian), *ES,* I, 81-87. By joining most eastern denominations in repudiating the Gregorian reform, the Orthodox churches of the embattled Rus areas found their traditional calendar an important weapon of self-preservation. Through celebrating holidays ten or more days later than the Catholic and Uniate churches, the Orthodox priesthood most graphically demonstrated to the masses the line of separation between the two denominations. See the older, but still valuable, study by J. Schmid, "Zur Geschichte der Gregorianischen Kalenderreform," *Historisches Jahrbuch,* III, 388-415, 543-95, esp. pp. 546 f., 560 f. Jews were not directly affected by that controversy, although some of them may have been inconvenienced by having to respect different dates of holidays among

their divided neighbors. Only the folkloristic rule that Jews should abstain from studying the Torah on *Nitl* (Natale = Christmas), caused some puzzlement as to which of the two Christmases they were to observe. With their customary traditionalism, the majority of those who paid attention to this nonobligatory custom preferred to follow the Julian calendar.

30. The participation of the Jews in the defense of their cities against raids by Tatars and others is attested by both Jewish and non-Jewish sources. An interesting legal case is discussed, for example, in a responsum by R. Meir b. Gedaliah of Lublin, with reference to a Jew who did practice shooting under the supervision of a Gentile noncommissioned officer. The rabbi added: "This was at the time of disturbances in Volhynia on account of Tatar attacks. It has been a custom among the inhabitants of the frontier cities that everyone be on the alert with his weapon in hand, to participate in battle against the invaders, on orders of the prince or lords." See his *Resp.*, No. 43. In fact, we have some records of Jews joining enterprising peasant pioneers, especially the Cossacks, in their raids into neighboring Tatar, Moldavian, and even Turkish possessions. This entire aspect of Jewish life in southeastern Poland is connected with the rise of the fairly autonomous Cossack region, which will be discussed more fully *infra*, Chap. LXX.

31. *Arkhiv Yugo-Zapadnoi Rossii*, Part 2, I, 262; *supra*, Chap. LXVII, n. 31; and *infra*, n. 44. The essential unreliability of tax records as instruments for ascertaining the size of the Polish population has frequently been noted. An interesting debate on this score arose after the publication of P. Szafran's *Osadnictwo historyczne Krajny w XVI–XVIII wieku* (The Historic Settlement of Krajna in the Sixteenth through Eighteenth Centuries). See the Polish review of this volume by Z. Guldon in *KHKM*, X, 653–61; Szafran's reply thereto, entitled "Tax Inventories or Registers" (Polish), in *Zapiski historyczne*, XXXI, Part 1, pp. 53–71; and Guldon's rejoinder, "Observations on the Scholarly Usefulness of Tax Registers from the Sixteenth Century" (Polish), *ibid.*, pp. 73–79. That this shortcoming applies not only to Polish tax records but also to the more orderly registers of western Europe, has been emphasized by Z. P. Mombert in his "Über die geringe Zuverlässigkeit älterer Volkszählungen," *Jahrbücher für Nationalökonomie und Statistik*, CXXXIX, 745–51. But see the remarks thereon *supra*, Vol. XII, pp. 4 ff., 243 ff.

32. See the general survey of "The Pre-Partition Church Visitations as a Demographic Source" (Polish), in *Przeszłość demograficzna Polski* (Poland's Demographic Past: Materials and Studies), II, 3–45; and E. Vielrose's critical comments, "The Accuracy of Demographic Data Stemming from Pre-Partition Church Visitations" (Polish), *ibid.*, pp. 47–52. In contrast, West-European parish records have served modern demographers in very good stead. French scholars, especially, take legitimate pride in their pioneering achievements in this field. They have been successfully emulated by British and other students of historical demography. However, in Poland and Lithuania this type of research is only in its early stages, being hampered particularly by archival losses sustained in the historical storms which have swept over the country. See especially I. Gieysztorowa's pertinent observations in her "Demographic Studies on the Basis of Parish Registers" (Polish), *KHKM*, X, 103–121; her "Methodical Pitfalls Affecting Polish Investigations into [Parish] Rolls of the Seventeenth and Eighteenth Centuries" (Polish), *ibid.*, XIX, 557–603, with a

French summary; and S. Hoszowski and Z. Sułkowski's reasonable suggestions to future researchers in this field in their "Vital Statistics Based on Former Parochial Certificates (Project of a Unified System of Collecting Data)" (Polish), *Przeszłość demograficzna Polski*, IV, 3–20, with an English summary. See also Gieysztorowa's briefer study "Research into the Demographic History of Poland: a Provisional Summing-Up," *APH*, XVIII, 5–17. Moreover, the historical value of even the more exact and better-preserved registers of the nineteenth and twentieth centuries has frequently been questioned. See especially S. Szulc, *Dokładność rejestracji urodzeń i zgonów* (The Accuracy of the Registration of Births and Deaths). Here a leading statistician of post-War Poland has cast doubt not only on the ecclesiastical, but also on the government registers, which have naturally included records of Jewish births and deaths in modern Poland.

33. See *supra*, Chap. LXVII, n. 22; and *infra*, n. 51; S. A. Bershadskii, *REA*, II, 152 ff. No. 231; idem, *Litovskie Evrei*, pp. 330 f.; the list culled from this work by A. Gomer in his *Beiträge zur Kultur- und Sozialgeschichte des litauischen Judentums*, p. 11; M. Bałaban, *Dzieje Żydów w Krakowie*, I, 97 f.; and, more generally, C. Krawczak, "The Origin and Development of Building Codes in Poznań to the Year 1838" (Polish), *Studia i materiały do dziejów Wielkopolski i Pomorza*, IX, Part 1 (XVII), 31–56 (claims that the fires spreading "from the worst constructed Jewish quarter" gave rise to the city's zoning laws; p. 35); and particularly the very informative monograph by S. Waszak, "The Population and Residential Housing in the City of Poznań during the Sixteenth and Seventeenth Centuries" (Polish), *Przegląd Zachodni*, IX, Part 3, pp. 64–136, esp. pp. 111 ff. and Table XIII. See also M. Horn, *Ruch budowlany w miastach ziemi przemyskiej i sanockiej w latach 1550–1560 na tle przesłanek urbanizacyjnych* (The Building Movement in Cities of the Przemyśl and Sanok Districts in the Years 1550–1560 against the Background of Urbanization Programs). At any rate, the Jewish houses themselves, about which we often have more information than about the total number of Jews or of Jewish families inhabiting them, ought to become a rewarding subject of further detailed investigation from the architectural and social, as well as demographic, points of view. See also the additional data, *infra*, nn. 49 and 51.

34. The need for new methods to investigate the complex demographic problems before the nineteenth century has long been recognized. See, for instance, J. Duparquier's "Démographie et sources fiscales (à propos d'une communication d'A. Leroi)," *Annales de démographie historique*, pp. 233–240 (referring to A. Leroi's study, "La Population de l'Élection de Chaumont et Magny à la veille de la Révolution," submitted to the 88th Congrès National des Sociétés Savantes held in Clermont Ferrand in 1963, pp. 891–905). See also *supra*, Vol. XII, pp. 4 ff., 243 ff., with the literature cited there; and my brief sketch on "Population" in the English *Encyclopaedia Judaica*, XIII, 866–903.

35. T. Czacki, *O statystyce Polski* (On Poland's Statistics), reprinted in his *Dzieła* (Works), ed. by E. Raczyński, III, 2 ff.; idem, *Rozprawa o Żydach i Karaitach* (Discourse on the Jews and Karaites), new ed., Vilna, 1807, with a supplement on the life and works of the author by K. J. Turowski, esp. pp. 117 f. (also reprinted in his *Dzieła*, III, 138–270); W. Surowiecki, *O statystyce Księstwa Warszawskiego, Wykład w Szkole Prawa 1812 roku* (Statistics of the Duchy of Warsaw: a Lecture

at the School of Law, 1812 [1813]), reprinted in his *Wybór pism* (Selected Writings), ed. with an Intro. by J. Groywicka and A. Łukaszewicz, pp. 247–492, esp. pp. 454 ff., 476 ff. (relating to Jewish history and demography); and A. Pawiński, *Polska XVI wieku pod względem geograficzno-statystycznym* (Poland in the Sixteenth Century in Geographical-Statistical Aspects), Vols. I–XIII (*Żródła dziejowe*, XII–XXIII); A. Jabłonowski, *Lustracje . . . Wołynia, Podola i Ukrainy* (*Żródła dziejowe*, V); and other volumes in the same series. The latter two pioneers studied Poland region by region, not only from the demographic but also from the geographical and social points of view, furnishing much interesting source material for other aspects of life as well. They include occasional references to Jews.

Most important, however, have been the contributions since 1946. Among the pertinent writings, we need but mention here E. Vielrose, "Poland's Population from the Tenth to the Eighteenth Century" (Polish), *KHKM*, V, 3–49; I. Gieysztorowa, "Studies in the History of Poland's Population" (Polish), *ibid.*, XI, 523–62; supplemented with some comparative material from western Europe in her "Recherches sur la démographie historique et en particulier rurale en Pologne," *Ergon*, IV, 500–528; and her aforementioned essay in *APH*, XVIII (all with extensive bibliographies). Of considerable interest also are such systematic and methodological studies as S. Hoszowski's "The Dynamics of the Evolution of Poland's Population in the Feudal Period, From the Tenth to the Eighteenth Century" (Polish), *RDSG*, XIII, 137–98, with a French summary; W. Kula, "The Status and Needs of Investigations concerning the Demographic History of Old Poland (to the Beginnings of the Nineteenth Century)" (Polish), *ibid.*, pp. 23–109; idem, "The Needs and Possibilities of Historical-Statistical Investigations in Polish Scholarship" (Polish), *Wiadomości statystyczne*, III, 3–11. Drawn on a broader canvas are the studies by J. Halliczer, *Liczebność Polaków na przestrzeń wieków* (The Numerical Strength of Poles in the Course of Centuries in Connection with the Problems of Overpopulation and the Question of Emigration from Poland; Naval and Colonial Aspects); and Z. Pawlik, "Demographic, Geographic, Economic, and Social Problems of Population in Their Historical Evolution" (Polish), *RDSG*, XXVIII, 11–30, with a French summary. See also E. Buchhofer, "Die Entwicklung der Bevölkerungswissenschaften in Polen nach 1945," *ZOF*, XVII, 297–335.

36. See *supra*, Vols. XIII, pp. 148 ff., 162, 268 f., etc.; XV, pp. 34 ff., 394 f. nn. 43–44; Joannes Pileatorius' characterizations, cited from two MSS by S. Kot in his "Nationum Proprietates," *Oxford Slavonic Papers*, VI, 1–43; VII, 99–117, esp. VI, 2; Krzysztof Słupecki's correspondence with Gerhard Johann (Joannes) Vos (Vossius) in Vos' *Epistolae et clarorum virorum ad eum epistolae*, compiled by P. Colomesius, 1691 ed., I, 229 No. 185, 320 f. No. 295, 330 f. No. 308, 351 f. No. 334; II, 183 f. No. 252, partially reproduced in his *Opera*, IV, 212 No. 392; *supra*, Vols. XIII, pp. 407 f. n. 28; XV, pp. 62 f., 406 n. 73; and Chap. LXVIII, n. 26. On the early Ashkenazic settlement in Altona-Hamburg, see A. Feilchenfeld, "Die Älteste Geschichte der deutschen Juden in Hamburg," *MGWJ*, XLIII, 271–82, 322–28, 370–81; M. Grunwald, *Hamburgs deutsche Juden bis zur Auflösung der Dreigemeinden, 1811;* and *supra*, Vol. XIV, pp. 277 f., 407 n. 54. On the other hand, L. Lewin's comprehensive and detailed monograph on "Deutsche Einwanderungen in polnische Ghetti," *JJLG*, IV, 293–329; V, 75–154, covers several centuries and, because it frequently relies on evidence derived from connecting the names of Polish Jews with likely places of origin in the Holy Roman Empire, it inevitably leaves the question open

of when their bearers arrived in Poland. The individuals mentioned in the extant sources may be descendants of earlier settlers who had retained their ancestors' names for generations. More directly pertinent to our problem is I. Halpern's study of "Jewish Refugees of the Thirty Years' War in Eastern Europe" (Hebrew), *Zion*, XXVII, 199–215, reprinted in his *Yehudim ve-yahadut be-mizrah-Eiropah* (Eastern European Jewry: Historical Studies), pp. 197–211. However, the number of new-comers in 1618–48 could not have been very large, or they would have left many more traces in the existing documentation. Many arrivals of the stormy 1630s may have actually returned to their home countries, especially in the Habsburg posses-sions, when the military clashes there diminished in intensity in the mid-1640s, even before the conclusion of the Treaties of Westphalia.

37. See B. D. Weinryb, *Texts and Studies in the Communal History of Polish Jewry* (= *PAAJR*, XIX), Hebrew section, pp. 3 ff., esp. Nos. 1 and 2 and *passim;* L. Lewin, *Die Landessynode der grosspolnischen Judenschaft*, pp. 57 ff., 82 f.; M. Balaban, *Die Judenstadt von Lublin*, pp. 25 ff.; *supra*, n. 3; Vol. XV, pp. 101 ff., 413 f. n. 34; Chap. LXVII, n. 10; and *infra*, n. 38. The problem of the "fugitives [borehim]" was of sufficient gravity for the Council of Four Lands and the Council of Provinces to adopt, in 1623–24, a series of regulations as to how they, their fami-lies, and possessions were to be treated. See I. Halperin, ed., *Pinqas Va'ad 'Arba Arasot*, pp. 45 ff. Nos. 111–49, and other passages listed in the Index, p. 557 *s.v. Boreah;* and S. M. Dubnow, ed., *Pinqas ha-Medinah*, pp. 7 Nos. 24–25, 28 No. 117, etc. (see Index, p. 343). See also P. Dickstein's juridical analysis, "On the Fugitives [Bankrupts] in Polish and Lithuanian Ordinances" (Hebrew), *Ha-Mishpat ha-'ibri*, 1918, pp. 29–76; and *infra*, Chap. LXX, n. 16.

38. See A. Warschauer, "Die Entstehung einer jüdischen Gemeinde," *ZGJD*, [o.s.] IV, 170–81. From the outset the Poznań elders tried to limit the right to settle in Swarzędz to members of their own community who had enjoyed residential rights in Poznań for at least two years. But as early as 1624 they made an exception for a Jew from Wronik, who was allowed immediately to proceed there with his family, "because he is the victim of a fire and for other reasons." See D. Avron, ed., *Pinqas ha-Ksherim*, p. 4 No. 17.

39. See V. O. Levanda, *Polnyi khronologicheskii sbornik zakonov* (Complete Chron-ological Collection of Laws and Ordinance Relating to Jews, 1649–1873), pp. 359 ff. No. 304; I. Halperin, "The 'Rush' into Early Marriages among East European Jews" (Hebrew), *Zion*, XXVII, 36–58, reprinted in his *Yehudim ve-yahadut*, pp. 289–309; E. Vielrose, "Poland's Population" (Polish), *KHKM*, V, 7 ff.; P. Goubert, *Beauvais et Beauvaisis de 1600 à 1730. Un équilibre fragile, la démographie naturelle de Beau-vais avant 1750*, esp. p. 453 n. All references here to the life expectancy of Jews and non-Jews are extremely tentative. Hardly any studies have thus far been made concerning this aspect of life among the various ethnic groups in prepartition Po-land, and admittedly the source material concerning it is very scarce and tenuous.

40. See Sebastyan Miczyński, *Zwierciadło*, Chaps. xviii–xix; T. Korzon, *Dzieje wojen i wojskowości w Polsce* (A History of the Wars and Armed Forces in Poland), 2d ed. rev., esp. II, 64 ff.; B. T. Urlanis, *Vojny i narodonaselenie Evropy* (Wars and the Population of Europe: Human Losses of the Armed Forces of the European

Countries in the Wars of the Seventeenth through Twentieth Centuries, a Statistical-Historical Study), with the critique thereof by J. Duparquier in *Annales de démographie historique*, 1967, pp. 297–99. Both scholars agree, however, that probably more civilians than soldiers died from wartime contagions. The nexus between the spread of communicable diseases and the general deterioration of economic conditions (particularly those resulting in famine), even in times of relative peace, is stressed by M. Horn. See his "Epidemics of Contagious Diseases in Red Russia in the Years 1600–1647" (Polish), *Studia historyczne*, XI, 13–31, esp. pp. 30 f., referring in particular to the years 1600–1603, 1622–26, 1629–31, and 1641–42 and showing that a town like Krosno could lose 42.6 percent of its population in a single year, 1622. Even in the eighteenth century, despite some improvement in the prevention and treatment of communicable diseases, the devastating results of a plague are well illustrated by G. Bradt's description of "Die Pest in den Jahren 1707–1713 in der Provinz Posen," *Zeitschrift des Historischen Vereines für die Provinz Posen,* XVII, 301–328; and *infra*, n. 52. See also, for instance, F. Suwara, *Przyczyny i skutki klęski cecorskiej 1620 r.* (Causes and Effects of the [Polish] Defeat at Cecora in 1620), esp. p. 117, showing how greatly the Turkish victory contributed to the devastation of large areas of Podolia, not only by the soldiers but also by local hoodlums. As a highly vulnerable segment of the population, Jews probably suffered more than their neighbors from such belligerent actions. On De Najera's testimony, the numerical strength of the Spanish and Polish clergy, see *supra*, Vol. XV, pp. 186, 463 n. 29; as well as E. Wiśniowski, "The Numerical Strength of the Diocesan Clergy in the Polish Territories in the First Half of the Sixteenth Century" (Polish), *Roczniki humanistyczne* of the Towarzystwo Naukowe Katolickie of the University of Lublin, XVI, Part 2, pp. 43–77, with a brief French summary. The ratio of the clergy doubtless increased considerably under the impetus of the Counter Reformation and the proliferation of monastic orders during the reign of the first two Vasas and their successors.

On the impact of elemental catastrophies on early modern Poland and Lithuania, see A. Walawender's aforementioned *Kronika klęsk elementarych w Polsce i w krajach sąsiednich* (covering the period of 1450–1586), continued for the years 1648–96 by S. Namaczyńska in her first volume under the same title and subtitle. See *supra*, Chap. LXVII, nn. 23–24. Moreover, because of climatic fluctuations, the population bore the brunt of bad years both in poor harvests and in the spread of contagious diseases owing to atmospheric conditions. See G. Utterström, "Climatic Fluctuations and Population Problems in Early Modern History," *Scandinavian Economic History Review*, III, 3–47. This area of research, not yet sufficiently applied to East-European conditions, merits further examination, especially on the extent to which such climatic changes may have affected Jews, too. See also the more popular survey by R. J. G. Concannon, "The Third Enemy: the Role of Epidemics in the Thirty Years' War," *Journal of World History*, X, 500–511; and the additional data quoted *infra*, n. 51.

41. See B. D. Weinryb, "Private Letters in Yiddish of 1588" (Yiddish), *Yivo Historishe Shriftn*, II, 64 ff. Nos. vi–vii; L. Lewin, *Die Landessynode*, p. 40; Vol. XIV, pp. 268 f., 403 n. 45; Chap. LXVII, n. 23; M. Bałaban, *Dzieje Żydów w Krakowie*, I, 135. The question of lesser mortality among Jews in pestilences—a factor which seems to have contributed to accusations that Jews poisoned wells during the Black Death and other periods—cannot be proved from documentary evidence in Poland-

Lithuania. Nonetheless, chances are that the ritualistic and social factors mentioned in the text substantially reduced the number of Jewish victims in the recurrent plagues. On the other hand, as we recall, fires were even more common in the Jewish quarters than elsewhere, and may have caused many deaths in families who could not escape in time. However, all this is quite conjectural, and we rarely hear in the sources about persons actually burned in the conflagrations. The devastation of dwellings certainly was very great. For example, to cite a contemporary account, as a result of fire which struck the important city of Bełz in June 1637, its "market place, together with the city hall, three churches, two Orthodox sanctuaries, two gates, . . . the streets with the parks—all burned down and were destroyed, so that in the place of the city there was only an open field." No sooner did the Bełz inhabitants, including its Jews, begin to rebuild their houses, than in 1644 another fire devastated the city and converted it once more into an open field. Yet even in these cases we do not hear of numerous dead or injured. See M. Horn, "Jews in the Voivodship of Bełz," *BZIH*, no. 27, p. 37. Hence the demographic effects of fire were on the whole more indirect, causing mental anguish, loss of property, including foodstuffs, and the resulting undernourishment of both adult and youthful victims. But the ensuing retardation of the Jewish population growth appears to have been relatively small.

42. See L. Lewin, "Jüdische Aerzte in Grosspolen," *JJLG*, IX, 367–420; M. Balaban, "Jewish Physicians in Cracow and the Ghetto Tragedies (Fifteenth through Seventeenth Centuries)" (Russian), *ES*, V, 38–53; and other literature which will be considered in connection with the professional status of physicians in the Jewish community. That some of them enjoyed an international reputation was evidenced by the urgent invitations sent to two Jewish doctors in 1554 and 1606, respectively, by Hungarian leaders. See *supra*, Chap. LXVII, n. 5. Needless to say, not only Jews but also Christian nobles and burghers in the sixteenth and seventeenth centuries often studied at foreign universities like Padua. See, for instance, S. Windakiewicz, "I Polacchi a Padova," *Omaggio dell'Accademia Polacca di scienze e lettere all'Università di Padova*, pp. 1–34, esp. p. 33; and G. Lachs, "Alcune notizie sugli allievi polacchi presso la Scuola di Medicina di Padova," *ibid.*, pp. 275–328, esp. pp. 295, 324. However, most of the Polish Jewish students abroad were interested in medical training, whereas the majority of Polish nobles and burghers going to foreign schools were students of the humanities, particularly of Greek and Latin—subjects frowned upon by Jewish leaders.

43. See P. Szewachowski, "The Mortality of Jewish as Compared with Non-Jewish Infants" (Yiddish), *YB*, IX, 262–71; S. Waszak, "The Offspring of a Burgher's Family and the Natural Movement of Population in the City of Poznań at the End of the Sixteenth and in the Seventeenth Century" (Polish), *RDSG*, XVI, 316–84, with French and Russian summaries, esp. pp. 375 ff.; E. Vielrose, "Poland's Population" (Polish), *KHKM*, V, 5 ff. Szewachowski's statistical data also shed light on another intriguing problem. Some opponents of Jewish ritual circumcision, usually performed on eight-day-old boys, contended that this operation materially contributed to the weakening of the infants' constitution and led to infectious diseases, resulting in their greater mortality. A study made in Warsaw covering the years 1929–31, for which alone satisfactory data were available, revealed an astonishing absence of such consequences. In 1929, for instance, not one Jewish child aged less than one year was reported as

suffering from septicemia or purulent infection, as against 10 recorded Christian patients in that age range. In 1930, one Jewish boy and one Jewish girl aged 6–11 months, as against 6 Christian infants of that age or younger, were affected by these diseases. Only in 1931 were there two such Jewish boy patients aged between one and five months, and one aged more than six months, while no Jewish girls suffered from these ailments. At the same time, no fewer than 21 Christian infants (12 boys and 9 girls, mostly under the age of six months) were so affected. And, it must be remembered, the Jews constituted about one-third of the population of the Polish capital at that time! Evidently, the immediate negative impact of circumcision upon Jewish male infants was negligible, while its long-term medical benefits, both for them and for their wives in later years, have often been asserted by specialists. See Szewachowski, p. 263 Table 1.

44. See II Sam. 24:1, 15; J. Kleczyński, "Population Censuses in the Polish Commonwealth" (Polish), *Rozprawy* of PAU, Historical-Philosophical Section, 2d ser. V (XXX), 33–61, esp. pp. 36 f.; idem, "The General Capitation Tax in Poland and the Population Censuses Built upon It" (Polish), *ibid.*, pp. 240–62; L. Charewiczowa, "A Survey of Recent Monographs Relating to Polish Cities" (Polish), *KH*, XLII, 391–403 (critically reviewing a number of writings of the early 1920s); T. Opas, "On Ancient Fortifications of Privately Owned Cities in the Lublin Palatinate" (Polish), *KHKM*, XIX, 251–55; *VL*, VII, 50; Ber of Bolechów, *Zikhronot*, ed. from an Oxford MS with a (separately printed) English trans. by M. Vishnitzer (Wischnitzer), entitled, *The Memoirs of Ber of Bolechow (1723–1805)*, pp. 145 f. See also the suggested rearrangement of the extant fragments, and other pertinent comments, by A. Marmorstein in his review of that volume, supplemented by D. Simonsen's "Note" thereon, in *MGWJ*, LXIX, 121–22. According to Opas, Kraśnik was the most important of these privately owned cities in the Lublin palatinate. It is therefore of special interest to study J. Morgensztern's "Information on the Jewish Population of Kraśnik on the Basis of an Inventory of 1631" (Polish), *BZIH*, no. 32, pp. 27–42, 85–86, with an English summary. By way of contrast, Warsaw, the capital of the Polish Crown, had maintained its two-centuries-old exclusion of Jews, who are therefore, passed over in silence by authors like B. Grochulska in her "Population Statistics of Warsaw in the Second Half of the Eighteenth Century" (Polish), *PH*, XIV, 586–608. On the rapidly changing situation there, see *infra*, n. 47.

45. See W. Tokarz, *Galicya w początkach ery Józefińskiej w świetle ankiety urzędowej (1783)* (Galicia at the Beginning of Joseph II's Regime in the Light of a Government Inquiry of 1783), pp. 268 ff.; K. Koranyi, "The Mercenary and the Recruited Soldier" (Polish), *CPH*, I, 105–108; and other literature, mainly emphasizing the legal aspects, listed by J. Bardach, ed., *Historia państwa i prawa Polski*, II, 137 ff. See also *supra*, n. 40; and Chap. LXVIII, n. 53.

46. Understandably, the census of 1765 has aroused the curiosity of many scholars, although truly searching monographic studies of special areas did not begin to appear until a century after the event. We need but mention here the following publications: I. Kamanin, "The Listing of Jewish Settlements in the Southwestern Territory [of Russia] in 1765–1791" (Russian), *Arkhiv Yugo-Zapadnoi Rossii*, Part 5, II, referring to Volhynia, Podolia, and the Ukraine; F. Bostel, "Jews in the Lwów Area and the District of Żydaczów in the Year 1765" (Polish), *Archiwum Komisji His-*

torycznej of PAU, VI, 357–78; M. Bałaban, "The Census of Jews and Karaites in the Halicz Area and the Districts of Trembowla and Kołomyja in the Year 1765" (Polish), *ibid.*, XI, 11–31; H. Aleksandrova, "The Jewish Population in Belorussia in the Period of the Partitions of Poland (Historical-Statistical Studies)" (Yiddish), *Zeitshrift* (Minsk), IV, 31–83. More comprehensive were the studies aiming to analyze that census with respect to the entire Polish Crown, or even to the whole dual Commonwealth. See esp. J. Kleczyński and F. Kluczycki, *Liczba głów żydowskich w Koronie z taryf r. 1765* (The Number of Jewish Heads in the Crown According to the Lists of 1765), reprinted from the aforementioned *Archiwum*, VIII. The Polish studies were followed by Ch. Korobkov's twin essays, "The Statistics of Jewish Settlement in Poland and Lithuania in the Second Half of the Eighteenth Century (On the Basis of Data in the Official Registers)" (Russian), *ES*, IV, 541–62, and his more detailed "List of Jewish Settlements in the Vitebsk Gouvernement in 1772 (From Historical Archives)" (Russian), *ibid.*, V, 164–77; I. Schiper, "The Distribution of Jews in Poland and Lithuania" (Russian) in the *Istoriia evreiskogo naroda* (A History of the Jewish People, XI = *Istoriia Evreev v Rossii*, I), 108–121; J. Lestschinsky's succinct statistical tables in "The Jewish Communities in Poland (Ukraine) on the Eve of the [First] Partition of the Polish State" (Yiddish), *Bleter far yidishe Demografie*, I, 21–24; and N. M. Gelber's summary of other aspects in his "On the Statistics of Jews in Poland at the End of the Eighteenth Century" (Yiddish), *Yivo Shriftn far Ekonomik un Statistik* (Yivo Economic Studies), I, 185–88.

All these efforts were overshadowed by R. Mahler's detailed and painstaking work, *Yidn in amolikn Poiln in likht fun tsifern* (Jews in Old Poland in the Light of Numbers: the Demographic and Socioeconomic Structure of the Jews in the Polish Crown in the Eighteenth Century, Accompanied by a Volume of Tables). This work was briefly summarized, with some additional comments, by A. Eisenbach in his "Jews in Old Poland in the Light of Numbers" (Polish), *KH*, LXVI, 521–26; and, more fully, in the Polish version entitled "Jews in Old Poland in the Light of Numbers: the Demographic Structure and Socioeconomic Status of the Jews in the Polish Crown in the Eighteenth Century" by J. Lewinzon in *Przeszłość demograficzna Polski*, I, 130–80. This study was to be completed in the subsequent instalments of that annual, which was not done, perhaps because of the anti-Jewish reaction in Poland after the Six-Day War in the Middle East.

47. See esp. W. Tokarz, *Galicya w początkach ery Józefińskiej*, esp. pp. 176 ff., 335 ff., 353 ff.; A. K. Holsche, *Geographie und Statistik von West-, Süd-, und Neu-Ostpreussen;* W. Surowiecki, *Wybór pism*, pp. 247 ff. (estimating for the Duchy of Warsaw the presence of 277,474 Jews, including about 7,000 in the city of Warsaw; p. 471); H. Grossman, *Struktura społeczna i gospodarcza Księstwa Warszawskiego na podstawie spisów ludności 1808–1810* (The Social and Economic Structure of the Duchy of Warsaw Based upon the Population Censuses of 1808–1810; offprint of *Kwartalnik Statystyczny*, II, 1925; he considers the census of 1810, with its assumed 8.4 percent deficiency, much superior to that of 1808, which he regards as 28 percent deficient); and, with special reference to Jews, the twin studies by A. Eisenbach, "The Structure of the Jewish Population in Warsaw in the Light of the Census of 1819" (Polish), *BZIH*, nos. 13–14, pp. 73–121, esp. p. 82 Table (reviewing the annual figures for the city's total population in 1792–1813, which, after a decline in the early years, recovered its original strength in 1805; in contrast, the number of Jews increased steadily from 6,013 in 1793 to 14,601 in 1810, or from 8.6 to 18.1 per-

cent of the civilian population); and idem, "Distribution and Dwelling Conditions of Jewish Inhabitants of Warsaw in the Light of the 1815 Census" (Polish), *ibid.*, no. 25, pp. 50–86. Much can also be learned from the general data assembled by one of the outstanding statisticians of the late eighteenth century, A. F. Büsching, in his *Magazin für die neue Historie und Geographie,* 23 vols. esp. XXII, 36–414.

All these researches refer to the period after 1648, and although they shed some light on the earlier conditions as well, they leave a great many questions unanswered. Hence we must depend mainly on the pre-"Deluge" sources—deficient as these are in many respects—for analyzing the earlier Jewish demographic situation. That not all Polish researches, even those dealing with limited areas, contribute directly to estimates of the Jewish population, may be noted from the example of R. Szewczyk's dissertation, *Ludność Lublina w latach 1583–1650* (Lublin's Population in the Years 1583–1650), where the author claims that he found no satisfactory data on Jews (p. 14), though he mentions some figures relating to converts (pp. 107 ff.). See *supra,* Chap. LXVII, n. 36. In contrast, discussing the later period, W. Cwik was able to marshal considerable evidence on "The Jewish Population in the Cities of the Lublin Area in the Second Half of the Eighteenth Century" (Polish), *BZIH*, no. 59, pp. 29–62. See also J. Kleczyński's "Census of the Population of the Cracow Diocese in the Year 1787" (Polish), *Archiwum Komisji Historycznej* of PAU, VIII, largely based on local and diocesan church records; and B. Kumor's more recent analysis of "Unknown Sources Referring to Population Statistics for the Diocese of Cracow in the Eighteenth Century" (Polish), *Przeszłość demograficzna Polski,* IV, 21–59, with an English summary, esp. pp. 38 f. relating to Jews.

48. The size of the Jewish population in Poland and Lithuania at the end of the fifteenth century is given here in accordance with what was said about it *supra,* Vol. X, pp. 36, 317 n. 44. To be sure, this questionable figure, originally suggested by I. Schipper, has been rejected not only by B. Mark, as mentioned *ibid.,* but also by E. Friedman in his "On the Statistics of Jews in Old Poland" (Polish), *MZ*, III, Part 1, pp. 130–35, who believes that no more than 10,000–11,000 Jews lived in the whole Commonwealth at that time. However, this is decidedly an underestimate, though admittedly one which Friedman shares with Tadeusz Ladenberger (Ładogórski), a leading student of medieval Poland's general population. See the latter's *Zaludnienie Polski na początku panowania Kazimierza Wielkiego* (Poland's Population at the Beginning of Casimir the Great's Reign), with a French summary, largely based upon records of the collection of Peter's pence in the Polish areas. Despite Ładogórski's recently renewed arguments in support of his generally low estimates, in his *Studya nad zaludnieniem Polski XIV w.* (Studies on the Polish Population in the Fourteenth Century), his figures have been considered too low by almost all other competent students of Polish historical demography.

On the Commonwealth area and population in 1582 and 1634, see B. Baranowski and S. Herbst, "The Consolidation of the Large-Estate and Serfdom Structure" (Polish) in T. Manteuffel, ed., *Historia Polski,* I, Part 2, pp. 416–50, esp. pp. 416 ff. Here the authors include an estimate of ethnic Poles and Jews only for the period close to 1648—at which time, they believe, the total population of the Commonwealth reached some 10,000,000 souls, with the Poles amounting to "no less than 40 percent" of the population, while the Jewish population had risen to 5 percent. This ratio is not much higher than our postulated 4.5 percent. On the other hand, the estimates for the mid-sixteenth century tend to be rather vague. No one seems to have thoroughly investigated the data assembled in the Jewish census of 1550, in part reflected in the royal courtier Stanisław Lipnicki's "description of Jews residing in the royal cities of the palatinates of Sandomierz, Rus, Podolia, Lublin, and Bełz." This description and its location have long been known from W. Abdon's 1923 list in his study of "The Archive of the Crown Treasury in the Cracow Castle" (Polish), *Archiwum Komisji Historycznej* of PAN, 2d ser. II, 124–577, esp. p. 542.

The great variation in population estimates for that period came to the fore, at the very beginning of serious Polish demographic researches, in the controversy between Adolf Pawiński and Włodzimierz Czerkawski. Limiting themselves to the most easily ascertainable data for the three major provinces of the Polish Crown (Great Poland, Little Poland, and Mazovia), Pawiński estimated for the year 1578 a rural population of 1,700,000 and an urban population of 400,000, totaling 2,100,000 persons; while Czerkawski raised the figures to 2,400,000, 800,000, and 3,200,000, respectively. After a fresh review of these estimates, W. Kula took an intermediary position, postulating a total population of 2,700,000. See Pawiński's and Kula's studies cited *supra*, n. 35; and W. Czerkawski, "The Method of Investigating Poland's Population in the Sixteenth Century" (Polish), *Sprawozdania* (Proceedings) of PAU, 1897, Part 2, pp. 8–12. Other demographers are inclined to adhere to Czerkawski's higher figures, or even to raise them. Egon Vielrose, for example, accepted the total estimate of 3,200,000; while I. Gieysztorowa lowered the number to 3,100,000 for 1580, and raised it to only 3,830,000 for 1650. (These figures are not controverted by Z. Guldon's estimate of 2,809,000 inhabitants in the three provinces and a total of 6,473,000 in the entire Polish Crown in his "Poland's Population in 1629" [Polish], *Zapiski historyczne*, XXXIII, 43–52, with a German summary; the study is based on an extant official summary of the hearth tax of that year. See esp. p. 50 Table 4.) Gieysztorowa explained this relatively small increase of 20 percent in seventy years by the recurrent plagues, especially that of 1623–25, and the constant warlike disturbances. She might also have added the factor of progressive colonization of the southeastern provinces, which drained off some of the surplus population from western Poland. This factor operated even more strongly among the Jews. But no one has suggested a population larger than 10,000,000 for the entire Commonwealth in that period before the Cossack uprising and the Swedish-Muscovite invasions.

The estimate of 750,000 Jews in 1764 follows R. Mahler's painstaking computations and rather cogent arguments. This estimate comes close to the 780,000 postulated as early as 1812 by W. Surowiecki. The figure of 900,000 given by Tadeusz Czacki, like that of 620,000 calculated by J. Kleczyński and F. Kluczycki, is less convincing. But subject to the necessary corrections in the underlying computations, as argued by Mahler and others, their estimates may be reconciled with the best approximate figure of 750,000. See their studies listed *supra*, n. 35; and the independent summary of his own and other investigations by I. Schiper in "The Development of the Jewish Population in the Territories of the Old Commonwealth" (Polish) in the ed. by him *et al.* of *Żydzi w Polsce Odrodzonej* (Jews in Resurrected Poland), I, 21–36. Schiper's estimate of only 100,000 Jews in the entire Commonwealth in 1578, however, and of 450,000 in 1648, postulates a wholly disproportionate Jewish increase of 350 percent while the general population was increasing but moderately. Schiper's figure for 1578 (he also gives low estimates for the general population) is based entirely on the fragile data derived from the incomplete extant records of the capitation tax. His estimates should, in my opinion, be raised by at least 50 percent. On the general population of Poland-Lithuania in 1771, see M. R. Reinhard *et al.*, *Histoire générale de la population mondiale*, p. 229. This lengthy note and the corresponding computations in the text were fully formulated in the present form when B. D. Weinryb's *The Jews of Poland* reached me, immediately after its publication. This informative volume includes a very suggestive Appendix 3, dealing with the "Jewish Population in Old (Prepartition) Poland" (pp. 308–320, 394–98). After carefully reviewing the author's data and arguments—some of them quite significant in detail—I have found no reason for altering any part of the above presentation. I could not accept, in particular, his low estimates of 10,000 Jews in the dual Commonwealth around 1500, and 170,000 in Poland, without Lithuania, around 1648. Yet this continued difference of opinion ought to demonstrate to the reader anew how much must yet be done in Jewish population research on the early modern period before any kind of consensus may be reached even about total area figures, not to speak of many other, more detailed vital statistics.

49. See M. Traub, *Jüdische Wanderbewegungen vor und nach dem Weltkriege*, pp. 111 ff. Tables XII–XIII, XVIII–XX: my *Steeled by Adversity: Essays and Addresses on American Jewish Life*, ed. by J. M. Baron, pp. 280 ff. nn. 18–20; J. Gieysztorowa, "Recherches sur la démographie," *Ergon*, IV, 500 ff.; S. Ettinger, "Jewish Participation," *Zion*, XXI, 124; B. Rubshtein, "About the Number of Jews in the Grand Duchy of Lithuania in the Mid-Sixteenth Century" (Russian), *ES*, VIII, 20–28; S. Aleksandrowicz, "The Population of the Small Towns in Lithuania and Belorussia in the First Half of the Seventeenth Century" (Polish), *RDSG*, XXVII, 35–65, with a French summary. On the birth rate among the Polish peasants being as high as 45 to 50 per 1,000, see I. Gieysztorowa, "Studies," *KHKM*, X, 546 ff.; W. Kula, *Problemy i metody historii gospodarczej* (Problems and Methods of Economic History), pp. 455 f. On the other hand, the total birth rate of the Polish and Lithuanian population must have been considerably reduced not only by the aforementioned presence of a large celibatarian clergy but also by the indubitably lower fertility among the noble families, whose ratio in the population was as high as 10 percent. A smaller birth rate is indicated, if for no other reason, by the relatively late marriages customary in that class. According to Tadeusz Furtak's very tentative computation—in "Some Problems in the Historical Demography of the Polish Gentry" (Polish), *RDSG*, VI, 31–58, esp. pp. 47 ff. and Table 2a—Polish noblemen married, on the average, at the age of thirty-five in the sixteenth century, and at nearly thirty-one in the seventeenth and eighteenth centuries. The relative poverty of the large mass of dependent nobles (the so-called *golota* or *holota*), combined with their aspirations to a high standard of life, must also have contributed to diminished natality and increased mortality among members of that class. At the same time, the peasants, who usually amounted to more than two-thirds of the entire population, married at a much earlier age and were quite prolific, despite their hard life under the growing oppression of serfdom, which many of them considered God-ordained and immutable. See L. V. Razumovskaia, *Ocherki po istorii polskich krestian v XV–XVI vv.* (Sketches in the History of the Polish Peasants in the Fifteenth and Sixteenth Centuries), with the comments thereon by L. Żytkowicz in his "Polish Peasants in the Fifteenth and Sixteenth Centuries" (Polish), *PH*, LXII, 100–111; and E. O. Kossmann, "Zur Geschichte der polnischen Bauern und ihrer Freiheit," *HZ*, CCV, 15–45.

In his otherwise noteworthy study of "Jews in the Voivodship of Bełz," *BZIH*, no. 27, pp. 22–61, M. Horn comes to the surprising conclusion that in the years 1578–1629 the number of Jewish families in ten major cities of the Bełz province actually diminished by 44.6–55.6 percent. This conclusion seems wholly unjustified. True, that province had been the scene of numerous Tatar raids in the first decades of the seventeenth century. Combined with the recurrent epidemics and fires, these raids must have greatly inhibited the growth of the Jewish, as well as the general, population. Yet the same destructive factors did not prevent the Jewish population from increasing, in the following fourteen years (1629–43), by about 47 percent, in both the royal and the private cities of the area. See *ibid.*, pp. 44 ff. Tables 5, 6, and 8. Horn's underestimate of the size of the Jewish population in 1629 stems from his assumption that, on the average, a house owned or rented by a Jew had approximately 7 inhabitants. He thereby overlooks the widely attested phenomenon of excessively crowded Jewish quarters, partly imposed upon the Jewish inhabitants by the burghers' intolerance. While the situation in the medium and small towns of the Bełz province greatly differed from that in Poznań and other metropolises, we may readily assume that the space allotted to Jews there, too, was considerably restricted. Nor are we altogether certain that the tax collector clearly differentiated between the tax liability of the Jewish tenants and that of the Christian owners. On the other hand, Horn's estimate of the increase of the Jewish population by some 51–95 percent in the hundred and twenty years between 1643 and 1764 (p. 52), may be approximately correct. Though not quite as dynamic as in the southeastern provinces, the Jews' demographic evolution in Red Russia during the last prepartition century doubtless exceeded that in the western provinces.

50. See M. Łowmiańska, *Wilno przed najazdem moskiewskim 1655 roku* (Vilna before the Muscovite Invasion of 1655), esp. pp. 72 ff.; L. Lewin, "Die Judenverfolgungen im zweiten schwedisch-polnischen Kriege 1655–59," *Zeitschrift der Historischen Gesellschaft für die Provinz Posen*, XVI, 79–101; I. Gieysztorowa, "Studies," *KHKM*, X, 543 Table VI; Moses b. Naphtali Hirsch Rivkes, *Be'er ha-Golah* (Well of Exile, commentary on the *Shulḥan 'Arukh*), Amsterdam, 1661, Intro., in the excerpt trans. into English by Israel Cohen in his *Vilna* (Jewish Communities Series), pp. 41 ff. In his "Poland's Population," *KHKM*, V, 49 f., E. Vielrose actually estimated the total population of the three provinces in 1660 as low as 2,250,000, but he mentioned no figures for 1650. At that time the population must have been considerably larger than in 1572, for which he postulated a total of 3,200,000. More specifically, Jerzy Topolski estimates the following percentages of population losses during the mid-seventeenth century: for Mazovia, 64; Pomerania, *ca.* 60; Podlasie, 50; Great Poland, 42; Little Poland, 27. See "The Impact of the Mid-Seventeenth-Century Wars on the Economic Situation in Podlasie" (Polish), *Studia historica* in honor of Henryk Łowmiański, pp. 309–349, showing that the population of the province was reduced from some 250,000 to a little over 125,000 in the years 1650–62. The decline of the whole country's Jewish population by at least 100,000 is very likely, though estimates by contemporaries that no fewer than 60,000–100,000 Jews were killed by the Cossacks, and that the total number of persons who were killed or who emigrated to other lands amounted to 180,000 are doubtless too high. See the sources, cited by Schiper in *Żydzi w Polsce Odrodzonej*, I, 31 f. The full extent of the catastrophic losses sustained by Polish and Lithuanian Jewry in the years 1648–60 will be analyzed here in a later volume.

51. See B. Baranowski and S. Herbst in T. Manteuffel, ed., *Historia Polski*, I, Part 2, pp. 450 ff.; Stanisław Lipnicki's description cited by W. Abdon in "The Archive of the Crown Treasury" (Polish), *Archiwum Komisji Historycznej* of PAN, 2d ser. II, 542; *supra*, nn. 46–47. The instrument frequently used for estimating the size of the Jewish population in the respective cities—namely, the number of Jewish houses in a particular locality—is highly unreliable. Even without the specific restrictions imposed by cities upon the size of the Jewish quarter or the number of allowable Jewish dwellings, statistical computations derived from recorded housing "have always proved misleading." See P. Wolff, *Les "Estimes" toulousains des XIV et XV siècles* (a complementary Paris thesis). Nonetheless, in view of the paucity of other, more dependable materials, we must often make use of this resource for reaching some approximations of the number of Jewish inhabitants. See, for instance, the careful analysis of "The Housing Conditions in Poznań's Jewish Quarter on the Left Bank [of the Warta] within the City Walls in 1619" included in S. Waszak's "Population," *Przegląd Zachodni*, IX, 112, Table XIII. See also S. Aleksandrowicz, "The Population of the Small Towns in Lithuania and Belorussia" (Polish), *RDSG*, XXVII, 35–65.

Remarkably, no serious effort has yet been made to correlate the size of population with the area inhabited by it in the respective cities. This method served me in good stead back in 1928, when I tried to come to grips with the even more complex problem of "The Israelitic Population under the Kings," first published in Hebrew in *Abhandlungen zur Erinnerung an Hirsch Perez Chajes*, pp. 76–136; and recently included in an English trans. in my *Ancient and Medieval Jewish History Essays*, ed. by L. A. Feldman, pp. 23–73, 380–99. See also F. Lot's voluminous *Recherches sur la population et la superficie des cités remontant à la période gallo-romaine*, published in 1945–53. Such studies with respect to prepartition Poland are complicated by the presence of numerous *jurydyki*, within and outside the city walls, where the demographic situation often widely differed from that in the sections under municipal control. In the Jewish case, the residential restrictions and occasionally rigid boundaries of the Jewish quarters, which were forced to accommodate ever-growing numbers of inhabitants, has further aggravated the task of ascertaining relevant demographic data. Yet the paucity of precise data ought to encourage students to develop plausible hypotheses from a variety of approaches, which would hopefully add up into a series of converging probabilities.

52. See M. Bałaban, *Dzieje Żydów w Krakowie*, I, 103 following F. H. Wettstein's computation in his *Toledot anshe shem be-Qraqa* (A History of Famous Men in Cracow) reprinted from *Hamicpe*, I and III. The contrast between ordinary and plague years was equally sharp in a London parish during the period 1586–1605. A detailed and accurate recent investigation has shown that, during the three plague years of 1592, 1593, and 1603, no fewer than 2,809 persons died, as against the more usual mortality during twenty-three normal years, when the number of deaths totaled only 3,476. In fact, in the six-month period of 1603, 1,422 persons died (including 339 children up to four years of age, and 173 aged five to fourteen). Remarkably, men seem to have been more susceptible to contagion than women. Their ratio of deaths in plague years was 134.8 to 100 females, whereas in other years it was only 114.7 to 100. It may also be noted that the birth rate, according to these limited records, amounted to only 29.5 per 1,000 population, which seems unusually low. See M. F. Hollingsworth and T. H. Hollingsworth, "Plague Mortality Rates

by Age and Sex in the Parish of St. Botolph's without Bishopsgate, London, 1603," *Population Studies*, XXV, 131–46. No comparably exact data seem to be available for any Polish-Lithuanian area of that period.

53. We have no adequate information about sex ratios in the Jewish communities before 1648. But we may perhaps assume that the situation did not materially differ from that in 1764, when the census listings became detailed enough to enable modern investigators to compute reasonable figures for that relationship. According to R. Mahler, the records of three palatinates of the Polish Crown show an average ratio of 100.3 females to 100 males. Evidently, for occupational reasons, there was a major difference between towns and rural settlements. In the latter, the average ratio was only 92.4 to 100, whereas in towns females exceeded males at the rate of 103.7 to 100. Incidentally, the proportion of unmarried persons was extremely high. In ten palatinates the records seem to show that 49 percent of town dwellers and 50 percent of villagers were unmarried. This high ratio can best be explained by the presence of a great many children of non-marriageable age. But since these lists excluded infants below one year of age, the question is still quite moot. See R. Mahler, *Yidn in amolikn Poiln*, pp. 67 ff. and Tables XIX–XXXII, 71 ff. and Tables XXXIII–XXXVII.

LXX: SOCIOECONOMIC RESTRATIFICATION

1. The relationship between population movements and economic prosperity has long been debated. The World Population Conference, meeting in Rome from August 31 to September 10, 1954, received from a United Nations Committee, recruited mainly from American and French specialists, with Frank W. Notestein serving as rapporteur, a report about serious "Gaps in Existing Knowledge of the Relationships between Population Trends and Economic and Social Conditions." See its *Proceedings*, Vol. V, pp. 1013-29. This report was submitted to the Twenty-Sixth Session of the Conference, which was entirely devoted to a discussion of the "Inter-Relations of Population, Economic Development, and Social Change." Among the other papers there presented, the following are particularly relevant to our subject: S. Kuznets, "Under-Developed Countries and the Pre-Industrial Phase in the Advanced Countries: an Attempt at Comparison"; and B. Minc, "Transformations essentielles du taux de l'accroissement naturel de la population en Pologne," *ibid.*, pp. 947–70 and 971–93. In the case of Polish Jewry, the demographic upswing of the period 1500–1648, though followed by a sharp decline in the following dozen years, had lasting effects; its underlying factors continued to operate during the gradual recovery of Polish Jewry after 1660.

2. See *supra*, esp. Vol. IV, Chap. XXII; and Vol. XII. Regrettably, the immediate impact of population growth on Polish Jewry's economic diversification is difficult to ascertain because of the paucity of substantial, dependable data before the nineteenth century. We must also bear in mind the resistance to change characteristic of the generally traditionalist Jewish leadership; the preference a great many Jews had, for educational and cultural reasons, for living in close quarters in towns, rather than in small, isolated settlements among frequently unfriendly neighbors; and their fear of exposure to strong assimilationist and conversionist pressures in the new lands. Yet, in a relatively short time, the inescapable economic needs and appetites of the Jewish population enforced a gradual adjustment to the alien environment, which was made less exclusivist by its ethnically heterogeneous population.

3. See Giovanni Botero (J. B. Benesius), *Mundus imperiorum, siue de mundi imperiis libri quattuor*, new ed. Cologne, 1603, p. 26; G. Rzączyński, *Historia Naturalis curiosa Regni Poloniae, Magni Ducatus Lituaniae, annexarumque provinciarum*, Sandomierz, 1721, p. 61 n. 1; and other sources cited by R. Rybarski in his *Handel i polityka handlowa Polski w XVI stuleciu* (Poland's Commerce and Commercial Policies in the Sixteenth Century), I, 1 f. Rybarski sees the subsequent reappraisal of Poland's position, illustrated by David Hume's harsh comment (cited *infra*, n. 4), as a contrasting criticism. However, both the glorifiers and the critics were independently right; they merely reflected the changing realities of their respective periods.

4. J. Topolski, "La Régression économique en Pologne du XVIe au XVIIIe siècle," *APH*, VII, 28–49; D. Hume, *Essays Moral, Political and Literary*, Part II, 2: Of Refinement in the Arts, Oxford, 1966 ed., p. 283 (this title was adopted by the author

in 1770; the original 1752 title, Of Luxury, was more explicit). Hume intended to combat Bernard de Mandeville's view that the desire for luxury, though intrinsically a human failing, nevertheless could be of economic advantage to mankind. See *supra*, Vol. XV, pp. 52 f. In any case, in eighteenth-century Poland, the existing system aimed at promoting the *szlachta*'s luxurious way of living, could hardly be considered of general benefit to the country. Hume, like Richard Cantillon in his *Essai sur la nature du Commerce en général*, voiced the prevailing opinion of their mercantile-minded eighteenth-century compatriots. But his comments could not be applied to Polish Jewry, which never relinquished its important commercial function. In fact, with the diminishing resources and growing disorganization of the Commonwealth, the role played by Jewish commerce was even greater than before.

Although the problem of a European economic crisis in the seventeenth century was extensively debated in the historical literature in the late 1950s and early 1960s, the problem has not been altogether resolved. In addition to the studies listed *supra*, Vol. XIV, pp. 377 n. 49, 386 f. n. 1, see R. Romano, "Tra XVI e XVII secolo. Una crisi economica 1619–1622," *Rivista storica italiana*, LXXIV, 480–531; and, with special reference to the comparable conditions in Western Europe and in Poland-Lithuania, the Polish essays which appeared in quick succession in *KH*, LXIX and LXX: J. Topolski, "On the So-Called Economic Crisis in Seventeenth-Century Europe" (LXIX, 364–79); A. Wyczański, "On the Question of a Seventeenth-Century Crisis" (*ibid.*, 656–72); A. Mączak, "On the Crisis and Crises of the Seventeenth Century" (LXX, 53–68). See also the more general observations by M. Małowist in "Die Problematik der sozial-wirtschaftlichen Geschichte Polens vom 15. bis zum 17. Jahrhundert," *La Renaissance et la Réformation en Pologne et en Hongrie* (= *Studia Historica*, LIII), 11–26. In "The European Economy and Politics during the Sixteenth and Seventeenth Centuries. A Crisis or Retrogression?" (Polish), *PH*, LV, 1–21, M. Hroch and J. Petráč not only discussed that semantic problem but also rightly pointed out that, while the economic slowdown after the dynamic expansion of the sixteenth century had begun before 1600, it came fully to the fore at different times in the various Western countries during the seventeenth century. See also *supra*, Vol. XIV, pp. 377 n. 49, 386 n. 1. Of course, the Thirty Years' War had the greatest impact upon the Holy Roman Empire, but its effects were gradually felt in France, Holland, and England as well. Poland, on the other hand, may actually have benefited from that war; for instance, by the immigration of numerous Silesian weavers, who gave additional stimuli to the Polish textile manufacture. The new Jewish immigrants, too, contributed their share to Polish production and trade. Thus, the country did not really suffer from the spreading economic stagnation until its own great emergency of 1648 and after.

5. See P. Bloch, *Die General-Privilegien der polnischen Judenschaft*, pp. 12 ff. Arts. 1–7, 24 (23), 26 (25), 28 (27), 29 (28), 30 (29), and 33; and *supra*, Vol. X, pp. 43 f., 320 f. n. 53; and Chap. LXVII, *passim*. On the extensive Polish legislation concerning Jewish commercial rights in various parts of Poland and Lithuania, and the aforementioned constant Jewish struggle against restrictions demanded especially by competing burghers, see esp. I. Schiper's analysis in *Dzieje handlu żydowskiego na ziemiach polskich*, pp. 23 ff., 59 ff.

6. P. Bloch, *Die General-Privilegien*, pp. 18, 60 f. (German), 118 f. (Latin); John Sobieski's confirmation of the basic charter Arts. 23–24, reproduced by L. Gumplo-

wicz in his *Prawodawstwo polskie względem Żydów*, pp. 174 f.; Sebastyan Miczyński, *Zwierciadło Korony*, Cracow, 1618 ed., pp. 69 f. The story of the petty Jewish money trade in sixteenth- and seventeenth-century Poland has yet to be told in detail. This branch of Jewish business, usually conducted between lender and borrower, mainly in connection with the pawning of a small object, is rarely recorded in the sources, Jewish or governmental, except when it gave rise to litigation. The scattered references in the judicial and other records, even if assembled and carefully analyzed, would most likely produce few surprises. On the whole, this business was conducted along traditional lines, such as those analyzed in connection with other lands in our earlier chapters, particularly in Vol. XII. On the whole, the extant records mention the amounts due, without describing their origin or stating whether they included accumulated interest. As Jewish commercial activities intensified, the additional income provided by interest on outstanding loans from the sale of merchandise became a welcome sideline to whatever profits may have been obtained from the original sales. This combination of general commerce with banking was also characteristic of business among non-Jews, including leading patricians like the Boner family in Cracow.

7. Stanisław Sokołowski, *Quaestor, siue De parsimonia atque frugalitate* or in the simultaneous Polish trans. entitled *Szafarz, ábo O pohamowaniu vtrat niepotrzebnych*, Cracow, 1589; Marcin Śmiglecki, *O lichwie y trzech przedniejszych kontraktach* (On Usury and Three Foremost Contracts: Wiederkauf, Rents and Business Partnership: a Short Lesson), which appeared in three different eds. in Vilna and Cracow, 1596, and in a new, much enlarged form in Vilna, 1607 (its popularity was attested by its publication in four more editions between 1613 and 1641); B. Baranowski and S. Herbst, in T. Manteuffel's ed. of *Historia Polski,* I, Part 2, p. 468. On the medieval antecedents in Poland, see Z. Pazdro's analysis of "Usury in the Light of the Polish Synodal Legislation in the Middle Ages" (Polish), *KH*, XV, 449–503. The conditions in Zamość are well analyzed and documented by J. Morgensztern in her "Jewish Credit Operations in Zamość in the Seventeenth Century" (Polish), *BZIH*, no. 64, pp. 3–32 and its six statistical tables, as well as in her other pertinent studies listed *supra*, Chap. LXVIII, n. 49. As in other inflationary periods, especially if they were accompanied by a currency depreciation, the rate of interest was apt to rise rapidly, in order to compensate the lender for the reduced purchasing power of his capital. These adverse phenomena came fully to the fore only after the "Deluge," but they were already partially manifest in the first half of the seventeenth century. Before 1600, on the other hand, it was the speedy economic expansion, and the great acceleration of other commercial activities requiring capital investment, which had caused a shortage of funds, with a concomitant rise of interest rates. But none of these developments appeared simultaneously in all parts of the dual Commonwealth. Hence there were enormous local, regional, and chronological variations. A thoroughgoing analysis of the data, explicitly or obliquely recorded in the scattered sources, might well be a rewarding task for persevering researchers.

8. See *supra*, Vol. XII, p. 295 n. 45; and *infra*, n. 12. The literature on Jewish communal debts and their liquidation—which became the subject of extended negotiations and debates in the early Emancipation period in various lands, including Poland's three successor states—is very large indeed. We need but refer here to the following studies: M. Bałaban, "The Situation of the Cracow Community about

1700" (Polish), *MZ*, I, Part 2, pp. 413–28; J. Freylichówna, "The Problem of Liqui-
dating the Debts of the Community of Kazimierz [Cracow] after the Third Partition
(1795–1809) and under the Republic of Cracow (1817–1829)" (Polish), *ibid.*, III,
Part 1, 467–78; M. Laubert, "Die Schuldenregulierung der jüdischen Korporationen
in der Provinz Posen," *MGWJ*, LXVIII, 321–31; I. Galant, "The Indebtedness of
the Jewish Communities in the Seventeenth Century" (Russian), *ES*, VI, 129–32
(with special reference to Łuck); I. Schipper, "The Financial Ruin of the Central
and Provincial Autonomous Bodies of the Jews in Poland (1650–1764)" (Yiddish),
Yivo Ekonomishe Shriftn, II, 1–19; B. D. Weinryb, "Beitraege zur Finanzgeschichte
der juedischen Gemeinden in Polen, II," *HUCA*, XVI, 187–214, esp. pp. 209 ff.;
idem, *Texts and Studies in the Communal History of Polish Jewry*, esp. pp. 81 ff.
(English), 31 ff. (Hebrew). See also other sources, and the data referring to Jewish
communities in other countries analyzed in my *JC*, II, 68 ff.; III, 190 ff. nn. 25–32.

9. See J. Kądziołka's careful study *Finanse miasta Poznania 1501–1648* (The Finances of the City of Poznań 1501–1648), with a German summary, esp. pp. 136 f.,
147. This contrast between the cities and the Jewish communities will become
clearer in our general analysis of Jewish communal history during early modern
times, in a later chapter.

10. See B. Baranowski and S. Herbst in T. Manteuffel's ed. of *Historia Polski*, I,
Part 2, p. 466; B. D. Weinryb, *Texts and Studies*, Hebrew section, p. 31 No. 82.
Clearly, the genuine communal need to increase the flow of capital for Jewish businessmen so that they could expand their general trade, for the benefit of the community at large, did not prevent conflicts of interest among elders with respect to
their own or their relatives' private finances. On the other hand, there were cases
when a particular elder's credit was better than that of the community, and such
individuals were often persuaded to guarantee or actually cosign a communal bond.
See a number of illustrations to this effect culled from the records of the Poznań
kahal by M. Breger in his Breslau (Wrocław) dissertation, *Zur Handelsgeschichte
der Juden in Polen während des 17. Jahrhunderts mit besonderer Berücksichtigung
der Judenschaft Posens*, esp. pp. 23 ff.

11. See S. A. Bershadskii, *Dokumenty i materialy dlia istorii Evreev v Yugozapadnoi Rossii* (Evreiskaia Biblioteka, VII–VIII); A. M. Kurbskii, *Zhizn* (see *supra*,
Chap. LXIX, n. 27), I, 288; other sources cited by S. Ettinger in his "Jewish Participation" (Hebrew), *Zion*, XXI, 126; B. D. Weinryb, *Texts and Studies*, Hebrew section, pp. 32 ff., esp. Nos. 84–87, 90, etc. On the loan from Tuczyński and the subsequent complications, see *infra*, n. 15.

12. See B. D. Weinryb, *Texts and Studies*, Hebrew section, pp. 101 f. No. 225, 110
No. 245 and n. 318a; S. M. Dubnow, *Pinqas ha-Medinah*, p. 14 No. 72; I. Schipper,
"Polish Regesta to the History of the 'Council of Four Lands' from Archival
Sources" (Yiddish), *Yivo Historishe Shriftn*, I, 83–114, esp. pp. 85 ff.; and, more generally, idem, "The Financial Ruin," *Yivo Ekonomishe Shriftn*, II, 1 ff. The inter-
twining of private and public interests by leading individuals was also common in
non-Jewish societies of the period, including the bureaucracies of the various lands.
We recall how difficult it was to segregate the Polish kings' private property from
the royal domain. See *supra*, Chap. LXVIII, n. 86.

13. B. D. Weinryb, *Texts and Studies,* Hebrew section, p. 58 No. 95. The danger of excessive indebtedness by the community is well illustrated by an entry in the Poznań minute book of 1642. The elders suddenly realized the risk of powerful lenders unexpectedly calling their loans at once, "and it would be impossible to postpone payments even for a moment." They instructed their representatives not only to obviate such an immediate emergency but also to seek, at the forthcoming Gniezno fair, by whatever means they deemed appropriate, the adoption of long-term measures to prevent its occurrence. See the text in D. Avron's ed. of *Pinqas ha-Ksherim shel Qehillat Pozna* (Acta Electorum communitatis Judaeorum posnaniensium [1621–1835]), p. 82 No. 407.

14. See Z. Pazdro, "Usury in the Light of the Polish Synodal Legislation" (Polish), *KH,* XV, 470, 481 f.; the general remarks thereon by J. Bardach in his *Historia państwa i prawa Polski,* I, 320; M. Breger, *Zur Handelsgeschichte,* pp. 31 ff.; P. Dąbkowski, *Prawo prywatne polskie* (Polish Private Law), II, 564 ff.; S. M. Dubnow, ed., *Pinqas ha-Medinah,* p. 152 No. 631. It should be noted that communities sometimes tried to lower the prevailing interest rates. In 1595, before the economic stringency of the seventeenth century, it was possible for the Cracow community to include in its ordinance a provision that, even in loans to Gentiles, moneylenders should be satisfied with an income of 12 groszy per 100 zlotys weekly. This was the equivalent of 20 percent annually. Transgressors were threatened with severe excommunication. See M. Balaban, "Die Krakauer Judengemeinde-Ordnung von 1595 und ihre Nachträge," *JJLG,* X, 296–360; XI, 88–114, esp. X, 311 f., 313 n. 1; and the additional, largely procedural, antiusury provision adopted in 1604, *ibid.,* XI, 107 f.

15. See the texts in B. D. Weinryb's ed. of *Texts and Studies,* Hebrew section, pp. 32 ff. Nos. 84, 89–90; and Weinryb's remarks in the English section, p. 44. The reichstaler at that time was, for the most part, equal to about 4 zlotys. But the rate of exchange was never quite stable, especially since the Polish mints had generally discontinued issuing coinage of their own, and the country was flooded with inferior coins, both from Prussia and from the Baltic seaports. There were also some clipped coins in circulation, some of them cut by the governments themselves during the Thirty Years' War. See A. Szelągowski, *Pieniądz i przewrót cen w XVI i XVII wieku w Polsce* (Money and Price Fluctuations in Sixteenth- and Seventeenth-Century Poland); *supra,* Chap. LXVIII, n. 40; and Vol. XII, pp. 231 ff., 388 ff. nn. 6–7.

16. See I. Halperin, ed., *Pinqas Va'ad 'Arba Araṣot* (Acta Congressus Generalis Judaeorum Regni Poloniae), pp. 16 ff., 22 No. 74, 45 ff. Nos. 111–18, 146 No. 343; *supra,* Chap. LXIX, n. 37; also in L. Lewin's "Neue Materialien zur Geschichte der Vierländersynode," *JJLG,* II, 15 No. lvi; and D. Avron, *Pinqas ha-Ksherim,* p. 213 No. 1270. It is of interest to note that such a major, almost epoch-making, reform was voted by the members of the Council of Four Lands only in general terms, and that they left the actual formulation to a single rabbinic member. Perhaps for this reason its author felt obliged to warn the readers that they should not take these provisions lightly, "for we have debated them at great length, and the heads of the academies, who were here at the fair with us, agreed to these statements but, after passing the resolution, they had to depart in their respective directions. Thus I remained here alone and drafted these statements in writing at the order of the heads of the provinces who accepted them and upheld them, thus stating in their own

minute book." That is why the passage quoted in the text, censuring the communities for borrowing on interest, is noted by Falk ha-Kohen in a personal way. Nonetheless, the summation of the laws to govern moneylending on interest, published in the same year by Falk ha-Kohen in a special tract (*Quntras*), was frequently reprinted and extensively commented on by later rabbinic authorities. See Halperin's comments in his *Pinqas*, p. 23. On the antecedents of the evasive doctrine of the *Heter 'isqa* (Permissiveness of Business [Partnership]), and similar debates in Polish ecclesiastical circles in the thirteenth century, see *supra*, Vol. XII, pp. 192, 338 f. n. 70; and Z. Pazdro, "Usury," *KH*, XV, 455 f.

17. See M. Breger's *Zur Handelsgeschichte*, pp. 23 ff. The class of agents was not limited to money brokers. As a matter of fact, almost every branch of business and many private relations between individuals required some mediation by informed middlemen. Outstanding among such specialists were the marriage brokers, who arranged many marriages in the Jewish community. In some respects the transfer of funds involved in dowries, resembled business loans and was governed by similar laws. However, on the whole, the community looked with greater equanimity on marriage brokerage, because it contributed to the fulfillment of the commandment of procreation. There was also a remarkable discrepancy between the commissions of marriage versus money brokers. The Lithuanian Council—which, in 1623, somewhat more generously than many local communities, allowed a money broker a one-half percent commission—placed marriage brokers on a par with agents who brought together parties for the purchase of real estate, including synagogue seats, and allowed them to charge 40 groschen per 100 guilders, or one and one-third percent of the dowry agreed upon. Remarkably, in its protective device for the marriage brokers the Council went so far as to declare a broker's promise to the parties that he would charge them no commission, to be null and void. "All of it should be considered mere chat, and he [the broker] has to be paid as if he had never made that promise." See S. M. Dubnow, *Pinqas ha-Medinah*, p. 8 Nos. 34–35. On marriage brokerage in general, see the forthcoming analysis of Jewish family life, in a later chapter.

18. Mordecai b. Abraham Yaphe, *Lebush 'Ir Shushan* (Garment, the City of Susa; a commentary on Joseph Karo's *Shulḥan 'Arukh*), on Ḥ. M. lxviii end; Philip Bloch, "Der Mamran, der jüdisch-polnische Wechselbrief" in *Festschrift . . . A. Berliner*, pp. 50–64, esp. pp. 62 ff. No. 2. Another copy of a *mamran* is to be found in A. Gulak's comp., *Osar ha-Sheṭarot ha-nehugim be-Yisrael* (Thesaurus of Deeds Frequently Used by Jews), p. 215. On the medieval antecedents of bearer instruments according to Jewish law, see *supra*, Vol. IV, pp. 213, 348 n. 82; and my "The Economic Views of Maimonides," in *Essays on Maimonides*, ed. by me, pp. 202 ff.; also reprinted in my *Ancient and Medieval Jewish History: Essays*, esp. pp. 204, and 484 n. 151.

19. F. Lütge, *Strukturwandlungen im ostdeutschen und osteuropäischen Fernhandel des 14. bis 16. Jahrhunderts* (= *Sitzungsberichte* of the Bayerische Akademie der Wissenschaften, Phil.-Hist. Klasse, 1964, No. 1), esp. pp. 15 ff., 28 ff.; E. Horn, "Legal and Economic Situation of the Jews in the Towns of the Halicz Province" (Polish), *BZIH*, no. 40, pp. 32 ff.; and *supra*, Chap. LXVIII, n. 58. These major routes were supplemented by many regional roads. For Lwów and the east, for

example, see those enumerated by M. Bałaban in his *Żydzi lwowscy*, pp. 93 f. n. 1; and A. Wawrzyńczyk, *Studia z dziejów handlu Polski z Wielkim Księstwem Litewskim i Rosją w XVI wieku* (Studies in the History of Poland's Commerce with the Grand Duchy of Lithuania and Russia in the Sixteenth Century), pp. 26 ff.

The export trade in grain, lumber, oxen, and other major articles had, of course, important implications for domestic economy and policies, all of which affected the Jews. See A. Mączak, "Export of Grain and the Problem of Distribution of National Income in Poland in the Years 1550–1650," *APH*, XVIII, 75–98 (showing that, like Amsterdam, Gdańsk enjoyed at that time a continuation of low food prices and high profits from trade and industry, a circumstance which favored businessmen, including Jews, in other localities as well); idem, "The Export of Grain and the Problems of the Polish Balance of Trade in the Sixteenth through Eighteenth Centuries" (Polish), a paper submitted to the *X Powszechny Zjazd historyków polskich* (Tenth General Congress of Polish Historians), held in Lublin in September 1968; and M. Horn, "Trade in Oxen in Red Russia in the First Half of the Seventeenth Century" (Polish), *RDSG*, XXIV, 72–88, with a French summary, esp. p. 86, concluding that Poland's annual export of oxen may well have reached 60,000 head as suggested by the contemporary Łukasz Opaliński. See also such important monographs as S. Mielczarski, *Rynek zbożowy na ziemiach polskich w drugiej połowie XVI i pierwszej połowie XVII wieku* (The Grain Market in Polish Lands in the Second Half of the Sixteenth and the First Half of the Seventeenth Centuries: an Essay in Regional Divisions), with French and Russian summaries; arguing, on the example of the western provinces, where the rural population outnumbered that in the cities by a ratio of 1.7:1 in royal Prussia, and up to 8.2:1 in Mazovia, that the more urbanized regions consumed larger quantities of the grains produced and left smaller surpluses for export (pp. 180 f.). This factor operated, of course, even more strongly in the less urbanized, and less industrialized, eastern and southeastern regions, which became major granaries for export. Additional light is shed on this broad subject by J. M. Małecki, *Związki handlowe miast polskich z Gdańskiem w XVI i pierwszej połowie XVII wieku* (The Commercial Connections of the Polish Cities with Gdańsk in the Sixteenth and the First Half of the Seventeenth Centuries); A. Wyczański, "Tentative Estimate of Polish Rye Trade in the Sixteenth Century," *APH*, IV, 119–31; M. Małowist, "Les Produits des Pays de la Baltique dans le commerce international au XVIe siècle," *Revue du Nord*, XLII, 195–206; idem, "Poland, Russia and Western Trade in the 15th and 16th Centuries," *Past and Present*, no. 13 pp. 26–41. See also some of the older studies analyzed by L. Koczy in his "New Sources for the History of Poland's Commerce on the Baltic Sea" (Polish), *RDSG*, VI, 179–213.

Of great general importance are the aforementioned comprehensive studies by R. Rybarski, *Handel i polityka handlowa Polski*, including the enormous amount of statistical data tabulated in Vol. II; and J. Rutkowski's even broader *Historia gospodarcza Polski* (Economic History of Poland); or in the French trans. by M. Rakowska of the first ed. of this work, entitled *Histoire économique de la Pologne avant les partages*.

20. The almost incredible figures for meat consumption in the Middle Ages and early modern period were documented by G. Schmoller in "Die Historische Entwicklung des Fleischconsums sowie der Vieh- und Fleischpreise in Deutschland," *Zeitschrift für die gesammte Staatswissenschaft*, XXVII, 284–362; G. Adler in *Die*

426   LXX: RESTRATIFICATION

Fleischteurungspolitik der deutschen Städte beim Ausgang des Mittelalters, esp. pp. 18 ff.; and in the comparative study of medieval and late nineteenth-century conditions by R. Martin in his "Der Fleischverbrauch im Mittelalter und in der Gegenwart," *Preussische Jahrbücher,* LXXXII, 308–342, esp. pp. 308 ff., 322 ff., showing how the prices of beef in stable, late nineteenth-century German pfennigs rose from an average of 14 pfennigs per kilogram in 1451–1500 to 33 pfennigs in 1601–1625. After various ups and downs, it rose again, to 46 pfennigs in 1821–30, and to 121 pfennigs in 1892. In other words, during the entire sixteenth century, the rise totalled 134 percent, while in six decades of the nineteenth-century it amounted to 165 percent. The earlier price rise had, of course, greatly whetted the appetites of the Polish exporters. See also F. Lütge's remarks in his *Strukturwandlungen,* pp. 29 ff. Incidentally, it appears that medieval Jews, too, were great consumers of meat. This may well be reflected in the 1308 provision of the city council of Frankfort on the Oder permitting the 10 Jewish butchers in the city to slaughter up to 2,500 oxen a year. See Schmoller, pp. 290 ff.

21. See Isserles' glosses on Joseph Karo's *Shulhan 'Arukh,* Nos. 123, 1, 124 *passim,* 132, 1; *supra,* Vols. IV, pp. 162 f., 317 n. 14; XII, pp. 27 f., 258 n. 24; Sebastyan Miczyński's *Zwierciadło,* cited by K. Bartoszewicz in his *Antysemityzm,* p. 86. On the importation of wine from Hungary and Turkey, and its high prices, see esp. K. Pieradzka, *Handel Krakowa z Węgrami w XVI wieku* (Cracow's Trade with Hungary in the Sixteenth Century), esp. pp. 96 ff.; and other data cited *supra,* Chap. LXVII, nn. 54. Interesting data on the fur and wax trades were assembled by Rybarski in his *Handel,* esp. II, 62, 82, 101, 338 f.; and A. Wawrzyńczyk in her *Studia,* pp. 43 ff., 46 ff. A more comprehensive listing of articles in which Jews traded on a large scale both domestically and internationally is furnished by I. Schiper in his *Dzieje handlu,* esp. pp. 71 ff., 91 ff.

22. S. A. Bershadskii, *REA,* I, 276 ff. No. 285; and *infra,* n. 30. On other early Polish-Jewish visitors who went to Leipzig for commercial reasons, see I. Schiper, *Dzieje handlu,* pp. 42 f. These visits became much more frequent and mutually profitable as the number of Polish and Lithuanian Jewish traders increased and the Leipzig fairs gained in international importance. On the period after 1664, for which extensive local documentation has become available, see the mutually complementary studies by R. Markgraf in his Rostock dissertation, *Zur Geschichte der Juden auf den Messen in Leipzig von 1664–1839;* and M. Freudenthal in *Leipziger Messgäste. Die jüdischen Besucher der Leipziger Messen in den Jahren 1675 bis 1764.* See also Markgraf's observations on "Der Einfluss der Juden auf die Leipziger Messen in früherer Zeit," *Archiv für Kultur-Geschichte,* V, 363–76, claiming that Jewish traders must have lived in Leipzig as early as the thirteenth century. He also shows that, after the Leipzig fair had recovered from the wounds inflicted upon it by the Thirty Years' War, Jewish visitors increased from an annual average of 415 in 1675–80, to 488 in 1684–90, and 834 in 1691–1700 (pp. 322, 324 f.). Its attraction may well have been considerable before the war, too.

23. See S. M. Dubnow, *Pinqas ha-Medinah,* p. 69 No. 321. Even the few examples cited from archival sources by A. Wawrzyńczyk in her *Studia,* pp. 105 f. n. 13, relating to non-Jewish entrepreneurs, probably are not quite representative of the whole trade. Of interest also is a Tatar carter's recorded charge of 25 groszy daily for a

waiting period up to five days, and of one zloty per day (or 20 percent more) thereafter. See also *infra*, n. 32. On the insecurity of Jewish travelers and transport workers, note the following examples cited by M. Bałaban in his *Żydzi lwowscy*, pp. 400 f. In one case, in 1616, a newlywed couple were traveling with three sleds containing their trousseau, wedding gifts, and home furnishings, as well as merchandise for opening a store in Jazłowiec; quite close to their destination they were attacked by highwaymen, who killed them and their coachmen and removed the sleds with all contents. In another case, in 1628, some Jewish merchants entrusted their goods to a professional Armenian wagoner, who apparently conducted a regular caravan with several armed peasants. But this did not prevent robbers from murdering the Armenian and his armed men and capturing the whole transport. Occasionally, even noblemen participated in such holdups. In the 1620s two notorious brothers operated in the vicinity of Lwów, often cruelly murdering travelers and appropriating their goods. After one such assault, the hoodlums whom the brothers employed were captured and executed, while they themselves went free. Such examples can readily be multiplied.

24. R. Joel Sirkes, *Resp.*, Ostrog, 1834 ed., fol. 11bc No. 27; M. Bogucka, "Merchants' Profits in Gdańsk Foreign Trade in the First Half of the 17th Century," *APH*, XXIII, 73–90, esp. p. 81 Table V; M. Balaban, *Die Judenstadt von Lublin*, pp. 8 f., citing the decrees of 1521 and 1530 from archival sources. Most of the grain naturally was consumed at home. According to Adolf Pawiński's computation, the total exports of grain from the three major Crown provinces and the bishoprics in royal Prussia totaled 74,642 tons, of which Gdańsk handled 86 percent. In contrast, domestic consumption amounted to 414,897 tons in the rural districts, and 112,854 tons in the towns. See A. Wyczański's "Observations on the Consumption of Victuals in Poland in the Sixteenth Century" (Polish), *KHKM*, VIII, 373–81; and, in an abbreviated form, in his "Tentative Estimate of Polish Rye Trade in the Sixteenth Century," *APH*, IV, 119–31. As we shall see, Jews played a relatively small role in the production of grain, unless they happened to serve as arendators of large estates; but they controlled much of the sale and shipment to remote destinations. On the enormous share of the Dutch in trade and shipping in Gdańsk, see the noteworthy statistical data for 1476, 1530, and 1583 marshaled by J. Schildhauer in his "Zur Verlagerung des See- und Handelsverkehrs im nordeuropäischen Raum während des 15. und 16. Jahrhunderts. Eine Untersuchung auf der Grundlage der Danziger Pfahlkammerbücher," *Jahrbuch für Wirtschaftsgeschichte*, 1968, No. 4, pp. 187–211; and "Der Seehandel Danzigs im 16. Jahrhundert und die Verlagerung das Warenverkehrs im nord- und mitteleuropäischen Raum," *ibid.*, 1970, No. 3, pp. 155–78.

25. I. Halperin, *Pinqas Va'ad 'Arba Araṣot*, pp. viii No. 11, 33 No. 94; A. Ackermann, *Geschichte der Juden in Brandenburg A. H.*, pp. 58 f.; S. Stern, *Der Preussische Staat und die Juden*, I, Part 1, pp. 44 ff., 119 ff.; Part 2, pp. 1 ff. esp. Nos. 1 (1650) and 4 (1658); idem, *Josel of Rosheim* (English trans.), pp. 170 ff.; M. Breger, *Zur Handelsgeschichte*, pp. 19 ff.; and the sources quoted in the notes thereon; and *supra*, Vol. XIV, pp. 286, 410 n. 62.

26. Siegmund von Herberstein, *Selbst-Biographie, 1486–1553*, ed. by T. G. von Karajan in *Fontes rerum Austriacarum*, I, 67–396, with comments thereon by

F. Adelung in his *Siegmund Freiherr von Herberstein, mit besonderer Rücksicht auf seine Reisen in Russland geschildert;* B. Mandelsberg, "From the Economic History of the Lublin Jews in the First Half of the Seventeenth Century" (Polish), *BZIH*, no. 26, pp. 3–27, with an English summary, p. 121 (in this essay, part of a Master's thesis prepared under the direction of Majer Bałaban, the young author, afterward slain by the Nazis, connected the Lublin court judgment of 1641 with the growing mercantile crisis in Poland, which also accounted for the aforementioned discriminatory law of 1643 forbidding Jews to sell goods at profits greater than 3 percent, while non-Jewish traders were allowed markups of 5–7 percent; see *supra,* Chap. LXVIII, n. 38); Andreas (Andrzej) Cellarius, *Regni Poloniae magnique ducatus Lituaniae omniumque regionum iuri polonico subiectorum novissima descriptio,* Amsterdam, 1659; J. M. Małecki, *Związki handlowe miast polskich z Gdańskiem;* and Z. Guldon, *Związki handlowe dóbr magnackich na prawobrzeżnej Ukrainie z Gdańskiem w XVIII wieku* (Commercial Connections of the Magnates' Possessions on the Right-Bank [of the Dnieper] Ukraine with Gdańsk in the Eighteenth Century). Many of the conditions described here had already existed in the preceding two centuries.

The international fairs held in Lublin and Jarosław were of major Jewish communal interest, because of the stated sessions there of the Council of Four Lands. The three annual Lublin fairs, which were held on February 2–18, during two weeks around Pentecost, and from October 28 to November 15 (for a time there was also a fair beginning on August 15, but it was discontinued in the seventeenth century), accounted for fully two-thirds of all entries in the city records around 1500. As to volume, the city's long-distance trade, especially with Cracow, Vilna, Poznań, and Gdańsk, amounted as early as 1528–31 to 45 percent of its entire commercial transactions, compared with regional exchanges of but 26 percent, and local trade of 25 percent. See H. Samsonowicz, "Lublin's Commerce about the Year 1600" (Polish), *PH*, LIX, 612–28, with a French summary, esp. pp. 615 ff., 620. This extensive trade with distant localities was facilitated not only by Lublin's central location but also by a long-established network of roads, which of course also encouraged travel for other than commercial reasons. See L. Białkowski, "Lublin on the Old Commercial Highways" (Polish), *Pamiętnik lubelski,* III, 288–93; M. Zakrzewska-Dubasowa, "A Contribution to the History of the Lublin Fairs" (Polish), *Annales* of the Marie Curie Skłodowska University, Lublin, XX, 59–74, with Russian and French summaries; and J. W. A. Wagner, *Handel dawnego Jarosławia do połowy XVII wieku* (The Commerce of Old Jarosław to the Middle of the Seventeenth Century). See also S. Lewicki, *Targi lwowskie od XIV–XIX wieku* (Lwów Fairs from the Fourteenth to the Nineteenth Centuries); and, more generally, M. Haubrichówna, *Wolnice, czyli wolne targi w miastach polskich* (Free Fairs in the Polish Cities to the Beginning of the Seventeenth Century); and H. Samsonowicz, "The Fairs in Poland against the Background of the Economic Conditions in Europe during the Fifteenth and Sixteenth Centuries" (Polish), *Europa–Słowiańszczyzna–Polska* (Europe–Slavdom–Poland: Studies in Honor of Kazimierz Tymieniecki), pp. 523–32; supplemented by his succinct observations on "Poland in the European Economy of the Late Middle Ages" (Polish), *Pamiętnik* of the X. Powszechny Zjazd historyków polskich (Proceedings of the Tenth Congress of Polish Historians, held in Lublin in 1968), I, 104 ff.; and W. Rusiński's "The Role of Polish Lands in the European Commercial Exchanges in the Sixteenth through Eighteenth Centuries" (Polish), *ibid.,* pp. 165 ff.; as well as the aforementioned comprehensive works by M. Rybarski and J. Rutkowski.

27. I. Halperin, ed., *Pinqas Va'ad 'Arba Araṣot*, pp. 24 f. Nos. 78 and 80, 38 ff. Nos. 103 and 107, 46 No. 111, also citing a significant comment by R. Menaḥem Mendel Krochmal in his *Ṣemaḥ Ṣedeq* (Righteous Offshoot; Resp.), Amsterdam, 1675, p. 68 No. 183; S. M. Dubnow, *Pinqas ha-Medinah*, pp. 85 ff. Nos. 404, 422; 93 f. No. 443. Not surprisingly, the post of market judge at the Lublin fairs during the Council sessions was most widely sought after. In 1620 no candidate was willing to accept a similar appointment at the less glamorous Jarosław fair unless he was also promised that office at the February 1621 fair of Lublin. This condition was accepted by the Poznań community. See Halperin, p. 36 n. 99. Other communal delegates, too, often appeared at fairs to negotiate with the respective municipal administrations in cases affecting the rights of Jews to display goods and sell them. Certainly, such negotiators might have prevented the untoward developments which thwarted the joint endeavor of the four Lithuanian Jews to sell a large consignment of merchandise in Gdańsk (see *infra*, n. 28). But negotiations of this kind were merely a part of the general political and diplomatic activities of the so-called *shtadlanim* (spokesmen), whether acting as semiofficial representatives of communal organs or in a private capacity.

28. S. Arnold and M. Bogucka, "The Formation of the Multinational Gentry Commonwealth (from the Middle of the Fifteenth to the Third Quarter of the Sixteenth Century)" (Polish), in T. Manteuffel, ed., *Historia Polski*, I, Part 2, pp. 78–146, esp. p. 138; S. A. Bershadskii, *REA*, II, 112 No. 216; L. Koczy, *Handel Poznania do połowy wieku XVI* (Poznań's Commerce to the Middle of the Sixteenth Century), esp. pp. 63 f., 255 (claims that Jews "discovered" the trade with northern Germany after 1550), 268 ff.; A. Wawrzyńczyk, *Studia*, p. 103; S. Miczyński, *Zwierciadło*, p. 34; K. Bartoszewicz, *Antysemityzm*, p. 89. See also J. Janáček, *Dějiny obchodu předbělohorské Praze* (The History of Commerce in Pre–White Mountain Prague), esp. pp. 66 ff. (incidentally mentioning a reciprocal sale of Hebrew books); and, more broadly, Jan M. Małecki, "Le Rôle de Cracovie dans l'économie polonaise aux XVIᵉ, XVIIᵉ et XVIIIᵉ siècles," *APH*, XXI, 108–122. On Polish Jewry's role in maintaining, with royal support, the significant trade between Poland and Silesia, despite the animosity of local merchants, see *supra*, Vol. XIV, pp. 248 f., 396 n. 24.

29. Sebastyan Miczyński, *Zwierciadło*, Chap. XI; K. Bartoszewicz, *Antysemityzm*, pp. 100 ff.; V. Avron, ed., *Pinqas ha-Ksherim*, p. 102 No. 519; M. Bałaban, *Żydzi lwowscy*, p. 399. The elders went so far as to threaten any agent who obtained credit for fraudulent merchants outside of Poznań, with the loss of his rights of citizenship and with public denunciation of his misdeeds. To enlist the cooperation of local businessmen, the elders emphasized that, if such misdeeds were allowed to occur, all Jews might be barred from the Gdańsk trade. See also Avron, p. 94 No. 482. Similar provisions were adopted by the Cracow community in its famous ordinance of 1595. See M. Balaban's "Die Krakauer Judengemeinde-Ordnung von 1595 und ihre Nachträge," *JJLG*, X, 296–360; XI, 88–114, esp. X, 311 f. On Poznań, which was in many ways, the focal point of Poland's western trade, and its Jewish businessmen, see B. D. Weinryb's *Texts and Studies*, *passim*; L. Koczy's older analysis of "Studies in the Economic History of the Poznań Jews before the Middle of the Seventeenth Century" (Polish), *Kronika miasta Poznania* (Chronicle of the City of Poznań), XII–XIII; his more comprehensive study of Poznań's commerce to 1550, cited *supra*, n. 28; continued by M. Grycz in his *Handel miasta Poznania, 1550–1655*

(The Commerce of the City of Poznań, 1550–1655). Of independent value still is not only J. Leitgeber's *Z dziejów handlu i kupiectwa poznańskiego za dawnej Rzeczypospolitej Polskiej* (On the History of Poznań Commerce and Merchants in the Old Polish Commonwealth) but also the aforementioned very well-documented *Obraz historyczno-statystyczny* (The Historical-Statistical Image of the City of Poznań in Times Past) by J. Łukaszewicz, published in 1838.

30. See F. Lütge, *Strukturwandlungen im ostdeutschen und osteuropäischen Fernhandel*, pp. 30 ff.; *supra*, n. 22; M. Bogucka, "Amsterdam's Baltic Trade in the First Half of the Seventeenth Century" (Polish), *Zapiski historyczne*, XXXIV, Part 2, pp. 7–33; idem, "Merchants' Profits in Gdańsk Foreign Trade in the First Half of the 17th Century," *APH*, XXIII, 73–90; and, more generally, M. Małowist, "Poland and the Price Changes in Europe in the Sixteenth and Seventeenth Centuries" (Polish), *KH*, LXXVIII, 315–19. See also, from the Dutch side, N. W. Posthumus's *Inquiry into the History of Prices in Holland*, esp. Vol. I: Wholesale Prices at the Exchange of Amsterdam, 1609–1914; *supra*, n. 24; and Chap. LXVIII, nn. 35 and 37.

31. M. Bałaban, *Żydzi lwowscy*, pp. 39 f., 467. See the theretofore generally overlooked entries in *Akta grodzkie*, X, Nos. 1364, 1399–1400, 1423, 1561, 1566–68 (referring to Joseph Nasi's business transactions in 1567–70, including his visit to Lwów in August 1570); and other sources, analyzed by Z. Świtalski in "The Reasons for the Withdrawal of the Turkish Jews, Refugees from Spain, from the Levant Trade of the Polish Commonwealth in the Last Years of the Sixteenth Century" (Polish), *BZIH*, no. 37, pp. 59–65, with an English summary, pp. 109–110; *supra*, n. 21; Chap. LXVII, nn. 51 ff., 54, 55. To be sure, Kaffa, the former Genoese colony on the Black Sea, after her occupation by the Tatars, did not completely lose her commercial importance for the trade with Poland-Lithuania. Yet, the great shift of the center of gravity from the Levantine to the Atlantic trade, and Lisbon's control over much of the importation of oriental goods to western Europe, would have undermined Kaffa's formerly dominant role, even if the city had remained in Genoese hands. See M. Małowist, *Kaffa—kolonia genueńska na Krymie, 1453–1475* (Kaffa—Genoese Colony in the Crimea, 1453–1475), with a 30-page French summary; R. M. Della Rocca, "Notizie da Caffa," *Studi in onore di Amintore Fanfani*, III, 265–95 (with seven documents from the Venetian Archives). See also the fuller treatment of the status of the Jews in that area, in the forthcoming Vol. XVII.

32. See M. Bałaban, *Żydzi lwowscy*, pp. 419, 430, and the documentary section, pp. 17 f. No. 16. The lack of an easily available linguistic medium of communication between Poland and the Balkan peoples (only a few Tatars, Karaim, and other residents were familiar with the Turkish language, while hardly any Turks knew Polish or Latin) was an additional obstacle to commercial transactions. Sephardic Jews at least had the advantage of easily communicating with their own coreligionists; they also could quickly acquire a working knowledge of Italian, a language understood by many Ottoman businessmen, both Muslim and Christian. See B. Baranowski, *Znajomość Wschodu w dawnej Polsce do XVIII wieku* (Knowledge of the Middle East in Old Poland to the Eighteenth Century), esp. pp. 32 ff., 53 ff. See also S. Kutrzeba, "Polish Commerce with the East in the Middle Ages" (Polish), *Przegląd Polski*, CXLVIII, 189–219, 462–96; CXLIX, 512–37; CL, 115–45, esp. CL, 137 ff. On Lwów as the most important Polish center of that trade, see Ł. Chare-

wiczowa, *Handel średniowiecznego Lwowa* (Commerce of Medieval Lwów); and *supra*, Chap. LXVIII, n. 34.

33. See, in particular, the vast materials—to a large extent based upon archival documents—assembled and well analyzed by A. Wawrzyńczyk in her *Studia z dziejów handlu Polski*, esp. pp. 19 n. 6, 21 f., 38 n. 1, 47, 114 n. 2. Several interesting court cases involving Jews, then mostly in conflict with burghers, and the presence of quite a few wealthy Jews in Brest, Pinsk, and other cities, are briefly documented *ibid.*, pp. 77 n. 5, and 108 f.

34. See the sources cited by A. Wawrzyńczyk in her *Studia*, pp. 21 f., 23 f. On the centers of the Russo-Polish trade in Lithuania, especially the speedily developing city of Mogilev, see H. Łowmiański's twin essays, "Mogilev's Commerce in the Sixteenth Century" (Polish), *Studia Historyczne* (Historical Studies in Honor of) *Stanisław Kutrzeba*, II, 517–47, esp. pp. 523 ff., 525 n. 2 (on the aforementioned Jewish merchant Affras [Ephraim] Rachmaelovich), 527 (on the five local fairs), 542 (claiming that local Christian, rather than Jewish, traders developed the local commerce); and "Mogilev's Economic Structure about 1600" (Polish), *RDSG*, VIII, 37–91, esp. pp. 60 ff., 88 ff. See also S. Aleksandrowicz, "The Small Towns in Belorussia and Lithuania," *Rocznik białostocki*, I, 63–130; and, more generally, J. M. Kulischer, *Russische Wirtschaftsgeschichte*, Vol. I, esp. pp. 420 ff.

35. Jean de Bleranval de Laboureur, *Histoire et relation du voyage de la Royne de Pologne et du retour de Madame la Mle [Maréchale] de Guébriant*, Paris, 1647, II, 225; F. D. S. (abbé), *Relation d'un voyage en Pologne fait dans les années 1688 et 1689* (in *Bibliothèque russe et polonaise*), III, 30, both cited, together with other interesting excerpts, by S. Frydman (Zosa Szajkowski) in his "French Reports on the Jews in Poland-Russia from the Fifteenth to the Beginning of the Nineteenth Century" (Yiddish), in *Yidn in Frankraikh* (The Jews in France: Studies and Materials), ed. by E. Tcherikower, I, 16–32, esp. pp. 17 f.

36. See the data analyzed by M. Bałaban in the extensive Chapter VI of his *Dzieje*, pp. 142 ff., esp. pp. 208 f., mentioning a number of Jewish owners of shops in Cracow-Kazimierz, in addition to those enumerated by Sebastyan Miczyński (Bałaban deals, however, more with residential and family relationships of the particular merchants, rather than with the details of their occupational activities; he includes, for example, brief genealogical tables of Izak and Samuel Jakubowicz, mentioned in the text, from which it appears that they were not related to each other; pp. 161, 202); idem, *Żydzi lwowscy*, pp. 405, and *passim;* I. Schiper, *Dzieje handlu żydowskiego*, pp. 94 ff., 99 f., 106 ff.; idem, "Jews in Tarnów," *KH*, XIX, 229 f.; B. D. Weinryb, *Texts and Studies*, pp. 40 ff., 48 ff., 61 ff., 81 ff., 99 ff., and the corresponding documents in the Hebrew section (shedding more light on communal regulations and controls, rather than on actual practices); A. Mączak, "La Compagnie orientale anglaise (Eastland Company) et le commerce dans la Baltique dans la seconde moitié du XVIe siècle," *APH*, XXIII, 91–104; J. Wojtowicz, "Samuel Edwards' Business Enterprise in Toruń in the Seventeenth Century" (Polish), *RDSG*, XIV, 203–244, with a French summary. To be sure, even these specialized monographs on non-Jewish firms may indirectly shed some light on Jewish mercantile activities, too. Even for West-Prussian Toruń, which at that time embraced but a

tiny Jewish community, Wojtowicz, in reviewing the pertinent archival data of 1645–54, surprisingly found that no fewer than 91 of the 194 transactions concluded by Edwards during that decade involved Jews as either buyers or sellers (pp. 225 f.).

As against these descriptions of non-Jewish business ventures, only W. Pociecha's *Abraham i Michał Ezofowicze, działacze gospodarczy XVI wieku* (Abraham and Michael Ezofowicz, Business Leaders of the Sixteenth Century), stresses these men's economic activities. Most other biographical sketches, even of such leading business-men as Wolf Bocian (Poper), Saul Judycz Wahl, Salomon Calahora, and Izak Nach-manowicz (mentioned here in various connections), usually deal with their political and communal functions more than with their business pursuits. Many other studies of individual leaders are devoted for the most part to tracing their family connec-tions. Wahl, for example, has been much more the subject of scholarly debate with respect to the legend of his one-day reign as king of Poland than with respect to his historically attested far-flung and influential exploitation of salt mines and the distribution of that important product in both parts of the dual Commonwealth. See Schiper, *Dzieje handlu,* p. 108.

37. See *infra,* n. 53; *supra,* Chap. LXVIII, n. 38; Vol. XII, pp. 40 ff., 265 ff. nn. 38–42, and the literature cited there. Much interesting material comparing condi-tions in Poland with those in the Jewish quarters of German cities, from which most of the Polish Jews had originally come, is available in A. Pinthus, "Studien über die bauliche Entwicklung der Judengassen in den deutschen Städten," *ZGJD,* II, 101–130, 197–217, 284–300 (his original dissertation on this subject was described in its subtitle as a *stadtbiologische Studie*). Polish Jews doubtless benefited from the general decline of their archenemies, the burghers, and the concomitant transfer of much urban real estate to nobles, who often appreciated Jews as tenants, lenders, or agents. Cracow's example may not be wholly typical, because of the city's loss of status after the royal court moved to the new capital, Warsaw. But the tremendous rise in the nobles' real estate holdings in Cracow between the 1570s and 1668 must have been paralleled, at least to some extent, in other cities. See M. Niwiński, "The Class Division in Cracow Real Estate Ownership in the Sixteenth and Seventeenth Centuries" (Polish), *Studia historyczne* (Historical Studies in Honor of) *Stanisław Kutrzeba,* II, 549–84, esp. pp. 576 ff. and 579 ff., listing the noble owners of real estate by name. See also S. Waszak's studies of Poznań's housing conditions, cited *supra,* Chaps. LXVII, n. 22; LXIX, n. 33; and, on the relatively small Jewish par-ticipation in the building trades, and the reasons therefor, *infra,* n. 53.

38. See J. Morgensztern, "The Inventory of Holdings by the Zamość Merchant, Lejb Józefowicz (1675)," (Polish), *BZIH,* no. 70, pp. 57–72, with an English sum-mary; and R. Rybarski's otherwise noteworthy *Handel i polityka handlowa Polski,* I, 223 ff. Because of the dramatic changes after 1648, one cannot learn too much about the situation before that date from W. Rusiński's "On the Interior Trade in Poland in the Second Half of the Eighteenth Century" (Polish), *RDSG,* XVI, 113–51, with a French summary, esp. pp. 117 f. Of interest also are such regional studies as J. M. Małecki's all-embracing *Studia nad rynkiem regionalnym Krakowa w XVI wieku* (Studies in Cracow's Regional Trade in the Sixteenth Century), esp. pp. 21 ff., 32 f., 45 ff., 144 ff., 199 ff., 206 ff., 212; his "Le Rôle de Cracovie dans l'économie polonaise," *APH,* XXI, 108–122; and J. Leitgeber's *Z dziejów handlu i kupiectwa poznańskiego.* Because we know so little about the Jews in the smaller towns and

hamlets, we must doubly welcome such a detailed monograph as A. Dunin-Wąsowicz Żaboklicka's *Kapitał mieszczański Nowego Sącza na przełomie XVI–XVII wieku* (The Burghers' Capital in Nowy Sącz at the Turn of the Sixteenth Century: Its Impact on the Economy of the City and Environment), with a French summary—particularly when it is read in conjunction with the economic data included in R. Mahler's recent ed. of *Sepher Sandz: the Book of the Jewish Community of Nowy Sącz* (Yiddish), esp. pp. 21 ff., 29 ff. To be sure, sometimes a singularly favorable geographic location catapulted even a smaller town into business prominence. This was, for instance, the case of Włocławek, which played a disproportionately significant part in international transport and commerce, because of its access to the Vistula in relative proximity to Gdańsk. More typical was the younger township of Włodawa in eastern Poland, founded in 1540. Usually in the possession of one or another Polish magnate, the town attracted a fairly large number of Jewish settlers. See the documents published and analyzed by B. D. Weinryb in his *Texts and Studies*, pp. 95 ff. (English), 221 ff. (Hebrew).

39. *Ibid.*, Hebrew section, pp. 23 No. 59, 142 No. 307 end. Although it stands to reason that Jewish peddlers in Poland did not play an economic role comparable with that assumed for a time by their counterparts in the United States and other western countries, their nearly total neglect in modern Jewish historiography is regrettable. See also, more broadly, M. Kosower's twin essays under the same title, "The Interior Trade of the Polish Jews in the Sixteenth and Seventeenth Centuries (Sources for the History of the Jews in Poland on the Basis of Rabbinic Literature)" (Yiddish), *YB*, XII, 533–45; and XV, 182–201. These sources are mainly concerned with certain legal and ritual aspects, such as the permissibility of consuming meat, butter, cheese, or wine acquired from, or held for a time by, non-Jews; the reliability of Jewish stamps attesting the ritual quality of particular foods; the validity and applicability of certain provisions in partnership and other contracts; the accuracy of reports concerning the death of a husband on a distant journey, with respect to his wife's right to remarry. Yet they incidentally furnish some telling illustrations of daily business practices. They also supply some documentation for Jewish peddlers in small towns and villages, suppliers engaged in the dangerous pursuit of accompanying Polish armies on their military expeditions, especially to Muscovite lands, and a variety of internal squabbles among Jewish merchants. They also illustrate, more graphically than the pertinent enactments by the central and provincial Jewish councils and the local communities, how greatly Polish and Lithuanian Jewry was affected by the anticompetitive spirit of their Christian neighbors. The same Jews who were engaged in a perpetual struggle against the burghers' efforts to limit Jewish residential rights and restrict competition from Jewish merchants and artisans, often tried to keep other Jews from settling among them, underselling them in the open market, or luring their traditional customers away from them. In all that, we must particularly regret the habit of many responsa writers to concentrate so intensely on the legal aspects of the problems under review, that they fail to mention the names of the persons and the localities involved; the dates of the events described, or of the decisions rendered; the specific kinds and quantities of goods traded, and the prices charged; and other details which were not juridically relevant, but which alone help convert legal abstractions into historical realities.

40. Jan Ostroróg, *Monumentum pro comitiis regalibus sub illustrimo principe*

Casimiro Rege Poloniae pro suae Reipublicae utilitate congestum, new ed. by T. Wierzbowski, esp. p. 30; Marcin Kromer, *Polonia sive de situ, populis, moribus, magistratibus, et republica regni Polonici libri duo,* Cologne, 1577; and in L. Kondratowicz's Polish trans. entitled *Polska, czyli o położeniu obyczajach, urzędach Rzeczypospolitej Królestwa Polskiego,* esp. pp. 49, 62, 74 ff.; Andrzej Frycz Modrzewski, *De republica emendanda,* Chap. XVI, in his *Opera omnia;* and in the Polish trans. by Cyprian Bazylik, 2d photo offset ed. with an Intro. by J. Krzyżanowska in his *Dzieła wszystkie* (Collected Works), I, 158, 160; Sebastyan Fabian Klonowicz, *Worek Judaszów* (The Pouch of the Judases), *passim;* and E. Horn, "Legal and Economic Situation," *BZIH,* no. 40, p. 35. See also *supra,* nn. 3–4; Chap. LXVIII, nn. 53, 66, and 72; and the various early modern publications and other sources briefly analyzed by A. Popioł-Szymańska in "The Views of the Gentry and the Burghers on Poland's Interior Trade from the End of the Fifteenth to the End of the Seventeenth Century" (Polish), *Roczniki historyczne,* XXXVII, 39–83, with a French summary, esp. pp. 41 ff., 48 ff., 53, 66.

41. See *supra,* Chap. LXVII, n. 5; and Vols. XIII, pp. 89 f., 355 n. 30; XV, Chap. LXV. Of considerable interest in this connection are the economic views held by a number of contemporary Polish writers, reproduced by E. Taylor and S. Zaleski in their ed. of *Merkantylizm i początki szkoły klasycznej* (Mercantilism and the Beginnings of the Classical School: a Selection of Economic Writings of the Sixteenth and Seventeenth Centuries), trans. into Polish by C. Znamierewski, with an Intro. by E. Lipiński; and E. Lipiński's analytical *Studia nad historią polskiej myśli ekonomicznej* (Studies in the History of Polish Economic Thought). See also *infra,* n. 43.

42. S. Arnold and M. Bogucka, "The Economic Prosperity of the Cities" (Polish), in T. Manteuffel, ed., *Historia Polski,* I, Part 2, pp. 107–146, esp. pp. 116 ff.; B. Baranowski and S. Herbst, "The Multinational Commonwealth" (Polish), *ibid.,* pp. 454 ff.; S. Inglot, "Lew Sapieha's Business Affairs 1588–1607" (Polish), in *Studja z historji społecznej i gospodarczej* (Studies in Social and Economic History) dedicated to Franciszek Bujak, pp. 165–226, esp. pp. 201 ff.; A. Pawiński, ed., *Źródła dziejowe,* VIII, 80 No. 5, 84; M. Bałaban, *Dzieje,* I, 146; J. Morgensztern, "Regesta," *BZIH,* no. 47, p. 121 No. 46 (reads the names in the Báthory privilege as Nadida and Telatyn); and, more generally, R. Rybarski, *Wieliczkie żupy solne w latach 1497– 1594* (Wieliczka's Salt Mines in the Years 1497–1594); K. Pająk, *Wieliczka, stare miasto górnicze* (W., an Old Mining Town: a Monographic Sketch); A. Keckowa, *Żupy krakowskie w XVI–XVIII wieku* (The Cracow Salt Mines from the Sixteenth to the Eighteenth Century), with a German summary, esp. pp. 316, 424 ff.; W. Osuchowski, *Gospodarka solna na Rusi Halickiej* (The Salt Industry in the District of Halicz in the Seventeenth and Eighteenth Centuries), esp. pp. 68 ff.; E. Hornowa, *Stosunki ekonomiczno-społeczne w miastach ziemi halickiej w latach 1590–1648* (The Socioeconomic Conditions in the Cities of the Halicz District, 1590–1648); together with her study "Legal and Economic Situation of the Jews in the Towns" of that area in *BZIH,* no. 40, pp. 3–36, esp. p. 30 (also pointing out that Jewish participation in the various phases of the salt business continued into the seventeenth century, notwithstanding the promulgation of various decrees curtailing Jewish rights in this area); H. Łabęcki, *Górnictwo w Polsce* (Mining in Poland: a List of Polish Mines and Refineries from the Technical, Historico-Statistical and Legal Standpoint). See also A. Keckowa's biography of *Melchior Walbach,* which underscores

the inadequacy of the existing descriptions of the business careers of Jewish merchants in the dual Commonwealth.

The identity of the places where the Calahoras and Hadidah (or Nadidah) exploited the salt deposits is still uncertain. However, the misspelling Telatyn for Delatyn would by no means be unusual. The same kinds of error even appear in the contemporary documents relating to the family name Delatyński, derived from that town. See P. Dąbkowski's *Zwierciadło szlacheckie* (A Mirror of Nobility), p. 107 n. 1. According to an excerpt published by J. Morgensztern (p. 122 No. 52), an accounting made on March 12, 1581, after the death of Jakub Rokosowski, showed that the well-known Jewish merchants Ezdra and Jeleń (Zvi Hirsch b. Moses Dokter) received 6,000 and 2,584 zlotys, respectively, as their share in the revenue from the Wieliczka and Bochnia salines and from various arendas. The excerpt does not specify, however, how much these merchants had invested in the salt mines or what their relationship to Rokosowski was.

43. See *supra*, Chap. LXVIII, n. 68. The Jewish share in the exploitation of the salt mines may also explain the expulsion of Jews from the small town of Uście Solne (about 1610). In this connection, some Christian traders doing business with Jews under the jurisdiction of local nobles, were also severely fined. See Z. Daszyńska-Golińska, *Uście Solne. Przyczynki historyczno-statystyczne* (Uście Solne: Historical-Statistical Contributions to the History of a Small Town on the Vistula. An Archival Study), pp. 120 f.

The relative absence of Jewish entrepreneurs from the metallurgical phases of mining may perhaps be explained by the fact that the few Polish-Lithuanian silver and copper mines were *regalia*, as a rule exploited for the king by a few favorite merchants or aristocrats. Some of them also were quickly exhausted, calling forth, as early as 1622, a Polish tract by Wojciech Gostkomski on "Ways for Improving the Damaged Gold and Silver Mines in the Most Worthy Kingdom of Poland," reproduced in J. Górski and E. Lipiński, comps., *Merkantylistyczna myśl ekonomiczna w Polsce* (The Mercantilist Economic Theory in Poland in the Sixteenth and Seventeenth Centuries), pp. 129 ff. But few contemporaries realized that the best long-term method of accumulating precious bullion was to increase the country's own productive capacity, which, by satisfying certain domestic needs and stimulating exports, would result in a favorable balance of trade, leaving annual surpluses to add to the store of gold and silver. See J. Goldwagner's Polish "Discourse on the Present Price of Money," *ibid.*, pp. 331 ff. The far more important output of iron and iron products, on the other hand, was widely scattered among small enterprises which often employed villein labor unavailable to Jews, except those who were employed by the landlords as administrators or agents in charge of a variety of functions. Nonetheless, the Polish Jews' role in the Commonwealth's mining, large or small, deserves further investigation.

44. See M. Bałaban, *Dzieje*, I, 314 ff. Among non-Jews, too, merchants often helped individual craftsmen, even in smaller towns, to establish themselves in their particular line of business. See the examples cited by A. Dunin-Wąsowicz Żaboklicka in her aforementioned study, *Kapitał mieszczański Nowego Sącza, passim*. Regrettably, the full text of the statute of the Cracow Jewish guild of furriers as approved by the communal elders in 1613 is not available. The excerpt, published from the communal minute book by F. H. Wettstein in his *Qadmoniyot mi-pinqesa'ot yesha-*

nim (Antiquities Gulled from Old Minute Books; reprinted from *Oṣar ha-Sifrut*, IV), No. 8, and summarized by Bałaban, deals mainly with aspects relevant to the communal organization as such, especially the payment of membership dues, election of officers, and appointment of guild officials, rather than with rules relating to the training of apprentices, required qualifications of journeymen and masters, and the like. It is evident, however, that not only were master artisans obliged, as members, to pay a *szeląg* (shilling, a varying fraction of a silver grosz) per week, in addition to a smaller farthing (*pieniądz*) of each zloty of their earnings, but the merchants, too, had to pay the same percentage of their earnings.

45. Most of our information about the detailed operations of Jewish craftsmen comes from the period after the "Deluge," when the number of Jewish artisans, and the ramifications of their output, assumed significant proportions. About the earlier stages, we learn more from the prohibitions imposed upon Jewish craftsmen by city councils, or from the agreements reluctantly concluded by the municipalities with the Jewish communities, than from sources stemming from the artisan quarters themselves. Fortunately, the existing partial evidence has often been reviewed. See esp. M. Kremer's complementary essays, "On the Study of Craftsmanship and Craft Guilds among the Polish Jews in the Sixteenth to Eighteenth Centuries" (Hebrew), *Zion*, II, 294–325 (with a good review of the earlier literature on this subject); and "The Participation of Jewish Craftsmen in the Christian Guilds of Old Poland" (Yiddish), *Bleter far Geshikhte*, II, 3–32; B. Mark, "Jewish Artisans in Feudal Poland" (Polish), *BZIH*, nos. 9–10, pp. 5–89; idem, "Jewish Craftsmanship in the Renaissance Period" (Polish), *Odrodzenie w Polsce* (The Renaissance in Poland), I: Historia, pp. 303–308 (part of an interesting discussion on the wide-ranging paper by M. Małowist submitted to a Scientific Session convoked by the Polish Academy in 1953; see below in this note); M. Horn, "Jewish Craftsmen in Red Russia around 1600" (Polish), *BZIH*, no. 34, pp. 28–70, with an English summary, p. 172; idem, "New Details concerning Jewish Craftsmanship in the Bełz Province around 1600" (Polish), *ibid.*, no. 55, pp. 85–92, with an English summary, p. 118; and, particularly, M. Wischnitzer's "Die Jüdische Zunftverfassung in Polen und Litauen im 17. und 18. Jahrhundert," *VSW*, XX, 433–51; and his comprehensive *A History of Jewish Crafts and Guilds*, esp. pp. 206–275.

For this reason we must deduce a good deal from the general conditions of the Polish crafts and guilds, which had had a rather rich history since the end of the Middle Ages. See esp. M. Małowist, *Studia z dziejów rzemiosła w okresie kryzysu feudalizmu w zachodniej Europie w XIV i XV wieku* (Studies in the History of the Crafts in the Period of the Crisis of Feudalism in Western Europe in the Fourteenth and Fifteenth Centuries), chiefly reviewing the developments in Flanders, England, and Holland; idem, "Polish Crafts in the Period of the Renaissance" (Polish), *Odrodzenie w Polsce*, I: Historia, pp. 261–98; idem, "L'Évolution industrielle de la Pologne du XIVe au XVIIe siècle (traits généraux)," *Studi in onore di Armando Sapori*, I, 571–603; I. T. Baranowski, *Przemysł Polski w XVI wieku* (Polish Industry in the Sixteenth Century), posthumously ed. by K. Tyśmieniecki; and J. Rutkowski's comprehensive *Historia gospodarcza Polski*, 4th ed., or in the French translation of the first ed., *Histoire économique de la Pologne*, esp. pp. 165 ff. With respect to the contrast between the incipient decline of Polish crafts and the simultaneous expansion of Jewish craftsmanship, see, for instance, A. Wyrobisz's remarks on "Problems of the Decline of Crafts and the Economic Crisis of the Cities in Poland: Sixteenth or Seventeenth Century?" (Polish), *PH*, LVIII, 132–38; with M. Horn's succinct comments thereon in "A Contribution to the Discussion on the Economic Crisis of the Nobles' Commonwealth in the Sixteenth and Seventeenth Centuries" (Polish), *ibid.*, pp. 668–69; and *infra*, n. 53.

46. Alliances between Jewish craftsmen and *partaczy*, as well as with Tatar and Greek Orthodox artisans, were quite frequent. Such instances were recorded in Lublin, Rzeszów, Tarnów, Chrzanów, Sandomierz, Nowy Sącz, and in the Lithuanian cities of Vilna and Grodno. See B. Mark in his "Jewish Craftsmanship" (Polish), *Odrodzenie w Polsce*, I, 304 f.; and *supra*, Chap. LXVIII, n. 37.

47. A. Wawrzyńczyk, *Studia z dziejów handlu Polski*, p. 85; *supra*, Vol. XII, pp. 58, 273 n. 58. In Lithuania, where the population was far more heterogeneous, intergroup restrictions in the industrial field often were considerably relaxed. Even in relatively intolerant Vilna, the municipal and guild administrations had to make allowances for ethnic and religious disparities. See K. Chodynicki's "On the Denominational Relationships in the Vilna Guilds from the Sixteenth to the Seventeenth Century" (Polish), *Księga pamiątkowa* (Memorial Volume) *Oswald Balzer*, I, 117–31; *supra*, Chap. LXIX, n. 28.

48. See the apprenticeship agreement of 1650 first published by F. H. Wettstein in his *Qadmoniyot mi-pinqesa'ot yeshanim;* here quoted from M. Wischnitzer's *A History of Jewish Crafts and Guilds*, p. 286, App. vi; the statutes of the barbers' guild quoted *ibid.*, pp. 214 f. (see *infra*, n. 57); another apprenticeship contract (Nov.–Dec. 1645), between a silversmith and the parents of a youth, agreeing on the boy's training for three and a half years, reproduced by Wettstein in his "Tales from Days of Old" (Hebrew), *Ha-Zofeh*, IV, 166–86, esp. pp. 178 f. (quoted from the Cracow minute book); and J. Rutkowski, *Histoire économique*, pp. 171 f. If the 1650 contract is typical of similar agreements elsewhere, the fee paid by the parents of an apprentice almost equaled the wages of a young journeyman. Moreover, according to the contract, the master artisan could employ his trainee at half the usual wages—or for as little as 7 zlotys per annum—when he was ready to become a journeyman. It stands to reason, therefore, that many Jewish masters were tempted to impart their skills to upcoming young men, despite the fear of training future competitors. In addition, some may have defied other restrictive Jewish guild regulations, such as that of the barbers' guild in Cracow, which allowed each master barber to have only one apprentice at a time. Curiously, apprentices were forbidden by the statutes of that guild to marry local girls, "in order not to place additional burdens on the community." See Wischnitzer, *A History*, p. 215. Some of these practices resemble those employed in the Polish guilds of the period, on which see Z. Pazdro, *Uczniowie i towarzysze cechów krakowskich od drugiej połowy XIV do połowy XVII wieku* (Apprentices and Journeymen of the Cracow Guilds from the Second Half of the Fourteenth to the Mid-Seventeenth Century).

49. See R. Isaac Jacob b. Yuzpa Sorazina, *Resp.*, printed at the end of R. Asher b. Yeḥiel's *Resp.*, Venice, 1607 ed. end, fol. 1d, cited by B. Z. Katz in his *Le-Qorot ha-Yehudim*, p. 25 No. 4; M. Bałaban, *Dzieje*, pp. 309 f.; and, more generally, A. Chmiel, *Rzeźnicy krakowscy* (Cracow Butchers), esp. Chap. IV dealing with the

Christian guild's struggle with outsiders, including Jews. See also G. Adler, *Das Grosspolnische Fleischgewerbe; supra*, n. 20; and Vol. XII, pp. 68 ff., 276 f. nn. 1–7.

50. See M. Bałaban's graphic description of the 1607 incident in his *Żydzi lwowscy*, pp. 473 ff. The provisions of the 1485 agreement between the Jewish community and the city council of Cracow, its subsequent modifications, and the new agreements at the beginning of the seventeenth century—all under royal supervision—are briefly analyzed *supra*, Chap. LXVIII, nn. 43–44. Similar difficulties were encountered by Jewish butchers and slaughterers in many other communities as well.

51. See M. Bałaban, *Dzieje*, pp. 322 ff.; Sebastyan Miczyński, *Zwierciadło*, Chapters VIII–X; K. Bartoszewicz, *Antysemityzm*, pp. 85 ff., 93 f.; Bałaban, *Żydzi lwowscy*, pp. 470 ff. A regular Jewish guild of tailors was recorded in Lwów as early as 1627, although no details of its statutory provisions or functions are available. See M. Horn, "Lwów's Artisan Population and Its Struggles in the Years 1600–1648" (Polish), *Zeszyty Naukowe* of the Wyższa Szkoła Pedagogiczna in Opole, XXI, 69–124. See also the other valuable studies by this author, mentioned *supra*, n. 45; and *infra*, nn. 53 and 59. It is only to be regretted that his monograph on the crafts in the districts of Przemyśl and Sambor, announced in his 1967 comments in *PH*, LVIII, 668 f., as being prepared for publication, seems not yet to have appeared in print. For the time being, see K. Arłamowski, *Dzieje przemyskich cechów rzemieślniczych w dawnej Polsce* (A History of the Przemyśl Artisan Guilds in Old Poland); and, on the considerable variety of local Jewish crafts, M. Schorr, *Żydzi w Przemyślu*, pp. 62 ff.

52. I. Halperin, *Pinqas Va'ad 'Arba Araṣot*, p. 17 No. 49; S. M. Dubnow, ed., *Pinqas ha-Medinah*, pp. 34 Nos. 139–40, 69 No. 324, 74 No. 360, 178 No. 728; I. Sonne, ed. (from a MS located in Rome), " 'Ordinances Pertaining to the Prohibitions Arising from the Sabbath and Holidays' by R. Meshullam Feivish of Cracow" (Hebrew), *Horeb*, II, 236–46 (also reproduced by Halperin in the "Supplements" to his *Pinqas*, pp. 483 ff. No. 922); E. Feldman, "Where and for Whom Were the Regulations Forbidding Work on Sabbath by R. Meshullam Feivish of Cracow Composed?" (Hebrew), *Zion*, XXXIV, 90–97, with an English summary, p. iv; and another statute, issued in 1602 by the community of Włodzimierz (Vladimir) of Volhynia, reproduced from an Oxford MS by H. H. Ben Sasson in his "Statutes for the Enforcement of the Observance of the Sabbath in Poland and Their Socioeconomic Implications" (Hebrew), *Zion*, XXI, 183–206, with an English summary, pp. iii f., esp. pp. 195 ff.

Feldman correctly argues that the Sabbath statutes were most likely proposed by a rabbi living in a newly developing eastern community, where Jewish arendators in charge of the magnates' latifundia had many temptations to break the Sabbath. Rural occupations are, indeed, most directly alluded to in the "Ordinances." Of course, the superscription in the Roman MS referring to R. Meshullam Feivish as a Cracow rabbi, may have been added by the copyist, writing after 1599, when the scholar really headed the community of the ancient capital. But Feivish may well have formulated the "Ordinances" while still residing in Brest-Litovsk. In 1590 the Central Council of the Jews of the Commonwealth (which, until 1623, embraced the Lithuanian communities), found this eloquent and detailed document sufficiently applicable to the Polish Crown, to confirm it as a country-wide enactment, as it did a few years later with the antiusury laws prepared by Joshua Falk ha-Kohen.

Certainly, Jewish artisans of the western Polish cities had enough difficulty in eking out their meager existence, in view of the Christian guilds' sharp opposition and the competition of numerous "interlopers." Some of them may indeed have tried, surreptitiously, to circumvent the Sabbath rest provisions of Jewish law, just as they far more openly disobeyed enactments by kings, palatines, or city councils. True, religious observance—closely supervised by the Jewish community with the strong support of public opinion, which was less unanimous about adhering to hostile enactments by outside authorities—was more difficult to breach. Fear of divine retribution in this world or in the hereafter must also have served as a strong deterrent. Yet occasional lawbreakers do appear in the sources; for instance, the Poznań tailor who, after receiving payment for his work, refused to perform it. After repeated transgressions of this kind, he was deprived of his residential rights and ordered by the Jewish elders to leave the city, together with his family. See D. Avron, ed., *Pinqas ha-Ksherim*, p. 5 No. 19.

53. See M. Horn, "Jewish Craftsmen in Red Russia around 1600" (Polish), *BZIH*, no. 34, pp. 28–70; idem, *Rzemiesło miejskie województwa bełzkiego w pierwszej połowie XVII wieku* (The Urban Crafts in the Province of Bełz in the First Half of the Seventeenth Century: Problems of the Economic Crisis of the Nobles' Commonwealth in the Seventeenth Century); idem, *Skutki ekonomiczne najazdów tatarskich z lat 1605–1633 na Ruś Czerwoną* (The Economic Effects of the Tatar Raids on Red Russia in 1605–1633); W. Trzebiński, "From Studies in the History of the Building of Private Towns in Poland in the Enlightenment Era" (Polish), *Prace* of the Instytut Urbanistyki i Architektury, V, 83–123; B. Baranowski and S. Herbst, "The Multinational Nobles' Commonwealth" (Polish) in T. Manteuffel, ed., *Historia Polski*, I, Part 2, pp. 450 ff.; C. Krawczak, "The Origin and Development of Building Codes in Poznań" (Polish), *Studia i materiały do dziejów Wielkopolski*, IX, Part 1 (XVII), p. 35; *supra*, n. 37; and Chaps. LXVIII, n. 85; and LXIX, n. 33; and, more generally, M. Gębarowicz, *Z dziejów przenyslu budowlanego XVI–XIX wieku* (From the History of the Building Industry in the Sixteenth through Nineteenth Centuries). Moreover, M. Małowist's complaint of 1953 in *Odrodzenie*, I, 273 (see *supra*, n. 45), that the history of the building trades in prepartition Poland had not yet been satisfactorily investigated, still holds true today, despite the newer studies by Gębarowicz, Waszak, Krawczak, and others.

Yet it seems that Jewish participation in these industrial pursuits was also hampered by the apparent inability, or unwillingness, of Polish Jewish capitalists to enter the real estate market in any major way. This was in sharp contrast with the great role Jewish businessmen played in the upbuilding of many Western cities in the nineteenth and twentieth centuries, as well as with their fairly active share in real estate transactions in medieval Germany, Spain, and England. See *supra*, Vol. XII, pp. 40 ff., 265 ff. nn. 38–42. It should also be mentioned that Horn's thesis about the enduring effects of the early seventeenth-century warlike disturbances in the province of Bełz has been disputed by A. Wyrobisz. With the aid of a statistical table covering twelve towns, this author has shown that their housing facilities had steadily dropped, from 650 in 1578, to 404 in the decade 1618–28, to 292 in 1629–35, and 145 in 1650. He has concluded, therefore, that the Tatar raids were not the cause of the economic recession, but rather the result of the economically induced weakened resistance of the local population and government. See his "Problems of the Decline of Crafts and the Economic Crisis of the Cities" (Polish), *PH*, LVIII, 132–38; and Horn's reply *ibid.*, pp. 668–69, cited *supra*, n. 45.

We must bear in mind, however, that the special archival records pertaining to real estate transactions have been largely neglected in modern research, especially in so far as they relate to Jews. In her "Notes on the Sephardim in Zamość" (Polish), *BZIH*, no. 38, esp. pp. 75 ff., J. Morgensztern has shown how much information about Jewish house ownership in Zamość during the first half of the seventeenth century could be derived from the local Acta Advocatialia, even though these records are but partially preserved. Of course, dealing mainly with real estate transfers, the documents tell us little about the workers who built or renovated these houses. However, the mention of brick buildings alongside wooden ones, and the record of one Moses Abramowicz paying 4,200 zlotys for a house (*ibid.*, p. 78), shed revealing light on both the Sephardic and the Ashkenazic settlers in the city. Clearly, similar careful studies of pertinent archival records extant in other Polish-Lithuanian cities would help fill an important lacuna in our knowledge of the economic history of Polish Jewry in the prepartition period. See also C. Krawczak's study on the building codes in Poznań; M. Horn's noteworthy lists of Jewish houses in the province of Bełz in *BZIH*, no. 27, esp. pp. 40 ff. Tables 2–15; and stray reports in many monographs on individual Jewish communities.

The artistic and communal aspects of Polish synagogues and other Jewish buildings will be discussed in another chapter. Here we need concern ourselves only with the economic aspects of Jewish craftsmanship involved in erecting dwellings, shops, and other structures, and supplying their interior decoration. Even in the case of synagogues, we are not entirely certain that some of them were not built by, or with the aid of, Christian personnel. In the case of the celebrated Lwów synagogue, erected in 1582 by Izak Nachmanowicz, we definitely know that the architect was a Christian immigrant, Paolo Felice (Paweł Szczęśliwy) of Rome. However, it appears that especially in the smaller towns, where most of the famed "wooden" synagogues were later found, the work was performed by local Jewish builders and carpenters and decorated by talented members of the community who may have remained anonymous even to their distant contemporaries. Most of these workers doubtless considered such labors a matter of religious devotion even more than one of earning a living.

54. See Z. Rajewski, "The Problem of the Early Medieval Work in Gold in Polish Lands" (Polish), *Wiadomości archeologiczne*, XX, 3–22, with Russian and English summaries; *supra*, Vols. III, pp. 218 f., 339 f. n. 58; XII, pp. 57, 272 f. n. 57; *infra*, n. 57 (on the later Jewish workers in gold in Leszno); B. Baranowski and S. Herbst in T. Manteuffel, ed., *Historia Polski*, I, Part 2, pp. 455 f.; Krzysztof Opaliński, *Satyry* (Satires; in the early editions with the added subtitle: Warnings Relating to the Reform of the Government and Customs in Poland), ed. with an Intro. by L. Eustachiewicz, p. 69 vv. 211–12; M. Bałaban, *Żydzi lwowscy*, pp. 429 ff., 482 ff. (raising the still-unanswered questions as to who was making and repairing the synagogue silver); idem, *Dzieje*, I, 324 f., 327 ff.; W. Łoziński, *Złotnictwo lwowskie* (Lwów Goldsmithery), explaining that, although the numerous complaints by the guild of Christian goldsmiths about Jewish competition would seem to indicate the presence of a number of Jewish craftsmen in this field in Red Russia's capital, direct evidence is very hard to come by. See also such general studies as Ł. Charewiczowa's *Lwowskie organizacje zawodowe za czasów Polski przedrozbiorowej* (Lwów's Professional Organizations from the Times of Prepartition Poland); M. Horn's "The Lwów Artisan Population" (Polish), *Zeszyty naukowe* of the Wyższa Szkoła Pedagogiczna

in Opole, Historia, XXI, 69–124; and N. Gąsiorowska-Grabowska, *Przemysł metalowy polski w rozwoju dziejowym* (The Polish Metal Industry in Its Historical Evolution).

55. See the statute of the Cracow barbers' guild, cited *supra*, n. 48; and *infra*, n. 57; and on Jewish printing, A. E. Harkavy, *Meassef niddaḥim* (Collection of Stray Items; reprinted from *Ha-Meliṣ*, XIV–XV), pp. 64, 84–89, 104–110, 121–29; *supra*, Chap. LXVIII, n. 6. The story of the Jewish printing presses in Poland and Lithuania and of their impact on the cultural life of the Jews, not only in the Commonwealth but in the entire Ashkenazic world, will be more fully discussed in a later chapter. For the time being we need but refer to the comparative material from the history of Polish printing in general. See especially, J. Muszkowski, "The Beginnings of Printing in Cracow: the Present State of Investigations and Actual Problems" (Polish), *Prace polonistyczne* of the Towarzystwo Literackie imienia Adama Mickiewicza, Łódź section, Ser. 8, 1950 [1951], pp. 9–58; C. Pilichowski, "From the History of Production, Trading, and Culture Connected with the Book in Poznań, 1570–1595" (Polish), *Przegląd Zachodni*, IX, Part 3, pp. 644–86 (showing, among other matters, that in those years 38 titles appeared in Polish and 85 in Latin, totaling 924 and 1,062 printed signatures, respectively; and that even in that late Renaissance period, the output, though overemphasizing religious issues, seems not to have included any writings pertaining to the Hebrew language); and the comprehensive survey of Polish printing in the respective provinces compiled by A. Kawecka-Gryczowa *et al.*, *Drukarze dawnej Polski od XV do XVIII wieku* (Printers of Old Poland from the Fifteenth to the Eighteenth Century), Vols. I–VI. See also her general analysis of "The Role of Polish Printing in the Renaissance Period" (Polish), *Odrodzenie w Polsce*, IV, 464–522. Often connected with printing was paper manufacturing, on which see, for instance, J. Ptaśnik's *Papiernie w Polsce w XVI wieku* (Paper Mills in Poland in the Sixteenth Century). Regrettably, we do not have sufficient data on the Jewish share in this economically minor, but culturally quite important, branch of Polish industry. See also *supra*, Chap. LXVII, n. 56.

56. On "The Legal Status of the Jews in Płock in the Sixteenth and First Half of the Seventeenth Centuries" (Yiddish), see I. Trunk, *Shtudies in yidisher geshikhte in Poiln* (Studies in Jewish History in Poland), pp. 25 ff. The fullest information on the attitudes of the Christian guilds toward Jewish associates is offered in M. Kremer's Yiddish study, "The Participation of Jewish Craftsmen in the Christian Guilds of Old Poland," *Bleter far Geshikhte*, II, 3–32. Understandably, the author had at his disposal data mostly from the period after 1650. Yet this essay has shed considerable new light on the relationships evolving between the Jewish craftsmen and their organized non-Jewish counterparts, and on the great regional and local differences, particularly between the eastern Lithuanian-Rus and the western Polish cities. Kremer has also shown how frequently Jews, as well as other religious and ethnic groups, were able to secure limited admission to the guilds as *kwartalni* or *suchedniarze*. These curious designations arose from the financial contributions paid quarterly or on certain designated fast days. Associates of this kind also had to assume certain duties of regular members, including pledges to avoid unfair competition, participate in the defense of their cities, and the like.

57. L. Lewin, *Geschichte der Juden in Lissa*, pp. 23 ff. The statutes of the Cracow Jewish barbers' guild were first published by F. H. Wettstein in his *Qadmoniyot mi-*

pinqesa'ot yeshanim, and in a partial English translation by J. R. Marcus, in *The Jew in the Medieval World: a Source Book, 315–1791* (also paperback), pp. 446–49. For the sake of comparison, see W. W. Głowacki, "A Poznań Surgeon's Pharmacy of 1528" (Polish), *Archiwum Historii Medycyny,* XXIII, 467–79; and his and B. Stępnicka's "The Surgeons' Statutes in Rzeszów" (Polish), *ibid.,* XXII, 567–75; W. Feilchenfeld in "Eine Innungsverordnung für die jüdischen Handwerker," *Zeitschrift* of the Historische Gesellschaft für die Provinz Posen, 1895, pp. 310 ff. See also *supra,* n. 45.

58. See M. Bałaban, *Żydzi lwowscy,* pp. 482 f., 485. Needless to say, such an absence of competition was quite rare in the larger cities. But it must often have occurred in smaller towns and villages, particularly in the underpopulated southeastern provinces.

59. B. D. Weinryb, *Texts and Studies,* Hebrew section, pp. 26 f. Nos. 69–70; English section, pp. 61 ff.; his "Studies in the Economic and Financial History of the Jews in the Polish and Lithuanian Cities in the Seventeenth and Eighteenth Centuries" (Hebrew), *Tarbiz,* X, 90–104, 201–231. For the emphasis on class struggle, see B. Mark's aforementioned studies, in *BZIH,* nos. 9–10; and *Odrodzenie,* I (*supra,* n. 45); and, with fuller documentation, I. Sosis, "Social Conflicts in the Jewish Communities of the Sixteenth and Seventeenth Centuries (Hebrew texts with Yiddish translations)" (Yiddish), *Zeitshrift* (Minsk), I, 225–38; and A. Eisenbach, "On the Problem of Class Struggle in the Jewish Society in Poland during the Second Half of the Eighteenth Century" (Polish), *BZIH,* nos. 17–18, pp. 129–70; 19–20, pp. 60–113, with English summaries, pp. 267 f. and 245, respectively.

As to the class struggle in the cities generally, Poland witnessed relatively few major artisans' revolts similar to those which frequently occurred in Germany. There were few repetitions of such uprisings as had taken place in Gdańsk in 1416 and Wrocław in 1418, when neither city was under Polish suzerainty and when the majority of both patricians and artisans were Germans. See J. Bardach, *Historia państwa,* I, 409. Exceptionally, artisans could take over the municipal council without a struggle. In the relatively small town of Przeworsk in the Cracow palatinate, where more than 60 percent of the population consisted of craftsmen, as against 13 percent of farmers and but 8.9 percent of traders, the artisans dominated the council. In certain years all seven councilors were recruited from that class. See M. Horn, "The Occupational Composition of the Przeworsk City Council in the Years 1600–1650 against the Background of the City's Occupational and Social Structure" (Polish), *PH,* LX, 270–90, with Russian and French summaries, esp. p. 286 Table 3.

60. See M. Bałaban, *Żydzi lwowscy,* p. 490. Regrettably, the large and varied class of intermediaries has not yet become the subject of detailed historical research. They not only performed the extremely important economic function of bringing together producers and customers, sellers and purchasers, landlords and tenants, and so forth, but also penetrated the more intimate sphere of family life by serving as marriage brokers (*shadḥanim*). The sources mentioning them are widely scattered, which is but another reflection of the great diversification of their services. Apart from engaging the attention of the various communal organs, central, regional, and local (see, for instance, the resolutions adopted by the Council of Four Lands in

1583, 1617, and 1624, reproduced by I. Halperin in his *Pinqas Va'ad*, pp. 3 No. 7, 33 f. No. 95, 50 No. 142, etc.), they were frequently treated in rabbinic responsa, homilies, and, particularly in the nineteenth century, in belles-lettres. Certainly, an effort to come to grips with the often complex problems of this class, which were generally aggravated in periods of economic crisis, would be eminently worthwhile.

61. B. Baranowski and S. Herbst in T. Manteuffel's ed., *Historia Polski*, I, Part 2, pp. 417 f.; *supra*, Vol. X, pp. 31 ff. Opportunities for the type of pioneering performed by Wołczko in the fifteenth century were now extremely limited, even in the southeastern provinces. Legally, as well as on account of the existing power relations, the *szlachta* alone was able to acquire the vast newly developing lands. Jews could make use of the new opportunities only indirectly, by helping the nobles to make these fertile lands highly productive.

62. S. Arnold and A. Wyczański in *Historia Polski*, I, Part 2, pp. 99 ff.; Z. Kaczmarczyk and B. Leśnodorski in J. Bardach, ed., *Historia państwa*, II, 13; A. Mączak, "Export of Grain and the Problem of Distribution of National Income in Poland in the Years 1550–1650," *APH*, XVIII, 75–98, esp. p. 90; A. Wyczański, *Studia nad folwarkiem szlacheckim w Polsce w latach 1500–1580* (Studies in the Nobles' Manorial System in Poland in the Years 1500–1580), with a French summary, esp. pp. 265 ff.; L. Żytkowicz, "From Studies of the Revenues from a Large Estate in Poland in the Last Quarter of the Sixteenth Century" (Polish), *PH*, LXIII, 505–514 (on the basis of several monographs by Alina Wawrzyńczyk). Kaczmarczyk and Leśnodorski rightly assume that the Jewish entrepreneurs, after employing the putting-out system among Jewish artisans, extended it to other *partaczy*. From here it was but a step to employing unskilled labor in both cities and villages to perform part-time work with tools and materials supplied by the employer. Unfortunately, we have no scholarly monographs dealing in depth with the early "cottage system" in Poland generally. Of course, original documentation is very sparse, since industries of this type, sharply opposed by the guilds, often had to be rather clandestine. Research in this field has also been hampered by the modern scholars' universally shared a priori view that the "cottage system" played an incomparably smaller role in early Polish industrial production than in the Commercial Revolution in Western Europe. However, a concentrated effort to secure dependable data on this significant problem ought to prove meritorious.

63. S. Arnold and A. Wyczański in *Historia Polski*, I, Part 2, pp. 99 f.; *Sbornik Russkogo Istoricheskogo Obshchestva* (= Journal of the Russian Historical Society), XLIII, 228. All these articles were, of course, significant objects of commerce, including the export trade, and have been mentioned here in various contexts.

64. Krzysztof Opaliński, *Satyry* (Satires), ed. by L. Eustachiewicz, IV, 8, pp. 209 ff., esp. vv. 10–12; M. Baliński and T. Lipiński, *Starożytna Polska pod względem historycznym* (Ancient Poland in Its Historical, Geographic, and Statistical Aspects), II, 728 f.; E. Horn, "Legal and Economic Situation of the Jews in the Towns of the Halicz Province" (Polish), *BZIH*, no. 40, pp. 29 f.; A. Kamiński *et al.*, eds. *Inwentarze dóbr ziemskich województwa krakowskiego* (Inventories of Landed Estates in the Cracow Palatinate, 1576–1700: a Selection from the Books of Reports of the Cracow Tribunal), p. 353; the grand ducal "Ordinance concerning castles, leaseholds,

and courts of Our Grand Duchy of Lithuania, both in the Vilna and Troki districts, and how the district governors, leaseholders, and officials are to conduct themselves," Polish text published by M. V. Dovnar-Zapolski in his *Ocherki po organizatsii zapadno-russkogo krestianstva v XVI vieku* (Studies in the Organization of the West-Russian Peasantry in the Sixteenth Century), Appendix, pp. 84–100, esp. pp. 92 f. (although undated, this decree is placed by the editor among others issued in 1567); F. Rawita-Gawroński, *Sprawy i rzeczy ukraińskie* (Ukrainian Affairs and Matters), pp. 193 ff.; *supra*, Chap. LXVIII, n. 56. On vodka and its still moderate consumption in the sixteenth and early seventeenth centuries, see Z. Kuchowicz, "Observations on the Consumption of Distilled Alcoholic Products in Poland in the Sixteenth Century" (Polish), *KHKM*, XIX, 667–78, with a French summary. The author emphasizes that only the introduction of a greatly improved technology lowered the price of the product sufficiently to make it accessible to the masses.

The importance of the liquor monopolies for the landlords and their representatives was from the outset quite substantial, but it naturally grew in proportion to the amount of consumption. On the legal and social aspects of the production and distribution of alcohol, and their impact on the Polish, Lithuanian, and Rus villages and towns, see M. Bobrzyński, "The Law of *Propinacja* [Liquor Monopoly] in Old Poland" (Polish) in his *Szkice i studia historyczne* (Historical Sketches and Studies), II, 32–97 (emphasizes that, unlike the villages, which to the end of the Polish Commonwealth were under the landlords' monopoly, the cities were usually free to dispose of the exclusive liquor rights as they pleased, except for the competition offered them by the nobles' *jurydyki* within their walls); and J. Burszta, *Wieś i karczma, rola karczmy w życiu wsi pańszczyznianej* (Village and Tavern: the Role of the Tavern in the Life of the Village in the Period of Serfdom).

On the other hand, Jan Rutkowski's valiant effort to come to grips with the occupational statistics of the village population in Poland was not very successful, and later scholars (for instance, L. Żytkowicz in his "Polish Peasants," *PH*, LXII, 103) have given up further efforts along these lines. Nevertheless, the subject is too intriguing and important not to receive further consideration in the light of our expanding knowledge of conditions in the villages of prepartition Poland. See also, more generally, H. Samsonowicz's *Rzemiosło wiejskie w Polsce XIV–XVII wieku* (The Village Industry in Poland in the Fourteenth through Seventeenth Centuries), esp. pp. 118 ff. (on flour mills), 149 ff. (beer and liquor industry); and more detailed studies such as J. Topolski's *Gospodarstwo wiejskie w dobrach arcybiskupstwa gnieźnieńskiego od XVI do XVIII wieku* (The Village Economy in the Possessions of the Gniezno Archbishopric from the Sixteenth to the Eighteenth Century).

65. I. Halperin, *Pinqas Va'ad 'Arba Araṣot*, p. 16 No. 46; S. M. Dubnow, *Pinqas*, p. 34 No. 140. This ritually inspired impetus to Jewish interest in agriculture had a long history behind it. As early as the thirteenth century, the Austrian rabbi Isaac b. Moses Or Zaru'a insisted on disqualifying cheese made by Gentiles (against the more lenient view held by R. Jacob Tam), "since this prohibition had been adopted in all lands of Canaan [Slavonic Central Europe]." See *supra*, Vol. IV, pp. 157 f., 315 f. n. 10.

66. See M. F. Vladimirskii-Budanov in *Arkhiv Yugo-Zapadnoi Rossii*, Part VI, I, art. 78; A. Pawiński, ed., *Żrodła dziejowe*, V, 132; and other sources cited by S. Ettinger in his "Jewish Participation in the Colonization of the Ukraine" (Hebrew),

Zion, XXI, 133 ff., 138 f. On the movement beginning in 1488 for the restoration of the royal domain, see I. Sułkowska-Kurasiowa, "The Revision of the Royal Donations around 1500" (Polish), *KH*, LXXIV, 289–97, with Russian and French summaries; and A. Sucheni-Grabowska's study, cited *supra*, Chap. LXVIII, n. 86. Despite this gigantic and remarkably successful effort, part of the royal domain was still controlled by the aristocracy. A telling example is offered by the Lubomirski latifundium, which as late as 1739 embraced 52 towns and 940 villages fully owned by, and 5 towns and 18 villages partially belonging to, the family. These properties, scattered over 9 palatinates, included major possessions in the three provinces of Volhynia, Kiev, and Bratslav (15 fully and 2 partially owned, 9 fully and 2 partially, and 14 fully owned, respectively). In addition Aleksander Michał Lubomirski had leased, in 1658–64, 8 towns and 99 villages from the royal domain. See A. Homecki, *Produkcja i handel zbożowy w latyfundium Lubomirskich* (Grain Production and Trade in the Lubomirski Latifundium in the Second Half of the Seventeenth and the First Half of the Eighteenth Century), pp. 13 ff. These data, though not quite synchronous, clearly illustrate the complications arising from such widely dispersed possessions. To be sure, we have no record that any Jewish leaseholder ever controlled an entire latifundium of this kind. But a number of them, especially Abraham Szmoiłowicz, simultaneously leased a considerable number of townships and villages belonging to different landlords. This situation often gave rise to conflicts of interest and other complications for the leaseholder, of which the extant sources vouchsafe us only occasional glimpses.

67. S. M. Dubnow, ed., *Pinqas ha-Medinah*, p. 35 Nos. 145–46; S. Ettinger, "Jewish Participation," *Zion*, XXI, 127. The Wroński contract is cited from the *Pamiatniki Kievskoi Arkheographicheskoi Kommissii* (Memoirs of the Kiev Archeographic Commission), I, Part 2, pp. 66 ff., by Ettinger in his "Jewish Participation," *Zion*, XXI, 133 f. See also *infra*, n. 70.

68. See A. Kamiński *et al.*, eds., *Inwentarze dóbr ziemskich województwa krakowskiego*, pp. 323, 347 ff., and the numerous data supplied in such regional histories as L. Białkowski's *Podole w XVI wieku* (Podolia in the Sixteenth Century: Socioeconomic Outlines); and D. Doroshenko's *History of the Ukraine*, trans. and abridged by Hanna Keller and ed. with an Intro. by G. W. Simpson.
From the enormous literature on Polish and Lithuanian serfdom, we need but quote here B. D. Grekov's *Krestianie na Rusi s drevneishikh vremei do XVII veka* (The Peasants in Rus from Earliest Times to the Seventeenth Century), 2d ed., Vols. I–II; or in the German translation of the first edition [1946] by H. Truhart and K. von Bergsträsser (Vol. I); and by H. Giertz (Vol. II), entitled *Die Bauern in der Rus von den ältesten Zeiten bis zum 17. Jahrhundert,* ed. and rev. by P. Hoffmann according to the 2d ed., especially I, 251 ff., 370 ff., and *passim*. This study sheds much light, not only on the southeastern provinces but also on Red Russia, which the author calls the Halicz (Galicia) Rus. Many new data and insights may also be derived from a retrospective analysis of the developments in Galicia after the Austrian occupation of that area in 1772–95. See esp. R. Rozdolski's detailed and well-documented study, *Stosunki poddańcze w dawnej Galicji* (The Conditions of Serfdom in Old Galicia). It includes numerous references to Jews, both in the analytical Vol. I and in the vast array of documents reproduced in Vol. II; see the entries in the Index, II, 424, *s.v.* Żydzi. Some of the more comprehensive recent

studies dealing with ethnographic Poland, rather than the Rus areas, have been cited *supra*, Chap. LXVIII, nn. 49–50. See also S. Šreniowski's "Signs of an Economic Recession in the Manorial-Serfdom System at the End of the Sixteenth Century" (Polish), *KH*, LXI, Part 2, pp. 165–96; and J. Rutkowski's stimulating *Studia z dziejów wsi polskiej XVI–XVIII wieku* (Studies in the History of the Polish Village in the Sixteenth through Eighteenth Centuries), selected and ed. with an Intro. by W. Kula, though more than half the space is devoted to problems of the eighteenth century. Of some importance for comparative purposes is H. Ludat *et al.*, eds., *Agrar-, Wirtschafts- und Sozialprobleme Mittel- und Osteuropas in Geschichte und Gegenwart*, though offering few data directly relevant to early modern Poland and its Jews. Incidentally, we may refer here to C. Warnke's "Bemerkungen zur Reise Ibrahim Ibn Jakubs durch die Slavenländer im 10. Jahrhundert" (*ibid.*, pp. 393–415), in supplementation of what was said *supra*, Vols. IV, pp. 217 f., 538 n. 57; VI, pp. 221 f., 434 n. 87. See also some of the studies reviewed by A. Mączak in his "Polnische Forschungen auf dem Gebiete der Agrargeschichte des 16. und 17. Jahrhunderts (1945–1957)," *APH*, I, 33–57.

69. See M. F. Vladimirskii-Budanov, *Arkhiv Yugo-Zapadnoi Rossii*, Part VI, I, Art. 92; S. Bershadskii, *Dokumenty i materialy*, No. 4; both cited by S. Ettinger in his "Jewish Participation," *Zion*, XXI, 132, 135; S. Kardaszewicz, *Dzieje dawniejsze miasta Ostroga*, pp. 117 ff. The exemption of the castle of Horochów (Gorokhov) in the Sanguszko contract of 1601 was probably owing to the fact that the prince continued to live in that castle and did not wish to suffer from any interference on the part of the two leaseholders. A considerable number of other such contracts are briefly summarized in Ettinger's essay, *passim*.

70. See especially S. M. Dubnow, *Pinqas ha-Medinah*, pp. 14 Nos. 73–75, 17 No. 87, 24 Nos. 104 and 106; Benjamin Aaron b. Abraham Slonik, *Sefer Mas'at Binyamin* (Benjamin's Portion; Responsa), Metz, 1776, fols. 19 ff. No. 27. "Acquired rights" (*ḥazaqot*) generally loomed very large in the controlled economy of the period. We recall that the very right of settlement in a city, and one's residential and working opportunities, greatly depended on the acquisition of a *ḥezqat ha-yishub* recognized by the community. See *supra*, Chap. LXVII, nn. 12 and 17; LXVIII, n. 80; and, on its ancient and medieval antecedents, *supra*, Vols. IV, pp. 71, 274 n. 91; V, 68 f., 321 f. n. 83.

71. See S. M. Dubnow, *Pinqas*, pp. 13 No. 66, 14 No. 74, 17 No. 87, 59 No. 284, 67 f. No. 308, 83 No. 404, etc.; idem, "Arendators' Contracts in the Seventeenth and Eighteenth Centuries" (Russian), *ES*, II, 105–111. These deliberations indicate that, much as they appreciated the economic advantages of the tenancy system and the Jewish share therein, some Council members sensed, as through a glass darkly, its potentially explosive impact on overall Gentile-Jewish relations of the period.

72. See the detailed description of Israel Złoczowski's unfortunate experience, and an excerpt from the original contract signed by Aleksander Zborowski on January 12, 1595, in M. Bałaban's *Żydzi lwowscy*, pp. 82 ff., Materials, pp. 42 f. No. 38. It appears that such arbitrary acts were rather infrequent. However strong-willed and powerful, most nobles doubtless realized that such acts would merely discourage any other businessmen, Jewish or non-Jewish, from entering into agreements with them.

73. See the anonymous poem, published in 1648 and reproduced by K. Wójcicki in his ed. of the *Biblioteka starożytna pisarzy polskich* (A Library of Old Polish Writers); Przecław Mojecki, *Żydowskie okrucieństwa;* Sebastyan Miczyński, *Zwierciadło,* Chap. VII; K. Bartoszewicz, *Antysemitysm,* pp. 45, 96 f.; S. Ettinger, "Jewish Participation," *Zion,* XXI, 110 f.; I. Sonne, ed., " 'Ordinances Pertaining to the Prohibitions Arising from the Sabbath' " (Hebrew) and the literature thereon mentioned *supra,* n. 52; Anzelm Gostomski, *Gospodarstwo* (Husbandry), Cracow, 1588, reed. with an Intro. by S. Inglot, p. 15 and *passim.*

74. M. Bałaban, *Żydzi lwowscy,* p. 190. Although it is very likely that Nachmanowicz employed some Drohobycz Jews in his business there, we do not hear about any of them being involved in those acts of violence against the peasants of the district. Yet the memory of the 1634 miscarriage of justice must have rankled many non-Jewish inhabitants of the area, and it may well have stiffened the resistance of the Drohobycz burghers to the admission of Jews to the city even after 1648. See J. Wikler, "From the History of the Jews in Drohobycz (From 1648 to the Fall of the Commonwealth); the Struggle of the Drohobycz Jews for Residential and Commercial Rights" (Polish), *BZIH,* nos. 71–72, pp. 39–61, with an English summary. See also *infra,* n. 81.

On petitions as a mild expression of peasant resistance, see J. Topolski, *Położenie i walka klasowa chłopów w XVIII wieku w dobrach arcybiskupstwa gnieźnieńskiego* (The Condition and the Class Struggle of the Peasants in the Possessions of the Archbishopric of Gniezno in the Eighteenth Century), pp. 221 ff. A collection of petitions and complaints circulated by Polish peasants was published by S. Szczotka in his ed. of *Lament chłopski na pany* (A Peasant Lamentation against the Lords). The title of the volume is taken from a lengthy poem written before 1622, which is reprinted there. To be sure, neither the poem nor the peasants' petitions reproduced by Szczotka contain accusations against Jews. Although doubtless partially reflecting the relative absence of Jewish arendators in the Crown provinces, the total silence about the Jewish aspects of exploitation is quite significant.

It appears that the Jewish leaseholders and even the communal leaders, both lay and rabbinic, did not fully perceive the dangers in the oppression of the peasant masses by their masters. Certainly, no Jewish voice was heard similar to that of Krzysztof Opaliński, who predicted, in one of his satires, that God would punish the Poles for no sin so severely as for the oppression of serfs. See his *Satyry,* I, 3; ed. by L. Eustachiewicz, p. 29. On public opinion in general, see also B. D. Grekov, *Krestianie,* II, 210 ff., and in its German translation, *Die Bauern,* II, 204 ff., which, though mainly concerned with the Rus, rather than the Polish, opinion of the time, opens vistas on the attitudes prevailing in eastern Europe as a whole.

75. W. Rusiński, "On the Interior Trade," *RDSG,* XVI, 125. It must also be remembered that, even in the provinces which after 1569 remained under the suzerainty of the Grand Duchy of Lithuania, there were but a few scattered large cities. Most of the smaller towns and hamlets embracing a population of under 5,000 souls, permanently retained a semirural character. See J. Ochmiański, "On the Problems of the Agrarian Character of the Towns in the Grand Duchy of Lithuania" (Polish), *Studia Historica* in honor of Henryk Łowmiański, pp. 279–93, esp. p. 290 Table I. The Jews thus had many opportunities to reduce their living ex-

penses and to supplement their income by at least part-time cultivation of the soil and small-scale animal husbandry.

76. See I. Sonne, ed., "Ordinances" (Hebrew), *Horeb*, II, 236–46; reprinted in I. Halperin's *Pinqas Va'ad 'Arba Araṣot*, p. 483; J. Bardach, *Historia państwa*, II, 309; *supra*, n. 73. Apparently the regulation that Christians were to be employed on a contractual basis, at least on the Sabbath, created no serious difficulties. A non-Jew had the advantage of speaking the language, or languages, of most of the arrivals at the station; and when it came to fisticuffs he was, as a rule, better able to take care of himself than a Jew, often recruited from a slumlike ghetto. See *infra*, n. 80.

77. See *Akta grodzkie*, ed. by O. Pietruski *et al.*, II, 70 ff. Nos. xlii and xlv; IX, 73 No. lvi; XIV, 147 No. 1204; 159 No. 1287; 215 ff. Nos. 1724, 1728, 1735, 1743; 357 Nos. 2704, 2709–710, 2718; and 377 f. No. 2868; S. B. Bershadskii, *REA*, III, 12 ff. Nos. III–IV, etc.; *VL*, I, 259; II, 20, 52; M. Bersohn, *Dyplomataryusz*, pp. 224 ff. Nos. 404, 406, 409–10, 414, 417–19, and 425; 239 f. No. 456; and other data cited by I. Schipper in his *Virtshaftsgeshikhte*, pp. 30 ff., 164 ff., 239 ff.; M. Bałaban in his *Żydzi lwowscy*, pp. 382 ff.; *supra*, Vol. X, pp. 45 f., 321 f. n. 55; and Chap. LXVIII, nn. 58 and 60. Leaseholds of public revenue were a more or less permanent bone of contention, not only between the *szlachta* and other classes but also between the Polonized German burghers and members of other ethnic groups. On the whole, the nobles fared better with Jewish or Armenian leaseholders and tax farmers than with their Catholic counterparts. On many occasions a nobleman was merely a figurehead to obtain the license from the government or a private lord, and he left the administration to a Jewish agent, who advanced all the necessary funds and shared the revenue with the nobleman in a predetermined ratio. This subterfuge became less common in time, however, and Jewish capitalists frequently appeared as direct bidders, even against impoverished noblemen. Of course, Jewish tax collectors, too, sometimes failed to meet their obligations. For one example, as early as 1466 the Polish dignitary Jakub Koniecpolski, governor [*capitaneus*] of Przemyśl, had to sue his Jewish tax farmer, Judah, for 50 marks allegedly owed him. See *Akta grodzkie*, XIII, 519 No. 6308.

78. I. Halperin, ed., *Pinqas Va'ad 'Arba Araṣot*, pp. 1 f. No. 1; Joel b. Samuel Zvi Sirkes, *Resp.*, Ostrog, 1834 ed., fols 20 d f. No. 61; J. Caro, *Geschichte der Juden in Lemberg*, p. 161 Note II item 3 (reproducing the Hebrew epitaph of Róża Nachmanowicz); M. Bałaban, *Żydzi lwowscy*, pp. 41 f., 205 (a Polish trans. and facsimile of that inscription), 169 ff., 175, 382 ff., etc. The famous 1580 resolution of the Polish Council was repeated and reinforced by a fine of 200 zlotys by the Cracow elders in 1595. It was, indeed, first published by Balaban from the minute book of the Cracow community in "Die Krakauer Judengemeinde-Ordnung von 1595," *JJLG*, X, 310 f., and has frequently been republished and commented upon. The text has also been translated into Polish, German, and Russian. See the references in Halperin's informative note on his reedition.

79. See K. Lepszy, "The Structure of the State in the Period of the Formation of the Nobles' Commonwealth" (Polish) in T. Manteuffel's ed., *Historia Polski*, I, Part 2, pp. 291–319, esp. p. 306; *supra*, Chap. LXVIII, n. 14; and *infra*, nn. 88 ff.

Understandably, the problem of *czopowe* engaged the attention of the Polish and Lithuanian Councils on many later occasions, too, whereas leaseholds of salines and mints were rarely discussed there; they also played an ever-diminishing role in the Jewish economy of the seventeenth century.

80. See T. Chudoba, "Problems of Warsaw's Vistula Trade in the Sixteenth Century" (Polish), *PH*, L, 297–321, esp. p. 300; the graphic description of manifold activities of tollmasters, culled from Lwów archival records, in M. Bałaban's *Żydzi lwowscy*, pp. 47 ff., 62 f., 382 ff.; and his briefer German sketch, "Isaak Nachmanowicz, ein polnischer Jude des XVI. Jahrhunderts," in his *Skizzen und Studien zur Geschichte der Juden in Polen*, pp. 5–10; and the examples of the use by Jewish scribes (even those employed by noble toll collectors) of Hebrew and Yiddish for entries in the records of toll revenues, assembled by R. Mahler in "A Contribution to the History of the Economic Relations of Lithuanian Jews with Poland in the Sixteenth Century (Hebrew-Yiddish Custom House Registers from Bielsk Podlaski and Łuków, Written in 1580)" (Yiddish), *Yivo Historishe Shriftn*, II, 180–205, with an English summary, *ibid.*, pp. viii f. (Incidentally, a similar phenomenon of "Hebrew-Yiddish Documents Relating to Censuses of Jewish Population in Poland during the Second Half of the Eighteenth Century" is illustrated in Mahler's Yiddish essay in *YB*, III, 208–222.) Yet rarely do we hear of complaints against this practice such as that submitted in 1614 by an Armenian merchant against the Lwów Jewish scribe David. See Bałaban, *Żydzi*, p. 387.

81. See M. Bałaban, *Żydzi lwowscy*, Materials, pp. 23 f. No. 21, 121 f. No. 91; *supra*, n. 22; and Chap. LXVIII, n. 48. Because of his connections with the king, Izak Nachmanowicz the Younger often enjoyed full cooperation of royal officials. We recall their violent reaction to a peasant delegation during Wladislaw's sojourn in Lwów in 1634. See *supra*, n. 74. However, the peasants' major grievance—that Izak had imposed a tax of 30, instead of 2.5, groszy per lan (= 16.7 hectares, or about 42 acres) —was unjustified. They apparently were unaware that this tax had indeed been raised to 30 groszy, or one zloty, per lan. See J. Bardach, *Historia państwa*, II, 148. At the same time, like other tollmasters, Izak was not immune from judicial prosecution or mob assault. On one occasion (on October 15, 1637) he was actually condemned to death in absentia by Poland's supreme tax court, the Crown Tribunal in Radom. The judges themselves evidently did not take their sentence too seriously, however, and five years later condemned Izak to banishment only, for another default in payments to the Treasury. All along, he continued in his accustomed ways of doing business, despite ever-increasing legal complications. He was, of course, subject to purely economic failures; indeed, his career ended in bankruptcy, and he disappeared from the scene in 1646. See Bałaban, *Żydzi lwowscy*, pp. 192 ff., Materials, pp. 129 f. No. 100.

82. Joel Sirkes, *Resp.*, Ostrog, 1834 ed., fol. 51bc No. 27; M. Bałaban, *Żydzi lwowscy*, Materials, pp. 23 f. No. 21. We must also bear in mind that Jews, however powerful, often found it difficult to secure justice in controversies with Polish potentates. Rare indeed was the case when Izak Nachmanowicz the Elder actually held a Polish noble in custody. Also unusual was Stephen Báthory's intervention on· another occasion (in 1578), forcing the district governor Mikołaj Herburt of Lwów to appear before him as defendant against a Jew; the king empasized: "the

official and the Jew are both the king's servants" and as such equal before the law. See J. Caro, *Geschichte der Juden in Lemberg*, p. 32.

83. Nicholas Copernicus, *De moneta cudenda ratio*, Cracow, 1517, revised in 1526; J. Dmochowski, ed., *Mikołaja Kopernika Rozprawy o monecie i inne pisma ekonomiczne* (Nicholas Copernicus' Tractates on Money and Other Economic Writings); K. Lepszy, "Attempts at Political Reforms and the Struggle of the Middle Gentry with the Magnates" (Polish) in T. Manteuffel, ed., *Historia Polski*, I, Part 2, pp. 214 f.; B. Baranowski and S. Herbst, "The Multinational Nobles' Republic" (Polish), *ibid.*, pp. 466 f.; I. Halperin, *Pinqas Va'ad 'Arba Araṣot*, pp. 1 f. No. 1; S. M. Dubnow, *Pinqas ha-Medinah*, pp. 15 f. No. 81; *supra*, n. 10; Chap. LXVIII, n. 40; and Vol. XIV, pp. 231 ff., 349 f. n. 7. Several other writers likewise suggested a variety of reforms, which were frequently discussed at the Diet and in other official circles. Sigismund I enlisted the aid of leading Cracow businessmen like Jan Boner and Jan Turzon in seeking thoroughgoing changes in Poland's fiscal and monetary policies. However, all attempts at major reforms were defeated by the resistance of the nobles, who feared damage to their class interests. See Z. Sadowski's twin studies *Rozprawy o pieniądzu w Polsce pierwszej połowy XVII wieku* (Treatises on Money in Poland during the First Half of the Seventeenth Century, Selected, Introduced, and Annotated); and *Pieniądz a początki upadku Rzeczypospolitej Polskiej* (Money and the Beginning of the Decline of the Polish Commonwealth), with English and Russian summaries. See also the literature cited in the next note.

84. No systematic, comprehensive, up-to-date analysis of the entire fiscal structure and administration of prepartition Poland and Lithuania is as yet available. The material is admittedly widely scattered, incomplete, and very difficult of access. Not surprisingly, the part played by Polish and Lithuanian Jews as taxpayers in the dual Commonwealth and its political subdivisions, or in their own communities, is even less known. The very meaning of technical terms like *sekhum* (the equivalent of a property tax collected by Jewish communities from their members) is differently interpreted by various scholars. For the time being we must be satisfied with such partial studies as those by B. D. Weinryb in his "Beiträge zur Finanzgeschichte der jüdischen Gemeinden in Polen, [I]," *MGWJ*, LXXXII, 248–63, esp. pp. 250 f.; "II," *HUCA*, XVI, 187–214; his "Studies in the Economic and Financial History of the Jews in the Polish and Lithuanian Cities in the Seventeenth and Eighteenth Centuries" (Hebrew), *Tarbiz*, X, 90–104, 201–231; and his "Studies in the Communal History of Polish Jewry," *PAAJR*, XII, 121–40 and Hebrew section, pp. vii–xlvii. Most of the sources consulted by this author, however, date from the period after 1648, and must be used with considerable discernment in drawing conclusions for the earlier period. See also the comparative data analyzed in my *JC*, Chap. XV in Vols. II–III. On the dual Commonwealth in general, see such partial studies as J. Rutkowski, "The Polish Fiscal System under Alexander Jagiellon" (Polish), *KH*, XXIII, 1–77; and A. Pawiński, ed., *Skarbowość w Polsce i jej dzieje za Stefana Batorego* (The Polish Fiscal System and Its History under Stephen Báthory). Some monographs pertaining to the financial administration of certain cities will be mentioned in the following notes. A particular lacuna in the general historiography of this subject consists in the nearly total absence of studies comparing conditions in Poland with those in other European countries of the time.

None of these difficulties can be overcome, however, until more solid bases are found for critically evaluating the data given in the fiscal sources. We remember J. Kleczyński's reservations concerning the reliability of the records of the capitation tax in Poland as a means of computing population. Similarly, M. Horn has pointed out how misleading tax records can be for ascertaining the occupational structure of any area. See J. Kleczyński, "The General Capitation Tax in Poland and the Population Censuses Built upon It" (Polish), *Rozprawy* of PAU, XXX, 240–62; M. Horn, *Ruch budowlany,* esp. p. 16; and, more generally, Z. Guldon's "Observations on the Scholarly Usefulness of the Tax Registers" (Polish), *Zapiski historyczne,* XXXI, Part 1, pp. 73–79 (in connection with his aforementioned debate with P. Szafran); *supra,* Chap. LXIX, nn. 31 and 44; and other sources cited *infra,* n. 94. But these obstacles are not insuperable.

85. A. L. Feinstein, '*Ir tehillah,* p. 15; I. Sułkowska-Kurasiowa, "The Revision of Royal Donations around 1500" (Polish), *KH,* LXXIV, 289–97, with Russian and French summaries; J. Bardach, ed., *Historia państwa,* II, 145; A. Wyczański, *Rozdawnictwo dóbr królewskich za Zymunta I* (Sigismund I's Dissipation of Crown Property); B. Baranowski and S. Herbst, "Multinational Nobles' Commonwealth" (Polish) in T. Manteuffel, ed., *Historia Polski,* I, Part 2, p. 557; R. Solomon b. Yeḥiel Luria, *Resp.,* Lublin, 1599 ed., fols. 28d ff. No. 35; *supra,* Chap. LXVIII, nn. 86–87; and *infra,* n. 88. The inexhaustible variety of Polish-Lithuanian taxes was owing not only to the ingenuity of legislators and tax collectors but also to the anarchical variety of bodies empowered to impose new taxes. The result was a chaotic fiscal situation, which even contemporaries could not completely fathom and whose reconstruction by modern historians has been extremely difficult.

86. See the text of the royal circular addressed to the Cracow Jewish community, which was made chiefly responsible for raising the entire sum of 60,000 zlotys and delivering it to Wisemberg in M. Bersohn's *Dyplomataryusz,* pp. 132 f. No. 238; also M. Bałaban, *Żydzi lwowscy,* Materials, p. 141 No. 110; and *infra,* n. 95. Similar orders were issued to the communities of Lwów and Lublin (*ibid.,* p. 134 Nos. 239–41), and undoubtedly also to that of Poznań, which owed the king a special debt of gratitude for the two favorable decrees addressed to it on March 9 and May 2, 1633. See the texts reproduced by J. Perles in his "Geschichte der Juden in Posen," *MGWJ,* XIII, 327 ff. nn. 8 and 10.

87. See, for instance, Stephen Báthory's decree of August 4, 1576, summarized by J. Morgensztern in her "Regesta," *BZIH,* no. 47, p. 126 No. 81; Nathan Neṭa Hannover, *Sefer Yeven Meṣulah* (Deep Mire: a Chronicle of the Massacres of 1648), Venice, 1652, partly reproduced in A. Kahana's *Sifrut ha-historiah ha-israelit,* II, 295–318, esp. p. 314; in the Yiddish trans. by W. Latzky-Bertoldi, with a Supplement by I. Israelsohn and an (introductory) Investigation concerning the Period of Chmielnicky by Jacob Shatzky, or in A. J. Misch's English trans. entitled *Abyss of Despair,* p. 41; S. M. Dubnow, *Pinqas ha-Medinah,* pp. 40 No. 189, 49 No. 233, 145 No. 607, 158 No. 660, 186 No. 743; M. Bersohn, *Dyplomataryusz,* pp. 37 No. 32, 100 No. 149. Although Báthorys' decree refers only to Krzemieniec and mentions a preceding deliberation of his Council, it appears that this was no real innovation, and that the tax exemption of rabbis, reaching back to pre-Christian antiquity, was fairly universal in the dual Commonwealth, too. Examples of exceptions from the

rule of law and subsequent exceptions therefrom can easily be multiplied. Many contemporaries, especially the beneficiaries of the exemption, found the system highly appealing, though it undoubtedly added to the confusion prevailing on all administrative levels.

88. K. Lepszy's classification in his "The Structure of the State" in T. Manteuffel, ed., *Historia Polski*, I, Part 2, pp. 305 f.; B. Baranowski and S. Herbst, "Multinational Nobles' Commonwealth," *ibid.*, pp. 556 ff. A somewhat different classification is offered in J. Bardach's *Historia państwa*, pp. 306 ff. See also *supra*, nn. 78 and 79. The names of the different imposts, their character, and amount, differed from time to time and from area to area. Their mere enumeration would require more space than is warranted here. We shall see that in the Jewish case the gap between assessments and actual payments was at times quite large, and rarely were such arrears fully paid' up in subsequent years.

89. S. Weymann, "The First Laws Pertaining to the General Poll Tax in Poland (in the Years 1498 and 1520) against the Background of the Then Prevailing Fiscal System" (Polish), *RDSG*, XVIII, 11–74, with French and Russian summaries, esp. pp. 12 f., 23 ff. (discussing some of the reform projects and the views of leading political thinkers), 28 ff., 63; *supra*, nn. 3–4, 40; and Chap. LXVIII, n. 66. According to Weymann, Jews were not subject to the poll tax of 1520, but were supposed to pay a lump sum of 2,000 zlotys instead. A record of 1521 indicates that the Jews of the palatinates of Red Russia, Bełz, Podolia, and Lublin were expected to contribute 1,100 zlotys. While other arrears were for the most part treated complacently by the Treasury, the Jews' failure to deliver the last 80 zlotys of that sum prompted the government to shift the burden of making good the balance to certain named individuals. See O. Balzer, ed., *Corpus iuris polonici*, III, 629 f. No. 251. The origin of the Council of Four Lands, its antecedents before 1580, and the extent to which the government's fiscal needs contributed to its ultimate realization, will be discussed in a later chapter in connection with the great changes which took place in the organizational structure of Polish Jewry.

90. The early assessments and payments usually engaged the attention of the Polish Council and are, for the most part, reflected in the documentary excerpts assembled by I. Halperin in his ed. of *Pinqas Va'ad 'Arba Arasot*, pp. 5–9, and *passim*. They are also recorded in the early resolutions of the Polish Diet of 1581–1607 as reproduced in *VL*, II, 1030, 1251, 1306, 1354, 1385, 1416, 1444, 1540, 1555, 1583, and 1646; and in such communications by the secretaries of the Treasury as that by Jan Firlej in 1603, reproduced in M. Bałaban's *Żydzi lwowscy*, Materials, p. 51 No. 48. See also *ibid.*, pp. 341 f., mentioning that the receipt for the Jewish poll tax delivered to the Treasury in 1593 was signed by Sigismund III in person.

The gradual increase of the annual assessments to 70,000 zlotys in the 1650s, and 100,000 zlotys from 1660 on, brought about by the tremendous needs of the Treasury in those critical years, must have appeared extremely burdensome to the Jewish communities, whose fate was then hanging in the balance. It is not surprising, therefore, that whatever other payments the Council may have made to special recipients, the head of the Treasury generally received varying smaller amounts. According to reports submitted in 1662 by Jan Kazimierz na Krasnem Krasiński in behalf of the Polish Treasury, for the Diet's approval, he had received the full amounts of 70,000 and 100,000 zlotys only in 1659 and 1660, respectively. In 1650 the collection had totaled only 53,465 zlotys and 6 groszy, in lieu of the anticipated 70,000. In contrast, in 1656 and 1658 the receipts dropped to but 3,000 and 2,000 zlotys. M. Bersohn, *Dyplomataryusz*, p. 208 No. 365. It is possible, however, that Krasiński listed here only the revenues received directly by the Treasury, and did not mention various, probably larger, payments, made by the Jewish Council to specifically designated recipients.

91. See *VL*, II, 358; I. Halperin, *Pinqas Va'ad*, p. 8 No. 24 and n. 3 thereon. By 1764 each side blamed the other for the breakdown of the system. The government stressed the weaknesses and abuses which had crept into the operations of the Councils, but it glossed over the underlying shortcomings of Poland's growingly anarchical sociopolitical structure and its ever more inefficient and corrupt bureaucracy. An analysis of these complex factors must be relegated to a later volume, dealing with the eighteenth century.

92. See M. Bersohn, *Dyplomataryusz*, pp. 123 f. No. 238; J. Bardach, ed., *Historia państwa*, II, 307; L. Lewin, *Die Landessynode der grosspolnischen Judenschaft*, pp. 57 ff.; J. Caro, *Geschichte der Juden in Lemberg*, pp. 43 f.; M. Bałaban, *Dzieje*, I, 372 ff.; *supra*, Chap. LXVIII, nn. 22–23. Equally disagreeable was the Cracow community's having to pay 15 zlotys annually to the Augustinian convent in Bochnia for the use of the Jewish cemetery, the ownership of which was under litigation as late as 1619. See Bałaban, pp. 373 f. Quite annoying must also have been the indeterminate nature of the *kozubalec*. From time to time Jews had to appeal to courts or the university rector for protection against excessive demands by the unruly youngsters. In their complaint of July 17, 1647, the Jewish community of Cracow claimed that students of the Corpus Christi school had "extorted a *kozubalec* from Jewish merchants planning to go to the fair of Jarosław by disturbing them four weeks in advance, notwithstanding the rector's injunction of several years ago, against students exacting these horrible and unjustified payments, under the penalty provided for the disturbance of public order." Pupils of another Cracow school collected illegitimate tolls from the transporters of wine and other goods. *Ibid.*, pp. 371 f. Such exactions, far beyond any agreed arrangement, were not infrequent in other communities as well. A good general summary of the great variety of taxes paid by Polish Jewry in the prepartition period is offered by R. Mahler in his *Toledot ha-Yehudim be-Polin*, pp. 157 ff.

93. See M. Bałaban, *Żydzi lwowscy*, Materials, pp. 112 f. No. 84, 125 ff. No. 96; J. Kądziołka, *Finanse miasta Poznania 1501–1648* (Finances of the City of Poznań, 1501–1648), with a German summary, esp. pp. 38 ff., 58, 72 ff., 81, 84 f. including Table 26; *supra*, n. 82; J. Perles, "Geschichte der Juden in Posen," *MGWJ*, XIII, 294, 450 f., etc.; L. Lewin, *Die Landessynode*, esp. pp. 57 f., 70 n. 10, 72 n. 18.

94. See M. Bałaban, *Dzieje*, I, 80 f., 87, 90 ff., 95 ff. In Lwów there was a prolonged litigation over the question of whether the Jewish poll tax freed the Jews from all municipal taxes, including the portion of the real estate tax derived from their use of municipal land (in the suburbs as well as in the city), and from the specific levy for the defense of the city against Tatar raids, as the Jews contended; or only from imposts on persons and houses, according to the interpretation of the city

council. The case was finally decided by Wladislaw IV on March 31, 1642: the king canceled all purported arrears owed by Jews to the city; but for the future the Jews were told to pay the muncipality 200 zlotys annually in property tax (*szos*), in addition to "rents" for their land and their cemetery, and one-fifth of the municipal water tax and war contributions. See Bałaban, *Żydzi lwowscy*, pp. 345 ff.; Materials, pp. 112 ff. Nos. 84 and 86, 125 ff. No. 96. These examples give us but an inkling of the important part played by Jews in the municipal finances of their localities, despite the royal privileges which exempted Jews from municipal taxation because of their obligations toward their own autonomous community. Unfortunately, this important historical area has thus far remained largely unexplored. Much more work is yet to be done before the widely ramified and variegated patterns of general municipal financing in Poland and Lithuania can be clarified. Notwithstanding the difficulties inherent in such research, a fuller examination of the fiscal relationships between cities and Jewish communities would help fill an important lacuna in our knowledge of the economic and political history of the dual Commonwealth and its Jewries.

Some material has become available in local monographs such as the aforementioned studies by C. Krawczak, S. Waszak (with special reference to housing), and particularly J. Kądziołka, mentioned *supra*, n. 93 and Chap LXIX, n. 33, all of which are based upon Poznań sources; R. Zubyk, *Gospodarka finansowa miasta Lwowa w latach 1624–1635* (The Financial Management of the City of Lwów in the Years 1624–1635); W. Adamczyk, *Gospodarka finansowa Lublina w latach 1569–1589* (Financial Management of the City of Lublin 1569–1589); supplemented by the *Rejestr poborowy województwa lubelskiego z roku 1626* (The Register of Tax Collections of the Lublin Palatinate in the Year 1626), ed. by J. Kolasa and K. Schuster; the similar publication of the *Rejestr poborowy województwa krakowskiego z roku 1629* (The Register of Tax Collections of the Cracow Palatinate in the Year 1629), ed. by Wanda Domin *et al.* (both under the general editorship of S. Inglot). Incomplete and unreliable as many records of this type are, a careful examination of whatever Jewish elements, especially names, are found in them might prove quite rewarding.

95. See M. Bałaban's *Dzieje*, I, 378 ff. The total cited in the text does not include the largest item, 60,000 zlotys, which the Cracow community acknowledged it owed to the royal secretary Jan Wisemberg. It promised to pay this amount in three installments of 20,000 zlotys each on March 31, 1644, January 7, 1645, and January 7, 1646. It appears that this debt referred to the 60,000 zlotys which Wladislaw IV had in 1643 asked the Cracow community to collect from the other Jewish communities in the realm and deliver to Wisemberg on January 6 (or rather January 7, since the 6th was a holiday), 1644. See *supra*, n. 86. The general fiscal and welfare activities of the Jewish communities in Poland and Lithuania will be more fully discussed in later chapters. For the time being, suffice it to refer to my *JC*, Vol. II, Chaps. XV and XVI, and the sources listed in the notes thereon in Vol. III, which, published more than thirty years ago, are of course no longer up to date.

96. B. Baranowski, *Powstania chłopskie na ziemiach dawnej Rzeczypospolitej* (Peasant Uprisings on the Territories of the Former Polish Commonwealth); and, especially for the eighteenth century. J. Topolski, *Położenie i walka klasowa chłopów*, pp. 252 ff. Deeply impressed by the havoc wrought by the Ukrainian peasant uprising of 1648, Count Albrycht Stanisław Radziwiłł vastly exaggerated when

he contended that the peasant wars in Poland were generally much more severe than those anywhere else. See his *Pamiętniki* (Memoirs), ed. by E. Raczyński, II, 391; and *supra*, Chap. LXVII, n. 78.

97. See the rather overapologetic summary by K. E. Franzos, "Juden als Kirchen-Pächter," *ZGJD*, [o.s.] IV, 373–78 (with some slight documentation from an eyewitness account of the massacre in Umań during the Gonta uprising in 1768, and from some later folk songs); and the considerable material accumulated by J. Shatsky in his introduction to W. Latzky-Bertoldi's Yiddish translation of Nathan Neṭa Hannover's *Yeven Meṣulah*, the main Jewish chronicle recording the massacres of 1648. See especially pp. 32* ff. See also the additional data in S. Ettinger's "Jewish Participation in the Colonization of the Ukraine" (Hebrew), *Zion*, XXI, 124 ff., with an English summary, p. i.

98. The assertion of Anna Dembińska that Jewish capitalists contributed much to the spread of Polish culture in Volhynia is but partially justified. See her *Wpływy Kultury polskiej na Wołyń w XVI wieku* (Influences of Polish Culture on Volhynia in the Sixteenth Century). Only indirectly, by helping the Polish or Polonized magnates to develop their latifundia agriculturally and commercially, may Jews have unwittingly also helped to spread Polish life patterns in the eastern provinces. But they themselves staunchly adhered to their own traditional mores, which appeared equally alien to both the Polish and the Rus populations.

99. See the texts of Chmielnicki's Polish letters and instructions, reproduced in *Dokumenti Bogdana Khmelnitskogo* (Bohdan Chmielnicki's Documents, 1648–1657), compiled by I. Kripiakevich and I. Butich, pp. 23 ff. Nos. 1, 2, 4, 5, 6, and 7; and, more generally, the numerous biographies of Chmielnicki, such as G. Vernadsky, *Bohdan, Hetman of the Ukraine;* L. Vynar, "The Question of Anglo-Ukrainian Relations in the Middle of the Seventeenth Century," *Annals of the Ukrainian Academy of Arts and Sciences in the U. S.*, VI, 1411–18. See also E. Borschak, "Early Relations between England and the Ukraine," *Slavonic and East European Review*, X, 138–60. Polish attempts to reduce the influence of the Orthodox Church on the Rus population within the dual Commonwealth; the antecedents of, and the negotiations leading to, the Union of Brest of 1596; the counteraction of the patriarchate of Constantinople, acting in alliance with the Muscovite authorities, to keep the faith alive, as exemplified by the aforementioned visits of the Antiochian patriarch Joachim and the Constantinople patriarch Jeremias in Kiev in the 1580s; and Patriarch Theophanes' intervention to keep the Cossacks from aiding the Polish army during its crucial battle with the Turks at Cecora in 1620—are all briefly described in Z. Wójcik's *Dzikie Pola w ogniu* (The Wild Steppes in Flames), 3d ed., pp. 61 f., 91 f.; *supra*, Chap. LXIX, nn. 3, 19 ff., 29–30. See also the mutually complementary studies by K. Chodynicki, *Kościół prawosławny a Rzeczpospolita Polska. Zarys historyczny 1370–1632* (The Orthodox Church and the Polish Commonwealth: an Historical Sketch, 1370–1632); and F. Titov, *Russkaia pravoslavnaia tserkov v polskolitovskom gosudarstve v XVII–XVIII vv.* (The Russian Orthodox Church in the Polish-Lithuanian State in the Seventeenth and Eighteenth Centuries).

100. The etymology of the designation "Cossack" still is obscure. See W. E. D. Allen, *The Ukraine: a History*, new ed., p. 68; M. Hrushevsky, *A History of Ukraine,*

ed. by O. J. Frederiksen, with a Preface by G. Vernadsky, p. 103. The derivation from the Turkish word *quzaq*, suggested in the text, illustrates how intertwined the predominantly Slavonic Cossacks, whether residing in the Zaporozhe or the Don River and Riazan areas, were with their Tatar and Turkish neighbors. The earliest known occurrence of the term has been traced to a passage in a thirteenth-century manuscript located in the Marciana Library in Venice. Other references recur in the fifteenth century. But the term becomes unequivocal only in the complaints about Cossack attacks by the inhabitants of the Genoese colony of Kaffa in 1449 and by the Crimean khan in 1493. See M. K. Liubavsky, *Ocherk Istorii Litov-sko-Russkavo Gosudarstva do Liublinskoi Unii Vkliuchitelno* (A Sketch of the Lithunian-Russian State up to the Union of Lublin), p. 226; and, particularly, G. Stökl's searching study, *Die Enstehung des Kosakentums,* especially pp. 39 ff., 53.

No less complicated has been the problem, frequently discussed with partisan fervor, of the heterogeneous composition of the Zaporogian Cossack settlement. The most plausible reconstruction is offered by W. Tomkiewicz in his "On the Social and Ethnic Composition of Ukrainian Cossackdom around 1600" (Polish), *PH*, XXXVII, 249–60, citing among other sources Sigismund III's expostulating reply to the sultan, pointing out that Tatars, Russians, Turks, Rus, and Moldavians (as well as Poles, of course) were all members of that uncontrollable group (p. 256). From time to time one found there Armenians, Greeks, Serbs, Dutchmen, Englishmen, and Germans. On early Jewish relations with the Cossacks, see the brief essay "Jews-Cossacks at the Beginning of the Seventeenth Century" (Russian), *Kievskaia Starina*, 1895, No. 4. See also, more generally, V. O. Golobutsky (Holobutskyi), *Zaporozhkoe Koza-chestvo* (Zaporogian Cossackdom); the succinct yet comprehensive history of the land and people by Z. Wójcik, *Dzikie Pola w ogniu;* and, even more broadly, W. H. McNeill, *Europe's Steppe Frontier, 1500–1800.*

101. See A. Jabłonowski, *Historya Rusi południowej do upadku Rzeczypospolitej Polskiej* (History of the Southern Rus to the Fall of the Polish Commonwealth); and other sources cited by Z. Wójcik in *Dzikie Pola;* D. Boretsky's *Protestatsiia*, ed. by P. Zhukovich in *Sbornik statei po slavyanovedeniia*, III, cited from O. Ohloblyn's English translation of D. Doroshenko's *A Survey of Ukrainian Historiography: Ukrainian Historiography, 1917–1956 (Annals of the Ukrainian Academy of Arts and Sciences in the U. S.,* V, Special Issue), pp. 35 f.; and numerous other writers through the ages reviewed by Doroshenko in his *Survey.* See also the succinct analysis of both primary and secondary sources, in the main relating to the sixteenth century, and emphasizing the Ukrainian and, to a lesser extent, the Russian literature on the subject, in I. L. Gordon's informative Yale University dissertation, *Revolutionary Banditry: an Interpretation of the Social Roles of the Ukrainian Cossacks in Their First Rebellions, 1590–1596*, pp. 318 ff.

102. Guillaume Le Vasseur le Sieur de Beauplan, *Description d'Vkranie, qvi sont plvsievres prouinces du royaume de Pologne. Contenvës depvis les confins de la Moscouie, iusques aux limites de la Transilvanie. Ensemble leurs moevrs, façons de viures, et de faire la Guerre,* Aroüen (Rouen), 1661; Geronimo Pinocci's dispatches home, as well as Wojciech Giżycki's letters to him, reproduced by A. Grabowski, comp., *Ojczyste spominki* (Ancestral Reminiscences in Writings Pertaining to Old Poland), II, 102 ff.; and cited by S. Ettinger in his "Jewish Participation" (Hebrew), *Zion*, XXI, 124 f.; Moses Rivkes, *Be'er ha-golah* (Well of Exile), on *Shulḥan 'Arukh,*

Ḥ. M., 346, 5, cited by H. Graetz in his *Geschichte der Juden,* 3d ed., X, 60 n. 1; M. Weinreich, ed., "A Jewish Song Regarding Shabbetai Ṣevi [*Shain nai lid fun Meshiaḥ* = A Beautiful New Song about the Messiah]" in his *Bilder fun der alter Yiddisher Literatur* (Studies in the History of the Yiddish Literature from the Beginnings to Mendele Moykher Seforim), pp. 219–52; J. Shatsky's intro. to the Yiddish trans. of Nathan Neṭa Hannover, *Yeven Meṣulah,* pp. 41* f.

Beauplan's relative indifference to the Jewish aspects of the Cossack uprising, and to the general life of the Jewish community in the Ukraine (particularly in the Zaporozhe, his detailed topographic description of which has served modern scholars in good stead), may be explained by his background. Born and long residing in Dieppe, Normandy, he had had practically no contact with Jews before he came to Poland as a young engineer. Among his numerous tasks was the building and rebuilding of the fortress of Kudak, designed to stem the Cossacks' bloody incursions into Tatar and Turkish lands, raids which generally hindered Poland's efforts to maintain amicable relations with the rulers of these countries. An excellent and generally accurate observer, the engineer, upon his return to France, published his *Description* in 1651, at the height of French and European interest in the Cossack uprising. It immediately became a best seller, reappearing in several French editions and in a number of other languages; it has since served as a major source of information on conditions before 1648 in the Ukraine, where Beauplan spent the most productive seventeen years of his life. It is to be regretted that his few references to Jews, such as his statement that they held the keys to the Orthodox churches in order to enforce the payment of the prescribed fees by the peasants (1661 ed., p. 17), give us a completely one-sided picture. Even after settling in Rouen in 1652, where he may have been in contact with the flourishing New Christian community, Beauplan saw no reason to alter or supplement his data on the Ukrainian Jews in the subsequent editions of his book. See also *supra,* Chap. LXIX, n. 20.

103. See A. Jabłonowski, *Żrodła dziejowe,* XX, Intro. p. 84; O. Baranovich, *Zaludnienie Ukraini pered Khmelnichchinoiu* (The Population of the Ukraine before Chmielnicki); S. Ettinger, "Jewish Participation," *Zion,* XXI, 120 ff.; *supra,* Chap. LXIX, nn. 46 and 50; and Vol. XV, pp. 275 f., 505 f. n. 20.

104. Colonialism having become a dirty word in recent years, the pioneering services rendered to the Ukraine by its Polish and Jewish colonizers have been greatly obscured by modern biases. The somewhat more balanced view of the Ukrainian situation, as presented by the German historian S. Gargas in his *Volkswirtschaftliche Ansichten in Polen im XVII. Jahrhundert,* pp. 44–85, has found few sympathetic followers. Even in the Western Hemisphere, despite its heritage of having utilized the more or less forced labor of the native Indian or mestizo population and even the outright slave labor of Negros imported into the Americas, more stress has been laid in the existing literature upon the oppressiveness of the Polish regime than upon the simultaneous pioneering achievements and cultural advances of the mass immigration, which was promoted by the early capitalist methods of production and distribution. Nor must we forget that, in its more advanced phases, modern capitalism (whether one thinks of it as but an intermediary step toward a socialist society or as the most effective and progressive form of social organization), with its concomitant growth of liberal ideas in both economics and politics, had inherent forces which ultimately led, almost simultaneously in the early 1860s, to the emanci-

pation of the slaves in the United States and of the peasant serfs in the Ukraine and the rest of Russia.

As we have seen, and shall see again, in various contexts, Jews played a disproportionately great role in many phases of the capitalist evolution. On the more specific aspects of these evolutionary forces in the Ukraine, see also the broad analysis by W. E. D. Allen in his *The Ukraine: a History*, pp. 64 ff.; O. Halecki in his *Borderlands of Western Civilization: a History of East-Central Europe;* and the contributors to the *Cambridge History of Poland to 1695*, ed. by W. F. Raddaway *et al.* While thus stressing certain similarities between Western and East-European historical evolution we must not minimize the numerous dissimilarities, however, as does, for instance, B. Stasiewski in his plea for fuller consideration of East-European history in relation to that of Western Europe. See his "Zum Begriff der osteuropäischen Geschichte und Kirchengeschichte," *Theologische Zeitschrift*, IV, 324–40.

105. D. Kaufmann, "David Carcassonni et le rachat par la communauté de Constantinople des Juifs faits prisonniers durant les persécutions de Chmielmicky," *REJ*, XXV, 202–216 (basically applies to the earlier period as well); *supra*, Chaps. LXVII, n. 7; LXIX, n. 23; Z. Wójcik, *Dzikie Pola*, pp. 116 f.; Szymon Okolski, *Diariusz transakcji wojennej . . . w r. 1637* (Diary of the Belligerent Proceedings . . . in the Year 1637), p. 193; and other data cited in W. Tomkiewicz, "On the Social and Ethnic Composition," *PH*, XXXVII, 258 f. The relations between the Krymchaki and both the Cossacks and their enemies, the Tatars, have not yet been fully clarified. Anthropologically, too, this remarkable segment of Polish-Lithuanian Jewry has presented one of the most intriguing problems of East-European Jewish history. Very likely some of the Krymchaki were descendants of the original Khazar inhabitants of the Crimea and its vicinity, although their Khazar ancestors had disappeared from the scene of history since the twelfth century. Some of them seem to have reappeared in the Crimea under Tatar domination as professing Jews, even receiving special "Letters of Privilege Given by Khans to the Krymchaki," according to I. Kaia in his Russian article under this title in *ES*, VII, 102–103 (referring to charters of 1597 and 1742). See also S. Szapszai, "Karaites in the Service of the Khans of Crimea" (Polish), *Myśl karaimska*, II, 5–22.

The problems of the relationship between the medieval Khazars and the Polish-Lithuanian Krymchaki and Karaites have often been discussed, though rather inconclusively. See esp. A. Zajączkowski, "On Khazar Culture and Its Heirs" (Polish), *ibid.*, n.s. I, 5–34, esp. pp. 26 ff.; idem, *The Karaims in Poland*, esp. pp. 12 f., 37 ff.; I. Halperin, "A Few Words about the Karaite Dispersion in the Middle of the Seventeenth Century" (Hebrew), *Gelber Jub. Vol.*, pp. 35–38 (reproduced in his *Yehudim ve-yahadut be-mizraḥ Eiropah*, pp. 401–404), with special reference to a diplomatic mission sent by the khan in 1660–61; J. Czekanowski, "Anthropological Problems Relating to Karaim" (Polish), *Myśl karaimska*, n.s. II, 3–23 (with reference to the sociological investigations by Michał Reicher); A. M. Pulyanov, "Toward an Anthropology of the Karaim in Lithuania and the Crimea" (Russian), *Voprosy Antropologii*, XIII, 116–33. Also of some interest in retrospect are the few fragments dated shortly before Russia's annexation of the Crimea in 1783 and published by J. Mann in his *Texts and Studies in Jewish History and Literature*, II, 444 ff. To the literature on the generally complex Khazar problem listed *supra*, Vol. III, 323 ff. n. 30, one may add a considerable number of more recent publications, especially in the Soviet Union, on which see I. Sorlin, "Le Problème des

Khazares et les historiens soviétiques dan les vingt dernières années," *Travaux et mémoires* of the Centre de Recherches d'histoire et civilisation byzantines, III, 423–55. The forthcoming comprehensive volume by Professor Omelian Pritsak of Harvard may shed much new light on the entire historical evolution of the Khazar people.

106. See Z. Wójcik, *Dzikie Pola*, pp. 24 ff. and *passim*; I. R. Gordon, *Revolutionary Banditry*, esp. pp. 98 ff., 175 ff.; F. Babinger, "La Date de la prise de Trépizonde par les Turcs," *Revue des études byzantines*, VII, 205–207, and the sources listed there.

107. See S. Kryczyński, *Tatarzy litewscy; próba monografi historyczno-etnograficznej* (Lithuanian Tatars: a Tentative Historic-Ehnographic Monograph); M. Horn, *Chronologia i zasięg najazdów tatarskich na ziemie Rzeczypospolitej Polskiej w latach 1600–1647* (The Chronology and Extent of the Tatar Raids on the Lands of the Polish Commonwealth in the Years 1600 to 1647); and B. Baranowski, "The Genesis of the Cossack-Tatar Alliance in 1648" (Polish), *PH*, XXXVII, 276–87. Baranowski rightly points out that, despite their perennial hostility and the Tatars' deprecation of the Cossacks as mere "robbers and highwaymen," the two groups had sometimes joined forces in looting the more civilized, wealthier areas of Poland and Lithuania. During their alliance in 1648, the Tatar khans regularly spoke of their "Cossack brothers." See also such specific monographs as Baranowski's twin studies, *Polska a Tatarszczyzna w latach 1624–1629* (Poland and the Tatar World in the Years 1624–29); and *Stosunki polsko-tatarskie w latach 1632–1648* (Polish-Tatar Relations in the Years 1632–48); and, on the somewhat later period, Z. Wójcik, "Some Problems of Polish-Tatar Relations in the Seventeenth Century: the Financial Aspects of the Polish-Tatar Alliance in the Years 1654–1666," *APH*, XIII, 87–102. Jewish-Tatar relations in the former Genoese colony of Kaffa and elsewhere will engage our fuller attention in connection with the story of the Jewish settlements in the Black Sea area in forthcoming chapters.

108. The greatest permanent achievement of Erich Lassota von Steblau's mission was his *Tagebuch (1573–1594)*, ed. by R. Schottin, which contains valuable information, unavailable in any other source, on the Zaporozhe in the late sixteenth century. Similarly, because Poland's foreign policy had in the early 1600s concentrated on Muscovite and Livonian affairs, the Thirty Years' War exerted only an indirect influence on the evolution of Polish-Cossack relations. See G. Gajecky and A. Baran, *The Cossacks in the Thirty Years' War*, Vol. I: 1619–1624. See also A. Dziubiński, "The Trade in Polish and Rus Slaves and Its Organization in Sixteenth-Century Turkey" (Polish), *Zeszyty Historyczne* of the University of Warsaw, III, 36–49; I. Halperin, "Capture and Redemption of Captives in the Time of the Persecutions in the Ukraine and Lithuania, 1648–1660" (Hebrew), *Zion*, XXV, 17–56; and, more generally, W. Czapliński, "The Subject of Tatar Raids in Poland in the First Half of the Seventeenth Century" (Polish), *KH*, LXX, 713–20; and the literature listed *supra*, n. 102.

109. See B. Baranowski *et al.*, comps., *Upadek kultury w Polsce w dobie reakcji katolickiej XVII–XVIII w. Wypisy źródłowe* (The Cultural Decline in Poland in the Period of the Catholic Reaction in the Seventeenth and Eighteenth Centuries: Ex-

cerpts from Sources), *passim*. Although not free of anti-Catholic bias, this collection of excerpts furnishes a graphic illustration of the cultural decline and the growth of obscurantism among both the intellectual leaders and the masses of the period. The Jewish intellectual reaction will be discussed in a later volume.